OVERWORLD

Confessions of a Reluctant Spy

Larry J. Kolb

BANTAM PRESS

LONDON · TORONTO · SYDNEY · AUCKLAND · JOHANNESBURG

TRANSWORLD PUBLISHERS
61-63 Uxbridge Road, London W5 5SA
a division of The Random House Group Ltd

RANDOM HOUSE AUSTRALIA (PTY) LTD
20 Alfred Street, Milsons Point, Sydney,
New South Wales 2061, Australia

RANDOM HOUSE NEW ZEALAND LTD
18 Poland Road, Glenfield, Auckland 10, New Zealand

RANDOM HOUSE SOUTH AFRICA (PTY) LTD
Endulini, 5a Jubilee Road, Parktown 2193, South Africa

Published 2004 by Bantam Press
a division of Transworld Publishers

A catalogue record for this book is available from the British Library.
ISBNs 0593 051017 (cased)
0593 053591 (tpb)

Printed in Great Britain by
Clays Ltd, Bungay, Suffolk

1 3 5 7 9 10 8 6 4 2

Papers used by Transworld Publishers are natural, recyclable products
made from wood grown in sustainable forests. The manufacturing processes
conform to the environmental regulations of the country of origin.

For my mother and father,
For Aleen, and for Bob,
And for Miles.
All dead now.
Except in my dreams.

And for Muhammad,
Who may live forever.

CONTENTS

OVERWORLD

A mile of clean sand.
I will write my name here, and the trouble that is in my heart.
I will write the date & place of my birth,
What I was to be,
And what I am.
I will write my forty sins, my thousand follies,
My four unspeakable acts. . . .
I will write the names of the cities I have fled from,
The names of the men & women I have wronged.
I will write the holy name of her I serve,
And how I serve her ill.
And I will sit on the beach & let the tide come in.
I will watch with peace the great calm tongue of the tide
Licking from the sand the unclean story of my heart.

—EDNA ST. VINCENT MILLAY

Paris, April 1st, 1922

The world I grew up in was slightly different from the world you grew up in. My father was a senior United States intelligence official, or, if you prefer the lurid: a spymaster. I grew up all over the earth, and from when I was very young I had spies for uncles. By the time I was eleven, I'd learned to sit on the stairs in the dark and listen to my father and his men downstairs drinking into the night and saying things they thought no one else would hear. I grew up knowing secrets. I grew up knowing my family's telephones were monitored, our mail was intercepted. I grew up understanding everyone has the capacity to betray.

And I grew up loving my father, but certain I didn't want a life like his. By my twenty-third birthday, I'd been recruited by the CIA, said no thanks, and set out to lead an entirely different sort of life. Yet I write this in a safe house. A safe house on a beach in Florida, where, at the moment, a gentle rain is falling.

I am here, to put it simply, to hide and wait. That seems the only thing to do until my lawyers and the State Department have finally made a deal with a certain foreign power that has announced it wants to have a word with me. Until I'm satisfied I'll be safe and immune when I sit down with its authorities to help them make sense of various perplexing matters apparently of vital national importance to them, to help them, as they've written repeatedly in their propaganda and their demands for my cooperation, "winnow falsehood from truth."

When the sun comes out, I like to cross the dunes to feed the gulls and watch the waves roll in, collapse at my feet, and drain backward into the sea. I stand on the edge of America and face due east. Africa. Turn a little to the left and I'm facing Europe. Hard right is South America. It's been nice to think nothing but one unbroken stretch of water separates me from so many places, so many possibilities. My life is nothing now if not rich with possibilities. And if not all of them are good, well, I know it's never been otherwise for anyone.

On this beach, I live in a big house that doesn't look big. Do you know the sort of house I mean? From every single point, it hides most of itself. Outside, it looks nothing special. My father taught me not to draw attention to myself in times like these.

I have a deck and a pool, but so do most houses along this stretch of coast. Inside are Spanish tiles, wooden beams and shutters, and white plaster walls that change colors throughout the day. It's comfortable enough, a good place to read, to listen to the wind and rain, to wait.

I don't know my neighbors. We've shaken hands. We wave occasionally, shout hellos; but that's as far as I let it go. Down the coast road a way and across the bridge, on the mainland, is a growing little town—which I visit at least a couple of times a week, to have a meal or buy supplies, groceries, books. An hour or so by highway through swamps and piney woods is a bigger town. It's not a metropolis. But it's got an airport, things to do, a nightlife. Whenever one of my lawyers or anyone else needs to see me, that's where we meet; and that, for now, is the farthest boundary of my shrunken universe. I spend much of my time now dreaming of another world.

There are some who would argue my journey to this beach began on a summer's morning in New York, when Miles Copeland casually introduced himself to me. He was the CIA's first covert political operative, and he may or may not have been a friend of my father. Miles once told me that between political forces there will always arise problems that cannot be resolved by politicians—constrained as they are by their highly principled public images. And that a problem such as these is best solved by a mysterious gentleman from afar who bounds onto the scene, does whatever needs to be done, and disappears. This beach is where I've disappeared to.

One rainy Heathrow afternoon, we were next in line for takeoff and I was bound nonstop to a hero's welcome in far New Delhi, when the Boeing 747 into whose front seat I was strapped was pulled over by a speeding police car, then boarded by two deceptively courteous detectives who took me off the plane, questioned me for hours, and let me go. Can that really be? Yes. It happened. And it was the first tug I felt of the currents that left me washed up like driftwood on this beach.

How, I ask myself, did I get from there to here? From the bowels of Heathrow and the King of Saudi Arabia's palaces and billionaires' jets, from boxing with the Pope and kissing the rosy red tip of Saddam Hussein's nose, from secret meetings in the White House and in the winds and dust of the Khyber Pass, from speeding through Paris with my wife's cousin Dodi en route to shower his favorite belly dancer with hundred-dollar bills, to a hermit's life in this house on a beach in Florida?

I arrived here after a month on the run, hiding, being scared. Do you know what it feels like to go to bed every night in a different place with a different name, afraid you won't live through the night? You look around the cheap motel room, assess its layout, and, just before you go to sleep, you say to yourself, if tonight's the night they get me, they'll come through that door there, or that window, and there'll be at least two of them, and I'll barely have a chance—but everything's fine, go to sleep.

Sometimes, sitting here in torpid isolation, it all seems so improbable. What things I saw and did! What amazing things I was *allowed* to see because I could be useful. What things I did to prove just how useful I could be. Nothing seemed impossible back then. Can that busy, jet-lagged fellow really have been me?

During the long gray rains that come this time of year, I've had plenty of time to sit inside and ponder. I watch the weather and reflect. I try to make sense of the extraordinary people and events that brought me here. I try to winnow falsehood from truth.

Outside, the rain has passed and the sun is coming out. Soon steam will rise from the sand, black skimmers will work the waves for fish, and when the air is warm and soft and perfect the gulls will begin to cry. I've come to know this place too well. I stare out past dripping palmettos to the sea and long to fly across it. There are so many places I want to go, so many things I want to do. I know I wasn't meant to stay here forever, trapped in memories like some demented keeper of the flame.

Inside this house on a beach in Florida, I look forward to the great day someday soon when my lawyers, my government's lawyers, and my interrogators will sit down with me at a long table in a room without a window. When they will set up stenography machines and lights and video cameras to record my story, and one of them will look at me and say, "Start from the beginning."

In the beginning, I was born the son of a spy. That's a crucial piece of evidence, and I've already decided I must withhold it from the interrogators.

PART ONE

THE SPY WHO LOVED ME

1 | PORTRAIT OF MY FATHER

DIGGING UP A DEAD BABY

My father told me he was born on a dirt floor in a shack in Georgia, and that he'd memorized so many lies about his birth date that he wasn't even sure anymore when he was actually born. I was born in 1953, in a hospital in Norfolk, Virginia, where my father was temporarily assigned to the War College to teach a class called Sophisticated Assassination.

I have a photograph of him standing in front of a War College blackboard, wearing one of the soft gray cardigans he used to wear, pipe in his left hand, and in his right a pointer he's using to indicate something that—like much of the rest of his life—was just out of view. But I remember nothing of the year we lived in Norfolk, nor of the next two years in Washington, D.C.

My earliest remaining memory begins on the deck of the United States Navy destroyer the USS *Breckenridge*. Somewhere in the Pacific Ocean— somewhere between Seattle where my mother and I embarked and Japan where we were heading. My father had gone by plane and was already in Japan.

It was raining. The clouds were gray. The deck was gray. The ship's rail was gray, and so, except for whitecaps, was the sea beyond it. I was wearing a harness and crossing the unsteady deck on the end of a chain.

We had a rough passage. My mother spent nearly the entire three weeks seasick in her bunk. That left me at the mercy of the young Japanese fellow my mother called "our cabin boy." He could've yanked me around on that leash, but he was kind and gentle. He let me make it to the rail to look down at what I wanted to see: the guns on a lower deck. Then he led me back to our cabin, where he turned little pieces of paper into origami animals. He made a crane, showed me how to make its wings flap, then he handed it to me. And that's where it ends.

The next thing I remember is my father's smiling face in an ocean of coolie hats. He was standing on the dock beneath the ship and waving up at my mother and me. I remember red earth beyond the dock, and watching with my mother and father as a crane lifted our new car out of the ship's hold and onto the land. I remember my father signing some papers and passing them out the window of the car before we rode off together to our new home—and the beginning of my long tangled journey into my father's secret life. Memory is a dream. Certainty is an illusion. But this is how it comes back to me now.

It was 1957.

We lived in southern Japan in an American compound.

We ate T-bone steaks and hot dogs in our backyard, shopped for American clothes and toys in an American store, watched American cartoons, drove an American car, and I peed in the kiddie pool at the American club with other American kids.

George Washington was on the fronts of our dollar bills and Honest Abe Lincoln was on the fronts of our fives. But the backs of our bills were not green; they were yellow. Yellowbacks. Occupation scrip. My father was part of what he called "the Army of Occupation." My father was a spy.

Our end of the island was crawling with Americans in uniform—GIs, jarheads, airmen—but there were also plenty of American civilians around, and they, like my father, went to work in suits and ties. His suits tended to be gray, his ties dark blue or black. My father was six feet tall, his eyes were blue, and his hair was either light brown or blond, usually blond, depending on how much he'd been in the sun lately.

He called his office "the shop" and he told me what he and his men did there was mostly boring paperwork. Reading and writing reports. Sending and receiving TWXs, pronounced *twixs*. But the truth was that what he did most of all was travel. Sometimes he was gone for days that seemed to me like weeks, and other times for weeks that seemed like months. TWXs were the root of all evil. When I heard my father casually telling my mother he'd received a TWX, usually he was leading up to telling us he was going on TDY. TDY is an intelligence and military acronym for Temporary Duty Away. The key word being *Away*.

The TWX machine was a gray steel beast in my father's office that periodically hummed and chattered and spat out yellow messages, short or long, typed all in CAPS, coded or not, sent from afar. Some TWXs came in pairs, one written in the clear, authorizing travel and expenditures and the like, and its counterpart coded, detailing the operation the travel and expenditures were in aid of. TWXs received by day were bad enough. But when a TWX came in the night and was too important to wait until morning, it could rip my father right out of my life without him even saying goodbye.

The signs of his abrupt departure were usually already clear by the time I made it to my bamboo chair at our breakfast table, but I'd still ask my mother hopefully, "Where's Daddy?"

The answer too often was "TDY." I pined for him whenever he left, especially when he left in the middle of the night without giving me my marching orders. We were at war and I needed marching orders when I was going to be the man of the house.

According to the few contemporaneous files kept by my father, or about him by others, which I've managed to get my hands on, he'd spent the last several years in the States training intelligence officers and working staff jobs at headquarters; Japan was the first place he'd been operational in nearly a decade. Officially, the territory over which he took responsibility on the day he landed there was limited to the southernmost islands of Japan, the Ryukus. But notations by my father's boss the deputy director back in the States say he soon discovered my father was the best man he had in the Pacific. After that, when problems popped up anywhere near Japan, the deputy director sent my father to take over. He seemed to spend a lot of time on TDY in what he called Formosa, which we call Taiwan, and in Hong Kong, Korea, and the Philippines.

The longest he was ever gone from me on TDY was three weeks, and the day he came home, looking tanned and happy and bearing a neat-o pearl-handled six-shooter for me, was the first day he ever told me anything about his work, other than the boring paperwork.

"I'm sorry I was gone so long," he said.

"Me too."

"I've been in Manila, in the Philippine Islands," he said, and then he handed me a mahogany cigar box and let me hold it. "Careful," he said.

"What's it say?"

First my father showed me the seal branded onto the lid of the box. "This is the Seal of the President of the Philippines," he said. Then he read me the vague but very grateful inscription engraved into the little silver plaque beneath the seal.

"The reason I had to be away so long," my father said, "was I was with the President of the Philippines. He's a good ally of the United States and he had a problem. Some people wanted to kill him."

"Really?"

"Yes."

"Was it Communists?"

"Yes," my father said. "It was Communists."

"Wow! Did you get them?"

"Yes. I got them. Don't worry. I'll be at home for a while."

Even if it wasn't clear to me then who my father was, I was thoroughly conversant with who he was up against. The Communists. The Reds from Moscow and Peking. The Main Threat. Our enemy.

Khrushchev said "We will bury you," but my father just laughed at that. Everybody knew we were technologically and scientifically superior to the Communists. Until one day, a few months after our arrival in Japan, the Russians proved they were ahead of us, and then kept reminding us of it, every ninety-six minutes.

Beep—beep—beep—beep—beep—beeeeeeeeeeeeeeeeeeep.

"What the hell is that?" said my father the first time we heard it on our television. We were all together in our living room. My mother and father and me.

I can close my eyes and see my mother sitting there on the green-striped couch. She's tall, tanned, dark-haired, good-looking, and wearing her cat's eye glasses, which somehow didn't look incongruous then. A tall glass of bourbon and ginger is beside her on one of the two round, shiny tables that once a week made our house smell like Brasso. My father is on one knee in front of our enormous television cabinet trying to make the snow disappear from the pictures on our tiny television screen.

"A-flat," said my mother.

"Yeah, but what the hell *is* it?" Then suddenly it dawned on him. He'd known all day.

It was *Sputnik!* Both Eisenhower and Khrushchev had announced plans to launch "artificial satellites" into space. The Space Race was on. And we'd always assumed we'd win it.

But for more than a year we'd been trying, and failing, to fire into orbit a tiny satellite which was no bigger than a grapefruit and weighed less than four pounds. Now the Russians had succeeded in launching a satellite bigger than a basketball and weighing more than a hundred eighty pounds into orbit. It was traveling at more than ten thousand miles an hour, circling the earth every ninety-six minutes. It had four long antennas through which it beamed to us clear evidence that we were behind. Beep—beep—beep—beep—beep— beeeeeeeeeeeeeeeeeeep.

The Communists had made it into space, and America was reeling. We tried, but still couldn't get our grapefruit into space. A month after *Sputnik I,* the Russians successfully launched *Sputnik II.* This time their artificial satellite weighed more than a thousand pounds, and inside it was a living passenger, a dog named Laika. We were inferior. Suddenly my father and my uncles and mother all had a sense of, if not doom, urgency at least, and they tried to keep it from me but I could feel it too.

Beep—beep—beep—beep—beep—beeeeeeeeeeeeeeeeeeep.

My father left for the shop every morning at dawn. He had a gun, which most days he wore in a shoulder holster under his suit coat. But sometimes he left it in his sock drawer. I wasn't allowed to touch the gun when he left it in the drawer. But I did.

He had scratchy cheeks when he kissed me, and he smelled like aftershave when he left for work and pipe tobacco when he got home—usually with one or two of my uncles in tow. I had lots of uncles, and mostly they were men who worked for my father. When my father or my uncles brought files with them from work, which was almost every evening, they took them straight into my father's den. In there, in a corner, was a gray steel safe with a combination dial on the door. When my father opened it to put the files in was when I got to see the other things in there. Those usually were: another gun; more files in Manila folders with a word stamped on them in the color of dried blood; and stacks of yellowbacks, greenbacks, and yen.

When I asked my father what was the word stamped on the files, he said, CLASSIFIED. When I asked what the money was for, all he said was "Work."

I knew what the gun was for.

My father was a secret policeman—something vaguely like Broderick Crawford, the policeman who wore suits in my favorite television program, *Highway Patrol*. Every afternoon, it came on Armed Forces Television at four, and I watched carefully for clues to what men like my father did when they weren't trying to act normal in front of their sons.

Once the files were locked inside the safe, it was time for cocktail hour, which was a sacred ritual hosted by my mother. Spying and counterspying are high-stress jobs. Hi-balls eased the stress, and my father and my uncles loved hi-balls.

I had an uncle George who flew in from Tokyo in his F-100 to surprise us at dinnertime sometimes, tell me great stories, and drink hi-balls. Bourbon and water. I had another uncle George who was skinny and pale and always looked to me like he still felt bad about something he'd done long ago. Gin and tonic. I had an uncle Ken who favored old-fashioneds, and an uncle Jim who went for Scotch, straight up. I had an uncle Glenn, and a lot more uncles too.

Who were they? Looking back, I wonder why the ankle holsters weren't more of a clue. I know now they were one of the finest collections of case officers, eavesdroppers, envelope steamers, inquisitors, second-story men, black-mailers, escape artists, getaway drivers, and fully licensed con men ever as-sembled on the face of the earth. It's funny the things a kid remembers, or, I mean, that an adult remembers from his days as a kid. I remember pocket contents. I suppose I thought every American kid saw saps and shivs and brass knuckles whenever their fathers' friends emptied their pockets in search of the bubble gum they'd brought them. Judging by some of my uncles' pocket contents, I'd have to say probably at least a few of them had special gifts for making you see things their way.

I remember a nice Canadian uncle who brought out surgical gloves, a little roll of duct tape, a pocketknife, alligator clips, and two spare magazines of bullets when I stuck my cap gun into his back. "Hands up! Okay, empty your pockets. Real slow now, pardner."

They were watchers, listeners, fixers, buggers, burglars, bagmen, interrogators, polygraphers, safecrackers, photo analysts, photo doctorers, pencil pushers, graph plotters, gunrunners, sheep-dippers. They were even seducers, and elicitors, and code clerks, and forgers. They were codebreakers and talentspotters and reports officers. And a few of them were the uncles every kid has who can make quarters come out of his ears. But one thing they were not was spies. Not a one of them. Not if you asked them.

I think it's because spies betray those closest to them that men like my father have never liked being called spies. They refer to themselves as "intelligence officers" and, to them, most spies are far away and duly removed at the ends of long strings of recruiters, handlers, and cutouts, and usually they are not heroes but something else entirely.

Calling themselves spies comes later to men like my father and my uncles. After they've loosened their sphincter muscles enough to gain a bit of perspective. Only then, when they're retired and drunk, or retired and telling true tales to their grandchildren, or both, will men like my father admit that, "Yes, I suppose that, in a certain way, you could say that I was once a spy." As I sit here now remembering my father, deep in the throes of his retirement, saying those very words to his grandson, it occurs to me that I could now say about the same words of myself—equally guardedly, and not to my interrogators. Fuck them.

After cocktail hour was dinner.

Dinner was for feeding uncles, or distinguished visitors from afar. My mother and Teruko and Yoshiko, her helpers, my friends, would get busy feeding shrimp cocktails, T-bone steaks, baked potatoes, white asparagus, and apple pie à la mode to a succession of uncles, Japanese police and intelligence chiefs, American Marine colonels and Air Force generals, and our recurring guests Generals Wei and Chang from Taipei—who always arrived together, usually bearing hand-carved toys for yours truly, and had nothing whatsoever good to say about the dirty Red Chinese.

When they finished eating, my father and his guests would disappear into his den for a while to talk shop. I wasn't allowed in on that, but judging by what I picked up at the table, I'd have to guess what they spent most of their time talking about in there was trouble the Communists were causing us in Japan and all over the Pacific. There were Chinese agents, Russians attachés, Communist sympathizers, labor organizers, opposition leaders. Troublemakers all of them, and what they were doing mostly, besides making life hell for us in general, was trying to convince the Japanese to kick the American military out of Japan—which we'd won fair and square.

Convincing Japanese not to like Americans wasn't all that hard. We were the good guys, I knew that. But, every Saturday when my father was at home, he and my mother and I climbed into our light-blue 1957 Chevrolet Bel-Air and drove right past the tall, gray seacliffs where, a dozen years earlier, when the Emperor's men had told the people that the American soldiers were coming and they couldn't hold them off any longer, ordinary Japanese from our island, hundreds of them, then thousands of them, men and women and children, had thrown themselves off the cliffs because they thought Americans were monsters.

"Really, Daddy?"

"I'm afraid so."

Our Saturday drives began at the Caltex station, where we gassed up and my father paid with our ration card. Then we drove on yellow dirt roads past the cliffs to where we could either turn toward the beaches or into the hills. The beaches were beautiful, rocky places. But I've seen enough of sand and water lately, and on the Saturday I'm seeing now we went up into the hills.

My father was at the wheel, watching his mirrors for cars that stayed behind us too long, I was in the middle, and my mother rode shotgun. Though, actually, the only gun in the car was my father's pistol. It lay on the floor where my father could reach it, under the lip of his seat—tucked inside a triangular leather case which was the color of caramels. A bullet was in the chamber. The safety was on. An extra clip was stuffed down a slot on the side of the case. It was wonderful. My father was back, it was just the three of us, and we were a family.

I had a brother, but he was seventeen years older than me and already away at school when I was born. He lived in Colorado now, with the rest of my family—all from my mother's side. My mother and I and my distant brother were pretty much the only family my father had.

When he was five, he went fishing with his father, who fell out of the boat into the river and drowned before my father's eyes. He made it through fifth grade and then ran away from home and started working as a field hand. Then he got word his mother, his brother, and his sisters all died. When the Second World War came, he lied about his age so they would let him join the army. He started as a private and his dream was to someday be a sergeant. But soon he was assigned to an intelligence unit. In intelligence, class and education are not as important as thinking clearly. So, by the end of the war, he was a colonel on the staff of General Eisenhower. My father wasn't in the army anymore, but he was still an intelligence officer.

We drove past gray stone shrines with Japanese writing on them, women walking beside the roads carrying clay jugs on their heads, water buffalo, rice paddies—terrace after terrace after terrace of muddy water and green shoots climbing up the mountainsides, and men and women in coolie hats working in paddies in water up to their ankles.

When we finally stopped, in a little clearing somewhere way out in the boondocks, my mother brought out our picnic basket and we sat on a big white rock in the sunshine and ate fried chicken and the deviled eggs she'd made that morning and wrapped in wax paper. Then my parents ate potato salad while I fed mine to a line of ants, and I drank Bosco while my mother blew on her coffee between sips, and my father put a cigarette in his mouth and lit it. I can still hear the sounds his steel-gray Zippo lighter made each time he flipped it open, lit it, shut it.

My father smoked Camels. Back then they didn't come in a filtered version. The logotype was printed on the paper near the end of the cigarette that came out of the top of the pack. That was the end most people put in their mouths. But my father smoked with the maker's mark out, so it would burn away faster, leaving one less trace of him. That was a sign of his training.

But I didn't realize that until years later when I read it in one of the spy novels my father read voraciously. Intelligence officers read spy novels, I think, because they give them a sense of resolution which their real-life cases seldom do. Who was it that said the difference between real life and fiction is that fiction has to make sense? I can't remember just now.

In restaurants my father always sat with his back to the wall and facing the door, and you can bet the place we'd stopped for our picnic was both carefully sited to give my father a commanding view and so far out that no one could've found us anyway. Little things like that were natural to me, but I didn't notice them. It would be a few years before I started to become conscious of my father's tradecraft, and years after that before I could get him to talk about it.

On that Saturday up in the boondocks, when my father finished his cigarette, he sang to me. There was something beautiful about my father's voice. Something clear and pure, but complicated. He sang to me all the time, and to himself even more. I'm not trying to tell you my childhood was like growing up as an extra in a musical about singing spies or anything like that; but my father liked to sing, and when people heard him they would stop and listen.

If you had heard him that afternoon singing, *Goodnight Irene, goodnight Irene / I'll see you in my dreams,* you would've believed there really was an Irene who my father loved more than anyone else. And, a few verses later, when he sang the refrain, your heart would be breaking because you knew you were listening to the saddest man in the world.

When my mother started packing up the picnic basket, that was my cue to start bugging my father to take the turn into the village on our way home.

There were—I pointed out to him—all sorts of fun things we could do in the village if only he would take a few extra minutes out of his busy schedule so we could go there. We could look for Lucky, the three-legged dog. We could watch the glassblowers melt Coke bottles and blow them into vases suitable for genies. We could stop and talk to the shopkeeper my father knew. And, if we were fortunate with our timing, we might even be able to stand outside and listen to gamblers inside cheering and groaning while a poisonous snake fought a mongoose.

Of course, one of the real reasons I liked the village so much was you could watch Japanese kids, and grown-ups too, squat and shit right in the middle of the streets. They did it wherever and whenever they felt like it. But I'd learned to leave that out of my pitch.

My father kept me in suspense until the last minute. Then he took the turn to the village.

We went into the shop and my father was chatting in English across the counter. He wasn't facing the counter head-on, but obliquely—so he could see the man behind the counter and the front door at once.

An old and raggedy man came in and said something in Japanese to my father.

My father smiled, took some yen out of his pocket, handed them to the raggedy man, and then went back to his conversation.

Which the raggedy man soon interrupted.

"I wonder what he wants," my father said, in the tones he used for thinking out loud.

"He wants you to move our car back a little bit," I said.

"He's right," said the shopkeeper.

And that was when my mother and father learned I could hold up my ends of secrecy pacts and conversations in Japanese. On our way home, I told them how—whenever my father was at work and my mother was off playing golf or at one of her ladies' luncheons—Teruko and Yoshiko, and Ewao, our gardener, and his son, Ukio, spoke to me only in Japanese.

I said this began when Teruko heard me mimicking her conversations with Yoshiko, and that Teruko and Yoshiko told me then that they would be my *nay-sans*—and that meant my big sisters—and they would teach me to talk like them and this would be our secret project until I'd learned it. And I told my father and mother when I really started to get the hang of it was when Ukio started coming to play with me, in Japanese, and when my mother started letting Teruko take me into town, to the back streets, where you barely ever saw an American.

There were split curtains hanging in doorways, paper windows, bright paper lanterns, cotton banners blazing with kanji—not a roman letter anywhere in sight—and mysterious, delicious smells wafting down the streets and alleys. Set me down in the middle of all that and, to this day, I will feel quite at home. Japan was imprinted on me early.

"I'm so proud of you!" my father told me on that long-ago Saturday. "I can't wait to tell your grandmother *my* son Larry can speak Japanese!"

It was still light in half of the sky, but the moon was already up, and I watched it chase us home through the wispy trees. After dinner and my bath, I put on my pajamas and brushed my teeth with Ipana, my father hugged me and kissed me good night, and then my mother tucked me into bed, helped me say my prayers, read me a story, kissed me, closed my mosquito netting around me, and said "I love you" as she stole out of my room.

Then I lay there in my bed thinking about cowboys and Indians in Colorado. Which was all the way across the world, and was where my grandmother lived. And my brother. My parents spoke of him often and there were framed pictures of him around our house. But to me my brother was like a distant god and I grew up like an only child.

My grandmother and my brother lived with my real uncle and my real aunt in a big white mansion on three hundred acres of land, just on the outskirts of Denver—where my aunt yelled at my uncle, my uncle ranched, my grandmother made egg custards and read the Bible, and my exalted brother did impossible things I knew I'd never be able to live up to. Every week or two we got a letter from my aunt, whose name was Aleen, mostly about the latest accomplishments of my brother, whose name was Jerry.

To hear my mother tell it, he'd always been a perfect child. He loved to go to church. He was an Eagle Scout. He never missed a day, or even a single customer, on his paper route. When he was twelve, he got a greyhound, which of course he trained to run so fast that it won the national coursing championship, whatever that was. He was a natural horseman, and he sang with perfect pitch, whatever that was. The year before I was born, when he was sixteen, my uncle started teaching him to shoot a rifle. And the year after I was born, he won the NRA National Championship. Smallbore—200 Yards—Any Sight. Which meant my brother was the best shot in the country with a twenty-two. And weren't my parents proud of him!

Now he was just out of college and already knew how to fly an airplane. Next the son of a bitch was going to learn to fly helicopters.

To hell with him, Daddy. I can speak Japanese!

Officially, on the census rolls and things like that, my parents and I lived in that big white house in Colorado too. I'd been there enough. I even had my own room, in spite of the fact that in Japan I kept having to consult photographs when I wanted to remember what home really looked like. Beside my bed, I kept a picture of the bunkhouse where the cowboys who worked for my uncle slept, and another of the rugged stretch of land out behind the fishing creek, where I figured there was plenty of room for a whole tribe of Indians to hide out. Every night that I could, I lived in that bunkhouse with the cowboys.

My uncle had bought the grand old house from a U.S. Senator, and my aunt had promptly filled it with silk wall coverings, crystal chandeliers, and antiques. At which point my uncle took to every month or two leaving the side door open to let his favorite billy goat in to drive my aunt crazy. My uncle's name was Watt Redfield, and he owned the Redfield Gunsight Company, which manufactured the best rifle scopes anywhere—preferred by Olympic shooters and sniper-assassins the world over. In the winter, when it was too snowy to practice shooting outside, Uncle Watt would set up a target range inside the house so he and my brother could keep shooting.

It's not every boy that has a rifle range inside his house, but I had one in mine. It had to be exactly fifty feet long, because that was the distance used for indoor smallbore matches. It was a big house, but it took lots of quirky twists and turns, and because of the distance specification, that meant Uncle Watt and my brother Jerry lay on their stomachs in the front sitting room and fired through the parlor, the dining room, a corner of the kitchen, and into the back entrance hall—where the bullet trap was.

When they were shooting, Aunty Aleen had to lock herself and the dogs in the basement, or upstairs. Which was one of the reasons Uncle Watt loved winter rifle practice so much. Its other allures included the wailing of the hounds, the clouds of gunpowder wafting through the house, and the great clang the bullet trap made each time a round slammed into it.

With intrigues and deception swirling around him in ways he feels but doesn't understand, the child of a spy in a foreign land needs a safe place he can return to in his mind. That was mine. Home sweet home. My oasis of sanity. My bedrock.

Basically, as soon as my mosquito net was shut, I started trying to go to Colorado. But some nights there was atmospheric disturbance, and I couldn't make the trip. In the room of the halfdream, somewhere between falling to sleep and consciousness, I lay under my net and had the most terrible fears about what my father and mother were really up to. Saturday drives in the country; picnics; my proud parents; kisses and bedtime stories. All that love, and still I didn't trust them. Not entirely. Not always.

Something inside my buzzing head sensed everything going on around me wasn't quite as safe and innocent as I was being told. They *say* when I'm asleep they stay here and protect me, I thought, but how do I really know that? What if they go out when I'm asleep? Why is my father gone so much? Where did he really get all that money in the safe? What if, when I'm asleep, my father and my mother go out and leave me here alone, and what they really are is *robbers?*

I lay in the dark, listening to faint sounds of clinking glasses and ice cubes and my mother and father and uncles talking and chuckling, working myself into panics.

Teruko and Yoshiko were out most evenings with their boyfriends, and with my parents as suspects I couldn't exactly seek out facts and comfort on this subject from them. So, during many bedtime hours of the fifth and sixth years of my life, I grew increasingly convinced that after I fell asleep I was left alone—while my father and my mother, and often my uncles too, went out into the night and did mysterious and dangerous things.

By the light of day, my night fears were buried, my father was my hero, and I loved and trusted him and my mother. But I was right, of course, in a way, during those terrible nights.

My father *was* out doing dark and mysterious things I couldn't have even imagined back then. And my mother *was* in on it. There are, of course, exceptions, but one thing I can tell you about spies' wives is: They know. There are limits to what they know; most of them don't know all the details; but their husbands tell them a thousand times more than the security manuals say they're supposed to. It's lonely work, and frightening, and everyone needs someone to share their fears with.

One night my panic turned into asthma so bad that I woke up the next day in an oxygen tent. I was lying in a bed somewhere, and my father was smiling at me through a clear plastic wall. Where am I? I asked, and my father said we were in the American Dispensary, and I was breathing rich pure oxygen.

The mahogany cigar box sits now atop my desk here in Florida. As with all important religious objects, it carries a certain measure of mystery within its majesty. Its contents include my father's government ID card, with his stern work face staring out at me, his dog tags and medals, credentials which gave him access to offices of various friendly intelligence services, his short-snorters from the war, a couple of curled and yellowed photographs, and the long, lugubrious letter which during his retirement he wrote to his family trying to explain and reconcile for us the secret world we'd always known he lived in and his even secreter world we'd just discovered. Nine pages, on eight-and-a-half-by-eleven paper, handwritten, over time apparently, for it's rendered in five different inks. It ends, *I thought I had done the right thing at the time, but since then I've often thought and worried about these things. How's that for a long sad story? Love/ Dad.* The real question, though, isn't how he explained it to us, but how he explained it to himself. And as to that, there are few clues.

There was so much I didn't know back then.

For example, I had an uncle Bill, my father's friend Mr. Bill Tharp, who lived on the other side of the island from us in a place where lots of other Americans lived too. We lived on the East China Sea. They lived on the Pacific Ocean. I knew Uncle Bill was so rich that he owned his own airline.

What I didn't know was that Bill Tharp's airline was only cover, the compound where he lived was the Chinen CIA base, Uncle Bill was in charge there, and in the CIA he was a legend.

In the early days of the CIA, one of Bill's cryptonyms had been Oscar Zachariah. That was how he signed his cables for a time. Or sometimes just O.Z. Certain of the cognoscenti in Washington cleared to read his cable traffic took to calling him Oz. Which soon became The Wizard of Oz, and then was truncated into just The Wizard. Which fit perfectly well, because he could make people disappear and, if they were lucky, reappear someplace else entirely. Most important, he could do this both in the material world and on paper. No one was ever better at these dual black arts than Bill Tharp.

I knew, vaguely, that everyone on our island said Uncle Bill must be making himself a fortune because his airline, Flying Tigers, was getting so busy. But I didn't know that from his shiny headquarters The Wizard was running most of the CIA's operations in the Pacific and Southeast Asia. A story from a newspaper on our island during the time we lived there, which my mother saved and gave to me years later, reports that owing to his excellent relationships with humanitarian-aid organizations based in Washington and Geneva, Uncle Bill had won his airline contracts to fly rice and other humanitarian supplies to needy recipients all over Asia. What I didn't know, and apparently the reporter didn't either, was that Uncle Bill's airline flew rice in three varieties. Plain rice was blankets, medicines, or food—sometimes even including rice. Hard rice was ammo or weaponry. Soft rice was people—including refugees, spies, or even armies that didn't exist flying off to fight in wars that weren't being fought and consequently couldn't be found in any newspaper. Eventually, Flying Tigers and its sister carrier CAT merged most of the aircraft in their fleets and began flying under the catchy new name Air America.

Which brings us to the AMPO Crisis. 1960 now. Far away in Tokyo, where my father was on TDY, the deadline was almost up for a Diet vote on whether to renew the AMPO Treaty, which was what kept American military forces in Japan. Prime Minister Kishi, who is now said to have been not only a war criminal but also a CIA stooge, delayed the vote as long as he could because he knew he didn't have a majority. Meanwhile hundreds of thousands of protesters surrounded the Diet building, whipped up, my father told me years later, by Communist agitators. When the moment for the vote finally came, Kishi had opposition politicians forcibly carried out of the legislative chamber and then he called the vote.

The AMPO Treaty was ratified by a landslide. Kishi signed the treaty.

And even I knew that pissed a whole lot of people off. There were more anti-AMPO protesters now than there had been before the vote. Even way down where we lived, suddenly there were crowds outside the gates of our compound waving banners, and screaming at us, and spitting at our car when we drove in.

After the AMPO vote my father came home and sang "Ghost Riders in the Sky" to me. Then he vanished again.

I was six, and even I knew President Eisenhower was coming next week, Japan was seething, and now there was big trouble over an American couple's missing baby.

The strangest thing was my mother said my father wasn't on TDY. He was here, just hadn't had time to come home. My mother insisted he wasn't gone, he was busy looking for the missing American baby.

Three days after my father disappeared, and sometime before dawn, something woke me up when my father came home with Uncle George. As I think I mentioned, I had two Uncle Georges—regular Uncle George and skinny Uncle George—and I mean now skinny Uncle George, with his pale ecclesiastical face and his slim dark suits, with the stovepipe pants I sometimes still marvel at in photographs.

All I remember with certainty of their apparel that morning is they were wearing suits and they were rumpled. But, as I picture it now, Uncle George's suit is black and my father's is gray, and they're wrinkled all to hell and gone. They haven't shaved or slept. They sit down across from me at the kitchen table.

My father's hands shake as he lights a cigarette.

Teruko shuffles out in her pink terry-cloth robe. It's my mother and me who are wearing kimonos. My mother tells Teruko everything is under control and why doesn't she go back to bed and get some sleep.

One look at my father, though, and you know everything isn't under control.

My mother starts up the electric coffeepot. She sets out place mats. Napkins. Knives. Forks. Spoons. Butter. Apple jelly—my father's favorite. Mine too. What's wrong? I ask my father—but he won't say. He has a sort of crazed look in his eyes. Where have you been, Daddy? Are you all right?

He doesn't speak until my mother set cups of coffee in front of him and Uncle George.

Thanks, says my father.

Thanks, Jean, says Uncle George. Your coffee is delicious as usual.

My mother raises a frying pan over her head like a tennis racket and says she'll have some toast and bacon for them in a few minutes.

What's wrong, Daddy?

He looks up at me, fakes a smile, and says he's just decided it's time for me to drink my first coffee. He gets a cup and pours some for me. Black. Just like his.

Then my mother says Wait!, and swoops in to add cream and sugar.

Okay, now try it, she says. And I do.

As carefully as the Pope's food taster over dinner at the Borgia's, I take a sip. And it is so awful that twenty years will pass before I ever touch another drop of coffee.

We eat bacon and eggs and toast, and I drink Bosco while my father and skinny Uncle George pour down coffee and ignore my questions. Through this whole excruciating parade of manners, I keep trying, but they tell me squat.

Then Uncle George says, Thank you, that was delicious, and goes to the couch and falls asleep.

What's wrong, Daddy?

My father turns to my mother and me, looking like maybe he's ready to let it out. But then for a long moment he's silent. When he finally speaks, he does it quietly, sadly. He says they've just come from digging up the body of the baby. He says for three days the baby's mother claimed her Japanese houseboy ran away with her baby. But then, at two in the morning, the baby's mother had finally confessed to my father: The houseboy was the baby's father; she had smothered the baby and buried it in her garden, so her husband would never see the baby's face grow part Japanese. My father looks away from us and goes on in horror about the digging, about holding the poor baby. It was a boy. He was beautiful. Named Brady. So small, and so blue. A little blue baby.

My father shivers like he has to take a leak, and then his eyes are clearer when he looks at me. He says he's going to have to trust me now to keep all this a secret. Because, if the Communists or the Japanese find out what happened, the whole country is going to blow.

I feel important. I've been allowed into my father's world.

He turns to my mother and says Bill Tharp already has the baby's mother and father on an airplane heading to Honolulu.

Bill Tharp, the Wizard, could make anyone disappear.

I was eleven, and we were in the Rhineland, creeping through fog on the autobahn in our enormous Chrysler, just my father and me, when he told me the Cold War had made Germany the world capital of espionage. "These days, seventy percent of all the intelligence product in the world originates in or passes through Germany," he said. He drove cautiously through the fog. German drivers roared up behind us flashing their lights, then pulled into the passing lane and paused to shake their fists at my father before zooming off. They didn't know who they were shaking their fists at. Of course, I wasn't so sure either. But, when we moved here a month earlier, my mother had proudly told me my father had gotten a promotion, was now the deputy director, and was running every station and every intelligence officer his organization had in Europe and the Middle East.

By then, as clueless as I still was, I did know at least a little about my father's line of work. Including that at some point not long after he'd become an intelligence officer he'd come to specialize in counterespionage—the darkest and most subterranean corner of the thoroughly dark and subterranean intelligence universe. Who would you rather have to spy on? Fat generals and blowhard politicians, or seasoned spies? Counterespionage services don't just catch spies, they also run their own agents, many of whom are tasked with infiltrating enemy intelligence services.

In London, where we'd just moved from, I'd learned from reliable sources that my father was a master practitioner of the essential but often neglected art form known in the intelligence community as "liaison." He built relationships with his counterparts in the intelligence, counterintelligence, and national police organizations of wherever we lived, and with lots of other people he thought he should get to know. He made them friends. Brought them home for dinner. Sent congratulatory notes whenever one of them did something good. Sent flowers to their wives on their birthdays. Took their kids with me to the circus. Sent cases of booze if he couldn't make it to a party. Picked up almost every check.

"Sometimes," my father liked to tell me, "a little diplomacy is required, and that's usually where I step in." There'd never been a time diplomacy between the allied intelligence services was needed more than it was just then.

The Soviets were at the height of their power, and ahead of us scientifically and technologically. They'd launched the first man into space. Yuri Gagarin, a *cosmonaut*. What a cool word, when we first heard it. But how frightening. The Soviets' rocketry was better than ours, and that meant they could deliver nuclear warheads to our great cities and our fruited plains. One of the few things I clearly remember of the four dull years we'd lived back in the States after Japan is the air-raid drills in school in which we were taught to hide under our desks with our heads between our legs, so that—as a big kid in my fifth-grade class liked to assure us—we could all kiss our asses goodbye.

After Gagarin's flight, the Soviets had had the balls to build a wall right across the center of Berlin and then sit there in their tanks with their engines idling, staring at us. And there was nothing we could do about it.

Relations between the American and British intelligence services were at an all-time low. The year before our arrival in London, one of MI5's highest-ranking officers, Kim Philby, had defected to Moscow and announced he'd been working for the Soviets since before he'd joined British intelligence. That same year, there'd been an enormous sex-for-secrets scandal involving a British cabinet member, a showgirl, and a Soviet attaché. The Americans weren't exactly impressed with the British security services, and in our inimitable American way we'd made sure they knew that. Yet we needed to hang together like never before. It was time for a little diplomacy.

From the files—an entry by the director about my father: "He absolutely excels in command relations and in rapport with high-level officials, both foreign and U.S. nationals. This has been extremely beneficial and productive."

In England, our little American house was so cramped we didn't have many dinner guests. So my father usually staged his snake-charming act in clubs and restaurants. But a few weeks before we were to leave for the next stop on our sold-out world tour, he brought his best British friend to our home for dinner.

Sir Ranulph R.M. Bacon was the deputy commander of Scotland Yard. Note that, according to my father, in most intelligence, counterintelligence, and national police services, it's the deputy who actually runs things—because the top man is a political appointee. Note also that, according to my mother, who seemed somewhat agog, Sir Ranulph was the holder of the hereditary title passed down all the way from Sir Francis Bacon. At our front door, Sir Ranulph told me to call him Sir Rasher, like everyone else.

Over dinner, he looked at me and said, "Now, Larry, do you know what your father does? Do you know why you moved to England?" I started to say something, but Sir Rasher interrupted. "The answer is," he said, "your fine father is the first American Ambassador to Scotland Yard."

Extract from the files, dated 19 June 1965: "He has developed particularly outstanding working relationships with British police and security agencies. In doing this, he had to overcome serious difficulties from a marginally effective relationship between his predecessor and these agencies. The effective new U.S.-U.K. cooperation has resulted in greatly improved counterintelligence coverage of our interests in the U.K. and is reflected in the fine results being achieved in counterintelligence operations which require British assistance. The morale of all personnel involved has improved markedly since his arrival."

By the time we arrived in Germany, in the summer of 1965, I knew too that when the CIA was established a few years after the war, several other American intelligence and counterintelligence services had also been formed. The CIA got all the press and the other agencies flew under the radar. No one ever even heard of most of them, and my father told me that was just the way they liked it.

But there were turf wars—between rival American agencies, and between the American and British services, the American and French services, and others who should have been on the same side—but instead spent much of their time deceiving and betraying one another. For deceiving and betraying are what spies do best. When official lines of communication between them grew cold and formal, or broke down entirely, they kept speaking to my father— sharing information, offering advice, talking out of school. And the result, I've been told, was my father had a better grasp of the big picture than almost anyone else. That was why he was moving up in the world.

In Wiesbaden, a small and leafy city on the Rhine, we moved into a big old house with apple trees in the back garden. The day after the movers left, my little brother Billy—seven years younger than me, born in the States the year after we left Japan—and I watched the sweepers search our house for bugs. The men were from my father's new office, and that was the first of many times we would see them at work in this house. Our lives had been fairly relaxed in London. Here we seemed to be on a heightened state of alert.

A few days after we finished unpacking, my father brought home an unexpected guest for dinner. This was my father's old friend Herr Dickopf, who slyly poured me beers, loved my mother's cooking, and smelled slightly of pigs.

Herr Dickopf was a pig farmer, and the president of Interpol. As well as the chief of the Deutsche Bundeskriminalmt, the German equivalent of the FBI. Over dinner, my father told us that, with his fingers on so many controls, Herr Dickopf could prove very handy when it came to getting agents out of jams.

Herr Dickopf came back to see us often. It's called liaison, by God, and if only the President of Interpol would be so kind as to drop by my house here in Florida for dinner and a little liaison every month or so for a while, I'm sure we could work something out. I'd sweep the house for bugs and cameras, make certain no one's listening on the stairs, and after dinner we'd sit beneath the potted palms in the living room and drink and talk.

Eventually I'd get around to mentioning the annoying little matter of the Interpol Red Notice that's been filed against me. Apparently, certain powers that be want to get their hands on me so badly they've invoked their rights as signatories to various Interpol conventions. Now I'm subject to arrest at any border crossing. So I walk the beach. Stalling. Avoiding my interrogators. Listening to the ocean slurping away at the shore. Remembering.

If you look at my current passport, you'll see: no stamps. But if you'll look at this one, United States of America Passport No. Z5122852, issued to me at the United States Embassy in London, you will find 218 entry stamps, from all sorts of interesting places, and all dated within the first seven years after the passport was issued. And that's just half of it. I had a second U.S. passport, also in my name, and also of the tourist variety, which the United States Government, in its wisdom, saw fit to issue so as to aid me in misleading foreign officials regarding the true nature of my travel patterns.

The point is when I arrived here I'd been moving all my life, but I am no more. I spend my days now on the cusp between the ocean and the land—where I find seaweed plastered to my windows after storms and once I found a fish in my front yard, and where last month I saw a palm tree uprooted from the land and floating away on the tide.

Not long after we got to Wiesbaden, my father bought an old gray Volkswagen. He said it was "only transportation" to drive to his office so he could leave our big-finned Chrysler for my mother.

But, recently, while waiting at a bus stop on Hainerberg Hill for nearly half an hour, I'd amused myself by counting cars, as boys will do, and come to the conclusion that about one in every four automobiles on the streets of West Germany was a Volkswagen. Back then there was pretty much only one kind of Volkswagen. The bug—the model co-designed by Adolf Hitler.

My father almost always dressed in quiet clothes. He spoke in clear, even tones, without an accent. My mother told me that, before I was born, he'd worked very hard beating every trace of Georgia out of his voice. Once, back in the States, when I'd asked him to put a bumper sticker on our car like my friends got their fathers to do, my father had said, "That goes against all my training. I don't want anything that draws attention to myself."

It seems to me now that was about the first time my father had ever mentioned his training to me. And that was the end of it. He didn't elaborate then. Though I remember that, years later, when I asked him about that old car, he said, "You want to have a car that blends in. But it also should have plenty of power in reserve in case you need it." He didn't say why it should blend in, or why it might need all that extra power. But that was implicit, and my father never really got explicit about such things.

He got new tires for his Volkswagen and souped up the engine, and it was in that car that one night my father and I drove to Frankfurt to watch Muhammad Ali fight Karl Mildenberger for the heavyweight boxing championship of the world.

The ring was set up outdoors in the middle of a soccer stadium.

Probably, for a time after we arrived and found our seats, my father's eyes never stopped scanning the crowd. Then he settled down to watch the spectacle unfold.

Ali appeared, glowing in his own personal halo as a spotlight followed him down an aisle to the ring. He looked as beautiful and dangerous as a young god. He looked like he knew it, too. After he stepped through the ropes, he got down on his knees in his corner, lifted his gloves to just in front of his face, and prayed. I'd never seen anything like him.

My father and I sat in a crowd of Germans slowly singing *Mil-den-berg-er, Mil-den-berg-er, Mil-den-berg-er, Mil-den-berg-er*—in that wonderful, slow, rhythmic, drunken way they sing at soccer matches. My father sang along with them. I screamed myself hoarse for Ali before the fight even started.

If you were casting a handsome, charming, secretly vicious Nazi spy for your next B-movie, Karl Mildenberger just might be your man. He was the reigning European heavyweight champion; he was left-handed, and one tough German.

Years later, I would hear Ali telling a reporter Mildenberger had a very awkward style and was at the time the slipperiest opponent he'd ever faced. But the night of the fight all I had to go on was my father's commentary. He didn't think much of Ali. Or Clay, as my father called him. As most of my father's men knew, not long after World War II my father was the U.S. Army heavyweight boxing champion.

Referee and judges and fighters introduced. Instructions to the fighters. Touch gloves. Seconds out. Then it began.

Ali shuffled.

Ali swiveled. When Ali got his hips swiveling just right, he could dance around the ring with his hands at his side and nobody could hit him. Every punch missed by half an inch. No need to expend the energy to make them miss by more.

Ali jabbed and flurried.

Ali coasted.

Ali struggled—driving the Germans and my father wild.

Ali taunted them between rounds. They bayed for his blood.

Ali got hit. Hard. Again. Who is this fucker? Ali slipped away. The crowd sang *Mil-den-berg-er, Mil-den-berg-er, Mil-den-berg-er.*

Ali got in trouble in the corner. No room to swivel there.

Ali clowned to mask the symptoms of his distress.

Ali parried. Round after round. The crowd sang on.

Ali charged out and unleashed a jolting right-hand lead.

Ali circled.

Ali saw his moment. Ali flurried.

Ali finally TKO'd Mildenberger in the twelfth round.

As we filed out of the stadium, my father was making fists and rubbing his knuckles the way he did when he started remembering his own time as a boxer. From there, he usually moved on to crouching and throwing soft hooks at me. Then teaching me to cover up and fight back. But not that night.

He put his hands into the pockets of his windbreaker and looked at me with a gleam in his eye.

He said, "I think I could have taken that draft dodger."

He was serious.

I told him he was crazy.

I met this kid named Leonard. My mother wasn't fond of him. But it wasn't because he was Mormon, the first Mormon kid I'd ever known. Leonard was dangerous.

He was almost fifteen. Two years and then some older than me, but he seemed much older, even though we were in the same grade.

Leonard's precociousness was not without precedent in Wiesbaden's American community. As most of my friends knew, it was from the fabled halls of our school, Wiesbaden Junior High, on Hainerberg Hill, that a U.S. Army truck driver by the name of Elvis Presley had a few years earlier plucked a pretty fourteen-year-old eighth grader by the name of Priscilla Beaulieu. She was an Air Force colonel's daughter, and by now she was living in Elvis's mansion in Memphis, under the protection of Elvis's mother, who was helping Priscilla with her Bible studies—or some such unlikely cover story.

One evening Leonard and I went downtown.

First we stopped in the record shop at the bottom of the green hill that flowed down into the city from the American compound we lived in. Right before my eyes—while I was listening to "Norwegian Wood"—Leonard kyped a 45. He slipped it right into his raincoat pocket. If I could see that through the window of the listening booth, why couldn't the salesman, who was closer than I was to Leonard and looking almost right at him? And why was I the only one who was nervous when we left the shop?

I wish I could help you see the Old World charm that was all around us as we made our way through the city. Wiesbaden was a beautiful old spa town, a resort where the Rhine met the green Taunus Mountains on the edge of the wine country. Because Wiesbaden had served mostly as a base for hospitals during the war, it had gone relatively unbombed. Which was why General Eisenhower had made it his headquarters when he arrived in Germany. Unlike nearby Frankfurt and about every other German city I'd seen, Wiesbaden was not still rebuilding.

Leonard and I made our way past the Belle Epoque architecture of the *Kurhaus,* which housed the thermal springs for which kings and princes had been coming to Wiesbaden for centuries, and the *Spielbank,* the casino, where my father did a lot of his liaison work and in which, a hundred years earlier, to the year, Feodor Dostoyevsky had lost three thousand gold rubles on a single spin of a wheel of fortune, wiping him out, and prompting him to speed-write a novel set in Wiesbaden and its casino. That, too, I'd learned in our school. But Leonard wasn't interested in architecture or literature. Just beyond the grand, red *Hauptbahnhof,* the main train station, he led me into a *Trinkhalle.* Germans would sell beer to any kid who could reach the counter with his money. Even to a fourteen-year-old Mormon kid whose parents were so strict they didn't drink caffeine, let alone alcohol.

This was my first time in a bar without one of my parents. Leonard bought us a big brown bottle of beer, popped the swivel cap open, took a swig, and passed the bottle to me.

I took a little sip. Leonard took a long pull. I took a little sip. Leonard took a long pull. Pretty soon the bottle was empty.

Our next stop was an *Apotheke,* where Leonard kyped a little yellow jar.

"What's the Vaseline for?"

"You'll see."

It was getting dark, and we were heading into the neon heart of the city.

Leonard announced we were on our way to the legendary Crazy Sexy.

I'd heard of the Crazy Sexy but wasn't sure what it was. I thought it might be a nightclub. I'd never been to a nightclub. Maybe it was even a strip club. Whatever the Crazy Sexy was, Leonard claimed he'd been there before.

In fact, it was a bordello.

The entrance was in an alley off Mainzer Strasse. Two ladies of the evening were leaning against the wall beside the entrance. A couple of shills were working the door.

I wasn't convinced they were going to let us in.

I wasn't convinced I wanted to go in.

But Leonard was insistent.

He started toward the door.

And just then I saw someone—across the alley, standing in the shadows, as still as an Indian.

I knew him. He was dressed up like a German tonight, but he was American. Worked for my father. I'd seen him around the office.

Had he seen me?

"I'm getting out of here," I said to Leonard, with a note of urgency. Then I left him in that alley and booked all the way home.

And before I got there, a helicopter was circling overhead. I immediately concluded my omnipotent father had received a phone call from downtown, then ordered up a helicopter to follow me, and that he was going to go batshit on me when I got home. But that wasn't so. When I got home, my father was asleep.

I don't think his man even saw me.

What was he doing down there?

Was he on his own time, out to have a little fun? I doubt that.

More likely he was tailing someone, or waiting to meet a source.

Spies see some very unusual places.

My father tried to play golf every weekend he could. But sometimes, when he said he had to squeeze in a little extra work, on our way to the golf club we'd stop for an hour or two at his office—a squat white building which happened to have once been Gestapo intelligence headquarters for the Rhineland.

Inside my father's private office, which was a big room in the very center of the building, and had no windows, I remember an American flag on a wooden staff in the corner. And near that on the wall a photograph of President Johnson.

Behind my father's desk were two tall file cabinets, forged of the same thick battleship-gray steel his safes at home were made of. The front of each drawer had a combination dial on it and above that a T-shaped card hanging through a little metal slot. The cards were made out of the same sort of thick, puffy paper beer coasters were made of. One side of each T-card was green and the other was red. When my father unlocked a drawer, he turned the T-card around and hung it with the red side facing out. Open. The green side meant the drawer was locked and secure. He was meticulous about the T-cards.

On the floor beside the file safes were two steel waste cans. One had no markings, and one was marked BURN BAG.

Atop my father's desk, which was a big gray steel thing, along with three telephones—one of them red with no dial, the other two black with dials and lots of buttons—he kept the cigar box and, beside it, the misshapen, purple kiln-fired ashtray I'd made him in art class in sixth grade in London. Between steel bookends were two books: *Crusade in Europe,* by Dwight D. Eisenhower; and *Masters of Deceit,* by J. Edgar Hoover. Each was inscribed by its author with a note to my father. I have the Eisenhower book now, and no idea what happened to the other one.

On those Saturdays and Sundays, I would sit in one of the visitors' chairs in front of my father's desk with my feet in the other and read *Sgt. Fury and His Howling Commandos* comic books while my father sat across the desk smoking his pipe, smiling at me occasionally, and reading files.

The files were kept in Manila folders, and they don't make 'em like they used to. Back then, a Manila folder wasn't creamy white, it was brown, and it seemed to contain wood chips so large that in places you could still see the grain. And back then, a Manila folder was almost as thick and strong as cardboard.

Most of the pages clamped inside his files were what my father called "flimsies." Grayish-white paper you could see through, even thinner than airmail stationery. As my father read the files, he occasionally underlined a passage with a red grease pencil. He never left the room unless all the T-cards on all the drawers were green. He never let me see inside the files or told me what was in them.

Most of them were marked CLASSIFIED, like the ones I'd seen at home. But my father would sometimes pull files marked SECRET or TOP SECRET out of a safe. Those were somewhat thrilling to me.

One Saturday he let me hold a TOP SECRET file, look at all the rubber stamps, routing marks, and scrawled initials and dates on the folder. But he wouldn't let me open it. One should never underestimate the dogged lengths to which an intelligence officer will go to protect secrets.

But on the particular Wiesbaden Saturday I'm remembering now, I was thirteen, and in my father's office, and had just asked one too many times to see inside a classified file—to be allowed to see just one page of our government's millions of pages of secrets.

"Look," my father snapped at me, "I'm not going to show you, and you are not going to see." He calmed down a little bit. Not a lot. "I swore an oath of secrecy, and that's one reason I'm not going to show you. The other is it isn't safe for you, or several other people you've never even heard of, for you to know what's in these files."

The look in his eyes was fierce. This was a side of my father I'd never seen before, and I remember it made me feel like running out of the room. I don't mean to imply he hadn't been pissed off at me before. But this was different. This was institutional. In a real way, it wasn't just my father getting in my face. The man who sat before me now, leaning across the desk toward me, was speaking on behalf of the entire United States intelligence establishment, which didn't take kindly to kids willing to breach security procedures on a whim.

I realize now what my father said next came from one of his training lectures. For, beyond deceiving and betraying, another thing spies are awfully good at is churning out more spies. And I realize now my father was trying to protect me, not to attack me. But it didn't feel that way then.

"If you ever find yourself across from an interrogator," he said, "demand a lawyer. Even if you know they won't let you have one. Demand him anyway. Demand to eat. To drink. To call your embassy. To see a doctor. Do anything you can to stall. Because I'm a realist and *I* know, if *you* don't know, that eventually you'll tell the interrogators everything you know. That, unless you've stalled long enough to give them a chance, you'll kill every poor agent out there whose name or circumstances you've been allowed to blow."

He leaned toward me. "So it's my job to make sure my own men know as little as possible. No more than what they need to know, and the less the better. That's the way it works around here. So cut this crap, and I don't want to ever again hear you moaning, 'Come on, man, just let me see one secret. Who am I gonna tell? It's not like it's gonna hurt anything.'"

One black-green night which shimmers still in my memory, I was walking blind down the stairs to raid the refrigerator when I heard my father and Herr Dickopf down in our living room quietly saying things they thought no one else could hear.

I stopped, sat down on the stairs in the dark, and listened.

The acoustics weren't great. But the later it got and the more they drank, the louder they talked. That night I learned some very interesting things about Herr Dickopf.

For example, I learned he was an Abwehr officer during the war. Which is to say he used to be a Nazi spy. And forty minutes later—for already I knew the soul of surveillance is patience—I further learned that, in the middle of the war, he'd fled to Switzerland, changed his identity, and sat out the rest of the war dealing in diamonds and gold.

After that, when my father was home and countermeasures were lax, I sat on those stairs—one step below the landing, on the softest spot I could find on the carpet runner—night after night, listening to bedtime stories about my father's secret world.

The primary activities of a counterespionage agency are identifying spies, then either watching them, often while feeding them subtly false intelligence, arresting them, or turning them. Making them your own. Which is often crucial, because one of the best ways to identify spies working against you is to penetrate an enemy intelligence service. But that can get very sticky. Once a man who was your enemy and now professes to work for you goes back amongst your enemies, how can you ever know again who is actually doing what to whom?

From what I heard, apparently, my father spent much of his time analyzing patterns of irregularities to catch spies and saboteurs. And apparently, there were enemy agents operating all around us all the time, and often when you caught one you didn't let him know he'd been caught. There were plenty of things to do instead.

Examples:

You put running tails on him, 24-7.

You liaised with the locals to make sure he wasn't one of *theirs*.

You cross-referenced his K-As and put every one of them under surveillance until you found his midwives.

You read his mail and found his drops.

You traced his money.

And, if he made you, or as soon as he even suspected, you let the bloodhounds pick him up and take him to a quiet place, and then you sent a high priest in to read him Robert's Rules of Order. That way, if he refused to be played back, you just might be able to roll up his whole string. Or, if he was a compromising soul, you could double him, play him back to the other side. That is to say, you could induce him to defect.

Most defections weren't like in spy movies. Usually defectors stayed in place for as long as they could. The moment a Communist government official or military or intelligence officer wittingly provided genuine informtion to a Western intelligence service, he was classified on our books as a defector. The first things we always asked defectors were: Do you know of plans for war against the West, or of Communist spies working in the West? The secondary questions, if time and opportunity allowed, usually concerned order of battle, troop strengths, the status of weapons development and deployment, and political structures—who was really pulling the strings on the other side?

There were soft targets and there were hard targets. There were witting sources and there were unwitting sources. Among the witting sources were disaffected sources, compromised sources, ideologically motivated sources, and financially motivated sources. There were TWXs and there was Commo. There was TOP SECRET and there was SECRET, and before you traded with the host services you'd damn well better double-check to make sure that latest SECRET wasn't SECRET-NOFORN.

I knew the terminology and the grammar years before I understood its meaning and its consequence; some of it I still don't understand. I was crafty and I wasn't dumb, but I also wasn't shaving yet.

There was a tall blond American who'd been to dinner at our house a few times and was the American Air Attaché to Finland. Which meant he was a spy. I was twelve now and no longer appointing honorary uncles, but he would have been a likely candidate a few years earlier.

One night I was sitting on the stairs listening to my father and the attaché talk about routine signals intercepts, and a few nights later I was on the same step listening to my father and another man talk about the attaché. At first, I thought he must've defected. That's how badly they were talking about him.

But then I learned the attaché was not in Moscow but Washington.

And had been flown there in a hurry, along with his wife—just hours after two of my father's men photographed the attaché slow-dancing in a bar in Helsinki.

With a man.

Who also happened to be a Russian talentspotter.

And I never saw the American Air Attaché to Finland again. Those stairs were my education.

One night I listened to my father downstairs drinking hi-balls with his right-hand man Chuck, who my father told me was "the best electronics man in the business."

Chuck had an angelic smile, a flattop, and big muscles. He carried skeleton keys, lockpicks, little screwdrivers, and a tiny soldering iron in his front right pants pocket—where I kept my lunch money. Chuck was always nice to me, and he didn't make me call him Mister, or sir, or anything like that. He let me call him Chuck, like a couple of his kids did too.

When I ran into him, I liked to say, "Here's Chuck, Best Electronics Man in the Business!"

It had a nice ring to it, and sometimes I said it again and again. "Here's Chuck, Best Electronics Man in the Business!" But I would never say that in front of other people unless they were in the know about what sort of business Chuck and my father did. By then, I was already a coconspirator.

Chuck was a Catholic, and the Pope said no rubbers, so he had a lot of kids, and he let us go up into the attic with him and play while he worked on his ham radio. I thought it was just his hobby, but I'm not so sure of that anymore. One day I was heading up to the radio room with my father and Chuck and his son Steve. Chuck and my father had some cans of beer and a church key and were going to sit together while Chuck chatted to people on his radio.

At the door of the radio room, Chuck brought out his keychain and was about to open the door. But I stopped him and said, "How about if you show me how to pick a lock?"

Chuck glanced at my father in a way that meant, Should I?

My father shrugged his shoulders. Why not?

The next thing I expected to see was Chuck doing something cool like in the movies. A flick of the wrist, a shy grin, and the door would open and we would go inside.

What Chuck actually did next was remove all his skeleton keys and lockpicks and lay them out side by side on the floor in front of the door. Then he got down on his knees, complaining that if he'd known he was going to pick a lock, he would've brought knee pads.

At this point, my father told me that normally for a lockpicking operation you would post lookouts at each end of the hall. Because, when you're discovered down on your knees in front of a lock with a tool in your hand, there's not much you could be doing but breaking and entering.

The lock Chuck set to work on was relatively simple. Round tumbler, flat key, teeth on one side only. But if you'll think about every time in your life you've ever had to call a locksmith to help you open a door, you'll probably remember sometimes he got the lock open in a minute or two, and other times he spent maybe twenty or thirty minutes grumbling and assuring you it doesn't usually take him this long. Now consider that professional locksmiths, who open several locks a day, couldn't be any slower at it than intelligence officers, who are only human and don't get nearly as much practice. Ergo: Spy-versus-spy lockpicking isn't like in the movies.

While Chuck kept saying things like "Come to Papa," my father kept telling me Chuck was one of the best lock men he knew. After about ten minutes, Chuck was grinning with victory and he had us inside the radio room without the benefit of a key.

Back to me in the dark in the stairwell, listening. Chuck, the Best Electronics Man in the Business, had just come back from a month of TDY in Turkey. Or at least that's where he'd told me he was going before he left. He and my father were always going to Turkey. We had listening posts there, just across the border from the Soviet Union. It was good to hear Chuck's voice again.

My father said, "Last week, I went to Hungary to bring out a defector. He's a professor who's known me quite a while. He likes me, and he said he would only come out if I went in to get him."

My father paused just long enough to take a drag on his cigarette. "I went by underground railroad," he added, and, when I was sure he wasn't going to say anything more about it, I crept back up the stairs, got back into my bed, and imagined a secret train and a tunnel all the way from Germany to Hungary.

I was thrilled.

And it got even better. I remember I sat straight up in bed when it dawned on me that what my father was actually talking about was something like Harriet Tubman's Underground Railroad, which I'd learned about in history.

When we'd arrived in Germany, some of my new friends' fathers were generals and diplomats, but *my* father was a *spy*. And that was a fact which, once confirmed, had always afforded me a certain measure of prestige in the halls of my junior high school, at Little League practice, and on the golf course overlooking the Rhine—where, on weekdays, I competed ferociously for my friend Scott's allowance and, on weekends, when my father was around, I caddied for him.

My father the spy. None of my friends had ever really understood what that meant, and I hadn't tried to explain it. How could I? No one would've believed that my father was a spy but nothing like the spies in *The Man from U.N.C.L.E.*, every American kid in Germany's favorite television show, which was the latest word on international spy heroes and techniques. Nor that my father was also nothing like the spies in *Goldfinger*. Or *Secret Agent Man,* which everyone was singing that year.

> *There's a man who leads a life of danger.*
> *To everyone he meets he stays a stranger*
> *With every move he makes,*
> *Another chance he takes.*
> *Odds are he won't live to see tomorrow.*
>
> *Secret Agent Man.*
> *Secret Agent Man.*
> *They've given you a number.*
> *And taken away your name.*

As I was painfully aware, my father didn't have a wetsuit or a spear gun. In fact, he wasn't even all that great of a swimmer. How could I tell my friends about things like the dead baby, or that my father's gun didn't have a silencer? They did keep guns with silencers in his office, and I'd shot one. But the truth was silencers weren't even called silencers. They were called suppressors. How could I tell them that, or about the mountains of dull paperwork my father labored his way across almost daily in his office? Would anyone believe me if I told them I had it on good authority from a man who should know that the soul of every intelligence organization is its registry, its files?

I was fairly certain my father couldn't withstand hours or days of torture without breaking. In fact, I could drive him pretty much to the edge of insanity just by scraping the tines of my fork across my plate in a certain way over dinner. I'd never seen a woman like Pussy Galore, nor a shiny silver Aston Martin DB5 with a bulletproof rear window, passenger-side ejector seat, and machine guns. In fact, the car I'd scientifically deduced was my father's spy car was a 1951 battleship-gray Volkswagen that looked like hell but could fly like the wind. No one I knew would've believed a word of the truth—until this. *My father! Smuggled across the Iron Curtain! And back! By partisans, at great danger to themselves and him—especially given that he couldn't speak a word of Hungarian and could barely get a waiter to bring him a beer in German—to keep an appointment with a defector!* That night in my bed, it hurt really badly when I finally realized I couldn't tell a soul. And I haven't ever since. Until you.

Owing to severe limitations placed on my forward listening post in the stairwell by several operational factors—including an inexperienced case officer with no direct supervision, budgetary constraints that precluded use of sophisticated recording equipment, acoustical challenges within the target site, and the absence of anyone to spell me when I got bored or my butt got numb—my collection product was sporadic at best. Vital clues were often missed entirely or not recognized until too late. I got shards of information, little pieces of a puzzle, but never saw the whole picture.

I know now that the same could be said of almost any front line intelligence operation ever mounted anywhere. The information is almost always incomplete. The files are almost always ripe with code names and other obliquities no one has yet deciphered. But I didn't know that then, and I was frustrated as hell that I could never quite get to the bottom of a story from beginning to end.

The closest I ever came began one night when I heard my father unlock the front door, and then the unmistakable voice of Father Saxby—our young rector at Saint David's, which was the Episcopal church we attended down on the Pfalzerstrasse. Was he one of my father's men? They were talking very quietly.

"Thanks for waiting up for me." I acolyted for Father Saxby on certain Sundays. I knew both his pulpit voice and his whisper voice. He was always whispering instructions to my friend Scott and me when we screwed up. There was no mistaking Father Saxby that night.

"What's going on?" said my father.

"Well, I really don't know what to do." After that, a long pause. My father could wait out anyone's long pause. Finally, Father Saxby said, "One of my parishioners has come to me and confessed. He's an American serviceman. Stationed at the base. He's got a wife and children. But he's also got himself a German girlfriend, who's pregnant. But that's not all he came to confess to me about. He told me, as his priest, that the German woman had come to him and threatened to go to his wife and tell her everything unless he got her certain information she wanted about his work. This German woman works for a company in Mainz. But he's decided she's an East German agent. Of course, he didn't decide that until after he'd given her information. Not just once but twice. And some documents. Then she disappeared. And part of me wants to turn him in," said Father Saxby, "but the other part of me knows that would be a violation of my vows."

Like every true spy story, this one was fundamentally a tragedy. Father Saxby's choice was simple: to serve my country or serve my God, to betray my father or betray myself. Spying is an exercise in betrayal. It's that simple.

Father Saxby was as torn as I'd ever heard anyone. He believed in America, but he also believed in the sanctity of confession. He was talking to my father like a penitent to a Father Confessor. I am in trouble, Father. What do I do?

For my father, that was easy: Betray your priestly vows, and tell me who it was and exactly what he did. My infinitely pragmatic father could become direct and blunt in an instant. But he didn't that night. His response to Father Saxby was delivered only after a long quiet pause for calculation, and was so subtle and nuanced I couldn't fully appreciate it until years later when I was introduced myself to the black art of elicitation.

The first thing of note was that my father spoke not to Father Saxby but to Harry. He made him a human rather than a priest who'd taken vows. He did everything he could to distance Father Saxby from priestly considerations, such as the centuries-old tradition of the church as a place of sanctuary. None of that aided my father's position, so he transformed Father Saxby into Harry. And not just Harry, but little Harry. He talked to him like a father would talk to his son.

And this, too, was calculated. For what the unlucky parishioner almost certainly didn't know when he chose to confess to his priest was that his priest was the son of William Saxby, the legendary big-city police commissioner and law-and-order man.

"Listen, Harry," my father said, "I think you know what you have to do. But if you don't feel comfortable, go home and think about it and come back here tomorrow night and we'll talk again."

The next night I was ready to man the stairwell upon Father Saxby's return. But he didn't come.

He did, however, on the following night. Whereupon my father welcomed him like a lost son. Took him to the couch, fussed over him, finally asked him if he'd made a decision. That night Father Saxby said very little. But I heard the crinkle of a paper as he passed it to my father. Exactly what was on the paper I don't know, and that's some of the middle part of the story I'm missing—that and whatever Harry Saxby went through between his visits to our house. Almost certainly the paper contained the identity of an American serviceman who'd betrayed his family and then his country; perhaps there were other details too. I heard the paper crinkling again as my father opened it, read it, then folded it and put it into one of his pockets. My father said, "You've done the right thing." Father Saxby left quietly.

A couple Sundays later, in between acolyting two services in a doubleheader, I ate breakfast in the rectory with Father Saxby and his wife. "It's a German Farmer's Breakfast," Mrs. Saxby said brightly, just after I'd raved about it like my mother had taught me to do. I remember there were eggs and lots of potatoes, and I remember sitting there as we ate it, thinking, *They don't know what I know,* and that made me feel good.

A Saturday morning. My father announced we were all going to climb into the Chrysler and drive down to Dachau. Oh, won't that be fun.

My little brother Billy was five now, a year older than I was when my mother took me to see Hiroshima. But apparently Billy still wasn't cleared for the full horror tour, with visual aids, my father had in store for me. It was probably by prearrangement that, when we parked outside the Dachau Concentration Camp Memorial, my mother took off with Billy, saying they would meet us inside later. But it could have just been my mother sensing my father's mood.

He stayed with me in the front seat of our car.

I have a feeling the next thing he did was take a nip from the hammered silver flask he sometimes took to football games. That would make sense, and something tells me it happened. But I have no concrete memory of it. What I do remember with certainty is my father going to the trunk of the car and bringing out a wrinkled grocery sack. That was back when grocery sacks were brown paper. Beside me again in the car, he pulled an old black photo album from the sack.

When Dachau was liberated by the U.S. Army in April 1945, my father was a Counter Intelligence Corps officer working out of G-2 headquarters in Paris.

He was a very young colonel and didn't want that to draw attention to him when he got to Dachau on the morning after it was freed. So he wore the silver bar of a first lieutenant and the insignia of the 42nd Infantry Division when he drove into the camp.

"I was the first trained investigator on the scene here," my father told me in our car. 'There would be an official investigation soon enough. But we wanted to know right away what happened here, and if there were any assets we needed to move."

He handed me the photo album and said it was mine now and to bring it with us.

I didn't open it.

I could tell he wanted me to wait until we got inside the camp. By the time we got out of the car, he was already starting to lose it.

He had, he told me later, intended to give me a thorough guided tour.

Most of the prisoners' barracks and other buildings had been removed, and where'd they'd been were now memorials and lawns. He managed to tell me where a few buildings had been, and he opened the album and pointed some of the missing landmarks out to me. But this was the first time he'd been back here.

Once we started to look at the small black-and-white pictures of piles of naked corpses and of my father, young and handsome in a uniform, amongst living men who looked like skeletons, most of his sentences just fell away because he couldn't finish them.

The crematorium was still there, and in the same building a gas chamber disguised as showers. We went into the showers, and my father didn't say a word.

I wandered into the crematorium by myself. The ovens were open and empty. They were shiny clean now. *Sauber.* Just like Germans like to keep things. I wanted to stay awhile, to think about what happened there. But when my father arrived and saw the ovens, he turned and walked straight out. He looked so bad that I went after him.

He walked trembling past the end of the crematorium building, made a point of detouring to pass through the gate that lied *Arbeit Macht Frei,* in curling wrought iron, and then went straight to our car. These were unspeakable sights and memories. And, indeed, from the moment he saw the ovens, my father didn't speak.

In his photographs, which I have in front of me now, the ovens are caked with soot and stuffed with ashes and charred bones. In this one, in the oven on the right, you can make out an entire rib cage intact atop hundreds of other bones.

And, on the next page, in the photograph on the top right, I can't stop staring into the face of the tall man posing for my father in front of the gallows. What's he thinking? He's still wearing his striped prisoner pants, which are too tight and too short. And that's an Eisenhower jacket he's wearing, with all the insignia removed. I believe someone's given it to him to keep him warm. Just in front of him, and he's staring down at it, is the stool they made you climb onto and then they kicked out from under you after they put your head into the noose. What's he thinking? I've come up with twenty different answers to that.

I remember heading back inside to fetch my mother and brother. I don't remember who drove home. But I do remember the rush of relief we felt almost an hour up the autobahn when my father finally said something. Something inconsequential, but speech nonetheless. After that, the rest of us weren't afraid to talk.

By the next day my father seemed to be back to normal. Singing to himself and everything. But the record shows within a fortnight he amended his last will and testament, adding this instruction: *Under no circumstances is my body to be cremated.*

A few weeks after Dachau, word floated up through the stairwell that we were moving temporarily to Berlin. Why, my father never told me. The only intelligence I could glean on the subject, during an intensive debriefing of my mother, was my father was going to have to be in Berlin on TDY almost constantly the next month or two for something important, and he'd decided to take us with him.

We moved into a two-bedroom apartment in the high-security American military compound at Tempelhof, hard beside the runways the American and British air forces had used to break Stalin's Berlin Blockade just after the Second World War. We were in a big, crowded city now. Living a few floors up. I remember long views out our windows.

It was in those temporary quarters, over breakfast on the morning after we arrived, that my mother told me my father's greatest fear now was that I would be abducted by someone hoping to trade me and my life for my father and the secrets he knew. We were eating pancakes or French toast. I'm not sure which. But it had to be one of them. Because I remember that when she told me, I spent the next minute or two staring at a bottle of Log Cabin maple syrup and trying to appear totally unconcerned.

Believe me, just being in the American Sector of West Berlin at the height of the Cold War surrounded by barbed wire and hordes of goose-stepping East German troops, just passing Checkpoint Charlie on the morning we arrived, just knowing my father was there to spy, had been exhilarating enough. Now this.

My father had been telling me for years to study hard and get good grades because the KGB had copies of every one of my report cards going back to kindergarten. "In fact," he liked to tell me, "you can be sure by now the Russians have got a file on you that's three feet thick." I used to say, you're kidding, right? He'd always said, no, he was serious, and eventually I'd known he was telling the truth. But there was a big difference between knowing you were being studied from afar and learning you might be abducted.

Berlin was tense. Everyone was on alert.

When the crew-cut American sweeper who'd searched our apartment for bugs this morning left, he'd said he'd be back the next day, and every day, to do the same thing.

Even Mr. Potter, our little black dog, was nervous. He sat at my feet, staring at me and refusing to take a piece of bacon out of my hand.

I felt like screaming, so I did.

"What are you talking about?" I screamed at my mother.

She spoke to me in the tones she reserved for calming. "You are one of your father's biggest vulnerabilities," she told me. "You and your brother, because he loves you both. The fear is that, if the other side got your father, he wouldn't cooperate. But if they got you or your brother, your father would do almost anything—he'd defect, he'd tell all his secrets, to save you."

I thought about that. I thought about being spirited under the wall, locked in some grubby cell somewhere with no comic books, and made to eat the lymph-node sausages my father had assured me were a Soviet culinary specialty.

The moral of my mother's story was be very careful. And from then on, she informed me, I was to have a plainclothes policeman accompanying me whenever I left the American fortress of Tempelhof without my father.

I stewed all day.

One thing I was fairly certain of was I was going to be the only American kid in West Berlin not allowed to take the cool tour of East Berlin all the other kids raved about. You got to go right through Checkpoint Charlie in a bus, stare at bloodthirsty East German soldiers, sometimes even evil Russians, and see just how crappy life was for the poor slaves who lived in the Worker's Paradise on the other side of the Wall.

Worrying about missing the tour was better than worrying about being abducted. But when my father got home—before he'd even put down his keys, which was always the first thing he did when he got home—I asked him if what my mother had said was true, if he was seriously afraid I might be kidnapped.

My father became very still for a moment. He turned away. Then turned back and looked at me as sadly as if I'd already been drugged and taken away.

"Yes," he said. "And if that happened, I'd be flown straight back to Washington, and I wouldn't be allowed to help you."

One gray spring afternoon a few days later, my father took me to the British Sector. He walked me through the Tiergarten and the KaDeWe department store and various streets and alleys, while he taught me to turn as if I'd lost my way and scan the crowd, the whole crowd first, before any individuals, and while he showed me how to maneuver myself into settings where even I'd be able to spot the two East Germans—a farm boy in a suit and an old gray hag—who it eventually became quite clear to me were following us.

"Those are just the ones who want to be seen," my father told me. "There are more. Always assume there are more."

That evening, back in our apartment after he mixed himself a hi-ball, he showed me how easy it was to bug a telephone, or a room. Back then, the smallest bugging devices were about the size of ladybugs. My father pulled a few out of his pocket and let me hold one. He said it was a microphone and radio transmitter all in one. Then he showed me where to look for bugging devices before talking openly in a room. If you remember how big most batteries were back then, you'll understand why, in those days, it wasn't as easy as in the movies to conceal a bugging device. It had to either be installed within something from which it could draw electrical current—such as a lamp or an electrical receptacle or a telephone—or it had to have a huge battery wired to it wherever it was planted.

"From now on," he said, looking at me over the top of his bifocals, "you'll be well served if for the rest of your life you assume every telephone call you ever take part in is monitored, and every piece of mail you receive has been intercepted and read before you read it."

Sometimes my mother was even cagier than my father. There was, she now revealed, historical precedent right in our own family for why I should be concerned. This was when she finally told me about my older brother's folly.

All these years, he'd remained the perfect son in every report I'd heard. And since the first time I could remember actually seeing him, he'd done nothing to dispel my belief he could do amazing things I'd never be able to match.

That first sighting was in Colorado. During our first visit there after Japan. My mother and father and I were staying with my aunty Aleen and uncle Watt in their big white house. Probably Aleen was yelling at Watt, or had within the hour. Probably Watt was dreaming of snow and indoor rifle practice. I remember I was excited because I was going to see my brother in person, instead of just seeing him in the photographs my parents had always kept around our house like little shrines.

I was sitting with Aleen and Watt downstairs. My mother and father were upstairs taking naps.

My brother announced his arrival by buzzing the top of the house in the airplane he'd just flown up from Kansas.

The chandelier started tinkling. "There's Jerry," announced Aleen. Jerry being my much-celebrated older brother.

By the time we made it outside, he'd climbed to about three hundred feet and was flying in tight circles over the house. He waved his wings at us when he saw us on the front lawn.

The first parts of him I actually saw were his arm, as it came out of a window on the side of the cockpit, and his face, to the extent it wasn't hidden behind his aviator sunglasses.

There was something in his hand, and he dropped it.

A little white parachute opened and started floating down toward the other end of the lawn.

My mother and father were with us now.

"It's for you, Larry," said my mother. "Run and get it."

I did. I ran all over hell and back under it, because the winds kept shifting.

Finally it came down on the other side of a fence and next to the barn where CB the palomino lived.

It was a chute he'd made with a big white handkerchief and some cord, and then attached it to an army-green canvas bag. In the little bag, once I got the zipper open, I found a tangerine, a new football, and a note from my brother saying he was early because he was so anxious to see me, and could I please tell someone to pick him up at the airfield.

He'd forgotten I couldn't read his loopy writing. So I didn't know what it said until my father read it to me. Then my father added, "The kid sure knows how to make an entrance," and we all went off in the car to get my brother. Nothing had really changed since then. He was still perfect.

All of which has nothing to do with my older brother's encounter with the KGB. Except that it makes clear why, when my mother told me about it, it came as a glorious surprise.

"He did *what*?" I said.

I made her repeat every detail.

It was in Denver. Three or four years before I was born.

My mother and father weren't married yet, but they would be soon. Jerry was my mother's son, and technically only my half brother. My father adopted him when my parents got married.

For one of Jerry's junior high school classes, my mother said, he was assigned to write a report on a country that interested him. He chose Russia. And, not satisfied with the information he could dig up in the library, he wrote a letter to the Soviet Embassy.

Now, the exact contents of his letter are debatable. But, whatever he said, apparently he laid it on a bit thick. Because, when my grandmother answered a knock on her front door one fine Denver afternoon, she found two men from the Soviet Embassy on her doorstep asking for my perfect brother.

"Why?" asked my grandmother.

"He wrote us and said he wants to defect," said one of the Russians.

My grandmother called the FBI.

My brother barricaded himself in the basement and waited with his BB gun.

The FBI arrived.

An international stare-down commenced.

Eventually the Russians beat it.

My brother swore he only asked for information to help with his school project. My brother will also swear to this day that this had nothing to do with my father.

Personally, I doubt the Soviet Embassy in Washington sent out two-man teams to assist every kid around the country who wrote them requesting help with his homework.

"What you're saying," I said to my mother, "is 'Jerry screwed up.'"

"Yes," said my mother.

"Oh, yeah," said my father. "He screwed up *royally.*"

I liked my distant brother, the fallen god, better already.

"So, you see," said my mother, "you really should take this quite seriously. You're going to have to be very careful."

I tried. But, after a few days, I just wasn't worried by the fact that someone might try to kidnap me. I had a German policeman with me whenever I left Tempelhof without my father. I felt safe when I stared across the Wall at the Brandenburg Gate and at Unter den Linden and wondered what it was like on the other side.

Everyone knew the Wall was there to keep East Germans from escaping to the West. But the official Communist explanation was the Wall was necessary to keep decadent Western influences out of East Germany.

I thought it was only a Cold War, like the one they advertised in the newspapers. Tank battalions, fighter squadrons, and legions of soldiers massed on both sides of the border. Always on alert. But not fighting a war. I didn't know then that all across Germany, East and West, for the intelligence and counter-intelligence services at work there, it was as real as war could get. That the Stasi had been abducting agents, kidnapping them in the West and holding them or killing them in the East. I thought all the fuss was silly.

But I've never heard of anyone else doing what I soon did.

While we lived there, my mother had to have a hernia operation. When she was eighteen, her father had died a few hours after what should have been a routine appendectomy. So, whenever anyone in our family was going to go under anesthetic, she gave us marvelous frightening speeches and we all said poignant farewells—just in case.

My father had never learned much about how to take care of Billy and me. But the night before our mother's surgery all he needed to do was take us out to dinner and then let us sleep in the same bed with him. I fell asleep worrying that the next day my mother was going to die, and then, from somewhere in the darkness behind me I heard a voice and someone running after me and I knew I was being abducted. Then a hand clamped down on my shoulder.

"Larry! Larry! *Larry!* Wake up!" my father said, and I did, and found I was on the sidewalk a hundred yards from our building, in my pajamas, running barefoot up a little hill toward a glowing streetlamp, and I had no idea why. My father led me back into the building, and upstairs and into bed.

Anyone can sleepwalk, but it takes the son of a spy to sleep*run*.

Perhaps the submerged fear was the key to the wild joy that gripped me out on the streets by day. What I felt when my father or the detectives drove me around showing me the sights was pure fascination, the way only a boy can feel fascination. I have a clear memory of standing at Checkpoint Charlie with a detective blowing on his coffee beside me, while I stared across the divide at an observation tower and the East German border guard atop it who was stand-ing perfectly upright and perfectly still and had his giant binoculars trained— I was quite sure—on me. My heart was pounding, but I remember trying to act cool.

Between me and the East Berlin I wanted to visit were a wall, tank traps, barbed wire, land mines, and border guards with orders to shoot to kill. Mean-while, ever since President Kennedy had said *Ich bin ein Berliner,* it had been the stated policy of the United States of America that we would defend the freedom of West Berlin with nuclear weapons if necessary. The stakes were apocalyptic and I knew it, and I was thrilled at the sight of any evidence of what was really going on.

My father showed me an apartment building that happened to be right on the boundary of the Soviet Sector, so the Russians had bricked up all the doors and windows and strung barbed-wire entanglements all over the roof, and the building itself had become a section of the Wall. When it came time to go, I didn't want to leave. I could've stared at that building forever. But I forgot all about it when my father drove me to another place beside the Wall and showed me a rusted iron door he said had once been the entrance to a tunnel used by our agents sneaking into the East.

Berlin was riddled with tunnels. Wherever you went, there were always new rumors you would hear about brave East Germans tunneling under the Wall to freedom. My father showed me a couple places he said it had actually happened. But he didn't tell me about the Berlin Tunnel of all Berlin tunnels.

It began in the Rudow neighborhood of the American Sector, only a cou-ple of hundred yards from the Soviet Sector, East Berlin. In a Rudow field, a new building, ostensibly a U.S. Army Quartermaster facility, was constructed. Once the building was up, tunnelers moved into the basement and began ex-tending a passageway toward the Soviet Sector.

Eventually the tunnel extended about five hundred yards. And, when the Americans were directly under their target, a Soviet military communications trunk, they quietly built a tap chamber, filled it with amplifiers and tape recorders and desks and coffee machines, and then tunneled upward to within a yard of the Soviet landlines. The whole operation was so secret that few in American intelligence had even been briefed on it. Still, the CIA decided to hand over the last yard of the job to the British Secret Intelligence Service, because SIS technicians were thought to be more likely to be able to actually make the tap without detection. An irony, that was. Because when the British were brought in, the tunnel was betrayed to the Soviets by a senior SIS officer. George Blake—who was one of the Cambridge ring of spies, a KGB agent.

But the CIA didn't know that, nor did the SIS. They tapped into twelve hundred communications channels, of which, on average, about five hundred were in use every moment throughout the eleven months the tunnel was operational. The take was enormous: four million hours of tape-recorded Soviet military telephone conversations. A gold mine, or so the CIA and its secret sharers, the SIS, believed.

Until Blake fled to Moscow and a Soviet defector informed the CIA that Blake had betrayed the tunnel even before it was completed. It became the conventional wisdom that the intelligence gathered through the tunnel was disinformation. That is, that the Soviets, knowing the lines were tapped, had used them to pipe bullshit directly into the West. Probably that was what my father believed while we were in Berlin.

But it's since emerged that the truth was even more Byzantine than that, and makes clear just how far rivalries between supposedly allied intelligence services can go. Upon receiving Blake's report, the KGB decided they'd rather protect their agent than warn the GRU, Soviet military intelligence. It wasn't KGB lines that were compromised, after all, it was GRU lines and other Soviet military lines. Sometimes a little diplomacy's required, and apparently there wasn't much of that between the KGB and the GRU. It was good intelligence, not disinformation, which flowed through the CIA's Berlin Tunnel.

I still don't know why we went to Berlin. Nothing I picked up in the stairwell afforded me a clue, and none of the few files of or about my father in my possession even mentions his temporary posting there. The Freedom of Information Act requests for documents relating to my father's career I've made to various governmental agencies have resulted in nothing more than polite letters concluding with phrases such as "This letter constitutes a denial of your request for information." I'm not going to push it. I'm in no position to push things right now.

I've satisfied myself with the answer that we moved to Berlin because moving was what we did. We moved constantly. I realize now that was part of a pattern I never broke on my own. In all my life, until I arrived on this beach, I'd never lived in the same place for more than three years.

I've finally seen how all the moving affected me in other ways as well. I feel at home almost anywhere. I pick up accents and languages. I adapt. I change shape, depending on where I am or who I'm with. And ever since I was a child, I've been up for almost anything. I close my eyes and look back on the night we left Berlin.

My mother and Billy and I were to travel by train through East Germany to the West.

My father had already flown from Tempelhof to Frankfurt, where he would meet us. For some reason, it had been deemed more secure for us to travel by train than by plane. And for us to travel without my father. I didn't understand the logic of that then. But I do now, and it isn't pretty. We were separated so that, if the Soviets or their friends happened to get us, my father wouldn't be there to trade himself for us.

No one had tried to snatch my brother or me in Berlin. So all this hubbub seemed a bit much. Still it felt cool to have West Berlin detectives drive us to the Bahnhof in a panel van with more Polizei right behind us in an unmarked car and to be whisked into the station and handed over to an American security team. I learned later there was more going on than I'd been told—that my father's organization had received intelligence that, as the next escalation in the intelligence war going on all around me, the Stasi might take a child of an American intelligence officer to serve as a bargaining chip or a sacrifice. And that, with that, Billy and I had become logical targets and jumped onto all the watch lists. But at the time it just seemed like a game to me.

On our way through the station, I turned suddenly and patted my pockets, like I'd forgotten something, and scanned the whole crowd first before focusing on any individuals. No one besides our own guards seemed to react to this. As far as I could tell, we were clear.

Somewhere toward the front of a long green train belonging to the United States Army and crowded with American troops and dependents, my mother and Billy and I had our own car, which we were not allowed to leave. The train pulled out a minute or two after we got on, and I remember that as the posters outside my window began to move I realized how much I would miss the exhilaration of just being in divided Berlin.

My mother had made us a picnic and we were eating dinner when we passed out of West Berlin and rolled through Potsdam, in the German Democratic Republic. I was finally on the other side of the Wall—which didn't just cut Berlin in half; it surrounded West Berlin.

We were carrying flag orders, written in English, French, and Russian and signed by the Commandant of the Berlin Brigade of the U.S. Army. That morning my father had told me the papers asserted our right to travel by rail without let or hindrance through the Soviet Zone of occupied Germany. There wasn't a word of German on our papers, and my father said, while that wasn't very practical, it was a political statement. Because, as a conquered nation, the East Germans technically had no authority over American troops or officials anywhere in Germany.

"So, as a matter of protocol," he said, "if there's a challenge to an American military train, it's the Russians who board. Never the East Germans." He paused. "Don't sweat it. You'll be fine. Even if the Soviets board your train tonight, our guards *will not* let them into your car."

Our guards were from the U.S. Army, but tonight they were wearing civilian clothes and black leather jackets. They stayed with us until we were settled in our car and then sat just out of our view, on the other sides of the inner doors at each end of the car.

We rode through the dark without stopping for nearly three hours. About all there was to see were shuttered railway stations we passed through and occasionally the headlights of automobiles lined up waiting to cross the tracks.

One of the first things you noticed when you moved to Berlin was that, at night, West Berlin was lit up like a Christmas tree while East Berlin was nearly dark.

As we pulled into Marienborn, I suddenly realized why.

Somehow it had become part of East Germany's Five-Year Plan to divert every kilowatt of electricity and every incandescent bulb and fixture not absolutely necessary in East Berlin to be deployed instead at the railway border checkpoint at Marienborn. It was just after midnight, but outside it was as bright as day.

When our brakes began to squeal, I saw tall fences, concrete guard towers, and searchlights—and two Soviet officers leaning against a wall smoking cigarettes. I knew they were Russians because they were dressed in the same uniforms I'd seen pictures of Yuri Gagarin wearing when he got a medal from Khrushchev. They soon slid out of view, and eventually we stopped in the middle of a glowing cloud of concertina wire and blinding lights.

I looked closely at our surroundings, at the tight loops of razor-sharp wire billowing around and over the top of the train, at the thirty-yard-wide stretch of minefield I could make out through the first two waves of wire, at the electrified fence beyond the mines, and I knew we'd come to rest in the very center of the Iron Curtain.

On both sides of the train, East German soldiers with machine guns and shepherd dogs and big rolling mirrors walked along slowly, checking under and between the cars for defectors.

This was exciting as hell, but routine, and I'd been told to expect it.

When they'd finished their inspection, three East German soldiers stood right below the window at which I was standing. Their guns were slung over their shoulders and they were wearing the uniform of the East German border guards—complete with shiny black boots pulled over their pants and reaching almost to their knees. Just the look for goose-stepping. A couple of them had acne, and seemed not much older than me.

They looked up at me for a moment, then stepped back a few yards to get a better look at the car. Our guards were out of sight. My mother and Billy were asleep in a little cabin. To the three enemy soldiers who were passing around a cigarette and watching me watch them, it looked like I was the only one in the car. I'd been told not to open a window, but I did. I'd never been good at following my father's instructions not to touch his gun when he left it in his sock drawer, either.

I stuck my head out and looked left and right. There were no Soviets in sight. The next-closest East German soldiers were about forty yards away, and walking beside the train with their backs to us. The three outside my window had no dog and they looked like nice enough guys. I could tell they were trying to keep their faces blank, but then one of them broke into sort of an ironic grin. I smiled.

And then something in me made me pick up the *Stars and Stripes* newspaper I'd already read, open it, put a *Time* magazine, a couple comic books, and a Baby Ruth bar inside, fold them all into one tight package, and then drop it out the window. One of the soldiers was already on his way to pick it up when I smiled again, quietly shut the window, and then sat down innocently in a corner where no one could see me—thus concluding my first covert political operation.

Years later, when Miles Copeland heard that story, he told me it only confirmed his suspicion that I was a natural-born propagandist.

1968 was the year we orbited the moon, and I was back in the States to watch it.

Three American astronauts read to us all from the Bible, live on television, while circling our nearest neighbor. "*In the beginning God created the heaven and earth,*" they began, and when they finished the scripture they delivered a message of peace to everyone down on earth. It was night in America, and it was when we watched the stark gray pictures of the surface of the moon sweeping by that we knew for sure we'd finally pulled ahead of the Communists in the Space Race. The Soviets were busy with other things that year, such as rolling their tanks across Czechoslovakia to crush the Prague Spring.

American network coverage of the Space Program was miles better than we'd gotten in England and Germany. During our four years Stateside after Japan, I'd watched every one of the Project Mercury launches live, and every splashdown and recovery, because my mother knew I loved it and let me stay home from school to watch television whenever there was going to be a launch or a landing. My space reporter of choice was Jules Bergman of ABC, and it wasn't hard to convince my mother I could learn more from him in a couple of hours than I could in a whole day of school. My mother had always believed in getting me out into the world "to see the things that are important."

During our three years in Europe, I'd missed every launch, and every spacewalk and reentry, of the Gemini Program. We'd seen bits and pieces of footage on the evening news and pictures in the newspapers, but nothing live, and nothing like the wall-to-wall TV coverage I'd come to expect back in the States watching the Space Program and the assassination of our President, followed two days later by the assassination of his purported assassin.

We moved home to the States just in time for me to watch coverage of the assassinations of Martin Luther King and Robert Kennedy, and of the night men first saw the dark side of the moon. Other than that, living back in the States was boring compared with living in exotic places surrounded by intrigues and Communist hordes. It'd felt the same way when we lived in the States after Japan, and then we'd gone back out into the real world beyond

America's borders. Something in me expected that soon my mother and father and Billy and I would be shipping out again. We'd be living thousands and thousands of miles from the protected shores of the United States, having adventures, seeing exotic things, and maybe we'd be kidnapped by Communist agents or torn to bits by an angry Japanese mob. I never expected it to end.

It wasn't that I hadn't been told, when we moved from Germany to the States, that we were going home for what was to be my father's last assignment before retirement. It just didn't ring true—probably, among other reasons, because we didn't even really have a home to go to. My uncle Watt had sold his gun scope company and his place in Colorado. I had no vision of where we would go after we moved out of our new government-owned mock-Tudor two-story house in Virginia, and I surely didn't put much thought into it. I was caught up in the small details of daily life. School. Homework. Baseball practice. Trying to save enough money to buy *The White Album*. Making new friends. My father was a spy and he was about to retire, but that was just another fact. Like wallpaper you've lived with for so long you don't even notice it anymore.

As always when we arrived in a new locale, my father dove into his liaison work. A river of spies flowed past our dining room table, and it seemed like half my old uncles came to dinner at least once during our first few months in Virginia. Uncle George came over all the time. Not the skinny one who worked for my father in Japan and came home with him on the morning of the dead baby. My other uncle George. My favorite uncle of all.

Technically, Uncle George wasn't even a spy. But we didn't hold that against him because his wife, my aunty Simone, was a spy—a highly decorated French Resistance operative, who'd fought alongside men in battle while dressed as a man, then she'd been recruited and trained for espionage and given the most dangerous job of all, radio operator. And how had she managed to transmit vital messages to the Free French and their leaders in exile in London without being caught by the Nazis who were constantly hunting radio operators? She was just a girl then, only twenty, but she smuggled a radio into the attic of the school building the Gestapo had made their area headquarters, and sent Morse code from there. The Gestapo never found out, because when their radio-detection trucks triangulated on their own building, they assumed the transmitter was one of their own.

Uncle George was a pilot not a spy, though he'd once lived for months with the French Resistance while they hid him like a secret treasure and slowly moved him northward across enemy lines to the Allies. My father had known Aunty Simone and Uncle George since the war, which to them could only mean the Second World War. Uncle George had managed to drop in for dinner with us at least once in every place on earth we'd ever lived.

Now he was about to retire too. He was still a fighter pilot, but he didn't actually do much flying anymore. Just enough to keep his hours up. He'd recently been made the Base Commander of Andrews Air Force Base. My father told me that was a high honor, traditionally awarded to an outstanding Air Force colonel as his last tour of duty. Part of the job was to see the President off each time he took off from Andrews in Air Force One and greet the President each time he landed there. The problem with this was he wasn't exactly a fan of our President, Lyndon Johnson.

"In fact, Larry," Uncle George said one night over dinner, "the President wouldn't know it—because I'm an Air Force officer and he's the commander-in-chief, so I show him perfect respect—but I can't stand the son of a bitch."

"Oh, George!" my mother said. "That's just because you're such a Republican."

"No, it's because he's such an asshole," Uncle George said. "Last month, they sent us this nice young steward from Ohio. Twenty-one years old, and just out of tech school, and such a great kid that for his first assignment as a steward they sent him straight to Air Force One.

"On the kid's first day on the plane," Uncle George went on, "I was right behind the President heading down the aisle, and the kid was just beaming with pride. He stepped up, introduced himself to the President, said how much he admired him and what an honor it was to be able to serve him. Then he stuck out his hand to shake the President's hand, and do you know what the son of a bitch did?" Uncle George didn't wait for an answer. "The President looked at that poor young steward and said, 'Get the fuck out of my way!'"

It had a certain admirable directness and simplicity. To this day, it remains my favorite Presidential quote. I was only fourteen, but I was six-one and I'd noticed adults were starting to swear a hell of a lot more in front of me. Which was a good thing, all in all. What I craved most at that age, I think, was raw intelligence, unfiltered information about life and what it was like to be and think like an adult. Myself, I'd always liked LBJ.

While NASA made its final plans to land a man on the moon, my father kept up his liaison rounds. When he wasn't bringing people home for dinner, he was visiting embassies and government agencies, catching up with old friends, making new ones, sharing information—and though I didn't realize it, in his way he was also saying his goodbyes and shutting down.

One day, when he went to the West Wing of the White House, he took me with him. I wore my Sunday-go-to-Episcopal-Church suit.

Owing to certain historical precedents in Dallas, President Lyndon Baines Johnson did not trust the Secret Service to keep him alive, and so had retained one of my old uncles, one Charles Sither, to advise him on personal security.

My father told me that hadn't gone down too well with the Secret Service but that Johnson had let it be known he slept better because of Uncle Charley. Eventually everyone learned not to mess with him.

Uncle Charley's Masterpiece. On a single morning planned and executed by Uncle Charley, uncredentialed men and women bluffed their way into Camp David and planted a bomb in the toilet in the bathroom of the President's cabin; a team of scuba divers swam across the Potomac and attached a detonator and one hundred ten gallons of Uncle Charley's favorite red dye to the hull of the Presidential yacht the *Sequoia*; and a bogus Air Force Reserve general talked his way into a private tour of Air Force One and planted a fake bomb under the pilot's seat.

Very enterprising, my uncle Charley. Maybe I should point out that he was an honor graduate of my father's Sophisticated Assassination course. After Uncle Charley showed heads of the Presidential security detail how he'd pulled it all off, it was hushed up. But the President heard all about it, and Uncle Charley and Lyndon Johnson had a regularly scheduled private meeting every morning.

According to the letters he'd sent to Billy and me in Germany, Uncle Charley's title was Special Assistant to the President of the United States. When the Secret Service regularly swept the White House for bugs, Uncle Charley's team was usually a few hours behind them finding bugs the Secret Service had missed. Or planted.

My father was here to say hello to Uncle Charley. A little diplomacy. But my father was also here to get me and a few others who'd never seen it into the working part of the White House. Uncle Charley gave us a guided tour which began in the Old Executive Office Building, wound all through the West Wing, and ended at the door of the Oval Office.

That day, my father had also brought my mother, my little brother, my older brother and his wife, and my father's protégé, Dick Beyea, and his wife. Dick would later go on to become head of Air Force counterintelligence, and after that to run the Intelligence Community Staff, which is supposed to coordinate the operations and reporting of all American intelligence services, and good luck to him. So all of them were there somewhere with us.

But they weren't there when Uncle Charley and I arrived at the door of the Oval Office. Maybe they were around a corner admiring a painting or a Remington bronze or a famous antique. Dick Beyea had a passion for such things and would hold forth on them. Or maybe they were still chatting with someone Uncle Charley had introduced them to. That would be just like my father, the liaison man, getting the entire life story of someone he'd just met.

Somehow it was just Uncle Charley and me who arrived together at that door.

Uncle Charley stuck his head through the door for a moment. Then he turned to me. "Larry, the President isn't in there right now. So why don't you walk in a couple of steps, stand all by yourself in the Oval Office of the White House, and imagine what it feels like to be the President of the United States all alone in there with the weight of the whole world on his shoulders."

I suppose a kid should be excited the first time he walks into the Oval Office. But the truth is I wasn't really. Maybe it was because I knew the President wasn't inside. The first thing I noticed was the wall was very thick, and the next thing was the room was much smaller than I'd imagined. Smaller than some of my father's offices had been. Uncle Charley had said a couple of steps, so I only went as far as the back of a couch.

The President's desk was across the room. I stood there for a moment staring at it, trying to imagine Abraham Lincoln sitting there, or Teddy Roosevelt. Or Lyndon Johnson.

The next thing I noticed about the Oval Office was it had several doors.

I noticed this when one of them opened, and in walked Lyndon Johnson.

He was all by himself. Carrying his suit jacket in his hand. His white shirt was wrinkled, and he looked like he did have the weight of the whole world on his shoulders. He looked so old and tired. He saw me, and just stood there looking at me for a second with that hound dog face of his. Then he quizzed me with his eyes—Who are you? He didn't speak, but I understood exactly what he was asking.

Part of me wanted to stand at attention and salute. Part of me wanted to shit in my pants. Part of me wanted to tell the President I was a poster child, here to have my picture taken with him, and I'd gotten lost from my minders. But it didn't take long for the training my father had given me to kick in. "Excuse me, sir," I said while heading for the door. "I didn't mean to disturb you."

Lyndon Johnson didn't say a single word to me. But that wasn't what I told my father in our car on the way out of the city.

"Did you speak to the President?" my father asked me.

"Yes, I did. I said, 'Excuse me, sir.'"

"And did the President speak to you?"

"Oh yes, he did. He said, 'Get the fuck out of my way!'"

My father was either fifty-one or fifty-three, depending on which public record you chose to believe. He was born in either 1914 or 1916. His birth certificate said the latter. But, then again, his birth certificate was issued in 1952 in a little courthouse in rural Georgia on the basis of an affidavit signed five days earlier by a doctor in Virginia. My father had been in the employ of the United States Government for thirty-five and a half years.

His rotation home was routine. It was policy that after three years overseas his organization's officers were assigned to the United States for at least two years. His new job was technically on a level with the one he'd had when we'd lived in Germany, but the reality was a letdown. Germany was the world capital of espionage and my father missed being at the center of the action. There was talk for a time about my father becoming the director. But the current director wasn't ready to step down. Regulations said that, unless my father moved up a grade, within another year he would have to retire. Then word came down that regulations would be overlooked if my father would accept the job of CIA station chief in Saigon.

He wanted to go.

Saigon sounded great to me too, until my father said my mother and Billy and I would have to stay in the States. My father would have to go alone, but he still wanted to go.

In his lifetime, he'd shifted so many times between various and assorted intelligence and counterintelligence organizations that transferring to the CIA would have come quite naturally to him. And it would have been a transfer.

If you've assumed that, during my childhood, my father's organization was the CIA, well, that would suit him just fine. And it would tend to prove his point that the CIA got all the press and captured the public imagination while more than a dozen other formidable, well-funded American clandestine services bugged and trip-wired their way around the world in total anonymity.

To hear my father tell it, it didn't really matter which service he worked for today. Forget every organizational chart of the American intelligence community ever dreamed up in Congress or the White House. Beneath the surface rivalries, American intelligence was run by a secret society, an old boy network of men who'd known and trusted one another since the war. Back then, every one of them had been in a different organization than he found himself in now. They were all still working toward a common purpose.

"There's something about the exhilaration of war," my father told my mother and me one night after dinner with Uncle George. "Something you can't understand unless you've lived it." He turned to me and grinned. "Larry, when the war had been over a few months, and normality had set in, your uncle George and I used to sit around in Paris and say to each other, 'It wasn't a good war. But it was better than no war at all.'"

My mother spent months moping around our house.

I didn't want my father to go either. And I told him so. I told him that, all through my childhood when he'd been so busy, we'd always known the date was coming when he wouldn't have to work anymore and he wouldn't be too busy for me anymore. All my life so far, when we went outside to play catch, he'd ended our games covertly. I cannot recall a game of catch with my father that he didn't end by throwing the ball long, way over my head. Whether it was a football, or a baseball, or a basketball, it didn't matter, my father could accidentally-on-purpose wing it past me. I'd run after it, wheel excitedly to whip it back to him, and discover he'd vanished. I fell for it every time. And I told my father I'd been told it wouldn't always be like that. So why in hell did he want to go off to Vietnam now to get himself killed?

I told him the only time I could remember hearing the words "CIA station chief in Saigon" on the nightly news had been in a sentence which also included the phrase "was killed today by his houseboy, a Viet Cong operative, with a hand grenade."

But my father wanted to go. And if it hadn't been for my mother locking herself in their bedroom, shutting out all the light, and falling into a depression that brought a doctor to our house a time or two, my father would've already let them cut him orders for Saigon.

They kept calling, whoever they were, and their calls seemed never to fail to excite my father.

There were lots of arguments behind my parents' bedroom door.

1969 was the year we landed on the moon and the year my father retired.

Forsaking the CIA's continuing inducements and the exalted position Chief of Station Saigon, he bought the only house he'd ever owned—in a beach town in Florida—and began living off his retirement pension. The spymaster was reduced to fishing off his dock, mowing his lawn, playing golf in pink pants with retirees. He was diminished, shrinking.

He'd recently controlled hundreds of agents at a time, but now the numbers of those under his command had dwindled to one; that would be me. Billy was exempt somehow, and my father increasingly demanded total obedience and loyalty of me. He almost never sang. He wouldn't answer my questions about his career. Except for when my father's old friends were passing through town, the secret world was something I didn't hear much about anymore.

Sometimes I went to bed thinking maybe it was my fault. Maybe I shouldn't have made all those great speeches about why my father shouldn't go to Saigon. Maybe that was selfish. Maybe we should've let him go, do what he was good at. He obviously didn't want to play catch with me in the front yard. He was dying of this place. If I put Bob Dylan on my record player, I could tune everything else out and go to sleep.

Drinking became my father's favorite hobby. He began having nightmares from which he woke up screaming, "I'm sorry. I'm sorry." Afterwards, he wouldn't say what it was he was sorry for. He'd sit on the edge of his bed in his boxer shorts, bare feet on the carpet, elbows on knees, chin in hands, staring at a memory. Then, after half an hour, or an hour, he'd settle back down into bed, have the same dream, and it would start all over again. When I was lucky, all I actually saw of these episodes was the glow of his cigarette tip while he sat in the dark between dreams.

I wanted to help him. I also wanted to kiss girls and feel their breasts—but I wasn't even brave enough to ask one out. How the fuck could I help my father?

When Jerry came to visit, my brothers and I mounted a covert action. Pure treachery. We went to our father's sock drawer and Jerry, our resident gun expert, removed the firing pin from our father's gun. Three weeks later, it had been replaced.

By day and late into the nights, I avoided the whole scene as much as I could. I got out of the house, made new friends, explored my new world. The town we'd moved to was about fifteen miles down the gently curving beach from Cape Kennedy. The gantries of the launch pads shimmered in the heat out over the water to the north of us. Most of my new friends were sons and daughters of NASA engineers, telemetry experts, rocket scientists, and the like. Ask any kid you met where his father worked and he was almost bound to say, "The Cape." I stopped asking, because I learned usually, after they'd answered me, the kids would ask back, "What about yours?"

We had rockets standing upright outside our public buildings in place of sculptures, and groups of rockets laid out horizontally in our parks to form rocket gardens. I enrolled in Satellite High School. How's that for a Space Age name? It would be the eleventh school I'd attended since first grade.

My mother rallied. She took Billy and me to Cape Kennedy to watch them launch *Apollo 11* to the moon. And after that she took Billy to every tourist trap in Florida to make sure he had something fun to think about.

Apollo 11 was special, of course, not only because it was my first launch but because it delivered men to the surface of the moon for the first time. Watching a launch can be the experience of a lifetime. But we saw launch after launch after launch until they became *almost* mundane. When they weren't launching men into space, they were always launching satellites—weather satellites, communications satellites, and spy satellites disguised as weather satellites or communications satellites. They kept busy, and the night launches were the best because it seemed like you could see the red glow of the second- and third-stage burns almost forever.

When manned launches happened to be scheduled during school hours, classes were brought to a halt so we could all watch the results of the local handiwork.

On the fourteenth of November, 1969, at quarter to eleven in the morning, a bell rang at Satellite, and the entire school, every teacher and student, all fifteen hundred or so of us, assembled in the courtyard. Then we were frog-marched out past the administration building, across the parking lot, past Publix and across A-1-A, to the beach. Where we stood together like so many lemmings, faced north, listened on transistor radios, and watched the launch of *Apollo 12*. Which, from where we stood, on that day, in that weather, looked like nothing more than a momentary orange fizzle against the dark gray sky. On our way back into school, I told the principal, "Thanks, man. That launch was really outta sight."

Five months later, we watched the launch of *Apollo 13*. Crystal-clear skies, bright sunshine, beautiful fire and smoke and steam rising against the rich blue sea and the boundless blue heavens.

My father may've been the only guy in town who didn't watch, or try to watch, either of those launches. He'd seen secret launches at Vandenberg in the Fifties and early Sixties. Seen one, seen 'em all. That was how my father looked at most things in those days on the beach. But *Apollo 13* was the moon-bound craft that malfunctioned, and when it did our astronauts seemed doomed. My father sat beside me on the couch in our family room for days watching live TV coverage while *Apollo 13* limped ever farther from earth, with its oxygen dwindling, and a whole bunch of NASA geniuses on the ground figured out a way *Apollo 13* could coast to the moon and then use lunar gravity to slingshot the capsule back to earth.

Times like that, when my father displayed at least a flicker of his old self, it only made me sadder afterward.

Given where we lived, there were almost always Russian trawlers off our coast. They looked like fishing boats, and probably they did catch fish, but they were also arrayed with big antennas and microphones and other devices that sucked up communications and telemetry emanating from the Cape. After my father told me what to look for, I saw them out there almost every day.

One night he and I were driving along the beach, heading south on A-1-A toward home. I remember he saw something out of the corner of his eye, then pulled off into a little stand of casuarinas by the shore and parked, facing out to sea.

A few miles out, helicopters were dropping bright pink flares. We couldn't see the aircraft clearly, could only tell what they had to be by the way they moved, or sometimes didn't move, while the flares sank slowly toward the sea. It was as bright as a pink sunrise out there in one little patch of sky and water, and behind the flares were low clouds mottled a reddish gray. Then we saw tracer rounds flowing out of a helicopter toward the water.

"They've caught a Soviet sub!" said my father. "Or maybe a trawler. SIGINT. Signals intelligence, whichever it is." God, was he happy! In the next moment he reeled off for me an experienced intelligence officer's assessment of what we were seeing. "It's not a training exercise," he said, "because, one, it's too close to such a vital facility to be an exercise. Two, we know the Soviets hang around out there, so we would never run a training exercise anywhere there's such a good chance they would observe it. Three, it's a holiday weekend, and no commander in his right mind would run a dangerous training mission on a holiday weekend. Not unless he wanted to be hung by his men. This," concluded my father, "is real."

And, for just a moment, I could see he ached to be out there. Or, at least, to have the power to drive slowly home and then calmly pick up a red telephone and within a couple of minutes learn every pertinent detail.

But he didn't. Not anymore, and by the time we made the turn into our street he was my sad, bored father again, telling me to please, for God's sake, close my window tonight because he didn't feel like paying to air-condition the whole goddamn neighborhood this month.

No oil slick or naval debris washed up on our beach, the same beach where a decade later the Space Shuttle *Challenger* and seven astronauts would wash up in thousands of little chunks. And there was no mention in our newspapers of what my father and I had seen out there. Just another unrecorded skirmish in a secret war hidden beneath the Cold War.

When Uncle George came to visit, he told me a story about how, when he got to Paris after the Normandy invasion, he met my father. "There he was," said Uncle George, "the baby-faced bruiser from Georgia. He happened to be from G-2 and therefore not the sort to be trusted, Larry. But I trusted him anyway. And, by the way, your father was one hell of a boxer. You should've seen him!"

By now my father was perking up. "My record was fifty-two and one," he said happily. "And the *one* was when I got disqualified for punching the referee!"

Next Uncle George told me about a night he and my father were out in a little French town in a restaurant filled with homesick American soldiers.

"There was a record player, but all the records they had were French. One of the GIs had heard your father singing once, Larry, and he offered to buy your father's dinner if he would sing his favorite song. So your father did. Then another guy offered to buy *my* dinner if your father would sing another song, so he did. Pretty soon, your father and I couldn't eat or drink another thing, and GIs were lining up to pay your father money to sing their favorite songs."

"It wasn't a good war," my father said, "but it was better than no war at all. One more for you too, George? Bring your glass over here. I'll pour." That night, after a lot more pouring, my father sang, and it was the first I'd heard him sing in a very long time.

Exiled. Living in memories. Waiting for something real to happen. It's the wrong way to live, I know. I walked a little more than three miles down my beach this afternoon, through a hot wind, heading south—toward Miami, Cuba, Panama, and the westernmost tip of Ecuador. "All of South America is east of Tampa, Florida." I remember Uncle George telling me that during his long ago visit to my father's house in Florida, in what seems to me like another lifetime that somehow I've warped back into. This morning in my own house I had nothing better to do than get out a map and check it out. Uncle George was right.

Now that I live here, I understand. My father had to be bored to fucking tears. I've got to get out of here.

5 | PORTRAIT OF MY FATHER
COMBING HIS HAIR

Spymasters deal in betrayal in every conceivable variety. They can induce it, stockpile it, fund it, sell shares in it, justify it to their in-house panels of psychiatrists board-certified in sophistry. I was still very young the first time my father told me, "Every man has the capacity to betray." Which is perhaps why, three years after we moved to Florida, when it came time for me to register for the draft and I told my father I didn't want to die in Vietnam, he saw the choice before me as a simple one between duty and betrayal.

"If you're drafted," he told me, "you must go."

I remember we were sitting out on our patio, looking out over the lawn to the dock.

"Muhammad Ali refused to go," I said, "and the Supreme Court cleared him."

"Fuck Muhammad Ali," said my father. Then he poured himself another drink. And on that happy note I left for college.

Someone at the Educational Testing Service in Princeton, New Jersey, had made an enormous mistake—twice. I'd been tested and retested and informed I was rather clever, which had come as quite a surprise to me. When word got out, people had started looking at me differently, then talking to me differently. That gave me a confidence I'd never had before. I'd been invited to skip my first two years of college, and back then that was rare. I'd been given a slide rule, a decrepit Volkswagen, a scholarship, and a book of stamps and sent barreling down the highway to study and await the selective service lottery. I'd gotten a job as a lifeguard, drowned like my grandfather before me, been brought spectacularly back to life, and now—after a few months in a hospital and then back at home—here I was back at school. That's when my mother called me and said, "You're not going to believe *this*."

Having grown up knowing all my father's immediate relatives had been dead since before I was born, I must admit to a certain measure of surprise when my mother told me my father's mother, his brother, and his two sisters were at that very moment seated in our living room singing drunkenly with my father.

My mother said the doorbell rang, she answered it, and there stood a group of people who said they were my father's family. My mother left them on the doorstep, walked into the bedroom, and reported this interesting development to my father. Who ran wild-eyed into the bathroom and locked himself in. "I don't want to see them," he said through the door.

They told my mother they were staying at the Holiday Inn on the other side of the river. She told my father that—when he finally came out of his hiding place.

He paced around the house a little while. Then he went out.

And six hours later they all came back drunk and singing and calling my father by a different name than my mother or I had ever known him by. That was hours ago, my mother said.

They were still going at it.

I could make out my father's whistling in the background.

"What are their names?" I asked my mother.

"Well," she said, "he calls his mother 'Mama.' And the rest of them . . . I'm not quite sure yet."

There was Lewis Jackson Kolb and there was Jack Cobb. My father was both of them and neither of them. Or my father was both of them and either of them. Take your pick. The trick to it, as I learned later, is to actually believe, to forget everything else except the version you're telling.

It went unspoken, but we all knew he'd betrayed them.

Apparently, there'd been operational issues, identity issues, other factors relating to his work. My father could've made some more cumbersome arrangement, or at least told them he had to go away. But for a resourceful young fellow just trained in the ways of spies, it had to be tempting to vanish without a trace, reported dead, and that was what he'd done to them thirty years before they showed up on his doorstep. Occasionally he'd sent his mother money, anonymously, and that had always made her suspect he was alive.

Having his old family again, and being caught red-handed, and then forgiven, somehow softened my father. "Who am I to judge?" he said the next time we talked on the phone about the draft.

Every American male born in the year I was born was subject to a national draft lottery to be conducted in the February of my second term in college. So when I left for school I knew that, depending on where my number came up, I'd either be called up for induction into the military sometime around my second year in college, or I'd get to stay in school.

When the day came, I had my draft card in my wallet and all my fantasies of splitting for Canada had drifted away. I didn't like it, but I'd decided that, if I were drafted, I would go. Go at least to my pre-induction physical and point out my flat feet, and my height, which technically was an inch and a half below the height that disqualified you for service, but maybe if I stretched. And if, after all of that, I were drafted, fuck it, I would probably go.

When the hour came, we all assembled in the TV room in our dorm—Algonquin Hall—where the cinder-block walls were painted institutional yellow and the TV set was bolted onto the wall, up high, close to the ceiling. Like we were in prison. Up on the TV screen, there was this gray-suited shorthair ready to spin a big Plexiglas drum with all our fates in it.

It looked every bit like *Dialing for Dollars,* the local-TV-station-weekday-afternoon-programming staple in which, after a big buildup, they pulled a telephone number out of a hopper and dialed it, and if they happened to dial you and you were watching and answered the phone, you could win yourself some serious money. The prize kept building up until someone won. Sometimes it got up to as much as two or three hundred bucks. But today the prize was slightly different.

The lower your number the greater your chance of being drafted. There were 365 numbers to be assigned. Generally, if your birth date was assigned a number between 1 and about 90, you were almost sure to be drafted; if you drew between about 91 and 130, there was a good chance you'd be drafted, but it wasn't certain; between about 131 and 180, you might be called up, but probably not. Over about 180, and you were very likely safe. This was the Devil's Arithmetic, and we knew its every permutation.

We'd seen the same show the previous year, though without the same morbid fascination— then our own lives hadn't been on the line. One thing we knew from last year was there was no need to listen to the crazy motherfucker up there on the screen spinning the drum and calling out the numbers. They had graphics to provide the grim details. So, before it started, one of our number had carried in his record player and cranked it up. We weren't going to be able to make it through this without our music. About when I walked into the room, Country Joe McDonald and the Fish were singing, *Yeah, come on all of you big strong men, Uncle Sam needs your help again / He's got himself in a terrible jam, way down yonder in Vietnam.*

Then the shorthair started spinning the drum, slowly, with a big smile on his face like the devil himself enjoying the hell out of this. The dread was building, then the numbers started coming up. Within the first few minutes my suitemate got number 32, and knew immediately he was fucked. He screamed and quivered and flopped around on the floor like a fish on land for a while, then sat up and started sobbing right there in front of all the rest of us. I never liked him anyway.

He was an asshole, another genius chosen out of the vast American high school populace to be a guinea pig student like me. Except he was a physics major, who'd made straight As since first grade, rode all over campus on his unicycle while wearing a long black Dracula cape with red-satin lining, and he bragged about the true fact that he hadn't brushed his teeth since he was seven. He stank. He was about six-two and a hundred sixty-five pounds, at least five pounds of which were zits, frizzy black hair that fell halfway down his back, and food that had been accreting between his teeth since the Kennedy Administration. As soon as his number came up, he hated me even worse than he'd hated me before. "Sorry, man," I said, suddenly feeling sympathy for him while he paused for a breath between his tears. "Fuck you!" he said back to me.

I thought I might console him by telling him my father said every young man should spend time in the military because it builds character and discipline, but it didn't seem like a good time to say all that.

"Fuck you!" my suitemate said to me again.

After that, all I could think was, Well, Mr. 32, I've been wanting a new suitemate since the day I met you.

I look back on it wondering, could I really have been that callous that day? Yes. Should I be ashamed of it now? Probably. We were all on edge.

I sat there watching the screen, feeling doomed at first, but growing more and more confident as my birthday kept spinning around and around the drum and getting passed over, while I sang along with almost everyone in the room and John Lennon: *All we are saying is give peace a chance.* And finally my number came up. 252. My suitemate was going to die and I was going to live. I'd dodged a bullet, a hail of bullets and napalm, and a conflict with my father, who'd aligned himself with the shorthairs on this issue which, to almost every American male coming of age back then, was a fault line between father and son. I called my father, collect, to tell him my number, but he said he already knew. He'd watched it live, just like me, and the best part was he sounded relieved.

In her weekly letters, my mother reported my father had started diluting his drinks again, had thrown away his pink golf pants, and the lime ones, and was wearing the grays we'd always known him in. He was coming back to life.

Then he wrote me himself, saying that during my next school break he wanted to take me to Georgia to meet my family. I could hardly wait.

I was driving. North on 95.

I'm hungry, I said. Let's pull off in Jacksonville and find something to eat.

Or that was the gist of what I said. I don't remember exactly. As I sit writing this, I can't even confidently tell you what color pants I'm wearing without looking down to make sure.

Let's press on to Brunswick, my father said. I know a little place up there that's got good food.

But I was driving, and I was hungry, and I turned off into Jacksonville.

No! said my father. And something about the way he said it said he meant business.

I started to turn around.

Then he sighed, and said, What the hell? Let's go downtown.

It was early evening, as I vaguely remember it now, but it might have actually been afternoon or morning. I don't remember what time of year it was, or what the weather was like. I'm fairly certain it wasn't pounding down with rain—because I remember my father looking out the windows and pointing things out along the way. He was happily saying things like There's the movie theater we used to go to, and over there, on that corner, that used to be a bank.

I don't remember the name of the restaurant we went into, or what street it was on, or much about what it looked like inside. All I remember is the wall my father sat with his back to was cream colored, there was a neon sign above him which gave parts of the wall a faint yellowy glow, and he sat across from me in a booth, with one eye on the front door, and carefully checked every face coming inside. But I've never forgotten the story he started telling me there, while he finished his coffee and waited for his change.

"Early in the war," he said very quietly, "when I was a young special agent in the Counter Intelligence Corps, I came here undercover, and it was the scariest time in my life.

"Do you remember Asa Candler?" my father asked, a little louder now.

"Of course," I said.

Asa Candler was my father's friend during the war. In Georgia, the Candlers were famous. Two generations before my father's friend, the alpha Asa Candler had founded the Coca-Cola Company.

"Well," my father said, "Asa was the only man on earth who knew where I was or what I was doing.

"And do you remember," my father said, "J. Edgar Hoover used to send me a Christmas card every year?"

"Yes."

"It all started here," said my father.

Then he stopped and thought awhile.

"Let's get out of here," my father said next, after his change had come back and he'd laid down a tip. "This place gives me the shivers."

He didn't tell me the rest of it until we were out of Dodge, back on the highway and nearing the Georgia line.

"One of the things an intelligence officer does is what we call talentspotting. I was already in the CIC, but Asa spotted me as an up-and-comer. Recruited me to work for him. Promoted me. Made sure I was first in line for every important opportunity. He was an officer, from a great Georgia family, and I was an enlisted man. Also from Georgia, but poor as dirt. Asa and I became great friends anyway. After awhile we knew each other so well that we called each other Asa and Jack. We only used our ranks in front of others, or to give each other shit.

"Asa kept getting promoted, and he made sure I did too. But in the CIC, outside of its internal structure, rank didn't matter. CIC special agents didn't wear uniforms or rank insignia. A special agent could be a major or a corporal, and nobody on the outside would know the difference. We were all just special agents. And that way a sergeant who was investigating a dirty general couldn't have the general pull rank on him and order him to get the hell out of his office. We all had the power of arrest. Equally.

"I was working out of Fort Benning when the Japanese bombed Pearl Harbor. Suddenly we were in the war. And suddenly there was a new imperative to protect our harbors. I was transferred to Jacksonville. One month after Pearl Harbor, I was Special Agent in Charge, Jacksonville Station, Counter Intelligence Corps."

I remember my father pausing at that point. I think he was deciding whether or not to tell me the rest. Then he went on.

He said, "It wasn't long before we discovered there was a group of German-American Nazis operating in Jacksonville. They were cooperating with German intelligence. We decided to try to send someone in to infiltrate them. And eventually we decided I was the best man the CIC had for the job. I was perfect for the part.

"I was a young Southerner. A Georgia boy, from a German-American family. So was the leader of the target group. An infiltrator doesn't want to have to learn an entire life story all that different from his own. He wants to memorize a new name, another birth date, and a few other details. But that's all. The rest he's got to be able to draw from his own experience if he's going to be successful under pressure."

What my father said next, I can still hear him saying like it was last night, and not half my lifetime ago. "The pressure is tremendous," he said. "It takes a special kind of person to go in alone and insinuate himself into a tightly knit group of people."

He paused a moment to let me ponder that.

Then he said, "I met a few members and let them know my folks were German too. Eventually they took me to a meeting, and I joined the Nazi party right there that night. We had meetings three or four times a week. We all wore brownshirt Nazi uniforms with swastika armbands. At the beginnings and ends of our meetings, we stood at attention, stuck out our arms, and saluted a big red-white-and-black Nazi flag. Then we said *Heil Hitler!* to each other, took off our armbands, and slunk off into the night."

My father kept talking.

This was a miracle, the first time he'd ever opened up to me about his career.

He said, "I got to know the leader of the group. Made him my friend. He liked me, trusted me. He made me his lieutenant. I was second in charge. He had a great big picture of Adolf Hitler on the wall behind his desk in our office. He wore a little mustache just like Hitler's. I grew one too. Goddamnit, he used to scare me! We were planning a big sabotage operation. We were supposed to go out to the beach and rendezvous with a German submarine, to meet some agents sent in from Germany. But instead one night the FBI swept in and rolled us all up."

I said, "What do you mean?"

My father said, "They took us down. Arrested us. All except for me. They killed me. Right in front of some of the group. And that's why they never found out I betrayed them."

"What happened to them?"

For a moment, my father didn't answer. He looked, of all things, ashamed.

He finally said, "Some of them were executed. Some of them were sent to prison. But they all left friends and relatives back home in Jacksonville. Who knew me. And that I was killed that night. If one of them saw me alive, they'd know. They'd understand everything. That's why I never set foot in Jacksonville again."

As I drove us into Georgia, he told me the arrests that night crippled an even bigger Nazi sabotage operation, and that J. Edgar Hoover publicly took all the credit for it. But he didn't forget my father, or Asa Candler. Hoover brought them to Washington, introduced them around, said good things about them to the right people. "After that," my father said, "Asa and I were rising stars."

Within a couple of months my father was an officer. He and Asa were transferred together, first to Atlanta and then a year later to Washington, D.C.— where Asa Candler would be made the A-2, the Chief of the United States Army Air Force Counter Intelligence Corps, and my father its Executive Officer, the deputy who actually runs things.

He didn't seem to want to stop talking. Especially about Asa.

Nine months after they got back from their meetings with Hoover in Washington, Asa told my father to learn to fly an airplane. My father did that in Atlanta and Myrtle Beach. Then he went down to MacDill Field, in Tampa, posing as an Army Air Force bomber pilot.

Posing is the right word. He'd had only enough time to learn the basics before he had to hurry off to Florida.

The problem was B-26s kept falling out of the sky.

One a day in Tampa Bay.

They were crashing in clear skies and good weather.

B-26s were hot planes. Temperamental as fighters, but as lumbering as the big bombers they were. B-26s had much faster takeoff and landing speeds than other bombers. B-26s stalled viciously.

Crews were calling B-26s Widowmakers.

Crews were requesting transfers in droves.

It wasn't really one per day, but close enough that crews were singing "One a day in Tampa Bay" and going AWOL. More than thirty B-26s flying out of MacDill went down in the last few months of 1942, and more than sixty in 1943.

MacDill was a main training base for B-26 crews, but B-26 training was going on at other places at the same time. B-26s were crashing at other training bases too. But not at nearly the same rate.

That, said my father, was just the sort of pattern a counterintelligence officer looks for.

One every month or two at Maxwell Field; two or three a year at Langley; one a month at Barksdale. One a day, sometimes even two a day, in Tampa Bay.

Find the pattern of irregularities.

Week after week, my father flew out of MacDill as a B-26 copilot. Posing and praying over Tampa Bay and the Gulf of Mexico, and over the bombing range at Avon Park. Posing, watching, and listening in the crew rooms and the barracks and the hangars at MacDill.

"And finally we got him," said my father. "It was sabotage. A German-American maintenance crew chief was bringing down those planes. We arrested him right there in the hangar. Asa came down from Atlanta and we took him down together.

"And then," my father went on, in the tone he used for cautionary tales, "the powers that be in the overworld decided to cover it all up. They decided it would be better for morale if no one knew what one German agent had done to us right in our own country. So they wrote it all off to design flaws and poor training procedures. And that was the end of that."

When we got near Milledgeville, my father took over at the wheel because he knew the way.

How are you supposed to feel when you're nineteen years old and just meeting your grandmother and uncle and aunts you'd thought long dead? What are you supposed to think of the son and brother who turned his back on them all? I hadn't really thought about that up to then.

I'd been away at school and had only heard about it secondhand. Mostly from my mother. But also from my little brother—who'd already met our relatives from Georgia and pronounced them very friendly.

Other than inviting me up here, my father still hadn't said much of anything to me about his old family. And he didn't seem all that anxious to get started now. As we drove into Milledgeville, Georgia, my father became a local history expert and tour guide.

You wouldn't believe it to look at this crumbling little town today, now that all the major highways and rail lines had passed it by, but Milledgeville, my father informed me, was the capital of Georgia during the Civil War. And, as such, it was the prime target on Sherman's march through Georgia to the sea. Nowadays, the largest employer in Milledgeville was the Central State Hospital, formerly known, in less euphemistic times, as the Georgia State Lunatic Asylum. Back then it was the largest lunatic asylum in the world. My father had dug up information for me about everything in Milledgeville, except his family.

Milledgeville, he told me, was the home of the great southern writer Flannery O'Connor—who'd set many of her stories here and had died here eight years earlier, all too young.

And Milledgeville was the home of Mrs. Francis Gary Powers, while her husband the famous U-2 pilot was imprisoned in Russia for spying. Early one Berlin morning in 1962, the Americans and Soviets traded spies: Rudolf Abel for Francis Gary Powers. They walked slowly across the Glienicker Bridge from opposite sides of the Havel River, passed each other at the midway point where a white line divided East from West, and were free. And, as fate would have it, at that very moment, which was still the middle of the night in Milledgeville, Mrs. Francis Gary Powers, who hadn't been kept fully abreast of the secret negotiations that freed her beloved husband, was at home, dead drunk, and in bed with a solicitous neighbor from down the street. Whose wife soon showed up with a shotgun. Prompting Mrs. Powers to call the police. Who showed up at roughly the same time as representatives of the news media began arriving to record the poignant reaction of Mrs. Powers to the dramatic release of her husband the famous spy.

The CIA had a hell of a time keeping that out of the news, my father said. A television reporter tried to film a statement from her, but she kept falling out of her chair.

Maybe up here there's something in the water that makes you folks crazy, I told my father. Maybe that's why a little place like this needs the world's largest insane asylum.

He stopped somewhere and bought some flowers.

Then he checked himself in a mirror, straightened his collar, carefully combed his hair.

In barbershops all over the world, I'd watched, when they'd finished cutting my father's hair, his barbers trying to comb it. And it never looked quite like my father until he took the comb from the barber, dug the fine-toothed end into his forelock, and, while sweeping his hair back and to the side, turned his wrist just so.

From the look on his face now, I could see he was still feeling shame for what he'd done to his family. Part of him looked just like he always had. But another part of him looked like a little kid trying to get back into the good graces of his mother. I felt sorry for him just then.

My memory gets sketchy here, and I'm not sure why.

I remember my father took some turns and headed down a residential street with telephone poles and scrubby pine trees lining the road, and red clay showing through worn patches in front yards.

He pulled into a driveway in front of a little red-brick ranch house, shut off the engine, whistled nervously for a moment, then said to me, "They're just good country people."

And I remember the front door opening and out of the house streaming three smiling women my father the spymaster had compartmentalized right out of his life. And mine. They were my aunts and my grandmother, and I'd never laid eyes on them. My new aunt Wilma was the first to the car. She was pretty, blond, about fifty, and wearing a nurse's uniform. In those days, nurses didn't wear the sort of uniforms they wear today—which to us back then would've looked like toddlers' pajamas. In those days, a nurse wore a white blouse, white skirt, white nun hat, white stockings, white wedge-soled shoes, and my aunt Wilma was wearing all of those things except the hat. She was my father's baby sister, she smelled good, and this was her house.

My grandmother lived here too, and she was the next one to the car. I have a photograph which shows she was wearing a billowing orange housecoat covered with Hawaiian flowers. Her eyeglasses had thick black frames, and the lenses were tinted somewhere between brown and pink. Her hair was white, and it had been teased and then sprayed.

She walked up to me just as I got out of the car and, in a sweet high voice, she said, "I believe you must be my grandson Larry."

I gave her a hug, and it didn't feel as weird as I'd thought it might.

Next came my new aunt Theodora, also known as Dokie. She moved slower than my grandmother. Dokie had diabetes and wasn't well. Dokie was married to a bootlegger, who, my father said, was "reformed, and now a model citizen."

We all hugged and said hellos. They hugged me first. Then my father hugged them all, for a very long time. And then we went into the house, and about thirty seconds later my father had a thick Georgia accent. Inside, I met my uncle Charles, who was once my father's little brother. He had a flattop and wore a potentially embarrassing pocket protector with a mechanical pencil and two or three pens in the front pocket of his shirt. His hair was the coppery-blond color of my father's whiskers.

I remember that, as fast as I could, I got away from Uncle Charles and sat down next to my grandmother on the couch. She was seventy-six years old, and there was something wrong with her eyes that made her wear her dark glasses rain or shine, inside the house and out. She and I sat there talking for a while, just the two of us, while she dipped snuff and occasionally spat, quite delicately, into the brass spittoon that stood just beyond the end of the couch.

"Now, Larry . . ." was how she began a lot of her sentences, and the way she said Larry, it had at least three syllables.

It wasn't long before I was drawling right back at her. It rolled off my tongue quite naturally, and seemed to be the thing to do up there.

No one would have guessed that twenty years later, after my grandmother had gone blind and outlived most of her children, I would be the talk of Green Acres Nursing Home in Milledgeville, Georgia—for every week or so for years sending her a postcard from someplace like Nairobi one week, Monaco the next, New Delhi the week after that, then New York, Belfast, Beirut, Macao, and her guess was usually about as good as mine as to where I'd show up next.

My new aunt Wilma came out of the kitchen and delivered a plastic glass full of something dark and mysterious to my grandmother, saying, "Here's your tonic, Mama." Then Wilma turned to me and said, "How 'bout you, Sugar? You want sweet tea, or a nice cold Co-Coler?" I remember I opted for the Coke, and that by the time my father and I left Georgia a few days later I was certain that not a single Georgian could say Coca-Cola.

After a little bit, my grandmother asked me what time it was, and I told her.

She said presently my kinfolk was gonna start arrivin' from miles around to meet me. And so they did. Later that day, and the next, I met first cousins, second cousins, great-uncles, a third cousin, and other blood kin who'd driven in from all over the county to meet me. I wish I could remember them better, but it's about when that second wave of my new relatives starts washing over that my memory really begins to blur. I do remember we got along well and that having a whole new secret family to meet didn't seem all that strange to me. Ever since I was little, I'd been on the move and meeting new people at every stop. The trick to getting on with them fast was to use the side of you that was closest to whatever they were like.

I remember eating fried catfish, fried chicken, fried shrimp, fried ham, fried grits, fried hushpuppies, fried okra, fried sweet potatoes, fried tomatoes, deep-fried oysters, corn fritters, pecan pie, and boiled peanuts, and pretending I loved it all. Then washing it down with sweet tea—which is iced tea laced with more sugar than they put in tea anywhere else on earth, with the possible exception of Morocco.

And I remember, on the last afternoon of our visit, driving way out into the country with my father and his mother and sisters to see the oak tree under which once stood the shack where each one of them except my grandmother was born.

I'll never forget the happy way my father's eyes lit up when he saw that tree.

"Our house was right here," he sang out, and we all got out of the car and walked around in the dust.

Pretty soon, Wilma said she could tell Dokie was feeling poorly. So we didn't stay all that long. But, at least for a moment, I stood in the shade of that oak with my father. And I've always been glad I did.

It was a little old frame house, he told me.

He told me this the next day, while he and I drove home to Florida.

His first memory, he said, was watching his father drown, in the mouth of the Dog River, near where it fed into Mobile Bay, and his second was of sitting on the riverbank watching men drag the waters for his father's body.

But after that, almost all his early memories were centered around that little house in the country.

There were cracks in the floors, except in the room with nothing but dirt for a floor. There was no electricity. No phone. No plumbing. An outhouse. Nearly sixty acres of fields to work. And, with my father the man of the house now, he was the one that worked them. He and his mother and a mule.

"From the age of seven, I worked like a Trojan," he said. "I worked so hard I was an old man at fifteen."

I drove and he kept talking.

It was in that house that he and his mother and his sisters and his layabout brother lived—except for the occasional month or two when my father ran away from home and got work as a field hand. And it was in that house that, when my father was almost fourteen, he watched his mother doctor the family Bible, subtracting four years and some from the date of his birth, so she could get the certificate she needed from the county to send her son off to get a job in the Civilian Conservation Corps.

The CCC was a Roosevelt New Deal project for the poor, my father said.

He stayed in a CCC camp for almost a year. Whites living on one side. Negroes on another. Everybody working together. He loved it. He had a life of his own, and could still send money home to his family. He worked up in a forest service tower, spotting fires. It was the easiest job in the world. But one day, up in the tower, his appendix burst. Two men carried him down the ladder. It was the worst pain he'd ever felt. Afterwards, his friends told him he screamed the first half of the way down, then he passed out. While he was coming out of anesthesia, he talked too much and the doctor figured out how old he was.

He was sent home.

To the little house where, a few months later, his mother created an all-new birth record for him. She changed his date of birth again and gave him a new first name to boot, just in case the Army recruiters had access to CCC records.

He joined the Army. After basic training, they sent him to Cooks and Bakers School. But that was a really bad idea. He graduated and they made him a cook. Soldiers threw his biscuits back at him.

So they sent him to Traffic School and made him an MP. He was the best traffic cop his sergeants had ever seen. Didn't just make traffic stops. Changed the road signs, retimed the stoplights, rearranged the parking lots. Traffic started to flow a lot better.

So they gave him some tests and then made him a detective. He was better than any of them at that too.

They gave him more tests, and when the results came back a general wrote a letter that sent him straight to G-2.

First stop: the Military Intelligence Training Center at Camp Ritchie, Maryland. Later he went to CIC Officers School in Chicago, my father's beloved Chicago, where he and a couple of dozen other students practiced spy-versus-spy maneuvers—on the streets, and the elevated trains, and in the alleys and hotels and bars and museums and grand department stores—amongst the totally unsuspecting population.

It was a friend of his from G-2 that a few years later my father dressed up in an infantry uniform and sent out to the little house in the country to officially and with great regret inform my father's family of his death.

Was that at the same time as when you disappeared from Jacksonville? I asked. Was that why you had to do it? To protect them, and yourself?

Just say, Yes, I thought, *and I'll find you Not Guilty.*

No, said my father. It wasn't like that at all.

Somewhere on our way home, I don't remember where, I asked him about his nightmares.

"Was it your lost family you kept waking up screaming about? Was it them you kept apologizing to?"

My father turned away from me and stared out the window.

Finally, he said, "No. It wasn't them. It was a guy right out of intelligence training. We were both young. But the poor guy was even younger than me. He was new. Nothing more than a courier, really.

"He got drunk and forgot the password he was supposed to give me. I'd never met him. I didn't know who he was. We were in a dangerous place. I told him, 'Don't move!' and I asked again for the password. But he laughed, and said he couldn't remember, and tried to push through the door."

Something terrible was building in my father's voice.

"I was young then, too," he said. "And I didn't know what to do. I stood there for an instant, torn between betraying my instinct and betraying my orders. Then I did what I'd been told to do.

"I shot him.

"I killed him."

My father was crying now.

He said, "I still see his face at night."

Like most kids my age, instead of getting a real job when I finished college, I paddled a canoe from near Atlanta to Miami, rode a horse across Afghanistan, crossed Lapland by reindeer sled, traversed the moonscape of northern Iceland, and people actually paid me to do some of those things. Not much, but enough to keep me going, and one step ahead of my father's ambition of seeing me gainfully employed.

After a virtually tentless childhood, I'd slept in blue tents, orange tents, reindeer skin tents, mountain huts, lean-tos, and, for the past three weeks, in a cave halfway down a yellow cliff on the face of the Grand Canyon—but this evening my postprandial conversation with my father wasn't going as well as I'd hoped.

There I stood, cramped inside a phone booth, all six feet six inches of me, staring out over the South Rim, and explaining to my father that, yes, I did have three months before my next job, which was in the Alps, but I wouldn't be coming home right now, because last month in Albuquerque I'd met with an old friend who had a problem: Her daughter had left home and joined a cult. And, by the way, I'd agreed to join, find out what I could about it, report back on that, and try to get the daughter out.

"I guess spying runs in my family," I told my father. But actually I didn't consider what I was going to do even half as serious as spying. To me it was another adventure, and a favor for a friend.

"It could be very dangerous."

How could he possibly know more about bluffing his way into a cult than me?

"It's not like I'll be infiltrating the Politburo, Dad."

After a while, when he knew he couldn't talk me out of it, he wished me luck and made me promise to call him at least once a week.

The cult was based in a little town in the high desert in California. Thither I went.

———

While I braked and downshifted my way from Nevada into Death Valley, I decided I would tell them I was just a traveler in the wilderness looking for a place to stop and rest. That was true enough and, I hoped, sufficiently allegorical to appeal to whatever mind-set I might encounter when I got there.

I remember my ears kept popping, all the way down.

Once I hit bottom, the road soon became a straight two-lane strip of concrete with sage and stunted gray grass on both sides of it. For fifteen miles I didn't see another car or any moving thing. Then a convoy rose steadily out of the heat waves, heading toward me, crowding the center of the road, rattling my car as big rigs thundered past.

I climbed over a gray range of mountains and onto a desert plain.

It takes a special kind of person to go in alone and insinuate himself into a tightly knit group of people. It's lonely work, and terrifying. Though I replayed my father's words many times that afternoon, I thought that, when it came to infiltration, I would be a natural. It was what I'd been doing all my life. Arriving in new places, meeting new people, making new friends. Fitting in.

At a crossroads, I turned right, then climbed until the road leveled and I was in a dusty brown-and-yellow valley that stretched north as far as I could see. A ridge of crumbling brown mountains blocked the view to the east. To the west was the granite wall of the Sierra Nevada.

An hour up the only road, I arrived in the one-stoplight town I'd come to visit. I saw cottonwoods and evergreens, whitewashed wooden houses with little corrals behind some of them, and a grassy park with concrete picnic tables. It was evening. Low clouds were turning pink.

On the edge of town, I checked into a grubby little motor court. A "claptrap" was what my father would've called it. Night fell suddenly, unambiguously here. By the time I made it into my room, the only light I could see through the gauzy curtain was the white glow of the neon VACANCY sign out by the highway.

Of all my nights on earth so far, that was my worst, my loneliest.

By the dawn I was finally feeling sleepy, very sleepy. When I awoke, just after eleven, I put on a heavy sweater, my oldest surviving blue jeans, and mountain boots that had been resoled three times. Outside my window, fat snowflakes were falling and the ground was lightly dusted with snow. I headed out on foot.

Across from the traffic light, which was set on flashing yellow in all directions, stood an old gray stone building which, according to the signs out front, was the county courthouse, and the town hall, the sheriff's office, the jail, the library, and the historical society. On the lawn beside it, I found an elm which seemed to be the place for local kids to carve their initials into eternity.

I stood there reading the tree.

I stared up at the icy peaks.

I was seeing everything as if it were my last day.

Across the street was a cafe with a rusting white sign hanging out front. I pushed the glass door open and went in. The walls were lacquered pine. The booths were red vinyl. I sat at the counter.

Back then, I didn't need to put my back to the wall and face the door. The woman behind the counter was wearing a uniform with her name on a badge on the front of her blouse.

"Coffee?"

I still hadn't recovered from the coffee my mother and father concocted for me on that morning in Japan. "Do you have hot chocolate?"

She nodded, and I ordered some. Plus a ham steak, scrambled eggs, and toast and jelly.

When I'd finished all that, I asked for another mug of chocolate, then went to the rack beside the cash register and picked out scenic High Sierra postcards. I wrote and meticulously addressed cards to four of my friends. Then I dawdled back to the rack for more cards.

This time I got jackalopes.

I wasn't really thinking much about postcards. What I was thinking was *What the fuck am I doing here?* About all my friend had told me was that in this little town lived twenty-four young Americans, three-fourths women, one of those her rather lovely daughter, all led by a cowboy who'd shaved his head and told his followers to call him Swami. That was about all my friend knew.

"Swami!" she'd said. "Larry, what exactly *is* a swami, anyway?"

Neither one of us could answer that with confidence.

Leave! I heard my father whisper in my ear.

I finished all the cards, settled up, and laid down a tip.

But then I just sat there.

This was the first, but not the last, time I felt the fear and indecision I later came to understand was natural just before becoming operational. Later the apprehension would always seem to drop away as soon as I got down to work. But later, I never would've done what I was about to do then—march blindly into the problem. What I should've been about to do was reconnaissance. I should've observed the swami and his crew from afar for a day or two—taken their measure before I put myself in their control. I should've observed that most of the houses around town, the swami's included, seemed to have come out of the same cookie cutter, and contrived a way to get myself invited into someone else's house so I could learn its layout before I ever set foot in the swami's. With knowledge and planning comes confidence, and a measure of safety. But I didn't know that yet. I was working purely on instinct and emotion.

The cook came out of the back and dropped some coins into the jukebox. Freddy Fender began to sob a slow, sad Mexican lament. *I can't leave on that,* I told myself. So I counted knots in the pine walls. The next song was also Freddy Fender, in English this time, and even more lugubrious. But Patsy Cline sang next, something so magical that I got up and headed out the door to find the daughter and her swami.

He wasn't at all what I'd expected. At first, he was framed in the gray haze of the screen door of the yellow wooden house he lived in. Then he stepped outside to speak with me. A little gnomic fellow. Mid-forties. Pale. Almost avuncular. Calm as a cat thief, and dressed in jeans, a faded yellow cotton turtleneck, muddy cowboy boots.

He had, as reported in the letters that had brought me here, shaved his head. But not in the last three or four days. His face was worn, and wrinkled around the mouth and eyes.

He smiled, and actually said, "Howdy."

Then he looked at me with moist brown unshockable eyes, and I imagined he knew everything. He knew I was here to hurt him. He knew about my father's secret train. He even knew about the unpaid parking ticket I'd skated out on a month ago in Phoenix.

But when I spoke he seemed to have a childlike faith in me.

"Yes, sure," he said. "We'd love to have you visit with us for a while. Why don't you come back this evening, and you can meet everyone then." The air was soft and cool, and I smelled apple trees and hay and horse manure. The snow was gone.

"What time?"

"Six-thirty or so."

Smoke from someone's chimney drifted by.

"I don't mean to be rude," I said. "But what exactly is a swami?"

"A holy man." He sucked on a tooth, then turned to go back inside. "A spiritual teacher."

I suppose I'd better admit right now that I don't remember all of that. Not anymore. Not in all that detail. Back then, I was in the middle of the first of several journal-keeping phases of my life. I remember walking back to the motel, calling my mother and father from a pay phone along the way, then locking myself into my room and writing all about it. I wrote in my journal almost every day I was out there. Probably, it was how I worked out my fear.

I was careful, circumspect. I assumed the swami might soon be reading what I wrote. So there were things I danced around, or left out entirely, but what I put in my journal I got right. Which is why the story has been flowing out of me much faster in these last few pages, while I sit here writing in a little pool of light, at three in the morning in this house on a beach in Florida.

He walked into the living room, barefooted on the faded yellow shag carpet. He was dressed in the same jeans and turtleneck he'd had on earlier. There was no furniture in the room. He sat on the floor in front of us, then arranged his legs into a half lotus position and took a few deep breaths.

"*Om shantii, shantii, shantii, shantiiiiiiiiiii,*" he said, stretching out the last word an extra beat. Then he turned toward me and translated. "Peace," he said, "peace . . . peace . . . peace."

He looked around the room and smiled at everyone. And while he did that, a tall young fellow with a TV wrestler's chest and a TV wrestler's shaved head got up from the front row, filled a brass bowl with incense, and lit it.

Lighting ceremony complete, the swami started up again.

I allowed my eyes to creep around the room, taking inventory.

Apparently, this swami's spiritual teachings appealed more to women than to men. There were seventeen females, six males. Most of the girls were good-looking and in their early twenties. Four or five of them were absolutely beautiful. One was dumpy with blotchy skin and kinky hair, but you can't have everything.

All the guys looked young and fit and eager to please. Three of them had shaved their heads. The only beard in the room was on the face of the heretic who'd invaded them that night. He hadn't shaved in eleven months, much to the consternation of his father.

It was snowing again, and the swami's flock had smelled of damp wool when it wandered in, in little groups of two or three, brushing snowflakes from their sweaters, talking quietly, like they were in a church. A few of them had stopped and said hello to me.

Straight through two refillings of the bowl, the cowboy who became a swami sat and told us Bible stories, Hindu stories, stories of the Buddha, and of the alignment of the stars and the wisdom of "the adepts." He pronounced *adepts* like some people pronounce *Arabs. Ay-rabs. Ay-depts.* I wasn't sure who they were, but he seemed to think they were very wise indeed, and perhaps that he was one of them. An *ay-dept.*

I still had a lot to learn, but it seemed to me the essence of being a swami might lie in the capacity to make grand and mystifying statements with a straight face. No one could be taking these stories seriously. They had kind and gentle undertones but just didn't make any sense the way he jumbled them all together to make his points.

But I could tell at a glance that the swami was making sense to everyone there but me. They listened carefully. They gave judicious little nods—while incense filled my eyes and lungs and then my soul, and the holy man droned on. About the kinship of every living thing. And about the revolution that was going to sweep across this country sometime soon, you could mark his words on that.

Finally he stopped talking.

He sat back, head up, gut in, breathing deeply, like a boxer between rounds. Then he took a big gulp of air and licked his lips, and for a terrible moment I thought he was only just getting warmed up, and that there were hours more of his wisdom still to be shared with us that night.

But instead, he started chanting and they all joined in.

"Ommmmm shantii, shantii, shantii, shantiiiiiiiiiiiiiiiiiiiiiiiiiiiiii." They sang it over and over.

When they finished, they stood up and some of them stayed and chatted and others said goodbyes and started leaving for their houses. They didn't all live together, even though those were the days of California communes. That was something I didn't understand yet.

I'd seen studio photos of my friend's daughter on the wall of her dining room at home, and recently she'd mailed me little snapshots of the girl. I'd torn them up back in Phoenix. One of the women who hung around to speak with the swami before she left was young and honey-haired and beautiful, and probably my friend's youngest daughter—the one named Pamela. I liked the gentle look on her face, and the way she cocked one hip as she waited her turn to speak with the swami. But I showed no interest in her.

The swami sidled up to me. "I don't want you to waste your money staying in the motel anymore," he said. "Over by the highway, I've got a shed. It's got a clean cement floor and a bathroom with a shower. And there's an air conditioner you can turn on. I'd like it if you'd bunk in there until we find a better place for you."

"Thank you," I said. "You're very kind."

There were Townies and there were Halpernites. A Townie, to us, was anyone who lived in our little town in the desert but wasn't one of us. Halpernites, to Townies, were all of us, because some Townies knew the swami when he was just another drunken cowboy, and back then his name was Halpern.

In a town that small—Population 846, according to signs out on the highway—no business ever turned away a customer. But sometimes the smiles on Townies' faces fell away when they saw a Halpernite walk in. I'd been seen with Halpernites but didn't wear the strings of beads they wore around their necks, and the Townies weren't sure what to make of me. At first, they treated me better than a Halpernite, except when I was with one.

I worked my way in.

I made friends.

I felt the group's love.

I became a vegetarian, like the swami preached. I abstained from sex, like the swami preached. I practiced yoga every morning before dawn, on the wall-to-wall carpet of the swami's furnitureless living room. And each day, after yoga, when the swami shuffled in to lead us all in prayers, I prayed to Shiva, Rama, Jesus Christ, and Vishnu, just like the swami preached.

The snows on the day of my arrival were a fluke. The next afternoon the temperature had hit eighty-one, and two weeks after that, a hundred and four.

Day after day, an hour after dawn, when our yoga and our prayers were finished and the town had become a web of scorching streets, I marched out into the blinding sunlight and drove off with the swami's men thirty minutes down the two-lane highway to the Quonset hut where we all worked for several hours every day.

We were piecework glassblowers—making bongs, hash oil pipes, and crystal coke sets for a raging asshole friend of the swami who operated out of a post office box in Los Angeles, this hut, and a beat-up woody station wagon. Drugs, the swami said, were not for us. But drug paraphernalia, what could be wrong with blowing glass? We brought in the money that paid the rent and put wholesome vegan products in our stomachs.

Piecework promoted speed.

I could make a jumbo four-hole bong, with feet, in twenty-nine seconds flat, not counting cooling time. Cooling time was irrelevant. By the time my first bong of the day was cool enough to handle, I could make twenty more. No one in that hut took as much pride in his work as me.

The desert was hot; the hut was even hotter. Usually, by two or three, we'd sweated all we had to sweat and couldn't stand it in there anymore. So we said goodbye to our cretin boss—waved at him through the window of the air-conditioned sanctum from which he watched us work—and hit the highway. Late afternoons were free for religious studies and siestas, for private counseling from the swami, or, in my case, for surveillance, burglary, and drives up into the mountains to cool off and try to think straight.

Which wasn't always easy. Because every evening we went back to the swami's house, the big acolyte filled the brass bowl with incense, and lit it, and the swami preached to us. And in the morning it all started again. My life in the inferno.

Did the swami feel the heightened scrutiny everywhere around him? Did he sense the reason I habitually showed up for yoga several minutes early, the first intruder in his sleeping house? Did he notice that, sometimes when he went out, I was in the field nearby picking wild asparagus and waiting for him to exit so I could enter? Did he realize that, as crazy as I knew it was, his damn sermons were starting to make sense to me? That blackness filled my traitor's heart several times each day?

Sometimes it got chilly at night.

That's the only explanation I can think of for the local fascination with hot springs. Maybe in the winter it would make more sense. But I was there during the late spring and early summer, when our whole valley was hotter than the hinges of hell—to borrow the local expression. Still, almost every weekend, the swami took us all an hour up the highway to an Olympic-sized swimming pool filled with the hottest water you'd ever want to imagine lapping at your body. It was 128 degrees Fahrenheit. Steam rose off the surface of the pool in clouds so thick you couldn't see through it, but then disappeared by the time it had risen thirty or forty feet into the parched air. The swami said it was good for us. Good for us to stand in the bright sunshine, in the middle of the broiling desert, up to our necks in water so hot that the first few times we went there it took me more than ten minutes just to coax my balls beneath the water line. Meanwhile, the swami just dove in. And he wasn't the only crazy one. The place was usually packed. Hellcats from all over the valley brought their families there. They tanned themselves on deck chairs beside the pool, sucked down Cokes and sno-cones, then dove back in. Parents taught their kids how to swim in there. High school girls practiced synchronized swimming routines. The wading pool was filled with 112-degree water and laughing, peeing toddlers. And, to each and every one of them, the swami looked like any other joe in a bathing suit. That, I thought, was maybe why he liked the place so much.

"I need to go off walking for a few days."

No response. The swami didn't even move.

"Someplace up high where I can get used to altitude," I said. "I've got to get in shape for Switzerland."

He was sitting in the bentwood chair on his little porch.

After awhile, he looked up at me with a face filled with beatitude and trust.

The greatest dangers to a spy aren't physical, but psychological, said my father once. *It's just not easy for a man to intentionally befriend and then betray another man.*

"Is that all right with you?" I asked the swami.

"You may come and go as you wish."

There was a thump inside his house, and, while we turned toward that, I was certain once again that he knew everything. *Leave*, a voice inside me said. My own voice, not my father's. *Get in the car. Leave now, forever.*

But when I turned back to the swami, everything was fine. He brushed a flower petal off his shirt. "Where are you thinking of going?"

"Someplace high in the Sierras. Any suggestions?"

The swami told me about a trail he thought I might enjoy. And I might have, had I not left before dawn the next morning and, instead of climbing into the Sierras, walked east across the desert and into the low brown mountains that framed the other side of our valley.

I look down at the scar on my wrist. How on earth, I wonder, did I ever get from there to here? Somehow, my first swami, my first clandestine journey, and my invitation to join the CIA all came wrapped together. In view of where I sit now, and why, I must admit there is a certain symmetry to all of that. But it's not something I want to be discussing with my interrogators. I open the slats of my shutters and stare out toward a ship's lights on the sea.

No mention of this in my journal. But I remember that as I slogged up a switchback, Charles Manson was on my mind. He was on all our minds. Because the swami talked about him nearly every day. Manson had spent time in our town, and all around this desert, before his celebrated trial and incarceration.

There were still unindicted Manson Family members drifting around in the desert. Every once in awhile they'd stop in town for a day or two, and I'd see them in the park or in the general store and filling station. The first one I met spent half an hour telling me weird shit about force fields and how he and Charlie used to practice jumping out of moving cars in Death Valley, rolling themselves into balls as they fell and then letting their force fields protect them. He asked me if I had a car and wanted to try it with him. It was tempting. Who wouldn't want to learn to activate his own force field? But I said no, on both counts.

It wasn't clear whether the swami had known Manson or just liked to give the impression he might've. Sometimes the swami brightened up his sermons with statements such as: "Charlie did get off track a little, as we all know. But when it comes to the race war that's going to sweep across this country, old Charlie got that just right."

Of course, Elementals were also on our minds, and it was usually while I pondered them that any softness I'd developed for the swami hardened. He had every one of those poor fools believing Elementals lived out in the rocks. What wood sprites were to woods, Elementals were to our rocky desert. According to the swami, they looked like humans, only they were very, very short. They must be a bit like leprechauns, I gathered, except they didn't live in Ireland but in the rocks around our town, and they weren't mischievous but kept us safe from danger. I swear to God—some of the poor bastards I blew glass with kept their eyes peeled for Elementals while we drove down the highway to work. My new ambition was to pound so much shit and sandalwood out of the swami that he'd never scar another soul.

Halfway up a truly dismal slope, I finally found what I'd come to see: the abandoned mine shaft that was to be the swami's redoubt when the revolution came. This was the sanctuary he promised all of us after he got us good and scared.

I didn't need to duck, and the shaft seemed to be so well braced that I didn't worry much about accidentally entombing myself. Twenty yards in, I came to oil drums lining the wall on my left. The first ones I opened were filled with jugs of water. There were other drums filled with blankets, with lanterns and little stoves, with fuel, with rifles and pistols and ammunition, and with food. Two tons of corn and oats and beans and wheat all dried and sealed and waiting for hell to break loose.

I'd seen plenty of guns before. It was the food that held me. Fascinated me.

As apocalyptic stockpiles went, this wasn't just any food. This was Charlie Manson's food—seized and then auctioned off by the sheriff who arrested him, purchased and treasured by the swami. Half the Halpernites had been there at the sheriff's auction, and they'd told me all about it. A bill of sale was taped onto the lid of one of the drums.

I pried open every one of them and, at first, I was afraid to touch the food. Being that it had once belonged to Charles Manson. But then it occurred to me how stupid it was to be spooked by a barrel full of wheat reflecting in my flashlight beam. Pretty soon I was running my fingers through the grain, and when I moved on to a barrel of corn suddenly I knew nothing could stop me from eating some. I dropped a handful into one of the aluminum nesting pots I'd bought in Arizona. Whoever'd dried this stuff had done a thorough job. The kernels sounded like rocks hitting the pot.

After I banged the lids back onto all the drums, I went outside and watched the sun set over the Sierras while I cooked myself a freeze-dried dinner, then topped it off with popcorn. It tasted like any other popcorn. It was a little burnt and not all of it had popped. But I didn't mind that. Back home, I always asked my mother for the burnt, half-opened bits at the bottom of the pan when she made popcorn.

Run! I heard my father say.

And perhaps I would have. Or maybe not. I'm the dogged, persistent type. It's one of my greatest strengths, and one of my weaknesses—but I hadn't figured that out back then. I'll never know what I would have done.

When I got started the next morning, the sky was blistering blue. Even over the snowfields high in the Sierras there wasn't a single cloud. I followed yellow switchback after yellow switchback down the driest mountains I'd ever seen.

It started to go wrong when I thought I saw a shortcut. It was a little animal trail, the color of straw, amidst big coppery rocks. It didn't look all that steep, and it promised to deliver me across and down a talus slope and help me cut out two miles of switchbacks. I started down the pebbly little trail.

Way down in the valley, I could see the town. There had to be more going on down there than what I knew so far. What was I seeing but not seeing? What was the swami really up to? My friend's daughter was in Oregon on an errand for him and wasn't expected back for another two weeks, maybe longer. No one was sure, and it didn't really matter to anyone but me.

I kept moving down the steepening trail, and suddenly I was standing on nothing.

I was in the air, flying.

Only fifteen feet or so, and straight down. I landed on my heels, bounced, dropped a little farther, then came to rest on my feet, my butt, and my hands. Nothing hurt much anywhere. But when I got up and started dusting off my khaki shorts, I saw the sharp black rock I'd landed on had cut my wrist and half-severed the tendon just below my right thumb.

Inside my backpack, compliments of my father, I had a very small and very fine first-aid kit. I'd never noticed before that, in addition to a surgical suture set and several other handy items, its contents thoughtfully included a list of useful phrases in Russian. My wound wasn't bleeding much. But I knew if I didn't take care of it now I might well bleed to death before I got off this mountain. I became very calm. I sewed up my wrist as well as I could left-handed, then wandered down the slopes and around a black wall of cinder cones, across an ancient lava field, and toward my shed in the center of the inferno. I will not answer these questions without a representative. *Ya ne budu otvechat na voprosy bez predstavitelya.* It was so hot, and I had so far to go. I lost my hat in a shimmering black-and-silver lake that kept stretching out before me. I wanted to sit down and rest, but there was no shade. *Hat* spelled backward is *tah.* Where is my tah? I was afraid if I sat down I wouldn't get up. It was so hot. When evening came, on an unpaved road still six miles from town, I ran out of water, but kept going. Walking toward the lights. Until an old blue pickup truck screeched to a halt beside me.

The driver was a giant with a greasy Stetson smashed down over his hair.

In slow motion, I watched him put my pack in the bed and me in the cab. I wanted to teach him some useful Russian phrases, but apparently I'd lost those too somewhere along the way. I sang hysterically all the way to town.

He dropped me outside the cafe.

I was only half crazed. I knew I had to replenish my body with fluids and food. I went inside and drank a pitcher of ice water and about five Cokes. I didn't feel like eating, but I ate some pie anyway. On the house. They said they were going to throw it out if somebody didn't eat it tonight. That was a lie. They gave it to me as an act of charity, pure and simple, and may God bless them for it. I thought I'd healed myself by the time I left the cafe. I walked back to my shed thinking I was all right.

But in the morning I was sick.

Around noon, the swami's women took me from my cot in the shed to a brass bed in one of their homes. For days, they hovered around me in shifts, smiled at me, sponged fever off my forehead, changed my bandages and my sweat-soaked blankets, brought me soup and medicine. And when the poison in my blood made me too sick for them to handle, they raced me down the highway to the nearest town that had a hospital. Then at least one or two of them sat with me every day until I got out. I had never felt better looked after, or more treacherous.

Everyone agreed I needed a new regime. I said I couldn't stand blowing glass in that fucking Quonset hut anymore. Not every day. The swami decreed that from now on I'd blow glass only twice a week, and once a week I'd drive ninety miles up the highway to buy supplies. That suited me just fine. That would give me perfect opportunities to call home, and eat forbidden hamburgers.

Everyone further agreed I shouldn't live by myself in the shed anymore. The swami said I was to share a house with Philip—the burly acolyte, the lighter of the incense. I moved into Philip's tiny wooden house—which like half of the other houses in our town had long ago been hauled up the highway from a concentration camp called Manzanar.

"No one's ever been here as long as you without getting their mala." Philip—who was either my new roommate or my jailer—announced this to me one morning in our concentration camp quarters before we left for yoga.

Malas were the prayer beads, the strings of thick brown seeds the swami made by hand and gave his devotees. Malas were powerful magic—everyone knew that. Malas kept you safe. And malas were symbols of belonging.

Of all the swami's men, I'd always found Philip quite the stupidest. But not today. "Swami's still got his doubts about you," said Philip. "I can see it when he looks at you when you're not looking."

"It's just because he knows I'm heading off to Switzerland," I said. "He's waiting until I get back. That's all." I didn't believe it, though, and I didn't think Philip did either.

Usually I'd talk to my mother first. She'd tell me how she was, and then she'd tell me how my father was. He didn't talk much about himself while I was still out there in my fever dream of an expedition into the swami's desert kingdom. Aside from the fact that I was an untrained amateur, how many times had my father been through something like this? How many infiltrators had he tried to calm, tried to help hold themselves together long enough to get a job done? The thing that got me most about our conversations was he always seemed to know what was going to happen next.

For an infiltrator, said my father, *the most dangerous time is when he needs a friend.*

"You're a Halpernite, aren't you?" Her tone was somehow disappointed in me, like I was an old friend who'd let her down. But I didn't even know this green-eyed beauty who'd appeared behind me, smiling over my shoulder and looking at my plate.

"Well, sort of," I said. "I just joined."

I was sitting at the counter in a roadside restaurant thirty minutes north of the town where I lived, and where she lived too, I thought. I'd glimpsed her there a few times, and once she'd smiled at me on her way into the courthouse.

She widened her eyes in comic horror and pointed at my cheeseburger. "So why are you eating *that?*"

"To tell you the truth," I said, "I was sick. I'm still not really well. And you know how they say when your body is sick it knows what it needs, and craves that? Well, I crave beef. And that's why every day this week I've been sneaking up here to eat it."

She considered this at length, then grinned.

The place was almost empty except for us. She swung aboard the stool beside me. She told me her name was Sarah and I told her mine. We ate together, and a few times while we were talking her fingers came over and touched my hand, rested there a moment, then moved away. "I'm going to drive up into the meadows now, and take a walk," I said. "Would you like to come along?"

"No Halpernite nonsense?"

"I don't believe half of it myself," I said, and was rewarded with Sarah's smile. "Why should I try to sell it to you?"

She was tall and clear-eyed, maybe twenty-one or twenty-two, and her hair was shiny brown and pinned up in the back. Her frilly gray dress was high-collared, and it pinched in at the waist and then flared out and draped to her ankles. It gave her the look of a pretty schoolmarm in an old Western. The kind all the cowboys fight over by the last reel.

She climbed into her jeep and followed my car all the way out of the desert and up curling gray switchbacks to where the road ended. Or began, depending upon your point of view. And when she got there, all smiles, she was wearing hiking shorts, a faded peasant blouse, and mountain boots. Good trick, I said.

At the roadhead, we were already at nearly ten thousand feet. Above us, the peaks were white with fresh snow. We hiked toward heaven. Past cool green tarns and huge gray boulders, over talus fields and through meadows brimming with wildflowers.

Sarah called out their names. Lupine. Mule's Ears. Mariposa Lily. Larkspur. Phlox. Fireweed. Horsemint. Indian Paintbrush. Pentstemon. She seemed to know them all.

Just below the tree line, we stopped beside a stream to drink. The water was running high and fast and sparkling in the sunlight. On the edge, a gnarled pine was braced against the current. Almost all its roots were exposed, and I said one day soon it would break loose and go clacking down the streambed.

Sarah's cheeks were pink and happy and she said maybe I was right.

I told her about my father, and that because of him I grew up all over the world. And I told her that, since then, I'd just kept moving. I told her of strange lands I'd seen, and others I wanted to see. I said I'd crossed the Pacific on a leash, climbed the pyramids of Giza, and popped Charles Manson's corn. I wanted to tell her more, what I was up to here, but I stopped myself just in time.

In the gloaming, we made it back to the roadhead and she smiled at me and I pulled her against my side and kissed the top of her head goodbye. And after that, once or twice each week, we walked together in the mountains, then talked and stared at the stars and slept beside each other—naked, but chaste and modest, in separate mummy bags, in a meadow that smelled like flowers and damp earth.

Operational considerations. The many-faceted role of devotee, bong manufacturer, mountain man, swain, and dutiful son of a spy is not an easy one to carry off in the best of circumstances. But you should try adding to that the requirement of running a one-man surveillance operation through a tiny town where everyone knows everyone else and in and over the desert surrounding the town.

Every week, every one of them had a private session with the swami. The schedule never changed, but the places they met and their means of getting there were maddeningly unpredictable.

Sometimes the swami would pick one up in his truck or on his motorcycle, and together they'd ride off into the desert and come back an hour or two later. Sometimes they'd meet at his house and then head off on foot. Sally lived alone in a gabled Victorian house near the courthouse. Sally had money and was a busy woman, and for Sally the swami made house calls. Every Thursday afternoon at four.

Without a mala, I didn't qualify for private sessions. All I could do was inquire as to what they were all about. "The swami gives us special blessings for our individual spiritual needs" was Philip's answer. Philip could be a sanctimonious prick. "Or sometimes we just sit and talk."

Did the swami feel me gaining on him? Did he notice that, on certain Tuesdays, when he and the graceful Pamela roared off on his motorcycle, I was on the edge of town and on the highest rock, tracking their dust trail and trying to find just where in hell it was they went?

And, after many Tuesdays, once I'd finally found that place—a little patch of desert in the middle of a boulder field—did the swami know that when they next arrived I was also there?

That evening, even those beautiful mountains couldn't soothe me.

Walking toward our meadow, Sarah asked me what was wrong, and I said nothing. After dinner and not much talk, I lay down and closed my eyes and seethed. Until Sarah unzipped my sleeping bag and sat on top of me. She unclenched my hands, then kissed me lightly on my eyes and on my forehead. Her hair fell all around me. I felt her nipples tickling my chest. "I think you need to lighten up," she said.

Eventually, we zipped our bags together and stared at a riot of stars, until she entwined me in her arms and became still. In the morning, I skipped yoga. While we ate breakfast, I looked down into the valley and told Sarah what I'd seen the afternoon before.

They arrived, and parked the motorcycle at the base of the very rocks I'd climbed. From my grandstand seat, invisible in a black triangle of shade between two orange rocks, I could see their smiles and hear them talking, but couldn't make out all their words. They spread upon the desert floor one of the old green army blankets of my childhood—my father must have had a dozen of them.

The swami took off his shirt, then sat down, face up toward the sun, and folded his legs into a full lotus position. Pamela said something funny and walked over and leaned against a gray rock which was streaked with black.

Beside it was a little pump I hadn't noticed. Pamela began to crank the handle. She doused herself under the spout, then walked back, laughing in the sunshine, dazzling wet all over, yellow snakes of hair dripping diamonds. Her sundress was heavy now, sticking to her in places, and she held part of it out in front of her, carrying water.

She was beautiful and kind, and my friend's youngest daughter—which added to my fury as I watched the swami undress Pamela, and then expose his cowboy ass and dispense to her a special blessing for her individual spiritual needs.

"He preaches chastity," I said to Sarah. "And I just know he's screwing *every* one of them."

On our refrigerator, Philip had left a note saying he'd be gone for a week or two, visiting his brother, and don't touch his stuff. That would be no problem. I'd already been through all of Philip's stuff, had already read every page of the diary of his enlightenment. Philip's smoke bomb of a car was gone, and I had my doubts it would make it all the way to Colorado and back. But that was Philip's problem. That evening, before the swami preached, I heard Philip had gone to try to convince his brother the dentist to convince their parents that Philip hadn't gone crazy and to keep sending him money. Good luck, Philip.

I wasn't sure how many lucky Japanese-American internees our plywood and tar-paper house was meant to hold, back when it and a thousand identical relocation quarters were surrounded by barbed wire and searchlights and patrolled by soldiers with machine guns. It was crowded with just the two of us big guys living there. I dragged the mattress out of my bedroom and into the living room. Now I couldn't touch all four walls at once.

Two psychiatrists and a holy man walk into a bar. It was the jokes that told me Andy was my man. When my friend's daughter came back from Oregon, she brought with her the key to her own redemption. I had to tell someone. If I told all of them at once, they'd kill me. If I told the wrong one, they'd kill me. If I told the right one the wrong way, they'd kill me. I had no standing with the swami's flock. I didn't even have a mala. Andy had one, though, and when he got back from a month in the outside world, he was a different man. I hadn't known him well before he left, but on his first day back at yoga, he was like a clown at a funeral, and, at the workbench beside me, he told me joke after joke while we churned out the best damn hash oil pipes a man could make in less than fifty seconds. It was obvious the travel had done him good.

Andy was six years older than me. He was twenty-eight. He had a thin and thoughtful face, and brown hair, parted in the middle and flowing to his shoulders. His eyes were an accountant's cautious eyes and were set behind little silver-rimmed spectacles. For Andy, think John Lennon in granny glasses and you won't be that far off.

Poor Andy told me he had a master's degree in mathematics and another in psychology, and he'd once had a good job and a house on the ocean and a woman and a dog. But he had given all that up, for he'd been touched somewhere deep inside him when he first heard the words of the cowboy who became a swami.

I knew, though, if Andy didn't know it yet, that part of him—perhaps not a part of him he was fully conscious of—had realized there was something wrong with the equation he'd been handed. And I knew I was going to risk a talk with him sometime soon.

For those not sated by weekend trips to hell's swimming pool, all around the valley there were other places, secret places, locals went to satisfy strange urges to boil their own blood in water funneled straight from the volcanoes that smoldered beneath us all. Eight days after his return from Oregon, my new friend Andy took me to his secret spring.

It was ten miles out of town but less than a hundred yards from the highway. Still, you'd never see it from a passing car.

It was a little rill, carved by water through the bedrock desert floor. It looked a bit like the Grand Canyon except it was only about as wide as my shoulders and maybe six or seven inches deep. Most of it was as dry as a rill on the moon, but a trickle of water about four inches wide and an inch deep flowed down its center.

We followed the stream until we came to a spot where it widened out into a pool. It looked just about big enough for me to fit my body into. Andy told me to get in. I draped my clothes over a tuft of sagebrush and lowered myself into the hole. When my feet hit bottom, the water was just over my waist. Meanwhile, Andy lowered himself into another little pool, which was around a bend in the rill but only about six feet away from me. We squatted until the water reached our throats. I felt like a missionary in a pot.

It was so hot that suddenly it felt cold; my brain was receiving so many signals at once that my skin went numb.

From where I was, Andy looked like a man buried up to his neck in the desert.

"How'd you find this hellhole, anyway?"

"In the winter, it steams." Andy had already been through two winters here. Long enough to accrue plenty of residual loyalty to his swami. Was I about to be very foolish?

My journal contains no record of the rest of our conversation. I remember I realized what I was about to say could be dangerous, so I made him promise to listen with an open mind.

And I remember the essence of what I then made him listen to.

While the novice in me studied and surrendered, another part of me held out. It's that simple. Are you with me, Andy? I've tried, Andy, I swear to you I have, but I've just never been sure I really believed all this stuff. And if you'll think about it, like I have, Andy, you'll realize that you and I, and all the rest of us, just don't deserve to be made to believe in tiny men and women who live in the rocks and watch over us the chosen ones, nor in fish gods or Charlie's revolution or the divine necessity of chastity. And, while we're on the subject of chastity, Andy, let me tell you one more thing. . . .

Andy was quiet when I finished. I wish I could forget the terrible look on his face as he rose halfway out of the water, fingering the shiny brown seeds of his mala while he stared into my eyes. I was afraid I'd gone too far. Just think it over, I said. Think for yourself about it. And we'll talk more tomorrow.

That night every creak or rustle I heard outside the house was the swami's men come to get me. But in the morning, I was whole.

When Andy arrived for yoga, late enough to make me worry—we'd already finished *nadi sudi* and moved on to *vyaghrasana*—he slapped me on the back and winked at me, and I knew he hadn't discussed our conversation with anyone but himself. A lost look had settled over him by the time we climbed into his Datsun pickup to head to work.

When we turned onto the highway at the edge of town, I saw the swami. He was standing all alone, leaning on the top rail of a corral—and staring in at the horses like a cashiered sailor staring out to sea.

"Look!" I said to Andy. But perhaps he didn't hear me.

He drove on in silence for miles.

"I think I believe you," he finally said. "But I want you to prove it to me."

That was on a Tuesday.

And so it came to pass that, on the following day, in the evening, just after Sally left to meet us all in the swami's living room to get some more of that good old-time religion, Andy and I stole into Sally's house of five gables, carrying a tiny postage scale.

And that, the day after that, also in the evening, and this time just two hours after Sally's house call from the swami, we stole into her house again and, when I pulled back the mirror above her bathroom sink, Andy looked into Sally's medicine cabinet and yelped.

"Christ!" he said. "We don't even need to weigh it!"

On the middle shelf, folded into an entirely new shape, and with its cap glistening with a fresh coat of excess unguent, rested Sally's tube of contraceptive jelly.

Andy said how did you know? I said I didn't know. But I saw this a couple months ago when we were all over here watching TV, and I cut my finger and Sally sent me in here to get a Band-Aid. Remember? It didn't really register on me at first, because I knew she had a boyfriend when she first moved here. Before she met the swami.

"Moses Halpern . . . you are *busted!*"

Andy began to laugh after he said that. But I calmed him right down, told him to set the scale on the counter and, if for nothing more than the sake of the Scientific Method, we must complete our measurements. The truth was I didn't want him to have any doubts later.

That night Sally's spermicide would've cost one less stamp to mail than the night before.

Miles Copeland would teach me years later that, when it comes to fomenting a revolution, if you recruit the right man and give him all the tools he'll need, your job is done. Andy was the right man. And, once I'd armed him with the truth, he had a ferocity about him that made me proud.

The next morning he buttonholed Myra when we ran into her on our way to the library. "I want to talk with you," Andy said, so sternly that Myra led us straight through her little white picket fence and into her Manzanar house and put on a pot of tea.

Andy put it to her quite forcefully. "I *know*," he said, "what you've been doing with the swami."

Myra turned and walked into the kitchen, as if the pot were whistling, which it was not.

When she came back, her eyes were shiny.

"He told me I was such a terrible student," she said, "that the only way he could break through to my soul was through my body."

"I know," lied Andy.

Myra was the chubby, blotchy one with frizzed-out Little Orphan Annie hair. A tear rolled down her face and hovered just above her lip. "And he told me that I mustn't tell, because I was his only one."

"I know. I know." Andy gave her a hug. "I know, and it's all right."

"You're right," Andy told me once we were back outside. "If he's fucking her, he's fucking every one of them."

We walked a little way in silence.

"What's next?" I asked. I was no longer in charge.

"Group therapy," said Andy. And I knew then it was time to go say good-bye to Sarah.

Outside the door of the swami's house, in a whisper, I said to Andy, "Remember to take care of Pamela. Send her home to see her mother." Then I gave him the four one-hundred-dollar bills her mother had given me for her. It was more than I had to my name, and I'd grown quite attached to it—neatly folded into a secret recess in my wallet. But I had a five-hundred-dollar payday coming for four weeks' work once I got to Switzerland. That would be enough to keep me going a couple more months while I evaded my father's questions about a real job.

"I'll wait in my car for fifteen minutes," I said. "And if he comes before I leave, I'll honk the horn."

"Okay," said Andy.

"Take care," I said. "And give 'em hell."

"What can I do," said Andy, "except see the funny side of it?"

He shook my hand—a soul shake, such were the times—then went inside, where all the swami's flock were waiting.

A few minutes later, the swami roared up on his motorcycle, and I honked twice and waved at him, and he waved back—just before opening his front door and walking into a hellstorm of women scorned and men too long duped into celibacy. I was sorry I couldn't stick around to see the oppressed masses rise up against the tyrant. But, even at twenty-two years old and just concluding my second covert political operation, I knew enough to get out while the getting was good.

I imagine he knew something was wrong the moment he walked in, but that it took him a couple of minutes to fully grasp the magnitude of what everybody inside now knew. And that, by then, I'd already driven slowly beneath the flashing yellow traffic light and turned past the courthouse and the cafe, the little lawns and the cottonwoods, and I was safely out of town.

As I look at the scene now in my memory—as I pull back and up and watch my car speeding through the desert, heading north through mountain shadows toward the man my father had told me to go to when I needed to escape—it's clear to me that even then I already was a spy, or was predestined to become one. And that makes my reaction to what happened the next day seem somewhat inexplicable from here.

There's a man in an ice-blue turban I've been seeing in my dreams. I wonder if he'll be my interrogator.

The news—the long-awaited, oft-delayed, wholly expected, yet still quite thrilling news—is I am about to testify! It seems the Justice Department and the Government of India have made a deal. Frank Morse called and told me this morning. We're going to do it in Miami, in the federal courthouse, where I'll feel nice and safe. Frank's flying out next week to get me ready.

The strangest thing has been happening to me since Frank's call. I've felt wave after wave of the most vivid nostalgia. Not for people or events, but entirely for places. I've been to London, Tangier, Sydney, Shinjuku, Kowloon, smelled them, tasted them, recalled the minutest atmospheric details I would've thought long forgotten. But, as it turned out, they were only long suppressed. I've momentarily lost myself in each of them, and felt little jolts at realizing I was not there, but only here, and only daydreaming.

Soon I will be traveling.

San Francisco, viewed through the windows of Bill Tharp's yellow Gran Torino, was a far different city than any I'd seen before. It was to Bill Tharp that my father sent me from the desert. By now, of course, I knew that, back when I knew him in Japan, he was an airline tycoon who wasn't an airline tycoon. And earlier this afternoon I'd learned he was no longer the hale and tan Uncle Bill in a fine off-white linen suit I'd frozen in my memory.

He was an old man now. After more than thirty years in the FBI, the OSS, and the CIA, Bill Tharp had retired to a neighborhood of ranch houses with neat green lawns and flower beds, sprinklers twirling beneath hardwood trees, and the aroma of steaks broiling over charcoal in backyards. He was weary, but very kind, and doing his best to show me some hospitality. "I'll give you a little tour," he'd said when we got into his car, and soon we were heading out of the burbs and onto a highway that led along the bay and into the city. It was after we passed Candlestick Park that he began to forever change my perspective on cityscapes.

I still didn't know most of what I know about him now. I didn't know he was a CIA legend, the Wizard, the thoroughly ordinary-looking pensioner sitting next to me, his old eyes staring straight ahead on the road. My tour guide.

"Up ahead there," Bill said with a sweep of his hand inches from the windshield, "what do you see?"

I saw a curve in the road, around a steep slope covered with ice plant.

"I see a bottleneck," he said before I could answer. "Whenever I arrive in a city, I look at how many tanks per hour could move in on the main roads. This is a chokepoint that affects that."

We rounded the curve and saw the skyline of San Francisco against blue sky.

"And," he went on, "I look for the bridges, the television and radio stations, the power plants, the water supply, the telephone exchanges. Where are they? How many troops would you need to take them? How many to hold them?"

"God, the city is beautiful!" I said. "This is the first time I've ever seen the Transamerica Tower."

"It's actually a pyramid," Bill said. "The city *is* pretty, isn't it? Haven't you been here before?"

"I think I've been everywhere once," I said. *In fact, I left hell just yesterday,* I thought. "But I don't believe I've been to San Francisco since I was six."

Soon we were on an overpass, cresting into the city.

"In the CIA," said Bill, "we have what's known as the 'old boy network.' We try to recruit most of our people from inside it. That helps us keep our circle small and tight. Sons of intelligence officers usually make good intelligence officers. Do you know what I mean?"

I turned to look at him. "Are you saying what I think you're saying?"

"Probably," he said.

He drove on. Didn't say another word until we were downtown, idling at a traffic light.

We must have been in what I know now is called the Financial District. I remember a canyon of tall buildings lining the street, busy sidewalks, cars everywhere, horns honking. The street was in shadow except for golden light slanting in through the cross streets. In the intersection, glowing in the sunlight not twenty feet in front of us, were three men in hardhats. One of them was leaning into a jackhammer.

"Who are they?" Bill said. "Are they from Pacific Gas and Electric, like the uniforms say? Are they really working for the power company? Or are they working for the FBI, or maybe a Soviet or Chinese intelligence service, and here to splice into a telephone trunk? Larry, it happens. More than you would ever believe, it happens. There's a secret world all around us. You just don't see it unless you know where to look."

He drove on.

I saw places I'd seen in movies or on TV, and I said so.

Bill kept deflecting the conversation back to espionage. "I want you to try to see this city through the eyes of an intelligence officer," he said as he drove us slowly past Fisherman's Wharf. "Look at all the boats. Which one is the one that, most of the time, goes out fishing just like every other boat, but, four or five nights a year, it also rendezvouses with a Russian submarine or trawler?"

"Do you mean to bring someone in?"

"Someone or something. In or out."

I said I didn't know which boat it would be. And Bill said he didn't either, but we could be sure it was happening—somewhere nearby, if not here.

According to my journal, there was one cloud in the sky and it was floating just above Alcatraz.

Next, Bill drove me past the Soviet Consulate, which was a hell of a big building, and—to show him I was catching on to the theme of our tour—I asked if he supposed they needed room for so many employees just to arrange cultural exchanges and put visa stamps in passports.

A man came out of the building, and Bill asked if I thought he was heading out to meet a tourist who'd spent the day photographing scientists in town for a convention. Maybe, I said, or maybe our man is wearing that happy grin because he's off to meet his new lover—who happens to work for an American counterintelligence service.

Bill showed me an apartment building which looked like any other apartment building but had once been a hive of enemy spies. He drove me past an otherwise unremarkable hotel which at the beginning of the Second World War had housed the second-highest ranking Japanese intelligence officer in the United States.

When we came upon a drunk calmly picking through a trash can, Bill asked me to expatiate on what we might be beholding. "That," I said, enjoying myself now, "is either a bum looking for something to eat, or drink, or read, or an agent servicing his dead drop, picking up new instructions from his controller."

And with that, apparently I'd passed the aptitude test. Because now Bill sped up, made a few turns, and navigated us to a parking space in front of a little bar with a neon Michelob sign in the window. "Let's go into my branch office and talk," he said.

That was the most compelling evidence I'd seen yet that Bill Tharp was a seasoned intelligence officer who knew all the moves.

He sipped on his beer. I didn't know it then, but Bill had three months left to live. This was his last recruitment. "Your father and I are both part of that old boy network," he said. "Sons of intelligence men make good intelligence men. And the agency likes to hire them. They're easier to check out. Known commodities. Larry, because of your father, we've been keeping background files on you since the day you were born. So we know all about your life. And it would be a lot easier for you to join the CIA than someone from outside the old boy network. Do you get my point?"

"How would I go about joining?"

"Just tell me, and I'll take care of the rest."

"What would I do?"

It was a dark room. Bill had taken on a pallor that made him almost disappear in the deep shadows of our booth.

He said there were all kinds of things an enterprising young fellow could do in the CIA. He said most intelligence the CIA gathers is obtained not by spies but by CIA employees who sit around in capital cities all over the world reading newspapers and magazines and journals and reportingback on what they've read. He said the CIA employed every good linguist they could get their hands on. He said a CIA job was a cartographer's dream, that CIA's mapmaking department was bigger than any commercial map company. And he said that, for the sort of fellow who likes to sit around contemplating his navel or calculating how many angels can dance on the head of a pin, nothing could be finer than a job as an intelligence analyst in the CIA's Directorate of Intelligence.

None of that sounded all that interesting to me, and I told Bill that.

There is also, he said, in the tones of a salesman who'd known where he was actually steering me all along: the Directorate of Operations.

He said men like himself and my father were in operations. Field men. He said, if I joined the DO and I was even half as much of a charmer as my father, pretty soon I'd be a field man, and they'd have me out and about in the world dealing with important people.

Bill was old and exhausted, but his mind was still sharp. "Of course," he said, "for the first couple of years they'd dress you up like a bum and have you picking through garbage cans for messages from agents."

He got busy swirling his beer. My mind was racing.

Part of me was excited. Another part of me had known all my life this was coming and had hoped to put it off awhile longer.

"Please tell me," I said, "about your worst day ever in the CIA." And for some reason Bill did. He seemed to come to life as memories shifted into focus.

"My worst day ever in the CIA? That's easy. January second, nineteen fifty-five.

"Hands down, my worst day ever in the CIA was January second, nineteen hundred and fifty-five, in Panama City, Panama. I was the chief of station. The President of Panama was a guy named Chi Chi Remon.

"Old Chi Chi and I were great buddies. He was a good ally of the United States. And my job was basically to look after him. Keep him loyal and out of trouble. Chi Chi and I did everything together."

Bill took a sip.

"There was a security problem. So I had Chi Chi laying low. For a while, he and I sat around and shot the breeze and played cards every day. But, after about a week, Chi Chi couldn't stand it anymore. There was a big horse race and everybody in Panama City was going to be there. Chi Chi said he was going *with or without* me. So I went along. On January second, nineteen fifty-five."

Bill said, "I was sitting beside Chi Chi in the stands and someone called me to the phone." Bill paused. Then he said, "And when I went to the phone, they shot Chi Chi dead!"

Bill wrapped both his hands around his mug.

After a little silence, he said, "I *told* Chi Chi we shouldn't go to that racetrack!"

After another silence, I said, "Was there really a phone call for you?"

"What do you mean?" Bill looked at me. "Ah, bright boy! You could go far in this line of work. The line was dead. It was a setup. Somebody saved me."

"Who did it?"

"A bunch of guards with machine guns did the shooting. And Chi Chi wasn't the only one they got. A dozen others sitting around him also died. Later, they pinned it on the vice president. But he had nothing to do with it."

Bill stared into a private memory that seemed to be about eight inches in front of his face.

"I *told* Chi Chi we shouldn't go to that racetrack!" he said. He said it a couple of times while his eyes slowly came all the way back from Panama to me.

I drained my beer. "Did my father know you were going to ask me this?"

"Of course he knows," said Bill. "But don't talk to him about it on the phone."

"Of course not," I said. "I'll let you know as soon as I get back from Switzerland."

I wasn't as calm as I was trying to sound.

There are longer flights and I've been on them. But still it's a hell of a long way between takeoff from the waterfront beside San Francisco Bay to landing at the edge of the Kloten Woods outside Zurich. I spent almost the whole trip in my journal.

Over North America and the polar icecap, I wrote of my last few days in the inferno. Heading south over Greenland and Iceland and Britain, I described my day with Bill Tharp and sifted through my thoughts about working for the CIA. By the time a voice from the cockpit announced we'd made landfall over the Continent, I was dog-tired and thrashing, and when I fell to sleep, I'd tentatively decided I was going to say yes. Why not? I could always quit if it didn't work out.

Probably I would've said yes. Except that: while bumping in and out of airline sleep, falling toward Switzerland, out of my exhaustion or some untamable corner of my soul, there came to me a vision of my father's favorite cartoon. That changed things.

It was drawn by one of my father's men in Germany. On a sheet of eight-and-a-half-by-eleven paper. Across the top was written *THE INTELLIGENCE OFFICER, AS SEEN BY . . .*

Beneath that were three images.

The first one, headed *HIS WIFE,* showed an intelligence officer undressed and in a bed across whose top sheet was scrawled *UNDERCOVER.* Sitting beside him in the bed, as he puckered up to kiss her, was a knockout of a naked blond woman, with big cartoon breasts without nipples. On the nightstand beside them was an almost empty bottle of whiskey.

The second heading was *HIS BOSS.* The drawing beneath it showed the same intelligence officer lounging in his office, leaning back in his chair with his feet on his desk, watching the clock tick down toward five o'clock, his IN tray full of papers, his OUT tray empty.

The final image was labeled *HIMSELF,* and it depicted our intelligence officer in yoke and harness, dragging a big leafless tree up a steep hill. Beneath the tree were these words: *HAULING DEADWOOD.*

Apparently, this succinct deconstruction of the spy myth made a lot of sense to my father. Even back in Germany, in the world capital of espionage, while he was deputy director, and running hundreds of case officers and thousands of agents all across Europe and the Middle East. For he had this office joke mimeographed—purple ink, that unforgettable smell—and then distributed it to all his officers. He even pouched a copy to the director back in Washington.

Judging by the appreciations I heard in my stairwell listening post, my father and all the intelligence and counterintelligence hands he knew seemed to agree no outsider could possibly understand just how dull and seemingly pointless their jobs could be. The year-long stakeouts without a single sighting of the target. The endless writing of reports. The compartmentalization that often left them out of the loop when victory came, if it ever came. Hauling deadwood indeed.

Come to think of it, with the exception of liaison, especially when it coincided with cocktail hour, I'd seen nothing of my father's work which he seemed even halfway to enjoy. And in the long run his secret life hadn't exactly been a boon for him or his families. His adjustment to retirement was ugly. By the time I got through customs, I'd decided that tonight—after the dinner of raclette and baby potatoes I'd been dreaming of for weeks—I would not be heading straight to a pay phone to tell Bill Tharp deal me in. I had a month to think about it, after all. There was no need to be rash about this.

In the Berner Oberland, in July, it's not impossible to convince yourself that you've somehow found the natural center of the universe. Complete text of the postcard I sent my mother and father on my third day in residence in Lauterbrunnen: *I have never seen a more beautiful place.*

In the fairytale village of Lauterbrunnen lived about nine hundred souls. These were hale and pink-cheeked Swiss mountain folk, and nearly every one of them was named *von Allmen.* Rough translation: Everyman.

Their beautiful village is set at the entrance to an even more beautiful glacial valley. Picture Yosemite and the sheer rock wall of El Capitan, except make El Capitan eight miles wide and just as sheer and dramatic along its entire face. Then, for the other side of the valley, imagine the mirror image of this eight-mile-long vertical granite wall. Make these cliffs rise from the green valley floor straight up for more than half a mile on each side, and then add waterfalls—the tallest waterfalls in Switzerland lining the sides of the valley every mile or so to the end.

There, at the head of the valley, put the tip of a glacier—all that's left of the Ice Age monster that carved out this valley long ago. Above the glistening blue-green ice of the glacier put snowfields and mountains and, in the very center, framed perfectly by the sheer walls, put the wondrous snow-white crest of the Breithorn.

With that, you will have a rough approximation of the view out the front door and windows of the chalet that was my home for the month. It was small and built of rock and pine. With red geraniums in every window box. A brook passed not forty feet from my door. Beyond it, looking down the valley, were hayfields and green meadows, birch copses, spinneys of spruce, and there wasn't a building in sight.

What I really wanted out of life, I decided—by the end of my fourth night in the chalet—was a rollicking adventure. While many would see a job in the CIA as just the ticket for that, I thought I was perhaps uniquely qualified to know otherwise. Was I wrong? Most of my certainties at twenty-two were wrong. Still, I'm not so sure.

I do know I was wrong to believe I could stay, unscathed, in magical places like that forever. But I was young and walking ridgetops through clouds in intoxicating mountains. And when I thought back to the very few action-adventure passages in the very many true accounts of intelligence work I'd heard, or overheard, the lines that came back to me easiest were the ones like "They shot Chi Chi dead!" and "I still see his face at night."

Every morning, my new friend Krist von Allmen put a crate of Rügenbräu, the local beer, in the stream. In the evenings, we sat outside the chalet, sharing meals and drinking beers and talking about women, and places to walk, and places to climb, in the mountains. Friends would drift by and we'd drink more beers and tell lies, and when Krist got drunk he would yodel. Every few minutes one of us would be back in the stream plucking out more Rügenbräus. The bottles were brown, and ice cold when they came out of the water. On Rügenbräu, I learned enough Schwyzerdutsch to get along. Languages came easy to me, something Bill Tharp had already read in my file.

My job that month was leading American college kids around in the mountains.

Above the ledges at the top of the Lauterbrunnen Valley were vast green slopes, and trails that led through meadows and wildflowers, cowbells ringing everywhere, and across boulder fields and spurs, and snow-choked passes into the enormous mountains that surrounded us. We climbed straight up from Lauterbrunnen to Wengen, past deer and chamois in the morning shadows. We hiked to the north wall of the Eiger and past the Jungfrau. We swam in lakes with banks of snow still melting on their shores. We ascended the Schilthorn to Piz Gloria, the aerie where James Bond dueled with the evil Blofeld. We scrambled over scree and traversed a glacier. Owing to the wisdom and maturity of our leader, we stuck religiously to every switchback.

Some days, all along the way, I tried to convince myself I was still weighing two equal possibilities in my mind. Down one road, I would join the CIA and underline flimsies in red grease pencil for the rest of my life. Down the other, I wouldn't. I told myself I hadn't decided yet.

But when I flew back to San Francisco, I told Bill Tharp no. Thank you very much, but no.

I have no actual memory of telling him that. Likewise, I don't remember calling my father that night and saying: "Don't worry. I've got it all figured out. I have a plan. You'll see." But it's recorded in blue and white, complete with quotation marks, in my too-serious handwriting of the time, and I cringe every time I read it now.

I doubt it did much to improve my father's confidence in me when I got home, a couple weeks later, and told him the reason I wouldn't be joining the

CIA was I'd decided to become a businessman—and that the business I'd chosen was selling dreams.

Anyone could see it was an untapped niche market, I explained. There had to be plenty of pent-up demand. While outlining my plan to my father, I used every term I could remember from the one business text I'd read—or I should say *skimmed*—in college.

In a rainstorm, hours above Lauterbrunnen, I'd started thinking of all the storms I'd walked through, paddled through, ridden through, in the past couple of years. Then I'd started remembering people I'd met along the way. So many of them—especially the ones who seemed the most successful—when they'd heard where I was going, or how, or why, said they wished they were going with me. The word they used most often was *dream*. A wistful look came over them and they said something like "If you could only know how I dream of an adventure like that!" It seemed as if, to get where they'd gotten, they'd given up something they hadn't known they were giving up. Now they pined to get it back, but didn't know how. "And so," I told my father, "I've decided to sell them back their own dreams."

I'm sure it sounded then just as naïve and stupid as it looks now when I read it.

Years later, my mother told me that, that night, my father said to her, "I think he's gone apeshit." Probably he was right. But I set up my first business anyway—organizing and operating, and sometimes personally leading, adventure tours in the wilds. Today there's a whole adventure-tour industry. But, back then, almost no one else was doing it. And, five months after I'd told my father about my business plan, I'd managed to get a story about my new enterprise on the front page of *The Wall Street Journal*.

Another clear indication, Miles would say years later, that I was born to be a propagandist.

"Ah, wilderness!"—the *Journal* story began—"Businessmen head the pack of those seeking exotic vacations, says Larry Kolb, president of Wilderness Travel Inc." Read on and you would learn that, if you were looking to sail the Galapagos or the Maldives, or to walk through the Swiss Alps to the Matterhorn, or through the High Himal to Mount Everest, or to cross a little corner of Greenland by dogsled, I was the man to see. Larry J. Kolb, purveyor of dreams.

I've always been decisive. Which is to say I haven't always thought things all the way through before deciding on them. Which has probably made my life more interesting but also leads to the fact that the hard way is about the only way I've ever learned anything. The hard way was certainly how I learned to run a business. But this is not the story of my first adventures and false starts in commerce. Nor of what fun and pure terror it is to climb into the basket of a hot-air balloon in the Berner Oberland and rise above the Alps, not knowing whether the winds that day will carry you to Germany or Italy or into the face of a mountain.

What's relevant here is my father got behind me. He bought a stack of papers and proudly sent clippings to several people, mostly spies who'd known me since I was young. Maybe there was more to be said for selling dreams than he'd originally thought.

I'm quite certain he didn't give a damn when I told him yak butter is pink and in the Himalayas the Sherpas melt it in your tea as a substitute for milk. He started rooting for me anyway, and that felt good.

I moved to New York. I'm not sure why. I can still see my father standing outside at the airport in Florida, waving goodbye to me over the top of a low chain-link fence as I walked toward the plane. "Good luck," he said. "You can do it."

Eastern Air Lines, nonstop to LaGuardia. I had, until then, spent just one day of my life in Manhattan—years earlier, with my mother and father and Billy and Mister Potter, on our way home from Germany.

Imagine my pride when, toward the end of my first week in the city, I spotted, gleaming in the window of a headshop at Broadway and 71st, a hash oil pipe which it was immediately clear to me I'd made in a Quonset hut in the desert. There was a certain way I twisted the carbon rod when I pulled it out that gave my pipe feet a distinctive look. And no one else turned a lip quite like I did. I had no doubt this pipe was my work. Oddly, it had lasted longer than the effects of my other endeavor in the desert. Pamela had gone home to her mother, my old friend. But it didn't take completely. Eventually Pamela had gone back to the swami. Never underestimate the power of a swami to talk his way out of almost anything.

Finding your way around in the city was simple. At least in midtown and uptown. Learn the logic of the grid and after that there wasn't much you couldn't find.

So this must've been very early on. I was at 57th and Park, standing in the middle of Park Avenue, on the sidewalk at the end of one of those concrete and flower bed islands. I asked a woman which direction it was to Madison Avenue.

You've got to be a rube to be at 57th and Park and ask directions to Madison.

"You must not have spent much time around here," she said.

"No. I'm new here. And you're from England."

"From London, yes."

"So what brought you here?" I didn't know yet that only a rube or a lunatic would try to chitchat with a total stranger, the way you might talk to someone you met beside a stream in the mountains.

"I work for the J. Arthur Rank Organisation," she said. "We make films." Her hair was dark brown, and rich and shiny.

"I know."

"How do you know?" Her voice was confident and wispy at once.

"Because I've owned J. Arthur Rank stock since I was eleven. And not just a little of it. I laid down my entire life savings and bought two hundred dollars' worth when I found out they make Bond movies."

"Well, yes, you're absolutely right," she said. She was older, but actually quite good-looking. Was she ten years older than me? Twelve? At twenty-two, either one seemed like a lot to me. But she was very well put together, in a fuzzy gray suit I wasn't smart enough to recognize as Chanel.

"Madison is *that* way," she said. "But if you'd like to walk a few blocks *this* way with me, I know just the place to get the perfect map for you."

She was wearing heels and her skirt stopped above the knee.

As we walked, toward wherever we were walking, there was something wonderful about her calves.

"Here we are," she said. "I told you it wasn't far."

Doorman. Judging by his uniform, at least a brigadier in whatever army he was representing. Maybe the Free French. His hat was reminiscent of de Gaulle.

Her apartment was like a place you see in movies. "Minimalism," she said. "Would you like an ice cube in your Campari?"

Her bra—I knew as soon as I saw it—cost more than all the clothes I'd put on that morning. It was lacy and sheer, bone white, and embroidered with a garden of tiny roses. Most of them were pink; a few of them were deep red. The label said it was made in France.

By the time we ate dinner, quite late, on her little balcony, I'd learned I prefer my Campari in a tall glass with soda and plenty of ice.

Sometime in the morning, she opened the curtains to let in the light.

Then she lifted an edge of the covers, and got back into bed and hooked an ankle over my hip. She ran a fingertip down my spine. "Listen," she said sweetly, sleepily. "I don't really have a map for you."

Long letters came from home. I sent back postcards.

A picture is worth a thousand words, I reminded my mother when she protested. It's important to contain certain highly fissionable grievances quickly, decisively, before they can achieve critical mass.

Five years had passed since my father's old family found him. My mother's letters reported he was still making frequent visits to Georgia to see them, and they were still good for him. As a child, he hadn't made it past fifth grade. Since then, he'd done everything he could to supplement his education. He'd never been to high school or university, but the year I was born he'd somehow earned a law degree and passed the bar exam. My mother reported he was now attending the local junior college, making straight As in classes such as economics, marketing, English composition.

One afternoon I walked into a restaurant, a creperie, on East 57th—dark wood, lots of black wrought iron, nice young waitresses in dirndls and lacy white blouses—and just missed a Muhammad Ali sighting. My friend Dan, the bartender, told me Ali had come in, looking like a million bucks in a two-thousand-dollar chalkstripe suit, had lunch with some businessmen, and they'd all left just before I arrived. The place was still buzzing when I got there.

Ali was still my hero.

This was worth a telephone call to my father. Who told me he'd changed his position on Ali. He was a hell of a fighter after all. Look at what he did to Foreman. Look at how he stood up to Frazier. Look at how long he'd lasted at the top.

I said how disappointed I was that I'd missed him.

My father said, well, I could always tell my grandchildren I'd seen the great Ali in the ring.

New York was like that. You could run into anybody. Or not. I'd met Baryshnikov my first week there. I didn't know who he was, or why everybody else I was with was gushing over him. I had no idea he was a defector, or I'd have been interested. Automatically suspicious of any man wearing knitted legwarmers, I'd ignored him so badly that he came over and talked to me. A few days later, I'd seen Jackie O. and John F. Kennedy Jr. standing on a corner hailing a Checker cab. Cheap thrill, New York style.

The clamorous sidewalks. Jackhammers. People rushing everywhere. Three-card monte. Laughable, toy-sized shopping carts in the grocery stores. Brownstones. Neighborhoods. Tenement hotels. The Plaza. Alpenglow on the sheer rock wall of the east face of Manhattan. Broadway staggering like a drunken sailor through the otherwise perfectly orderly grid of streets and avenues. Papaya King. Who knew a combination of hot dogs and papaya juice aided digestion!

Beautiful women all over the place. High fashion. Bums. Steam rising out of subway grates. Shadows half a mile long stretching across the park. Sky-high rents. For a thousand dollars a month, enough to pay for my parents' house in three years, I got myself a seedy one-bedroom on West 71st, with kitchen, bathroom, and partial view of the Empire State Building as seen through the legs of a water tank atop an adjacent building. My walls were thin, and my next-door neighbor was a Juilliard student with a violin, which he played constantly.

On average, I was only in town about two weeks a month. I loved the city, but found it so intense that, if circumstances ever kept me there for four or five weeks in a row, I'd start to feel the need to escape. Sometimes I could. I'd get on a plane and go to London, or Switzerland, or Florida. But sometimes I had to stay, and one night Jennifer gave me a ticket out of all the chaos and grime. That was her name—the good Samaritan without a map, Jennifer. Of the J. Arthur Rank Organisation.

She wasn't in town all that often either, less than me actually. But sometimes she'd call me up late at night to ask if I wanted to go out. One night we went to Studio 54. Got out of a taxi, walked up to the crowd—four people deep, begging to get in—and the velvet rope opened for us as soon as the guy out front saw Jennifer. Inside she ran into a girlfriend of hers, and realized she'd forgotten to bring the book she'd promised her. "Would you mind terribly?" she asked me. "Not at all. I'll go get it," I said. So Jennifer wrote a note on the back of her business card: *Please give Larry Kolb the key to my apartment. Jennifer.*

Her building was on a leafy side street a few steps from the East River. There were diplomatic plates on half the cars parked there. The doorman read the card, handed it back to me, and gave me the key without hesitation. I got the book and took it back to Jennifer and her girlfriend. And I swear the reason I kept the business card, tucked it neatly into my wallet, was I thought it would be nice to have Jennifer's office phone numbers in New York, London, and Los Angeles.

I took to calling her occasionally, in London, or California, just to say Hi. And it must've been while I had the card out during one of those calls that I noticed Jennifer hadn't dated her note. By the next week, I'd gotten up the nerve to visit her apartment. Only for about half an hour. But it went smoothly.

After that, when the city got to be too much for me, and I'd telephonically determined Jennifer was thousands of miles away, I went back. Probably five or six times over a year. For an hour or two, then half a day, once two nights and the day between them. I didn't feel particularly honorable about it or like myself for being there, but I also didn't sniff her panties or steal anything, and technically the meaning of the note was debatable. I worked out in my mind that, if Jennifer ever caught me, she wouldn't care; she'd find it hilarious. I loved the minimalism. The quiet. The big rooms. The fact that nobody knew where I was, or how to find me. It was my first safe house. And years later, when Miles Copeland heard about it, his eyes lit up with happiness and he asked me to tell him all about it again.

When a certain old boy from the CIA finally stopped calling my father in Florida—and later my mother told me he'd kept calling for a lot longer than I'd ever known—other old boys started calling with all-new propositions for my father. Mostly these involved money and lots of it for his expertise. My mother said she'd watch him hang up from those calls with excitement in his eyes and in his voice. "You'd never believe who that was," he'd say brightly. But then after a few minutes, for reasons unclear then and now, he'd slump again, resigned to his life sentence.

But he kept getting offers.

My mother thought it would be good for him to get busy again. So did I.

Sir Ranulph Bacon was retired from Scotland Yard and had joined the board of Intertel, a private intelligence service based in New York and London. "Tell your father, 'Come join our board,'" Sir Rasher told me when I had lunch with him at his club in London. My father said maybe.

Chuck, the Best Electronics Man in the Business, had taken early retirement and gone to work in industrial espionage—making ten times what the government paid him. For men who worked for my father, a job in industrial espionage had always been the payoff in their futures, if they wanted it. The work was like taking candy from a baby and no one's conscience seemed bothered. Given the dark things they'd spent years doing against even darker forces, what could be wrong with something as silly as stealing doll designs or photographing next year's automobiles?

Chuck got me on the phone one day and asked me to tell my father there was plenty of room at the table for him; all he had to do was say he wanted in. My father told me to tell Chuck he wasn't interested in formulas for plastic barf. "No, better yet," my father said, "I'll call and tell him myself." A chance to reminisce.

Charley Sither had stayed on in the White House well into Richard Nixon's first administration. In fact, as the record reflects, in seventeen pages of detail—National Archives, Watergate Special Prosecution Task Force Records, Witness Files, Box 25—as one of his last acts before leaving, Uncle Charley helped an old CIA hand named James McCord get a job with the Committee to Reelect the President, CREEP. Then, in the week before the Watergate break-in, which was led by McCord, Uncle Charley packed up his office, kissed his secretaries goodbye, and retired. That, according to my father, was either a miracle coincidence or highly insightful planning.

Uncle Charley was now the Chief of Intelligence and Security for an oil-man named Armand Hammer and his company, which was called Occidental. According to my mother, it was on Occidental letterhead that Charley kept writing my father offering him very well-paid work, either full-time or as a consultant. And it was from Occidental jets that Charley kept calling my father to personalize the pitch.

I only made it back home to visit my parents four or five times in those first two New York years. But I happened to be sitting in the den in Florida watching television with my father one night when Uncle Charley called. He was, he told me, at present about forty thousand feet above a Wild West shit-hole called Tashkent and heading toward Teheran. Next he told me the Secret Service still had photos of me posted at all the White House gates. Then he told me to tell my father to get off his ass and come out and have some fun and make some real money.

"They're just looking out for me," my father told me later that night about the offers he kept getting from Uncle Charley and others. "They're looking out for me like I always looked out for them."

He stopped for a moment, then turned to look straight into my eyes. "Don't you ever forget this," he said: "For an intelligence officer, *nothing* is more important than taking care of his men in the field." He said it just like I'd never told Bill Tharp no.

Then, after another moment's pause, my father went on. He was quite adamant about this. "No matter what any desk idiot from headquarters tells you, you've *got* to take care of your men in the field."

My younger brother Bill was away at school in Philadelphia. So, it was, as my father pointed out, just the three of us again, like the old days in Virginia and Japan, except now I didn't need to stop to go to the bathroom so much when we went out in the car. My father had never been willing to talk with me as calmly and openly about anything I wanted to talk about as he was during that visit. "That's because he actually enjoys being with you now that you're an adult," my mother told me one night after my father went to bed. "All that singing cowboy and model airplane stuff wasn't really his thing."

When I couldn't stay any longer, my father drove me to the airport.

A few months later, I reconstructed our drive in my journal.

I'd been home nineteen days.

It was the longest I'd been with my parents in years.

For at least the last week, we'd played hearts at the dining room table every night—sometimes until two or three in the morning. We'd had an uncharacteristically great time together.

I was leaving because I had to go to Greece.

Part of the life I'd decided to lead, rather than hauling deadwood for the CIA.

My father told me there were "people" he still talked to. And that, at the moment, there was a lot more going on in Greece than I would imagine. So I ought to tell everyone I met there I was Canadian rather than American. And I ought to lock my passport up when I got there and not take it out until I left. And, if anyone saw my address, I should say I'd been temporarily stationed at my Vancouver company's New York office.

My father gave me a little scrap of paper containing two names and two telephone numbers. Handwritten by him, in a soft pencil. He didn't have to explain.

I remember it was an unusually beautiful morning. There was something about the light, the way it was filtering through the haze. The sky was tinted green. There were no shadows.

When we got to the causeway, the surface of the water was like I'd never seen it before. Normally there was at least a little chop in the tidal flow, but now it looked almost like glass. I perked up and looked all around us. But natural beauty wasn't something you'd ever interest my father in talking about.

I stared at the sky and the water and we talked about golf. The British Open was coming up in a few weeks. My father liked Nicklaus's chances. I said Watson would win.

I said, the next time I came back, when it wasn't so hot, we'd have to play lots of golf. Maybe we should even take a trip somewhere special just for golf. Like we'd done once back in Germany.

My father said that sounded good to him.

I said, and when we finished playing golf, we could start writing down stories about his career. We'd been through that several times before. For as long as I could remember, I'd wanted to someday write a book. Maybe even books, plural. I'd start with one about my father, the daring spy, if only he'd tell me the stories. But my father had, as he reminded me again out on that causeway, sworn a secrecy oath. No stories.

I said, but what if we just wrote down stories of things he did during the war? Only the war. So long ago. And, for the first time ever, my father said all right, we'd do it. But they couldn't be published right away. Not for a long time.

On the mainland, the light seemed a lot less supernatural. I suppose the sun was breaking through.

My father had an appointment somewhere, and I said he didn't need to come into the terminal with me like he usually did. He stopped the car and got out and opened the trunk and I lifted out my fat black bag and set it down on the curb.

Probably, I told him I'd miss him and he told me he'd miss me too.

Maybe I also told him I loved him, and thanks for the ride, and I'd see him soon.

We shook hands, and he got back into the car and watched me until I made it to the door of the terminal with my bag.

Then he smiled and waved goodbye and drove off.

I never saw him again.

On September 1st, 1978, he had a cold and had been taking cold medicine. He drove off that night in his month-old new car. Went to Gaskins Drugstore. Or the Rocket Lounge. Or both. They shared a parking lot, in which his car was seen that night. On his way home, either his brakes failed or he missed a turn. A few hours later, two fishermen found his body floating in the river, not three hundred yards from our house.

PART TWO

PEERS OF THE REALM

Everything about it was wrong.

There was a certain way my father combed his hair. The mortician got it wrong. My father lay there, his hair combed straight back from his forehead in a way I'd never seen before, in a way that didn't even look like him. His glasses were off. Even when my father stretched out on the couch and fell asleep, he almost never took his glasses off. And what about the improbable way he was dressed? He lay there in a white shirt, open at the neck, gray slacks but no belt, and socks but no shoes. His forearms and hands were resting on his lap in a position he would never submit to.

"It's a husk," my mother blurted out as soon as we saw him. "It isn't him. He's somewhere else now."

It was my father's body, all right. I could see it in his nose, his lips, the little golden hairs on his hands.

I wanted to touch his hair and fix it. But I didn't know the secret way he combed it. I only knew how it looked when he finished.

I wanted to squeeze his hand. Or at least to touch him. But I was afraid he would be stiff.

"I love you, Dad," I said, as my mother and brothers and I walked out of the visitation room in the funeral parlor. I said it loud, and maybe a little bit crazy. I had to say it loud enough for him to hear me. Because we were already at the door and he was still lying there on the other side of the room.

Then it was the next day. Intermittent drizzle. We stood under an opensided tent. An American flag covering my father's coffin. Men in uniform and white gloves slow-motion folded the flag into a blue-and-white triangle of stars. One of them gave it to my mother. Taps played well by a military bugler. Twenty-one-gun salute. Seven riflemen; three shots each. Nothing special for my father. This was the military funeral every veteran was entitled to. The Episcopal priest spoke a few words. The Episcopal priest being my older brother Jerry.

There were wreaths and flower arrangements all over the place.

I dropped a red rose and a clod of dirt down the hole onto my father's coffin.

Then we all went home.

There were so many people that our house was crowded. My father's mother and his sisters and brother. My secret sister, the one I hadn't known about for several years: my father's daughter, six years older than me, who never lived with us, and who, in keeping with family tradition, a few years after my father died, disappeared on us. Watt and Aleen Redfield, formerly of Colorado. Cousins I'd never met and would never see again. A man, in his mid-forties, who told me he hadn't seen my father in thirty years, but that my father had been such a good influence on him he'd wanted to be here. A couple of spies, or, I should say, intelligence officers—old men with their wives.

That night, when they'd all left and it was just my mother and brothers and me, I sat alone in my old room, under my posters, going through my desk. My father had taken to using it for doing his homework. Stacked up inside a double drawer, I found his college papers and mine. Among many others, my English History paper on Oliver Cromwell and the Interregnum just beneath his English Composition paper on the day he marched into Dachau with the 42nd Infantry. Unfortunately, having sworn a secrecy oath, he left out the essential fact that he was undercover. Still, he made a hell of a case for why he hadn't been cremated in the last few days.

I couldn't stop thinking of the night my father died.

I was in Greenwich, Connecticut, that night. Visiting friends. A happy doctor and his happy wife, and their kids. The parents were older than me, the kids slightly younger than me. Somehow I'd become friends with all of them.

They'd lived in Greenwich as long as I'd known them. But now they'd bought a grand old house and were moving from a nice neighborhood to a very nice neighborhood. The moving trucks had come and gone, and my friends had started to unpack. Already they'd decided they wanted to move some heavy pieces to different places in the big house. Who better to call for help than a strapping six-six lad accustomed to hauling hundred-pound packs through the mountains?

Dinner around their kitchen table. Then hours good-naturedly cursing and complaining, and laughing, while we moved furniture from room to room to room. While decisions were being made. Then remade. And, when it was getting late, and a suitable setting had at last been found for the grand piano, they saw me to the back door and I said good night to everyone and headed out to my car.

I closed the door behind myself and stood there on their back step.

I had an hour's drive into Manhattan and needed to be up early the next morning.

I looked at my watch. It was about 11:20.

I looked at the yellow glow in the sky, and just then, not in my ears, but in my head, I heard a sound. Like rain splashing on a pond.

And suddenly I felt lonelier than I'd ever felt in my life.

So lonely that, after a few minutes, I opened the door and walked back inside and said I was too lonesome to leave, and, hey, let's move some more furniture.

I'd never done anything like it before, and I haven't done anything like it since. I stayed another hour. Until the feeling passed enough for me to go.

And three oblivious days later—after I'd been to Manhattan and Southampton and then driven down to Georgetown, where I was when my mother and my brothers finally got a message to me, and after I'd flown home to Florida—I learned a neighbor reported hearing a loud crunch and a splashing noise at 11:20, when my father's car crashed through a wooden fence and dove into the river.

He made it out of the car. Maybe he was thrown out. Maybe he climbed out and swam a little. He'd never been much of a swimmer, not after watching his father drown. And there was a seawall to contend with, in the dark, and a big bump on my father's forehead. I think he drowned while I stood on that porch in Greenwich.

Six years and a few months after I'd drowned. Did that, I wondered, make me the second or third in a long line of drowners? Or had I broken the succession forever?

In any event, I knew what he must've felt. Gray-black peace. That's what I was thinking about when I got into bed.

I've never told anybody this. I didn't think I ever would. Later that night, I got out of my bed and went out to try to sleep on the couch in the family room. Even though I'd discovered my father had been using my room to do his schoolwork, I didn't remember spending much time with him in there. I felt closer to him out on the couch where we used to watch TV together. Finally, I fell asleep; and I saw the green grass of the cemetery, and the yellow tent over my father's coffin, and the terrible machine, all straps and pulleys and counterweights, that slowly-and-ever-so-smoothly lowers the coffin into the ground. I watched it lower my father's coffin, and when it reached six feet down I heard locks unlocking and rusty hinges beginning to swing open, and then my father screamed when the trapdoor in the bottom of his coffin opened, and I heard him screaming all the way down to hell.

I think it was the next day that I started reciting the Lord's Prayer several times a day. In my head when others were around, out loud when I was in the shower or otherwise alone. For propriety's sake, I'd recite the whole thing each time. But the part I focused on, like a mantra, was *Our Father, who art in heaven.* And by Our Father I meant not God but my father, and my brothers' father—plural possessive—*our* father. And I hoped that if I could just say it enough times, over and over, it would be true, and our father would be in heaven not hell. That's a hope that's never left me.

I'd had it in my head for a few months now that when I got back here my father and I were going to sit together and write down his stories from the war. Something in me wouldn't let go of that. One midnight, I went methodically through the desk, momentarily convinced I was about to find a whole stack of my father's secrets, all neatly parsed and typed for English Composition 201.

Wrong.

But at the back of a drawer I found a yellow piece of paper I'd carried with me during my college summer in Europe with a backpack and a Eurail pass. It'd been unfolded and refolded many times, in many countries. It was grimy now, and tattered. I unfolded it.

Like many of the other American students I met that summer, I'd had with me a list of European contacts composed by my parents. This was mine. Most such lists were of distant cousins or old family friends. Invaluable resources for free showers and home-cooked meals. But my list, in my father's antique hand, and written with a fountain pen, consisted of the home and office telephone numbers of his friends: the chief of Scotland Yard, the head of Interpol, the CIA's top men in Paris, Luxembourg, Vienna, and Berlin. *Take flowers for their wives,* my father had written, and underlined it twice.

Contacts and a sense of how to deal with people. Those were the things my father left me when he died. I decided I needed to start using them. But it took me awhile to leave. I didn't realize yet that wherever I would go in the world, for the rest of my life, my father would go with me.

Living in New York had taught me I didn't need to go into the wilds to find adventure. Anything could happen in New York, anything at all. I came to suspect I'd been spending too much time in sleeping bags. When I finally said goodbye to my mother and left Florida, I'd shaved off my beard and decided whenever I could I was going to steer myself and my business out of the wilderness. My escape plan was that vague.

Posing as a celebrated tour operator, with a stack of photocopies of a certain *The Wall Street Journal* story to bolster my claim, I could always get myself a free airline ticket for a scouting trip to almost anywhere. And, when I got there, a free hotel room. So, after a lifetime of traveling, I armed myself with free airline tickets and the access my father had given me, and determined to use them to somehow reinvent myself.

But I wasn't sure how. The whole next year, I realize now, was research toward that end. On this beach, it's also the year I find I go back to in my mind, more than all the others.

I saw the Louvre, the pyramids, and Lenin under glass.

Moscow. Just off Red Square, a beer machine. Put in a few kopeks and out poured beer. Not—in the American way—into a paper cup, which might or might not descend in time. Into a glass. The same glass, unwashed, used over and over. Put in your money, watch the glass fill, drink your beer, lick the sides of the glass to get the last few drops, and then put the glass back for the next guy. I knew as soon as I saw the beer machine which side was going to win the Cold War. And I said so to the friend of a friend of my father, a man from our embassy, who was showing me around, guarding me, spying on me—whatever you want to call it.

In London, I lunched with a lord, another friend of a friend of my father, in the dining room of the House of Lords. Once we were slightly drunk on port, he walked me into the Lords' private water closet. And there, over the broad white urinal, hung an ancient sign—*Peers of the Realm.* They had a whole vaudeville routine going in that loo. Another lord walked in and stood beside us. "Larry, please allow me," said my host, "to introduce you to my fellow peer."

I saw silk bazaars, shanties, boardrooms, boudoirs—and what I wouldn't pay to see them again tomorrow!

I went back to Japan, thrice, in that year after my father died. In the Ginza, on my list: Tanakasan. Japanese-American, in his forties. Born in the States, but permanently relocated now. A nightclub owner with, I would've guessed, a sideline in the covert. "Your father was a very good man," he told me. "Let me know if you need *anything.*"

I remember sitting on a carved-stone verandah on Corfu, staring across the straits to the mysterious land of Albania. Maoist, and closed to the West. Closed to almost every nation. "Over there," said my host, another friend of my father, a Greek who spoke English like an Englishman, "it's still the Stone Age."

What was I going to do with my life? I wasn't sure. But I *was* still deluded enough to think we decide such things for ourselves.

In Torremolinos the sun was fierce by eight in the morning. Hot days by the sea. And in the sea. Then you ate outside, and drank red wine. For some reason, I think of Torremolinos often as I walk along my beach. But it's only another beach. I've actually seen quite enough of sand and water lately. Right about now, I'd trade all the coconuts and palm fronds in the world to see just one pine needle on fresh-fallen snow.

I went to a very cold place in winter. Bodø, Norway. On the Norwegian

Sea, eighty kilometers north of the Arctic Circle. Did my father have his own memory of such a wonderful journey to get him by during his own exile in the sun? These days, I go over and over it in my mind.

A day's ride north of Oslo, you're in Trondheim. Change trains in Trondheim. Eight hundred kilometers farther to go. I couldn't take my eyes from the window of my cabin. Deep winter woods and frozen rivers. Down in the valleys, ghost trees and ice sculptures. As we climbed the ridges, starlit snow on pine boughs. It was night nearly the entire way. But never dark.

At every stop, men and women in surprisingly elegant clothes came aboard. Waiting beside them on the platform were reindeer—frozen solid, skinned, beheaded, hooves lopped off, glazed with frost, standing on their backs with all four legs pointing to heaven. Porters loaded the reindeer into unrefrigerated freight cars, then we pulled out. It was the same, village after village. Until we reached Bodø.

Inside the station, Catrine. Beautiful, long-legged, flowing hair the color of whisky and water. Wearing boots and one of those sheepskin coats with suede on the outside, fleece on the inside and the collar and cuffs. I asked her, in phrasebook Norwegian, "Where is a good hotel?" She had the palest blue eyes. An angel's eyes. She answered me in lovely English. "What sort of hotel do you want?"

"A very warm one," I said. She gave me her gloved hand to shake and said her name was Catrine. She said she had to pass the hotel now herself, so she'd drive me there. Outside, it was the polar night. They hadn't seen sunlight up there in over a week. Whatever color her car was in summer, that night it was white. Snow was swirling all around us. "Or would you rather stay in a pleasant, warm farmhouse with me and my family?" she asked. I had a sudden vision of Catrine and a kind husband and a child or two. Given the time of year, I thought, Why not?

Past the edge of town, a house entirely white in the headlights. She swore it was made of yellow stone. Inside, the first one I met was Mari, the vision of Catrine. *Identical twins.* Where's the husband? Where are the kids? "It's only me and Mari," said Catrine. "Mari came to live with me when I divorced. Now she's my only family." Two calendar days later, it was still dark outside, still snowing. And now it was Christmas.

I search my memory and this is the point in the entire passage where the route seems most tenuous and unlikely. The question remains: How did I get from there to here? How the son of a spy could be recruited to work for the CIA, I understand. But I said no. After that, how the son of a spy who, on his father's death, inherited some contacts in the secret world, but no money, and no contacts in the social world, got where I got soon, I don't understand. I don't know how it happened, where it came from. I don't know if I sought it out, or it sought ought me. But somehow, soon, there I was, with so many contacts, so much access, that I would be talentspotted on my own. Not for who my father was, but for who I was. There would be no escaping spies for me.

I went to Scotland later that year, and instead of freezing in a tent on the slopes of Ben Nevis, I stayed warm in hotels. And froze on golf courses, the great links courses where golf began.

In Scotland, golf was Everyman's game. Played all day. Played into the night. Played on courses built hard against the sea across wild, heaving, broken land—common land, owned by everyone. And thus shared with sheep, dog-walkers, families on picnics, lovers on blankets. By lord mayors, train conductors, and fishmongers, playing together. There was something magical about it. And by the end of the week I knew what I would do next.

Just as back then almost no one was organizing adventure tours, back then almost no one was organizing tours of the great old golf courses of Britain. Soon I was. And I added a twist. We brought the beloved young golf star Ben Crenshaw along to play with you, and the greatest living American golf writer, Herbert Warren Wind, along to sit down beside you and Ben by the fire after dinner, have a wee dram of whisky with you, and tell you stories of the glorious links you'd played that day and the one you were going to play tomorrow, and of all the great champions who'd passed there before you. I was still selling dreams.

Six months into my new career, I'd transformed myself. Or been transformed. I'm not really sure myself how it happened so fast. Things fell into place all at once, that much I know. Now, when I wasn't off in Britain, I spent the winters at Palm Beach Polo Club, whose president and developer had taken a liking to me—and, I'm sure, to the famous golfers I could bring around—and had given me a beautiful place to live. Some sort of tax fiddle, I realize now. The townhouse he gave me was mortgaged by a corporation I nominally owned; he made the payments and, I think, in the end, he would've expected me to give the title back to him. But that went unsaid, and I didn't really care. I had the only set of keys, and a fine address I didn't pay a penny for. Prince Charles's house was a few doors down. And across the way and around the bend was the house of my new best friend Bill Talbert.

Bill was in his early sixties then, a grand old gentleman of tennis. Former Davis Cup captain, one of the greatest doubles players ever, a member of the Tennis Hall of Fame, and author of the best books ever written about how to play tennis. For the past several years, Bill had run the U.S. Open Tennis Championships in New York. And, for a time, Bill became almost like a father to me.

The first time we met, we played golf, and I birdied the last three holes and shot 72. That was low for me, but wasn't that big a deal. We were playing from the short tees and the pins were set easy. But Bill and I were partners, and that afternoon we won a nice pile of money from two princes of Wall Street. After that, I was the only person around Palm Beach he wanted to have as his partner when he played golf.

Bill had beautiful manners, and he knew everyone. Captains of industry. Wall Street barons. Politicians. Movie stars. Broadway stars. Sports stars. All the sorts of people you read about in newspapers.

Bill had done it all. He'd romanced Grace Kelly and run with Errol Flynn. He introduced me to Rockefellers, Luces, Bronfmans, Henry Kissinger, Walter Cronkite, John McEnroe, Joe DiMaggio, Henry Ford, Princess Grace and Prince Rainier. Among others. "Kid," said Bill to me when we met up with Mickey Mantle for a long night of drinking and barhopping across New York, "allow me to introduce you to one of the great swordsmen of all time."

It wasn't long before I was on backslapping terms with senators, congressmen, tycoons.

Bill taught me what to wear, and where, and when. He taught me where to buy it. He taught me what to say, and what not to say. And Bill made calls that opened doors for me.

Soon, I wasn't only organizing golf tours. At Bill's suggestion, and with his help, I started organizing golf and tennis outings for corporate clients, and acting as an agent for a couple of professional athletes.

Lunch with the chairman of Philip Morris. Or Nabisco. Or Seagram. Talk a little golf. Talk a little tennis. Promise to give Bill and his wife, the wonderful Nancy, the chairman's best wishes that night when I see them for dinner. Then talk a little business. Ask the chairman for, oh, seventy thousand dollars to organize an unforgettable golf or tennis trip to Bermuda or Scotland or Portugal for him and six or seven of his best customers.

Or ask the chairman to pay one of my clients twenty-five thousand dollars a year to put the name of the chairman's company on my client's golf bag.

Often enough, the chairman would say yes.

So I lived in Palm Beach now, and a nice apartment in Manhattan. And out on the North Shore of Long Island, at Luce Ends, a Luce family country house on Cold Spring Harbor, a guest suite seemed to be permanently reserved for me. On weekends I was a country squire.

There must've been days, even weeks on end, of tedium. There always are. Precious time given over to waiting in lines at banks and airline counters, packing and unpacking, catching up on paperwork, shopping for the suits and blazers I suddenly seemed to be wearing everywhere. But I don't remember any of that now. From here, it seems as if, not long after my father died, I blinked and found myself in an all-new world.

There was a woman now too, to complete my transformation.

I met her in Tokyo.

Sunday morning. A low gray sky. Puddles. Drizzle. Wet grass clippings filling the welts of my shoes. *Jan.*

She walked right up to me, stuck out her hand across the spectator rope, and introduced herself. She was confident like that, had a certain presence.

We walked a little way together, and talked. I think she told a joke. None of the things that would happen to us had happened yet, and we were happy just to be together for a moment and share a laugh.

Her eyes were blue and beautiful, as big as lakes.

Most of the gallery had come to see her. But they followed a respectful distance behind us, so we could talk. Very polite, those Japanese. Even in the presence of the most beautiful professional athlete in the world.

She was, if you will, the Anna Kournikova of her time. Except that, while Kournikova has, as I write this, never won a professional tennis tournament, Jan was winning often. And not just ordinary professional golf tournaments. Major championships too. She won three majors in a two-year stretch; and, most important, she was gorgeous.

I watched her for a couple of holes, and then said goodbye, and that I had to go look for some friends of mine.

Beth and Sally.

Who, by the time I found them, had finished their rounds and finished signing autographs. They took me into the clubhouse, and we ordered beers, and they introduced me to a prince, a golf-mad nephew of Hirohito. He was about my age, spoke perfect American English, and was very gracious. In short order, he told me to drop the formality and call him Tak like everybody else did.

The clubhouse was filling up. Soon Japanese ladies and gentlemen were milling around, bowing and scraping to the prince. Tak, my ass. To them, he was Your Imperial Highness.

For just a moment, a little gap opened up through the people, and I saw her at a table in the back.

The biggest star there, and eating all alone.

I excused myself, and walked over and asked her how she'd finished.

Though I already knew the answer.

You never ask a professional golfer what they shot unless you know the answer, and unless the answer will not distress them.

She told me, and I said, Good work, and then she asked me to sit down and eat with her. It's egg curry, she said, and it's delicious. There was a big platter of it in front of her plate. More than enough for her and me. I sat, and we talked, but I didn't eat. Curry sounded quite exotic to me, quite Indian and mysterious. In those days I was smart enough to stay away from mysterious Indian things.

She said she had to leave now, to take a shower, because a car would be there soon to take her straight to Narita. To catch a plane back to the States.

Goodbye, she said, and it was nice meeting you.

Don't go just yet. Please let me have your phone number. No, not your office number. Your top secret number at home.

She gave it to me. And I walked off, smiling, a little startled by what I'd done.

She had a fiancé, an oilman. Who flew her around in private planes and managed her money, when he wasn't making deals.

She had a little business empire. Her own clothing line. Several endorsement deals. Appearance fees. Outings. Print ads. Calendars. TV commercials. Tournament winnings.

I became her agent and we went all over together. To Australia, and back to Japan. To New York, and New Jersey, and Nevada, and Florida, and Georgia, and Texas. And to Beverly Hills, to shop for a dress, and then over the pass to Burbank, to *The Tonight Show* studio—and into her dressing room, and into hair and makeup, and the green room, and we even went together right up to the curtain.

"Man, you gotta get outta here *now!*" said the big black dude who looked more like a bouncer than a curtain-opener.

"Don't let go of me," she whispered to me. "I'm so nervous."

"*Now!*" said the black dude, flexing the muscles in his back.

The show was in a commercial break. A young comic had just come off the stage, looking like one of the walking dead in a Wilfred Owen poem. His lips were rubbery. His legs were rubbery. Someone was leading him slowly back toward the dressing room. He had the thousand-yard stare. He'd just finished his first appearance on *The Tonight Show* and come to realize his career as a comic was over.

As soon as the poor fellow shuffled out of the way, the black dude got back in my face.

"If you don't get out of here right now," he said, "when I open the curtain, everyone's going to see you. Get *the fuck* out of here!"

On the other side of the curtain, Johnny Carson was announcing her, whipping up the crowd, but Jan wouldn't let go of my arm.

"You'll do fine," I told her, and at the last second she let go, and I escaped just before the black dude pulled the curtain back—and the crowd laid eyes on her.

Wolf whistles. My God!s. Because she wasn't just one of the top three women golfers in the world, and she wasn't just good-looking; she was, as *Viva* magazine had called her in the very month I met her: *Jan Stephenson, the Australian Sex Bomb.*

The crowd went wild, and not so long after that I was in New York getting my back rubbed by Meredith Luce, when Jan called. The *femme fatale.* She was in distress.

Please come. I really need your help.

I went.

I dropped everything and flew straight to Arizona.

In her car, a little black sports car, at night, heading from Phoenix north into the mountains.

I was driving.

She was sitting still now, lost, with her hands wrapped over the knees of her jeans. I reached over and put my right hand over her left. She took my hand and pulled it to her heart. I was one ignorant young man then, but even I knew this was a woman who very badly needed a friend.

And we were just friends. But soon very intense friends. Because we were living in such difficult times, and living so close. In her third home, a little place in Phoenix. And then one night we went to a Japanese restaurant in Scottsdale. We shared a pot of sukiyaki, and I drove us home, and went to the guest room where I'd been staying. Until Jan called me to her door. And, from behind it, her hand reached out, and she pulled me in and, as she did, she flicked the lights off and the room was dark and we were blind. Nothing but touch and smell and sound and taste. With those alone she led me to her bed, and she was so naked that she stopped my breath, and we kissed, and we undressed me and held each other trembling in the dark, until we rolled over and her soft sweet hair tumbled into my face, and three months later we were married.

And six months later we were divorced.

But this is not the story of my tabloid divorce in hell. The details of which are not important here, except for three facts. First: I came out of it wiser but still quite trusting and naïve. Second: All around the world, Rupert Murdoch's newspapers announced that Murdoch's top muckraker, Steve Dunleavy, was writing a book about Jan and me, in which I would play the heavy; the publication of which book I dreaded every morning I awoke for the next two years. And, third: When all the *Sturm und Drang* was over, I was pretty much washed up in the golf and tennis business. Almost everyone supported Jan. She, after all, was the star. Of all the athletes I knew, only one of them stood by me.

It seemed I was going to need a new career.

9 | CHAPTER WRITTEN UNDER DURESS

The venerable Franklin P. Morse, Esq., formerly of San Rafael, California, Palo Alto, California, Cambridge, Massachusetts, and Las Vegas, Nevada—where, at the tender age of twenty-eight, he became general counsel to Howard R. Hughes and the fabled Summa Corporation, and who, since the widely reported death of Mr. Hughes, has served as counsel to and minister plenipotentiary for a short list of business moguls of various stripes and nationalities—now residing in Beverly Hills, California, and, after all of that, still quite young and remarkably fit and well turned out, has come and gone, taught me how to testify, traveled with me to the federal courthouse in Miami, and sat at my right hand and sometimes interposed objections while a special master deputed by the Government of India posited to me questions from afar. Most of which I duly answered.

"A witch hunt" was what Frank called the whole proceeding on the record.

But the result is I'm free to travel now. Not to leave the country yet. There's still some paperwork before I'll be safe in foreign jurisdictions. Apparently, it's bureaucratically simpler to loose the dogs than to call them off. But for now, at least, it's safe for me to travel in my own country.

I've just returned from California. Where I had a meeting with Frank, and then spent a couple of days with an old friend of mine.

The one athlete who stood by me after Jan.

Muhammad Ali.

Jan and I met him not long after I became her agent.

We went with him on a promotional tour of Japan.

He and I became great friends. I traveled the world with him for years.

Muhammad is the finest man I've ever known.

I love him like a brother and I've missed him.

Which has seldom been made clearer to me than just last week, soon after Muhammad and I got into a car to drive across Los Angeles to, of all places, Annette Funicello's house—which was in the Encino Hills. I'd never met her.

Neither had Muhammad. I wasn't sure why we were going there. Howard Bingham was driving. Howard is a photographer and has been Muhammad's best friend for years.

Over lunch in a suite in the Beverly-Wilshire, Muhammad had asked me where I'd been, what I'd been up to, and, in general, how life had been treating me. I believe he phrased it this way: "Where you been, stranger? What you been doin'? You gettin' any lately?"

We hadn't seen each other in a couple of years. Which was unusual for us. There'd been whole years in which we were together, on average, probably one day out of every three. And since then, until I moved to the beach, we'd seldom gone more than a month or two without seeing each other.

The answer to Muhammad's first question, of course, was that I'd been on the lam. Though I didn't tell him that, not yet.

"I've been in Florida," I said, "and what I've been doing is writing."

Writing all these pages I've been piling up, mostly in the night, as I sit at my desk and remember. And, recently, writing a detailed chronology requested of me by Frank Morse.

"Writing what?" said someone I didn't know.

There were a few people there I didn't know.

So my answer was guarded. "A book."

A white lie which led to complications later.

With my answer to Muhammad's third question, I managed to move our conversation in a new direction.

Until we got into Bingham's chocolate-milkshake-brown Camry. Just the three of us now.

Muhammad insisted I take the front seat, in deference to my legs, which are longer than his. While he was wedging himself into Bingham's backseat, Muhammad said this: "*Another* book about me. What you gonna call it?"

"It's not about you," I said offhandedly, and just then Bingham turned left onto Wilshire and told us to keep our eyes on the car with Texas plates already three or four cars ahead of us. We were supposed to be following it.

Bingham and I began chatting about L.A., where he's lived in South Central since he arrived there in the 1940s—a four-year-old boy, fresh out of Jackson, Mississippi. In the backseat Muhammad fell silent. He doesn't really demand all the attention, or talk all the time, as you might believe. Muhammad is a humble soul.

And he catnaps frequently. Always has.

We didn't hear from him for at least five minutes. For all I knew, he might've been asleep back there.

Until: Wham! My head and neck went flying forward. Due to the punch Muhammad had just leveled into the headrest I'd been leaning on.

Wham! Another one.

"Not about *me*!" said Muhammad, in high-operatic dudgeon.

I turned around and looked at him.

"Not about *me*!"

Whump! This time a left uppercut through my seat back and aimed at my kidneys.

"What you mean you writin' a book that's not about me?" Wham!

Muhammad's been the subject of more biographies than any other living person. So I suppose it was only natural that, when I said what I'd been writing was a book, Muhammad assumed it had to be about him.

Wham! A right to the headrest. Then Muhammad started flicking precision left jabs that stopped about an eighth of an inch from my eyelashes. One of them touched me gently. Muhammad moves a lot better than you would think, sometimes. He isn't always frozen by Parkinsonism. Not always.

"Not about *me*!"

Wham!

"What's it about then?"

"Actually, it's about me."

"Ain't gonna be much of a book."

"Shut up, fool!"

"Better make it about me if you want it to sell."

"Fuck you!"

"Stop the car, Bingham. I'm gonna kill him."

We were sitting at a little round table. In the lounge off the lobby of the New Otani Hotel, in Tokyo. Muhammad, Bingham, Jan, and me. We'd ordered drinks.

Japan is probably the one place in the world where the people don't mob Muhammad. This is not to say they don't love him. They do. They frequently pay him to fly over there and appear. But they don't mob him. Very polite those Japanese. Instead they surround him at a respectful distance and take pictures of him.

Muhammad Ali ga iru! When you hear that, someone has spotted Muhammad, and the cameras start coming out all around you.

But it was the dead of the afternoon and there weren't many people about. Most of the tables were empty.

We'd just come from a press conference. During which, while the president of Caesar's Palace read a list of Jan's accomplishments that year—when he got to "won Canadian Open, won World Ladies' Championship, set all-time LPGA scoring record . . ."—Muhammad interrupted, turned to Jan, and said,

"Sounds like *you're* the greatest!" Jan had met Muhammad only a few minutes before the press conference. I'd met him the day before, at LAX.

Now here we all were, jet-lagged and bored. With four hours to kill before the next appearance.

Muhammad turned to Jan and me, made big eyes at us, and said, "What were Abraham Lincoln's first words when he woke up from a three-day drunk?"

Jan didn't know. I didn't know. We shrugged.

Even Bingham shrugged, playing along.

"I freed the *who*?" said Muhammad, loud enough for everyone in the room to hear. Cameras started coming out.

"Now *you* tell one," said Muhammad, looking at Bingham. And Bingham did.

He told an elaborate joke about a courtship between two birds, which involved not only narration but a lot of pantomime and whistling of birdsong. Back then Bingham had a wicked stutter. So it took a while. But the telling only made you like him more.

"Now you," said Muhammad, this time to Jan. She told a joke about a beautiful genie in a wetsuit who arrived on a desert island to grant three wishes. Straight out of Jan's after-dinner-speaking repertoire.

"Now you," said Muhammad, looking straight at me.

This was about the first moment he'd ever really paid any attention to me. My hero was sitting about four feet across from me in a beautiful pinstriped suit, all eyes and ears. Staring right at me. My heart started pounding. If I didn't think of something fast, I was going to turn into stone, or a pillar of salt.

I didn't know any Abraham Lincoln jokes. Or boxing jokes. In fact, it seemed at the moment I didn't know any jokes.

Then one came to me. Together with a vision of Muhammad doing his crazy-man act while stalking Sonny Liston.

"Jack Nicklaus goes to Japan," I said quietly, and Muhammad drew closer so he could hear me.

"And, to show him how much they appreciate him coming to their tournament, on the first night he's in town, the sponsors arrange for a geisha girl to take him out to dinner. She arrives at his room, upstairs in this very hotel."

I looked up at the ceiling. Muhammad looked up at the ceiling, then back at me.

I went on: "She doesn't speak a word of English. He doesn't speak a word of Japanese. So they speak sign language. They go out to dinner. They get along fine. And they come back to his hotel room and get into bed and start to make love."

By now I wasn't talking so quietly anymore, and Jan told me later that, as Jack Nicklaus and the geisha got into bed, I started rocking back and forth in my chair like crazy people do.

"Just after they started to make love," I went on, "the geisha starts whispering in his ear: *'Shee ku,'* she says. *'Shee ku.'*

"He doesn't know what it means. But he figures she must be telling him how much she appreciates it. *'Shee ku,'* she says. *'Shee ku.'* He goes on, harder and harder, and pretty soon she's scratching his back, and moaning, and crying out: *'Shee ku! Shee kuuuuuuu!'*"

At that point I was rocking back and forth, with my arms spread-eagled and my fingers out like claws, and now everyone in the big room could hear me. And couldn't help looking at me—clawing the air and moaning.

"He's pounding on, harder and harder," I said, "and she's clawing at his back and moaning and screaming, *'Shee ku! Shee kuuuuuuuuuuuuuuuuuuuuuu!'*

"And finally they're finished," I said, quieter now.

"A week later, Jack's been leading the golf tournament since the first round. Everyone has been wonderful to him. No fans anywhere in the world have ever treated him better. He's got a five-stroke lead. He's in the middle of the fairway on the last hole. A hundred thirty-four yards from the pin. He throws up some grass to check the wind. He pulls out his nine iron. Swings. And his ball lands on the green, takes one bounce, and jumps straight into the hole.

"The fans go wild! In the grandstands, they give him a standing ovation. They're cheering, stomping their feet in unison, clapping their hands, shouting his name. And Jack is moved to tears.

"As he steps onto the green he decides he has to do something to let them know how much he appreciates them. He walks up to the hole, lifts out his ball, raises his arms to hush the crowd, and shouts: *'Sheeeee kuuuuuuuuuuuuuuuuu!'*

"And just then a little Japanese official walks over to him and says, 'Excuse me, Mr. Nick-russ. What you mean, "wrong hole"?'"

I'd finished on my feet, pretending to pick the ball out of the hole, and then raising my arms to the sky, bellowing *Sheeeee kuuuuuuuuuuuuuuuuu!*, and now I was the Japanese official bent over beside Muhammad, with my hand up to his ear, stage whispering the punch line.

Across the room, cameras were clicking away.

Muhammad and Bingham were laughing their asses off. They started to calm down, then looked at each other, snorted, looked back at me, and burst out laughing again.

Muhammad buried his face in his chest. Then looked up at me.

"You crazier than me!" he said. "Quiet, skinny white boy like you. So shy and polite. Haven't said two words around me since yesterday. Now it turns out you crazier than me!

"Tell it again," he said.

And I did.

"You *a lot* crazier than me!" said Muhammad. "From now on, anything you want to say to me, you got my attention. '*Shee Ku!*' That's your new name."

And indeed it was, for the next couple of years, until Muhammad gradually started calling me Larry.

A few weeks after we got back from Japan. In Muhammad's big white house in Hancock Park in Los Angeles.

The doorbell rang. Muhammad sent me to answer it.

At the front door, an old African man. And a young African boy.

"We are here," announced the man, "because—before I die—I wish to introduce my grandson to the great Muhammad Ali."

Muhammad said bring them in. And I did.

The boy carried a food offering, as is the polite African way.

A Big Mac in a McDonald's sack. Hours old.

Muhammad ate it. Then called someone to whip up some food for his guests.

Muhammad hugged the little boy, and kissed him, and did a magic trick for him.

"How long you been in America?" said Muhammad.

"Eight days," said the old man. "First we went to Chicago. But found you no longer live there. Three days ago we arrived in Los Angeles. Today we found you. Tomorrow we can go home."

After they'd had something to eat, Muhammad put them in his brown Rolls-Royce convertible. The old man in the front passenger seat. The boy in the old man's lap.

I got in the back. Muhammad drove forty minutes across town to the rundown airport hotel where they'd been staying. He hugged them goodbye. Kissed them. Told them to go with God.

On the ride back to his house, cruising up one of the broad, endless boulevards of South Central now, Muhammad told me, "Every one of us has an angel watching us every day. Every time we do a good deed, the angel makes a mark on one side of his book. Every time we do something bad, he makes a mark on the other side. When we die, if we've got more good marks than bad, we go to Paradise. If we've got more bad marks, we go to Hell."

Muhammad sucked in a breath, making the air whistle.

"Everything on earth we do, we do *right* in front of Allah and his angels. *Maaaaann,* that's heavy! That's powerful! Think of it.

"Can you imagine Hell? Mash your hand down in a fryin' pan. Feel your skin sizzlin' and burnin'. Now hold your hand there and multiply that times a thousand, and that's Hell. For eternity! Can you *imagine* that?

"I've done a lotta bad things. Worldly things," he said. "Gotta keep doing good now. I wanna go to Paradise."

Muhammad drove on.

Later that afternoon, he and I signed an agreement which gave me rights to act as his agent. Not his exclusive agent, but his agent, nonetheless. He signed it while buck naked, lying back in his bed. Then he walked sleepily to his closet and stepped into a pair of suit pants and the heavy combat boots he ran in, and wearing only those he went downstairs with me, and we announced to Marge Thomas, his secretary, that he'd signed the contract.

I was so happy I forgot all about asking Marge to call a cab for me before I left the house, and forgot about hailing one once I'd walked past the guard gate at the entrance to Fremont Place and hit the main drag. Some time later, when I found myself five miles along Wilshire Boulevard and at the door of the Beverly-Wilshire Hotel, which was where I was staying, I had no memory of how I'd gotten back to Beverly Hills. It felt like I'd floated, but, judging by the blisters on my feet and hands that night, I must've walked. While lugging my heavy briefcase, which contained, among other things, two signed originals of the contract I wished I could show my father.

A month or two later. In a working-class neighborhood on the edge of London. In a crowd.

I'd never seen so many faces in a single block.

We'd worked our way out of the car, through a multitude, and up some steps. Policemen were holding a door open for us. We were almost there.

A red-haired boy, about ten, and his beefy father were the only ones still blocking our way. The boy was right in front of Muhammad, staring up into his face.

Muhammad reached out to shake the boy's hand.

But the boy was frozen in awe.

"Go ahead, son," said the father. "This is your moment. Shake the hand that shook the world."

I knew I'd never forget it. I looked back to take it all in one more time.

On both sides of the street, the sidewalks were jammed with people. In all the windows and on the rooftops, people. And on the steps leading up to every doorway. Everywhere, more people. Even the street was chock-a-block. With people, and cars which had stopped dead when their drivers saw Muhammad.

Who was now through the doorway.

I tried to follow.

But two policemen held me back.

"I'm with Ali," I said. "Let me through."

The policemen kept a hold of me.

"Mr. Ali?" called one of them.

Everyone was calling his name. But this was the voice of authority calling. Muhammad turned around.

"Do you know this gentleman?"

"I've never seen him before," said Muhammad. Then he turned and walked away, and the hands around my arms gripped tighter.

A moment later, Bingham came back, scowling. He was wearing a khaki photographer's vest, carrying a couple of cameras, and nodding at the policemen. "It's okay," he told them. "He's with us."

Muhammad Ali, King of the World, calling on his adoring subjects.

He visited heads of state all over the earth, and it was they and their blushing families who were thrilled. World leaders didn't just meet Muhammad in state rooms in front of cameras. They took him and whoever came with him into their private residences to meet their dying mothers. They lay down on the floor with him to play with their grandchildren. They didn't want Muhammad to leave.

I read somewhere once that Benjamin Disraeli said, "The world is governed by very different personages from what is imagined by those who are not behind the scenes." Travel for long with Muhammad and you would know the truth of that. You'd see the Pope, a little man in a long white cassock, laughing and hopping up and down right in front of you, trying to reach an uppercut to Muhammad's chin. You'd see Indira Gandhi, the Iron Lady, secreting herself in a dark corner and covertly sniffing her armpits for stink. You'd see Idi Amin, in color-coordinated baby blue-and-yellow tennis clothes, flipping through the pages of a magazine at a newsstand.

Travel for long with Muhammad and you would also learn that he is not black and you are not white.

I learned this in the breakfast dining room in King Fahad's guest palace in Jiddah.

There were three of us eating. Muhammad, Jabir Muhammad, and me. Jabir is known in the press as Herbert Muhammad. Jabir is a son of Elijah Muhammad, founder of the Nation of Islam. The Black Muslims. Who had whites across America shitting in their pants in the Sixties. Jabir was Muhammad's manager for many years.

After Elijah's death, Jabir, like Muhammad, renounced the Nation of Islam and its racism, and embraced true Islam.

Jabir was short and round, and he could be warm and friendly, and very nice. But during business discussions, when he wanted me to give him more—and I don't mean more for Muhammad, I mean more for Jabir—he could turn into quite a pain in the ass in a hurry, and usually he'd justify it on racial lines. This sentence from an FBI COINTELPRO memorandum written in May 1968 is perhaps instructive: *Herbert Muhammad has been described as money crazy and one who will do anything for money.* Which perhaps explains why, sometimes when he was dealing with white folks like me, an ugly look came onto Jabir's face and the old Black Muslim phrase "white devil" still escaped his lips.

As it did that morning in Jiddah.

"He's not white," said Muhammad. *He* being me.

Muhammad usually went along with just about anything Jabir said.

Sometimes it seemed to me that Jabir treated Muhammad like he'd inherited him when Elijah Muhammad died. There was love there, but there was also something of a master-slave feeling to Jabir's attitude about their relationship. And Muhammad usually went along with it. I rarely saw him talk back to Jabir.

But this was one of those times.

"He's not white," Muhammad said again to Jabir.

"Look at that pitcher," Muhammad said to me. "That milk's *white.* Now look at yourself."

He took my hand and put it next to the milk. "If you ever turn white like that, better get to a hospital. Quick! Because you're about to be dead."

Now Muhammad put his forearm against mine.

"And *I'm* not black," he said.

In fact, I was at the moment somewhat darker than he was. Before we left for Saudi Arabia, I'd spent several days in Florida visiting my mother and lying in the sun. So, as I sat at that table in Jiddah, my skin was something close to cocoa brown. While Muhammad had spent almost all of the last three weeks in overcast Chicago and New York, turning a pale golden shade that was lighter than me at the moment.

"When people say 'white,'" Muhammad said, "they mean 'European.' And when they say 'black,' they're talking more about the lips and the nose and the hair than the color. A 'black' man can be almost any color."

I'd never seen it until Muhammad said it. It's changed my perceptions ever since.

As for Jabir, I don't think he was sure whether Muhammad was defending me or chiding me. Jabir was nice as pie to me the rest of the trip.

That afternoon in Jiddah we went to a mall—Muhammad, Jabir, Mahdi, Jack, me, our royal protocol escorts, and probably a few others I don't remember. Muhammad said he wanted to get out of the palace and see some real people. Which we did.

When they saw Muhammad they mobbed him. At first a few dozen, then a few hundred. Arabs and Filipinos and Africans and even some Europeans—Jiddah being Saudi Arabia's most international city. People kept streaming to Muhammad from all over the place. A normal day for Muhammad. Who loves it.

But they don't love crowds in Saudi Arabia. In fact, throughout the Kingdom, crowds are banned. Except at stadiums for soccer matches, at mosques for prayers and sermons, and, of course, at such places as a certain Jiddah plaza I'd once visited. I don't know its real name. But Halass Square was what the locals called it. *Ha-lass*—Arabic for "finished." Halass Square was where Jiddah held its public executions.

It was a regular event there, though I saw it only once. The crowd was huge and nervous when I arrived. In the middle stood the executioner and the condemned. The executioner was a brown-skinned Arab with a mustache and goatee. I remember thinking he looked like a very religious man, somehow. He was wearing a sparkling white *thobe* and a checkered red-and-white *ghutra*, which was folded across his head just perfectly. And I remember his hands were huge and looked very strong. He read the execution order to the crowd and to the condemned, who wore a dirty white thobe and was tied and blindfolded. The prisoner sank to his knees then. The men in the crowd began braying, and the women ululated—that fevered howl they make with their tongues—from under their dark veils. Then, with a single stroke of the executioner's curved sword, it was done. Thank Allah there'd been so many people in the way that once the head rolled away, I couldn't see it.

The royal protocol officers who'd come to the mall with us started talking anxiously among themselves as soon as a little crowd began forming around Muhammad. After a couple of minutes the crowd had grown and our minders told us we had to leave. Fast.

Which wasn't possible. Because word had gotten out. By the time we got within thirty yards of the entrance, there were hundreds more, mostly imported Filipino laborers, streaming through it into the mall, toward us.

We could've made it out of there ourselves—eventually. We were experts at it.

But the protocol officers called in the army. Took all the fun out of it.

From the moment the first radio call went out to when the soldiers arrived—in jeeps with belt-fed machine guns mounted in the back—took only about six or seven minutes.

They got us out of the mall and stuffed our shopping party into about half a dozen of the King's hundreds of identical dark blue Buicks. Then escorted us back to the palace, where our minders told us we would not be leaving again. Except to go to the King's Mosque. Or the airport.

A soothsayer once told Fahad he would die in Riyadh, which is the capital of Saudi Arabia. Since then, Fahad's done everything he could to stay out of Riyadh as much as possible. At the Red Sea port of Jiddah, seat of the Hijaz province, he built himself a palace that goes on and on. There were facilities for everything. Plenty to do there. If we didn't mind friendly, helpful, royal protocol spies accompanying us every step of the way.

But the next morning, Muhammad left before dawn for Mecca. Which is only about forty-five miles from Jiddah.

The royal protocol could hardly turn down Muhammad's request to go to Mecca to perform Umra.

In an episode at the Holy Mosque which was has been covered up ever since, at the Holy Kabbah, the black cube built by Abraham which is the holiest place in all of Islam, pilgrims, who had waited all their lives to circle the Kabbah seven times then kiss it, saw Muhammad arriving and rushed from the Kabbah to Muhammad.

Which pissed off even Muhammad. He'd been to Mecca many times and it had never happened to him before, he told me that night.

It's a full moon, I told him.

As I said, we were experts at moving through crowds.

For all the leaders he met, Muhammad loved the common people more. Wherever he went, he made sure to see them. And to let them have a chance to see him.

When his visits were announced in advance, the crowds were enormous. One day in Seoul, more than two million fans filled a city square to greet him. That was the record, Muhammad told me. But even if no one knew he was coming, within a few minutes of his arrival almost anywhere there'd be a throng.

In New York, one of Muhammad's favorite things to do was arrive unannounced in Times Square, pop out of a taxi or a limo, and then leave a few minutes later—once traffic had come to a standstill. Horns honking everywhere. Bus drivers out of their buses getting autographs. Passengers climbing out of taxis to shake Muhammad's hand. Swarms of people moving down the sidewalks and through the streets toward Muhammad. I saw him perform his Times Square trick many times.

For Muhammad the traveling never ended. He was on the road as much as he was at home. Making free appearances for charities. Or paid appearances for businesses. All over the world. All the time. Often he'd visit three or four different countries in a row, for three or four different purposes, before heading back to the States.

And even back in the States he stayed on the move. L.A. New York. Chicago. Philly. Vegas. Miami. Maine, if somebody there invited him and the cause was right. Or the money. Likewise South Dakota, Oklahoma, New Jersey, and Alaska. Muhammad could be anywhere on any given day.

Usually, after a couple of weeks on the road with him, I'd say goodbye and catch up with him someplace else a few weeks later. I was living in New York and London now. London's a far better place than New York for doing business with Africa and the Middle East, which were the major markets in the Great Muhammad Ali Sale-a-thon. For all the nearly unanimous love he received in the rest of the world, making deals for Muhammad in the States wasn't always easy. In his own country, our own country, you sometimes still heard "draft dodger" when Muhammad's name came up, or "nigger."

So, even when I wasn't with Muhammad, I spent a lot of my time in places like Dubai, Kuwait, Riyadh, Jiddah, Istanbul, Cairo, Lagos. Doing my best to make deals. Endorsement deals. Paid personal appearances. Just about anything respectable, and not inconsistent with Islamic principles, that would result in wire transfers into Muhammad's bank account. Eventually I set up my own company, which Muhammad endorsed and made personal appearances for.

Everywhere on earth he went, Muhammad was more than happy to plunge into a sea of people. Knowing that somehow he would come out safely on the other side. Or wherever it was he was trying to get to. Traveling with him, you'd better stay close, or you'd never catch up. Because the sea would part, just a little, for Muhammad. But not for you.

He moved through the crowds at the stately pace of the Queen of England working a ropeline. Except Muhammad worked without ropes. Signing autographs, signing autographs, signing autographs, signing autographs, kissing babies. Shaking hands. Posing for pictures with fans. Racking up good-deed points on the books of his own personal angel.

Signing autographs, signing autographs, signing autographs. Mighty sloppy work. Because he's being jostled. Building up ink marks all over his fingers. When it gets too wild for signing, dropping the pen and moving on. Through people pressing toward him from every direction. Arms and hands reaching out to him. Shaking hands, shaking hands, shaking hands. Giving high fives. People all over shouting his name. Trying to carry on conversations with him. Women swooning. Kids with banners. Parents with children on their shoulders, pointing at the great man. "*Welcome, Champ!*"

"*As salaam aleikum, brother.*"

Moving slowly through hysteria, Muhammad with his fist in the air leading a chant, "*Ahhh-leee! Ahhh-leee! Ahhh-leee! Ahhh-leee!*" Cameramen walking backwards, taping as Muhammad approaches.

Photographers on ledges, trying to get views. "*Over here, Muhammad.*"

Mugging for photographers. Kissing babies. Naming babies. More than once, in Muslim countries, I've seen fathers emerge out of crowds, pass their infants to Muhammad, and shyly but passionately tell him they've been waiting for him to name their child. And here is evidence that the crowd can cooperate, and has a conscience. For somehow they sense the moment, and back off just far and long enough for Muhammad to hold the babe in swaddling at arm's length, look at it in its totality, then draw it up to his face, peer into its eyes, kiss it, and then pass it back to its father—pronouncing it a Khalid, or a Muhammad, or a Yasmine, or a Bilal. So be it.

Sometimes a brave soul comes out of the crowd looking for a fight.

A play fight with Muhammad.

The challenger throws a few slow-motion punches.

Muhammad throws a few back. And, if the guy looks like he has the moves, Muhammad commands the crowd to give them some room. Again the sea parts. Miraculously forming a ring. "*Get him, Champ! Get him!*" If it's a young buck, Muhammad whips him. If it's an old man, or a kid, Muhammad puts up a good fight but eventually covers up and goes down on one knee. Conquered. And, as soon as he's up and shaking his opponent's hand, Muhammad's at sea again. Surrounded.

Moving on. Shaking hands, shaking hands, kissing babies, kissing ugly women. "The pretty ones'll always have boyfriends or husbands," Muhammad will tell you in a low rumbly drawl, later, when you're out of the crowd. "But the ugly ones have got nobody. They've got lonely lives ahead of them. Now at least they can always remember they've been kissed by Muhammad Ali!"

The kissing bandit loves new shoes. Black. 13EEE. Cap-toe Oxfords. He loves the look of them when they're gleaming new, or highly polished. Which is a pity. Because within fifteen minutes in a crowd his shoes are wrecked. Scuffed to hell. Trampled on. I used to buy him new ones every few weeks.

Moving on, moving on, kissing babies. "*Howyoudoin', Champ?*"

Muhammad feigns indignation. "*Did you call me 'Tramp'?*"

People are handing him jars of jam, homemade, just for him.

Handing him bouquets.

Sometimes, something somewhere gives, and a collective shudder passes through the crowd. Muhammad and everyone around him lurches a step to the left or the right.

Then relative order is restored.

And Muhammad is moving on.

Except Muhammad is busy dispensing love and funny faces and doesn't know which way he's supposed to be going.

Usually there's someone local leading.

But his voice is lost in a thousand other voices.

And Muhammad doesn't know him. So he follows his own people.

Maybe it's Mahdi out front. Or Bingham. Or me.

People are grunting and straining toward Muhammad from all around. At Muhammad, they will stop. But you, they will be more than happy to tear through to get at him. Out front, you've got to chop hands and arms out of your face and put your shoulder down and plow. There's no other way.

Nearing wherever you're going, if there's a gate or a doorway—anything that creates a funnel—that's probably where it's going to get craziest. Five or six people at a time have their hands on you, pushing or pulling. Dozens of people at once are screaming Muhammad's name or otherwise improvising last-ditch attempts to get his attention. Banners are waving. Cops are linking arms. Putting their backs into the crowd. Behind you, Muhammad is reaching up and over, soul-shaking, reeling off one-liners—"*I'm so pretty!*" "*I shook up the world!*" "*Be cool, fool!*"—blowing kisses, and waving goodbye.

Then suddenly you're through a doorway. And the crowd is down to half a dozen nicely dressed people, chuckling nervously—the reception committee—who lead you into a stairwell or a corridor or a freight elevator, or through a kitchen. While you hear someone on a loudspeaker saying something like "*. . . to join me in welcoming a true hero, the greatest boxer of all time, the one and only. . . .*" And then you get behind Muhammad while they lead him onto a stage, or into a hall or a ballroom.

To a standing ovation.

And, after the Lord Mayor has welcomed him and given him something shiny, Muhammad takes over.

Deadpan, he says: "That's *it?*"

He pauses for effect.

"All that production flying me across the ocean. All that strugglin' getting me through the crowd to bring me in here. And you give me this little medal?"

And now Muhammad breaks into verse.

> *I enjoy your city,*
> *I admire your style.*
> *But your pay is so cheap,*
> *Don't call me back for awhile.*

He stomps off a few steps. Then comes back grinning.

And gives, sometimes: a beautiful canned speech. Other times: one of the craziest speeches of all time. Off the cuff. From the hip. Straight out of his heart. Branching out in all directions at once. Standing in the wings, or sitting on the dais, it seems to you he's totally lost the thread of what he's trying to say. You're praying he knows where he's going with it, but increasingly convinced he's lost it. Then somehow, in just a few words, he brings it all back together exquisitely. And, even though you've heard him speak a thousand times, you listen carefully. For you've just remembered you're listening to a mind like no other.

When he's finished speaking and rubbing shoulders with the audience, and he's backstage signing autographs, now that he has more elbow room and time to write, he seldom signs his name without inscribing a message. *Service to others is the rent we pay for our room in the Hereafter* seems to be what he writes most often above his signature.

"All my years of boxing were nuthin'," Muhammad tells the reception committee. "Just God's way of giving me fame. So I can deliver a message."

Someone opens the door a crack to check the size of the crowd. The Beast is waiting. Bigger than before.

"Let's go," says Muhammad, perking up.

And when you're finally back in the car, moving on, and the last kids running outside your windows have dropped away, Muhammad puffs up his chest, and somewhere a tallying angel winces and reaches for his quill because he knows what's coming next.

"If you think *that* crowd was something," Muhammad announces, "wait'll you see my funeral. It's gonna be bigger than Rudolph Valentino's! There's going to be beautiful women lining the streets for miles! Fainting. Crying. Moaning. No reason left to live."

What you're hearing, of course, are echoes of Cash and Bird.

Cash is Muhammad's nickname for his father, Cassius Marcellus Clay, Sr. A wild man, womanizer, and braggart of biblical proportions. "*He* ain't the greatest," Cash says indignantly when someone says something good of his son. "*I'm* the greatest."

Bird is Muhammad's nickname for his mother, Odessa Clay. You'd have to look a long time to find a sweeter, kinder woman.

Once you know them, you realize that Cash and Bird have been warring inside their son forever. And that, as Muhammad ages, Bird is winning.

A s I look back, it seems impossible. All the people all over the earth I already knew. Somehow, not so long at all after I was just a student, I could get almost anyone on the phone. Or to agree to see me. Or to welcome me back to their country. And as I sit here in my living room beneath a potted palm, my bare feet on the couch, watching videotape of me back then, out and about in the wide world, in my twenties and looking like nothing more than a boy in a suit, I have to wonder how I managed it in so little time. Certainly, being allied with Muhammad helped. Enormously. But there were plenty of others around Muhammad who got nowhere. Who were dreaded, while I was invited back. How, then?

I'm not sure, but I think the answer may be: If you showed a bit of world-view rather than behaving like a tourist, if you bothered to learn a few sentences of the local language as soon as you arrived, so that, by the time you met the King or Prime Minister or just a delighted porter, you could greet him flawlessly in his own language, if you did not fawn but treated even the exalted like normal people who crawl around on the floor with their grandchildren, if you took flowers for their wives—you would be well remembered and welcomed back. King Hassan would invite you to return next month to play golf with him and his brother Moulay Abdullah at Royal Rabat. You would spend a steamy Ghanaian night drinking with the Queen of the Ashantis, and she would offer you your pick of Ashanti princesses to be your bride. You would piss again in the House of Lords beneath your favorite sign, eventually have so much access that you become irresistible to such people as recruit spies, and end up in exile on this beach—walking across wet sand and dreaming of another world.

In India, everywhere an honored man visits garlands are hung around his neck.

Inside a little Indian car, with springs like trampolines, we struggled through the everyday hullabaloo of Indian streets—men, women, children, animals, cars, carts, heat and dust—multiplied times ten because today Muhammad Ali was visiting.

In places the roadsides were fifty people deep.

Sometimes, for a mile or more at a stretch, our daring driver could only inch through the bedlam.

While a hundred beaming faces pressed at every window.

There's a special sweetness in Indian smiles.

Muhammad would smile back, wave, roll down his window a few inches.

Each time he did, a dozen hands reached in to gently touch his face or grasp his hand.

There's a special gentleness in Indian hands.

Those not close enough to touch craned to get a look at him.

Skinny boys climbed statues.

Thousands sprinkled rose petals on our car as it passed by.

Indian welcoming committees were huge. At every stadium, school, temple, mosque, market, or fork in the road we stopped to visit, we found them emerging out of crowds or lurking en masse in lobbies or reception tents.

War heroes. Campaign contributors. Star students. Cricket captains. Brownnoses. Blackmailers. All smiling and slightly nervous. It was easy to imagine anyone with any influence wheedling the schoolmaster or imam or whoever was in charge for the honor of being selected to garland the most distinguished visitor. Thirty, forty, maybe fifty times at every stop, Muhammad bent forward while one of the chosen stepped up to him and draped another long necklace of flowers around his neck and down his chest.

Every little while Muhammad was so weighted down with flowers, looking about like a horse that had just won the Kentucky Derby, that we took him aside and helped him lift the garlands from around his neck. We dusted pollen and petals off his hair and clothes. Then set him loose for more love and flowers.

One evening I dream of still, we pulled into the outskirts of a village.

The last stop of a busy day.

The *sirdar* himself supervises the opening of the car door. Then stands at the head of the committee ready to greet the great man.

Muhammad receives their garlands. Then walks toward a podium and microphone set atop a small platform.

He hears music crackling from ancient loudspeakers. He smells flowers around his neck and sweet smoke from cooking fires somewhere in the distance. He looks over the crowd and sees wide-eyed boys and festive lanterns hanging twinkling from huge trees.

Before the platform, he stops for a beaming girl who is holding out a ring of flowers. My friend smiles and bends down to receive one last garland.

All my dreams of India begin and end with garlands.

New Delhi. At a reception on the lawn behind Indira Gandhi's house. It was sweltering, but for some reason we were all standing around holding china cups and saucers and drinking hot tea.

There she was. The Iron Lady. Mother India. The Prime Minister of the largest democracy on earth.

Muhammad stood chatting with Indira. He was the focus of everyone's attention.

Politicians, captains of industry, ambassadors, and spies waited for their chances to shake his hand. And pose for pictures with him.

Waiters in long coats and elaborately pleated and starched turbans circulated through the guests. Bearing silver trays of tea and pastries.

I stood off to the side with Indira's son, Rajiv. My first words to him were "*Bohaat khooshee hooey apsay milkar.*" Which, I had it on good authority from a kindly protocol officer I'd met a day or two before, was Hindi for "It's an honor to meet you." I rushed it a bit when I said it to Mrs. Gandhi, blurted it out. But I got it just right for Rajiv.

A friendly fellow. Warm. Down-to-earth. He was an airline pilot, he told me. Until recently, when his mother drafted him into the family business of running India.

Muhammad caught my eye and grinned at me across the heads of shorter people. He stuck out his pinkie and took a sip of tea.

Rajiv seemed more than happy to let his mother work the crowd. While he stood back, chatting with me. Asking me questions about Muhammad. Answering my questions about India. I'm the curious sort. India is a curious place. I asked a lot of questions. I remember a bird twittering in a bush behind us and Rajiv stopping a moment to listen.

When I had to go, he gave me his phone numbers and telex address. I gave him mine.

Out on the street, a crowd was waiting.

A few months later, the next meeting that led me to this beach:

Muhammad and I were dressed like James Bond, in tuxedos, on the Croisette in Cannes. In the Alpes-Maritime. On the Côte d'Azur, in the South of France, at the edge of the Mediterranean Sea, where the beach is a garden of nipples. Bare-breasted women, young and old, beautiful and not—recline on the seashore. At the height of a sunny summer day, there are hundreds, maybe thousands, of them. Across the bay is a low green mountain ridge that slides into the sea. It looks like paradise.

Now, it was getting late in the afternoon. The beach had all but emptied out. Waiters were closing big pink-and-white umbrellas. The last sun worshipers were concentrated up on the dock which stuck straight out from the beach into the sea. It was actually a pontoon, which tells you how minimal the waves were.

It was another one of those scenes I knew I would never forget—as I strode importantly down the dock with Muhammad, in my tuxedo and opera pumps, trailing a hotel porter and three uniformed boatmen, running a gauntlet of about twenty women stretched out on deck chairs, wearing makeup, jewels, and bikini bottoms, their eyes and naked breasts staring at us like we'd just arrived from another planet.

At the end of the dock, we stood beneath a broad white sign. MARTINEZ in Art Deco letters. The crewmen loaded us and our bags onto a Riva—one of those wonderful wooden speedboats you see in the Mediterranean—and rushed us across sky-blue waters and out past a chalky yellow cape to rendezvous with the *Nabila*.

At 282 feet and 1,800 tons, she was, according to what I'd recently read in a book, "the most opulent modern yacht afloat," and the property of mysterious Saudi Arabian businessman Adnan M. Khashoggi. The richest man in the world, or so they said.

Muhammad had met him, but I had not. I'd been looking forward to this.

She was beautiful. Long and sleek and white. With her cabin lights glowing through the evening haze. Parked behind a communications pod and an array of aerials on the top deck was a helicopter. It was full size, but looked like a toy in comparison to the scale of the boat.

We stood about forty yards off her starboard side while, six feet above the waterline, like magic, part of her hull hydraulically slid open, revealing a tender bay—a door tall and wide enough for us to walk through together. Next emerged a teak-and-chrome boarding platform, which the Riva was soon tied up to.

Khashoggi's Italian-born wife, Lamia, greeted us as soon as we were aboard. A tall, chestnut-haired beauty in rubies and haute couture. She chatted pleasantly in perfect English, and led us into a salon.

Where there were more guests. Who apparently hadn't been expecting Muhammad Ali this evening. There was an air of pleasant surprise.

Then Adnan Khashoggi appeared across the salon.

He was as short as I was tall, had chubby, jolly cheeks, was wearing a white tuxedo, and was as deeply tanned as a man could be. He glowed as he moved toward us, chatting and joking with his guests along the way, dancing a few steps as he passed the musicians.

He welcomed Muhammad. Told him he looked great. Shook his hand. Hugged him. Hugged him again.

Then turned to me.

And, in Arabic, I told our host I was honored to meet him. "*Tschaaraft be ma riftak*" was what I said.

He answered me in Arabic. "*Ahlan wa sahlan!*" Welcome!

Then he switched to English. Called me: "Your Excellency."

He grabbed my arm. "Come! You look hungry." He pulled me to a steward who held out a golden tray while Adnan hand-fed me a spoonful of caviar.

As far as I knew, he didn't even know my name. But, when Adnan softly squeezed my elbow and asked if I'd been enjoying myself in Cannes, he fixed his gentle brown eyes on me in a way that made it clear whatever I had to say was the most important thing in the world to him. After we'd chatted a minute or two, he handed me the golden spoon, saying, "I'll leave you to it, Your Excellency."

And a moment later he was on the other side of the salon, introducing people. Then he was off again, on the move, walking in a cheerful rolling way which, for all his weight, somehow managed to make him seem robust instead of fat. Smiling an infectious smile. Laughing. Moving on. Chatting, in good English, his Middle Eastern accent modulated by American sounds.

I recognized a few of the guests.

Sir James Goldsmith. Or Jimmy, as everyone was calling him. Wall Street Raider extraordinaire. For years he'd been a subject of fascination to me. I'd read books about him. He was half English, half French. He had two wives and two households, at once, and a whole lot of money. Sir Jimmy smiled and put up his dukes, and took a couple of swipes at Muhammad's chin.

Next we were presented to Don Jaime de Mora y Aragón. Spanish nobility, and brother of the Queen of Belgium. I'd seen pictures of him in magazines. Which didn't do justice to Don Jaime's presence. He was maybe sixty-five, had dark brown hair, slicked straight back, a thick mustache and goatee, and was leaning on an ornate walking stick. He wore black pantaloons and a white mess jacket. A gold medal hung beneath his black bow tie. And in his hand was a monocle, with which he was soon carefully inspecting the most famous face in the world.

"It's true," he finally announced to everyone gathered around us. "Not a single scar! And very pretty!"

After awhile, Muhammad asked for a tour of the boat, and Adnan sent for the captain himself to do the honors. As he led us down long white gangways and into elevators and staterooms and suede-walled salons and through hydraulic doors with the first keypad entry systems I'd ever seen, the captain told us all this and more in a pleasant Italian accent:

The *Nabila*, 1,800 tons, 86 meters long, and drawing nearly five meters, designed by Jon Bannenberg, powered by twin 3,000-horsepower Nohab Polars, steel-hulled, completed in 1980 by the M&B Benetti shipyard in Viareggio, Italia, at a cost no one was sure because the shipyard went bankrupt in the process, but perhaps fifty million dollars, manned by a crew of forty, and equipped with SatCom, SatNav, Atlas Ecosounder, three radar systems, Vosper stabilizers, redundant anticollision systems, bulletproof glass, Agusta 109 helicopter, two 10-meter Rivas and a 6-meter Riva, had sailed out of Monaco harbor that afternoon bound southwest to Las Palmas in the Canary Islands, four days away—at her cruising speed of twenty-one knots—by way of the Straits of Gibraltar and the western coast of Morocco.

Her interior, by Sturchio of Roma, included four main salons, cinema, disco, swimming pool, Jacuzzi, sauna, solarium, gymnasium, hospital complete with operating room, dining space for a hundred guests, two main galleys, smaller galleys on each deck, and eight guest suites, all with king-sized beds and private baths, and telephones and gadgets which popped up out of nowhere by remote control.

"Damn!" said the soulful Muhammad, and "Get back Loretta!" said Shee Ku at his side—as, at the touch of a button by the captain, they beheld a television slowly rising out of the top of a burled wood cabinet.

Down in the engine room, and again up on the bridge, where most of the controls were not steel or brushed aluminum but gold, Muhammad signed autographs and posed for pictures with members of the crew. Then the captain showed us into an elevator and down a corridor and back toward the festivities. But first we passed Adnan Khashoggi, all alone in a little cabin, oblivious to us and talking on a telephone. *Who are you?* I wondered, not for the last time in my life, examining Adnan's face for clues. *What's your secret? How did you pull all this off?*

Back in the main salon, and spilling out onto the afterdeck, the party was heating up.

When we came back from our tour, there were half a dozen beautiful women there I hadn't seen before we left. Where did they come from? I was just starting to talk with one of them, a model from New York, when Adnan walked up and took her wrist in his hands.

"Everything alright, Professor?" he said to me.

"Have you met the Professor?" he said to her.

Then Adnan was off, huddled with Lamia and a grandee whose name I'd already forgotten, and laughing.

Adnan's father was a doctor. Court physician to King Abdul Aziz, the founder of Saudi Arabia.

Adnan grew up at court, in Riyadh. Playing marbles in the dirt with young Prince Sultan, who would later be Saudi Minister of Defense. And befriending young Prince Fahad, who would be King.

Adnan's father was also an entrepreneur. He brought electricity to Riyadh. Lit up the mud-walled palace of the King for free. Sold electricity to everyone else.

The court physician and owner of Saudi Arabia's first power company sent teenaged Adnan to Egypt, to Iskandria, which we call Alexandria and was once the seat of all the knowledge in the world, to attend Victoria College. There, all classes were taught in English, and boys caught conversing in Arabic were caned in fine English boarding school style.

At Victoria, one of Adnan's classmates and best friends was Crown Prince Hussein, latterly known as King Hussein, of Jordan. Another was Hussein's Hashemite cousin from Baghdad, the Crown Prince of Iraq.

When it came time for Adnan to attend university, his father, a practical man, decided Adnan could best serve his country by becoming a petroleum engineer. So he was enrolled in the Colorado School of Mines, in Golden, Colorado, where, upon his arrival, in a blinding snowstorm, Adnan noticed it was somewhat chillier than he was used to. He sent word to his father that he couldn't stand it, then sat by a fire and awaited further instructions. When they came, his next stop was Northern California. Where the climate was more agreeable and Adnan enrolled in Chico State University, chosen because it had a small community of Arab students.

At Chico, Adnan parlayed his modest college allowance into what seemed to be a fortune.

He made his first big score selling trucks, manufactured by the Kenworth Motor Truck Company of Seattle, Washington, to one of his father's patients back home in Riyadh—a construction tycoon named Mohamed bin Laden, who was so rich he used to loan money to the King.

When the deal was done, Adnan, who was about nineteen years old, maybe twenty, received a fifty-thousand-dollar commission.

With which Adnan hired a secretary to help him with his homework and his business letters. Bought himself a fancy car. Hired a chauffeur. Moved into a hotel. And threw a hell of a party.

After that, every day, he had his meals, and those of his friends and staff and neighbors, catered by the finest restaurants in town. When he'd send a bellhop out to bring him back a forty-five-cent pack of cigarettes, he'd give him a ten-dollar bill, or a twenty. When the porter returned with the goods, young Adnan would tell him to keep the change.

Anyone who spent money like that had to be a millionaire. The manager wasn't worried when his new best customer fell behind on his hotel bills.

Adnan's father had once shown him a handful of coins, and told him: "Throw these on the carpet, and you hear nothing. Throw them on the marble floor, and they make a noise. Always put your money where it can be heard."

Soon there were more deals. More trucks sold to Saudi Arabia. More checks.

Adnan was on his way.

And the host with most.

He befriended a young senator named John Kennedy. Entertained him in California, introduced him to pretty girls. The senator reciprocated in Washington and Palm Beach.

Life was good, and Adnan no longer had time for school.

He went home and set up for business, bringing American and European products and services to the Kingdom of Saudi Arabia. Got himself Riyadh's Post Office Box No. 6, which might be seen as an indication of how early he got in on what was to be the Saudi development boom. To his agency rights for Kenworth Trucks, he added the exclusive Saudi agencies for Rolls-Royce engines, Marconi electronics, and Fiat and Chrysler automobiles. Saudi Arabia needed these things. More checks flowed in.

On a sunny day in 1962, young Adnan was summoned to the palace of Crown Prince Faisal, who was running Saudi Arabia in the stead of his debauched brother King Saud.

Down in Yemen, royalist guerrillas were fighting to take back the country from the Communists. The royalists needed guns and trucks, and the House of Saud wanted them to have them. But not to be linked to their supply.

Covert Statecraft 101. Adnan's education was continuing.

Faisal gave Adnan a check for one million pounds sterling. Told him to get a specified number of rifles and trucks to certain parties in Yemen. From where the goods came or how they got there, Faisal didn't care, as long as no one knew Saudis were involved.

Adnan did what he was told.

Adnan's first masterstroke. Then he went to his old friend Prince Sultan, who was now the Saudi Minister of Defense, and gave Sultan the change from the million-pound check. Asked Sultan to give it to Faisal.

No, said Sultan, the rest is for you.

No, said Adnan, I did this for my country. For my King. Not for money.

After that, as torrents of oil money washed into the Saudi coffers, Sultan gave companies represented by Adnan almost every major contract as Saudi Arabia built itself a modern defense system.

Before he was thirty, Adnan had netted over two billion dollars in commissions by putting together American or European sellers and Saudi buyers of everything from trucks and towels to fighter jets, tanks, radar systems, schools, and hospitals.

People called him an arms dealer, but Adnan called himself a "merchant banker." Or, on headier days, a "merchant statesman."

He had palatial homes and business interests all over the earth. He traveled between them on this yacht and on a fleet of airliners more lavish than Air Force One.

That much I'd read in books and magazines.

The chubby little chap standing a few feet away from me with his arms around two of his guests was by now either the richest man in the world or doing a damned good impression of him.

Dinner was served in the round dining salon. Buffet-style.

"We have three chefs," Adnan announced as he handed Muhammad a plate. "One French. One Lebanese. One Chinese."

The buffet table was covered with golden platters bearing elaborate arrangements of charcoal-grilled salmon and lobsters and giant prawns and kofta kebabs and lamb on beds of rice, and pigeons in sweet pastry, and hummus and tabouleh and *khubz*—flat Arab bread—and dumplings, and caviar, and grapes and melons, and golden teapots and coffeepots from Arabia, and mounds of cakes and cookies.

At the big round table, the knives and forks and spoons were gold, as were the salad plates and underplates and finger bowls.

Across a lake of flowers in the middle of the table, I looked at Adnan.

A friend of a friend of my father had recently told me Adnan had been on good terms with every American president since Kennedy; he had a genius for explaining Arabs to the West and the West to Arabs; he'd been at various times suspected of engaging in covert diplomacy for Saudi Arabia, Israel, and the United States; and that made him always a target of the Mossad, the Saudi Mukhabarat, and the CIA.

I looked around the table, wondering who among us was a spy.

When we'd finished dinner, and after the belly dancer and the disco, after three A.M., Adnan asked us if we'd like to go back to Cannes "by boat or by chopper." Muhammad couldn't swim and was afraid of flying. I grinned at him. He chose the helicopter. Rising into the sky and heading back to France, I watched the yellow glow of the *Nabila* until it disappeared.

As Lord Privy Counselor to the King of the World, the more I saw of the powers that be, the more I knew they were just people—like everybody else.

Which was something I already knew about spies.

They're ordinary people, doing mostly very ordinary things. They're all around us. Which perhaps explains why, even after my father's death, I didn't seem to be able to avoid them. Not entirely. And never for long. There were the old friends of my father, just staying in touch. There were the others who, when I met them, I just knew. And there were a few who surprised me—like James and Al.

James wasn't an intelligence officer, but his life had been torn apart by them. And he had a secret.

Which, for reasons I hope were clearer to James than they ever were to me, he one day proceeded to tell me. As soon as I was alone, I wrote it down. In a hotel room in Montreal. My first night ever in Canada and, instead of seeing the sights, I was writing down a secret I'd heard that morning.

"I know your father was in intelligence," James said. We were in a rented car, driving from the airport to a venue.

James was in the sports business. Specializing in promotional events. He wanted me to retain his company. Weeks earlier, I'd told him my father had been in intelligence. I suppose that had been gnawing at James ever since.

"And I know he's passed away," James said. "But you told me you still know some people in intelligence. I expect you'll call them to check me out. And, in that case, they'll tell you something about my involvement with them. Which I'd rather tell you. Because it didn't happen the way they'll tell it."

Remember this: I was a boy in a suit. Why James concluded I had such powers, I'm not sure. Yes, I knew a few intelligence officers now risen to high places. But, like my father, when it came to classified information, my old uncles wouldn't have told me squat.

Wrong, James. Wrong, I was thinking.

"You're probably right," I said. "Go on."

"I haven't told this to anyone," James said. "And you can't either. Or I could go to prison for the rest of my life."

"Go on."

"Well, you know, I'm from Tennessee. And I grew up on a farm. My daddy taught me to hunt. From the time I was twelve, if I was out in a field and a squirrel ran by two hundred yards away, I could pick up my rifle, take one shot, and kill it. Hit the squirrel right in the head every time. I didn't miss. Shooting just came natural to me.

"In the Army, every time we had to go to the range to qualify with a rifle, I got an Expert rating. And I only got that because it's as high as the ratings go. The instructors always told me my scores were higher than anyone else on the post ever got.

"I was sent to Germany. Stationed at K-Town."

"Been there," I said.

"One Saturday night, some of my buddies and I rode into Heidelberg to drink some beer. We were in a bar downtown. There was this drunk German guy, and I got into an argument with him. All of a sudden all these Krauts were rooting him on, and my buddies were telling me not to take that shit, so we stepped outside and started fighting, and I punched him right . . ." James took a hand off the steering wheel, turned toward me, made a fist, and stuck it into his neck just below his chin, ". . . here."

After holding it in for so long, it must've felt good to confess. Maybe, deep down, that was why James told me all this.

"As soon as I hit him," James said, "I felt something in his neck give. Like his whole windpipe collapsed. Crumbled. He went straight down. Wasn't moving. Wasn't breathing. One of my buddies said, 'Let's get the fuck out of here!' and we *booked*.

"We drove back to K-Town. . . . Everything was normal there for about a week or so. Then one morning the sarge came into the barracks, just like usual, yelling, '*Drop your cocks and grab your socks, gentlemen.*' But then he told me to report to the captain's office, and the captain told me to report to the Intelligence office.

"The Intell officer told me I'd committed murder. And that the German police were looking for a tall, dark-haired GI, and they were closing in on me. He said the Army would give me up unless Intell protected me. He said, 'You've got two choices: You can go to a German prison for murder for the rest of your life. Or you can volunteer to go out on a mission for us, and be back here in less than a month, free and clear for the rest of your life.'"

After that, until James finished telling me, he never looked away from the road. Didn't turn his face to me even once.

He told me how he opted for the mission, of course. How Intell kept him isolated in Kaserne for a few days.

Until they put him on an Air Force plane. Set up with rows of seats and an aisle down the middle, like an airliner, but all the windows were covered so he couldn't see out. He was the only passenger, and he'd been told not to talk to the crew. He was allowed to stay in his seat or go to the bathroom in the back. At chow time, they brought him trays of food and took them away. They wouldn't let him near the cockpit. Wouldn't let him see or hear anything that might help him identify where he was heading.

The plane landed a few times to take on fuel, but they made James stay on-board.

After a day and a half of flying they finally got to where they were going. Which obviously was somewhere in Southeast Asia. He could tell from the look of the land and the locals. Maybe Vietnam, James thought, though he had no real way of knowing. They'd removed or painted over everything in the camp that might provide a hint.

It was during the Vietnam War. He might have been in Cambodia, or Laos. Except that, wherever he was, the U.S. had a well-paved airfield which it controlled, and a camp in the jungle right beside it. Probably he was somewhere in Vietnam, James decided. But he was never sure.

You can guess what they made him do there.

At his first briefing after he arrived, they told him he owed them fifteen targets.

And that, when he had hit them, he would be free.

"That's all they ever called them," James told me, sounding lost. "'Targets.' They never once referred to them as people, or gave them names. And they never called it *killing*. My job was *hitting* the targets."

It was always one target per operation, James told me.

A couple hours before an op, they'd sit him down in front of a topo map and tell him something like:

A Huey will drop you and your spotter here.

You'll proceed to this point. Which is atop a little hill overlooking this village. Your spotter knows the way.

Set up and wait.

At oh-eight-fifty, a blue Mercedes will arrive in the village. Or, other days, at other times—it was a jeep. Or, some ops, there was no vehicle involved.

The target will get out of the Mercedes. Or, the jeep. Or, will come out of the front door of this long house. Or, the back door of this hut.

This is a photograph of the target.

The target will be wearing a military uniform with these markings on the shoulder boards. Or, we don't know what the target will be wearing, but the target will be accompanied by the woman in this photograph. Or, by the man in this photograph. Or, the target will be buck naked and taking a shower.

Your spotter will help you identify the target.

Hit the target. Then leave.

You take one shot only.

If you miss, leave anyway.

Hoof it back to the insertion point and we'll extract you.

James said it went like clockwork every time.

Except once. When the target didn't show.

James said he hit fifteen targets in just under four weeks.

I asked him if he'd missed any.

James said: "I wanted to. But, like I already told you, I don't miss."

I asked him how it made him feel.

James said: "It wasn't like shooting anything else. One moment a man is standing there right in front of you inside your scope. A living man. And the moment you squeeze the trigger he's blooming pink blood and brains and falling dead."

James said they all had Asian faces. Most of them were in military uniforms, but he wasn't sure whose military. At least a couple of them were high-ranking officers with staff cars.

James said it made him sick. But he told himself it was a time of war. And they were the enemy. They had to be, right?

James said, when he'd hit his fifteen targets, Intell, or whoever it was Intell had turned him over to—that was never clear—kept their word and sent him back to K-Town.

Rereading it now, as I've written it down here, it seems fantastical. A whopper straight out of a thriller. But if your father had once taught a course in Sophisticated Assassination, and if you'd been there, in that car with us riding past bucolic Canadian pastureland while James told his darkest secret—if you'd seen James tell it, and heard the shame and sorrow in his voice—you would've believed him. It had the indescribable but unmistakable sound of truth. With an undercurrent of surprise. It must've been startling for James, hearing himself saying out loud things which for years he'd only allowed himself to think. Alone at night in the dark.

In those days, almost no one had heard of the Phoenix Program. The CIA and a long-since-incinerated list of other intelligence outfits no one ever got wind of culling thousands of suspected Viet Cong sympathizers and local and provincial leaders from hamlets and villages and towns throughout South Vietnam. One bullet at a time. I hadn't heard of it.

Still I had no difficulty believing U.S. Army Intelligence could reason: *We are at war. Here's a guy with a problem. And a talent, which could be very useful to us. Let's help him if he'll help us.* It was realism in a microcosm. And I'd learned all about realism from my father.

But in the end James's story turned worse than I'd expected.

He didn't even mention this at first. It popped out when I asked him what was the cover story to explain his absence when he got back to his old unit in Germany.

"Emergency leave. Death in the family," James said. Then he added this:

It was the same arrangement on the plane going back. Except this time there were two passengers. They were told to stay apart and not to try to speak to each other. Crew members stayed in the passenger cabin to make sure they didn't.

But it was a long flight.

And James had to pass the other passenger on bathroom trips. And the crew weren't as vigilant as they could've been. James and the other passenger managed to communicate. With gestures and nods, they established they'd each been shooting people.

Using the bathroom as their drop, they exchanged their real names and addresses back home.

Back in the States and out of the Army, they talked. Just once. And discovered they were both farm boys from the South; were both crack shots; had both gotten into trouble; had both been offered the choice of a foreign prison or wiping the slate clean by volunteering for a mission; and had both been told basically the same thing when Intell was finished with them.

What James remembered Intell saying to him was that he would never hear from them again. Unless he told someone, anyone, about his mission. If he did that, they said, they would notify the German authorities that they had finally identified that Heidelberg bar-fight killer—and James would go to prison. "The statute of limitations for murder is forever," one of them told him. "Don't fuck up."

"God Almighty!" I said to James. "Don't you get it? This was systematic. You were duped and used."

But James wouldn't hear it.

"No!" he said. "I thought about that. But the thing is *I know* I killed that German. I knew it the moment I hit him. From the way his neck crumbled and he just went straight down."

I said, maybe, maybe not. But what about the other guy, the other shooter? How did he get into trouble with the law?

Was it similar?

Do you know?

James wouldn't say.

James quickly became so fiercely protective of the second passenger, I decided they'd entered into a pact.

Years later, when I read about the Phoenix Program, I tried to find James. But he'd moved on. And, after that, when I learned about the twenty-one ways grifters can fake a death, I tried even harder. But James had done quite a job of disappearing.

So I've pretended here that his name was James, and I've altered his appearance and enough other things that no one will ever identify him. I've altered almost everything but the core of his story and what possessed him to tell it to the son of a spy.

James's story didn't consume me like it might've had I heard it at another time. I was living the life I chose, still pursued by the life that chose me. I see that now, but back then I barely even noticed.

I was busy chopping my way through crowds and trying to make a buck or two. I was living on airplanes and in hotel suites and, in between, in flats in London and New York—with a wide range of entertainment options.

I was meeting presidents and kings and dictators. I was enjoying the elaborate spectacle of Mobutu Sese Seko's birthday party for his wife; or, actually—and this part was said to be a Zairian state secret—for his identical twin wives. I was in the Bahamas, in Muhammad's last training camp, sitting around the rec room with Muhammad and Bingham and others, cheering on John Travolta as he danced around the room swinging Muhammad's wet jockstrap over his head. I was learning my reaction to gunfire—not good, when shots are fired in Muhammad's bedroom by his bodyguard when a riot of pissed-off sparring partners and spit bucket carriers breaks out a few hours before the last fight of Muhammad's career, and the bullets happen to miss me and my groin by less than six inches before ripping into a dresser and through a couple of Muhammad's shirts; when that happens, I learned, I don't handle it all that well. I was falling in love with beautiful women glimpsed across the room in nightclubs. I was meeting half the journalists on earth and learning how to deal with them. I was up late with Muhammad—in hotel suites, when everyone else was asleep, and after he'd had a catnap—talking about philosophy and religion and power and pussy. Of all Muhammad's favorite topics, and all mine, those were the ones which overlapped.

One morning in England. In Handsworth, an inner-city armpit of Birmingham, in the heart of the English Midlands, to be more precise. For three straight days, the crowds had been crazy.

Someone knocked, and I opened the front door of Muhammad's suite.

A grave-looking policeman and a graver-looking policewoman were standing there. Black uniforms. Bobby helmets. Grim smiles. "We'd like to have a word with Mr. Ali, please."

But Mr. Ali was half asleep, sitting on the couch.

"Can I give him a message?"

"We'd like to speak with him personally."

"Please wait here," I said. And half a minute later I was back. "He asked me to ask you to tell me whatever it is you want to say to him."

They looked at each other. Their grim but magic moment was disintegrating. This wasn't at all how they'd pictured it on the drive over here. They looked at each other again.

"All right," the man said, and then the woman said, "Someone's phoned in a threat to shoot Mr. Ali."

"Come right in!" I said. "Welcome! Always nice to have the police around. Let me go and tell Muhammad to expect you."

But just then we heard Muhammad's voice. A roar: "Good!"

Muhammad has a sneaky way of listening to everything going on around him.

Even when he's just sitting or lying around, amongst family and friends, there might be six different conversations quietly going on in a room and somehow Muhammad monitors them all. In total silence, and while seemingly close to gaga—until he hears something he doesn't like, and pops up and chides whoever just said it. Or he hears something that's wrong, and corrects it. Or he hears something he appreciates, and opens his eyes and applauds it. Then slips back into his shell.

When we went into the living room, Muhammad was standing in front of the window beating his chest like Tarzan. "Good!" he roared again. "Just let 'em try it!"

I closed the curtains.

There was a wild look on Muhammad's face which I knew well—but it seemed somewhat alarming to our visitors.

"Mr. Ali—" the woman began.

But Muhammad interrupted. "I'm Superman!" he said in the tones of a twelve-year-old braggart. "Bullets can't hurt me. They bounce right off me— ping! ping! ping! ping! ping! Most of 'em can't even hit me. They fly right towards me, feel my power, and then zoom off in another direction." He demonstrated this effect with his hands and his mouth—had imaginary bullets flying all around us.

Until he tired of that and moved on to: "*Bang!* Missed me. *Bang!* Missed me again."

The constables looked at each other. *Is he barmy?*

Then they turned to me for help.

But, in a flash, Muhammad calmed down. "I'm not worried," he said. "I appreciate you coming to tell me, but it's all in the hands of Allah."

Still, all day long, we had a huge police escort.

The Handsworth crowds were as tough as the police. A mixture of working-class whites, blacks with English accents, blacks with Caribbean accents, blacks with African accents, Rasta-men, Arabs, Pakistanis, and more. All of them nice enough on their own, perhaps, but they didn't seem to get along all that well together.

And that added to the tension which I felt, even if Muhammad didn't, knowing that any moment someone might be shooting at him.

When we left the newspaper plant—where Muhammad had just thrown the switch to start that afternoon's press run for a special edition, *Muhammad Ali in Birmingham*—there was a mob outside and the police were determined to help us escape them.

A policeman put Muhammad, Bingham, and me into a patrol car. Someone opened the gate the newspaper delivery trucks used, and we shot out into the streets like a bat out of hell. Flashing lights, siren—nur-neeee nur-neeee nur-neeee nur-neeee. The plan was to get away from anyone who might be following us and then rendezvous with the Rolls-Royce we'd been riding around town in for the last few days.

But our chauffeur had stopped too close. He was waiting no more than half a mile from the newspaper plant. People had recognized the Rolls, so there was already a small crowd waiting on the sidewalk beside it. And behind us, motorcycles and cars were gaining on us.

What the policeman driving us should've done was keep going, and make the Rolls-Royce chase us. But he didn't.

The policeman stopped right behind the Rolls.

Which bolted a couple hundred yards forward when our chauffeur saw the crowd suddenly pouring off the sidewalk.

The policeman zoomed forward and stopped behind the Rolls again.

We got out in a hurry and Bingham got into the front seat and Muhammad got into the back, then slid over to his right, to behind the driver, and a whole gang of people were catching up to us now, and, just when I'd climbed halfway into the backseat, they caught me.

I lunged headfirst into the car and into Muhammad's lap and chest. My calves and ankles and feet were still sticking out the door, and people started tugging on them now. Not because I was a rock star or anything like that. I knew they didn't give a toss about me. But they knew the only reason Muhammad Ali was still right there before their eyes was that I hadn't made it all the way into the car yet. So they wouldn't let go of me, and, as I landed, I grabbed the lapel of Muhammad's suit and started dragging myself in, and I gave my big strong friend my free hand and, in something like desperation, I said, "Pull me in."

Muhammad's response took just three seconds.

One Mississippi—Two Mississippi—Three Mississippi.

Yet it was crystal clear.

And he delivered it without uttering a single word.

In the first second, while he removed my hands from him, with just his eyes he told me he was the great Muhammad Ali, a product of his own invention, a man the likes of which no one would ever see again after he was gone, and that he and I might well be friends, in fact may have slept in the same bed together a couple of times when we were out on the road and there weren't enough beds to go around, but I owed him and his brand-new suit a bit of respect, they deserved to be treated with some dignity, and if I ever again laid my clammy white fingers on his lapel and pulled, he might well break my hand and then push me out the door and slam it on me forever.

In the second second, while he tidied his lapel, Muhammad widened his eyes and told me he loved me, and he looked at me tenderly like I was a stupid, gawky, white, rhythmless child, so clueless and truly pitiful the way I lay there flailing that he'd decided to impart to me a small but vital portion of his secret knowledge.

In the third second, he told me the reason I was able to hear all this in less than the time it seemed to be taking a small but spirited gathering of his fans to work my right shoe off was that, contrary to what I may have until then ignorantly believed, a second in itself is not an inconsiderable segment of time; rather, as every boxing master knew, a second is freighted with potential. In a single second a fighter can pivot, feint, slip a punch, start a punch, pull that punch, adjust, load up, throw a punch that chops a man down, and watch him fall. In boxers' time, a second is an eternity.

Even as Muhammad conveyed that to me, I remembered the first time I'd sparred with my father. Inside the ring, with a big man stalking and slugging you, a three-minute round goes by like an hour. My father and I were in a gym in Virginia, in protective headgear and big sixteen-ounce training gloves, which are supposed to diminish punching power but didn't seem to be working that day. Less than fifty seconds into the first round, I'd looked up at the clock wondering why the bell hadn't rung. Likewise, about twenty seconds later.

In the remainder of that third second of his discourse, Muhammad told me what I didn't seem to understand was that, in moments such as these, the idea is not to think fast, it's to think *slow*. It's not a technique, he said. It's a state of being. Look. Listen. Feel. Grasp the details. Concentrate your mind to detect the slightest glimmer of change. Of direction. Of speed. Of intent. Find patterns in the chaos. Measure arcs and distances. Calculate range and azimuth. Swivel, parry, watch the punch miss by a fraction of an inch. Don't waste the energy to make it miss by more. Embrace the paradox. Assess pros and cons. Don't panic. Find grace. Don't think fast. Think slow. Don't freeze. Relax. S-L-O-W. Find your opportunity. Quit flopping around here on my lap, fool.

And with that, Muhammad placed his hands on my shoulders, closed his eyes on me in utter boredom, and pushed me back out toward the crowd.

I got it.

Somehow I understood.

I thought as slowly as I could.

Felt.

Assessed.

Pulled one foot into the car.

Pulled my other foot out of my shoe.

And into the car.

Shut the door.

Then composed myself, straightened my tie, rolled down my window, and asked for my shoe back, please.

When it was returned, we drove away.

If there was a grand design in all of this, I didn't see it then. But these are all things that happened, and that I know affected me later. Led me to this beach. There were spies, and perhaps also assassins, all around me. My father's world was catching up with me, whether I wanted it to or not. While we wound through Birmingham—even though I knew Muhammad was right, whatever happened to us was in the hands of Allah—in the back of my mind I wondered if somewhere out there was a man with a rifle. And, if so, if he was as good a shot as James.

"You know," I said to Muhammad, who I still hadn't properly thanked for pushing me back out into the mob, "the most fucked-up thing about this day is, if there really is someone out there who's going to shoot at you, I can already tell he's going to miss you and hit me."

Then there was Al. Tubby little black guy with a James Brown permanent wave and a mustache. Always wearing a track suit. And a necklace with a big round medal that swung back and forth when he walked, and straddled the boundary between his chest and the upper reaches of his belly when he sat still.

Every day I ever spent in New York with Muhammad, it seemed like I always saw Al at least once. Hanging out in hotel lobbies waiting for us, or showing up at Muhammad's appearances. Or up at the barbershop in Harlem. Or waiting outside the magic shop when we came out. Somehow he always found us. He'd give Muhammad a big smile and a handshake, or a hug, or a *My Man!* Then he'd pretty much drift into the background, and eventually he'd disappear. The first few times I met the guy, he didn't even tell me his name. Just nodded at me when I introduced myself and shook his hand. Eventually he told me his name was Al. No last name. Just Al.

A breakthrough, nonetheless.

I don't think Al and Muhammad were all that close. They never seemed to have much to say to each other. But we always saw Al somewhere.

And almost every time we went to the vaguely baroque Upper East Side townhouse that was Don King's New York office, Al was there when we got there.

Who the hell is Al? I remember saying to Keith Ali, a friend of Muhammad from New Jersey, one day on the sidewalk outside Don's office. Or maybe I said it to Kevin Ali, Keith's twin. I never could tell them apart.

Keith, or Kevin, said: That's Reverend Al Sharpton. He's a minister and a New York civil rights leader. I said: I don't think he likes me. Or any of us, actually. Keith or Kevin said: He's all right. Reverend Al is Reverend Al.

He seemed to do a lot of listening, and not a lot of talking.

Even on the few occasions he went up with all of us to Muhammad's suite, Al just hung out. Listening more than talking.

Listening to Muhammad talking shit about whatever he'd been up to that day or the night before. Or listening to Muhammad talking seriously to reporters about how the world's great religions are all rivers, all carrying the same basic truths, through different lands, into the same sea. Muhammad saying Muslims and Jews and Christians all pray to the same God. "Allah" is a word, not a name. Nothing more than the Arabic word for God. So Arab Christians pray to Allah just the same as Arab Muslims do. Ain't that much difference between us. We shouldn't be doin' all this fussin'.

Even then, about all Reverend Al would say was *Preach!* or sometimes *Tell it, Brother Muhammad!*

I couldn't figure out what he was up to. But after awhile I stopped trying.

Reverend Al was just Reverend Al. Around so much of the time, and usually so quiet you barely even noticed when he was there and when he wasn't.

Then one afternoon I was in the Soup Burg on Madison Avenue at 73rd—a greasy spoon in miniature, just twelve seats, all stools, arrayed around a counter and a sizzling grill—sitting there eating a really nice cheeseburger and reading the sports section of the *New York Newsday* I'd found on my stool when I sat down. And when I finished with the sports and flipped the paper over to the front page, there was a big black-and-white photograph of Reverend Al looking shifty and a huge headline: THE MINISTER AND THE FEDS.

Under that, I read: "For the last five years, the Rev. Al Sharpton, Jr., one of the city's most vocal and visible black activists, has been secretly supplying federal law enforcement agencies with information on boxing promoter Don King, reputed organized crime figures and black leaders and elected officials, according to sources. And in a two-hour, wide-ranging interview with New York Newsday, Sharpton, 33, said he carried concealed microphones in briefcases and accompanied undercover federal agents wearing body recorders to meetings with various subjects of federal investigations. He also allowed the U.S. attorney's office for the Eastern District of New York to install a tapped telephone in his Brooklyn home."

Al Fuckin' Sharpton, I thought in surprise as I stared into his face. I should've known. Al Sharpton! Muhammad had always said the government had someone spying on him or, as he also liked to put it, that there was "a nigger in the woodpile."

Say what you want about the word *nigger,* but I had never heard it used more often than by my black friends. Such as, at the beginning of a phone call, "Whassup, nigger?" Or, at the beginning of a wife-to-husband exchange, "Nigger, get your ass into this kitchen *now!*" Or, the first time I met Jesse Jackson, one afternoon in Los Angeles, when Muhammad asked him a delicate question, and Jesse shot Muhammad a look that meant *Not in front of the Man,* and Muhammad said: "That's jus' Larry Kolb. He a honorary nigger. You can talk freely."

Al Sharpton, I thought again, in astonishment. Al Sharpton! There was a spy in our midst and you were it. Reverend Al, community leader, champion of justice and racial equality, spy. Sitting there so quietly, never saying much, always listening. Getting it all on tape. Spy!

I read on about how the Feds showed the good reverend a videotape of his good self meeting with an undercover FBI agent about setting up a cocaine ring. About how they'd sought out Al—the cocaine wasn't his idea. But once they'd compromised him in living color, next they told Al he was facing a long stretch of jail time, put the fear of God into him, and then they brought up Don King and told Al they might be able to help him out of his jam if he'd help them with their investigation into Don's boxing empire.

Portrait of Al Sharpton caught between the devil and the deep blue sea: spy.

And I read about how, after they got him a little bit pregnant, they were insatiable. Weren't satisfied with just information on Don and his business operations. Also demanded information on links between boxers and boxing promoters and organized-crime figures, and about voting scams and black leaders and record honchos and hit men. And Al delivered the goods.

Preacherman-spy.
I never suspected.

Outside, the entire sky is blue, and the sea is a slightly darker blue. The tide is in. A lizard hops off a swaying palm frond and casually crosses my window-pane. I wonder how much longer I'll have to stay here remembering.

Some of this remembering is starting to really piss me off.

12 | AWAITING THE SHEIKH IN THE GARDEN OF NIPPLES

I went to Cannes to seek my fortune.

Approximately ten days after I'd gone to Madrid to seek my fortune. In Madrid, there'd been complications. And an invitation to try again in Cannes.

So there I was.

Picture me: looking out a tall window from the best suite in, arguably, the best hotel in Cannes, guest of, arguably, the richest man on earth, waiting for fortune to call.

My phone rings: There's been another complication.

Mr. Khashoggi has been delayed, or so I am told by someone French in English. I may either wait for him another day or two here or meet him next week in New York.

That, as I would learn later, was the opening move in the process of "tension and release"—as named and practiced by Adnan's chief of staff, Bob Shaheen. Whose singular talent was creating a middle ground between schedule-driven Anglo-Saxons and a member of the feline, nocturnal tribe of Arabs to whom time is meaningless. There is no word in the Arabic language that carries quite the sense of urgency that *mañana* conveys in Mexico; and Sheikh Adnan bin Mohamed Al-Khashoggi typically arrived a couple of days to a week late in whatever place he was supposed to appear in next for meetings. Driving men in gray flannel suits to exasperation.

Back home, they had wives and boards of directors and executive committees to report to. Budgets and calendars to follow. Promises to keep. They arrived eager, impatient, ready to deal.

Then they began to wait.

As postponements mounted, they grew tense and probably a bit insulted. But they waited nonetheless.

Out of greed. Or a sense of destiny.

They waited until they were numb with waiting. And when they finally saw the great illusionist and high-wire artist Adnan Khashoggi, he so quickly re-enthused them, with his elaborate energy and charm and his vision of the great things they could do together, that they were putty in his hands.

Tension and release.

He got the better of them that way.

But I'd seen this act before. In Riyadh I'd once waited with Muhammad in King Fahd's palace for seventeen days before we saw the King. Each day a royal protocol officer had informed us we should stay close at hand because the King would likely see us within a matter of hours. And each night in our lavish quarters we'd watched on the television news the King's stately progress through Europe, meeting daily with a different head of state, and then the King's hunting vacation in Pakistan, and his fishing trip in the Arabian Gulf. Followed by his encampment in a black goat-hair tent in the desert in the Eastern Province, and his majlis in Jiddah. After all, the King avoided Riyadh like death itself. When we finally saw him, he told us that, when we'd arrived he'd heard Muhammad looked tired, like he'd been traveling too much, and so the King had decided to give us some rest.

And while we'd waited for our appointment with His Majesty Fahd bin Abdul Aziz Al-Saud, King of Saudi Arabia and Custodian of the Two Holy Mosques, I'd gone about in the *soukhs* and the cafes of Riyadh wearing a billowing long white *thobe* and *ghutra,* like Lawrence of Arabia, with a *mishwaq* in my mouth and prayer beads in my hand, learning patience and practicing the lingo, and meeting a frail old Arab man, a lawyer, who spoke sad but beautiful American English and told me of the days when he used to make his pilgrimage from Mecca to the Holy Prophet's Tomb in Medina, almost three hundred miles through the desert, on a camel's back. That was faith, he told me. That was thirst.

Together we drank several tiny cups of *qahwa,* the original coffee, imported from Mokha on the coast of Yemen. A pale golden liquid, served hot, and flavored with a couple of cardamom seeds floating on top.

As to waiting, he said, we have a saying here: *Al sabru al muftaah al faraj.* "Patience is the key to great victory."

Then he told me how it came to pass that, in the 1930s, when the British ruled the world and British petroleum companies had already sewn up all the oil rights in Kuwait and Bahrain and the other Gulf sheikhdoms, the Americans had beaten the Brits out of the vast Saudi concession.

It was not a matter of national character, he said, for as a whole the British are more skilled in courtly ways than you Americans, who are an impatient lot. But it so happened that the American agent was an uncommonly patient man, ideally suited to the slow sweet rhythms of Arabia.

When the American agent arrived here in Riyadh, at roughly the same time as the British agent, and they each announced to the appropriate authorities they were representing oil companies and they sought to meet King Abdul

Aziz about obtaining exclusive rights to drill for oil in the Kingdom—nothing happened.

Except that they waited.

And waited some more.

Until, after about eleven months of waiting around in their respective mud houses for word of an audience with the King, the Brit scarpered back home to London.

While the American waited.

Then waited some more.

Until one fine day King Abdul Aziz Al-Saud sent for the American agent. And they hit it off. And that was the beginning of the relationship that became the Arabian American Oil Company, later known as Aramco—the West's single largest source of oil.

I can wait until Mr. Khashoggi arrives, I said.

And I did.

A young man without much money or responsibility is absolutely free. He is a man with nothing, and everything. With little in the way of commitments or attachments—not even wondering anymore, each day, the location of the wife who'd left him, not even worrying anymore about his portrayal in Steve Dunleavy's coming book—he is free. To stay at home, or travel. To see new things. To seek his fortune. To dream of how he'll spend it. To walk the shore, and wait.

Day after day—lunch under an umbrella at a restaurant on the beach. Salad and prawns. Or a nice grilled fish. Then a swim, or a nap. Or a walk through the narrow, crooked streets behind the Croisette.

If I need something—"*If you need anything, really anything*"—I've been instructed to pick up a phone and call CO.DA.PA., the mysteriously named office whose sole purpose is handling Mr. Khashoggi's affairs around town, and those of his family and guests. Operators standing by, twenty-four hours a day. So if I want to go somewhere beyond walking distance, and I don't mind Mr. Khashoggi's intelligence machine knowing where I'm going, I ring CO.DA.PA. And a few minutes later a big shiny midnight blue Mercedes and a pleasant young Lebanese driver in a French suit arrive to take me wherever I want to go.

"Where I'd like to go now, Michel," I say, "is to a big electronics shop. Not a tourist shop. I want to go to a good, big electronics shop where the local people go. Do you understand?"

Michel says "Yes" and we start out and, on a main street leading up a hill through the town, Michel says this: "Do you know how in Beirut now that we have the war we have the Green Line which separates the Christian side of the city from the Muslim side of the city?"

It is a purely rhetorical question, for before I can answer, Michel continues: "Well, here in Cannes, this street is the Entrecôte Line. All the restaurants on this side of the street, and the town, serve beefsteak, and all the restaurants on that side of the street and that side of the town serve horsemeat. All the local peoples know it, but they don't tell the tourists."

I wish I could remember the name of that street. Because—having forgotten it—I haven't ordered a steak or a hamburger in Cannes since.

In the electronics shop, I bought myself a cordless phone. It looked like the sort you could buy yourself in the States with, if you were lucky, a two-hundred-foot range, so that you could talk to your broker while you were in your backyard relaxing. But here in Europe, you could buy them with an advertised range of fifty kilometers and, if you were lucky, get reception from even farther than that. Don't ask me why. Not everything is better in America.

Back in the Hotel Carlton, beside my bed, I wired my new phone to the hotel's phone. Just the way Chuck, the Best Electronics Man in the Business, had shown me long ago. Now I could wander. With a rubber-coated telephone antenna sticking out of my inside jacket pocket.

Aloneness has never bothered me. Outside the windows of my living room, looking a few floors down and then out, the now-familiar view: strollers on the sidewalk, cars creeping along the boulevard, palm trees and streetlamps in the median strip, an outdoor restaurant with big blue-and-white umbrellas, the beach, the dock, and the sea. Floating in the middle distance, fishing boats and yachts, and speedboats skipping across the waves. The whole scene was wonderful, especially late in the day when the world was changing colors.

After a week I'd lasted long enough to rate an invitation to Mougins, a village up in the pine forest above Cannes. Dinner at the Villa Nabila with Adnan's daughter Nabila and her sister Kim, who was visiting from Africa. Like most twenty-one-year-old girls, Nabila lived alone in a fine house set on several acres of land, with a staff of fourteen, including two bodyguards. Nabila had hunting trophies and Impressionist paintings on her walls and the hairiest little dogs you'd ever seen running around her feet.

Over red wine and many small courses I can't recall and a wild rice dish so complex and delicious I've never forgotten it, it happened that Nabila kept turning the conversation back to the subject of her cousin Dodi.

Dodi was the son of Adnan's favorite sister, Samira, and Adnan's archenemy and ex-brother-in-law, Mohamed Al Fayed.

Dodi, by all accounts available to me at that table, seemed to be a fuckup and the much-beloved black sheep of the family.

Dodi, according to Nabila, had won a Best Picture Oscar for the very first movie he'd ever produced. *Chariots of Fire*. And the next year had promised to take Nabila and a few of her friends to the Academy Awards. But when they got to California there were no tickets, at least not for Nabila and her friends. "Dodi went, of course," Nabila said, while beginning to laugh, "and his date, and he told me and my friends to get ready to go, not to worry, he would get the tickets, and he kept calling me all afternoon saying he would have the tickets, and of course my friends and I watched the Academy Awards, while wearing ball gowns, on television in my room in the Beverly Hills Hotel."

Nabila said that when she was about fifteen, on her birthday, Dodi had arrived and presented her a huge velvet box containing a fabulous set of jewels: a great big sapphire-and-diamond necklace, a matching bracelet, a matching ring, a matching brooch. Sweet, silly Dodi.

"Kim, do you remember," prompted Nabila, "what Baba said when he came in and saw all this?"

Baba meaning Adnan. *Baba*, Arabic for "father."

Kim said, "He said: 'Dodi-Dodi-Dodi! *What* are we *ever* going to do about you? I think it's time I teach you something about how to deal with women. The question, Dodi, is, after you give her all *this*, what can you possibly give her *next*? So you like a girl. Maybe you love her. You give her a bracelet. Then maybe someday a necklace. Or a ring. But not-all-at-once, Dodi!'"

Nabila said in a few days she and Kim were going to Paris, where Dodi was putting them up in the Coco Chanel Suite at the Ritz, and I was welcome to go.

Nabila was setting me up with her sister.

All through the evening, the three of us had been planning to go out after dinner. But now, approaching midnight, Nabila said she was tired, so maybe just Kim and I should go.

Which we did.

Kim was good-looking and seemed fun and down-to-earth.

We borrowed Nabila's car and driver, and went to Monaco.

When Kim was born, she told me, her mother was an eighteen-year-old unwed telephone operator named Sandra Daly, who lived in Leicester, England. Within a few months, Kim's mother gave her up for adoption, and Kim was adopted by a family that lived on the edge of the Sherwood Forest in an English steel town named Corby. Her new father was a Scot transplanted from Glasgow and her mother was from England—Robert and Chriss Patrick.

Her father doted on her, made her feel safe, and drove a crane twelve hours a day at the steelworks, and her mother worked in a shoe factory. When Kim was nine, her father got a contract to work at a steelworks in the Transvaal in South Africa. So the whole family, Robert and Chriss and Kim and her older sister Debbie, flew from Heathrow to Madrid to Luanda to Salisbury to Johannesburg to start a new life.

Even in Africa, ends didn't quite meet. Kim wore hand-me-down school uniforms. But when she was fourteen, she was informed by her parents and grandmother that her birth mother was now a rather wealthy woman, who had requested permission see Kim in London.

Her parents said she could go, and they would go with her. Word came back: not a problem. And, a few days later, just outside London now when a chauffeured Rolls-Royce picked them up to drive them into Belgravia, Kim soon came to understand that the central equations of her life had changed.

We were sitting on the sand in Monaco, looking at boats' lights out on the water, when Kim told me how, growing up, she'd always been taught not to touch anything that looked expensive. Because if she broke it she'd be in trouble.

So, when the Roller pulled up in front of her at Heathrow, she was almost afraid to get in. But she managed and, though she did her best not to touch anything during the first half hour or so of the ride into Belgravia, she soon noticed she was receiving so much deference from the driver that something told her to relax. "And by the last part of the ride," Kim told me with a giggle, "I was giving the royal wave out the back window to the poor peasants on the street corners."

Her biological mother, Kim soon discovered, was none other than the famous Soraya Khashoggi, who was one of the world's great beauties and reputedly one of the wealthiest women on earth, the wife of Adnan Khashoggi. Holy shit! It was like a fairy tale.

Adnan welcomed Kim into the family. In an Arab way, nothing official. Just loads of hospitality. Robert and Chriss agreed that, because of the opportunities for a better education and a more privileged life, which Soraya and Adnan could give her, Kim could stay in England part of each year to live with the Khashoggis and attend a fancy boarding school.

Suddenly Kim found herself out to dinner with all manner of other famous personages, oil ministers, presidents, movie stars she'd been dreaming about all her life. She could fly around the world in private jets at her whim or, more often, that of her mother or Adnan. She ate in the finest restaurants. She lived on yachts. Or in mansions, or hotel suites. She was sucked up to by sycophants who wanted to get close to the Khashoggis. Oh, it was quite something, really. But she still went home frequently to Africa to see her parents and her sister. "At first, I had a hard time figuring out who I was," Kim told me on the sand. "But then I decided I'm a Patrick, not a Khashoggi. Except when I want to get into a nightclub."

Then something happened between Kim and Soraya. Kim didn't say what it was. Only that she'd gone home to South Africa.

When she got there, she needed work. So she went to classes for a while and then got herself a job doing drafting and mechanical drawing in an engineering and construction firm. At first her firm worked on plans for apartment buildings and office buildings and the like. But then it got a contract to participate in the design and construction of South Africa's first nuclear power plant. The whole job was highly compartmentalized. Kim and her colleagues may not have known it, but the reactor they were developing wasn't just for the purpose of providing cheap, clean nuclear power to sunny South Africa. It would also be producing the uranium necessary to develop South Africa's first nuclear bomb.

Legally, Kim was still the daughter of Mr. and Mrs. Robert Patrick of Vanderbijlpark, Transvaal, South Africa. And she had the birth certificate to prove it. Everyone in Kim's firm had to get security clearances to work on this job. And Kim got one. She filled out all the forms, answered all the background questions honestly and, as to who her parents were, she told the truth according to her birth certificate. She received her security clearance and began doing highly classified design work.

It was all going swimmingly. Then one day Kim woke up and found a full-page picture of her pretty face on the front page of one of Joburg's daily papers—with the headline THE BILLION DOLLAR LOVE CHILD. Oh, weren't they all excited to learn that the stepdaughter of the richest man in the world, Mr. Fix-It, the arms dealer of all arms dealers, was living in secret right there amongst them in Johannesburg! And that the Rolls-Royce of the richest and most mysterious man in Joburg, Dr. Marino Chiavelli, arms dealer and friend of Arab potentates, picked Kim up at her flat every morning and drove her to work.

When Kim got home from work on the night of the day the newspaper story came out, she found her apartment had been tossed. Just like in the movies. Every book from her bookshelves was on the floor and opened. Every drawer in the entire flat had been pulled out, turned over, emptied onto the floor. Her mattresses and pillows were slashed. Her coffee was poured out on the counter.

Then a thin man from B.O.S.S., the Bureau of State Security, arrived on Kim's doorstep and escorted her down to headquarters. He was a wiry little Boer with a mustache, Colonel Someone or Other, who interrogated her for three days, threatened her, insulted her, tried to charm her, but then finally let her go. Since then, she'd stayed in South Africa. The night I met her was only her second night with any of the Khashoggis in about the last four years. A rapprochement was in the works.

When the sun came up, Kim and I were still in Monaco. We bought Dany, the driver, a new shirt and a toothbrush and a razor, and a stack of casino chips. We finally made it back to Mougins two days after we'd left. Look, I said be polite, don't fawn, and do take flowers for their wives. I didn't say anything about not stealing their women.

When the sisters were off to Paris, more waiting.

You turn right when you walk out of the Carlton and stroll down the Croisette, stopping in the little tabac to look at *Nice Matin* and *Le Figaro.* You buy yourself an *International Herald Tribune,* and walk past the pirate ship in the harbor and past the Palais des Festivals, site of the annual film festival and orgy, and you even pass the strings of electric lights where old men joyously play at their *boules.* On the far side of the old port is a comfortable place where you can have the best pizza on earth, straight out of a glowing stone oven, and slowly read your newspaper and drink some wine and contemplate the fortune you and Muhammad will make when you finally get half an hour or so with Adnan to explain to him why he should fund your project.

Al sabru al muftaah al faraj.

Walking back after dinner each night, you stay on the beach side of the street. Where you hope you might again see breasts, wet and glistening in the moonlight, then three desirable and entirely naked women, rising from the sea—as on your first night here. An auspicious omen, you decided. All those nights ago. So where the fuck is Adnan now? you wonder. You pass the Carlton and decide to walk a little farther, to go see Georges, the bartender in the Martinez.

A bronze Rolls-Royce. The Martinez doorman is holding the left rear door open for a couple you've been watching since they stepped out of the hotel—while you were crossing the street toward the hotel. Late fifties. European. Very old money. In fact, they look like royalty to you. Every hair on his silver head is perfectly in place and he's wearing possibly the finest suit you've ever seen. She's wearing something woolly and drab, but beautiful, and pearls. Their posture is perfect, assured.

As the lady gets into the car and you're passing by on its other side, the right rear window glides down and you hear: "Your Excellency!" And then, as someone in the car repeats it, louder now, your spirits rise.

Adnan!

He shakes your hand through the window.

He says, Hi. I just got into town, and I hear we're meeting tomorrow.

You say, I've been looking forward to it.

He says, Good night, then. I'll see you *mañana.*

Then the window glides shut, and you start into the hotel.

Your Excellency?

You walk back to the car window, which is open again. Adnan says, We're going out to dinner now, and afterwards to a club. Why don't you meet us there and have a drink.

And so it goes.

Tension and release.

The nightclub was up in the hills, and fairly packed when I arrived. Lots of beautiful young wood nymphs and their suitors. Attended by hip young waiters in slouchy jackets. Very theatrical lighting. Loud as hell. The man on the velvet rope had told me Adnan wasn't inside. There must have been several excellent reasons why I shouldn't be in there at that hour, which was closer to dawn than to midnight, waiting for a phantom, but none of them occurred to me at the moment. Just about as soon as I walked in and started working my way toward the bar, Marilyn Monroe began singing "Happy Birthday, Mister President" and a conga lines of waiters, waving lighted sparklers and carrying a tarte au chocolat topped with candles, shimmied by me en route to a distant table.

Next the DJ played the Rolling Stones and then the Gipsy Kings.

Adnan came in after my second shot of vodka, just as Louis Armstrong began singing "What a Wonderful World." With Adnan were the couple he'd picked up at the Martinez and several others. Lovely women. Well-barbered men.

When they saw the tan, enchanting smile of Adnan Khashoggi, the hostess and waiters began politely but very quickly rearranging the social order, apologetically cooing to guests about *une reservation,* relocating some to far-flung tables, deporting others to the bar, making the best tables in the room one big table where Adnan and his guests could sit comfortably, eat caviar, sip champagne, and, within reason, hear one another. There was a bit of a commotion as an obnoxious Romanian prince and his friends were marched off to Siberia, but otherwise the transition went smoothly.

My approximately two dozen new friends talked of monumental affairs. Such as how good dinner had been, and where they'd just flown in from. Out on the dance floor a truly magnificent girl glided by. Shiny-haired and slim. Maybe twenty or twenty-one. She raised an eyebrow and blew a kiss to someone at our table.

Adnan's doctor, whom I'd met on the boat, told me: With the Chief, you just never know, but tonight he promised we'll be here three nights. And Adnan's younger brother Amr, a bright and charming fellow I'd met in Madrid, told me in the last six days they'd been in meetings in Seoul, Tokyo, Los Angeles, Cairo, and, this morning, Paris. But mostly they'd been in the sky.

After a little while, Adnan came over and spent all of maybe two intensely charming minutes focusing his hospitality and his attention on me. Kneading my shoulders. Telling me he saw a lucky star hovering above me. And, just before he blasted off toward another guest, reminding me to call him when I woke up—to fix the time tomorrow afternoon when we would have our meeting.

But the next day, though I did call, there was no meeting. I was, however, invited to dine with Adnan.

Or, as it turned out, with Adnan and a cast of maybe thirty others. At a ritzy clip joint called Le Pirate. Which served terrific food and had a novel approach to dishwashing. After you finished eating, you threw your plates against the wall. Then your host was charged for the china. At Limoges prices. Over dinner, before he personally led the plate-breaking festivities, Adnan told me we would have our meeting the next day. And, after dinner, we went, nearly all of us, to the casino at Monte-Carlo, where Adnan—or the Chief, or A.K., or M'sieur Khashoggi, as various among us called him through that long night—got on a winning streak. Then celebrated.

And so it went.

The next day I was up by the crack of noon, and eating breakfast with a matched pair of frazzled businessman-supplicants I'd met at dinner the night before. A crisis summit, and I was invited, by virtue of my nationality.

Both of them were Americans and CEOs. One, of a construction company; the other, of what I don't remember. But they were both substantial companies. And these were both substantial men, seasoned executives, representatives of the highly organized American industrial bureaucracy. Who, having come this far to secure the assistance of *the* Adnan Khashoggi in opening the lucrative Saudi market for their companies, and having spent a jet-borne week seeing the Orient and the pyramids and the Arc Du Triomphe, had never quite been able to get down to brass tacks with Adnan. Not yet.

It was just beginning to dawn on them now that somehow they'd wandered off into a feudal court situated in an entirely different century from the one they were used to. They were simultaneously enthralled and lost. Too jetlagged, fucked-out, and dazed to know what to do next.

Which was an issue, because they'd just received word, and so had I, that Adnan had blown out of town. Straight from the casino, apparently. And was at the moment in Geneva. For God only knew how long.

So—said the voice of CO.DA.PA.—if you would like to catch up with Mr. Khashoggi, you should be on his seven-two-seven, which is flying this afternoon from Nice to Genève. There is space for you. And we've booked you a room in the Richemond.

What to do? What to do?

The CEOs were going to Geneva, they resolved. In unison. Drawing courage from one another.

I saw one of Adnan's valets out in the lobby escorting a caravan of porters and trunks and cases toward the front door. And then it dawned on me. Suddenly, all I'd learned while traveling through strange lands with Muhammad, kissing rings and lounging in silk bazaars and princely palaces, and all I'd seen and heard while waiting for Adnan and while I'd been with him in the last few days, came together and spoke to me.

Later that day, I wrote it down, something along these lines:

In the court of the Sheikh. Adnan Khashoggi is not a high-flying businessman, or a tycoon, an arms dealer, a merchant banker, a playboy, or a middleman. He is a sheikh. A desert potentate, who has outgrown the desert.

All life and activities revolve around the Sheikh. If the Sheikh decides to put off the board meeting because today he wants to water-ski, you water-ski. And, in so doing, you are well advised not to outski the Sheikh.

If the Sheikh decides that, after all, he doesn't want the foie gras his heart was set on yesterday, but instead he wants spaghetti, you climb onto his plane and fly to Rome. For everyone knows spaghetti is better in Rome than in Saint-Tropez.

But, sir, the board meeting. Herr Doktor So and So is here from Zurich. The bankers are here from London. The directors are here from New York and Riyadh and Hong Kong.

"Tomorrow. *Inshallah.* Tell them the board will meet tomorrow. And tell them *Yella! Yella!* We're going to Rome to eat spaghetti!"

Yella is the Sheikh's favorite word. And the first word he teaches every foreigner. *Yella* is Arabic for hurry, come on, hustle, let's go, I've rearranged your life for you and you don't even know it yet. *Yella* is the word from which the conquered Spaniards derived their word *Olé*—with which to beckon bulls to the final dramas of their lives.

When you work for Adnan, or you go to him to seek his grace and favor, you are not, as you might think, a chief executive officer or a line manager, a bagman, or a procurer of beautiful women. You are a courtier in the court of the Sheikh. Rewarded with wealth and prominence and astonishing luxury by a thankful Sheikh as long as you fulfill his needs. Banished to a forsaken corner of the Sheikh's realm when sight of you no longer pleases him, or you have outlived your usefulness.

All authority comes from the Sheikh.

Anyone of any importance, or unimportance, reports directly to him.

Only the Sheikh commands. By his carefree public manner and his laughter and his silence. By his nod, his smile, the merest gesture of his face. By the attention bestowed on him by each person in his presence, whether the Sheikh is speaking or listening, or ignoring. By the way everything around the room, each chair and pad and fountain pen, each face, each dinner plate and knife and fork is subtly aligned toward him.

The Sheikh is all that matters.

If you work for him, other courtiers seemingly more exalted than you might presume to tell you what to do. But, unless they have the fiat of the Sheikh on the precise matter at hand, you can quite safely ignore them. All employees within the Sheikh's flat-lined organizational structure are equal. Because all have access to the Sheikh's ear, and pocketbook.

He dispenses favor personally, in cash. And, if sometimes your inflows are not as steady as if, say, you could rely on a thing as mundane as a monthly paycheck, that is a trifle you are willing to overlook. Because when it rains it pours.

Even if you don't work for the Sheikh, but you just stand near him after dinner in a casino in Monaco, sometimes it pours.

"When A.K. wins, everybody wins!" says the Sheikh—as he passes out banded ten-thousand-dollar stacks of crinkling hundred-dollar bills to every MBA, valet, and general dogsbody, and even every guest, in his presence when the Sheikh pulls off a big score.

If you are a CEO from America, you don't act insulted, but take the money. Because there are cultural differences you don't fully understand. And, if you are me, you don't act insulted, but take the money. Because of those cultural differences, and because, well, ten thousand dollars is ten thousand dollars.

The Sheikh is never on time, if on time means on someone else's schedule. He is a one-man band and bottleneck. Nothing, no one, moves until he says so.

He rules over vast distances through favor, fear, and unpredictability. The Sheikh is everywhere and nowhere. He makes his presence felt in every corner of his empire through the certain knowledge, born of experience, that he might at any moment drop in on you or intercede in any matter—from the closing of a two-hundred-million-dollar financing to the ordering of a birthday cake.

The pace of life at court is languid. Except when it is not. Except when a long line of empty limos suddenly draws up outside or the chopper is revving up on the roof, and ever-packed suitcases and valises are being grabbed, while cries of *Yella! Yella!* fill the air. Generally, you work and travel in bursts.

In between, there is plenty of time for sleeping in, for drinking champagne and eating the finest meals as your daily fare. Most days you will find everyone—from the Sheikh's executives, still foolish enough to think themselves modern businessmen, to the lowliest errand boy who knows good and well he is a courtier, to the pilots who flew you here, and the beautiful women who came last week for dinner and haven't left yet, to illustrious visitors from afar—dining with the Sheikh at one long table. And, after dinner, you might work, though it is four A.M.

But, more likely, you will party, for the Sheikh loves to celebrate. And in the morning, and well into the afternoon, you will sleep, in one of the Sheikh's many palaces, or on one of his planes, or yachts, or in the finest hotel wherever you happen to be—the entire top floor of which the Sheikh has taken over.

If you are an American CEO of a substantial company, eventually Adnan will make a deal with you. But not until he's desensitized you to such tedious concerns as calendars and budgets and then politely picked your pocket. Yes, he'll tell you. I think this is a great opportunity for your company and mine. Of course, if we're going to represent your company in the Kingdom, we're going to need an expense account. Nothing extravagant. Let's say ten thousand dollars per day per product line. That should be enough to sort things out.

And if you are a tall, young American, still in his twenties, for God's sake, and looking for Adnan to fund your venture, get in line. But, first of all, consider: Your numbers are far too small to get Adnan's attention. Second: Adnan doesn't invest money. He spends it. Adnan doesn't fund your ventures. You fund his. That's the way it goes.

Even before I wrote all that down, I'd gotten on the phone to the voice of CO.DA.PA, and said, Thank you. But I think I'll just go home.

After all, I was already a member of one flying circus. No need to join Adnan's.

So how, then, did I end up knowing Adnan so well, linked to him in so many lurid press reports, and living on this beach?

Six months later, I rendezvoused with Kim in Switzerland where she was Adnan's guest, and two months after that we got married in South Africa and set up our household in Johannesburg. From which I commuted frequently. To London and Dubai and New York and Chicago, and several other places. Since the death of my father, a spy, I'd been floating and—I realized later—waiting for something to happen. And then one day it did. On a summer's morning in Adnan's apartment in New York, just as I was going, Miles Copeland, a spy, tapped me on the shoulder and introduced himself to me. That was the last moment of my youth, innocent and free.

PART THREE

THE GAME OF NATIONS

When I look back on the day I met Miles, the thing that strikes me is how casual it all was. He said, "Hello, you're Larry Kolb, aren't you? I've heard of you. I'm Miles Copeland, it's nice to meet you, Larry. I was just leaving too," and then he rode forty-six floors down with me in the elevator, and we walked out past the doorman on East 51st and chatted while we strolled six or seven blocks together through Manhattan. I remember the blue-and-white seersucker suit he had on that morning, and that his black-framed glasses looked just like my father's.

Miles was lanky in a way that made him look taller than he really was. He was in his late sixties then. White-haired. His face hadn't actually wrinkled much, just wilted somewhere along the way. He still had a quick energy about him, though, something about his brilliance coming through, and a spark in his eyes. In a way, he didn't seem old; he seemed eternal.

At a corner where I had to go one way and Miles said he had to go another, he gave me his card and made me promise to call him next time I was in London.

Miles A. Copeland/ 3 The Green/ Aston Rowant, Oxfordshire. In those days, there were lots of people stuffing business cards into my hands in the course of my travels all over the world and asking me to call them.

Usually I didn't. But I knew I'd call Miles.

He lived in England now, but he was originally from the South and still had a hint of a drawl. He was clearly all American, though slightly courtly in a way you only pick up by living in foreign capitals. And he had a mixing-with-the-help affability I'd already seen right there in the Olympic Tower elevator while he talked music with its white-gloved driver. Miles was obviously smart as a whip. I just liked him. All that, plus I knew he was one of the founders of the CIA.

When I checked around a few days after I met him, I learned that, long ago—before he joined the Army to fight in the Second World War, before a routine battery of officer candidate tests revealed he was perfectly suited to be an intelligence officer because he had a genius IQ almost off the scale *and* he was one hundred percent amoral—Miles had left home in Alabama, made his way to New Orleans, and become a professional jazz musician, playing trumpet in the Glenn Miller Orchestra. That was the path Miles chose. Everything that happened to him after that was an accident, or fate.

The next time I was in London, I called him.

Whereupon Miles invited me to lunch.

Two days hence. At Bentley's, in Swallow Street, off Piccadilly Circus.

I got there first. The dining room was upstairs. Old wood, and plush seats. Stylish, antiquated service, and, according to Miles, the best fish and oysters in London. I asked him to order for me, and I remember we ate Dover sole meunière, served off the bone, and drank a cool white wine. And I remember nary a word was said of espionage, nor of Miles's friends at the Central Intelligence Agency.

He was such a marvelous talker. Wise, funny, upbeat, moving deftly from topic to topic. But never taking over. I would've been happy to just sit there listening, but he kept drawing me back into the conversation. When I spoke, he looked right into my eyes, through what still seemed to be a pair of glasses he'd filched from my father.

I remember, during just that one lunch, talking about a visit Muhammad had made to a boys' club in Cairo, London during the Blitz, Adnan's business adventures in the Sudan, chaos theory, Igor Stravinsky, the glories of Beirut before the civil war, where to eat couscous in Paris, and the current state of affairs in the music world. Beneath the boring suit, which was as drab and unmemorable as one my father would've worn, Miles was still hip, still a jazzman. Silver-tongued, and one cool cat.

A few months and several lunches with Miles later, I was back in London again and he invited me to his home in St. John's Wood. Where I quite briefly met a rock star. Stewart Copeland—sired by Miles and drummer of The Police, who at the time were about the biggest rock band there was. Except for their hairstyles and the aging Miles had been through, Stewart looked to me to be about a carbon copy of his father. Both of them had the same bone structure, the same smile, the same sly intelligent eyes.

After Stewart had gone, I met Miles's wife of forty years, Lorraine. She was stomping water off her gumboots in the entrance hall when Miles introduced me to her. Lorraine was an archaeologist. In her sixties now, with smart, energetic eyes, gray hair in a Prince Valiant cut.

She said, "Sorry I'm late, boys. I'll just pop upstairs, and be down in a tick."

Miles freshened our drinks, and we sat in the living room. I remember the rich woodwork, club chairs, brocade, an antique table. Candlesticks. Easy conversation. Talking with Miles was always so easy.

If you looked at the picture on the bookcase, of Miles and Lorraine on their wedding day in London in 1943, at young, blond, beautiful, and innocent Lorraine in flowers and lace, it was somewhat hard to believe that at the time she worked for British Intelligence and her specialties were blowing up bridges and derailing German trains.

Miles had told me before that, after he'd tested his way out of the infantry and into intelligence, he'd started out in the Counter Intelligence Corps. Just like my father. But when I'd informed Miles of that coincidence, he'd volunteered that he'd never known my father. I believed him.

On this beach I've learned the record shows that, while my father was still operating in Georgia and Florida, Miles shipped out of Washington to Britain as part of the first CIC team dispatched to London. Which was where Miles met Lorraine. After they were married, Miles was off to France.

Find the pattern: The record also shows that for five months in 1945 Miles and my father both lived and worked in Paris. Both serving as CIC officers.

Miles said he didn't remember meeting my father. Maybe that was true.

Miles lived on the Champs-Élysées in a hotel. My father lived on the edge of town in a chateau he never stopped dreaming of.

Miles hung out with jazz musicians, and with Ernest Hemingway and the literary crowd. My father hung out with boxers and with Uncle George and I don't know who else. Hemingway was a fight fan, and fancied himself a boxer. My father told me he'd met him a couple of times, but I don't know where or when.

Both Miles and my father were stationed at G-2 headquarters, inside SHAEF. But my father outranked Miles by three grades and was CIC Executive Officer, the number-two man, running things day to day. So my father did most of his work right inside headquarters. Miles told me he was officially based at headquarters but actually spent most of his time at the Joint CIC-OSS Prisoner Interrogation Co-op. Whatever that was.

When the war was over, my father stayed on in Europe, while Miles went straight back to Washington. Maybe they said fond goodbyes. Maybe not.

My father stuck with counterespionage, the subtlest of disciplines, made to order for the darkest souls. Miles moved over to intelligence, which was probably more fun. He got himself assigned to the Strategic Services Unit, which was the new postwar designation for what was left of the Office of Strategic Services, the OSS. After a couple of years, the Strategic Services Unit was reorganized into the Central Intelligence Group, which was soon to be further transformed into the Central Intelligence Agency. Until the CIA, the United States had never really had a national intelligence service.

"Ready, boys. Sorry about that." Five minutes after she'd arrived in trousers and a dripping anorak, Lorraine reappeared downstairs in a white blouse and a navy skirt and a cardigan.

We drove to a little restaurant somewhere in North London. I don't remember exactly where. It didn't look like much, but they turned out really terrific food—sort of a London take on nouvelle cuisine. Tiny portions, beautiful sauces. One thing about Miles, he always knew where to find good food. Every time I ever ate with him, when he picked the place, the food was terrific and the staff knew, liked, and fawned over "our Mr. Copeland." That certainly was the case on that first of many nights I ate with Miles and Lorraine.

"Hell is the place," Miles informed us with a smile, "where the police are German, the politicians are French, and the cooks are British. But here they've made an exception."

Over that dinner Miles told me his first job in the Strategic Services Unit in Washington was keeping tabs on Nazis who'd fled Europe. This was really the first time he'd ever told me that much about his early days in intelligence. Nazi movements were regrouping in South America and the Middle East, so Miles quickly came to know a lot about both places. It was on the basis of his knowledge of Nazi penetrations in the Arab world that Miles was assigned to the brand-new CIA's brand-new Near East and Africa Division.

Miles said, after a time they told him he was about to become chief of station in Damascus, and that his blood ran cold at the news. He'd always pictured himself working in Paris and Washington and London. Maybe playing a little jazz on the side. Damascus!

But once he got there, Miles quickly learned to love it.

A couple days after his arrival in Syria, Miles's KGB counterpart, Igor Fedorenko, called on him to welcome him to town and inform him they were certainly going to have a lot of fun together. As, apparently, they did.

It was while he was stationed in Damascus that, in 1949, Miles conceived, planned, and aided his first coup. It was also the CIA's first coup d'état anywhere on earth. And it was such a success that, when Miles rotated home to Washington the following year, he was given the task of writing the CIA's first handbook on how to plan and orchestrate a coup.

Suddenly, Miles was the CIA's resident expert on covert political operations, the man to see if you wanted to learn the niceties of how to foment a coup or swing an election. Or even if all you wanted was to politely discredit a rising young European or Latin or Asian or Arab or African politician you'd discovered was secretly funded by the KGB or one of its proxies.

Eventually the CIA created a whole new department for Miles to run. They called it the Political Action Staff, and justified its existence under Presidential Directive NSC 10/2. NSC 10/2—signed by Harry Truman—authorized the CIA to expand from its original mission of gathering and analyzing foreign intelligence into undertaking covert operations, including covert political warfare, to further U.S. interests and "support indigenous anti-communist elements in threatened countries of the free world."

Or, as Miles put it that night, "If you'll pardon me, Lorraine . . . Larry, what I'm trying to say is the Soviets were ratfucking us all over the earth, so we decided to fight them back the same way. *Whatever* it took to get on with the pursuit of our own objectives, we were going to do it."

In the Fifties, Miles and Lorraine moved back to the Middle East, where Miles rigged elections, toppled governments, helped install Shah Reza Pahlavi in Iran and President Gamal Abdel Nasser in Egypt.

And in the Sixties, when Miles wrote a bestseller, no less than the most famous spy in the world, Kim Philby, stepped out of the shadows to offer his opinion of it. "I've known that intriguer for twenty years," Philby said live on Radio Moscow, "so I can say with authority that Miles Copeland's book, *The Game of Nations,* is itself a move in the CIA's monstrous game."

By the time he wrote that book, Miles had officially left the CIA and become, according to *Newsweek,* one of the ten highest-paid consultants in the world—providing Mideast intelligence to oil companies, banks, airlines, and other corporate clients. But he'd also remained in close contact with his old friends the Shah and Nasser, and with Jesse Angleton and Kermit and Archie Roosevelt. Kim Philby wasn't the first person to suggest Miles's consultancy was cover and he still worked for the CIA.

By now, Miles had moved to England and written another book. He was such a spellbinding talker and writer that he'd become well known in Britain—sought out to appear on TV or offer his opinion in the newspapers whenever a spy was caught or Mideast politics boiled over. He was known to be a friend of Adnan, of Jeanne Kirkpatrick, Vice President Bush, and others in the power structure. And he still traveled frequently between London, Paris, New York, Geneva, Washington, Cairo, and sundry other points in the Mideast. So suspicions about what he was really up to still abounded. With Miles, it was just never clear where his private interests ended and the CIA's began. At the very least he was, in the phraseology of the CIA, which seems to need to have a phrase for everything, a "well-informed private individual."

I had my suspicions too. But at that point, that first dinner with Miles and Lorraine, we were still months of persiflage and pleasantries from the day Miles would finally level with me. I remember that first night we also talked about the Copeland Tycoons, the Dead Sea Scrolls, and Kim, and me.

We talked about me because we always talked about me. Because Miles, ever the gracious host, would never dominate a conversation. He was always asking my opinion after he'd told a story, and always drawing little pieces of my own story out of me. It's just good manners.

And part of a process called elicitation. But I hadn't learned that yet.

"So how's Kim?" Miles said.

Miles had known Kim since before I met her. He knew the whole Disney version of her story.

"She's good," I said. "She's at home in Africa. Do you know about Kim and flying?"

"Nu-uh. Tell us."

"Well, the plan at first was Kim was going to travel with me almost everywhere I went. But it just didn't work out. Flying with her is about the most wrenching experience you could ever go through.

"A few years back, when she was still living with Soraya, she had two bad landings in a week. One day she was on a KLM flight into Schiphol. The pilot announced they couldn't get the landing gear all the way down, so they circled, bleeding off fuel while the runway was foamed and then the 747 skidded into Schiphol. Then, a few days later, Kim was in a plane that had to make an emergency landing in Kenya. That was enough for Kim. Ever since then, she's been petrified of airplanes. Loves helicopters. Hates airplanes.

"Still, she tried to travel with me, and it went all right at first. All right from her perspective. From mine, it was hell. One afternoon at Nairobi, Kim and I were sitting in the First Class section of a BA 747 about to leave for London. Of course, she was fidgeting and crying a little bit, and her palms were sweating, and all that was what I'd learned to recognize as just Kim's normal pre-takeoff routine. When the pilot started to roll for takeoff, she stiffened up, like usual, but then, as our speed increased, she unbuckled her seat belt and made a run for the door. A stewardess and I were all that stopped her from getting that door open. It's *that* bad.

"In Florida, where we were visiting my mother, I found a medical hypnotist who was a former pilot and said he could help Kim beat this. He was great. Spent hours working with her, and did a lot of good. Taught her to hypnotize herself right before each flight. But then one day we were flying from New York to Joburg. We stopped in the Cape Verde islands. Petted the three-legged dog that always meets the passengers at the bottom of the steps. Refueled. Then we took off. Kim was doing pretty good. Until something started to go wrong, and even I started getting scared. I was glued to my window, and not only could I feel we were descending, but we didn't seem to be turning back to the airport. I saw rocks and beach and coves and hillcrests, getting closer and closer, but still we didn't turn. Then we flew right over the top of a little pink hotel and a swimming pool full of tourists by the shore and began climbing again.

"Well, for God's sake, Lorraine, a moment later the stewards and stewardesses were skipping down the aisles giggling their asses off about it. It was the very last flight ever of a certain South African Airways pilot's career, he'd just buzzed the hotel he'd been staying in for the last twenty years, and that turned out to be the expiry date of the hypnosis therapy Kim had so far been able to fly on."

"So now," Miles said, "she's spending most of her time down in South Africa?"

"Uh-huh." In South Africa, Kim was still a little bit famous, and I doubted Miles and Lorraine knew the story. I told them at length about the headline in Johannesburg, and how it had prompted B.O.S.S. to take an interest in Kim, only to discover to their horror that they'd cleared her to work on the nuclear power plant that was vital to their nuclear weapons program. Leading her to extensive interrogation under suspicion of being South Africa's own Mata Hari. Or to be more precise, I said, the suspicion was that Kim was a spy working for an Arab intelligence service—a prospect made all the more concerning because it was the Israelis who were secretly helping South Africa develop its nuclear bomb.

"You see what I've been telling you," Miles said, while winking meaningfully at Lorraine.

Mr. and Mrs. Copeland weren't the sort to anxiously watch their guest and want to bolt out of the restaurant as soon as he finished his last drop of coffee. You know the type. We'd finished eating, but we sat around drinking wine and talking. The Copeland Tycoons was what Miles and Lorraine called their sons that night. The aforesaid Stewart, founder of and drummer in The Police; Ian, booking agent for The Police, R.E.M., and several other bands; and "our young Miles," manager of The Police and other huge acts, record-label owner, impresario, and movie producer. The three of them were making so much money that no one ever questioned how Miles Sr. bought all those Concorde tickets.

We talked about the latest adventures of the Copeland Tycoons for a while, and then Lorraine told me a story set once upon a time in Damascus when she and Miles were young.

Miles, of course, was officially working for the Foreign Service, but actually for the brand-new CIA, which wasn't even called the CIA yet. Lorraine, meanwhile, no longer worked for British Intelligence. She was a wife now and a mother and an archaeologist.

I suppose that, in view of the fact that every U.S. Government outpost around the world I saw during the Fifties and Sixties was furnished from the same endless stock of drab gray-steel desks and safes and cabinets, which were already ancient then, when Lorraine described the United States Embassy in Damascus in the fall of 1947, I should've pictured it filled with essentially the same props as had adorned my father's offices in my youth. But for some reason I didn't. Lorraine told it so vividly and romantically, and with so much obvious love of antiquity, that I couldn't help but see it like scenes in an Indiana Jones movie. And to this day that's how I remember the story Lorraine told that night.

I picture Miles in his office. Sitting at an old wooden desk. Sweating in a seersucker suit. The lighting is dramatic. Rich syrupy light, almost the color of amber, pours in through window slats—making most of the room a beautiful pattern of light and shadows.

By the white glow of the lamp on his desk, Miles is reading through flimsies inside Manila folders. Marking them with a red grease pencil. Still learning the lay of the land. It is, in fact, his first week on the job in Damascus. His first week anywhere abroad as a representative of the Central Intelligence Group.

The phone on his desk rings.

A secretary, who coincidentally looks and sounds just like one of my father's old secretaries, tells Miles there's a man in the lobby asking to see him.

Miles says, Send him in.

Into Miles's office walks a sly Egyptian merchant, wearing dusty old Bedouin robes and carrying a sack.

The man bows deeply. Says, My name, good sir, is Metropolitan Samuel and I possess a great treasure.

Then he reaches into the sack and pulls out a scroll.

It's obviously ancient. Or an incredible fake. The edges are already disintegrating. Powdery little pieces of it are floating around in the light.

Metropolitan Samuel asks, What is it?

Miles says, I'm not sure.

Miles wishes Lorraine were in town. If she were, he'd call her and have her take a look, give him her professional opinion, tell him what to do next. But Lorraine is at the moment in Birmingham, Alabama, obtaining the American citizenship she will need before she can be seconded to the United States Legation in Damascus.

Miles tells Metropolitan Samuel, I don't know what it is. But if you'll leave it with me I'll have it photographed and get an expert to study it.

Exit Metropolitan Samuel. Without his scroll.

In order to photograph it in optimum light, Miles and two CIG case officers who work for him take the scroll up onto the embassy roof and stretch it out. It's a beautiful day. Blue sky. Hot sun. But not too hot, thanks to a cooling breeze.

While one of the case officers sets up the CIG camera and document stand, the wind picks up, and pieces of the parchment begin peeling away. Miles and his men begin working faster. The scroll is delaminating right before their eyes. Whole passages of text are lifting off, wafting, slipping beautifully from side to side as they catch thermals and fly away over the cobbled streets and the ancient rooftops of Damascus. Up on that embassy roof in the oldest continuously inhabited city on earth, Miles runs out of film after thirty frames. There is still plenty of scroll unphotographed.

What is left of the parchment, what hasn't blown away forever, Miles puts in a drawer, and forgets.

Because Metropolitan Samuel never returns.

And because, by the time the photographs finally make their way to the American Embassy in Beirut, to be analyzed by a prominent scholar versed in ancient languages, and the learned man excitedly declares the text to be written partly in Aramaic and partly in Hebrew and to be a portion of the Old Testament book of Daniel, and by the time word makes it back to Damascus that the scroll is indeed a great treasure, unlike anything ever seen before, several months have passed.

And by now no one in the embassy in Damascus can find the scroll.

"I know I put it in a drawer," Miles said, taking over from Lorraine for a moment. "But what drawer? At the time, I was still new there. Still learning my way to the Men's room."

"Years later," Lorraine said, "a fragment of a Daniel scroll was found in an excavation at the caves of Qumran, where the rest of the Dead Sea Scrolls were found. But no extensive Daniel scroll was ever found. And that, Larry, makes my Miles not just the first Westerner ever to *see* a Dead Sea Scroll, but also the first Westerner ever to *lose* a Dead Sea Scroll."

We'd gotten here pretty early, and now it seemed likely we were going to close the restaurant down. We sat there and just kept talking and drinking wine, which was fine with me.

There were a few episodes in my past Miles never seemed to bore of. He'd charmed each of them out of me more than once already. Now he wanted Lorraine to hear about them. First he gave her his own brief, but arch, account of my nights in the stairwell in Germany. Made it sound like a hell of a lot more fun that it actually was. Then he told her about my adventure with the border guards at Marienborn on the night train from Berlin all those years ago. Next, my minimalist safe house in New York—paid for by the J. Arthur Rank Organisation.

Then Miles asked me to tell Lorraine about something I don't think I mentioned here earlier. My trip to the 1980 Open Golf Championship, which Americans call the "British Open." Miles didn't give a damn about golf, nor did Lorraine, but he sure loved this story. He'd made me tell it enough.

One day on the spur of the moment, while in Zermatt, I'd decided to leave right away to go to Edinburgh, just outside of which the Open Championship was to begin in a couple days.

I rented a car, drove to Edinburgh, got myself a room in a bed-and-breakfast, and the next morning drove down to Muirfield, where the tournament was being held. I bought myself a day ticket, walked in, and joined the crowd of about forty thousand others. I knew a few of the players, and they would've been happy to get me tickets, but no one knew I was coming and no arrangements had been made.

My old friend Herb Wind was there to cover the tournament. Hundreds of members of the press were there, and they were based in a big white tent not far from the first tee. I didn't have credentials to get into the press tent, but I knew Herb was inside, and I wanted to go in and say Hi.

There were a pair of policemen at the entrance of the tent, checking credentials. So my grand entrance into the 1980 Open Championship press tent was from the rear, where I pulled up a stake and shimmied in. It was a big tent, but it happened that, right before me when I climbed in, not ten feet away sat Herb Wind, the greatest living American golf writer, and beside him my soon-to-be friend, Pat Ward-Thomas, the greatest living British golf writer. And beside Pat was Dan Jenkins, the greatest living Texan golf writer, who was there writing for *Sports Illustrated* but was also a novelist, a wild man, and one of the craziest mothers on the face of the earth. Herb and Pat were Old School, had nothing in common with Dan, except all three of them were golf writers, and they'd staked out this corner of the back of the tent for themselves.

In the first minute after Herb introduced me to him, Dan Jenkins named me "Circus Boy." Said I reminded him of a little kid sneaking into a circus tent. They gave me my own desk. Now we were four.

The next few times I went into the tent, I pulled up the same stake and slipped in the same way. But each time I left I made sure to walk out through the entrance and speak kindly to the coppers on my way out. And the next few times I entered, I walked in right in the center of little packs of journalists as they came off the course.

By the second day, I had the policeman so well trained I could walk in by myself, and I was having a hell of a good time sitting with Herb and Pat and Dan and the rest of the assembled sporting press over in the tent's interview room while Jack Nicklaus and Tom Watson and other great and good golfers came in, sat before us at a table with a microphone, recounted their rounds of that day, and then answered questions from the press. Circus Boy wasn't writing for anyone, but after he got the hang of the lingo and rhythm the reporters used asking their questions, he seemed to ask more questions than anyone there. And that was a fact which Herb and Pat and Dan seemed to find hilarious.

At that point in my story, Miles stopped me for a moment, and looked at Lorraine and said, "You see what I mean?" I didn't know it then, but I realize now what he was getting at was this was a story about the sort of personality talentspotters dream of. Circus Boy had the born covert operator's love of the game—solving problems, getting in when he wasn't supposed to get in, making new friends, asking questions, making a general nuisance of himself until he had what he wanted, all in a friendly, innocent way.

"It gets better," Miles said to Lorraine. "Listen to this. Tell her what happened next, Larry."

What happened next was that, on the Sunday, the fourth day, Tom Watson won the tournament and that night, of course, Herb and Pat and Dan and all my other new brethren of the press went off to write their accounts of the tournament.

Meanwhile, in spite of my desk in the press tent, not actually having to write anything myself, I caught up with Ben Crenshaw, who'd finished second that day, and Ben took me to dinner in Greywalls, the tiny, elegant, old hotel that stands hard beside the tenth tee of Muirfield. The best part of that evening was actually that Princess Margaret was there having cocktails before dinner, and Tom Weiskopf, an American golfer, asked her what her father did for a living.

But what Miles wanted Lorraine to hear about was the dinner I had with Ben and his beautiful wife Polly and Tom Weiskopf and Tom Kite and Bill Rogers, and an agent by the name of Hughes Norton, and some others. None of the golfers at our long table had won that day, though a few of them had come close, and they drank a bit consoling themselves.

As we drank, Ben got busy inspecting the baffie and four other ancient wooden-shafted golf clubs a Muirfield member had given him earlier in the week. It stays light until nearly eleven up there that time of the year. When we finished dinner, the course was still shimmering with golden light, and little patches of fog were drifting in off the Firth. It was beautiful, and Ben decided nothing could be better than to go out and have a bash with his new old golf clubs and a hundred-year-old gutta-percha golf ball he'd also been gifted. Tony Jacklin caddied for Ben, and the rest of us followed. When Ben finished the tenth hole, his first of the night, Tom Watson appeared out of nowhere accompanied by his wife Linda, a jeroboam of champagne, and a bagpiper in a kilt and all the other regalia.

There was something magical about the light, the air, the skirling of the pipes. We were all walking around out there in the mist pretending we were Scottish and in another century, talking in terrible fake brogues, and then Tom Watson stepped onto the eighteenth tee and challenged Ben to a one-hole match back to Greywalls.

I'd never met Watson before. But suddenly, in the middle of the eighteenth fairway, when it came time for him to play his second shot, I found myself nominated to be his caddie.

Ben and Tom finished their match, which Tom won by a stroke, and for the next few days all my new journalist friends, every one of whom had missed it, were calling me for information on the most interesting part of the 1980 Open Golf Championship. Then I wrote my own story of that night, the only firsthand account, which Herb helped me get published in magazines all over the world, and since then it had been anthologized a few times.

"You see what I'm saying," Miles said now to Lorraine. "All of the rest, and he's lucky too. And what could ever be more important than that?"

It went on like that, off and on, for a while.

Drinks, or lunch, or dinner, whenever I was in Britain and Miles was there too. I was there a lot that year, passing through on my way to the Middle East or Asia. We saw each other maybe once or twice a month.

Sometimes we talked about intelligence. Miles certainly didn't hide his past, and he had a fine collection of intelligence stories. Bureaucracy stories mostly, not spy stories. We talked a little about Philby and Jesse Angleton and the Roosevelts. But Miles didn't live in the past, so we also talked about music and films and politics and how good-looking Princess Diana was. And of course we always also talked about me—where I'd been, where I was going next, whom I'd be seeing. What I thought about it all. It was flattering to have someone as brilliant and accomplished as Miles so interested in my opinions.

Then, one day at Heathrow, Miles finally got down to it. This was what happened:

I was on my way from New York to Dubai on business. Wasn't even staying in Britain overnight. But I'd told Miles I'd be passing through and would have half a day to kill. And he'd told me he'd meet me at the airport.

Which, in fact, he didn't.

When I entered the arrivals hall, just past Her Majesty's Customs at Heathrow, a man I'd never seen before, a youngish Lebanese man in a shiny suit, came out of the crowd, said, "Hello, Mr. Larry," shook my hand, handed me a plump Manila envelope, and left.

Inside the envelope, an interesting development: forty thousand dollars in four packs of used hundred-dollar bills. And a typed and unsigned note informing me of a change of plans and where I should go next.

It was one of the Heathrow hotels. I think it was the Post House, but I wouldn't swear to that. For some reason I just don't remember, and I didn't write it down.

As Mr. Gaston Thibodaux of New Orleans, Miles had taken a suite. He greeted me at the door. Lately, I'd been noticing that, when Miles became enthused, he often broke into almost-but-not-quite-silent, half-whistled, half-hummed little patches of jazz. He was just emerging from a solo now as he showed me to a chair in the living room.

"So now that we're not on the phone, and not in any of my usual haunts," he said, "sit down, and I'll fix you a drink and tell you what's *really* going on."

Miles poured me a Tab, which was all I said I wanted.

Then he slowly mixed himself a gin and tonic, sat down with it, smiled as he lifted the glass to his mouth. After a sip and a delighted smack of his lips, he looked at me and said: "You know, I really am a consultant. That's legit. But I'm also what I like to think of as a 'loyal alumnus' of the CIA. In which capacity

I'm called on from time to time to do jobs that need doing but the Agency wouldn't dare do. If you get the distinction.

"In other words," he went on, "you can take the boy out of the CIA, but you can't take the CIA out of the boy. Not entirely. No one ever *completely* leaves."

"Does that mean," I asked, "that the CIA this morning gave me an envelope full of money?"

Miles said, "Yes and no. But mostly no. That envelope," he said, "came from friends in the Gulf, and half the money is for me, and half for you. Because I'd like you to come back to England as soon as possible and spend a couple of weeks with me."

Miles said, "Larry, you're the only person I know who's spending time with the sort of people I was spending time with when I was your age."

Miles said, "The most important qualities of an espionage agent are not, as novels would suggest, cool under pressure or anonymity. Actually, only one quality is essential for a spy, and that's access to the target."

Miles said, "I've talked it over with some of my friends, and we all agree your orbit seems to regularly bring you into close proximity to several rather interesting potential targets," then Miles was saying something about Shakespeare and something about "a constant quest for portcallers and legal travelers," and at first I wasn't sure if he was quoting the Bard or had proceeded to other thoughts and, while Miles went on, memories of my father were streaming through my jet-lagged brain, and suddenly I was thinking, *Thank God, I'm finally being recruited again,* and then Miles was saying, "With all the access and cover you have, it's clear you were meant to work with me. And would you, please?"

Room service for Mr. Thibodaux and guest.

I remember Miles ordered lunch for both of us.

I remember eating avocado prawns with Marie Rose sauce, and that it was delicious.

While we ate, Miles told me that, when what we did was for the government, but only unofficially approved, we'd usually get our expenses in advance, usually from friends in the Gulf, whatever that meant, rather than directly from anyone in Washington. And that, when what we did was for commercial clients, we'd get paid, sometimes very handsomely, and he'd share it with me.

He said, "Whatever we get, we'll pay the expenses off the top, then split the rest. Fifty-fifty. All right with you?"

I said, "I'm in."

I don't remember all that much of the next couple of hours.

By the time I finished eating my lunch, all I wanted to do was go to sleep. But I managed not to.

I remember the mixing of several drinks, and a hunt for limes.

I remember Miles giving me something of an introductory lecture on the structure and function of an intelligence cell, instructing me to tell no one about what he and I were up to, and to trust no one.

I remember Miles telling me I must become so self-sufficient that I need not trust.

"For example, Larry," he said, "if you're going to need a passport, friends of mine in Washington can provide one. But if you take it, you'll always have the problem of having at least one human back there knowing what name you're traveling under. Or hiding under. And that creates an unnecessary vulnerability. When you get back to England, my friends and I will teach you how to take care of yourself, to get what you need on your own, to trust no one."

I'm certain there was more we talked about. But I don't remember what it was.

When we were through, Miles made a quick phone call, then told me his driver would be up in a minute.

A uniformed chauffeur arrived, went into the bedroom, and came out with a wheelchair.

Miles had been roaming around, full of life and waving his arms like Igor Stravinsky conducting a symphony through half our meeting, but suddenly he was a frail old man tucked under a trilby and a blanket in the chair.

"Wait," I said. "Don't let me forget your petrodollars."

I took the envelope out of my briefcase and pulled out half the money. As I extended it toward him, Miles swiped it out of the air. In an instant it was out of sight, nimbly buttoned into an inside pocket of his gray-wool suit jacket.

"See you, Larry," Miles said, and the driver pushed him out the door.

nside the Oval Office. President Reagan had his fist on Muhammad's chin, and there was a small crowd cheering him on—five or six of us who came with Muhammad, and at least as many more who seemed to work for the President. Everyone was laughing it up. I was simultaneously applauding the action, wondering what the Secret Service would do if Muhammad actually punched the President back, and trying to figure out which door I came in the last time I was here. When Uncle Charley sent me in.

And, in spite of the fact that we'd been advised not to blink because this was what they called a ceremonial meeting and that meant it could be over any second, I had one eye on the President and the other on the circumstances that took us there that day.

For a couple of years now, Muhammad's left thumb had been twitching. At first, only some of the time; by now, pretty much all of the time.

When I first saw it, I thought Muhammad was just tapping his thumb on the top of his beautiful Louis XIV desk in his study in Hancock Park—drumming to release a bit of nervous energy, as twelve-year-old boys will do. And make no mistake about it, Muhammad spent at least a few minutes of every hour behaving about like a twelve-year-old boy. But then I saw that, when he lifted his hand from the desk, his thumb kept up the beat. It kept it up in midair, flailing against nothing, and kept on when he picked up the *Los Angeles Times* to look for a story he wanted to show me. Tap—tap—tap—tap—tap. His hand wasn't shaking, just his thumb. Which kept rustling the newspaper. Then after awhile it stopped.

It came and went like that, on and off, for months, maybe more than a year, before we knew what it was. Sometimes it got so bad that in public Muhammad would slip his left hand into his pocket to hide it. Eventually his right thumb started twitching sometimes too. And he kept getting hoarse.

The word on the street, and in the nastier outlets of the yellow press, was that Muhammad had *dementia pugilistica.* Which is to say he was punch drunk. Gaga.

Anyone who knew Muhammad well knew that wasn't true.

Even when his thumbs were jumping, and he was losing his voice, and taking on the thousand-yard stare—those were his main symptoms at their worst—his mind was sharp.

To be fucked with at your peril.

As bad as Muhammad might look one moment, he could snap out of it in a flash.

Nobody knew what it was. And nobody was all that concerned. Least of all, Muhammad.

Who, after all, had stared down Sonny Liston, Joe Frazier, and George Foreman; had stared down the entire U.S. Government when it told him he could join the Army or give up everything and go to prison; had stared down Idi Amin one crazy night in Kampala when Amin pulled a gun on Muhammad and promised to shoot him if he wouldn't fight him the next day at high noon for the heavyweight championship of the world; had even stared down nine floors of sheer drop when he walked out onto the ledge of a building in Los Angeles to talk in a total stranger who was suicidal and out on the edge preparing to jump. As Muhammad knew better than anyone, his fate was all in the hands of Allah.

When a doctor at the UCLA Medical Center told Muhammad he had Parkinson Disease, no one in the public found out for nearly a year. It was one secret we managed to keep.

Then, one soft yellow midnight in the Indian summer of 1984, in New York, I sneaked Muhammad via an underground entrance into Columbia-Presbyterian Hospital. And registered him under the name Paul Jefferson.

Our famous Mr. Jefferson was there undercover, in a room at the end of a hall not many people walked down, for a week of testing under the direction of prominent neurologist Dr. Stanley Fahn, who was reputed to know more about Parkinson Disease than any other American doctor. I took up residence in the vacant room next door to Muhammad's.

I remember thinking, while he sat down with me to explain Muhammad's condition, that Dr. Fahn had the gift of seeming both jolly and serious at once. I understood what he told me about Muhammad's condition better after I'd supplemented our first long conversation by an hour spent alone with a medical dictionary and a couple of American Parkinson Disease Association pamphlets. With those I pierced the veil, arrived at what Dr. Fahn had said.

Muhammad didn't have Parkinson Disease. He had Parkinson Syndrome. Which meant he had some of the classical symptoms of Parkinson Disease, but not all of them. Muhammad's primary symptom was his tremor—which, at the moment, manifested only in his thumbs. Another of Muhammad's Parkinsonian symptoms was bradykinesis, which is a slowing down of motor functions, particularly automatic motor functions.

Dr. Fahn told me all of that in about those same words. This I extrapolated from the pamphlets—think of the bradykinesia as inertia. Muhammad at rest tends to remain at rest; Muhammad in motion tends to remain in motion.

Sometimes when you were standing around chatting with Muhammad and it came time to move on—for example, if you were in a hotel hallway waiting for the porter to open the door and let you into Muhammad's suite, when the door opened—everyone else would walk through it, but then you'd turn around and Muhammad would be back where you started, leaning a little bit in the direction he wanted to go, but you'd look down at his dusty, much-stomped-on shoes and they seemed to be glued to the floor.

That's because *you* walked through the door on autopilot. You didn't think, Okay, I need to step forward now, left foot first, then right, let's go. You just went. Automatically.

But for Muhammad it didn't work that way. Not always. Not reliably.

A Parkinson patient has to be taught to take that first step forward. A therapist puts a brick in front of the patient's feet and teaches the patient to consciously step over the brick. That gets them going, and once they're going they're going.

Now, stopping—or turning—that's something else entirely.

So let's say Muhammad had stepped over an imaginary brick to get started and was walking with you now. Following the porter. Who had just shown you through the dining room and the kitchen and walked you past the grand piano with the vase of fresh-cut flowers and now you were heading down a hallway toward the master suite.

When you got to the end of the hall, where the porter and everyone else turned left, for just a moment, and it was a terrible moment to see, Muhammad would keep going straight, like he was going to run smack into the wall in front of him. Because the left turn that happened automatically for you didn't happen automatically for him. Muhammad would keep moving straight ahead until he consciously made himself turn. With a bit of a lurch. At the very last moment. When it came to him that it was past time to go left and that hadn't happened—so now he'd better do something about it.

Dr. Fahn said that divide between the automatic and the deliberate was why Muhammad's symptoms could come and go so fast. The automatic versus the deliberate, a concept which stuck with me.

To me, what Dr. Fahn was saying meant that, when Muhammad nonchalanted his way through something, his motor functions were off. But when he put his mind to it, he was beautiful again. A big man moving with a grace like no other big man had ever shown.

So Muhammad could be standing on a sidewalk looking lost and sickly—hiding his twitching thumbs in his pockets—until a fan saw him and called out, "*Dance, Champ! Dance!*" And the transformation would be quite astonishing. When Muhammad put his mind to the challenge, suddenly he'd be dancing, swiveling, sticking his tongue out at his imaginary opponent, then launching into a dazzling blur of combinations. Naming the punches as he threw them. "*Jab. Jab. Jab. Straight right. Left hook. Right uppercut. Left cross. Straight right. Left hook. Overhand right. Stop the fight, ref! Before I kill this sucker! Jab. Jab. Straight right.*"

And then, when he was finished showing off, the energy and the happy glow would stay with him for a little while. Until he started looking frozen and sickly like before. And that was when my heart would break, again.

Dr. Fahn said Muhammad also manifested a certain degree of facial rigidity, which was another thing typical of Parkinson patients, and that in Muhammad's case it was exacerbated by photophobia. Which I'd already been made aware of, and was why in the last year or so I'd seemed to be forever asking mobile television crews to light Muhammad obliquely rather than from straight on. "If you want him to look really bad, just turn that spot on, shine it right into his eyes," I'd tell them.

Bright light, especially bright light at a shallow angle—such as when the sun was rising or setting, or when a cameraman switched on a spotlight mounted right on top of a handheld television camera—hurt Muhammad's eyes and created a band of pain across his forehead. Involuntarily tensing his facial muscles. Thus, the thousand-yard stare.

Then there was the matter of Muhammad's voice. Dr. Fahn said Muhammad had episodic functional aphonia caused by underadduction of his vocal cords. Which I came to understand meant sometimes Muhammad's voice was AWOL, or a croak, or otherwise fucked up, and other times it was fine. And that the cause was that, like some of his other muscles, Muhammad's larynx didn't always work well unless he put his mind to it.

It was while reading up on aphonia in one of the pamphlets that I discovered a clue to the origins of Muhammad's condition.

In the next room, Muhammad was playing with his bed. Pushing the buttons like a little kid. The motor was whirring almost continuously: Up-Down-Up-Down-Up-Down. Pause. Click. Whirrrrrrrrrrrrrrrrrrrrrrrrrrrrrr. Pause. Click. Whirrrrrrrrrrrrrrrrrrrrrrrrrrrrrr. Then, when he finally got tired of that, he faux-snored for a while. At ever-increasing volume.

This was a cry for help, and a pathetic one at that. A tacit admission by Muhammad that he was suddenly bored and would appreciate a little company. I carried the pamphlet I'd been reading into his room with me. He'd been given the same set of pamphlets but had devoted approximately zero seconds to reading them.

Muhammad said, "S'up, Bwana?"

"You know how people are always asking you to repeat yourself when you're talking on the phone?"

"Yeah?"

"Well, Jimmy Ellis once told me that's been happening since you were a little boy. That, for as long as he can remember, you've been impossible to hear on the phone."

"So?"

"And it says here that's one of the early warning signs of Parkinson's. That many times Parkinson's patients' families and friends remember the first times they had difficulty understanding them was on the telephone. Sometimes years before they became difficult to understand in person. Which means your Parkinson's didn't come from boxing."

"Now you a doctor too?"

That night Muhammad's voice was clear and strong. I remember thinking probably the rest was doing him good.

And I remember that, as soon as he'd dissed me, he changed the subject to something he'd rather talk about. Like all the fine women strutting around in Harlem, just a few blocks south of us at that very moment, and whether I thought we could get away with sneaking out for the night to get us a good meal somewhere. I could tell he didn't really want to go out. Just wanted to enjoy thinking about it.

Muhammad has an endless capacity to entertain himself. But he's generous with it. He'll share it with you. For a few minutes he led our conversation through all the wondrous possibilities of a night out on the town, and then he changed the subject back to his voice. What I'd found in the pamphlet interested him. But he never wanted you to be the expert on anything. *He* wanted to be the expert. And now he'd had a revelation: "Course my Parkinson's not from boxing!" he said—like I was a fool trying to convince him it was.

But actually I was in the midst of becoming convinced that it wasn't.

I was thinking of his voice on the night most of us first heard him, standing in a corner of the ring, in a riot of excited people in Miami Beach, just after Sonny Liston refused to get off his stool to fight him anymore. Still named Cassius Clay, still young and beautiful, skinny as a colt, standing there in shock at what he'd done, proud as a peacock and shouting it to the whole world: *I am the greatest of all times!*—those words composed of high tones and low tones, but in the midrange most of what you heard was just the hiss of air rushing across his vocal cords. Already, he had that breathy, whispery way of speaking. Even when he was shouting.

I didn't know much about the workings of the telephone, but at that moment I was hypothesizing that it wasn't exactly a high-fidelity instrument. Probably, it was best at midrange tones, which was what Muhammad was worst at. Thus the difficulty understanding him on the phone. And if he'd been like that since at least the time in his career when he swiveled so fast that he'd almost never been hit, his Parkinson Syndrome wasn't due to boxing.

Dr. Fahn told us Muhammad's cognitive functions were undiminished and that, compared to most Parkinson patients, his condition was mild. He said Muhammad would need to learn to adjust his lifestyle some, particularly to train himself to switch from the automatic into the conscious mode to initiate his motor functions, and that his voice and his tremor and everything else would be a whole lot better if he'd just take his medicine regularly.

So, this morning, in the Washington Hilton, Jabir and I made Muhammad take his pill. Made him show it to us on his tongue. Watched him swallow and made him wash it down. Then made him stick out his tongue and show us his mouth was empty.

Not that we didn't trust him, or anything like that.

Muhammad was still strong as an ox. Still traveling half a million miles a year. Still carrying his own suitcases to show how strong he was, or to keep himself strong, I was never sure which.

But he rarely took his medicine. He wanted to be the expert on when he needed it. Which, according to him, seemed to be roughly: never.

When Muhammad took his Sinemet he didn't shake. But he did spend the rest of the day nauseated and quietly grouchy and, deep down, itching for a fight.

Which is one of the reasons why, while we stood there shooting the shit with the President, I kept thinking that if he took one more swipe at Muhammad's face, or hit him in the stomach again, Muhammad might just hit him back. Fast and hard. And wouldn't that be interesting!

But part of my mind was still on what brought us there that day.

All hell broke loose while Muhammad was in the hospital. A few days after our clandestine arrival, somebody blew our cover. Leaked to the press that Muhammad was in Columbia-Presbyterian under mysterious circumstances. The news hit the wires and suddenly the lobby downstairs was wall-to-wall reporters. Who had no solid information but were writing all sorts of interesting things.

For example, this headline: ALI IN FIGHT FOR HIS LIFE.

Within hours, out on the sidewalk beside the hospital, a handful of fans began a candlelight vigil. The next morning, down in the lobby, more reporters from all over the earth were arriving by the hour. And, out on the street, there were more fans with candles. Competing for space with an armada of television trucks. Things were getting out of hand.

So Dr. Fahn and I held a press conference.

Standing room only.

We sat beside each other at a table covered with microphones and a snakepit of wires and cables, staring into klieg lights and television cameras and crouching photographers. Behind the cameras were rows and rows of reporters in seats and more reporters standing in the aisles and along the walls on the side and in the back. Holy shit! There was Jules Bergman, still the ABC News Science Correspondent, the space reporter of my boyhood. There were so many bright lights in our faces, it was hard to see anyone well. Somewhere in the pack—I could tell by his voice—was the wiry little shill from the *National Enquirer* who earlier that morning had materialized beside me on the sidewalk as I was heading to the pharmacy. He'd offered me a check for fifty thousand dollars for just one photograph of Muhammad in his hospital bed. There were more than a hundred of them out there now waiting expectantly, looking at Dr. Fahn and me.

We stared into the white haze and announced Muhammad had Parkinson Syndrome. But, unlike in the movies, no one immediately ran from the room to a pay phone to be first to file the scoop. They all wanted more information, such as what did the future hold for Muhammad Ali?

Dr. Fahn told it his way.

With a twinkle and a lot of charm, but in neurologyspeak. In spite of the fact that obviously less than ten percent of the assembled spoke it, or any of its known dialects. Most of them out there weren't science writers or medicine writers, they were national news reporters or sportswriters.

I sensed the medical lecture wasn't playing entirely well. Some of the questions were getting ugly. I was afraid the sports guys thought the doc was trying to baffle them with bullshit. I was afraid the headlines were going to be even worse the next morning.

So, when Dr. Fahn was finished, I told it my way.

I said, Look, Muhammad's upstairs doing just fine. He's:

Not hurting.

Not suffering.

Not out of it.

Not in danger.

Not coming down here so all of you can have a look at him and verify that for yourselves.

There are two reasons for that:

First, Muhammad's busy, undergoing all sorts of tests the good Dr. Fahn and his staff have dreamed up since we arrived here.

Second, if you know Muhammad, as I know a lot of you do, you'll appreciate that he's enjoying this three-ring circus he accidentally convened way too much to do something that might make it end. This morning, up in his room, when I told him I thought maybe we ought to go downstairs for a minute so everyone could see him and people would stop worrying about him, Muhammad looked at me and said, "You must be crazy." After that, he stood for a while at his window, looking at all the fans, and the reporters, and the TV trucks, and the traffic jam. Then Muhammad turned to me, held an imaginary microphone up to his face, and said in a news reporter voice, "Is Muhammad Ali alive? Is he dead?" Pause. Big, fake anchorman smile. "No word yet. Tune in tomorrow."

Afterwards, when most of the reporters did rush out of the room to file stories, a guy walked up to me and said he worked for the *New York Post.* "I've got a message for you from Steve Dunleavy," he said, and my heart stopped. The book! The book I'd almost managed to convince myself I'd stopped worrying about. The soon-to-be-published book about me committing evil deeds I hadn't actually committed, researched and written by Steve Dunleavy and already salaciously previewed and promoted in every one of his boss Rupert Murdoch's newspapers.

The book's been canceled, the *Post* reporter told me. Steve asked me to tell you we're sorry about all the hoopla about the book in the paper. When he started researching, he found out you were the good guy and so he killed the book.

I guess good news travels slow. Because, when I asked when it was killed, the guy said that must've been a year ago, at least. I was so surprised and happy that I didn't even think to ask for a retraction. Then the guy handed me a piece of paper with some phone numbers on it and said, These are Steve's private numbers. Steve said to tell you, if there's ever anything he can do for you, please call.

When I got back upstairs, I found Muhammad spruced up in the bathrobe and slippers I'd bought him, and padding down the hall with a pretty technician and a shit-eating grin on his face as she led him off somewhere for a test.

Picture him in a robe, and probably it's a big white terry-cloth robe with a hood and MUHAMMAD/ALI embroidered on the back in simple black letters, like he used to wear into the ring. But this wasn't any such robe. He'd arrived in New York with no robe, no slippers, no pajamas. Maybe he didn't even own pajamas. I'd never seen him in bed any way but naked. Which wasn't going to work in the hospital. So at Bloomingdale's I'd bought him a navy-blue cashmere robe with burgundy piping, cordovan leather slippers, and baby-blue pajamas. He looked a bit like Hugh Hefner now strolling down the hall toward me with a babe.

All day long, up there, they seemed to be taking Muhammad off to wire him up to machines. Sometimes I went with him, and he made Frankenstein moves at me while they attached the electrodes to him. But, now that the world knew where Muhammad was, mostly I stayed behind, sprinting back and forth between his room and mine answering phone calls. His room because there was a short list of names of people whose calls were to be put through to Muhammad's room, and those people usually managed to call when Muhammad was out. My room because, though the switchboard was supposed to take messages from everybody else who called, they apparently didn't have the heart to blow off the rich and famous. So they put calls from people whose names they recognized but weren't on the list through to my room.

Which was why, when President Reagan phoned, though he wasn't on the list, the switchboard put the call through to me. I picked up my phone and heard a very competent woman's voice saying, "Hello, Mr. Kolb. This is the White House operator. I have the President calling for Mr. Ali."

What a nice touch! was what I thought. How the hell was I supposed to know Reagan wanted more than just to turn on his Great Communicator voice, all quavery but kind and sincere in that special way of his, to say "Nancy and I just wanted to wish you a speedy recovery and good health." A lot more.

When I told Muhammad the Great White Father had called from Washington, he was anxious to call him back. We tried a couple of times, on the number the White House operator had given me, but never got through to the man. And each time the White House called us back, Muhammad was out having tests. So eventually the President sent an envoy to the hospital to speak with Muhammad in person.

But first we had another visitor of political note: Jesse Jackson. Who showed up with his posse at Muhammad's bedside when Muhammad happened to be there. Jesse was looking for a photo opportunity. Muhammad knew it, and I knew it, and eventually Jesse owned up to it. But Muhammad was disinclined to please. Said no a bunch of times. He was looking fine and healthy, and I thought it would be good for a picture of him to get out to the newspapers. But Muhammad was holding on to the mystery.

It happened to be about six weeks before the presidential election, and that was the year Jesse had run a strong primary campaign, surprising a lot of people. Now he was out, though, and coming up it was going to be Mondale for the Democrats against Reagan for the Republicans. I looked at Muhammad and said, "Why don't you two guys go downstairs and announce to all the press down there that you're forming a ticket to run for President together?"

And that Muhammad couldn't resist.

He got a suit and tie on in about two minutes flat.

We went downstairs, into the mob of reporters and photographers, and it's been said I look quite regal in the photo of Muhammad and Jesse and me that appeared the next day in newspapers all over the world. I think that was the same day that Floyd Patterson came to visit, dispatched by President Reagan to carry a private message to Muhammad, and an invitation to the White House.

And now there we were.

With the President.

Who'd just shown us spike marks Eisenhower's golf shoes left in the floor behind his desk.

Reagan was still occasionally probing Muhammad's defenses. And I suppose I should mention here that it had recently been reported to Muhammad that, during his long, unjust exile from boxing, when he was trying to get a license to fight somewhere, anywhere, California was about to grant him a license, until Governor Reagan had stepped in and said, "That draft dodger will never fight in my state." And when Muhammad had heard this a few weeks ago, he'd shot right back, "Yeah. But he didn't say 'nigger draft dodger.'" Which was another reason I kept thinking, if Reagan didn't cut it out, Muhammad might just hit back. He's a double-hearted soul. Always has been. Calling press conferences in the Sixties to pronounce all white people "devils," and then spending the next half hour downstairs doing magic tricks for a hotel lobby full of white kids and their parents. Right now, inside Muhammad's head, Cash was saying, *Enough is enough, son! Hit this son of a bitch!* and Bird was saying something sweet and patient. At that moment the possibilities were many. But then we were wrapping up, and Reagan coyly said he was sure the Vice President would like us to stop by and say hello. Might be a nice surprise for him.

Walking through the West Wing with Muhammad was a bit of a circus.

They must be jaded with all the important people that pass through there.

But Muhammad was stopping traffic.

Shaking hands.

Kissing secretaries.

Posing for pictures.

Doing the Ali Shuffle.

When we made it into George Bush's office, he shooed all but one aide out, closed the door, got right down to business. Said he wanted to talk to us about something important.

———

I know I'm not really getting ahead of myself—that isn't actually possible when I'm in the present and it's *all* in the past?—but it feels like it. Because what I'm going to tell you about next took place a few years after we walked into Vice President Bush's office.

I was in a safe house in the Miraflores district of Lima, Peru. All across the city, the electricity was out because the *Sendero Luminoso,* Shining Path, terrorists had blown up another electrical tower. Inside the house, the walls were whitewashed and rough. By candlelight, it looked like we were in a cave.

I was drinking with an American named Mike Timpani, a covert warrior of formidable credentials. About which, more later. Mike and I had been in touch by phone and fax and telex for months. But we'd met in person only a couple hours ago.

We had business to attend to, and a mysterious box to deliver. But first we had to drink. This was our getting-to-know-each-other heavy drinking session. Standard Operating Procedure in the secret world.

It happened that George Bush had recently stepped up from Vice President to President.

I said to Mike, "So the former head of the CIA is now the President of the United States. What do you think about that?"

Mike sipped his scotch, then smiled and said, "George Bush is one covert motherfucker. He is *still* running the CIA. He *never stopped* running the CIA."

Sounds about right to me, because now let's go back to one of the less ceremonial reaches of the White House. Where Vice President Bush laid this on Muhammad:

We'd like you to use your status as a respected Muslim to enter into a secret dialogue with the Ayatollah Khomeini. To try to procure release of the American hostages held in Beirut. And the British and Kuwaiti hostages. Plus the Saudi hostages, who are a huge secret; nobody knows Saudis are being held too. This will have to be done without any trace of White House support.

The Vice President handed me a business card. *Robert M. Sensi/Chairman, The Ambassador's Club/Republicans Abroad c/o Republican National Committee,* followed by an address in Washington, D.C., and telephone and telex numbers. Apparently the RNC was providing cover for American intelligence operatives. Bush said: Sensi is actually working for the CIA, and he'll get you whatever you need to do the job.

I remember that, up close, George Bush looked a bit older than I'd expected, like someone's rich grandfather maybe. Patrician, but in a friendly sort of way. And he spoke clearly, with none of the verbal fumbles he became famous for in public. Why the difference? Probably, I've decided, because this was his element—the covert. He could melt into it, survive in it indefinitely, steal across its surface without leaving a trace. He was one covert mother, all right, and he seemed like a guy you could trust.

It hadn't been all that long since my Heathrow meeting with Miles, and what I was thinking was, Holy shit! I haven't even gone back for training yet and already I'm going on a secret mission!

I kept looking at the Vice President, thinking, He's a friend of Miles and I wonder if he knows about Miles and me. Then Miles's words came back to me: *Trust no one.*

Miles said later what I did with Sensi's card when we left the White House was telling. Miles said he was impressed, and he saw this as yet another indication that I was a natural and he was a hell of a talentspotter. But then Miles further told me to forget it. And, in order to forestall any future temptation, to go straight to my safe-deposit box, open the plastic evidence bag, and wipe the Vice President of the United States's fingerprints off the business card which I had so far touched only by its corners.

And so I did.

Miles had told me stay outside and keep moving. Outside because outside isn't wired for sound, like you should assume every room you ever set foot in has been. Keep moving—even if you're not going anywhere, keep moving—because, though the microphones used for listening in from afar are amazingly sensitive, can pick up a whisper loud and clear from four hundred yards, they're also difficult as hell to aim. Once a listener has zeroed in on you, changing your position by just a couple of feet can make the difference be- tween being heard perfectly and not being heard at all. These days, for all I know, they probably have it worked out so that one big microphone, say, in a plane two miles overhead, can listen in to every conversation going on in a square mile of London at once and filter out all but the voices it wants to hear. But as of then, and that was 1985, what Miles had explained to me was the state of the art.

So that was my second lesson in tradecraft from a professional: If you've got to have a conversation that's got to stay secret, and you don't happen to have a soundproof bubble room in your basement, have your conversation outside and keep moving.

Which explains why, in my memory, sometimes I'm looking down on Bill Dewey's head of fine blond hair, sometimes I'm looking up at him, and some- times I'm standing almost eye-to-eye with him—and I'm always moving.

It was a Sunday afternoon in London. A little cold, a little damp. I think we were somewhere in Kensington, though I wouldn't swear to that. We'd just eaten in an "American barbecue" joint, and I remember Bill saying he thought the food was pretty good and tasted authentic, which was clear evidence Bill had lived in London way too long, at least when it came to judging American barbecue.

Bill's an American, and a lawyer, the senior partner in a big American law firm's London office. When everyone else was eating dessert, I asked him if he'd take a little walk with me outside, as there was something I needed to tell him. I remember we turned left when we stepped out of the restaurant, and I would've walked all the way around the block to keep moving. But, because

Bill is a gentleman and his wife and their friends were waiting inside, there was a limit to how far he was willing to go. That turned out to be about thirty yards from the restaurant, and it happened that, just beside the spot on the sidewalk where Bill planted himself were five red steps leading up to a little landing and a doorway that had been bricked over and painted black.

The reason we were out there was I trusted Bill, and late the night before I'd decided I wasn't quite sure I trusted Miles. Not yet. Not with my life.

So far, Miles and I hadn't even had that fortnight of training I'd promised him I'd come back for. He'd casually slipped me the advice on how to have a secure conversation while we were walking together in Regent's Park a couple of days earlier. He'd also made me nervous, the more I told him of my plans. Which were to visit a place Miles loved, and, in retrospect, I think maybe that was why he didn't seem all that concerned about my safety there. I realize now the problem was Miles was so damn good at playing that one-hundred-percent-amoral role of his. I just wasn't sure he took care of his men in the field.

Bill Dewey was another story. He'd come through for me before.

Bill's about six-four, and ten years older than me, but just as baby-faced as I am, and I remember we were both wearing navy cashmere overcoats that afternoon. Black, cap-toe Oxfords. Pencil-striped navy suits. To anyone watching us from a distance, we might've looked like brothers—except that, if we were brothers, Bill was the serene one and I was the junkie.

He stood quite still, calmly listening to me. I never stopped moving. I'd been professionally anointed in two articles of tradecraft and was hell-bent to use them both, and to maximum effect. Before I started talking, I turned around a couple of times, in different directions, ready to scan the whole crowd first, before any individuals. But the street was deserted. It was possible someone in a closed window somewhere in our line of sight—a lip-reader or a man with a motion picture camera—could see my mouth. Miles hadn't mentioned lipreading to me, but for some reason it came natural to me to consider that too.

So, while coursing up and down the five red steps, and from one side of the landing to the other, and back and forth across the sidewalk and over the curb into the street, time and again, while I talked to Bill, I also kept turning my head away from wherever it had been facing a moment before. Miles hadn't pointed out to me yet that one thing I definitely shouldn't do while attempting to have a secure outdoor conversation was draw attention by making a total ass of myself.

I told Bill that, contrary to stated U.S. policy that it wouldn't deal with the government of Iran or with terrorists, the U.S. administration would deal with them provided it could do so from a covert remove. To wit: I'd been in London two times recently and hadn't called Bill—though I always called Bill when I was in London—because the representative of the United States Government who was orchestrating our secret dialogue with Iran had told me not to call anyone I knew while I was here. I said that representative was named Bob Sensi, and he was an official of the Republican National Committee, and an employee of Kuwait Airlines, and an agent of the CIA, all in one.

I said that, here in London, Bob Sensi had introduced us to some mysterious Iranians, who were said to be close to the ruling regime in Teheran. The way this worked was they would send a car for us, and it would pick us up at our hotel and deliver us through a warren of little streets to a big white building somewhere in Belgravia, or close to it, I was never sure. It was an old house that had been converted into an office, and the brass plate beside the front door said CYRUS INTERNATIONAL. Mahdi said Cyrus International was a trading company owned by the Government of Iran.

It was quite a big place. Seventy-five people could've worked in there, easily, but, even during business hours, there were never more than three or four inside when we arrived there. All Iranian men, all wearing boxy French suits. The place was dimly lit and expensively furnished. Lots of antiques. I wouldn't say it was dusty, but somehow it had an air of not being used much.

These Iranians were always nice as hell, didn't seem fanatical at all. Sometimes when we arrived they'd sit with us in the *diwan,* the living room, and sip sweet hot tea with us. Sometimes they'd skip the *diwan* and take us and the tea cups straight to the boardroom. Which probably was once a dining room. You could've fit sixteen people around the boardroom table in there, but usually it was just a couple of our Iranian hosts on one side of the table and Muhammad and whoever'd come with him on the other side. Usually Sensi, Jabir, Mahdi. Sometimes me. Sometimes others.

We did this several times, and each time we made it into the conference room the idea was that Muhammad was going to talk with the Ayatollah Ruhollah Khomeini himself on the phone. It was a pale green bakelite telephone, which our hosts dialed with something close to reverence, but even though they always assured us this time would be the time, each time we tried, Muhammad ended up speaking with someone else who said he was the Ayatollah's representative.

The Ayatollah's representative, or whoever he was, was vague, spoke English, liked to stick to pleasantries, and whenever Muhammad would cut to the point and say it was un-Islamic to be holding the hostages in Lebanon and he was calling to try to arrange their release, the man on the other end of the line would politely inform Muhammad that Iran had nothing to do with prisoners held in the Lebanon.

I told Bill that, once, the Ayatollah's factotum had added: But, perhaps we do have some influence over the people who are holding these prisoners, and perhaps we could assist you with them. *That* was progress.

I told Bill that, according to our new friends from Washington and Langley, it was an absolute certainty that the Iranian Revolutionary Guard was ultimately in control of the fate of the five American hostages then being held in Lebanon.

The Reverend Benjamin Weir, Presbyterian minister. Peter Kilburn, librarian from the American University in Beirut. Reverend Lawrence Jenco, Roman Catholic relief official. William Buckley, U.S. Embassy official. Jeremy Levin, CNN's Beirut bureau chief.

I'd memorized all their names, and photographs of them. Each one of them had been abducted at gunpoint, in separate incidents, in Beirut during the previous fourteen months. Since then, they'd been feared dead until, just weeks earlier, Buckley had shown up on a videotape describing his captivity and urging the United States Government to take action to obtain his release and the release of the other Americans.

The last time we'd been to Cyrus International they'd taken us into the *diwan* and stalled, because, they said, Faraz, the one we needed to talk to, was delayed and we'd have to wait for him. Then, eventually, while we cooled our heels and drank hot tea, the phone rang, and one of the Iranians answered and told us Faraz was still out and would we mind going to his home to meet him? That's fine, let's go, Jabir said, and I figured this was just a typical Middle Eastern logistical screwup.

But I soon learned it was a bit of stagecraft.

The car the Iranians had sent for us was waiting now on the curb in front of Cyrus International, and it took us not to Faraz's home—if Faraz was really his name, which was doubtful—but to a tall white house right on Belgrave Square. There was a property company's HOUSE FOR SALE sign outside. Our driver said go straight in and all the way up.

The door was unlocked.

Mahdi went in first. He and I were about the same age. But, unlike me, he was a golden-brown black man from Mississippi. He lived now in San Diego, where he preached Islam and sold real estate on the side, when he wasn't traveling with Muhammad. "This place would go for eight or ten million dollars, easy!" Mahdi said happily.

"Whoooo-eee!" said Jabir, looking around at the grand proportions.

"Anybody home?" said Muhammad.

The place was empty. Bare white walls. No furniture.

There was a lift, but we took the grand staircase, which was beautiful old wood, elaborately carved, and got narrower and slightly less grand with each floor we climbed.

On the fourth story, a canvas dropcloth covered the floor, and there was Faraz. He was sitting all alone on a folding chair. There were two more folding chairs. One for the phone, which was plugged into a jack on the baseboard and was a modern-looking thing—no bakelite this time—and one for Muhammad to sit on while he spoke first to the Ayatollah's representative and then, briefly, to the Ayatollah Ruhollah Khomeini himself.

Or at least to someone who said he was the Ayatollah Ruhollah Khomeini himself. How the fuck were we supposed to know the difference?

I told Bill that the result of all this vetting seemed to be Khomeini had now agreed he would meet Muhammad in Teheran. That we'd been told to go home and wait, and we would get word when to go to Kuwait to wait again until Khomeini sent a plane for us.

I told Bill that the White House was only one of the parties behind all this, and that the Kuwaiti royal family had been funding the operation—through Kuwait Airlines—because there were Kuwaiti hostages, as well as American and British hostages, in Lebanon. I said the Saudi government was also actively interested, behind the scenes, because there were several Saudi hostages in Lebanon, a fact that had been covered up because it would be an embarrassment to the Custodian of the Two Holy Mosques.

And I told Bill that Muhammad and Sensi and some others would be arriving in London in a couple of days, and there would be a press release in which Muhammad would announce that, at his own expense, he was traveling to Teheran to meet with his Islamic brother the Ayatollah Khomeini to ask him to help arrange release of the hostages in Beirut. And—I said—the day after that, Muhammad and company would be leaving for Kuwait and I'd be leaving for Riyadh, where I was supposed to deliver a letter to Prince Turki, and then I'd be going on to Kuwait, and on to Teheran with Muhammad.

I remember that, at that point, I was standing on the sidewalk about a yard away from Bill, looking into his eyes, and for a little while now I'd forgotten to keep moving.

"So, Bill," I said, "if anything goes wrong, I wanted you to know what's really happening and where I'll really be, and to please make sure the truth gets out."

He said he would, and then we went back into that shitty barbecue joint.

Before he left for Kuwait, Muhammad spent two days in London working the phones—calling Teheran, calling Damascus, calling Cairo, and Riyadh and Beirut and Tripoli, calling anyone he thought might be able to help get the hostages freed.

Then something good happened: Jeremy Levin was released.

The next day a representative of the Islamic Jihad told a reporter in Beirut that Levin had been let go as a gesture of goodwill in response to an appeal by

Muhammad. The Arab press picked this up, reported it widely. But when Levin surfaced in Damascus, he announced he'd escaped. Levin was a representative of CNN—and it was his unlikely story the Western media picked up.

The Arab press coverage suggested Muhammad had convinced his friend Syrian president Hafez el-Assad to procure Levin's release. But Mahdi told me the release was an inside deal, orchestrated by the Iranians, their way of showing Muhammad they were dealing in good faith, and that they respected him.

I wasn't there when the news arrived. I was in the Kingdom of Saudi Arabia delivering a message to His Royal Highness Prince Turki Al Faisal, who was chief of the Saudi intelligence service, the Mukhabarat. This was Jabir's idea, and it was pure liaison. Turki was a friend of Muhammad's, and I'd met him a couple of times while traveling with Muhammad in Saudi Arabia. The letter I gave Turki was of monumental unimportance. Its sole purpose, between the lines, was to convey to the Saudi power structure this message: Muhammad Ali is doing this for you too.

Turki was a prince, but not the sort of prince that lorded over you. He was friendly and easy to get along with. He *got* the message. And I remember that, when word of Levin's release came in, all of a sudden there was genuine hope in the air. It felt like we might be about to accomplish something good.

From Kuwait, Mahdi told me they'd been in touch with Teheran, and been told it would be at least a couple more days before we left for Iran. And Mahdi said the Iranians had promised they'd give us at least twenty-four hours' notice before they sent the plane to Kuwait.

I stayed in Saudi Arabia that night.

But the next day I was sitting in my hotel room, and my phone rang, and when I answered it Mahdi said: "Kolb, we've got a problem."

The problem, Mahdi said, was Muhammad's press statements saying he was seeking the Ayatollah Khomeini's help getting the hostages released, coupled with the release of a hostage soon thereafter, had been made to look like proof Iran was behind the kidnappings in Beirut. Consequently, word had suddenly come down that Muhammad would be wasting his time visiting Teheran—because Iran had nothing to do with the hostages. But perhaps Mr. Ali should go to the Lebanon to meet directly with the parties actually involved, and perhaps in that case we may be of some small assistance from behind the scenes, the Ayatollah's representative had added.

"So, Kolb," Mahdi said, "you've got a problem. Because I'm calling you from Beirut, and I don't know how you're supposed to get here."

Two years earlier, sixty-three people had been killed by a truck bomb that destroyed the U.S. Embassy in Beirut, wiping out, among others, every officer and employee of the CIA's Beirut station. Six months after that, 241 U.S. Marines were killed by a truck bomb that vaporized their Beirut barracks. Three months later, President Reagan pulled U.S. troops out of Lebanon. Now that almost all of the Americans were gone from Beirut, the few who remained were being systematically snatched off the streets. Beirut was a war zone where more than sixty thousand people had been killed in the last nine years.

"So, Kolb, we're here," said Mahdi. "Come on up, if you can figure out a way. And, if you tell us when you're coming, probably I can get Muhammad to come to the airport to help you get in."

Shit!

How the hell was a six-foot-six, blue-eyed, American white boy like me supposed to even be allowed onto a plane to Beirut at a time like this? Did airlines even fly from Saudi Arabia to Beirut?

I didn't even know that.

But, in the end, it was no problem at all. When I called the Lebanese consul general in his office in Jiddah and told him I was a friend of Muhammad and that I needed to get to Beirut, for which I didn't have a visa—the consul general said *Ma fi mushkila,* No problem. "In fact," he said, "I'm going to Beirut myself, and I'll deliver you personally. Where is Mr. Ali staying?"

"The Sunnyland Hotel."

"Oh, yes. You mean the Summerland Hotel," the consul general said, and the next day he did indeed accompany me on a plane bound to Beirut. With a visa conveniently stamped on a thin, white piece of paper, which somehow reminded me of the flimsies in my father's files.

Most of the institutions and public buildings in Beirut had been destroyed years ago. Two years earlier, the President-elect of Lebanon had been assassinated even before his inauguration. I wasn't even sure Lebanon had a government anymore. If it did, and it was like the last governments, it was a Christian government. But the consul general was a Muslim, late thirties, maybe early forties, spoke excellent American English. I wasn't sure who he was taking orders from, if anyone, in Lebanon. I wasn't even sure he was Lebanese. For all I knew, he might've been a Saudi and only an honorary consul. Something about his demeanor made me think it prudent not to ask.

Whoever he was, he was smooth, and he set me at ease.

MEA still offered commercial flights into Beirut in those days. Thrilling flights, which came in low over the Mediterranean, real low, and my flight was made even more thrilling when the consul general told me this angle of approach was to make the plane a more difficult target for surface-to-air missiles.

By the time our wheels chirped on the runway, the only things about the consul general that seemed clear to me were that I was real glad to have him with me, and he had not, as he'd told me, actually planned a trip to Beirut this week anyway. He wanted to meet the great Muhammad Ali.

Which was fine with me.

The runway was surrounded by tanks.

Likewise the airport terminal. Inside it was insane, but the consul general had the juice to get us through quickly. Once we got outside, everything seemed calm.

If I'd known you could drive from the airport to the hotel without crossing the Green Line, which was the divide between Muslim-controlled West Beirut and Christian-controlled East Beirut, I would've been a lot less concerned about my arrival.

In front of the Summerland Hotel, the consul general said he didn't want to inconvenience anyone now, but he would call me and then come back sometime to meet Muhammad, if that would be all right. Fine, I said. But I never heard from the consul general again.

"Maybe he was an angel," Jabir said later, and he was serious.

"Maybe he was a Mukhabarat agent," Miles said later, and he too was serious.

The Summerland was five-star deluxe, on the beach, and remarkably intact. If you closed your ears, or listened only during the lulls, you could've been in a hotel in Abu Dhabi. We were sitting around a table on a balcony—Muhammad and Jabir and Mahdi and me—eating fruit and yogurt, the runny white kind the Arabs give you.

In the distance, something exploded, and then we heard bursts of automatic gunfire. Then silence. Then more chattering of guns. Jabir said, "That was nothing. You should hear it later in the day. Yesterday, we had some crazy Arab up here who told us there's some rule that's not written down that says they won't fight in the morning. So the womens can go out shopping. The fighting's supposed to start at noon. But I've heard booms every morning."

"So," Jabir went on, "this man told us that he, and everybody else who lives here—by now they can all tell the difference between the way an incoming shell whistles from the way an outgoing one whistles. I said he's crazy, but he said, no, if you listen right, you can even tell when a shell is headed toward you, or going some other place. So, when they hear a shell, they listen and they know to hit the floor, or they've got time to get into a basement, or just to go on eating."

"Just like me," said Muhammad. "I can tell. And I'm gonna keep eatin'."

I said, "I know this guy from England. From Manchester. His father owns a newspaper there. I think you met him once, Muhammad. Anyway, he went to

London to study to be an actor. That was all he wanted to do with his life. He finished at acting school, and then went to an audition. Got himself a part as the understudy to the lead in a big Shakespeare play in the Drury Lane.

"He learned the entire part. But then his father phoned him and told him he was going to stop supporting his acting career. It was time to get his ass back to Manchester to join the family business. So my friend went home and worked in the newspaper. I think that was where you met him, Muhammad. And he tried to forget about his dreams of the stage."

Somewhere, something else exploded. This one was louder, and reverberated. We stopped for a moment and listened. Even the birds on the edge of the balcony stopped for a moment and listened. Muhammad put his spoon down.

Jabir said, "I don't know about you, but I don't think I could ever get used to that."

Muhammad and Mahdi smiled.

I went on. "So my friend was doing a pretty good job of learning about the newspaper, and forgetting about acting, until one day he was in his flat and his phone rang and it was the director of the Shakespeare play, and he said, 'The lead's broken his leg, the understudy's out with the clap, and we don't have anyone else to do the part. Do you still remember it?'

"My friend said, 'Of course I do,' and the director said, 'That's good, because we need you here tonight. We booked you on the next flight. Get on it, and we'll pick you up at Heathrow.'

"My friend was so happy! 'If I just remember the first line,' he told himself, 'the rest all flows out quite naturally.'

"So he recited the first line: 'Hark, a cannon doth roar!'

"He said it again, 'Hark, a cannon doth roar!'

"And all the way in the taxi on the way to the airport, and on the plane to London, and in the limo they'd sent to rush him to the theater, he repeated the line.

"'Hark, a cannon doth roar!'

"'Hark, a cannon doth roar!'

"He played with it. Sometimes he whispered it: 'Hark, a cannon doth roar.' Sometimes he boomed it out: '*Hark, a cannon doth roar!*'

"All the way into the West End, he said it over and over. 'First line's the charm,' he told himself when the car pulled up behind the theater. 'If I just remember that, the rest all flows out quite naturally.'

"He said it again and again while they were rushing him into the dressing room, and throwing him into his costume, and slapping makeup on him— 'Hark a cannon doth roar!'

"'Hurry, hurry, hurry!' they said.

"'Hark, a cannon doth roar!'"

"'Hark, a cannon doth roar!'"

"The play had already started. He could hear dialogue coming from on-stage, and he could almost hear the anticipation of the audience. They knew what was coming next. His opening speech. Shakespeare's famous soliloquy on a cannon. The greatest reverie on war ever written, and the first line, as I'm sure you know, Jabir, is 'Hark, a cannon doth roar!' He said it to himself under his breath again and again while the director was pushing him out onto the stage, and as he reached his mark he heard an enormous BOOM! He jumped two feet into the air, turned back to the director, and yelled, 'What the fuck was that?'"

Mahdi started up his celebrated donkey laugh. Jabir said: "You one crazy white man," and Muhammad bellowed: "Welcome to Beirut. *Sheeee kuuuuuu-uuuuu* is here!" Hearing this, Bob Sensi of the CIA walked onto the balcony.

For all his venality, Jabir was also a true believer and a preacher, and it was he who'd taught me the five pillars of Islam, years earlier. There are five things a Muslim must do.

Shahada. To become a Muslim, you must make a declaration of your faith in front of at least one Muslim witness. *La illaha illa Allah, wa Muhammadur rasullah.* "There is no god but God, and Muhammad is his messenger." Say that twice in front of another Muslim and you are a Muslim—no other formalities required.

Zakat. Give at least two and a half percent of your income to the poor.

Haj. Make a pilgrimage to Mecca at least once in your life during the Haj season, which is the twelfth month of the Islamic calendar—which is a lunar calendar.

Sawm. Fast each year, from dawn to dusk, throughout the holy month of Ramadan, the ninth month of the Islamic calendar.

Salat. Pray five times each day. The first prayer is just before sunrise; the next is just after noon; after that, midafternoon; then, just after sunset; and the last required prayer of the day is during the darkness of the night. All prayers are made facing the Holy Kabbah in Mecca, the black cube built as a temple by Abraham long before the Prophet Muhammad made it the central focus of Muslims everywhere. A Muslim may pray alone if necessary, but it's better to pray in a *masjid,* which is the Arabic word for "mosque," among other Muslims, if you can, and that's why all over the Muslim world you see so many mosques built so close together.

"Kolb, get ready. We're going to a masjid," Mahdi told me—waking me from a nap in a chair. "It's supposed to be the masjid the Hizballah leaders pray at."

I wondered how he knew that.

Arriving in a car with Muhammad was the same whether you were in London or Jakarta, or in Beirut pulling up outside the Imam Reda Masjid. As you slowed, voices rose, and excited faces filled every window.

Getting out of the car was never easy. While it was still gliding to a stop, you had to move quickly to get a door open before too many people were in the way.

Mahdi opened the door and sprung out and started chopping. Not really polite, chopping in front of a masjid. But what was he supposed to do? Hands and arms were reaching in from everywhere. People were shoving, pulling, yelling.

Then Muhammad was out, and signing autographs, signing autographs, shaking hands, hugging children. Just like everywhere else on earth. Everything seemed so normal. Someone handed Muhammad a bouquet, and from somewhere—a boom box or a public address system—we heard the first strains of "Black Superman."

All over the Third World, they seemed to play this everywhere Muhammad went. And when they tired of the recorded version, choirs wailed it and brass bands played it. It's a bouncy tune, somewhere between bubble-gum rap and reggae. We'd heard it so often we'd never forget it. And even there in Beirut, a city under siege in the middle of the Lebanese Civil War, word had somehow gotten out that Muhammad Ali was coming to the masjid, and someone had brought this tape to welcome him.

Suddenly, from much louder speakers, the muezzin began chanting the *adhan,* the call to prayer, and someone else shut off "Black Superman," and Mahdi stopped chopping, and the people weren't so much crowding Muhammad now as escorting him, escorting all of us, en masse, into the masjid. I'd been through this so many times before, and if anything was different that day I didn't feel it.

We left our shoes in one of the piles at the door—lots of sandals, not many shoes—and headed into the congregation. Muslims pray in rows, shoulder to shoulder, so the devil can't come between them. When a Muslim arrives in the masjid, he gets in the row next to whoever arrived just before him, regardless of wealth or station. Islam is about humility before God, submission to God's will. When one row fills up, another one forms behind it. We were all lined up, facing the Kabbah, hundreds of Lebanese Shiites, plus Mahdi, Muhammad, Jabir, me. Maybe Bob Sensi was there, maybe Hirschfeld, too, but I don't remember. Like everyone else there waiting for the prayer, we were on our knees but sitting, with our haunches resting on our feet. In front of us and behind us were more rows of worshipers, with enough space between them for prostration. Waiting for the prayer always felt to me very peaceful, and like being part of a big family.

When the imam rose and began leading the congregation in the prayers prescribed thirteen centuries earlier by the Prophet Muhammad, I did what Ali had told me to do the first time I went to a masjid with him—I copied the positions of the Muslim praying next to me while I prayed whatever prayers I wanted to pray, to whatever God I wanted to pray to, because there's only one God, no matter what you call him.

When the congregational prayer was over, we got our shoes and someone led us to a little room to meet the imam. He told Muhammad he knew absolutely nothing of the whereabouts of the four remaining American hostages. "I'm sorry, but this is not a question of compassion," the imam said, quite pointedly. "This is a political matter. Not a religious matter."

And with that we headed back out onto the street, where the crowd seemed to be waiting for Muhammad. This wasn't Saudi Arabia or the Gulf, where most of the crowd would be dressed like characters out of the Bible. Before it became a war zone, Beirut had been the most cosmopolitan city in the Arab world. Paris on the Mediterranean. Most of the men in the crowd were wearing pants and shirts. A few of them had draped red-and-white checked keffiyehs—like the one Arafat always seemed to wear—over their heads.

The first sign I saw anyone in the crowd holding had a big photograph on it of Muhammad wearing a tuxedo and a ruffled shirt and a black tie with a red carnation in his lapel. Beside the photo, someone had written, WELCOME CHAMP! There were more signs—six or seven of them total, all handwritten, all welcoming Muhammad. That night in my hotel room, I wrote that one of the signs said: WELCOME/TO OUR BRAVE/MUSLIM BROTHER/MOH'D ALI!

We could see the signs above the crowd and on the far side of the car—the dark blue Mercedes, we were trying to get to—while every man who'd been in the masjid with us tried to greet Muhammad personally. "*A salaam aleikum,*" about five hundred people said to Muhammad, one or two or three at a time, as he passed between them, shaking hands, shaking hands, smiling, answering "*Wa aleikum salaam. Wa aleikum salaam*" behind my shoulder and Mahdi's steady plowing.

At the car, an impasse. There was no fucking way we were getting the door open unless they wanted us to, and they didn't want us to. Someone in the crowd started to chant, "*Ahhh-leee! Ahhh-leee! Ahhh-leee!*" and soon the whole crowd was chanting and Muhammad had his fist up in the air and was leading the chant, and it was about then that he resorted to the standard car-door-opening fallback procedure.

Usually, if Muhammad would climb onto the roof of the car, so everyone could see him at once, and he'd lead the chanting, or he'd make faces and wave at everyone and blow kisses or throw some punches, after a few minutes of that, if he asked really nicely for everyone to move back, and he waved his arms in a way that made everyone understand, the people would move back a few steps so we could get the doors open, and then they would part in front of the car just enough for us to drive away.

I remember Mahdi steadying Muhammad as he put a foot on the rear bumper, and then Muhammad stepping alone onto the trunk, and then starting up onto the roof of the car, and all the while the Welcome signs were dancing and everyone was chanting "*Ahhh-leee! Ahhh-leee! Ahhh-leee! Ahhh-leee! Ahhh-leee!*" And I remember a couple of photographers rising up out of the crowd behind us, standing on crates or something, just about as Muhammad made it up onto the roof and began leading the chant.

He was having a great time up there: "*Ahhh-leee! Ahhh-leee! Ahhh-leee!*" The photographers were shooting away. They were pros: motordrive cameras; rapid-fire; finish one roll and pick up the next camera hanging around your neck and keep shooting. Muhammad was mugging for them with his fist in the air, leading the chant, and it was just then that the signs behind Muhammad, which were mounted on top of sticks, were spun around, and on the other sides of all the signs were giant photographs of the Ayatollah Khomeini, dressed like a character out of the Bible, beside lovely slogans such as OUR JIHAD/IS AGAINST/THE GREAT SHATAN! and DEATH TO THE USA! plus more of the same in Arabic or Farsi, or whatever the hell it was written in.

"Tricky devils," Jabir said while we strained to get a car door open, and I think it was about then all of us started getting an uneasy feeling about just what we thought we were doing in Beirut.

The next day, those photos—said to be of Muhammad Ali leading a rally in support of the Ayatollah Khomeini—were in Arab and Iranian newspapers. But, like the truth about Jeremy Levin's release, we never saw them in any Western press.

I remember, at the first checkpoint we came to on the way back to the hotel, Arabian pop music playing on the radio of the little wreck of a car next to us. A woman wailing something you could tell was sad but wonderful, with drums and violins whipping her into a frenzy. Every note was discordant and in a minor key, and beautiful somehow. Then we heard a gunshot over the music, and answering fire, and then a storm of gunshots, and then the squall was over and all we heard now was the wailing woman and the violins.

When the Arab gunmen manning the checkpoint saw Muhammad, every one of them came out from behind the sandbags and barbed wire and rubble they'd piled up in the intersection. They were boys in dirty brown uniforms, with keffiyehs around their necks. They smiled at Muhammad and shook his hand through the window, holding their Kalashnikovs casually in their left hands. Their leader was a wise old veteran of maybe nineteen years on this planet, and it was he who personally waved us through with a smile of welcome after he'd come back to shake Muhammad's hand a second time.

Mahdi was sitting beside me. In certain moments, like this one, when he had glasses on, with his spare, angular frame, his neat suits, his closely trimmed goatee, he could look so much like Malcolm X that it was spooky. "You okay, Kolb?"

"I'm fine," I said. Back in the hotel, Mahdi had told me the Iranians had given Muhammad no password, no recognition code, when they sent him here and told him to wait until the people holding the hostages contacted him. So what I was thinking about while we drove on was, *Who is it we're waiting for?* Bob Sensi didn't know Beirut, its factions, who the key players here were. He had with him a pack of photographs of Iranian leaders, to help identify people Muhammad might meet in Teheran. He had one photograph of a Lebanese leader, Nabih Berri, of Amal—who so far hadn't returned Muhammad's phone calls. Assuming, that was, that Muhammad had even called the right number. How do you get the telephone numbers of the leader of a secretive Islamic society—a phantom who never sleeps in the same place two nights in a row? If his representative contacted you, how would you know he's for real? It's not like these people's faces are known, or they carry credentials.

Three blocks later, another checkpoint.

In East Beirut, a single Christian militia controlled the entire sector. Down here, in West Beirut, dozens of Shiite and Sunni factions fought each other for turf. Neighborhoods changed hands overnight, which was when the heaviest street fighting went on. Meanwhile, almost every neighborhood we passed through seemed part war zone, part moonscape, part construction site, and part major city trying to go on living like nothing unusual was happening. Couples were out strolling, women were out on their balconies hanging laundry, school kids were playing in the rubble, merchants with long feather-dusters were tending their shop fronts, and a whole lot of people were going places in their cars.

Almost every day in Beirut, a car bomb went off somewhere.

Every time a big car rumbled up beside us, I looked out to see who was driving. But how the hell are you supposed to recognize a suicide bomber, anyway? Everyone seemed so normal. Listen to Muhammad: "Are you scared? Don't be. It's all in the hands of Allah."

It was rare to see a building that didn't have at least a few battle scars. At least one out of every five buildings I saw was an abandoned shell or not really a building anymore, just a pile of rubble. Some blocks were all rubble. At a corner, Muhammad got out on the sidewalk and did magic tricks for some kids—while I got out and examined a white concrete wall.

Boxy, modern architecture. A metal window frame, the kind that swings outward—the kind I remember from our house in Wiesbaden. This window frame had swung outward, permanently, and there wasn't a shard of glass left in it. Behind it, though, still hung white venetian blinds. For the first foot or so from the top, they looked the way venetian blinds are supposed to look. But below that they were total chaos. Signal and noise.

A thick green vine was climbing up a crack in the wall toward the window. Beside it was a concrete beam still precariously holding up the four floors above it, though the beam had taken a direct hit from a shell or a rocket. Whatever it was, it punched a big, jagged hole through the beam. Through this hole, I could see the rusted steel-rebar rods that were originally evenly dispersed through the beam to support it. Now only one rod was unbroken, and was all that was holding up the building. Which was rather thrilling, because a couple of floors up a family was living, and on the balcony children were looking down at Muhammad and laughing at his tricks.

I still dream of that wall, that beam, those kids.

When you hear your first shell whistling overhead, it's not like you could mistake it for anything else. "This one is coming from the west," our driver told me calmly when I got back into the car. "It will pass over, *Inshallah.*" Everyone was getting into the car now. Everyone except Muhammad, who had to make sure we all saw he wasn't fazed by cannon fire. "Get in here, Champ," Jabir commanded, and Muhammad got in and we sped off.

I remember, down on the Avenue de Paris on the Corniche, a waiter standing outside a sidewalk cafe. The place was deserted, but there was still hope. The waiter was polishing glasses.

Back in the hotel there was a promising new development, and its name was Isa. Six feet, three inches tall. Two hundred thirty pounds of ripped muscle. Head shaved bald. A black man with a gentle look in his eyes, and skin that wasn't black. Isa was a killing machine trained by the United States Army. In those days, his name was Cleven Holt. Now he was Isa Abdullah Ali.

He gave Muhammad a hug when we got into the lobby, and I remember that made me think maybe they'd met before I got to town. But Muhammad gives a lot of hugs to strangers. Isa came up to Muhammad's suite with us—also not a clear indicator, because Muhammad invites a lot of strangers to his rooms. I don't remember ever finding out when Muhammad first met Isa, or how, and I wonder about that now.

Isa was about my age, or maybe a little older. He had a pair of dark glasses strapped around his neck, and was wearing an olive-drab T-shirt and camouflage pants. I quickly came to the conclusion that, if Isa was on our side, that was a good thing. Because Isa seemed to be the only person I'd met in Beirut so far who was willing to talk substantively to us and had a clue what was actually going on out there in the darkness of the night.

Maybe friends of the Ayatollah had sent Isa to us. Maybe Bob Sensi had summoned Isa. If so, I had a new appreciation of Bob Sensi. Or had Isa, as he told me, come to us on his own? He said he'd heard about Muhammad's peace mission and wanted to help.

Welcome, Isa, whoever the hell you are. I'm not in charge here. In fact, I'm only here because I couldn't stand to not be here. I almost missed it, and who'd want to miss Beirut with the only traveling companion who might just be able to keep my white ass out of trouble? But my question, Isa, if you're inclined to answer it, is who's doing what to whom around here and, assuming Muhammad was willing, who would he have to blow to get the hostages released?

Isa took me for a walk on the beach, and he kept moving the entire time we talked. Good tradecraft, according to Miles.

The beach was deserted, save for a pair of brave old women in bikinis and gold-framed Cartier sunglasses. Christians, probably. According to Mahdi, there was an unwritten truce banning military operations at the Summerland. The hotel was nowhere near full, but I'd already determined its guests included Lebanese Shiites, Lebanese Sunnis, Lebanese Christians, Syrians, Greeks, Germans, Cypriots, Tunisians, and a pack of clueless Americans. The hotel was on the southern outskirts of Beirut, and it had its own generators and ample black-market fuel to keep it running during the frequent blackouts in the rest of the city. The Summerland was a miracle. The real Beirut was a couple of miles north of us.

I don't know who Isa thought I was—and, at that point, I'm not sure who I thought I was—but Isa seemed to like me, seemed to trust me, in a small way. He told me he was a member of the Amal militia. That made Isa the original American Mujahideen.

So how did a soul brother from the projects in Washington, D.C., make it to Beirut to fight alongside his Muslim brothers in a holy war?

Isa told me he'd served in the U.S. Army. Somewhere in Asia. Maybe it was Vietnam, or Korea, I don't remember. He said he felt rootless and abandoned when he left the Army and went home to Washington, until he found himself reading a Quran and converting to Islam. Then he heard about the slaughters in the Palestinian refugee camps Sabra and Shatila, on the south side of Beirut, and he knew he had a purpose. That was when Isa joined Amal. *Amal* is Arabic for "hope."

I had no knowledge of precisely what sort of training Isa had undergone in either of the two armies he'd joined. But something about him distinctly reminded me of my father's men.

Isa had a loud voice. He spoke very quietly while he walked beside me on the sand, telling me of just a few of the many mysterious forces one must deal with in Beirut. He spoke of the Pasdaran, which is the true name, the Farsi name of the Iranian Revolutionary Guard—Khomeini's secret army. "The Pasdaran," Isa said, "is here but not here. Ditto the PLO. Here but not here. Then you've got the Syrians, who are here and proud of it. Amal. Hizballah. Dozens of other Shiite and Sunni militias. The Christian Lebanese Army. The Druze. And the Zionists."

The Israelis held South Beirut, and it seemed to be only during their incursions into West Beirut that the Muslim factions all came together to fight a common enemy.

"But what about Islamic Jihad?" I said. "The ones who announced they freed Levin out of respect for Muhammad. Are they controlled by Teheran? Who has the hostages? Where are they?" Isa kept walking, silently, alongside me. North, toward the Casino du Liban, which was perhaps the most spectacular casino on earth, was still in business, still serving gourmet meals, still staging stunning shows. This was one weird place.

Isa finally said, "I've told Ali, if you all want to talk about the hostages, a man you should meet with is Ibrahim Amin. Ibrahim's been to Iran. Ali said he'd meet him, but I don't know if his heart's in it. Man, you can help us all out if you'll get him to have that meeting."

"So why do they trust you?" I said, and that I thought was the key question. Just who the hell was Isa Abdullah Ali, anyway? Was he a private or a general among the holy warriors? And if they trusted him, should we also trust him?

Based on the information available to us at the time, there was no way to know. The most important terrorist leader in the Islamic world could've walked into the Summerland and had tea with us and we would not have been able to distinguish him from just another fan delighted to be in the presence of the great Muhammad Ali.

"They trust me because I've proved myself to them," Isa answered after a long pause for self-assessment. "In the streets."

In his way, Muhammad was still proud and optimistic because of the release of Jeremy Levin. But I think he was also starting to get the feeling nothing good was going to come of staying in this weary place any longer. One day in Beirut felt like a month anywhere else. Day after day, we went to more masjids and talked with more imams. No more trick photography outside the masjids. But no help, either. Maybe Muhammad had already served his purpose here and was no longer required.

I remember, at dusk, watching a flock of birds, thousands of them, an amorphous dark cloud, shapeshifting, swirling, over the darkening hills. And I remember, night after night, back in Muhammad's suite, meeting with university professors, battle-hardened boys, relief workers, militia members, a bus driver, and the projectionist from a cinema that was still showing the latest in Hollywood action-adventures down in West Beirut. He offered us free tickets and reserved seats, and in a movie I'd once seen spies meeting their contacts in reserved seats in a movie theater, but we didn't go.

Every one of the fans of the great Muhammad Ali who ventured to his hotel made suggestions, and more than a few of them hinted majestically how they alone could be the key to solving the problem. Sometimes money came up, or U.S. citizenships, but most of the visitors just seemed to want to help. Or hang around with Muhammad. Hard to know the difference.

Still no word from Nabih Berri. Or Hafez el-Assad, who'd always seemed quick to take or return Muhammad's calls from London—but not Beirut. Muhammad was talking about going to Damascus next to see Assad, but that wouldn't be happening if he didn't return our calls. Back in Teheran, the Ayatollah's representative never seemed to be around the phone anymore.

But somewhere out there, in chains and blindfolds, were Americans, Brits, Kuwaitis, Saudis. Muhammad told every one of his visitors, "Go tell whoever you've got to tell: Release these men in the name of God."

By the third night, cannon fire seemed normal to me. And Isa was still chipping away.

"Okay, we'll go," Muhammad finally agreed. Jabir agreed. We all agreed. We were going to a secret meeting with Ibrahim Amin. Muhammad had agreed to meet him days earlier, but Isa had kept saying Ibrahim couldn't come to Muhammad. That had been the hang-up until now. Now we were going to a secret meeting with an Iranian-trained Shia-fundamentalist leader of the Hizballah, in the middle of the night, in a safe house, somewhere in the wilds of Beirut. Holy shit!

That night—after a long delay, by the time we left it was like one in the morning—two dusty black Mercedes picked us up at the hotel. I wasn't about to get into a car to head into Beirut at night without Muhammad. But there wasn't enough room in the car he and Jabir and Sensi and the driver and Isa were already in.

Isa climbed out of the car—where he was riding shotgun. I said: "I'm not going without Muhammad. We can pile on your laps." Isa said: "Get in the other car. You'll be fine. Just do it," and then he gave me a look that meant, Trust me.

I got in the other car, with Mahdi, and a driver in a keffiyeh plus a boy with weapons and ammunition hanging all over him and a cigarette dangling from his mouth. His name, he said, was Karim. We stayed right behind Muhammad's car. A few blocks past the first checkpoint, his car and ours both turned a corner and screeched to a halt, simultaneously, right beside a beat-up Volkswagen bus and a Chevy. No time for goodbyes. "Go now! Yella! Yella!" We switched vehicles in a hurry and peeled out. In the Chevy, our new companions were a driver and two gunmen. Hussein and Rasool and Mustafa, or so they said. Hello, gentlemen.

I presumed we'd just been handed over by the Amal to the Hizballah. But maybe that was just me trying to put a Western sense of shape on things. Probably the truth was less neat than that. At the next corner, Muhammad went one way and we went another. "It's all in the hands of Allah," I told Mahdi. I'd thought he'd be pulling out his hair about now, but he seemed fine. Sleepy, but fine. He said he'd been through exercises like this one in Libya going to meetings with Qadhafi. "Relax, Kolb. And don't disgrace yourself when they put the blindfold on you. That's next."

Hizballah, the Party of God. Who were these people? On the surface, at best, Hizballah was a militant political organization of Lebanese Shiites dedicated to using all means necessary to drive Israel out of southern Lebanon. Beneath the surface, according to the United States Government, Hizballah was a fanatical, bloodthirsty, worldwide terrorist organization funded and controlled by Iran.

Whoever they were, they knew how to give you a breathtaking car ride. Our driver seemed genetically indisposed to turning smoothly. He accelerated up to every corner and then skidded around it, leaning on the horn, while Rasool and Mustafa stuck their faces and machine guns out their windows, ready to shoot up any surprises around the corners. We careened around maybe a dozen corners like that, I lost count. Then, for four or five blocks the driving became quite dignified. Until we stopped in front of an old and narrow three-story house. No blindfolds. Muhammad was just going in the door.

"*Al-hahmdulillah!*" said Mahdi. "Kolb, we are blessed by God tonight."

The house was mildewed and decaying, but was once a rich man's villa. That was clear. Oriental carpets. Antiques. Blackout curtains. Just a couple of lanterns for light.

Arabs are very hospitable people. There's always something for guests to drink, and usually some food. Even in a safe house that was commandeered and cleaned up only this evening, and will be abandoned again before the morning prayer. The friendly fellow pouring the juice and walking around with a platter of dates turned out to be Ibrahim Amin. Political leader and deputy chief of the Hizballah worldwide terrorist organization—that was how I had to see it.

Muhammad asked him to release the hostages, and Ibrahim Amin said he'd never seen the American prisoners, didn't know where they were, or who had them. But he also said, while he had no control of the situation, he understood the Americans and British and Kuwaitis and Saudis and French would all be released when a certain group of more than two hundred brave Palestinians held by the Zionists were released. There was a list, in Arabic, typed. Someone else handed it to Muhammad. Ibrahim Amin wasn't the sort of fellow who passed out his own fingerprints. Jabir stuffed the list in his pocket.

Muhammad was confident he had fans everywhere. "Never been to Israel," he said. "Maybe that's where I should go next. The land of milk and honey. Become the first Muslim-American special envoy to Israel." Sensi got up, stepped over to Muhammad, bent to his ear, whispered something, then something more. Muhammad nodded. Sensi went back to his seat.

"Do you give me your promise," Muhammad said, "that, when our Palestinian brothers are released, the Americans held here will be released? And that, until then, the Americans will be protected?"

There's a special Arab smile that means, *I'm sorry, it's out of my hands,* and there was a flicker of that smile across the face of the political leader and deputy chief of the Party of God just before he said to Muhammad, "Yes—*Inshallah*—yes."

Now it was Jabir whispering in Muhammad's ear.

"You tell him. From me," Muhammad said to Jabir.

Turning the screw was Jabir's specialty.

"Ali wants you to arrange the release of another American now," Jabir said. "As a symbol of Allah's boundless mercy and compassion, and as a sign that you are the man we were directed here to meet."

No response. Only the smile.

"Well, we should go now," Isa said. And we did.

This morning, before I drove across to the mainland, I had to look up Ibrahim Amin's name to make sure I'd remembered it properly. But not Isa's. No one else I met in Beirut stayed with me like Isa Abdullah Ali. Who was he, and was he on our side or theirs? The army fatigue coat he'd worn to our meeting that night made Isa look suspiciously like just another burnt-out Vietnam vet. Was anyone we met in Beirut for real? We didn't have enough information to know. Then.

But now I know.

Twelve years after I last saw Isa in Beirut, this report drifted in to me:

SUBJECT: Isa Abdullah Ali

a/k/a Kevin Holt, a/k/a Cleven Raphael Holt, born Cleven Holt, 1951.

Isa Abdullah Ali, soldier, radical Muslim, jihadist, now wanted for questioning about terrorist activities. Grew up in a housing project in Washington, D.C. After serving honorably in the U.S. Army, converted to Islam and joined the Shiite paramilitary group the Amal militia. Subsequently, Isa Abdullah Ali joined the militant Islamicists Hizballah, and became the bodyguard of Muhammad Hussein Fadlallah, Hizballah's spiritual leader, who was for many years a leading suspect in the hostage-taking in Lebanon of the 1980s. Isa Abdullah Ali developed a high profile and became a trusted member of several Shiite militias. However, when the purity of the original Hizballah movement in Lebanon and Palestine became corrupted by the intelligence apparatus of the Islamic Republic of Iran, Isa Abdullah Ali spoke out against the murder and kidnapping of innocent civilians in Lebanon and elsewhere. For that, Isa Abdullah Ali was accused of being an American agent, then was isolated, interrogated, tortured, and imprisoned by a group of Iranian-backed Shiite militias. Eventually he was cleared and released, and he rejoined the fighting. Subsequently, Isa Abdullah Ali was ambushed, raked by machinegunfire, and left to die on a West Beirut street with fourteen bullet wounds in his abdomen. After he was saved, by a group of his Hizballah brothers in arms, who dragged him out of the street and forced a doctor at gunpoint to bring him back from the brink of death, Isa Abdullah Ali was stabilized and sent back to the United States for surgery. Upon his recovery, Isa Abdullah Ali secured employment picking up trash at Howard University in Washington, D.C. While Isa Abdullah Ali remained employed in Washington, D.C., former USAID official Joseph Cicippio, who was kidnapped by Hizballah, in Beirut, Lebanon, on September 12, 1986, was released after more than five years in captivity and returned to the United States. Upon his release, Joseph Cicippio told an American interviewer: "One day Isa stepped into my office and told me that I was about to be kidnapped. I should've listened." Joseph Cicippio reported he was abducted shortly after the warning he received from Isa Abdullah Ali.

The day after our meeting with Ibrahim Amin, a Lebanese boy showed up in the Summerland to shake the hand of the great Muhammad Ali and inform him Sheikh Amin had a suggestion for us. A suggestion which, when the boy elaborated, proved to be out of the fucking question: a trip to the Bekaa Valley. Hizballah's stronghold—where training camps turned out new terrorists every week, and where Jeremy Levin reported he'd been held with the other American hostages. Muhammad and Jabir said, yes, sounds great, we'll all go to the Bekaa Valley.

But it never happened. It didn't happen the next morning, when we were first scheduled to go but Jabir said he was feeling poorly. And it didn't happen that afternoon, either, when Muhammad was too tired to go. Nor again the following morning, when cars showed up a third time to take us to Baalbek.

Operational consideration: How do you cut short a partly successful but ill-conceived and dangerous secret mission to Beirut?

Mahdi and I both knew Muhammad well enough to recognize the signs when he was saying yes but what he meant was no. Likewise, as to Jabir. Neither one of them was crackbrained enough to go into the Bekaa Valley during that open season on Americans accompanied by a gang of thugs who looked just like those nice folks outside the masjid with the Khomeini portraits and the cameras. That much Mahdi and I recognized. And that neither Muhammad nor Jabir was willing to admit it to the other one.

By day, we were now continually on alert for a deployment into the Bekaa Valley which was never going to happen. And by night, in this netherworld where everything important happened by night, we were learning certain problems inherent in dealing with the very dangerous, very clever, very security-conscious wraiths who run terrorist organizations. No one had released another hostage, some of our visitors were looking increasingly menacing, and Nabih Berri was avoiding us.

Down in the coffee shop, over lunch, Mahdi and I dissected these and others factors, and then Mahdi said, "Kolb, we've got to get out of here!"

How did we make it out of Beirut alive?

Jabir, who secretly wanted to leave, had more influence on Muhammad than any other living person at the time. And vice versa. The road home had to go through both of them.

We might still be there today, acting brave and resolute, if Mahdi hadn't, shortly after lunch, gone into Muhammad's bedroom and said, "Listen, Ali, I know you think we're making progress here, and you can sure be proud of getting Levin released, and all. And I know you want to stay here until we've done more good things. But, between you and me, Ali, I just came from Jabir's room, and he seems to be a little bit scared by all this, but doesn't want to show it. I think he's afraid things might be getting out of control around here, and he's only staying out of respect for you. I know you'd like to stay, Ali, but why don't we go—for Jabir's sake?"

The moment Muhammad reluctantly agreed to leave Beirut, for Jabir's sake, Mahdi flew down the hall to Jabir's room, where I'd been providing covering fire, ready to intercept any incoming phone call and chatting with Jabir about women, one subject always sure to hold Jabir's attention. A moment later, Jabir reluctantly agreed to leave Beirut—for Muhammad's sake.

The rest of our visit to Beirut felt pretty much like being fired out of a cannon. No traveling party of well-intentioned Americans ever packed faster. An hour after we'd decided to leave, we were in the near-total madness of Beirut International Airport, where babies wailed, and women ululated, and the walls were pockmarked with gunfire, and Bob Sensi pulled out a credit card and told the man behind the ticket counter, "We'll take the next flight to anywhere, please."

Which was how we came to go to bed that night in Cyprus.

I don't know what you're expecting," Miles said, "but most intelligence work is dull and routine rather than clandestine. Espionage is used only as a last resort, if the desired information can't be obtained through open sources. We'll get to forgery, assassination, bugging, blackmail, smuggling, white slavery, and how to use your cyanide capsule later"—Miles grinned, and took a long pull on his gin—"but, for now, before you even learn to encode a report, you're going to have to learn to write it first in a style which is up to the U.S. Government's standards for dullness and verbosity. We'll get started on that tomorrow morning. Now, for God's sake, get me another drink and tell me more about Beirut!"

I told him all about it, quietly, to the extent I thought I should while amongst other patrons in the bar of Brown's Hotel in Mayfair. When I was finished, I said that, while I was in Beirut, I'd wondered a few times where Miles lived, where Philby lived, what really happened there.

Harold Adrian Russell Philby, popularly known by his nickname Kim, was recruited into the British Secret Intelligence Service, the SIS, also known as MI5, at the beginning of the Second World War. He rose quickly through its ranks and, by 1949, had been posted to Washington to serve as Britain's principal liaison to the CIA and the FBI. Philby was now in the secret heart of the West's secret war against the Soviet Union, and many believed he would soon be promoted to chief of the SIS. Yet, through all of that, Philby was an officer of the KGB.

If it hadn't been for the flight to Moscow of his old SIS colleagues Guy Burgess and Donald Maclean, Philby may well've never come under suspicion and he likely would've become SIS chief. Even when he did come under suspicion and was recalled to London, and became the subject of intensive investigations in London, Cambridge, Washington, Vienna, Istanbul, and every other place on earth he'd ever lived, worked, or stopped to have a cigarette—Philby survived the scrutiny. No one could prove he worked for or had sympathies for anyone but Britain. He was that good. Philby was officially cleared, and that was announced by no less than British Prime Minister Harold Macmillan on the floor of Parliament. Then Philby announced he was leaving the intelligence service and moving to Beirut as a correspondent for *The Observer* and *The Economist*. But, even in Beirut, he was actually still secretly performing services for the SIS. And the KGB, of course.

Then one night in 1963 he disappeared from Beirut, and when he turned up in Moscow and the KGB announced he was their man, had always been their man, was their man for several years even before he joined the SIS—Philby became the most famous spy in the world. And who was the last Westerner to see Philby on this side of the Iron Curtain? Why, Miles Copeland, of course. That much I knew. "So tell me, Miles, what really happened?"

After we'd made our way into the dining room of Brown's and ordered, and after Miles had questioned me in a little more detail on certain aspects of my visit to Beirut, he leaned forward in his chair and said, "Kim and I were old friends. We'd been friends for quite a while by the time I left the CIA and set up my private shop in Beirut. Of course, I was going to contact Kim, but he didn't even give Lorraine and me time to settle in before *he* contacted *us*. Kim just showed up for dinner one night with our old friends from Damascus days Sam and Eleanor Brewer. Sam was a reporter for *The New York Times*.

"In fact, Larry," Miles said, "one of the main reasons I'd moved to Beirut was to keep tabs on Kim for Jim Angleton."

Miles meant James Jesus "Jesse" Angleton, head of the CIA's counterespionage department. On this beach, I've learned Miles and Angleton were so close and had been friends for so long that, in 1949, on the eve of his departure for a CIA mission in Europe, the famously reserved Angleton stayed up into the night in Washington tenderly drafting a holographic Last Will and Testament, in which he asked that mementos and bottles of good spirits be given to a small circle of his friends: Allen Dulles, Richard Helms, e. e. cummings, Ezra Pound, and Miles Copeland.

"The British had cleared Kim," Miles went on. "Jim was now about the *only* person in British or American intelligence who still thought Kim was a Soviet agent. So, in addition to providing intelligence to oil companies and banks and my other private clients, while in Beirut I also lived off a huge entertainment allowance Jim gave me to use to keep tabs on Kim.

"The irony of this, Larry, was that both Jim and I considered Philby among our dearest friends. Both of us had known him since 1942, when he spent months in Washington and London training American intelligence officers. Kim taught counterespionage to both Jim and me. We'd both liked him from the beginning, and we'd both spent a lot of time with him during his liaison stint in Washington.

"As I said, Jim believed Kim was working for the Soviets. I *didn't*. But I *was* willing to suspend my disbelief and keep an open mind and, with the expense allowance Jim gave me, Lorraine and I became one of Beirut's most prominent couples. Of course, we almost always managed to throw our dinner parties on nights I knew Kim would be available.

"I couldn't tail Kim myself, of course," Miles said, "because he knew me. But I *did* make arrangements with a friend of mine in the Lebanese Sûreté to have his watcher teams subject Kim to occasional surveillance, and report back to me anything of interest.

"Well, of course, the reports I got back were that Kim was practicing his old tradecraft. Shaking off his tails. And along the way he'd lead the Sûreté watchers through some very strange parts of Beirut indeed, places like the Armenian Quarter, and way out at the beginning of the Damascus Road—the road you would've taken to Baalbek, Larry. Eventually we found out Kim was keeping a secret flat out there on the top story of a strange little building.

"Well, by now, even *I* was beginning to suspect Philby," Miles said. "But he was far and away the best espionage agent I ever saw. He'd covered himself. Why did he have a safe flat? Well, as soon as he recognized he'd been tailed all the way to the neighborhood where he kept that flat, he made sure to let us tail him right up to the flat, and let us discover it. Then he let us discover he was carrying on a lurid affair with Eleanor Brewer and the flat was their love nest.

"With that, the heightened suspicion all melted away. *Of course* a trained spy would use countersurveillance measures on his way to meet his mistress. *Of course* he'd keep a secret flat in an out-of-the-way part of town.

"But, anyway," Miles said, "Eleanor divorced Sam, married Kim, and one fine evening in January 1963, Lorraine and I went to Kim and Eleanor's house to collect them to go to a cocktail party. Kim came to the door with Eleanor, said he had to go out to meet a source, and that if Lorraine and I would be so kind as to take Eleanor along, perhaps he'd be able to meet us at the party later."

"Well, that was the last I ever saw of Kim," Miles said. "He slipped out of Beirut that night on a Soviet freighter, and Lorraine and I were left to hold Eleanor's hand until we could figure out where Kim was. Meanwhile, Eleanor, Lorraine, and I were all doing our best to help the British and American services piece together everything Kim was *really* up to all the while he was in Beirut. Then Kim surfaced in Moscow, and sent for Eleanor, and she went. It was all very patrician and gentlemanly the way it was handled in the end."

Next came the part I liked hearing best: For several minutes Miles told me how much Kim's disappearance had eaten him up, and that was a relief to me. He said most of his friends from the SIS and CIA suddenly hated Kim. "But how could I hate him for being a double agent when we were doing the exact same thing to the other side? Larry, I'm truly sorry I never got to see the old bastard again. He was probably the best spy of the century. The way he kept one step ahead of the hounds for years was a masterpiece.

"A lot of my artist friends were coming out for Kim, saying if they were ever forced to choose between their friend or their country, they hoped they had the courage to choose their friend. Well, Larry, I almost felt the same way. But my country always has to come first. That's just the way it is."

I remember looking into Miles's glasses, my father's glasses, thinking, So Miles *does* care about his friends, he *does* have a heart, and he's a patriot first—and all that came as quite a relief.

Across the tablecloth from me, Miles was still working on his Dover sole. In one hand, half a lemon wrapped in gauze; in the other, a fork. "You know, Larry," he said, "I lied. I didn't mean to, but I did. I told you the first thing we were going to work on, in this fortnight plenary session dedicated to passing the torch to Larry Kolb, is writing reports. But it just occurred to me that, since we've been talking about Kim, we should use that as a case study to talk about cover. Right here and now.

"Intelligence officers work in terms of cases. Just as a detective calls whatever he's working on a 'case,' intelligence and counterintelligence officers also work cases. Thus the term 'case officer,' and the importance of writing skills in intelligence. When a new man is assigned to an ongoing case, he 'reads himself into the case,' devouring file after file. One fact leads to another fact, and another file, and in order to have the comprehensive understanding necessary to think effectively about a case, a good intelligence officer spends even more time reading reports, and charting facts, than writing reports."

"Until now," I said, "I'd never quite believed my father's protestations that most of the work he did was dull paperwork."

Miles said, "Intelligence is also *taught* in terms of cases. If you were a CIA trainee, one of the first things you'd do is begin studying old intelligence cases. And, incidentally, Larry, the first case you'd probably study is the Allied invasion of Europe—because it encapsulates *all* the functions and operations of a modern intelligence organization.

"Hitler knew the Allies planned to invade the Continent sometime in 1944. The Abwehr's job was finding out precisely where and when. If Hitler and the German high command had known just a couple weeks in advance that the invasion would take place on or about the sixth of June on the beaches of Normandy, we might be living in a very different world today. So the Allied intelligence services did everything they possibly could to keep the Abwehr from learning our true plans, and to confuse the German high command about the real meaning of whatever true facts they did happen to know. We fed the Germans totally fake plans, and half-truths, and truths that were misleading, all to keep them guessing as to the meaning of what they knew, or thought they knew. You know the quote: Churchill said, 'In wartime, blah blah blah blah, truth should always be attended by a bodyguard of lies.' While we were lying to the Germans, to distract them we also created as much hell for them on psychological, political, and logistical fronts as we could. Larry, as they teach the new recruits at Camp Peary, essentially all the work of modern intelligence services can be inferred from the D-Day case: One group is working to learn the plans of the other, while the other is doing everything possible to hide the truth and confuse and demoralize the enemy.

"So," Miles said, "that's the first case everybody studies, at least the last time I heard. Now, what can we learn from the case of Philby in Beirut?"

"We can learn about cover, and the only cover you're ever really going to need to worry about, Larry, isn't the sort of cover you read about in spy novels. In books, cover usually means a false identity. When a CIA case officer who happens to be an American named Bill Johnson flies into Moscow with a passport and a whole batch of support documents saying he's an Irishman named Danny Macdonald, that's cover, and Bill Johnson had better hope his cover is real good. That sort of cover comes with a legend—a backstory—which may have to hold up to enormous scrutiny. So the legend is 'backstopped,' or 'authenticated,' which means it's supported by falsified documents which are not only in the possession of the person working under cover but have been inserted into the public record and all the records of all the places and organizations the legend specifies the agent has passed through in his entire fake life story.

"So, Larry, they've got all sorts of cover specialties they can give you classes in: Official Cover, Diplomatic Cover, Non-official Cover, Journalistic Cover, Commercial Cover, Military Cover, Cover for Status, Layered Cover, Documenting Cover, Aging the Cover.

"Fabricating and authenticating a cover can be a very elaborate exercise. But none of that matters at all to you, Larry. Because you're going to use the best cover of all: natural cover. Which means you're going to be who you are. There's no legend to authenticate. And the best thing about natural cover is the person using it isn't worried about remembering his cover identity. Under interrogation, there's no alias or fake life story to remember. All a person using natural cover has to remember is what the CIA calls Cover for Action, CFA. And that's where Kim Philby in Beirut comes in. Even under natural cover, an agent needs a cover story, or a cover operation, some way of misleading the target and the security services protecting the target as to what the agent is really doing.

"Although the British had cleared him, Kim knew he was still under suspicion in Washington, and he probably assumed he was also still under suspicion in London. So he knew he would be under at least spot surveillance while he lived and worked in Beirut. So how could he keep up his work for the KGB—which he *did* keep up while in Beirut—and get away with it? CFA.

"Why was Kim using countersurveillance tradecraft? Because he was sneaking around with another man's wife. That's CFA. Why did Kim keep a secret flat in a strange part of town? It was a love nest. CFA.

"Of course, Larry, it was only later we learned that top-floor flat of Kim's wasn't just his love nest, it was also a safe house. The windows of Kim's flat were in line of sight of the bedroom window of a KGB code clerk's flat more than half a mile away. Kim was using the place to send black-light messages to his Moscow handlers. Cover for Action."

When we finally left, after cheese and port and coffee, the whole dining room was empty save for a pair of lovers at a small table on the other side of the room.

The next morning. Miles and I were back at Brown's. Which, as London hotels go, is about as Old World elegant as they come. Fine antiques, old dark wood, open fireplaces, staff hovering everywhere like you're in Buckingham Palace. Miles and I were upstairs in a big suite sitting across a Queen Anne table from each other. Flat white light and the sounds of Mayfair were pouring in through the windows Miles had opened onto Albemarle Street. He kept threatening to get down to teaching me the boring art of writing in U.S. Government bureaucratese. But he didn't seem to want to do it any more than I wanted him to.

He'd already told me what we were going to be doing wasn't a case study, or an exercise. Miles had been given a job to do, I was going to help him do it, and I suppose that made Miles a practical man. The job was for Adnan. Miles had already told me that too, and it probably explains why, even when we started to work, Miles's digressions all tended to involve Adnan.

"Report writing is a highly valued talent in the intelligence world," Miles said. "Adnan first came to the attention of the CIA because of the quality of his reports."

What Miles told me then, launching our first digression of that morning, was that, in the 1960s, the "Dynasty reports" began arriving anonymously at the U.S. Embassy in Riyadh. These reports argued the strategic importance of the Arabian Peninsula and Persian Gulf, and they were so perceptive and innovative that the CIA became determined to learn the identity of their mysterious author, who had identified himself only as "Dynasty."

The reports were so sophisticated that the CIA feared they might be the work of an American think-tank genius who'd sold out to a Saudi interest. The newly formed Saudi Mukhabarat had been delivering the reports to our embassy and trying to pass them off as its own work. But eventually it was determined the Dynasty reports were the work of Adnan and his staff of lawyers, economists, and political scientists.

Next Miles told me that, since the Sixties, starting with Kennedy, Adnan had been on friendly terms with every American president. And I told Miles that an old friend of my father had told me that Adnan's friendship with President Kennedy began while Adnan was still a student and Kennedy was a young senator, and that their relationship evolved primarily out of whoring together. And that, when I'd asked Adnan about this, he'd said it was essentially true, except that the women were models, not whores, and Kennedy called it "chasing pussy."

I told Miles about how Adnan told me he'd once shown up at Kennedy's house in Palm Beach with a beautiful English model, and Kennedy had promptly stolen her. " 'He was just like us Arabs,' Adnan said—and now Adnan was holding both hands out in front of his lap, like he was pointing a fire hose, while he told me, 'Always carrying it around in front of him. Oh, she was a beautiful girl! So beautiful! The next time I saw her was at Kennedy's inauguration in Washington. He sent a plane to London to fly her there.' "

Miles now diverted our conversation to Adnan's private airplanes. And Adnan's yachts and houses and apartments—all the things Adnan had purchased with just some of the proceeds of the transactions he brokered during his first few years as a businessman connecting Saudi Arabia and the West.

"Of course," Miles said, "no one would ever doubt Adnan enjoyed those possessions. But the fact is his playboy lifestyle is more cover than anything else. Adnan started acquiring these things only when he realized they were the entry stakes to the world he wanted to deal in. He told me that, not so long after he left school to open his first offices in Riyadh, he chartered a yacht and sailed it to Sardinia—where he happened to dock between Aristotle Onassis's yacht, the *Christina*, and King Constantine's yacht."

Miles said, "Well, Larry, Adnan said to me, 'Suddenly Onassis and Constantine were my neighbors and I saw that they were members of a very small club of people who talked and socialized only with one another. About the only way to penetrate it was if you could meet them on their own ground.'

"Thus, Larry, the boats and aircraft and parties—which, you've seen with your own eyes—Adnan uses more than anything else for making contacts."

As I already knew, and as Miles reminded me now to make his point, while the whole world seemed to be enjoying the spectacle of Adnan Khashoggi spending some of his money, it went largely unreported what he did with most of the rest of the proceeds of his first big scores.

What he did was spend hundreds of millions of dollars trying to make his corner of the Third World self-sufficient in food production. As a young citizen of the world's richest country, per capita, Adnan couldn't fail to notice the enormous contrast between the wealth destined to be his and the poverty in so many of the countries surrounding Saudi Arabia. *I foresaw an ocean of envy, boundless in its demands for such assistance as the rich among us, according to the Quran, are supposed to give to the poor,* Adnan wrote once. *Give the poorest peoples of the Third World enough to eat and to shelter themselves, and enough extra money to give them some hope, and they will be far more inclined to peace than if they live as beggars seething against rich neighbors.*

Adnan acquired huge tracts of land in Egypt and the Sudan and Kenya. Poor countries, located next to rich countries. Then he bought verily half the cattle in Arizona and shipped them to some of his new lands. He acquired modern agricultural machinery, and irrigation systems, and seeds and fertilizers, and hired Western experts to help his people learn to produce enough grains and vegetables and beef to feed East Africa and the Middle East. And in the end, his project failed.

Not because of climatic conditions, or lack of capital, but due almost entirely to political factors. Assets were nationalized. Concession rights and export licenses were withheld while power shifted from one minister to another. Tariffs were imposed between neighbor countries while their bureaucrats squabbled. It was while this, his most ambitious project yet, circled the drain that Adnan first saw the political dimensions of the problem he'd rather idealistically set out to solve.

Thus, Miles said, the genesis of the document we were finally about to get to work on.

Some months earlier, Miles and Adnan had written a white paper setting out Adnan's contention that the key to lasting Mideast peace lies in economics, and proposing that—to end the cycle of despair, violence, and reprisal—rich countries, including not only the United States but also the Arab oil states, should establish a "Marshall Plan" for all the needy countries of the Middle East, including Israel.

Adnan's plan provided that, after its initial capitalization, the program would be funded primarily by taxes on all Middle Eastern oil exports. This, Adnan said, would effectively decrease the burden then borne under the Camp David Agreement entirely by American taxpayers. Every country dependent on a stable Middle East would be in a position of having to share the responsibility and expense.

Made sense to me, at least the way Miles laid it out that morning.

And, according to Miles, it also made sense to Ronald Reagan. In a recent meeting in the White House, Adnan had praised Reagan's outline for Mideast peace, but added that an economic perspective on the problem was missing from the Reagan Plan, as originally drafted.

Miles said Reagan had been so taken by Adnan's Mideast Marshall Plan idea that he decided to make it a key element of the Ronald Reagan Mideast Peace Plan. "Larry, what we're now about to do," Miles said, "is fuse the Adnan Khashoggi Mideast Marshall Plan into the Ronald Reagan Mideast Peace Plan. And the best part," Miles said, "is a deal is in the works. The Israelis, the Egyptians, the Saudis, and the White House, at the highest levels, are all secretly willing to go along with it."

Under the plan which Miles and I then started drafting—in consultation with Adnan and someone from the National Security Council Miles kept slipping into the bedroom to telephone—the Arab states would acknowledge Israel's right to exist behind secure borders; Israel would acknowledge the Palestinian people's rights to a sovereign homeland including the West Bank and Gaza and access to Jerusalem; and the United States, Great Britain, France, Germany, Saudi Arabia, Kuwait, the United Arab Emirates, and Adnan personally would all make up-front contributions to a fund which would be named the Mideast Peace Fund. Adnan was pledging a hundred million dollars of his own money.

Miles and I got high just talking about it. But when it came down to the actual work: Shit! The original draft of the Ronald Reagan Mideast Peace Plan we were working from was sixty-seven pages long. Adnan's original white paper was fifty-five pages.

The original Reagan Plan was written with an institutional tone plus a bit of majesty, sort of as if the Wizard of Oz had written it. Adnan's white paper was scholarly, but colorful, and a lot of it was written in the first person from the point of view of an Arab speaking directly to the President.

We were working on an old IBM Selectric typewriter, with no memory, and every page on which we made a mistake, usually almost at the bottom of the page, had to be retyped before we could move on to the next page. It wasn't quite like being a monk painstakingly copying an illuminated manuscript, but, compared to the best technology available even then, it felt like it.

Miles and I would talk about what to say, sentence by sentence. Then I did most of the typing and Miles did most of the interrupting, though I did my share too. Because of the boredom. Any excuse for a digression would do.

Before we'd finished the second page, we spent ten minutes talking about the ball-and-claw feet on the table we were working at. And, not many pages later, I remember Miles asking me, "So how's Kim? She's here, isn't she?"

"Uh-huh," I said, still typing. "She's here, and yesterday we went out to dinner at the Guinea Grill and then ran into Dodi and Valerie Perrine in a dark corner at Tramp. Today, Kim's with her sisters and Soraya. Tomorrow she's going home. But she'll be back in a week. *Jesus Christ*, Miles! Look what you made me do!"

"Start again," said Miles.

Day 3. Page 31.

In response to the suggestion that the United States has been dealing softly with the Saudis because of hope it would obtain cooperation on oil pricing, it should be pointed out that up until 1973, it was the United States itself which urged the Saudis to raise oil prices in order, assertedly, to permit Iran to earn enough foreign currency to pay for the arms it needed in order to become a credible military force. After 1974, pricing . . .

Only about thirty or forty more pages to go, single-spaced.

"You know, Miles," I said, "one day when I was in Cannes, staying in the Carlton—where Adnan had already been putting me up in a suite for more than a week—I was packing my bags, just about to check out, when someone knocked on my door. I opened it, and there was a Frenchman standing there. A nice-seeming guy in his thirties who introduced himself as the manager from Van Cleef and Arpels just down the Croisette. He said he'd been referred to me by the hotel manager.

"'May I come in and show you some things?' he said.

"'Sure,' I said, 'come on in.'

"So I let this guy in, and he had a big gray morocco-leather display case, which he opened, and inside it were all sorts of jewels. Diamond rings. Sapphire rings. Ruby earrings. Diamond chokers. Necklaces. Pendants. He showed them all to me, put a few of them in my hands, really seemed to want me to like them, and I said, 'These are all beautiful. Very nice. Thanks for showing me.'

"Then the guy said, 'Would you like any of these?'

"'Well, this one is very nice,' I said. 'Perhaps my mother would like it.' And what I was holding up was a beautiful blue necklace which he said was diamonds and sapphires.

"'How much is this one?' I said.

"'This one I could give you for only . . .' I can't remember exactly what he said in francs, Miles, but, in dollars, I remember it worked out to about fifteen thousand bucks.

"I said to him, 'This is very nice, but I don't have that much cash with me, and I don't want to put it on a credit card.'

"He said, 'But, sir, you don't understand. If you would like anything here, you can charge it to your room.'

"Well, Miles," I said, "at this point, I'd known Adnan for all of about two months. I'd seen him only three times, never alone, and he'd repeatedly put off the meetings he'd agreed to have with me. He'd just put me up in this suite— one of the best suites in Cannes, I was told—for something like ten days while I waited for him to arrive for a meeting."

"Tension and release," Miles said.

"And what I started thinking then, Miles, was surely I wasn't the only person waiting in a hotel room somewhere on the face of the earth for a meeting Adnan was late for. You know how it goes. Every week or two he's in New York, Paris, Manila, Riyadh, Cannes, Marbella. And probably, in almost every one of those places, almost every day of the year, somebody is waiting for Adnan—as his guest. And every one of those guests has full signing privileges for all the champagne and caviar and meals he wants, and apparently also for all of the jewelry he wants to put on his hotel bill.

"I didn't take anything. I wish I had now, but I didn't. But some people must.

"So, what I've been wondering ever since, Miles, is just how much money does Adnan really spend in a day, a month, a year?"

Oh the sloth and joy that question unleashed! Miles and I must've spent the next five hours then, without writing a word of what we were supposed to be writing, while we worked on legal pads and a calculator estimating Adnan's average daily expenses.

THE HOMES. Adnan owns and maintains homes in Riyadh, Jiddah, Paris, Cannes, Mougins, Monaco, Marbella, New York, Kenya, London, and the Canary Islands. In at least 3 of those places—Mougins, Marbella, and Kenya—he has at least two homes. Probably he has one or two more stashed away which we haven't heard of yet—but we make no allowance for those here. Each of Adnan's homes has a staff of at least 10, including majordomo, butler, chef, waiters, chambermaids, drivers, and security personnel. Some of the homes, including Marbella, New York, Riyadh, and Kenya, have much larger staffs—between 25 and 100 people each. In Marbella, in addition to human inhabitants, there's a barn full of Arabian stallions to feed and care for. In Kenya, there are thousands of animals fed nightly at the viewing sites. Including all staff compensation, pantry expenses, laundry expenses, automobiles, electricity, maintenance, insurance, property taxes, and incidentals appurtenant thereto, but excluding any applicable mortgage payments, for the Homes . . . .$38,000 PER DAY.

THE AIRCRAFT. The hardware utilized by Adnan's Flying Circus includes a DC-8, a DC-9, a Boeing 727, a Gulfstream, a Dassault Falcon, and an Agusta helicopter. Probably there are more aircraft we are not aware of, but we make no allowance for those here. Almost every one of these aircraft is in the air daily. Often when Adnan and his guests cross an ocean in the DC-8, the 727 or the DC-9, or both, are in hot pursuit, carrying staff and baggage or ladies-in-waiting. When the DC-9 and 727 aren't being used as chase planes, they're used instead by members of his family, or his executives, or a variety of satraps, princes, and dictators to whom Adnan loans the planes. When Adnan is cruising, the Agusta is kept busy flying between the *Nabila* and the shore. When the *Nabila* is in harbor, Adnan often uses the Agusta to avoid those nasty drives between his homes and the airports where his jets are waiting. Including fuel and other direct operating costs, plus a maintenance reserve equal to fuel costs, pilot and crew salaries and benefits, landing fees, aircraft parking fees, flight-planning services, galley expenditures, insurance, and incidentals, for the Aircraft . . . . .**$125,000 PER DAY.**

THE BOATS. Adnan's watercraft include the 282-foot *Nabila*; the 157-foot *Khalidia*; two ten-meter Rivas; three six-meter Rivas; plus a miniature submarine for the enjoyment of Adnan's children and guests. There may be additional vessels, but we are not aware of them and make no allowance for them here. Irrespective of her official port of call, which is Brunei, the *Nabila*'s main base of operations is the 300′-long concrete dock Adnan had built for her at the Puerto José Banus in Marbella. She cruises the world throughout much of the year, and is regularly seen in Sardinia, Portofino, Monaco, Antibes, Cannes, Saint-Tropez, Ibiza, the Bahamas, the Philippines, and Brunei, among other ports. When the *Khalidia* is not in use as a support vessel for the *Nabila*, she is used by Adnan's children or guests. Including fuel, maintenance reserves at the industry-standard rate, captains and crews, ships chandlery, harbor fees, dockage fees, dockside auxiliary power, navigation services, tenders, demurrage, ship-to-ship, ship-to-shore, and ship-to-satellite communications, the fresh-cut flowers you seem to always find in almost every cabin of the *Nabila* and the *Khalidia*, insurance, and incidentals, for the Boats . . . .**$65,000 PER DAY.**

THE WARDROBE. An illusionist, high-wire artist, and prestidigitator as proficient as Adnan the Great needs an impressive wardrobe. Adnan's tailor, a rich man in Paris, annually makes Adnan about 150 new bespoke-tailored evening jackets, business suits, some with epaulets, dress suits, smoking jackets, morning jackets, capes, overcoats, and short-sleeved tropical business suits, in various silhouettes to suit the waxing and waning of Adnan's waistline. The suits are shipped to Adnan's central wardrobe facility in Marbella, along with shirts custom-made by Sulka, Lancel, and others, and handmade shoes from cobblers in London,

Milano, and Rome. Including dry-cleaning charges, except at his Marbella ranch, where Adnan has his own dry-cleaning facilities, and excluding shoeshining costs, because shoeshining is handled by valets accounted for elsewhere herein, for the Wardrobe...$2,000 PER DAY.

THE CIRCUS TROUPE. Adnan never goes anywhere alone. Whether by plane, yacht, or motorcade, he takes with him a support staff, including his chief of staff Bob Shaheen, a doctor or two, a masseur, a lawyer or two, sometimes a seer, at least one secretary, Adnan's personal barber, one or two valets, at least one procurer, and 3 or 4 general flunkies tasked with solving the annoying day-to-day problems of Adnan's simple Bedouin lifestyle. Including all salaries, bonuses, social benefits, and incidentals, for the Circus Troupe ....$18,000 PER DAY.

We kept at it, in elaborate detail, through The Hotel Stays ($16,000 per day); Everyday Meals ($12,000 per day); Entertaining ($45,000 per day); Guests in Waiting ($14,000 per day); The Personal Offices ($24,000 per day); Family ($28,000 per day); Philanthropy ($40,000 per day); Miscellaneous ($50,000 per day); right up to

TOTAL $477,000 PER DAY.

"And that," said Miles, "isn't a bad per diem at all when you consider Adnan is essentially a covert operative for the Saudi royal family—has been ever since he delivered that first secret shipment of trucks and rifles to the royalists fighting down in Yemen."

And that was as far as we could take that digression.

Dignity seemed to require that we get back to work now. But the new Ronald Reagan Mideast Peace Plan was so big and so boring to us that instead we set to work on the cover letter Adnan would be sending to President Reagan with the finished plan. Typing now:

It is essential to point out that neither any other private citizen nor I ever "represented" King Fahd or any other member of the Saudi royal family. By unalterable custom, however, senior members of the family or of the government make extensive use of trusted citizens to probe, to convey attitudes, and to carry out various confidential tasks, but they do not take responsibility for them. Instead, they observe the rule of Somerset Maugham's Ashenden: "If you do well you'll get no thanks and if you get into trouble you'll get no help." I've been honored to enjoy access to King Fahd and other members of the royal family, but always "through the kitchen door." Such an avenue has given me a confidentiality of relationship, which has made

*me an "expert" on the king's and prince's thoughts and fears, but does not
qualify me as a "spokesman." Under present circumstances, such a position
is of particular value: There happens to be a wide gap between what His
Majesty thinks privately and what he may say in official contacts. . . .*

"You know, Larry," Miles said, "none of that is bullshit, either. Not only has
he been the Saudi royal family's unofficial emissary to America, but since as far
back as the Sixties A.K.'s also been the agent for quiet peace initiatives between
the Saudis and Israel.

"At first, most of his contact with Israelis was liaison with Mossad officers,
to exchange messages. But, by the Seventies, he'd graduated to secret meetings
with Menachem Begin *while* he was Prime Minister. It was Adnan who carried
to the Israelis the signal from Sadat that Egypt was ready for peace with Israel.
And, Larry, three or four years ago, Adnan hosted Ariel Sharon in Kenya, and
delivered a secret proposal from King Fahd for peace with Israel in exchange
for Muslim control of the Dome of the Rock.

"It didn't fly. But Adnan introduced Sharon to Numeiri in the process, and
then arranged for Numeiri to allow Sharon to use the Sudan to stage a rescue
operation for Jews trapped in the Ethiopian famine. They were airlifted right
out of Khartoum!"

Miles stopped now, grinned, then went on with his story.

"A.K. told me that, when Arafat heard about the rescue and that A.K. was
behind it, Arafat put out word that he was furious at Adnan for helping Israel.
Well, Adnan said he'd never met Arafat, so he went to see him, to talk it over.
Adnan walked into Arafat's office and saw Arafat was wearing his gun on his
belt. So Adnan said, 'Shoot me!' Then they laughed and kissed cheeks, and held
hands like Arabs do, and since then Adnan's been carrying peace offers back
and forth between Arafat and Shimon Peres."

As I remember it, it was just about then that the phone rang, right there in
the dining room, not the bedroom like always before, and Miles answered and
said: "Adnan! Speak of the devil!" Next Miles was nodding his head up and
down and saying, "Okay, Heathrow not Gatwick. Right?" And then he
said, "Larry's here with me, you know. I should bring him along, don't
you think?"

Then Miles said, "Okay, see you, A.K.," and then he put down the phone
and told me we were going to Germany.

I remember that, when we got out of Adnan's little Falcon at Hamburg
Airport, the sky was bright but entirely white. It was a strange shadowless day.

We were in Germany, according to what Miles had told me on the plane, to sit in on a meeting with Adnan and some friends of his from the Middle East and then write up a little report that would grow out of the meeting. Who these friends of Adnan's were, or what was to be discussed, Miles didn't know. Or at least he said he didn't.

While we rode into the Free and Hanseatic City of Hamburg in a dark Mercedes Adnan sent for us, neither Miles nor I had any idea that someday this little meeting we were about to attend would be investigated, reinvestigated, and more misreported, misunderstood, and infamous in America than probably any other conclave of our time save the Appalachian Conference. If we'd known, it would've been a great chance for Miles to teach me how to wear a wire. There was no security for the meeting. Adnan didn't even have one of his famous jabber tapes rolling. It was all so casual. Just another day in Adnan's life.

Adnan was already there when we got to the suite. Hello, Adnan. Hello, Dr. Nicole—Adnan's doctor from Paris. Hello, Nael, you son of a bitch—Adnan's brother-in-law, from Lebanon. That was the full extent of the people I knew there.

"Hello, Manoosh!" Miles sang out. "Didn't expect to see *you* here. Larry, meet Manucher Ghorbanifar, arms dealer, rogue, raconteur, and former officer of the Shah of Iran's dreaded secret police, the Savak. In fact, Larry," Miles said, "Manucher is the only Savak agent ever to flunk a CIA polygraph test. Which I always interpreted to mean he's one of the good guys, the one and only man once in the employ of the Peacock Throne who knows the truth from a lie, and right from wrong."

Ghorbanifar was Iranian, probably in his fifties. He was big and solid, with a bald head and thick, black eyebrows and a black-and-white Vandyke mustache and beard. He was wearing a dark business suit, an immaculate white shirt, and a Hermes tie. But I couldn't stop thinking he looked like a character straight out of *The Merchant of Venice*. The only thing missing was a pair of tights.

Hello, Mr. Ghorbanifar. Nice to meet you.

There were a couple of others Iranians there whose names I don't remember, plus an Iranian named Hassan Karrubi, whose name I also didn't remember and I had a hell of a time finding this morning, because in almost all of the congressional reports written about this meeting, he's known only as "the First Iranian."

Next I shook hands with David Kimche, who was officially the head of the Israeli Foreign Ministry at the time, but who, Miles informed me a few minutes later on our way to a bathroom break, was actually Israel's leading intelligence officer. "In fact," Miles said, "David and I've known each other for years, and he's as good as they get. Philby's tradecraft *may* have been better than

David's, that's debatable, but as far as overall understanding of how intelligence works, David has a better view of the big picture than any other intelligence officer anywhere on the earth. He may be the best spymaster who ever lived." Miles wanted to make sure I understood I'd just met a legend.

The next guy I met was Al Schwimmer, to whom Adnan introduced me as Professor Kolb. Schwimmer was another old friend of both Miles and Adnan. He was an Israeli and an arms manufacturer, arms procurer, and arms dealer.

Hassan Karrubi and I seemed to be about the only guys in the room who didn't know all the others there.

Welcome to the old boy network. We will now discuss a matter of potential interest to thinking people everywhere in the United States, Iran, Saudi Arabia, and Israel.

First up: the new guy, Hassan Karrubi.

Ghorbanifar introduced Karrubi as a confidante of Ali Akbar Hashemi-Rafsanjani, one of the most powerful men in Iran, and probably its most moderate leader.

Karrubi spoke of the need for an intermediary who could act as a bridge between Iran and the United States to convince both sides it was in their mutual interests to prevent a Soviet domination of Iran. "Of course," Karrubi said, "there are great risks involved in an Iranian even taking part in a meeting with representatives of Israel. But we are willing to take this risk because of the greater risk if we allow the Soviets to continue to penetrate and influence the Iranian military and the Iranian political elite."

The problem—as Ghorbanifar explained it when Karrubi had finished—was that due to the embargo the United States had imposed years ago on trade with Iran, the Iranian Air Force found it increasingly difficult to obtain spare parts and ordnance for use in the American-made fighters and other American aircraft sold for two decades by the United States to the Shah. Without access to American parts and to ammunition that could be fired from American-made planes, the Iranians, who were locked in a death struggle against Saddam Hussein's military forces, were becoming increasingly reliant on Soviet aid. At first, the Soviets had covertly provided the Iranians spare American parts, which the Soviets had purchased through intermediary trading companies in the Far East and elsewhere. But now, Ghorbanifar said, the Soviets were increasingly pressuring the Iranians to replace their American aircraft and weaponry systems with Soviet-made planes and weapons to be bartered for Iranian oil.

A Soviet-influenced or Soviet-controlled Iran surely is not in the interest of the United States or any of us here, Ghorbanifar said. Which is why Karrubi was there representing certain moderates within the Iranian political power structure and within the Iranian military, who'd secretly indicated that, if they were to receive a gesture of good faith from the United States, they would influence the Ayatollah Khomeini to soften his position on the United States. In fact, Ghorbanifar promised, "in exchange for the sale to Iran—at a fair market price, I might add—of various aircraft parts and TOW missiles, I have been promised that our friends in Iran would arrange for the release of the four American hostages now held in Lebanon."

This sounded a lot like a song I'd heard before.

Here's where Adnan came in. He said that in recent meetings in Washington, he'd been told that if the American government was going to participate in this venture in hopes of procuring the release of the hostages, it would have to be structured in such a way that there would be no trail of arms, or goods of any kind, leading from the United States to Iran.

So, Adnan said, while Schwimmer nodded in confirmation, it had been arranged that the actual goods could come from the Israeli government and other Israeli sources, and be transported directly from Israel to Iran. Then, Adnan said, to make up for the depletion of the Israeli missile reserves, the Americans had promised they would quickly sell a like amount to Israel.

This is one form of what's known in the darker reaches of the arms trade as a triangulation.

But arms trading and missiles and spare parts and hostages took up very little of the conversation that day. Most of the time was spent thinking, and talking, in grand and hypothetical terms, about a strategic opening between the United States and Iran—as a means of blunting Soviet attempts to dominate the world's third-largest oil producer. It felt like a geopolitical symposium, a meeting of intellectuals, not the makings of an arms deal. No concrete numbers or business terms were even discussed. It was all very hypothetical and altruistic, and it didn't take very long before everyone was shaking hands and saying goodbye.

Later, in one report Miles and I read, the investigators made it sound like right after the meeting Adnan and Ghorbanifar and Kimche locked a certain unnamed rogue CIA officer and his apprentice into a dungeon and fed them nothing but scraps of bread and thimbles of gruel until that certain rogue CIA officer had finished writing up the conspirators' dark plan. But what really happened was Miles and I flew back to England, and back to that fucking Selectric typewriter, and the next day wrote up a white paper based on the meeting.

Our little work—titled "Adnan Khashoggi's Views on the Possibilities of a Strategic Initiative Between the United States and Iran"—wasn't about an arms deal. It focused almost entirely on the Soviet threat to Iran and the many good reasons to take advantage of what was apparently a secret peace offering proffered to the White House by certain powerful Iranians who seemed to be far less strident than Khomeini.

For me, more than anything else, writing, and typing, that damned paper was more clear evidence in support of Miles's contention that the writing part of secret work is dull and routine, all too prevalent, and feels like it never amounts to anything. When Miles and I flew to Geneva to give our work to Adnan, who said he'd be sending it to the President in care of his national security advisor, Robert McFarlane, we both thought we'd never hear about it again. After Adnan had read through the paper with us, he took us to a hell of a dinner party and then Miles and I flew back to England.

We had no idea then that the vaguely contemplated transactions we'd written up would ever come to fruition, that months later a wild-ass Marine colonel would force the whole thing out into the open by stealing Adnan's fifteen-million-dollar bridge loan which funded the sale and sending the money to the Nicaraguan Contra rebels, that Miles and I had written the initial plan for what would become known as the Iran-Contra Affair.

Once the story broke, I remember Miles and me watching in wonder as the news unfolded. Every day we learned rich new details about things like a hot-looking secretary named Fawn slinking out of the White House with documents stuffed down her panty hose, Nelson Bunker Hunt and Ross Perot adding little wrinkles such as shoulder-fired Blowpipe missiles and the Contras to our plan, and what Ollie North was really up to way down there in the subbasement of the West Wing, all while our fearless Vice President Bush was perpetually "out of the loop."

Back in London now, just arrived from Geneva and that dinner party with Adnan. We're in another suite at Brown's. A higher floor. A slightly different view out the Georgian windows. A different antique table. Brown's has always been a favorite place for visiting Gulf royalty to stay. "Who the hell is paying for this, Miles? Friends from the Gulf?"

I asked, but Miles wouldn't say.

It wasn't that he actually cared whether I knew who was paying. Miles was using it as an object lesson. Operational security is built on compartmentalization, discipline, cell theory. The members of one cell don't know the identities of the members of any other cell. Communications between cells is indirect and anonymous.

But before we went deeper into all that, Miles felt the need to break my spirit—and he did it through adventures in parsing and typing. First, we finished the new Ronald Reagan Mideast Peace Plan, or, at least, our version of it, the version Adnan would send to the White House. That took four days, and by the end of it I was ready to take a sledgehammer to the typewriter.

Let's get out of here and find some lunch and then have some fun, was what I was thinking. But we had lunch in the suite, and right after that Miles taught me how to write a field report, what to include, what not to include.

Include: everything relevant about the target or situation being reported on. Who (with one exception), What, Where, When, Why? Remain objective. Stick to raw information. Don't filter it, interpret it, massage it, evaluate it, or make assumptions. EEI means Essential Elements of Information. If you have your own evaluation of the raw facts you've collected, send it in a separate document.

Do not include: confidential source identification. This is the exception under "Who" above. In all your reports, from the field or elsewhere, use a code name and no other characterization for every confidential source of information provided in a report. Identify and characterize such source only in a separate document or message, and store and transmit that document or message separately. The one form of field reporting in which the intelligence collector is expected to state the collector's own evaluative judgment is in such separately transmitted source identification and characterization reports. Such a report typically includes the collector's personal assessment of the credibility, reliability, and usefulness of a source.

"For now, Larry, assume your field reports won't be intercepted, that you and I will be the only persons ever to see them. We'll get to encoding, and disguising, and transmitting your field reports later. Today, learn to write them *en clair*.

"Sit down now, Larry, and write me a field report on the conversation you've just had with confidential source Miles Copeland about writing field reports and protecting sources."

I did.

Miles read it.

"Try again, Larry. Make it better this time."

I did.

Miles said, "Okay, this is marginally acceptable. For now, it'll do. But what about the source information? Who is this source of yours 'Mrs. Samuel Gompers'? Does she have any idea what she's talking about, and should we trust her?

"Sit down again, Larry. Write it up. Let me see it."

I did.

Miles read it.

"This is great, Larry," Miles said. "Just the ticket. Except your confidential source Miles Copeland will very likely soon be dead. Whatever possessed you to put confidential source identification information right here on the same table as your field report on the information the confidential source provided you?

"Let's start again," Miles said. "From the very beginning."

We did.

"Okay," Miles said hours later, "this field report isn't bad at all. Everything's there. Everything's objective. Now count the words."

I did.

"Nine hundred seventeen."

"Write it again," Miles said. "Say the same thing but cut it to six hundred words. Stick to the facts and don't rhapsodize."

I did.

"This is still too long," Miles said. "Try again. As you're working, count the words in your longer sentences. Cut any sentence that's twenty-eight words or longer into two sentences. Once per page, I'll allow you a sentence longer than twenty-seven words but less than forty words. Kim Roosevelt and I once determined shorter sentences make shorter field reports. It matters. Eventually you're going to have to encrypt your reports. Encryption is time-consuming. Try again."

I did.

"This is shorter," Miles said, "but some of the essential information is missing. Try again."

You get the picture. More than anything else, what Miles was teaching me that day wasn't just writing, and typing, but an all-new way of thinking, and acting, and controlling myself. By the next day, he'd finally lowered my expectations. Miles's recruiting pitch had sounded good, all right, but what I'd actually signed on for was a life of hauling deadwood.

Only once I'd realized that did Miles say: "We're not going to give you a comprehensive course, Larry. And that's not just because it's unlikely you're ever going to need to know much about blowing up bridges or disarming nuclear bombs. Obvious professionalism can be as undesirable in spies as in prostitutes.

"The major intelligence services all used to give their agents extensive training. But then they realized that often did more harm than good, that an agent who practiced countersurveillance measures every day on his way home from work eventually was going to arouse suspicion.

"The KGB were the first ones to realize this, Larry, and for years it gave them an advantage over the Western services. The Soviets actually taught their agents less rather than more. So when their agents came under spot surveillance—and almost everyone with access to sensitive materials or facilities is subject to routine spot surveillance—they didn't display mannerisms which betrayed them, and subjected them to full surveillance. Almost no one can beat full surveillance.

"So all we're going to teach you, Larry," Miles went on, "is what you're going to need to know to understand the process of collecting and communicating useful information, to recognize traps, and to get yourself and whatever you've got across borders or other checkpoints. The rest you're just going to have to accomplish with ordinary skills, and common sense, and all that access. You'll do fine."

"But first," Miles said, "there's something really important I've got to do."

Whereupon he got up from the table, went to the sitting room, and plopped down on the couch for a little nap.

Miles came to, went off somewhere for a minute, and then came back and we discussed some basics.

The three pure-intelligence functions of a modern intelligence organization are collecting information, only a small percentage of which is collected clandestinely; analyzing the information that's been collected; and shielding the organization and its secrets against penetration. Because of the culture of secrecy every intelligence organization fosters, there is a fourth function, which doesn't technically fall under the definition of intelligence, but for which modern nations tend to use their intelligence services: conducting covert operations, doing whatever a nation's leaders feel must be done without fear of exposure.

There's a difference between intelligence and espionage, and it's that intelligence can come from many sources, most of them overt or public, while espionage is conducted by spies and the intelligence professionals, the case officers, who manage them. A CIA officer isn't a spy, or even a CIA *agent*.

Spy novels and the media have managed to confuse the American public about the meaning of those terms so thoroughly that even many in our government don't understand the terminology. A CIA agent is a spy. A little Latvian janitor who's been co-opted and who, for payments of three hundred dollars per week, all cash, delivers to his handler the nightly contents of the admiral's wastebasket, is a spy. If his handler happens to be a CIA officer, that little Latvian janitor is a CIA agent.

It would be pretty simple understanding the difference between intelligence officers and agents, except that certain American security services have done their best to confuse everyone. The FBI and the Secret Service give their professionals the title Special Agent, which many in the media often shorten to just agent. While the CIC existed, both Miles and my father—not to mention Asa Candler, Henry Kissinger, and J. D. Salinger, for that matter—were at one point in their lives all CIC Special Agents. But officers of the American and British intelligence services are not agents, and God help you if you get it wrong in front of them. Because agents are spies, and spies are traitors.

Any intelligence case begins with the target. The target could be an individual, an organization, a country, an intelligence service, a situation, anything really. There are many means of producing intelligence, and covert means should be looked at only as the last resort. One of the other ways of producing intelligence is called gaming, and Miles stopped pacing now, and sat on the couch and told me all about it.

The American intelligence community's use of game theory to produce intelligence estimates began in the State Department's Game Room, which later became the model for the CIA's Peace Game Center. Miles was a key player in the early days of both facilities. His role: Nasser. No American knew Egyptian President Gamel Abdel Nasser better than Miles Copeland did.

In the Game Room, the players consisted of individuals, such as Miles, each of whom was an expert on one national leader. The players included in any given game depended upon which countries were actively involved in the situation or trend to be analyzed. One day, Miles might be playing against experts representing de Gaulle, Eisenhower, Khrushchev. Another day Anthony Eden and David Ben-Gurion.

The players had the benefit of the latest intelligence, received hourly from the CIA, the State Department, and the Pentagon, while they "gamed out" international situations—trying to think like the leaders they represented.

The rules of the game were simple: 1. Moral judgments are relevant only when they are consistent with the recognized moral standards of the country and leader involved. 2. It is assumed every national leader's first objective is to stay in power or, if he cannot, to retire from power with a minimum of personal loss. 3. It is assumed that, after his own personal interests, a national leader acts in his country's best interests as he sees them, rather than in the interest of the world at large.

The object of the game was to predict each interested nation's next move and the outcome of the trend or situation under analysis. Miles was so good at it that John Foster Dulles used to make special trips to the Game Room to, in Dulles's words, "watch Copeland's Nasser act."

"Our results weren't infallible, of course," Miles told me. "Because chance is such an important factor in real life. But the Game Room performed remarkably well. And one thing we came to see the more we studied it was just how important domestic political considerations invariably are in the formulation of any country's foreign policy. Probably, more moves on the international game board than not are actually domestically driven than anyone looking dispassionately at the problem of international game theory could rationally accept.

"It was in the Game Room, Larry," Miles went on, "that I hit upon a principle that's guided me ever since: I see life as a game. Not in a frivolous sense, but in the serious, strategic sense of our Game Room. If you treat life as a game, you gain several advantages. Chief of which is that you can take every event as it comes without having to label it as good or bad. And if you accept life's experiences without labeling them, you can enjoy almost anything.

"So, Larry, I'm telling you about the Game Room, first, to suggest you look at the things we're about to teach you as a game. That will make it easier for you. And, second, because I want you to see the importance of understanding the target. Whoever or whatever the target is. Once your target has been identified, there's nothing you can do to further your case better than preparation will further it. Study the target in advance. Read the files, whatever files are made available to you. Read the literature, whatever books and articles on the subject you can find. Once you know the basic facts and all the available details, you'll start to see the nuances as you learn new facts. You'll develop an intuitive sense of what fits and doesn't fit. That's when you're ready."

A knock on the door. Miles answered, and in walked a sturdy Englishman in a sweater and shirt, no necktie, a red anorak. Immediately he reminded me of a policeman, someone who'd walked a beat until he graduated to plainclothes work. "We're ready, sir," he said to Miles.

Miles introduced me to my new minder, who looked to be about sixty, and who may or may not have been a copper. I didn't ask, but I will always think of him as one. He said to me, "I'd like to take you for a little walk now, if you don't mind, sir. Right this way, please." Miles said he'd leave us to it.

When we got out of the hotel onto Albemarle Street, the copper told me there were watchers covering us. "You lead, sir, wherever you want to go, we'll go. Take your time, sir. As long as you want to walk, we'll walk. Then, when we stop, I want you to point out all the watchers to me."

"How many of them are there?"

"Oh, I wouldn't know, sir."

"Do you mind?" I said, and with that I slipped off the copper's red anorak. Handed it to the doorman. Asked him to be so kind as to send it up to the Professor's suite. I thought I was good.

When we'd gone a way, up Albemarle Street, through Bruton Place, and then the little park in Berkeley Square, and up Curzon Street, past Geo. F. Trumper, barber of royalty and purveyor of fine gentlemen's toiletries, and past the White Elephant Club, and I turned in to the Shepherds Market and wound my way onto Piccadilly and stopped there, the copper said, "Keep going. I want to give you a fair chance, sir."

So I kept going, up Piccadilly, and through the tunnel under Duke of Wellington Place and into Green Park, and, of course, several times along the way, I turned as if I'd changed my mind or forgotten something, and scanned the whole crowd first before focusing on any individuals, and I paid special attention to everyone coming out of the foot tunnel under Duke of Wellington Place, a classic choke point if there ever was one. Then I stopped. On a footpath in Green Park.

"Now, sir, who's following us?"

"The woman in the Burberry mac and the green scarf who just came out of the tunnel. And that chap over there, the one sitting on the bench now."

The copper pulled a little walkie-talkie out of his trousers pocket then, and said, "Raise your hands."

The woman in the Burberry mac and the scarf raised her hand. The man on the bench didn't. But four others did—three men, one woman. The copper pointed them out to me.

"Well, fuck me and the horse I rode in on!"

"Yes sir. I understand what you're saying, sir."

Three of them were a little way in front of us rather than behind us. "How'd they beat us through the tunnel?"

"I imagine, sir, they jumped the railings and crossed through the traffic.

"The point is, sir, what Mr. Copeland wanted me to get across to you is, you'll never beat good watchers. That was just a straightforward tail job. I don't suppose you've ever heard of a 'rolling tail'?"

He stood there for a moment, drawing circles in the air. "It's something like a wheel, sir. You see, the watchers are watching from in front. And I don't mean they're watching you over their shoulders. They're coming toward you, and when they've walked past you, they circle round and come at you from the front again, only this time in a different coat, with a different walking stick, or no walking stick this time. Different wig. Different way of walking. Different person entirely, by the look of them.

"That's the way it works, sir," the copper went on, "and they've got stationary watchers too. You walk by them, they call in your location and direction. Pass you on to the next stationary watchers. So the point Mr. Copeland asked me to make to you, sir, is that you're never going to be able to reliably spot every professional watcher that's been deployed against you. So don't ever believe you've managed that, sir."

I knew he was right.

"And, of course, sir, just standing here having this conversation isn't exactly secure. There's no one within fifty yards of us, sir, so you might think we're secure, talking quietly, real calm like, sir. But the truth is a listener with a good microphone could be listening to every word we're saying, sir. Or someone could be filming us, and once they've filmed us, all they've got to do is show our conversation to a lip-reader and, Bob's your uncle, they know everything we've said.

"I was supposed to get a cab now, sir, and deliver you to Mr. Copeland in Eaton Square. But since you've already conveniently led us this far in the right direction—it was uncanny, sir, was what I was thinking, like he was just willing you toward him with his mind—we're already most of the way there. So I suppose we ought to just walk the rest of the way. If you don't mind, sir."

"Let's go."

Miles was waiting for us on the corner where Upper Belgrave flows into Eaton Square. After the copper handed me off, Miles led me into Eaton Row, where he stopped in front of a mews cottage and rang the doorbell.

A beat later, a buzzer sounded, and the lock clicked and Miles and I went in. We climbed a dimly lit revolving staircase and emerged two floors up in a darkened bedroom, two walls of which had been taken over by circuit boards and electronic devices. There were two MI5 men and an American up there.

They welcomed Miles like an old friend, and me like I couldn't be all bad if I was with Miles.

Miles and I, and one of the Englishmen, went one floor down to the kitchen to brew a pot of tea and chat, and then we took a tray of tea and biscuits back upstairs to share with everyone.

After we'd had a cuppa, civilities first, the American showed me a chart, a diagram of a house. Somewhere in Eaton Square, according to the chart, but it didn't give a house number. Almost every room in the house was bugged. In every room that had a phone, the phone was hot-miked. Normal phones, Miles said, when the handset's in the cradle, they turn off. When a phone's been hot-miked, it's always on, even when the handset's in the cradle the microphone in the mouthpiece is transmitting. In most of the rooms without phones, hidden microphones had been installed.

One of the MI5 men looked like a movie-star spy. He was slim and tan and silver-haired, and wearing a fine gray suit with pencil stripes. He looked like the sort of fellow with a gold cigarette case in his breast pocket, engraved with the initials of his father.

"From here, Larry," the movie star said, "all of our recordings go to the Tower of Babel, which is the service's name for its transcription centre. Where all telephone intercepts and microphone circuits are transcribed. Taps and bugs, I mean. We call a 'bug' a microphone circuit, even though our friend Mr. Copeland insists on calling it a 'sneaky.' In spite, I might add, of our continuing requests that he desist. We've been considering formal action if he doesn't." He smiled a movie star's smile.

"So the point is," Miles said, "from now on, think of every room you're ever in as a potential recording studio. Never say anything on your telephone, or in your hotel room, or in an office, or in an elevator, or a car, that you don't want everyone to hear. Think of every hotel room or strange bedroom you're ever in as a movie set. Even if you've searched for hardware, it's pretty damned hard these days to know when anything is secure—now that camera lenses and microphones have been reduced to something approaching microscopic."

After a few more minutes, we said goodbye and left them to their listening. I remember that, while Miles and I gyred and gimbled down the stairs, turning and turning, I was thinking, whoever it was they were listening to, the poor sod didn't have a chance.

Back in the suite at Brown's.

Miles said, "There are witting agents and unwitting agents, and at first every agent should be an unwitting agent.

"Let's say, for example, the target is a file that's kept in an office in a government ministry building in Whitehall. You know which ministry, which building, which department, which bureaucrat seems to be responsible for the file. But you don't know his telephone number, or the location of his office, you don't even know what floor it's on. You don't know if he keeps the file in his personal safe in his own office, or he leaves it to his secretary to keep in her safe. For that matter, you don't even know his secretary's name. You don't know if the file stays in the same place all day, or if it's handled by several people daily, moves around the office during the day, and is only locked up in the safe at night.

"You do some homework and identify a junior executive, a confidential secretary, a messenger, a cleaner, and two girls from the typing pool, all of whom work in the same department as the bureaucrat who seems to be responsible for the file. Each one of them has potential to become your agent. But before you go about determining whether they have existing vulnerabilities you can exploit, or you go about creating vulnerabilities to exploit when you recruit them—you'd better find out first if they can actually be of any use to you. No point telling fat Sally from the typing pool she's the most beautiful woman you've ever laid eyes on if she's never heard of the file and doesn't have access to it.

"So, once you've identified your likely candidates, the first thing you've got to do is feel them out in a way that doesn't arouse their suspicion. This oral feeling-out process is one of the core techniques of espionage, Larry. It's much more important than you could ever imagine at first. It's known as elicitation. Elicitation can be used to get important information from an unwitting source. Or it can be used to interview potential agents to determine whether they might be suitable for recruitment.

"Elicitation is going to come easy to you, Larry, believe me. Because you may not know it, you may've never given it a name, but it's something you're already very good at. The ability to relate to and empathize with almost anyone, to genuinely like almost anyone and see their point of view—all that's essential to effective elicitation. And you have all that by the ton, Larry."

Miles looked over my shoulder.

I hadn't even known the copper was in the bedroom. But now he stepped out of it, saying, "'Ello sirs," and sat down beside me on the couch.

"Elicitation is the subtlest form of interrogation," the copper said. "It can be applied to either friendly or hostile subjects, and its objective is to obtain information from them without their realization they've served as sources. Elicitation, sir, is an indirect form of interrogation, characterized by the use of subterfuge, an apparently casual conversation shaped in such a manner as to obtain the desired information without the subject becoming aware of a deliberate attempt to gain information of intelligence value.

"Now, I probably don't need to tell you, sir, because Mr. Copeland says you're already a genius at this, even if you never knew it, but sometimes to get secrets or confidences out of someone you have to tell them secrets or confidences of your own. You might think of it as an ice breaker, or as a trade. But, of course, sir, in our work, you can't just tell them *real* secrets. And you can't really tell them made-up secrets. Not if you're ever going to meet them again, because those made-up secrets don't hold up. So, sir, as our Mr. Copeland taught me a long time ago, what you've got to tell them is 'nothing, and lots of it, with an air of great secrecy.'"

Now the copper laughed at his own joke, and I'd seen him smile a lot, but that was the only time I ever saw him laugh.

"There *is* one thing I can tell you, sir, which maybe is beyond your ken, at least consciously. And that is what we call the negative approach to elicitation. What our studies have shown, you see, is that when the subject is a tough nut— and I don't mean he's being evasive because he knows we're interrogating him, because he *doesn't* know, but when it's just his nature not to say too much— well, we found that nothing works better toward getting our questions answered than a negative approach. What you do, sir, is say something like 'No one here could possibly know where those records go after your office has processed them.'

"And you'd be surprised, sir, when you put it that way, how many people want to prove you wrong."

That night the copper took me to a pub in the West End, and just before I walked in, he stood out on the sidewalk with me and told me my name was Piet Jensen, that I was from Amsterdam, and I had twenty minutes to get someone to buy me a pint, and get that same someone to tell me his name, his birth date, what political party he voted for in the last general election, what he does for work, and the names of his wife and kids, if any.

Well, I didn't know anything at all about Amsterdam, except that they serve hashish in bars there and there's a district where naked ladies sit in windows waiting for customers, none of which I'd ever seen. I'd been through Schiphol a few times, but never gone into the city. So I picked my target and introduced myself to him, saying I was Pete Jensen, from Amsterdam by way of Chicago, where'd I'd lived since I was two, and what are you drinking, mate, let me buy you a jar. I got all the information the copper had challenged me to get, and more, and it didn't take me twenty minutes.

I know English people are reserved, think Americans who say "Have a nice day!" to total strangers are nutters. But I'm good at this. I've been making friends with total strangers all my life. Travel like I always had until I washed up on this sunny strand and you've got to learn to fit in. My new mate bought the second round.

An hour later, another local. I remember the copper and I walked right past the big revolving New Scotland Yard sign on our way to our second drinking establishment of the night. Outside the front door, standing right under the name of the proprietor, the copper gave me a new name and background and a seemingly only slightly-more-complicated assignment. What I didn't know was the copper had a confederate inside, a blond, crew-cut American who interrupted me in the middle of my spiel, called me by my real name, told me drunkenly that we went to high school together. But I dealt with it and kept up talking to my target, until the copper, who'd been hovering at the bar rail listening, got my eye and gave me a signal that meant "Meet me in the loo." Where he said, "Bloody 'ell, sir! We can stop right 'ere. Because you're already better at this than I ever was!"

And, the next morning, when the copper met Miles and me for breakfast in the suite, and told Miles about our pub crawl, Miles said, "I told you he's a natural."

After breakfast, the copper said to me, "Goodbye, sir, and good luck," and then took his leave, and Miles went straight back to how to get that file out of the ministry building in Whitehall.

"So, you've done your elicitation, Larry. Slowly and cautiously, you've learned the file does travel around the office most days, while different people read it, or work on it, and it's only locked up at night. You've also learned the file does frequently pass through the typing pool, and each of the typists is occasionally left alone with it in there, right next to a Xerox machine. And you've determined that, of the two typists you've identified, one of them is happily married and has a family and is relatively secure, and the other one is lovelorn and broke and has a four-year-old daughter she's not sure how she's ever going to be able to afford school uniforms for.

"Well, you can guess, Larry, which one becomes your agent. But you don't just approach her and tell her the truth, that you work for the KGB and you'd like her to steal a top secret file for you. You build up a relationship with her. Very slowly. Maybe it's a friendship. Maybe it's a romance. Maybe it's a friendship she hopes might become a romance. The key is that she comes to rely on you for something. For a couple of nice dinners out every week that she could never afford otherwise, for helping her out whenever she needs someone to watch her child, for telling her she's beautiful, for small loans every now and then—whatever it is you can make her need.

"Once she considers you her friend, and you've built up some credits in your favor by doing things for her, you still don't tell her you're from the KGB and ask her to please go betray her country for you now.

"But what you might tell her, Larry, for example, is that you work for an insurance firm and your boss has been pestering you to get an inside track on underwriting the account for her ministry. 'It really would help me,' you say to her, 'if you could get me a directory of all the employees in your department, and their addresses and phone numbers, so that we could get a head start on analyzing the risk. If I could just get that, my boss would get off my back, and I might even get a promotion.'

"Well, you're not really asking her for much, are you? And even if she realizes that, technically, you're asking her to commit a security violation of the sort the security officers are always warning everyone in the office about, she'll very likely be able to rationalize to herself that it's such a small and trivial violation that she just doesn't have the heart to refuse you, her friend. It's not like you're asking her to steal a top secret file or anything like that.

"You can see where this is going, can't you, Larry?" Miles said. "Typically, this is the first sort of task given a new agent—the theft of a classified telephone directory, or any small item the recruiter can present a plausible reason for wanting. Whatever it is, it should carry a very low security classification.

"Your agent, not even witting she's an agent yet, wrestles with her conscience, but then decides to do as you've asked her. She removes the directory from her desk at the end of the day, slips it out of the office, which she's not supposed to do, delivers it to you, then worries herself sick about it. For the next two nights, every sound she hears from her bed is the security officers about to knock on her door. But instead, you give her the directory back, she carries it into her office and slips it into her desk, and starts to feel very silly indeed about all the worrying she's been doing. She's now a little bit pregnant.

"The next time it's easier. And the time after that, easier still. Even though it's something slightly more classified you've asked her for, she gives it to you. Because you're her friend and she needs your friendship, or because your boss at the insurance agency's been giving you bonuses for all the good information you've been coming up with, and you've been splitting those bonuses with her. She's dependent on you now.

"By the time you ask her for the file, which is top secret, after all, and of no conceivable use to an insurance company, she realizes, of course, that she's an agent, and is involved in some sort of espionage. You've desensitized her conscience, carefully, slowly; but now her sense of patriotism kicks in. Even though she needs the money, most people just aren't willing to betray their countries without a strong ideological reason. So she confronts you: 'You've been lying to me! Who are you *really* working for? Where is all this information *really* going?'

"Larry, this is where your secondary cover comes in. You still don't say to her, 'You're right, I'm a KGB officer, and you've been betraying Britain.' You say to her you work for another British government ministry which has been tasked with oversight of her ministry, and you're an investigator they've assigned to probe her ministry's security measures. Or, if you don't think something like that will fly, you tell her, 'You're right, of course, I am an intelligence officer. I work for Canadian intelligence, and I'm sorry I've deceived you all this time.'

"Well, Britain and Canada are sister countries. They even share the same queen, don't forget. With all this money and attention flowing in to her, your agent really doesn't see why diplomatic niceties and technicalities should keep the Canadian government from seeing the file.

"You see, Larry," Miles said, wiping his glasses now, "the way to recruit agents is slowly, sympathetically, and so that, when they finally realize they're spying, they have no idea who they're really spying for. Most spies don't know for which intelligence service they're working."

It came to me right then that, if truth be told, I didn't know for certain either. *Who the hell is paying for this suite, Miles?* I wanted to know, but wasn't going to ask again.

He put his glasses back on. "So she gives you the file. Now you own her," Miles said, with a lot of joy and a bit of sadness in his voice. "Agent-recruiting is one thing, and it's based on trust and friendship. Agent-handling is something else entirely. The key to agent-handling is control. Probably your girlfriend from the typing pool will never set eyes on you again after she gives you the file. Unless you meet her one last time to introduce her to her permanent handler, who'll soon set up a whole new structure for dealing with her. It's called regularizing the contact. There's a reason the British services call agent-handlers 'controllers.'"

That afternoon I formally met the blond, crew-cut American asshole who'd interrupted me in the second pub the night before. "Larry," Miles said, "this is John. He's from Texas, and he works in the embassy, where his job description is Human Toolchest. You'd be amazed at the things John can do, Larry. John can do almost anything that needs to be done, except recruit an agent. He scares them all off."

Miles left then, and after I got over being mad at the new guy for interrupting my demonstration of bullshit artistry the night before, he actually turned out to be pretty nice.

He was chewing gum and his jaw never stopped working.

He was about forty—maybe seven or eight years older than me.

He was a twitchy son of a gun. Not too tall, not too short. Not handsome, or ugly. But twitchy, and his skin was tanned but mottled and his hair was short and blond but patchy. He seemed to run on higher-octane fuel than most of us humans.

He sat down in the chair across from me in the sitting room, started tapping his feet.

I said, "Miles means the American Embassy, doesn't he?"

"Yeah."

"The American Embassy here in London?"

"Yeah."

"Could you take me to your office there?"

"Nah. Maybe Miles will. I won't."

"Your name's not really John, is it?"

"Nah."

"You really from Texas?"

"Yeah."

"Mind if I call you Tex?"

"Whatever floats your boat."

"Okay, Tex, when we're done today, would you let me go with you to Grosvenor Square and watch you go into the embassy, past the guards and all?"

"That'd be all right with me. You *might* not be as dumb as you look." He had the palest blue eyes, like certain Labrador retrievers. "You done now?" he said. "Gonna let me talk?"

"Fire away."

He stood up now, moving toward the window, on patrol. "Life is all about escape routes," he said. "Don't forget that. Ever."

He didn't stay in front of the window for long. He turned around and said to me, "The moment I walked in here, I checked the doors, the windows, the street below us, took in every possibility. Escape routes are only escape routes if you know they're there. Plan. Prepare. Do your reconnaissance.

"I'm from West Texas originally," he went on. "Out near El Paso. But I once lived in the hills above San Diego. Of course, I studied all the roads leading in and out of my neighborhood, and taught my wife to vary her routes every time she left. Which, I might add, she almost never did." He shook his head. "People are lazy. They grow complacent. But I did the homework and asked her to vary her routes, even if she didn't. I knew every road in and out of the neighborhood we lived in for miles, every twist and turn. Every option. Every shortcut. I always figured if someone came to get me, I'd know the roads out better than they did."

There was something about Tex just on the verge of paranoia. You could see it. Almost smell it. But the thing was, when you heard him talking, he was so sincere about his thoughts, and so confident he was right, you came around to his way of thinking. He was reasonable and logical, everyone else was stupid and lazy. His life force was stronger than ours, because he tried harder. Tex wasn't the sort of guy you'd ever want to spend a lot of time in the same room with. But he held your attention. There was no denying that.

"And every morning that I lived there," Tex said, "I got up at first light and ran. Up the mountain. Around the mountain. Down the mountain. Of course, I was keeping myself fit. But I was also doing recon. Learning my environment better than anyone else would ever know it.

"Now, if you're wondering why someone might come to get me, don't ask. But the point is, I'm aware it's a possibility. If the day ever came when they did come for me, and I sensed there were too many of them or they were too well organized for me to escape by road, I'd also have the hills. I was quite certain no one could know the slopes and trails and hidey-holes in those mountains behind my house better than I did. No one."

Something about Tex told you this wasn't just a nice story he'd made up to illustrate his theme. He'd lived on the run. Deep down he was still running. Tex the Human Toolchest was at the moment pacing around the dining room. I could hear him but couldn't see him. "I loved my house," he said. "Really loved it. Adobe. Old wood beams. Barrel tiles. Two acres all of my own. It was nicer than anything I'd ever thought I'd own. Looked for all the world like something a Spanish conqueror had built there a hundred years earlier and it hadn't been changed since. Even the swimming pool looked old. So, of course, I was prepared to protect it, if I could.

"Well, I'm sure you've seen the fires they have out in Southern California," Tex said while reappearing in the sitting room. "As soon as I heard about them, I developed a plan for protecting my house. I kept emergency suitcases packed for my wife and kids. Clothes, food, medicines, plenty of money, and even water inside. I kept the cases stored in a cabinet in the garage, where I could load them, along with my wife and kids and dogs, into the station wagon and send them down the road at a moment's notice.

"But if a fire came, I was going to stay as long as I could. Hosing my house, my trees, by brush, keeping everything wet and cool as long as I could. Sometimes that's what it takes to keep a fire off, to make it choose your lazy neighbor's house instead of yours.

"Well, you've got to recognize your own strengths and weaknesses," Tex said. "The unexamined life isn't worth living. Knowing how dogged I am, I realized I might get carried away up there protecting my house too long. So that, by the time I was willing to leave, give up and let the fire take it, there'd be no safe route left for me to make it off the property.

"Which," Tex said, deadpan, "is why I kept four scuba tanks, rigged together, and a regulator and weight belt in the storage room beside my pool. I figured I could last underwater for a little more than four hours. And I figured that had to be long enough for the fire to roll over the house, take it, and then pass on. Life is all about escape routes."

With that, he went to the window again and looked down on the street. He said, "Let's get out of here," while he was already heading toward the door. I followed. Once we were out on the sidewalk, his first objective seemed to be to contradict everything the copper and his friends had warned me of just the day before.

"Miles told me you spent yesterday with the watchers. I'm sure those assholes did their best to impress upon you how unbeatable they are. They're good. There's no doubt about it. But you can bet they also stacked the deck against you to make a point. True, you're not going to be able to beat six well-trained men working as a disciplined surveillance unit. Let alone that fuckin' Ferris wheel they probably told you about. But did they tell you how many watchers it takes to run the Ferris wheel? Twenty minimum. More like forty to make it really work. What are the odds forty watchers are ever going to be assigned to follow you?"

He answered his own question, "Slim," and then kept talking. About how, if I ever got into trouble it almost certainly wouldn't be because of an elaborate surveillance operation. But because one or two of the wrong people happened to see me doing something suspicious.

So, anything covert I might need to do, I needed to plan it carefully first and use some simple principles every field man learns. Tex could only teach me the basics, he said, and after I understood them it would be up to me to use my own imagination and resourcefulness to make them work wherever I was.

To avoid casting suspicion on yourself, Tex instructed, avoid suspicious meetings. An American consular officer bumping into a Soviet nuclear physicist in the men's room during intermission at the Bolshoi is one thing, and suspicious enough that it will likely cause stepped-up surveillance on both of them. But the same American chancing upon the same Soviet twice more in a year will lead the Soviet to a charming little interrogation cell in a basement off Dzerzhinsky Square, still warm with the blood of its last guest.

Cutouts prevent contact or recognition between people who're involved in the same undertaking but don't know each other and don't need to. Cutouts can also be used to limit contact between persons who do know each other but, if seen together, might arouse suspicion. Used properly, cutouts don't even know from whom they're receiving or to whom they're delivering.

Let's say, Tex proposed, that you're in Indian country now, and you've got something you need to get to Miles, but you're not willing to carry it across the border. Not with all the security you saw at the airport coming in. Well, we've got specialists that can handle things like that. But you never know if they're under surveillance, or if they're working both sides. So, whatever it is you have to give them, you don't give it to them directly. You load it in a dead drop and signal that it's loaded.

In this case, assume the location of the dead drop and the loaded and unloaded signals have already been established and both you and the cutout are aware of them. The dead drop could be anywhere, as long as it's easy to get to, in the sort of place both you and the cutout might normally be seen, and inconspicuous, or so obvious that it's hidden in plain sight. And the dead drop could be anything, really, as long as it's a reasonable place to hide something until someone else can pick it up. It could be a plastic bag taped to the back of the cistern in the second stall in the Gents' loo in The King's Arms pub, just like in the movies, or the space behind a loose brick in the churchyard. It could be the hollow of a tree. *Dubok* is Russian for "oak tree," and also the KGB term for "dead drop."

"You speak Russian, Tex?"

"Yeah."

"Any others?"

"Yeah."

"Such as?"

Tex ignored my impertinence and went on with the lesson. Your dead drop could also be, for example, the front desk of a busy hotel. Leave a package or an envelope with the concierge, give him a small pourboire for his trouble and attentiveness, and ask him to hold the package until the arrival of Mr., or Mrs., or Miss, whatever the preestablished name is. Or, if you don't want to risk security cameras in the hotel recording your transaction with the concierge, mail the envelope or the package to the hotel, marked PLEASE HOLD FOR THIS GUEST'S ARRIVAL.

Once you've loaded the dead drop, you signal that it's ready for servicing. The signal could be almost anything. A chalk mark on a certain lamppost. A certain symbol sprayed onto a certain wall that is already covered with graffiti. A flowerpot moved into a certain windowsill. A red carnation carelessly left in the lapel of the suit jacket you send to the dry cleaners. A classified ad in *The Times*. It could be almost anything, as long as it's simple, inconspicuous, and preestablished. The cutout services the drop, collects your package, and delivers it, probably to another drop. That way the cutout doesn't know who he picked up from or who he's delivering to.

Once you've loaded the dead drop and signaled that it's loaded, you're done. Unless there's an unloaded signal to watch for. It's an added complication, but it can be used to give the sender peace of mind that his package has been received. Peace of mind can be very important in the field.

Tex and I were rounding into Grosvenor Square, at the far end of which was the American Embassy. On top of it perched a huge gilded eagle, wings spread, attempting to fly off with the ugliest building in London. For a moment I thought Tex was going to take me to the embassy. But instead he led me to a tourists-and-shoppers' restaurant in Oxford Street. I don't remember the name of the place, but it was vaguely reminiscent of Scotland and cattle, I think, and I'm certain the decor was suffused with the sort of warm red Fellini might've painted over an entire movie set. We sat in there on red velvet seats, at a red table, with our backs to red wallpaper, while Tex told me where all the exits were and how he'd scoped them all out while we'd walked into the restaurant and while he was busy with the pretext of asking the waiter if we could please have a different table. Then all we ordered, to the disgust of our Italian waiter in his tuxedo, were a couple of pots of tea.

"I'm repeating all these basics," Tex told me, "because I want you to understand how important the principles are. If there were a standard way to teach you countersurveillance and escape and evasion, I would. That would make it easier for both of us. But if there were a standard technique, the other side would learn it and it would never work again. So what you have to do is learn to think through the problem, and then to improvise.

"One of the first considerations is your appearance. This is the place where I'm supposed to teach you disguise. You can dye your hair, of course. Cut it differently. Wear a beard and glasses. Funny clothes. But the fact is, you're one tall drink of water, and whether we dress you up in a blue suit or a white suit, or a baseball player's uniform, or a surgeon's scrubs, you're still going to stand out, head and shoulders above the crowd—as the cliché goes.

"Anyone who knows your height is going to spot you. With a couple of exceptions, which you should think about. First, it appears to me you're all legs. Like Big Bird. You don't actually look very tall while sitting. Then you stand up, and up, and up. So sit. At a table. Maybe in a wheelchair. Or in a car. Or on a bench. You're less likely to get spotted while sitting, or lying down, than standing. Which isn't the case with everyone.

"Second, there *is* a way you can shorten yourself while walking. Just bend your knees enough and your head will come down six or seven inches. Hell, you can bend your knees and then stoop like an old man and come down two feet if you want. But that's just going to draw undue attention. If you keep your shoulders over your hips while you're bending your knees, from the waist up it doesn't look unnatural. Practice it in front of a mirror, walking back and forth. Once you've got the gait down, you can disguise the fact that you're bending your knees by covering them—wearing a long raincoat or overcoat or cape that comes to your calves. That's just something to keep in mind. I've seen it work before."

We chatted on, and drank our tea, and right before we left came the point at which I finally realized all those friendly chats I'd had with Miles since almost the moment I met him were elicitation sessions. We were good friends, no doubt, but he'd also been compiling a file on me.

Tex said, "Miles told me you told him about how your father used to time it so he could punch through yellow lights, and then turn right away, so if another car was tailing your car the tail car would have to speed up and follow you through the same light." I didn't even remember telling Miles about that. Next Tex said, "And Miles also told me your father taught you to vector watchers into terrain where there's only one way for them to go unless they want to turn around and lose you. Like a cattle chute, is how I think of it. And Miles said the watchers also noted with some approval how you led them through Bruton Place, which is about as good as a tunnel, and then through an actual tunnel. Good instincts. But the problem is, Big Bird, you didn't go far enough. Now let's get outta here."

For the next two days, in Oxford Street and Regent Street and the Haymarket, and Covent Garden, and in Hyde Park, Tex taught me how to live with watchers. First off, if you don't happen to have any surreptitious plans for the moment, you might want to make them show themselves just so you know they're there, but you don't even have to do that. As long as what you're doing is innocent, let them watch. The more innocent things you do under the eyes of the watchers, the more brownie points you build up.

Don't ever get cute. Don't make eye contact with a watcher. Don't play cat and mouse with the watchers. Don't send a bottle of wine to their table across the room. Remain oblivious and go on doing whatever you're doing.

If it becomes your task to create a dead drop, and you're in an urban setting, site it someplace near where there are lots of busy people around for a courier to blend in and out of. Make sure there are multiple routes in and out of the drop site, and that at least one of them includes features suitable for flushing watchers into sight. Make sure the site is a logical place for both you and the courier to be.

If you've got to elude a watcher or watchers, there are certain escape and evasion techniques you can utilize. E&E. Whatever you do, keep it natural. Create an innocent cover for every one of your actions, and for every place you go.

The longer the watchers aren't suspicious you're trying to lose them, the better off you'll be. When you want to suddenly reverse your direction on the sidewalk, do it next to a postbox. Drop something in the box just before you turn around. Or step into a phone booth like you're going to make a call, pat your pockets for a coin, swear at yourself for not having one, and then walk back the direction you came from. If you want to look around, stop at a corner like you're momentarily lost, then do it. These are old tricks, but they also happen all the time in real life, and the watchers just won't be sure. Especially if you've built up points for good behavior in the past.

Escape routes are everything. Walk into a department store, or a hotel lobby, or a movie theater, and while the watcher's floating outside—doesn't want to betray himself by following you right in—step out the back door. Pronto, and then keep moving, down the alley or up the street, into another alley or doorway. Keep turning. Keep expanding, exponentially, the possibilities of where you may've gotten off to. It helps if you've cased the area in advance. Whatever you do, keep it innocent-looking.

Through those two days, Tex watched me loading, unloading, and siting dead drops, walking down stairs into tube stations and then straight up more stairs and out on the other side of the street, then drifting away in the crowd, and strolling casually into hotel lobbies and then out side doors and into taxis which I exited just as we got around corners architecturally propitious enough to provide blind spots; and rushing into department stores or restaurants and into Gents' loos I stayed in so long that, if they were still on me, eventually one or both of Tex's two tame watchers from Michigan and Louisiana, or so I was told, would venture in to see if I was still there. I made a game of it, and it was glorious fun, even though Tex wasn't always pleased with my work.

When I did good I was Scholar—which was my nickname in college, and no one I knew nowadays even knew about that, so how the hell did Tex know it?—and when I failed, I was Big Bird, as in "Nice try, Big Bird. But you just screwed the pooch. Let's try it again, and if you don't get it right this time, I'm going to strip you naked and wrap your entire body in duct tape and let you pull it off. Hair by hair."

I got better at it, I suppose, and it came easier once I started to realize the key to it wasn't the deftness of my moves but how well I'd thought them through in advance. I taught myself to start at the objective and think backwards from there. Tex kept increasing the complexity of what he wanted me to be able to do.

Next stop: brief encounters.

Sometimes a cutout isn't the solution. Sometimes you need to meet face-to-face with a source or agent to rekindle their trust in who they're dealing with. Or maybe you've got to pass something to a certain contact, and a dead drop hasn't been preestablished. Maybe no courier is available. Whatever the reason, you resort to what's known in the trade as a brief encounter. The objective is to engineer the meeting so that it's unseen by watchers, but to make it look so innocent that, even if it's seen and filmed, it looks entirely above suspicion.

The meeting appears to be accidental and unplanned, but the key to the whole thing is meticulous planning. Objective. Where. When. Recognition signals. Bona fides. Abort signal. Contact procedure. Delivery method. Cover for action. Fallback schedule and site, or sites. Both participants have got to have every one of these elements down cold before they venture into a brief encounter. And on their way to the accidental meeting, they also need to make sure they're clear of watchers. It's a very elaborate dance for a contact that will last less than half a minute.

Tex drilled me in the principles and then watched me bluff my way through five brief encounters in a single morning. Then he delivered me back to Miles in time for lunch. "Look," Tex said, very quietly, just before we got back to Brown's, "there's an exercise coming up that you don't know about yet, and I just want to warn you the rules of the game will say the watcher team is allowed only five members. But they'll try to fuck you. What they'll do right about the time they start after you is call the Metropolitan Police and put out an APB on you, give a fake name and your description with instructions to every policeman in London to report a sighting, and to follow but do not approach the subject. Then the watchers will be talking to each other and listening to the police band while they hunt you. So think it through, and don't get cocky."

Back in the sitting room in the suite in Brown's, Miles said, "I hope you enjoyed your time with John, Larry, because he's had you doing things you may never have to do again in the rest of your life. While we still have the Human Toolchest in our midst, why don't we talk about a couple of other things no one's ever been better than John at, which you also will probably never have to do.

"First of all," Miles went on, "let's assume you've elicited the hell out of the ladies of the typing pool, and the janitors, and the file clerks, and the confidential secretaries, and the junior and senior executives of the ministry office you need to get that file from. And it is the purest office in the history of the world: Its entire staff is devoid of human frailty. You've even tried provocations, but no one has risen to the bait. You've got nothing on anybody. You also can't get your hooks into a thief willing to steal the file for you. But you happen to have been in the office the other day on a pretext, and you saw the file and a vulnerability in the way it's handled, and you've been instructed to get it at all costs."

Miles turned to face me. "You work for the KGB, Larry, and you figure they'll haul you home and shoot you if you don't get it anyway, so you may as well take the risk." Now he turned to Tex. "So, John, how does Larry go about stealing that file?"

Tex didn't like this turn in the conversation. I could see it on his face, and I took it as a sign of deficiency in me he'd spotted along the way. "Well, this isn't really the place to be learning to steal anything. We don't really have the sort of props or setup here necessary to do a run-through, Miles. And it's not your job to steal it yourself, Scholar. It's not recommended. It's highly unrecommended. So all I'll say about it is pretty similar to what I've told you about everything else.

"Do your recon. Plan. Prepare. Think it through. Be opportunistic. Know your escape routes. Act natural. Act like you own the place, in fact. Beneath your calm, be hyperaware. And when you're actually doing whatever it is you've planned, don't move fast, move slow. So slow that you do it right the first time and you're sure of it. Because the way to get caught is to rush through it, and when you're done a tiny question nags at you, so you open the door again to make sure you turned off the lights, or you go back and check to make sure you shut the cabinet drawer all the way—and that's when your train wreck begins."

After a little pause, Tex looked at me and spoke again, in a tone so penitential it made it clear he was sorry for even telling me as little as he'd just told me about burglary. "What I'd thought Miles was going to ask me to talk to you about now is passports."

"Right," Miles said, and while Tex got up and paced about the room, Miles said, "You know, Larry, I told you when you came back for this, we'd teach you about passports. Of course, we have friends in the embassy and back in Washington who could give you a passport if you need one. A passport in any name you want. But passports are traceable, and once you have the name and nationality someone's traveling and hiding under, you're a step closer to finding him. So there's no reason you should want to trust anyone in the embassy or in Washington to know your work name. Because that creates an unnecessary vulnerability. We've already talked about it before, Larry. In this world you want to trust, if not no one, at least as few people as possible."

"And some bureaucratic buttplug in Washington isn't exactly the sort of guy you want to put your trust in," Tex said, plopping down beside me as he said it. The first thing I noticed was he wasn't fidgeting. It was like his supercharger had flamed out all of a sudden. He didn't fall asleep or anything like that. But for once he was sitting there calmly, looking rather like a normal person.

"So anyway, Larry," Miles said, "the key to beating a system is understanding the system. Once you understand it, you can almost always devise a way to beat it. And when it comes to issuing United States passports for private use, the State Department sees fit to issue them by mail to any American citizen who fills out the application and submits it with a check, his signature, two photographs, and either his previous passport or his birth certificate. No other form of proof of citizenship will do."

"And that's the flaw in the system," Tex said. "If you've never applied for a passport before, they don't have a photograph of you on record. When you submit an application by mail, since you don't have a previous passport, all you have to submit as evidence you're an American citizen is your birth certificate. Which isn't a photo ID. So they've got nothing to compare the photos you've submitted with a known photograph of the applicant. They don't have easy access to driver's license photos or other databases. That's hard to believe, but true. So I'm not suggesting, Scholar, that you break the laws of the United States, but escape routes are everything, and a nice fresh escape passport can help you along your way."

"So, Larry," Miles said, with a twinkle in his eye now, "if a guy who happened to live in New York needed a new U.S. passport with his face in it and someone else's name, he might want to head over to Hoboken or Newark and start eliciting, and keep eliciting, until he finds a nice, broke, morally flexible male American citizen who's about his age and has never even thought of traveling out of the country. Then he might want to help that nice fellow obtain his birth certificate and fill out the first passport application of his life, thoughtfully providing him the photos to be included with the application. And then he might want to pay that fellow five hundred dollars when they drop the application in a mailbox, and promise him another two thousand dollars when the passport comes back in the mail—provided that, when the fellow from New York comes out to pick it up, it's still sealed in the envelope it was sent in."

"And," Tex threw in, "you might want to warn your new partner in crime that if he ever tells anyone about this, you'll make sure he's the one that catches hell, not you."

After that, Tex gave me a little talk about how to stay alive on the run, which I replayed often on my way to this beach. Then Tex and I said goodbyes, and I haven't seen him since—except in my dreams.

The next morning Miles told me that, contrary to popular myth, there is an unbreakable code system: the one-time pad. It's unbreakable because it's based on totally random relationships, and it's used once and then never used again. Oh what a wondrous thing a one-time pad is, to hear Miles tell it, and I was sold. But when I saw a one-time pad, I refused to carry one. Ever. To me, it just didn't seem like there was any way possible to disguise it satisfactorily. It was a code key, and though Miles and I tried, we never came up with a way to make it look like anything else. I had zero confidence I could smooth-talk my way past a customs official or a policeman who'd just had a look at this little pad of paper and asked me to explain it to him.

So much for the one-time pad Miles had planned to give me.

We spent the rest of the morning and all of the afternoon in the reading room of the British Museum. Which is just down the hall and around the corner from the mother of all code keys, the Rosetta stone. The British Museum Reading Room happens to be where Karl Marx invented communism. But Miles and I passed our time there in the company of an obscure metaphysical poet one of whose lesser but longest works became the basis for our code.

For years, I'd been memorizing poetry—little masterpieces I carried with me everywhere, to keep me company when I'd read every book I brought and still had thirty-seven hours to kill before the next flight out of Ougadougou. Even that afternoon in 1985, book codes weren't as foolproof as they used to be, now that codebreaking agencies had scanned almost every edition of almost every book published in the last two hundred years into their databases. Thus the obscure poet and the original manuscript of one of his lesser and, importantly, unpublished works. Miles and I figured probably no one but us and a few curators had seen these lines of verse in a very long time.

I would carry our code in my head, and Miles would keep the only written version of it. That's all I'm going to say about our code.

Back in the suite the next morning, Miles taught me how to disguise encryption as columns of trade statistics, budget projections, or the like, and we established the addresses and fax numbers to which I might in the future mail or fax encoded messages intended for Miles but addressed to Mr. M. Arthur, Mr. M. Chester, or Mr. M. Alan. Any one of them would suffice. And how could I possibly forget it—*Who was the only American President with three first names? Chester Alan Arthur.*

Then Miles told me the rules of the exercise which would be the culmination of all this and would take place the following day.

I would have all the rest of today to case locations and develop a plan for a brief encounter with Miles, which could take place anytime during daylight hours tomorrow, and during which brief encounter I had to successfully pass to Miles the file my poor trusting girlfriend from the ministry in Whitehall had filched for me. The watchers were on their honor not to watch me today, so I could be free to case possible locations. By the end of today, I was to deliver to Miles my written meeting plan for tomorrow. And by zero-dark-thirty tomorrow, I could be sure the watchers, a maximum of five of them, would be in and outside my hotel ready to catch me sneaking out under cover of darkness. No watchers would be allowed to follow Miles unless they encountered him in the course of tailing me.

But I should still probably allow myself plenty of time to lose my own watchers before attempting to make the meeting, Miles suggested, and then he gave me the file. Which sure enough looked like a real ministry file, and was bulky enough that I wasn't going to be able to stuff it into my pants or under my sweater.

It was right then and there that I did for the first time what I'd been trained to do through all of the last several days: I committed a slightly subversive act, somewhere between cheating and taking advantage of a flaw in the system. I wrote my meeting plan down, in code, before I left the suite, told Miles I'd hidden the file in the bedroom and that I was going out now and I'd be back by four to give him my plan and pick up the file. Then I went downstairs with the file in my briefcase, and the plan in an envelope—which I gave to a hall porter along with the not-inconsiderable sum of five pounds for taking the envelope and the meeting plan straight back up to the suite and delivering it to Miles. "Make sure he opens it and reads it." "Not a problem, sir. I'll see to it." By then I was gone.

London was where I first tasted freedom.

When I arrived there with my parents, the Beatles ruled, our Sweet Prince JFK was recently blown away, Carnaby Street was in full bloom, Mods and Rockers were at it in the streets, the amazing newspapers were full of pictures of naked girls and reports of the Profumo sex-and-spies scandal, my father was moving up in his world, and due to certain logistical considerations I would either have to forgo playing Little League baseball or be allowed to take public transport home.

London was deemed by my parents safe enough for me to try. What I had to do was take the 154 bus from Ruislip to Harrow-on-the-Hill. Change to the 258, to Harrow & Wealdstone. There, get on the Bakerloo Extension of the tube, where the Underground was overground. Three stops north and I was in Carpenders Park. Or if I got on the express instead of a local, I could go to Watford Junction and take a local back to Carpenders Park.

At the little kiosk in the station there, if I had sixpence I'd buy a Crunchie. And if I had a shilling, a Crunchie and a Rollo. English chocolates beat the hell out of the Hershey bars and Snickers I'd been raised on. Ten minutes' walk along The Mead to a high concrete wall and signs that said "Ministry of Defence Property KEEP OUT." We lived on the other side of that wall.

I was only eleven, but after I'd established my ability to find my way home from the baseball field behind the American school in Ruislip, my parents gave me the freedom of the city. Let me travel anywhere I wanted to go, by bus or tube, as long as I called home or my father's secretary first and said where I was going. The Bakerloo Line would take you straight to Piccadilly Circus, and from there you could get anywhere.

I saw the Rosetta stone and the Crown Jewels and the Changing of the Guard and the dome of St. Paul's and even the clock of all clocks at the Greenwich Observatory all by myself, and it was thrilling. The Bakerloo Extension wasn't even on the London Underground map I taped up on the wall above my bed in Carpenders Park. I can give myself little chills now just by pulling that map out and poring over it here in the night in Florida. On the map, the Bakerloo line ends at Harrow & Wealdstone. That shows how far out I had to go to get home.

It was all a very long time ago, even then, but one thing I remembered was the locals of the Bakerloo Extension were usually almost empty. If you took an express all the way to Watford Junction, the cars might be pretty full. But if you were riding the local to Hatch End or Carpenders Park, you'd often be the only one in your car, trundling along to that glorious music of wheels and tracks. Then you'd get out and walk home all alone.

It was all rushing back to me now as I sat alone in a train car somewhere on the Bakerloo Extension, watching once-familiar landscape become suddenly familiar again. I felt like crying, or screaming with joy, and why the hell had I let myself come back to London so many times without bothering to come out here? No one was following me. That much I was sure of. I was the only one in the car I was riding in. The cars on either side of it were empty. I'd already ditched the cover of the folder marked MOST SECRET before I got out of the West End, and made sure there was nothing like an electronic beacon buried in the pages I was carrying.

I was carrying them now not in my briefcase, which I'd stored at the

Waterloo Station, but inside one of the two identical black duffel bags I'd bought along with a change of underwear and a space blanket and a torch and a toothbrush and a few other things before I left the West End. I'd left by taxi and bus and tube, and even before I was out of Central London I'd been relatively sure no one was following me.

At Carpenders Park, I got off the train feeling like the last man on earth. No one else got off there. The little station was deserted. The kiosk was closed. Across the street, I went into the newsagent to buy a Crunchie. There was a woman behind the till, but not a single customer around. Walking all the way up The Mead, I didn't see another soul. Then, on the other side of the wall, I arrived in Little America, where the kids in the backyards and their mothers looked at me suspiciously. I wanted to tell them I wasn't a stranger, that this was my neighborhood too. But I couldn't. Or I wouldn't. Something in me didn't want to break the spell by talking.

I walked past the house where our neighbor Roy White died in his bed of a heart attack, and on to the spot in the road where the pale yellow Della Murra ice-cream van would come to a stop with its calliope calling us and half the kids in the neighborhood, all Americans, would run out with our sixpences or shillings to buy ourselves 99 Flakes or ice lollies.

Della Murra was Italian for something, we weren't sure what, but I swore to my father it meant Daily Manure. The ice-cream seller was a swarthy and borderline-chubby young Italian, who smiled a lot but wouldn't give us credit, and had the hots for Elke, the German au pair who lived inside our house and helped take care of Billy and me. We had the hots for her too.

Billy was only three when we rode with my mother to the airport to pick Elke up on her first day in England. "Oh, Mommy, she looks like a movie star!" Billy said, and we were both smitten immediately.

I walked all the way around the circle, took in all the other twenty-four houses in the compound, before I let myself look at our little house. Upstairs, the curtains were open in my room and I could see my wall, my door. Right below it, I almost expected to see my mother in the kitchen window, waiting to hear how I'd done at baseball when I came in the front door. And it could be my father was in the living room watching the BBC.

After a little while I realized I was standing dead still a few steps in front of our door, and barely breathing. That was when I made myself turn away and walk slowly back to the station. No one followed me. I got off the Bakerloo Line at Baker Street Station and rode the Circle Line one and a half times around London. No one was following me. I disembarked at Victoria.

Victoria Station has always been sacred ground to me. The first time I was ever there was with my father. He was wearing a raincoat because it was misting outside, not because of the pigeon that shat on him from the rafters. The pigeon shit didn't actually hit my father, just his coat and his glasses, and once he'd wiped off his bifocals he told me when a bird shits on you it's good luck. And I could share in it too, because look at my shoes.

Ever since then, I'd felt like Victoria Station was a lucky place for me. No one paid any attention to me while I milled around the station listening to the arrival and departure announcements or while I sat in the railway canteen nursing a milky pot of tea and slowly eating a couple of prawn sandwiches. When the station was starting to empty, I checked one of the duffel bags at the Left Luggage window, then milled around awhile longer until I quietly slipped onto the last platform on the left side of the station.

I don't remember the platform number, and I think it's changed since then. But I knew the platform fairly well. Almost ten years earlier, during my mountain boy years, I'd come to this station planning to take a night train to the coast, only to learn the next train to where I was going wasn't scheduled to leave until the morning. But it was already conveniently sitting in the dark on the last platform on the left. With all its doors unlocked, I soon discovered. Well, I'd had a railpass and a mummy bag and not much money with me, and nowhere else to stay, so you can guess where I slept that night. And four or five other nights during other months of my years as a mountain boy.

After I got the hang of it, I learned to find the sleeping cars, where you didn't have to sleep on the floor, and the train workers wouldn't bother you in the morning as long as you hadn't gotten under the covers or messed anything up and you sat up and made yourself look presentable when you started to hear doors slamming and shoes scuffing down the corridors.

So I spent the night before my brief encounter with Miles beneath a space blanket inside a First Class cabin in the train on the last platform on the left in Victoria Station. And at 8:06, I left the train and carried my duffel bag down the platform to the W. H. Smith shop inside the station. I stood for a moment before a stack of books and slipped the Left Luggage ticket into one of them.

When Miles walked in at 8:11 and went to the newspaper shelves, asking for the *International Herald Tribune,* I was squatting in the aisle looking at something on the lowest shelf. When Miles saw me, I said, "The new Jeffrey Archer. The bottom one in the stack. Page one sixty-seven." Then I left the shop, and left the station, and Miles went to Left Luggage with the ticket and picked up the file. That night the copper and captain of the watchers called me in my hotel room just to say, "That was super, sir. Really super." And that was the end of it, the sum total of my training in the dark arts.

A couple weeks later, as a sort of graduation, Miles sent me to the Continent on a little job. The details of which are unimportant here, except to note that, as I began my infiltration, I was scared, this was not a game, I was the son of a spy, and it wasn't Miles's advice but my father's that was resounding in my head.

18 | A UNIFIED THEORY OF THE SECRET WORLD

At first, the secret work was as modest as befit my meager skills, total inexperience, and overconfidence. Miles occasionally would ask me to deliver a package to someone somewhere—a few times in exotic places, but usually just two blocks from the White House, in the Willard Hotel, each time to the same silver-haired, flattopped man in a neat gray suit.

I was to check in, call a phone number in Houston and give the sum of my room number plus the day of the month to whoever answered, then go to my room and wait with DO NOT DISTURB hanging outside on my doorknob, and not to leave for anything, until the man knocked and took the Manila envelope from me without even as much as a secret handshake. Waiting there— the second time I waited almost two full days—seemed more like a test than anything else. But Miles swore it wasn't. He said sometimes the guy just couldn't break away. I never found out who the guy was or who he had to evade to make his collection run.

There was a certain Libyan I might meet in the course of a journey with Mahdi and Jabir to visit Muammar Qadhafi, and, in that event, I was to get as close as possible to the mystery man, eat beside him if I could swing it, and look at the fingers of his right hand. Are there tobacco stains? Small scars? Those were the days when Kremlinologists went into spasms of joy over every nuance of every lapel pin, smile, frown, or runny nose in photos of the wheezing, wizened gang of kleptocrats propped up atop the Red Square reviewing stand at the May Day parade. So I took it seriously. And, as it turned out, yes, there were three thin, roughly parallel white lines, skin that wouldn't tan, near the base of the Libyan's right thumb. We got on pretty well. Sat together drinking little glasses of hot and very sweet mint tea, while he smoked a Gitanes. He told me he used to be a soldier, but now he managed some state farms—and his dream was to retire to a farm of his own in Tuscany someday.

That's it. All I know. I reported to Miles and never heard another word about the guy.

I also did some daring floor-plan work. Apparently the CIA mapmaking department, which both Bill Tharp and my father had told me about, was doing its best to map every square foot of our planet, even indoors. I don't know; I only assumed that was who Miles was supplying the plans. But I did recognize that, whoever wanted them, there was a pattern to their requests.

If I told Miles I'd be going someplace like Japan or England or Germany, Miles would say, "Have a nice trip" or "Write if you get work" and that would be the end of it. But, if it were anyplace in Africa or the Middle East or South Asia I was heading to, usually Miles was interested. Within a few days, he'd get back to me with a shopping list of Intelligence Requirements, items that would be of interest to our friends should I happen to chance upon any information about them while in the target country. By "our friends," I mean Miles's friends— because I didn't know them, or even exactly who they were. By "happen to chance upon," I mean that literally, because Miles warned me not to engage in anything tomfool or deceptive to gain information about items on the list. With the exception only of floor plans.

I don't mean to imply I did anything as bold as cracking safes and stealing blueprints. About all I had to do, if I ever found myself in a building on my list, was get lost on my way to the bathroom. Then count my calibrated thirty-inch steps between the doors and the windows and other features I noted and memorized as I bumbled along my way. Sometimes there were specific questions I'd been given. Like: *At the end of the hall on the right is a double door. How many locks does it have, and what kind are they?* or *Does it open inward or outward? What is beyond that door?* It wasn't even the slightest bit nerve-racking. I never went into a building I wasn't invited into. And, beyond getting lost on the way to the pissoir, I never did anything more devious than ask a protocol officer or a friendly guard to lead me up onto a balcony, or onto the roof, so I could take an overhead picture of the beautiful gardens or the skyline of the city. Along the way, of course, I got to see more of the buildings. But they were palaces, or sports ministries, or private homes—not exactly high-security nuclear weapons facilities I was breaching. The expression "hauling deadwood" often came to mind.

And, in between those infrequent assignments from Miles, what did I do? I lived my life. Staying in South Africa or New York or London with Kim. Sending postcards to my grandmother back in the Green Acres Nursing Home in Milledgeville. Sending cards and letters to my mother back in Florida. Trying to make a buck. Traveling some with Adnan. Traveling more with Muhammad.

I have this strange and beautiful memory of a day in Cairo. At the airport. It seemed to be afternoon, but it might've been morning. We didn't know. Or care much. We were jet-lagged, and wouldn't be staying there. It was Muhammad, Lonnie, Bingham, Jabir, Mahdi, Mustafa, Kim, and me. Maybe one or two others I've forgotten. We were on a PIA 747 bound for Karachi, just stopping in Cairo for fuel. Except that, when we were all fueled up, and they tried to tow us away from the jetway, we went nowhere. For quite a while, we went nowhere.

The reason for this was not immediately clear to us in the First Class cabin. Did not become clear until the pilot opened the doors because it was getting very hot in there, and I went out the front starboard door, stood on the platform someone had rolled up to the plane, and I peered out ahead of us. To see that the little truck trying mightily to tow us away from the gate was smack in the middle of an oil slick, all four tires spinning in the ooze. Anywhere else, this would've seemed quite improbable. But this was Cairo, where chaos is the norm. About a dozen Egyptians, all in baggy laborers' clothes, were standing around in the blue-gray cloud of the little truck's exhaust, pointing at the oil and the spinning tires and at the big green-and-white plane and trying to figure out how to move it.

"Get a load of this!" I said to Muhammad, and in a moment he was beside me on the platform. Where, for a couple of minutes, nobody noticed him. A few people saw him and nodded at him. But what I mean is at first nobody recognized him. They nodded at him like he was just a regular passenger, just like me. Then I heard the first excited strains of *Muhammad Ali Clay*. Muhammad Ali is the most common name on earth. So, in the Middle East, they tag onto that his father's last name—which they pronounce *Claw-é*. And that's how they reveal they mean not just any John Smith, but *the* John Smith, if you follow my drift.

So, anyway, suddenly happy shouts of *Muhammad Ali Claw-é!* were filling the air, and everyone was looking up at us, and Muhammad was standing there beside me in his smelly socks with his fly half unzipped and sleep all over his face, smiling and waving down from the platform like the Pope from his balcony.

In nothing flat the right side of the plane was engulfed. Dozens. All men. Then more than a hundred. All men or boys. All laborers. And still more arriving. Where they were coming from, I didn't know, but this was Cairo. Don't ever bother trying to figure Cairo out. It's not possible.

Muhammad pulled a red silk handkerchief out of his pants pocket and made it disappear. Then reappear. Powerful magic. Suddenly they understood he was a wizard. And suddenly they realized they'd delayed him long enough, and more than anything else what the crowd wanted was to help the great man make his way to wherever he was going, for what surely must be important work beyond their fathoming.

Several of them unhitched the little truck and pushed it out of the way. That left just the crowd, the plane, and a rope.

When I think of a line used to tow aircraft, I think of the long, flat nylon tethers I've seen used at private jet terminals in the United States. But this was Cairo, and it was a rope. A dirty, gnarled, and frayed rope, as thick as my thigh—like something you might see tied to a decrepit old battleship rusting away in the back of the port of Mombassa, or the like. *That* sort of rope.

They tied it to the hardpoint in the nosegear, and suddenly they all looked like our opponents in a game of tug-of-war. The crowd versus the plane. Quickly all of the slack went out of the rope. In my mind, I also see a camel. A camel they tied onto the rope, helping them pull. But it seems likely that's a trick of my memory. On the other hand, it was Cairo, and I can't entirely rule the camel out. How heavy is a fully fueled and loaded Boeing 747? How many men does it take to pull it? I don't know, but that's at least how many were out there now. Pulling. Suddenly I was reminded of drawings I'd seen of ancient Egyptians tugging on ropes, dragging huge blocks of stone up the sides of pyramids.

And suddenly we were on our way.

Next stop: Dubai. For an hour of duty-free shopping inside the gleaming new airport. I remember that, just before the glass electric door whooshed open to let us in from the tarmac, Kim said, "This place looks nice. Could we come back sometime?" and I said, "Sure," and I meant it; but, well, lately I haven't been doing much traveling.

Inside, Kim went straight to the Cartier counter and tried on a pair of gold-framed sunglasses, but I could tell that was cover, what she was really doing was covertly checking out the price on the gold Cartier lighter identical to the one I'd once bought her at the very same spot. In that terminal you could buy almost anything, caviar, silks and perfumes, bolts of cashmere suiting cloth, Sony Trinitrons, haute couture, gold bars, diamond rings, Swiss watches, for less than you'd ever find them almost anywhere else.

Most first-time visitors to Dubai, knowing it's an Arabian city-state on the Persian Gulf, assumed it was another tiny sheikhdom awash in oil. But, though it's surrounded by the vast petroleum reserves of Abu Dhabi, Qatar, Oman, and Iran, Dubai itself had about as much oil per capita as Egypt—which is to say, not much. Yet Dubai thrives in a way Egypt hasn't since the Ptolemys. It's a booming commercial and banking center and a very wealthy city, principally because Dubai is the world capital of gold smuggling, though this is officially known there as "reexport of precious metals."

Far from being a crime, in Dubai it's the most respectable of industries. Each year the government releases official precious-metals reexport statistics along with the emirate's other leading economic indicators. Dubai's laws encourage entrepreneurs and businessmen of all stripes while the state, at least officially, takes only a very small piece of the action. Import duties on cigarettes, booze, *booze!*, and cars and perfumes and gold and other luxury items are so low that, for example, the emirate of Dubai, population one million if you stretch it, is the world's largest importer of Swiss watches. Of course, some of those watches are "reexported," but most of them are sold in the many soukhs and jewelry shops in the city of Dubai, and in the airport duty-free shopping center they'd just herded us into off that PIA milk run.

When we got back onto the plane, I told Kim that I wished I could take her right now into the town for a night, and in the morning show her the *dhows* in the Creek and the port, looking for all the world like vessels so antiquated Sinbad himself may have sailed one. And that what she would never guess was that those charming little wooden boats were warships. At war with several nations, but primarily with the State of India—whose peculiar regulations concerning the import and export of gold and silver and the hoarding and trading of foreign currencies have long driven its good citizens to crime, and created Dubai's smuggling industry.

I was losing Kim now; she was pretending to listen, but the engines were starting and her mind was on other things. I wanted to tell her how I'd been to Dubai probably twenty times before one of my Indian friends there trusted me enough to show me what the place was really all about, how he took me to his gold vault.

Which was in the dusty port, and looked not unlike a standalone two-car garage. Except that, when you slid open the door and went inside it was filled with gold. Hanging on all the walls and from all the ceilings: gold chains, gold necklaces, gold chokers, gold rings, gold saucers, gold foil. But all that was just tinsel compared to the gold bars.

Mostly they were ten-tola gold bars, the size preferred by both hoarders and jewelry craftsmen in India. In this little shed of his, my friend had at least a thousand gleaming ten-tola bars neatly stacked on pallets. Each one of them was about 3.75 ounces of gold, .999 purity, worth give or take a thousand dollars in Dubai. Thrice that in India, according to my friend. He had even more of them still inside the cardboard boxes they'd arrived in, two hundred bars, sixty-two pounds of gold, to the box. On the boxes were the trademarks of various European banks. My friend handed me a ten-tola bar. "Take one," he said. "A souvenir."

There were a lot more little sheds like this one at the port, and, yes, my friend told me, they almost all contained gold. The locks on the sheds I saw didn't look like much, and there seemed to be very little security around. But that didn't matter, my friend said, because all the gold vaults in the port were under the protection of the gold king and no one would ever rob him.

Every night, *dhows* laden with gold bars and jewelry and gemstones and gunnysacks filled with U.S. dollars and other contraband leave the Creek or the Dubai port and ply their way up the Arabian coast toward the confluence of Iraq and Iran, or through the Straits of Hormuz and across the Arabian Sea to Pakistan or India, mostly India. Probably almost daily a Dubai *dhow* is involved in a shoot-out with an Indian government patrol vessel somewhere along the west coast of India. There are heavy losses in this secret war. But most of the dhows get through, and either rendezvous with the gold king's high-speed tenders or go all the way in to the Kerala shore to unload their cargoes. Sometimes they land just so the dhow's captain, its *nakhoda,* can sniff his native land. But usually it's so they can take on cargo for the trip back to Dubai, fugitives, undocumented workers, spies.

Once the gold makes it to Kerala, it's divided up and moved to Mumbai—which is what we call Bombay. Some of it goes by car, by motorcycle, on foot, by rickshaw, by truck, by taxi, but mostly it goes by train. On almost every train from Kerala to Bombay, if you looked hard enough—though that wouldn't be a good idea—you'd likely be able to find somewhere between twenty and a hundred gold smugglers with twenty to a hundred suitcases, each bearing a few pieces of gold meticulously wrapped inside the folds of trousers and shirts and underpants. Ten-tola bars. Gold hoops, earrings, finger rings, chains, bangles.

Indian trains are as packed with humanity as any trains you'll ever see.

Several times each day in the dusty stations of Kerala, the smugglers melt into the crowds of passengers and stand peacefully amidst the chaos waiting to board a Mumbai express. When the train grinds to a stop, they shoulder their way through the multitudes onto the train and into unreserved compartments. Where, once they find seats, if they find seats, like almost every other Second Class or Third Class rail traveler in India, as soon as they sit down they loop a strong metal chain over the handle of their suitcase to tie it to the wooden seat. And thus the Dubai gold makes its way piece by piece to Mumbai.

I would've liked to tell Kim all of that, and how the gold vaults, the dhows, the smuggling routes—all of it—was controlled by one man, the gold king, an Indian Muslim. And, of course, had I known it at the time, I also would've liked to tell Kim that she and I would one day come to know the gold king. But Kim was holding on to the armrests of her seat now, for dear life, and we were on our way again. To Pakistan.

Which, as you may have heard recently, is about the most dangerous place on earth.

When we got to Karachi, we flew straight on to Lahore, where we were welcomed personally by Nawaz Sharif, Governor of the state of Punjab. He was a friendly young fellow, only a couple years older than me, and he gave us lots of garlands and other party favors, and flattered us shamelessly, and, when I asked, he told me Punjab means "five rivers." We all thought he must have a bright future. Indeed, not long thereafter he was elected Prime Minister of Pakistan, twice; and not all too long after that he was kicked out of office and thrown into prison. Where I understand he may now be writing a book.

From Lahore we flew to the capital, Islamabad. Which is a master-planned, modern city, nestled in green mountains. I remember Space Age white buildings all over the place. The only other city I'd ever seen that resembled it in a way was Brasília. Islamabad is the capital, but Rawalpindi, which is right next door, is the army headquarters, and it was there that we went to dinner in the big, white British Raj–style house of General Zia ul-Haq—who had taken power in a military coup ten years earlier and quickly made quite a name for himself in the world press by arresting and then hanging Prime Minister Zulfiqar Ali Bhutto. General Zia was now also President Zia, poppy cultivation and opium production had more than tripled all across Pakistan, but so too had U.S. aid to this country, which was now America's biggest ally and arms conduit in the fight against the Soviet invaders doing their best to hang on across the border in Afghanistan.

Oh how lavishly they greeted us! Garlands from the President, the head of the Pakistani Senate Ghulam Ishaq Khan, from the Defence Minister, and from a whole queue of grinning army generals. Even the American Ambassador, a nice fellow named Arnold Raphel, hung garlands around the necks of each and every one of us—while I flattered everyone in the room with a pulse, in Urdu, and Muhammad did magic tricks, until things settled down for a grand but boring state dinner.

What we didn't know while we sat there eating with them, and talking with them about mosques and shrines and cricket scores, was that they were all ghosts. Or would be soon enough. A few months after that dinner, General Zia and Ambassador Raphel and just about everyone else in that dining room with the exception of Ghulam Ishaq Khan and us—Muhammad's party—climbed into the President's C-130 transport plane for a short flight home to Rawalpindi. But they all died when the plane crashed and exploded—or exploded and crashed, no one was ever sure which—a few minutes after takeoff. At first a bomb was suspected, but I believe later theories turned to nerve gas pumped into the cockpit and passenger cabin.

Whatever the exact methodology, it was a sophisticated assassination—the sort of thing my father and Uncle Charley would've studied carefully. The chief suspect was one of the sons of the late Prime Minister Zulfiqar Ali Bhutto, a dutiful son honoring his father.

Ghulam Ishaq Khan took over as President, but would be run out a few years later. Though, uniquely enough by Pakistani standards, he would live through it and avoid incarceration.

When we left Islamabad—which is in the foothills on the southwestern slope of the Himalayas—if we'd flown just a few minutes to the east, we would've been over the disputed border with India, over Kashmir. Where Pakistani and Indian army units were fighting then, and are still fighting today, at breathtaking heights in what was then a secret war, which almost no one ever heard of in the West until the combatants on both sides went nuclear. But we flew instead to the northwest—inside an old silver propeller plane that looked exactly like something Steven Spielberg would've picked for Indiana Jones to fly across the Himalayas in. I remember looking out a window on the right and seeing mountain peaks, close by and higher than us. And the same thing out the window on the left. We were flying through a pass, hitting air pocket after air pocket. Bouncing up and down.

I was sitting next to Muhammad. Who was flapping his forearm up and down with his palm facing the floor—pretending he was bouncing our plane like a basketball. Muhammad also kept announcing to everyone on the plane that we were about to crash, which seemed quite reasonable and prophetic, but wasn't pleasing anyone except Muhammad. Kim was especially charmed by all of this. Kim was sitting with Lonnie, and Kim was crying now, and hyperventilating, and Lonnie was holding her hand. I should've been sitting with Kim. But the plane was so small and the seating so tight that Muhammad and I were together in the only two seats we could actually fit our legs in. Kim looked ready to make a run for it, but she and Lonnie were shoehorned into their places. Likewise Mahdi, and Jabir, and Bingham, and Mustafa. None of them looked too happy, the old plane was surging and thrumming and rattling like it was about to break up, and as Muhammad pointed out we were all about to die. Then we landed in Peshawar.

Muhammad stepped out of the back door of the plane into a shower of rose petals sprinkled by little kids in embroidered vests and sparkling-white *shalwar kameez*, the combination of really-long shirt and matching pants every man and woman in Pakistan seems to wear. Before he'd walked ten paces up the red carpet that was stretched out before us, Muhammad had already taken on half a dozen garlands. Not all of them were floral. One of them was an enormous tinsel thing that dominated all the others and made him look like he was wearing an aluminum-foil shirt. It's quite a nice look if you have the build and confidence for it, and I told him so.

Peshawar is the capital of the North West Frontier Province. We went straight from the airport to the Governor's Mansion for garlands and lunch, and then we all got into cars and drove about thirty miles through the Tribal Areas up to the Khyber Pass—where Muhammad was greeted rapturously by droves of Afghans who were said to be refugees but were armed to their brown teeth and looked just like mujahideen to me. In fact, I know now, they were a tribal council of elders of the mujahideen and their special guests.

Most of them had left weapons at the entrances to the enormous tent in which Muhammad was to speak and pass out food donations. But when he said, "Your cause is a great cause. Your war is a just war. Your jihad is my jihad. And if you give me a gun and permit me to participate in the war in Afghanistan, I will take part wholeheartedly," soon guns of all sizes and descriptions were conjured out of the turbans and sleeves and pantaloon legs of the hundreds of Afghan men and boys seated on the acre of carpets in front of us. Holy shit! was what I was thinking, but Muhammad just went on talking, and no one stood up to lead us over the pass and into battle, which was fine by me.

Muhammad passed out that very small portion of the four tons of milk powder I'd arranged to send there that hadn't been stolen en route, and then we said goodbye and drove back to Peshawar.

In the gloaming, we drove to a rickety old auditorium where Muhammad spoke to a polite crowd of a few hundred Muslims, all of them men except for Kim. She sat with me on a bench in the back while three rows in front of us sat a nice fellow in a white crocheted skullcap. He was one of the few Arabs in the audience and I don't think I paid much attention to him then, but I do now when I watch videotape of that speech. There he sits, listening politely, not eight feet in front of me, younger, yes, and not quite ready to set the world on fire, but all the same his name is Osama bin Laden.

Afterwards, I went out for a stroll on my own. Peshawar is a very ancient city—Alexander the Great, Genghis Khan, and Marco Polo had all been there before us. I wandered into a bazaar which looked like it had been there forever, and into a narrow, open-fronted building that from the outside seemed it might be a place to buy carpets or dates and pomegranates. Or batteries for my Walkman, which was what I actually wanted.

Inside, when my eyes adjusted to the light it was like Ali Baba's Cave. No batteries. No dates or pomegranates. Carpets, yes. A stack of them in a corner on one side of the room. Also porcelain vases, silks, a glass case of wristwatches, a whole wall covered with daggers shaped like crescent moons, another wall and the ceiling hung with hand-beaten copper trays and jugs, and coffeepots whose ornately curved spouts, like the gleaming oil lamps displayed beside them, suggested homes for genies. In the deep shadows in the back of the room I could just make out the stocks of rifles, maybe fifty of them, hanging on the wall. Beneath them was a brazier which was smoking and giving off just enough light to make the rifles' reddish-brown stocks but not their barrels visible.

Probably it was because I was staring toward the guns that the first words I heard inside the shop—spoken by a thin, young black-eyed fellow in a mud-colored turban who'd been lurking quietly since I entered—were: "You come, sir, for firing?" I hadn't answered yet when he spoke up again and said, "My name, sir, is Young Honest Ali, and I will be pleased, sir, to accommodate your test firing of any of the many fine weapons on the wall."

As it turned out when he switched on the bare bulb hanging by a cord from the ceiling, there was a much broader selection than just the rifles I'd first seen. The gunmetal was dulled and absorbed the soft light emitted by the coals in the little brazier. Which explained why I hadn't seen the pistols or the machine guns or the hand grenades also hanging on the wall and from the ceiling.

Young Honest Ali pulled down an armful of guns, and then he opened a cigar box containing fountain pens, took one of those too, and turned and marched into the darkness, saying, "Come, sir. This way. Follow me." Off we went, through a warren of back rooms groaning with weapons, a whole Devil's larder of them.

Peshawar is the largest conduit for arms in the world. In Peshawar you can buy every Soviet, American, British, or Chinese gun, grenade, launcher, missile, mine, cannon, conventional bomb, or weapon of nearly any kind whatsoever small enough for five men or less to carry. If they don't have it now, they can get it for you by tomorrow night. What Dubai is to gold, Peshawar is to weapons, and a healthy portion of the arms the U.S. funneled into Pakistan for delivery to the mujahideen in Afghanistan actually flowed not west but east, into Kashmir. Where, after all, for the same cause of Al-Islam, mujahideen were fighting another enemy almost as big as the Soviet Union.

Another portion of those arms never made it to either war, but remained in Peshawar for sale to gunrunners from all over the world. And in addition to the dazzling selection of foreign arms available in Peshawar, if you weren't hung up on buying guns manufactured by the OEM and you'd like a nice discount, sir, you could also select from the many excellent knockoffs made in the village of Darra Adamkhel, which is in the Tribal Areas near Peshawar.

"Welcome, sir," said Young Honest Ali, "to the Peshawar Smugglers' Market."

Now, *this* was more like it. Just the sort of thing I'd had in mind when Miles recruited me.

But so far the jobs I'd done for the talented Mr. Copeland were nothing to write home about. In fact, my one covert act during this entire trip to Pakistan was an act of covert editing and typing I'd done at the request of Muhammad and Jabir, nothing for Miles.

Our hosts had asked Muhammad to sign a letter, and not just any letter, but "Muhammad Ali's Open Letter to the Pakistani People" for publication in newspapers all over the country. It was a stout and meticulous epic of a letter, and when Jabir and Muhammad read it they saw it included several pointed opinions about domestic Pakistani political issues they knew nothing about. When I read it, I realized also that it had been written by a highly educated American, not our Pakistani hosts as had been implied. So, in the dead of the night in the back office of the Lahore Hilton, after a hunt for a typewriter of suitable font and point size, I'd rewritten it, and retyped it, careful to replicate the paper and layout of the original document in such a way that, we hoped, after Muhammad signed the new letter the changes wouldn't be noticed until it was too late to change them back. And it had worked. It was the revised and toned-down letter that appeared in Pakistani papers over Muhammad's signature. That had pissed off quite a few people.

But I didn't deserve to die for it.

So, why, when Young Honest Ali finished leading me up the outside stairway onto the rooftop, did he and about a dozen of his friends all lift AK-47s and fire them with wild abandon straight up into the night sky? From whence, my too-logical Western mind concluded immediately, all those bullets must soon rain straight down on us. Or someone nearby.

But next, nothing happened. No one cried out in agony or dropped dead from a bullet hurled back at us from heaven. Up there on the rooftop, cooking fires were going and there were maybe forty or fifty charpoys. A *charpoy* is sort of a cross between a low bed and a hammock. It consists of a wooden frame with legs which lift it maybe eight or ten inches above the ground, and it's strung with webbing usually made of leather in Pakistan and of rushes or hemp in India. No mattress. You sleep on the webbing, and every night hundreds of millions of Pakistanis and Indians do just that in charpoys lined up side by side by side, sometimes acres of them in neat rows, under the sheltering sky. Which, at the moment, was not raining bullets.

So Young Honest Ali and his friends lifted their guns and launched a new and more prolonged burst of happy gunfire into the night. "Joy-shots" is what Lawrence of Arabia called them in *The Seven Pillars of Wisdom*. All over the Muslim world, rifles and machine guns serve as something like the equivalent of party noisemakers in America or Europe. Probably, at any given moment somewhere in the Islamic world, at least one fool is rapturously squeezing off a brace of joy-shots aimed roughly at himself and whoever he's celebrating with.

What I wanted to do was wince and cover my head and tell these crazy assholes to cut it out. But something told me this was a time and place to act brave. *No, really, you're too kind. You've made enough fuss about my arrival already. Thank you. Thank you. Nice to meet you too. An honor, really.* In fact, I said those last two sentences to them right then in Urdu. But that only prompted huge smiles and reloading and more joy-shots.

Then the guns came down and everyone stood still to give Young Honest Ali a fair chance to ply his trade.

"We have here, sir, for your firing, a fine selection of weapons. All from the vast stores of the Americans and Russians and our brothers the mujahideen. Whom I believe you have met today, sir. We have seen you on the television this evening, sir. No mistaking such a distinguished gentleman as yourself, sir. Normally we charge dearly for the firing. But you, sir, may fire for free. No charge for the firing, sir. And should you wish to make a purchase, you will scarcely believe the price we will give such an honored guest."

Young Honest Ali handed me an AK-47 and said, "Please, sir, you fire now."

I wasn't about to fire it up into the air, and I didn't see any direction I could fire it without maybe hitting someone. The alley below us was filled with men and boys, and donkey carts, and dogs, and piles of spices, and some really-serious-looking chain-fed antiaircraft guns mounted on tripods. This roof was crowded with people, as was the one on the other side of the alley.

I balked.

Young Honest Ali took the AK-47 from my hands and passed me an older rifle with a long yellow stock. "Here, sir, try this one," he said. "Lee Enfield three-oh-three. British rifle."

"Where? I'll hit someone."

"No, sir. You won't. Fire that way, sir. Through the lane and into the field. No one is there, sir. They all know to stay away."

The gap he wanted me to fire through was about fifty yards out and, because of a roofline that got in the way, about six feet wide at the most. In marksman's terms, the equivalent of the broad side of a barn.

"No."

"Look, sir. AK-74 Shorty Assault Rifle. Just like in *Scarface*, sir. You must fire it. No charge. You are our guest. Fire that way, sir."

I just stood there like a moron. So one of Young Honest Ali's friends showed me the gap to fire through. He aimed a Kalashnikov down the alley and through the gap and into the field and then squeezed off one round. It looked like fun, but what Young Honest Ali and his friends were running up against was all the gun safety rules my father had drummed into me before he'd let me fire his gun.

"Please, sir, you must fire something. Be our guest. Try this, sir." That was when Young Honest Ali showed me the first weapon of the night that looked safe for me to handle. The gold fountain pen. Which turned out to be the gold-fountain-pen-.22-caliber-single-shot assassination weapon.

Young Honest Ali opened it, loaded it, pointed it for me at a little mud wall on our end of the rooftop. At the moment, there was no one between the wall and me. He kept it pointed to the wall while he handed it to me. The wall had bullet holes in it already.

"Squeeze here, sir."

I did. And with an almost-silent *pffffffffft*, it fired and I actually heard the bullet smack against the wall.

"Low velocity, sir," said Young Honest Ali. "Excellent for stealth killing."

"How much does that cost?" I said.

"One hundred rupees, sir."

I put it back in his palm.

"For you, sir, our honored guest, fifty rupees."

"I'll give you eighty rupees for two of them," I said.

Young Honest Ali backed up a step and looked me over, saying, "Must be ninety rupees, sir."

"Seventy," I said, starting toward the stairs, wondering if they'd grab me if I tried to just walk away now.

"Okay, sir, for you: two diabolical Peshawar pen-guns for eighty-five rupees. Do we have a deal?"

"Done," I said. "One for me and one for Miles."

"Who, sir?"

"Miles."

After Young Honest Ali had led me back down the stairs and through the armory to the cigar box to pick up the second pen-gun, no ammo, thank you, he led me out to the street and shook my hand and I asked him where I could buy some batteries.

"I will show you, sir," said Young Honest Ali. "This way."

Then he led me down the street past two or three narrow shopfronts and stopped at a little stand attended by a young-but-one-eyed Pathan with a thick brown mustache and dark brown hair cut in a style reminiscent of the early Beatles. On the stand were what looked like Christmas puddings and fudge and brownies.

"This, sir, is not batteries. But I think it will interest you, sir."

I love England but I hate English pudding and cakes, especially the ones stiff with fruits and nuts and raisins they force on you at the holidays.

"Do you know what this is, sir?"

"Blood pudding?"

"No, sir. Semtex, disguised as pudding."

"Oh!"

"And this one, sir?"

"Fudge?"

"No, sir. This one is hashish. You can tell by the color, sir."

"Batteries?"

"This way, sir. A little farther for batteries."

Once I got my batteries, I said goodbye and walked out of the bazaar alone, realizing I might be hard-pressed to find pomegranates here, but every one of the little buildings all around me was filled with arms. And then I remembered riding through San Francisco with Bill Tharp while he told me, "There's a secret world all around us. You just don't see it unless you know where to look."

I was in the mood for an epiphany, and it was right then that I began trying to connect the dots. Trying to build a unified theory of the secret world, if you will. All these years later on this beach, I'm still at it.

When I have these thoughts, usually I start there in Peshawar. Walking down an ancient street with two diabolical single-shot assassination weapons in the inside breast pocket of my silk suit. Which often leads me from Peshawar to thoughts of James. Crack shot, dupe, assassin. Where does he fit in?

Or sometimes I head from the arms bazaar straight back to Beirut, to Bob Sensi and Isa Abdullah Ali.

What am I to make of this? Sensi had been paying for everything with an American Express card and a Kuwait Airlines air travel card. After we left Beirut, he kept doing the same while continuing to work with Muhammad, even going to Israel with him, trying to get hostages released. Until one day in London, Sensi was arrested and charged with embezzling from the Kuwaiti government.

He was extradited and put on trial in federal court in the United States. His defense was he was a CIA agent and the expenses he paid for with Kuwait Airlines funds were sanctioned by the CIA and funded by Kuwait under a secret agreement with the White House. The CIA sent a representative to court to stipulate Sensi was a CIA agent but further testify that the CIA had no involvement in or knowledge of our mission to Kuwait and Beirut. What was that Miles told me? *Trust no one.*

And what about Isa? What was he really up to? Whose side was he on? I already mentioned that, after the Lebanese Civil War, it emerged that during his time in Beirut Isa had actually been trying to prevent kidnappings of Westerners. So what am I to make of this news story:

DATELINE: SARAJEVO, Bosnia-Herzegovina (CNN)
HEADLINE: U.S. troops in Bosnia step up security against terrorists
SUBHEAD: "Extremist" American being sought

Tighter security took effect Wednesday at NATO installations in Bosnia, including the Tuzla headquarters for U.S. troops, following reports that militant Muslim groups might be planning attacks against NATO forces.

U.S. troops also have been warned to be on the lookout for a U.S. citizen with close links to such groups. The command of the NATO-led peace mission said it had distributed leaflets to guards and security officers alerting them about a man known as Kevin or Cleven Holt. He's also identified as Isa Abdullah Ali.

The pamphlet described Holt as an African-American in his thirties "who has expressed sympathies for extremist causes."

A senior NATO official, speaking on condition of anonymity, said the alert was raised Tuesday after Holt attempted to enter a NATO compound in Bosnia in the previous 24 hours. The compound was not identified, and no further information on Holt was released.

For whatever it's worth, my money's on Isa Abdullah Ali. Funny how, even as they burn him and brand him a Muslim extremist, they deny him his Muslim name. Where does Isa fit into the broad pattern I'm searching for? That's still not clear, and probably never will be.

I spend a lot of time these nights thinking about my buddy Mike Timpani.

I told you earlier a little bit about the first night Mike and I actually spent together in person—drinking in a candlelit safe house in Lima. Candlelit because the Sendero Luminoso kept blowing up electrical towers and power stations all over Peru, and especially around the capital.

I picked Mike up at the Aeropuerto Internacional Jorge Chavez and took him to the great little hotel we stayed in, the El Condado, which a few years later was blown to smithereens by a Sendero Luminoso bomb. We had business to do—airplanes to sell, airplanes to appraise, a mysterious box to deliver, quite a few mysterious Peruvians to glad-hand—but first we needed a drink and a place to talk and for that Mike had kindly arranged an alternative location.

Who the hell loaned us this place, Mike? He never quite said. Ask Mike if he worked for an American intelligence agency, and he'd say things like "Not me. But I know some people who do."

Ask Mike if, as promised before we came down here, he had a telephone number to call if we got our asses in a sling while within the territorial jurisdiction of the Republica del Peru, and he'd say, "Yes." Ask him who it was precisely that would be coming to rescue us, and he'd say, "You never know until you call. Usually it's Americans, though. But you always hope it's Israelis. Israelis do a lot of our unofficial ass-kicking for us. As sort of a professional courtesy. No one can save your ass like an Israeli can save your ass."

You'll remember that was the night I asked Mike about George Bush, and he gave me a very specific answer. But ask Mike something as specific as whether the CIA was the American intelligence agency he didn't work for but he knew some people who did, and he'd get vague again. Which, of course, was what he was supposed to do.

Whoever he was, Mike was a covert warrior of formidable if mysterious credentials.

We'd started out on the four minibottles of scotch Mike cadged off the Eastern Air Lines stewardess who'd liked him on the flight on the way down. But next we moved on to the tall black bottle of pisco we found in a kitchen cupboard. On pisco, anything can happen. And what happened that night was that Mike started telling me his story. Not all of it certainly, and not the classified parts, he was careful to say, but enough of the story that you could read some of the rest of it between the lines.

He was a nice-enough-looking fellow. Dark hair, medium build. That night he was wearing a Black Watch Plaid button-down-collared shirt with khaki pants and lace-up black leather shoes that looked like business shoes on top but had Vibram soles. You see shoes like that nowadays all the time, but not back then. And he looked to be about my age. In fact, he was about two years older than me.

Mike was born in Lansing, Michigan, in 1951. But he and his family soon moved to Indiana, then Washington state, then Oregon. In Monmouth, Oregon, his father was a prison warden and Mike was an altar boy and a star of his high school football team.

When he achieved the minimum age, he went to Salem and joined the Highway Patrol. He was on a motorcycle making what he thought was a traffic stop one day out on the interstate, when the passenger of the car he was trying to stop stuck a gun out the window and took a shot at him. "I was just leaning down to reach something in my boot," Mike said, "and if I hadn't done that just then, I would've been hit." As it was, the bullet only grazed the back of his jacket. But by the end of that day, Mike had decided, *What the fuck? If people are going to shoot at me, I might as well join the Army.*

Which he did. But he was rather vague that night as to exactly what he did during his first years in the Army. Even though I've tried recently to reconstruct it, I'm not sure. I believe he was an enlisted man at first. I remember he told me that in the beginning he was a foot soldier and he did most of his training at Fort Bragg. He may have been a Ranger, I'm not sure. But at some point he went to Oregon State University, where he played football again, and after that he became an Army officer.

He went into training to become an Army pilot. After he learned to fly fixed-wing aircraft, he moved on to helicopters. He was perhaps for a time a Cobra pilot in the 82nd Airborne Air Cavalry. That, too, is a little murky. Because it was sometime around then that Mike slipped over to the dark side.

In the wake of the helicopter crash in the Iranian desert that scuttled the American hostage-rescue raid on Teheran, U.S. Army Special Forces developed an elite helicopter unit of their own, capable of striking undetected under extreme conditions in the most hostile environments around the world. It was called Task Force 160, and Mike was soon a member and the U.S. military's highest-rated night-vision helicopter pilot—capable of doing some very remarkable things undetected, under cover of darkness.

Task Force 160 first saw action in 1983 when Ronald Reagan sent Special Forces and Marines units to invade Grenada, restore democracy there, kick

Cuban ass, give the Marines something to smile about because their Beirut barracks had just been blown up a few days earlier, and evacuate the American medical students stuck on the island paradise whether they wanted to be evacuated or not.

It was supposed to be pretty simple. The assault was supposed to begin under cover of darkness. By the time any defenders could see what was hitting them, most of the resistance on the island was supposed to have been taken out by Task Force 160 and a team of Navy SEALs. Then, at first light, the Marines and others would land triumphantly, the locals would joyously wave American flags at them and blow them kisses, and democracy and Marine Corps honor would be restored, thank you very much.

The first Mike heard of any of this was on a weekend when he was recalled from leave and told to get his ass halfway across the country to Fort Bragg within a few hours. At Fort Bragg, they told him he'd been chosen to lead the initial air assault of Operation Urgent Fury, the American invasion of Grenada. He and the other pilots he'd be flying with quickly drew up a plan, the key to which, of course, was that the air assault was to take place about half an hour before first light.

Some of Task Force 160 was flown to a forward staging area in Barbados. But Mike's team would fly directly from Fort Bragg with its helicopters in the belly of an Air Force C-130, which would land without lights at the Grenada airport. Mike's team was to roll its matte-black AH-6 helicopter gunships out of the belly of the Air Force beast and launch the attack almost immediately after the C-130 landed.

"Let's have some more of that pisco," Mike said. "This is the part you won't believe."

Mike snoozed most of the way from Fort Bragg to Grenada. He woke himself up when he felt the plane beginning its approach to the airport. He glanced out a window.

"And the fucking sun was coming up!" Mike said.

"What?"

"The dumb-ass Air Force at Homestead had flight-planned us from Fort Bragg to Grenada and forgotten there was a one-hour time difference between East Coast time and Caribbean time."

"So why didn't you abort, reschedule for the next morning?"

"It was too late. The Soviet bird was coming over in a few more hours."

"The what?"

"The Soviet spy satellite. We had too many ships too near Grenada. There wasn't time to disperse them. The Soviets would know what was up and warn the island. So the order came down: 'Go anyway!'

"By the time we landed, the sun was over the horizon, the invasion had already begun, SEALs were pinned down on the beach because we hadn't taken out the Cuban gun positions we were supposed to, and we were under heavy fire even before we got the belly of the plane open. They had to drop Rangers on the airfield by parachute just to secure the area enough for us to get into the air."

"Wait a minute. That part about the Air Force at Homestead fucking the whole thing up—did that ever come out?"

"No."

"How do you know it's true?"

"Trust me. We got to the bottom of it."

"I bet you did. So the whole meticulously planned invasion was screwed up by the noncombatants at Homestead?"

"Right."

"Holy shit!"

"Right."

"Are any of the Air Force geniuses who perpetrated this FUBAR still breathing?"

"I don't know and I don't care."

"So what happened next?"

What happened next was that Mike and his team—no longer the tip of the spear as had been planned—rose into the air and attempted what had been their original mission, an assault on the defenses around the Governor-General's Mansion. But the intelligence that had said the defenders would be lightly armed was wrong. Mike's team came under heavy fire almost immediately, and matte-black helicopter gunships make excellent targets against the bright pink light of the rising sun.

Black Hawks went down. An AH-6 went down. Mike was hit, shot to hell, and probably everyone else in his team was too. They stayed in the air, re-grouped, tried to help out around the secondary target, the radio station—where they managed to provide enough cover to allow a Black Hawk to hover while a commando team fastroped to the ground. Meanwhile, in the city, which was supposed to be the site of a parade about now, three SEALs were missing.

Mike and three other pilots volunteered to fly into the city to find the missing men and bring them out. On their way into the city, word came in to Mike by radio that the three missing SEALs weren't in the city. They'd never made it there. And now they were in the ocean swimming as fast as they could away from the island because there was so much fucking gunfire coming at them. One of them kept swimming, injured, seven miles out to a Navy ship and banged on the hull until they heard him and pulled him out of the water. The other two swimmers were less mobile and under heavy fire, until Mike's chopper and another chopper found them and rescued them.

The commendation Mike received afterwards said he'd displayed the highest level of bravery and heroism ever displayed by an American military man. Mike didn't tell me that, but I learned it later.

After Grenada, Mike decided, *What the fuck? If people are going to shoot at me like that, I might as well get out of the Army and go over to the really dark side.*

But before I go there, usually I ask myself, what can Mike's joy ride in Grenada add to my unified theory?

I've decided it's that secret warriors are human and therefore as subject to human frailty as everyone else. In other words: Even in the secret world, shit happens. That's why the People's Revolutionary Army of Grenada and a handful of Cuban army regulars and military advisors can get their chance to slice up by day an overwhelming American military force primed to invade by night. That's why a nineteen-year-old West German kid in a single-engine Cessna can fly across the Iron Curtain, evade several squadrons of MiGs, in fact evade the entire vaunted Soviet air defense system, and make it all the way to a pinpoint landing in Red Square. And it's why a shitfaced truck driver can steal an Army plane, fly it across Washington, and crash-land it onto the White House lawn. Never underestimate the roles of chance and the human factor in determining the secret destiny of the world.

"Now, if you can manage to actually fly it by night," Mike said, "there are a lot of really cool things a night-vision helicopter gunship pilot can do.

"First of all, you're flying around in the dark in a totally black helicopter that nobody on the ground can see. You've got night vision goggles on. You've got head's-up display, which means you never have to take your eyes off your target to look at your instrument panel because all your instrument displays are hovering right between you and the windshield so you can look at them and look through them at the same time. You've got forward-looking infrared radar—thermal imaging—so you can find the hot spots, the muzzle flashes, the warm bodies hiding behind walls, the jeeps hidden in the jungle with their engines still ticking. And you've got a helmet-mounted gunsight which automatically aims your Gatling gun, or your machine guns, or your rockets, whichever you pick, right at whatever you're looking at. Once you acquire a target, all you've got to do is keep your eyes on it, and then you fire your weapons by voice command. No fumbling for a joystick or a button.

"And you're up there in the dark in the middle of the night making one hell of a lot of noise, waking every motherfucking Communist in the village up. They're scared to death. They run out of their huts into the jungle with their guns blazing, firing blindly into the sky, because they can hear you but they can't see you. And you smoke 'em."

"Does it make you feel bad, killing them, Mike?"

"No. I *hate* Communists."

After he left the Army, Mike officially went to work for the United States

Council for World Freedom, a nongovernmental organization run by retired U.S. Major General John Singlaub which somehow obtained 501(c)(3) tax-exempt status from the Internal Revenue Service and was funded ostensibly by contributions from Bunker Hunt, the Coors family, and private contributors in Saudi Arabia. Officially their mission was to deliver nonlethal humanitarian assistance to the Nicaraguan Contras in their bases in Honduras and Costa Rica. Mike and another American pilot participated in a *Soldier of Fortune* article about their delivery of an ancient medevac helicopter to a Contra base in Honduras.

"Yeah," I said, "but what were you really doing down there, Mike?"

For whatever it's worth, General Singlaub has since written a memoir in which he states that, after he left the Army, Mike went to work for the CIA flying air operations for Contra leader Eden Pastora. But there must be some mistake. Because, like Mike had already told me, he didn't work for any American intelligence agency but he did know some people who did.

Mike wouldn't tell me that night who he worked for, but he did admit he lived for a couple of years with the Contras in the jungles in Nicaragua and El Salvador and Honduras and Costa Rica. And that he did fly helicopters there, and not just beat-up twenty-five-year-old medevac helicopters with red crosses painted on their sides. He also flew a matte-black, state-of-the-art, night-vision helicopter gunship which must've come from somewhere, but the U.S. Government never officially deployed any such aircraft against the Sandinistas or their brothers in arms in El Salvador. During this time, Mike had long wild hair and a different name and a pet panther he found in the jungle when it was a baby. He adopted it, kept it in his tent with him, took it up with him into the night sky to wake every motherfucking Communist in the village up and shoot them. The Contras, who knew they didn't know Mike's real name anyway, named him El Pantera.

With all this shooting of Communist motherfuckers, I think I need to point out here that Mike's a gentleman, a great guy, one of the best people I've ever known in my life. I've seen him do some very honorable things—at times when no one would've known or cared really if he'd done the opposite.

Anyway, we ran out of pisco and made a beer run. And when we got back to the safe house, Mike was suddenly worried about ears in the light fixtures. He led me out onto the balcony and we sat down on the floor with our backs against the concrete wall. "Look," he said, "you've asked me so many times to tell you specifically something cool I did in a helicopter that, just to shut you up, I'm going to tell you the coolest thing I ever did in a helicopter. But you've got to swear to me you won't tell this to anyone until I'm dead. Either until somebody smokes me or I die a natural death."

"Okay. I swear. Is this gonna be classified?"

"Not the way I'm gonna tell it. But that doesn't mean it's safe for me to have anybody hearing about it. I don't need anybody coming around to smoke me because of you shooting off your mouth about it."

"Okay. I swear."

"There was this bad guy. He was a Communist leader, or a terrorist leader, take your pick, operating in a country we didn't have much access to."

"What country?"

"I can't tell you. But to help you narrow it down, I can tell you I've flown night-vision helicopter ops in Europe, the Middle East, Africa, Central America, the Philippines, and Korea.

"This motherfucker lived in one of those places and he was the enemy. We couldn't get to him. We only had a few men on the ground in his country, and there was no way we could get them over the big wall around the compound he lived in. Even if you could get over the wall, he had security forces out the wazoo.

"Now, in the city in which this bad guy lived, at precisely one in the morning for thirty nights in a row, a guy on a motorcycle, a big loud, juiced-up motorcycle with no fucking muffler on it, pulled out of a shed on the edge of town, drove through the city at exactly thirty-five miles an hour, loud as hell, taking the same route every night right past the walls of the bad guy's compound on his way to the other side of town. Until, on the thirty-first night, there was no motorcycle.

"But on that night, at precisely one in the morning, a matte-black night-vision helicopter gunship with no fucking muffler on it passed over the roof of the motorcycle shed on the edge of town, then proceeded at exactly forty-two feet above the streets and thirty-five miles an hour along the same route the motorcycle had driven every recent night before it. As the helicopter approached the bad guy's compound, the pilot activated his helmet-mounted gun sight, selected a rocket, locked his eyes onto his target, said one word—'Fire!'—watched the destruction of the home of a hard-to-kill-but-now-dead enemy motherfucker, then continued along the rest of the motorcycle's usual route to the other side of town, and proceeded over the nearest border."

"Holy shit!"

"Yeah, but wait. That's not the best part," Mike said. "The best part was, for the next forty-five nights in a row, at one in the morning, the motorcycle pulled out of the shed and rode the exact same route as before. I think they call it Cover for Action. Don't they, Scholar?"

"How the fuck did you learn that nickname?"

"Doesn't matter," Mike said. "Let's go back to the hotel before we pass out."

But before we go on, what can be inferred from the story of the motorcycle and the gunship? I've decided it's that it's usually only an intelligence service's failures most people ever hear about, pick over in the newspapers, watch Senators bleating about on television. The success stories are seldom revealed.

There's a secret history of the world and most of it's never been read. It resides in vaults, meticulously maintained by the world's intelligence services in Washington and Moscow and London and Paris and Teheran and many other places secret warriors work. It is our collective unconscious, compiled in the secret histories of individual events and campaigns written by the secret historians—the only surviving accounts of what really happened versus what we were told happened, or what we were never told about at all. But even what you could find in the vaults is only trace evidence, clues. In *The Book of Disquietude,* Fernando Pessoa wrote: "Everything stated or expressed by man is a note in the margin of a completely erased text."

But back to Peru now. Mike and I had aircraft to inspect the next morning in hangars at Callao, and aircraft to try to sell the next day. Indeed, before we left, we managed to sell three Boeing 727s to a new Peruvian domestic airline.

And we had to go to the home of the just-retired Prime Minister of Peru, who kept rabbits in a blood-streaked hutch in his neatly trimmed backyard, and inside the retired Prime Minister's study Mike stood at a giant map of Peru with a pointer and laid out for the assembled—all Peruvian, all mysterious, all distinguished-looking—the basics of a plan for exterminating the Sendero Luminoso.

And after that we had a mysterious box to deliver. It was about four feet wide, four feet deep, and two feet tall—about the height of a computer tower. In fact, it was covered with the same sort of hard, almond-white plastic that computer skins are made of. It had all sorts of data ports and jacks for telephone lines flowing in and out. It was a device of some sort for monitoring telephone communications between certain preselected numbers. If a call went out from Juan the Maoist Motherfucker's home number to the take-out ceviche stand that had already been cleared, the device ignored it. But if Juan the Maoist Motherfucker called Carlito the Suspected Maoist Motherfucker's home number, the device monitored the call in real time, and recorded it too, of course, in case Max the counterintelligence officer was in the shitter when the call went out. That was about all Mike could tell me about the mysterious box.

What was my role in all this? I was the guy with the access. The connections. I could bring all these people together, get their attention.

And what was Mike's role? Well, he didn't work for an American intelligence agency but he did know some people who did. In fact, when we left Lima and flew together back to Miami, Mike introduced me there to an old friend of his by the name of Félix Rodríguez. Who quite famously did work for the CIA.

Félix was wearing Che Guevara's Rolex on his wrist. Félix had removed it himself after managing the hunt for the famous guerrilla leader and then either executing Che himself or ordering a Bolivian soldier to do it. It's unclear who actually pulled the trigger. Félix is understandably vague as to this. But Félix will admit that, just as is written in a vault somewhere in Virginia or Washington, D.C., after he removed Che's watch, he also removed one of Che's fingers and mailed it to *Commandante Fidel Castro/Habana/Cuba.*

There's a story going around about Adnan. That, late in 1968, soon after Richard Nixon won the White House, Adnan flew out to San Clemente to congratulate his old friend who was now the President-elect and also to convey to him the best wishes of Prince Fahd bin Abdul Aziz Al Saud, who is now King Fahd. When the meeting in Nixon's private study was over, the story goes, Adnan stood up and accidentally-on-purpose forgot his briefcase, which happened to contain one million dollars in hundred-dollar bills. A little gift from the House of Saud to the new American President in hopes he would see things their way from time to time in the course of his administration.

That story, I can tell you unequivocally and from personal experience, is false. No briefcase ever made will hold a million dollars in hundreds.

On the other hand, fill a briefcase with large cut-and-polished gems of the highest quality and it will carry four hundred million dollars—which isn't bad if you might someday have to leave your country in a hurry and in the very same week that every one of your bank accounts on earth is frozen. Rubies, emeralds, diamonds, and sapphires, in that order, are the world's most portable wealth. Flight insurance for dictators.

Khashoggi family lore: In her apartment in New York while she is the First Lady of the Philippines, Imelda Marcos is entertaining Lamia Khashoggi. At some point, Imelda bids Lamia to follow her into a bathroom. Now, Lamia is a woman not unaccustomed to displays of wealth. But, when Imelda lifts the lid of a Louis Vuitton vanity case filled to the brim with loose diamonds and rubies, Lamia swoons and goes down hard.

Apparently Imelda carried the family jewels with her everywhere on earth she and her husband went. And while this might be taken as an indication of their venality, I should point out the Marcoses were not Americans or Europeans and there are historically many good and legitimate reasons for the elected leaders of Third World countries to keep a portion of their nation's treasury under their personal custody and control.

Oft times when a Third World head of state leaves his country, someone else, a not-democratically-elected usurper, takes over. If he's schemed well and made the right alliances, the usurper now has control of all the country's institutions, all the cash and gold in its vaults, all the soldiers in its barracks, all its military arsenal, and all the government's foreign bank deposits. What's the rightful-but-now-deposed head of state to do? If he wants to regain control of his country and save his people, who are living under desperate conditions now and praying for his return, he needs a war chest.

Which is why it's traditional for Third World leaders to stash huge amounts of their countries' funds and of their political parties' funds offshore in their own names. Sure, a lot of times it's venality. But it isn't always. And that's something difficult, I think, for anyone used to living in as stable a place as America or Western Europe to understand.

In 1986, when Ferdinand and Imelda Marcos left the Philippines after accepting their old friend Ronald Reagan's offer of safe haven in the United States and a home in Hawaii, it was reported that U.S. military personnel confiscated a case filled with gems from Imelda as she boarded the U.S. Air Force plane that would fly her and her husband into exile. By some inexplicable oversight, there was no fashion reporter on the scene at the runway, so it went unreported whether the confiscated case was Louis Vuitton. Still, there can be little doubt that the family jewels took a big hit at that moment. But, in the course of her travels around the world as First Lady of the Philippines, Imelda had quite prudently stashed some of her most valuable stones in bank vaults, or in the hands of trusted friends. At least that's what I was told when I was initiated into the honorable and secret trade of supplying gems to kings and despots.

It began in my office, on East 57th Street, in New York. There were these two guys, whose names aren't important here. Let's call them "Schlemiel and Schlimazel," because that's what they liked to call each other when they were giving each other shit. Both of them were Americans. One of them was an American from Israel, where apparently Schlemiel and Schlimazel are the butt of all jokes.

They were gem dealers, big-time gem dealers from 47th Street. Not Hasids. No black hats and curling sidelocks. Schlemiel and Schlimazel looked and dressed like anybody else, which is quite important at a certain level in the secret world of gems. What they told me on the day I met them was that Imelda Marcos had probably the finest gem collection in the world. Worth hundreds and hundreds of millions of dollars.

It hadn't been seen, they said, since Imelda and her husband left the Philippines. But recently, at the highest level in the gem trade—a small circle of dealers who, like Schlemiel and Schlimazel, dealt only in the most important stones, and bought from and sold to only the world's wealthiest people— there had been rumors that Adnan was quietly selling off stones for Imelda. If,

Schlemiel and Schlimazel said, I could get Adnan to sell to us instead of other buyers, I could make millions.

"Go for it," said Miles later that day when I called him in Oxfordshire. "And don't forget to send me my share."

But when I flew to Spain to discuss the story with Adnan, he told me it wasn't true. "I don't know anything about this gem collection," he said. "You know, there's a problem over some buildings in New York, and because of that I haven't even been allowed to speak with the Marcoses for the last several months." Adnan and I strolled around in his garden for a while, talking about nothing in particular. Then his eyes lit up and he grabbed my elbow and said, "But since you've come all this way, maybe I can help you with some others. President Mobutu is a buyer, and maybe also a seller. He'll be in the South of France in a week or two. And perhaps I can find you someone else who wants to sell."

Later that afternoon, I was in a hotel down in Marbella with Schlimazel, who'd come with me to Spain, but I hadn't taken him with me up to Adnan's ranch for our meeting. So, anyway, Schlimazel was sitting next to me when my phone rang and it was Yann Gamblin calling. Yann was a Frenchman, a photographer for *Paris Match*, and Nabila's boyfriend of the moment. I'd seen him up at Adnan's earlier that day.

"Larry," Yann said. "I heard you speaking with Adnan about big diamonds today. He doesn't know I'm calling you, and let's keep it that way. But, look, I have a friend in Paris who wants to sell a big diamond. Forty-something carats, D-flawless, emerald cut. Beautiful. I just called him and got all the information. My friend's a banker selling it for his client. No one's seen the stone yet. You can have the first shot at it. Talk with your friends and let me know if you're interested."

"Bingo!" said Schlimazel. "Plausible deniability. Anonymity. This is how it works. This is the deal. I can smell it."

It was another world Schlemiel and Schlimazel then escorted me through as we chased the 41.72-carat, D-flawless, emerald-cut Golconda diamond quietly for sale by a banker in Paris, and as we chased around the world after Adnan so he could casually introduce us to friends of his who might be sellers, or buyers, and as my new friends showed me the inner workings of the gem trade in New York and Amsterdam and Antwerp and Geneva.

But then, I like other worlds. Hasidic Jews walking around 47th Street with briefcases in one hand and Bagel Nosh take-out sacks in the other hand. It's usually the Bagel Nosh sack the diamonds are hidden in. A wire-thin Israeli named Zve upstairs in his office. Once you get past all the security doors and locks, and you'll only get past those if your face is known and accepted, Zve's actual office is literally about the size of maybe two or three phone booths. But rent's not cheap and that's plenty of room for Zve and his little safe and his wheel, on which he cuts many of the finest fancy-colored diamonds in the world.

Assuming the clarity, cut, intensity, and carat-weight are equal, and that it came by its color naturally, a canary-yellow diamond is worth scads more than a white diamond. And a blue diamond is several times rarer and several times more valuable than a yellow one. Next up is pink, which is much rarer and more valuable than blue. After pink, you're in the realm of green and red, which may be the realm of fantasy. No one is sure if green or red diamonds actually exist in nature. It may be, I was told, the only examples of them ever sold were irradiated, cooked, by fraudsters. A cooked fancy-colored diamond of any color is only worth about as much as a comparable white diamond.

As to white diamonds, they can be beautiful. But they became objects of desire and value a couple centuries ago when they were truly rare. Back then, diamonds were to be found only deep in the jungles of Brazil, and in riverbeds and tiny mines in India. The old Indian mines were centered around a market called Golconda, from which came the finest diamonds in the world. Back then the worldwide production of gem-quality diamonds was only maybe two or three pounds a year.

But late in the 1800s, enormous veins of diamonds were discovered in South Africa. Later in Namibia. Then in the Belgian Congo, latterly known as Zaire. Then Guiana. Then Arkansas. Then Siberia. The truth is there were now so many beautiful white diamonds that they were intrinsically worth about as much as ugly brown diamonds, which are also known as industrial boart. Industrial boart is used all over the world in grinders and saws and drill bits, and the market price for the stuff is about five dollars per carat. The only way De-Beers has managed to keep up the myth of the scarcity and value of white diamonds is by hoarding more or less the world's total production, and only letting stones out slowly.

Still, the smartest gem collectors know white diamonds aren't truly scarce. So they stick to rubies, emeralds, sapphires, and fancy-colored diamonds, which are scarce, and to Old Mine diamonds, also known as Golconda diamonds. Golconda diamonds are truly scarce, because the mines there played out long ago. And there's something special about Golconda diamonds.

The reason cut-and-faceted diamonds can be so beautiful and sparkly in the first place is that diamond is the only gem material that is single-refractive. Single-refractive means light can only pass through the stone in one direction. That's not the case with rubies or emeralds or sapphires, which are beautiful in their own ways but are double-refractive. The principal object of modern diamond-cutting is to position the facets in such a way that they reflect and concentrate light upward, toward, and through the table, the flat spot on the top of a diamond. No one's sure why, but Golconda diamonds have a special intensity and fire to them. Set a D-flawless Golconda diamond next to a D-flawless diamond of identical shape and weight from anywhere else, and you'll see the special fire inside the Golconda. Probably the most famous Golconda diamond is the Koh-i-noor, the Mountain of Light, and it is aptly named.

Schlemiel and Schlimazel didn't deal in common white diamonds or medium-quality rubies and sapphires and emeralds, which other dealers weekly sell by the thousands to jewelry makers all over the world. Schlemiel and Schlimazel and their buddy Zve the cutter called such stones "commercial quality" and to them that meant junk.

In the world they dealt in, transactions are in cash. Ownership is anonymous. Dealers will loan their stones to other dealers who say they have customers who might be interested. This is called memo. A memo is a cryptic little receipt signed by whoever is taking away a stone. No deposit is required. You might not be able to discern it from the language of a memo, but the deal is you can do anything you want with the stone, take it anywhere on earth, show it to anyone you want, claim it belongs to you, sell it, keep it for yourself, or bring it back. If you don't bring the stone back by the date specified on the memo, you have to pay the price specified on the memo by that date.

Beyond memo, almost nothing is written down. Complicated contracts are made orally and then finalized only with a handshake and one word, "*Mazal!*" If the dealers have a dispute among themselves, they don't take it to the courts. It's decided by a council of elders, whose decision is final. Secrecy is paramount. That's how it's always been in the diamond trade and remains today.

Few outsiders have ever seen the way it really works. They are not invited or encouraged. Yet somehow Schlemiel and Schlimazel smuggled me effortlessly into their world and I saw it all.

Even for wealthy, respectable dealers on the up-and-up like Schlemiel and Schlimazel, smuggling is sometimes a necessity. We were flying all over the world all the time with millions of dollars' worth of stones on us, sometimes in chartered jets but more often in airliners. Insurance paperwork had to be filed every time a stone was moved to a new location. Move twenty stones at once and that's twenty separate insurance filings required.

When a dealer takes a stone of significant value into almost any country in the world, he has to either pay import duty on the stone upon arrival or post a bond guaranteeing the import duty will be paid if the dealer doesn't leave the country with the stone by a specified date. Such a bond is called a carnet, and it must be issued by a recognized insurer or underwriter. It gets very complicated and time-consuming dealing with the paperwork of moving stones across borders. But the reputable dealers must do it, and if they don't do it their insurers come down on them.

Except sometimes a stone will come along at the last minute, a stone that's perfect for whoever you're about to try to sell to, and you'll take it on memo, and there just won't be time for all the bureaucracy before you've got to leave. That was what happened to Schlemiel and Schlimazel and me one morning in the Old Town section of Geneva over coffee with another dealer. "Damn if this isn't a beautiful ruby," Schlimazel said, "and I think our customer might love it." Customers are anonymous in conversations between dealers, of course. In no time, a price was fixed, a memo was written and signed, and off we went with the ruby, plus a sweet fancy-yellow diamond Schlemiel had come up with while Schlimazel was haggling over the ruby.

We were supposed to catch a flight to Nice early that afternoon, but we weren't going to make it because of the time we were going to lose on the insurance paperwork and the carnets for the two new stones. So, solid citizens that they were, Schlemiel and Schlimazel decided we would charter a Lear jet so we could leave later and still get to where we needed to be on time. The charter service, punctilious Swiss, told us the absolute drop-dead time by which we had to be on board and taxiing toward the runway if we were going to make it to our appointment, which happened to be with Adnan and Mobutu Sese Seko, one of the biggest diamond collectors in the world. This was an appointment Schlemiel and Schlimazel didn't want to miss, yet, as the drop-dead time approached, the last two carnets still weren't in hand. At which point, Schlimazel said, "Fuck it! We're going anyway! I'll do the stones!"

Schlemiel said, "Band-Aid?" and Schlimazel nodded, and that was all I knew until we were on the plane and over the Alps.

There, Schlimazel showed me the undocumented fancy-yellow that happened to be inside a pop-out ring he was wearing. Personal jewelry worn by its owner is exempt from import duties and carnets. Even a known dealer with a stack of carnets and a case full of stones can't be required to declare a stone he's wearing in what seems to be his personal jewelry. So dealers carry pop-out rings, which are gold rings that look normal but are so flexible that if you know where to push you can pop different stones in and out of them within seconds.

But by then I already knew all about pop-out rings, and I'd already noticed the fancy-yellow on Schlimazel's hand. "So where's the ruby?" I said. "Under a Band-Aid somewhere?"

"Yes," said Schlemiel. "But not just somewhere. Schlimazel has an enormous schlong, a fact which everyone in the trade knows. So sometimes even competitors invite him on selling trips at the last minute when a stone comes up and there's no carnet. In a lot of these countries, the customs agents are bastards when it comes to us dealers. They make us strip and show them everything, *everything*. Schlimazel's schlong is so big he can hide impressive stones behind it under a Band-Aid. Sometimes they even make me lift my balls to show them there's nothing under there. But when Schlimazel pulls down his underpants and they take one look, it scares them, and right away they say, 'Put it back!' "

A few nights later, in fact on the night of the day after I strolled down the beach in Cannes with twenty million dollars in gems, one of them a pigeon-blood red Burma ruby recently affixed to Schlimazel, I went to a party on the roof garden of Adnan's penthouse in Monte Carlo. It was a clear, starry night, and there was a warm breeze that smelled of the sea. Down below us, I could see the lighted cabins of cruise ships and warships and yachts, all so small and perfect from these heights that they looked like toys.

Adnan was working the floor, flitting here and there, chatting and joking with his guests. He was wearing a white smoking jacket over a black silk shirt with a Nehru collar. Lamia swirled in just then wearing jewels and one of the couture creations that were her trademark. It was bright orange silk, with a long, tight skirt and wave after wave of ruffles that seemed almost to sprout into wings at her shoulders. It reminded me of the Sydney Opera House, and it would have looked ridiculous on almost anyone else. But as tall and elegant as she was, and with all that confidence of hers, it was startling and beautiful. Adnan took her hand and led her to me.

"You look terrific," I said as she offered me her cheeks. I smelled perfume and powder as I kissed her. *"Hello, Larry,"* her hot, moist whisper thundered in my ear.

Then Adnan grabbed my arm. "Come!" he said, his merry face reflecting lights from a row of torches burning along the wall. "We will introduce you to Swamiji."

Adnan pulled Lamia and me toward a round-shouldered man dressed in a long white silk robe and white sandals. He had skinny wrists and ankles but was otherwise quite fat. His hair and beard were long and wild and black, and he looked like he might've slept in his robe. There was an inch-wide smudge of red paste centered low on his forehead, and hanging from his neck almost to his stomach was an intricate strand of heavy gold beads. A mala, but a rich man's mala. At the bottom of the necklace was a rectangular gold locket engraved with a single Sanskrit letter.

"Your Holiness," Adnan said, "this is Larry Kolb. He is married to Kim, Soraya's daughter."

"Yes, yes. I have heard of Kim," Swamiji said, smiling at me. His voice was deep and mellow, and he had an Indian accent. He seemed to be in his late thirties, and he was leaning on a tapered black cane with an ornate silver knob on top.

"And I have heard of Swamiji," I said.

"Hello, Larry Kolb," said Swamiji.

"*Bohaat khooshee hooey apsay milkar,*" I said, and at that the smile contorted from the holy man's face, and, at first, the sounds he made were so deep that either he was choking to death or belly-laughing. Adnan and Lamia had no idea what I'd just said, and I was starting to question it myself.

"Did I say it wrong?" I asked when Swamiji finished wiping his eyes.

"No, no, no," he said. "It. . . ." But then he started snorting and giggling, and between spasms, he unleashed little bursts of Hindi to another Indian who was standing a few feet from us. That one was about the size of a jockey and was dressed in a gray suit, white shirt, blue tie.

While picturing him in racing silks, I asked him if I'd gotten the words wrong. "No, no," he said, wobbling his head the way Indians will. "His Holiness said he finds it very funny to see a giant fellow like you wearing a Western suit and speaking Hindi. The accent, everything, was right. That made it funnier, you see."

About now, Swamiji's face was taking on the serene, holy look he strives for.

"You're a long way from home," I said to Swamiji. "Do you enjoy traveling?"

"Life is a journey," he said, and it struck me then that might be the most predictable line I would ever hear.

"Come!" Adnan said, taking Swamiji's elbow and leading him away with Lamia. "I see the guest of honor." The guest of honor was a famous Indian lawyer by the name of Ram Jethmalani, and I met him and chatted with him. But, for God's sake, let's not talk about Indian lawyers right now.

So, anyway, after a bit I strolled back over to the little Indian jockey. I wanted to know more about Swamiji. I'd heard he was close to the Sultan of Brunei, Mobutu, Elizabeth Taylor, and all sorts of others. In the press, Swamiji was billed as Adnan's guru, but I'd also heard that wasn't quite the true story.

"Who is this Swamiji?" I said to the jockey.

He looked reverently for a moment toward Swamiji. "His Holiness is one of the five spiritual kings of India," he said. "He has hundreds of millions of followers. He is so loved in India that when people see him coming they lie down in the street until he passes by. The cane he carries, it is a symbol of his power."

So that was how I came to meet Swamiji, aka Chandraswami. But we'll come back to His Holiness later.

Not so long after that party, United States Attorney Rudolph Giuliani puffed out his chest on my television screen in New York and announced he'd just procured indictments, in New York of all places, of Ferdinand and Imelda

Marcos for looting several hundred million dollars from the Philippines, and Adnan for helping them conceal their assets through a series of sham transactions. "These indictments show that no one is above the law," Giuliani said. But there was actually a little more to it than that.

Well, it wasn't long at all after the indictments that the Paris banker Schlemiel and Schlimazel and I'd been trying for a couple of months now to hammer on the price of the 41.72-carat, D-flawless, emerald-cut Golconda diamond he was selling quite suddenly and precipitously dropped his price. Provided, he stipulated, that the sale would be confidential and quick. He didn't know all sales of important diamonds to dealers are confidential. He didn't know what we meant when we closed the deal—a little more than four million dollars in certified funds in exchange for the stone, inside the Port Franc duty-free zone at Geneva Airport—and shook hands with him one by one and said, "*Mazal!*"

Soon after the indictments, I tried to reach Adnan. But he'd vanished. When I finally reached him, by sending faxes addressed to Adnan to every fax number on earth I knew he had, Adnan contacted me. Not in person. Through a lieutenant.

"The Chief," said the lieutenant, "wants intelligence. Find out what's really going on in Washington. Why is this happening?"

What I found out, through Miles, was certain elements within the CIA were thoroughly torqued with Giuliani for including their old ally Adnan in the indictment, and with Reagan and Bush for letting it happen. Adnan's old friends asked me to give Adnan their best wishes, but they didn't have much else for me.

However, working on my own for a few days, I did discover something that got my attention, and that I was sure would interest Adnan and might be useful to him.

I called the lieutenant. "I've got to see Adnan."

"It's not possible."

"It's got to be possible. I've found what he's looking for. You know what I mean."

The next day the lieutenant called me back and told me to proceed to Paris, where one of Adnan's planes would pick me up.

"Fine," I said. "Where is Adnan?"

The lieutenant didn't respond.

"Where am I going? Antarctica, or the tropics? How should I pack?"

"Don't tell anyone," the lieutenant finally said, "but A.K. is at the Mena House. You're going to Egypt."

So off I flew to Paris with a bona fide in my briefcase.

At Le Bourget, where Lindbergh landed, I climbed aboard Adnan's DC-9 and into the king-sized bed in the back. I thought I'd be traveling alone, but then some others came on the plane. Two men, two women, all Americans. Then another American. The only one of them I talked to at first was a handsome, still-youngish lawyer in a blue suit, by the name of Frank Morse. The famous Frank Morse, who at the mere age of twenty-eight had somehow become Howard Hughes's general counsel.

And that, in its way, was fitting, because in the secret world that's all around us, only certain planes have landing rights and this was one of them. Douglas DC-9, tail registration VRCKO, Victor Romeo Charlie Kilo Oscar, registered in the simultaneously sunny and shady jurisdiction of the Cayman Islands. Recently, to throw off the hounds whenever Adnan was aboard, his crews had been filing false flight plans for this plane, then after takeoff calling air traffic control and advising them of new routes and destinations. But that was baby stuff compared to the legendary night in 1973, during which, at Heathrow, Adnan had sneaked Howard Hughes in a baggage van past Her Majesty's Customs and Immigration officials and smuggled Hughes onto this plane. At four the next morning, Hughes and six of his aides deplaned in the dark at the end of a runway in Freeport, the Bahamas, and twenty minutes later Hughes was ensconced in the penthouse of the Xanadu hotel. By then, the plane was in the air again, on its way to Mexico. For months, almost no one knew how the mysterious tycoon had left London, or where he'd gotten off to.

Charming fellow, Frank Morse. Bright as hell. Quick. An excellent dancer. There was a short delay for some reason. Captain Jerry came out of the cockpit and told us air traffic control had told us to hold for twenty minutes, maybe longer, and he was going to open the door so we could have some fresh air. After a few minutes, I looked out a window and saw Frank Morse and his girlfriend Rio had gone outside. They were waltzing in front of the wing.

Once the door was closed again, and we were almost under way, I said to Theresa, or David, or whoever it was looking after us in the cabin that day: "I think I'm going to take a nap now. How long's it going to take us to get to Egypt?"

That's when I learned Adnan had slipped out of Cairo the night before. We were going to Spain.

Adnan answered his front door by himself. No entourage. Minimum staff to cook and clean. Adnan was on the lam, and the fewer witnesses around the better. Frank and the other Americans weren't with me, were still on their way here from Malaga airport. Adnan had had me cut out of the pack and delivered here separately. It was just him and me.

"Come," he said. "Yella!" He led me through the living room to the broad white terrace out back. He sat down at a little table, with his back to Marbella and the Mediterranean, and I sat across from him. Looming in the distance to my right was the Rock of Gibraltar, and over the shoulder of the man who'd made his fortune bridging two cultures, across the sea, on the horizon, the hazy brown ridge I saw was the mountainous coast of Morocco, the tip of Africa, the edge of the Arab world.

"It's better we talk out here," Adnan said. "What is your news?"

"Do you remember your first meeting with Rudolph Giuliani?"

Adnan looked perplexed.

"Well, no."

"This is what I learned," I said. "Something like a dozen years ago, when Giuliani was a young lawyer in private practice in a firm in New York, one of his clients was John Tumpane." Adnan's eyes grew very interested just then.

John Tumpane was a lawyer who happened to own a large construction and logistical services company which operated in Saudi Arabia and Libya and Iran and Spain and several other places. Adnan knew all that because he'd brought the Tumpane Company into the Kingdom of Saudi Arabia as its exclusive agent.

Together Adnan and Tumpane had made tens of millions of dollars each. But at some point Tumpane had tried to break its contract with Adnan. Which was contrary to Saudi law. In Saudi Arabia, commission agency rights are exclusive and for life.

Adnan had sued Tumpane, and eventually won.

"So," I told Adnan, "at your deposition in the Tumpane lawsuit, it was Giuliani who asked you the questions for Tumpane. And apparently you did an excellent job of slipping and sliding, talking in poetic Arab terms, and Giuliani never got anything useful out of you. You showed him up in front of his client. And when you and your lawyers walked out of the deposition, Giuliani turned to John Tumpane and vowed, 'Someday I'm going to cut A.K.'s nuts off for how he treated you today.'"

"How do you know this?" Adnan said.

"I can't tell you from whom I learned this," I said. "But I do have this check to show you, as proof that my source was there in the room that day." The check I showed Adnan then was the canceled check that Tumpane Company had eventually paid to Adnan's company Triad Marketing to settle the lawsuit. Adnan looked at the check, both sides, carefully. It was only for six hundred thousand dollars. Pocket change. All this trouble was over that?

"What did Giuliani say again?"

"He said to John Tumpane, 'Someday I'm going to cut A.K.'s nuts off for how he treated you here today.'"

"Oh boy," said Adnan, followed by "Well . . . he's trying."

Quite ironic, I was thinking, if Giuliani indicted Adnan as a favor for a friend, since all Adnan was accused of in the indictment was doing a favor for a friend. Somewhere here there must be something useful, a corollary applicable to my unified theory, but I lost the thread when Adnan stood up. "Yella! Come with me."

He led me back into the house and into the control room, where he reached out his hand without saying a word, and the young Lebanese chap on duty gave him an envelope containing five thousand dollars in hundred-dollar bills. Adnan passed it to me without looking inside. "That's for your expenses," he said, taking my elbow and pulling me close. Then he lowered his voice: "They'll be here soon. After I meet with them, take the Concorde to New York with the lawyers, listen all the way, and then tell me what they talked about."

Just then, the Lebanese fellow manning the control room got excited and said, "Look, sir! On CNN!"

There were a few television screens built into the wall, and on one of them was Imelda. She was in Manhattan, wearing what appeared to be a ball gown, climbing the courthouse steps through a mob to surrender to U.S. Marshals and pay her five million dollars bail.

Next they cut to a grainy black-and-white photograph of a woman and a man getting out of a car. *Doris Duke,* said the caption. The man was tall and silver-haired and wearing ArisTotes, the wide-sided sunglasses made popular by Aristotle Onassis.

"I know them," I said. "He's Franco Rossellini." Next on the screen was footage of Imelda the day before. "What's this all about? I haven't seen any news for a day."

"Didn't you hear?" Adnan said. "While you were traveling I guess, this great American woman paid the First Lady's bail."

The next day we were all still in Marbella. No quick Concorde flight from Paris back to the States. At least not yet. Adnan and the lawyers were in heavy session, and I slept through it. Until Adnan sent for me, and met me in the piano room, where he introduced me to another one of the Americans who'd been on the plane. Michael Hershman. A clean-cut American, if there ever was one. He looked about forty. I assumed he was a lawyer. But Adnan said, "Mr. Hershman used to work for American Army intelligence, and now he's looking into my case."

"That's right," said Hershman.

"Tell Mr. Kolb what you learned," Adnan said.

"First off," said Hershman, "this indictment is a can't-lose proposition for Giuliani. No one knows it yet, but he plans to resign in a couple of months. So he takes all the glory of the indictment on television, and if the case is lost at trial all he has to say is 'Look, I did my part. I can't help it if my successor dropped the ball.' And," Hershman went on, "Giuliani has been attempting to bring this indictment for several months. But the White House always blocked it. So he waited until a crucial time in the campaign, three weeks before the election, and then he told Reagan and Bush that if they didn't allow him to go ahead with the indictment, he would call a press conference and complain that the White House was interfering with the criminal justice system to protect its friends."

"Bold!" I said. "Positively J. Edgar Hoover*esque*."

"Right," Hershman said. "It takes brass balls to blackmail a sitting President of the United States. But it appears to me that Giuliani's got 'em."

It's funny you should mention balls, I thought, but I didn't say it, because I knew Adnan wanted to ponder the information I'd given him before he told anyone.

Months later, while still on the lam, Adnan called me from Riyadh. Said, "Bring me more intelligence."

So I went to see Franco Rossellini.

Somehow Franco was all these things at once: aristocrat, man of the masses, stereotypical Italian film director, eccentric artist, hilarious raconteur, vicious gossip, slob, fashion plate, ladies' man, flaming queen, and world-class walker. His uncle Roberto Rossellini had raised him and taught him to make movies; his aunt Ingrid Bergman was but the first formidable female in his life. Since then, his dearest friends had been Maria Callas and Imelda Marcos and Doris Duke, not to mention his cousin Isabella Rossellini. It was a rare paragraph Franco spoke without including at least one of those famous names. In a single sentence he could manage to deify and excoriate his closest friends and family.

But somehow the overall effect was kind of charming. When I'd first met Franco, at a Park Avenue dinner party a few years before, he'd arrived carrying a long silver cigarette holder and a sleek black cane and dripping an opera cape. Over dessert, we'd discovered we had a mutual enemy, and Franco had invited me to his apartment the next afternoon. "We'll compare notes about this horrible man. No, better yet, we'll plot a *murrrrrrrr-der*," he'd said.

The night that I visited him on the mission for Adnan, like most of the other times I'd been to Franco's apartment on West 56th, he was wearing an old white T-shirt, wrinkled pants, and white tube socks. No shoes. The bottoms of his socks were gray with grime from padding along on the hardwood floors. "Oh, my dear, it is *so* good to see you!" Franco said, with the air of a man in an opera cape. "Where is Khashoggi? Imelda and I have been *dying* to know. And his lawyers won't tell us *anything*."

"Adnan's in a safe place," I said. "In the Middle East. How is Imelda?"

"Of course she is terrible. *Terrible!*" Franco said, throwing his hands in the air. "Her husband is dying, and they make her come here like a common thief."

A sly look crossed his face for a second. "Imelda may be a thief. But never a *common* one. Oh, my dear, I tell you this is a monstrous thing. Monstrous! *Where* in the Middle East?"

I started to speak, but Franco just kept on going. "You know, the arraignment was just a *circus.* But Imelda walked through the mob like an empress."

Franco leapt from the couch now. Tilted back his balding, crew-cut head. Then, all the way across the living room, and back, he mimicked Imelda's walk.

"And when it was over," he said, lowering himself back onto the couch, "she got in the limousine with Doris and me to ride to the helicopter to go out to Doris's estate in New Jersey, and President Reagan kept calling and calling the car and Doris was just *furious!* She told me to tell him to stop calling. Can you imagine? Telling the *President.* . . . Well, Doris can be so rude, and I have better manners than that, and, after all, the President is a *friend.* So I told him, 'I'm sorry, the First Lady isn't available right now,' and he said to me, '*Wellllll* . . .'" Now Franco rearranged himself, and for a moment he became Ronald Reagan: "'I just wanted to tell my friends Imelda and Ferdinand that I'm sorry about . . .' And just then of course Doris rips, *rips,* the phone out of my hand and says to the President, '*She doesn't want to talk to you!*' and *slams* the phone down. On the President! Can you *imagine?*"

Suddenly Franco's arms stopped waving and he was perfectly calm. "Shall I have Enzo bring us some espresso?"

"Please." It was while we were sipping coffee that I asked, "Why did Mrs. Duke pay Imelda's bail?"

"Oh, my dear, you don't really *believe* this, do you?" Franco picked up a cigarette and a short black cigarette holder and joined them. "Doris barely *knows* Imelda. Before this performance of New York, they have only met a few times. Imelda is *my* dear friend, and Doris is *my* dear friend. I am the only link between them. And Doris is so *cheap!* Impossible! Doris didn't pay a penny until Imelda sold a diamond and someone sent the money to Doris's banker."

I laughed my ass off then. Because it had finally come to me that Schlemiel and Schlimazel and I had funded Imelda's bail. There'd been no hint of deceit in Adnan's face that sunny afternoon in Spain when he'd told me he knew nothing about selling Imelda's jewels.

That discovery I kept to myself. It was what I learned next that I reported back to Adnan.

Franco lowered his voice now. He said, "Last week, Doris and I went out to dinner with Niarchos. Stavros had come from Washington—a private dinner at the White House the night before. And he gave us a message for Imelda from the President. He said to tell her he's sorry about all this. But there is nothing he can do about it."

"What do you mean?" I said to Franco. "He can pardon them all."

"Well," Franco said, "Doris's lawyers have been working on this thing of the pardon. But Niarchos asked, and the President said he *cannot* do it. But, you know, he is the most powerful man in the world! If he wants, he can walk ten miles across the sand without leaving a footprint." Franco's face brightened then. "So we can all pray it will be a Christmas surprise, and this whole stupid thing will finish. And, oh, my God, how Imelda is praying! You cannot believe it if you should see her house in Honolulu! My dear, I tell you it is *filled* with statues of the Madonna."

A perfect Oxfordshire morning. It was one of those rare, glorious days you're certain there could be no better place in the world to be than the English countryside. The air was crisp. The sky was bright blue, with just a few baggy white clouds in the distance. From inside the chauffeured gray Mercedes Miles had sent to pick me up at Gatwick, I watched low stone walls and hedgerows racing by, and sunlit green and yellow fields and meadows and gentle hills that seemed to roll on forever. After more than an hour of traveling through that wonderful landscape, we turned off into the village of Aston Rowant, glided past the common green, and stopped on the gravel driveway of the ivied-brick cottage which was the home of Mr. and Mrs. Miles A. Copeland.

"Hey, Larry!" Miles was opening his front door, escorted by his enormous guard. A bullmastiff. "This is Delilah. Don't let her worry you. She looks ferocious, but she's about the sweetest dog you'll ever meet."

Miles led the gentle Delilah and me down a hall and into his book-lined study.

Miles was dressed for comfort: a well-worn tan cashmere cardigan, a white dress shirt, unbuttoned at the neck, gray wool trousers, brown leather shoes with soft rubber soles. His eyes were alert and his voice was still as full of energy and fun as ever. But every movement—walking, turning, lowering himself into his high-backed armchair—looked painful. "Ever since my car accident," Miles said, not the first time I'd heard it, "this damn arthritis is killing me."

Enter a pleasant, middle-aged Englishwoman bearing tea on an antique silver tray. She was dressed like a librarian, an effect completed by the glasses hanging on a chain around her neck. Miles introduced her as his secretary, and I remember I thought that was odd. Because I'd never heard of her before. *Who are you selling me to now, Miles? Or who's vetting me?* We talked a moment. Then she set the tray down on a low table and left.

I sat on a sofa across from Miles and poured two cups, milk in first. Then, for a moment, Miles and I talked about why the English, who couldn't cook to save their souls, could make such a fine pot of tea, while the French, who cook like wizards, always screwed up tea. It's an insoluble mystery, we finally decided.

My journal, begun that very night, records that I'd come there at Miles's request, my expenses to be reimbursed out of our fund, but that, beyond that, there'd been no indication of how we might profit from what Miles had called me there to discuss. While I drank more tea and tried to break through my jet lag, Miles debriefed me about my visit with Adnan in Marbella and what I'd told him.

Miles had always said Adnan's playboy life was only cover—that deep down Adnan was a serious statesman and a valued friend of the United States. Miles was furious about Adnan's indictment. "When Adnan and King Faisal came to Washington in 1966," Miles said, "Faisal and Johnson posed for the press and did their thing while A.K. so impressed the right people in behind-the-scenes meetings that the U.S. Government *completely* overhauled its posture toward the Saudis. Up until then, Washington's answer to every Saudi request for sophisticated military hardware was automatically no, because no one could see they had any use for it other than blowing up Israel. You know, Larry, it's not an exaggeration to say that, if it weren't for Adnan, the Soviets would control the Arabian Peninsula."

We caught up until I started yawning and Miles moved over to his desk and got back to work on what he'd just been starting on when I arrived.

Smearing some politician somewhere. I don't remember his name. Actually, I do, but I'm going to change it here, though Miles was about to make sure no one in our part of the world has ever heard of him.

"Come sit over here," Miles said after a few minutes, pointing to a wooden chair where I could sit behind his desk with him. "You look a bit too pooped for us to get started. But you might as well watch and learn."

Objective: Miles gingerly typed onto his computer screen, *to embroil Ahmed Dajani in a scandal of sufficient moment to topple him from his position of power in the government of the Hashemite Kingdom of Jordan.*

Miles said, "Where did I put that file?" He looked around the room. "There it is. On that table." I knew by the way he said it he wanted me to bring it to him. I did, and got to practice my upside-down reading along the way.

The "file" was a stack of dog-eared papers, probably two or three hundred pages. Private investigators' reports on a certain Ahmed Dajani, rising Jordanian bureaucrat.

While I delivered the stack to Miles's desk, he was telling me, "What I have to do now is create a parable of good and evil. Something so basic everyone in Jordan can grasp it. And the problem is, I skimmed through some of these this morning. I haven't seen it all. But I'm not sure it's what we need."

Delilah lay on her back at her master's feet, racing her paws through a dream.

Miles handed me about half the stack and said, "Find something useful." Then he put the rest of the pile in his lap and started skimming through it.

A couple minutes later, he said, "This isn't much good unless you want to know what Ahmed Dajani ate for breakfast on his vacation in Hawaii."

"I haven't found anything either. What *did* he eat?"

"We *really* don't need surveillance reports and photographs of a family man on holiday with his wife and kids. What we need is to catch him putting the squeeze on a government contractor. Passing secrets to a foreign agent. God, where'd they get this junk?"

Minute-by-minute surveillance logs and telephoto pictures of the Dajani family's idyllic progress through tourist spots in Honolulu, Los Angeles, and New York. Copies of Ahmed Dajani's hotel bills. Credit bureau reports. Telephone bills. A couple of California real property deeds in the names of two of Dajani's friends. That was about it.

"But we don't have time for a new investigation," Miles said. "Which means I'm going to have to work from whole cloth."

Now Miles departed for a few seconds, into a glassy-eyed patch of jazz. Whistling, humming, very quietly, totally absorbed.

Then he snapped out of it and turned back to me.

"Time for a little alchemy, Larry," he said, eyes twinkling. "Time to turn lead into gold, *molehills* into *mountains*."

Then he froze.

After a moment, he said, "But first I've got to make a phone call. It's always best to start with something *real*. We need at least a few well-documented facts. To which we'll add, of course, a few well-documented half-truths, and a lot of well-documented absolute bullshit. We also need to know: Does this have to hold up forever? Or just through a few weeks of headlines?"

Miles picked up his phone and dialed, Delilah rolled over, and a moment later Miles broke into his zesty Southern-fried Arabic. His grammar was fine, as far as I could tell, and I'm no expert on that, but I was sure his accent was straight out of Muscle Shoals.

After a minute or two, he hung up. Said, "He wasn't home."

Then Miles froze again. Genius at work.

Next he looked at me and said, "Maybe I can just weave in these dates we know Dajani was in California and New York."

He pointed me to one of the bookcases. "On the bottom shelf," he said, "there's a tall thick book with no name. Coffee table size. The cover is shiny black. . . . To your left."

"This one?"

"Bring that here."

I set the book in front of Miles.

He said, "Open it." The cover was heavy, and every effort except typing seemed to hurt his hands. "This," he said, "is an FBI file on the hunt for Edwin Wilson."

Wilson was a former CIA officer, an expert on clandestine arms acquisitions and transfers, who'd found he could make a whole lot more money selling plastique and other ordnance to the Libyans than he'd made while a CIA official. His defense, when he was arrested and charged with shipping explosives to Libya, was that, after he officially retired from the CIA, he'd continued to work for them in an unofficial capacity, and that what he'd done he'd done with their knowledge and at least their tacit approval. Sounded familiar.

I said, "How'd you get it?"

Miles said, "A friend of mine in Washington used it for some research he was doing. When he was finished, he bound it and gave it to me."

Miles said, "Look here," then started flipping through the pages.

Agents' reports on surveillance of Wilson in Libya. Requests to the NSA for transcripts of telephone traffic. Wilson's bank statements. Wilson's tax returns. Wilson's property deeds. Wilson's medical records. Wilson's birth certificate. Interviews with informants. Psychological profiles. Background reports from field offices in every town in America Wilson ever lived in.

"That's how it's done," Miles said. "Have a look."

I pulled the book to my lap.

"Notice all the clutter," Miles said.

There was a lot more of it than I would've expected. Notes scribbled in the margins, underlined passages, initials, signatures, filing stamps, distribution stamps, classification stamps, clearance stamps, coffee-cup rings. "That's how a real file looks," Miles said. "Amateurs forget the clutter."

While Miles went to the loo, or somewhere, I read from the Wilson file. And when Miles came back, he stopped at the bookcase and pulled out a binder.

Inside it, he showed me, were several style guides. Instructions distributed to secretaries and typists and others creating documents in the White House, the FBI, the CIA, the State Department, the Justice Department, and various other U.S. Government agencies. Detailing the formats to be used for letters, memoranda, reports, cables, travel expense requests—all the paperwork that keeps bureaucrats fat and happy. And annotated with the precise time periods during which each style guide was valid. One doesn't want to forge a letter dated 1983 in a format that was discontinued in 1979, or on stationery that wasn't used until 1987.

Next Miles brought out an accordion file. From which, like a magician, he extracted little stacks of crisp genuine sheets of letterhead from: The White

House; the Federal Bureau of Investigation; the Central Intelligence Agency; New Scotland Yard; Interpol; the U.S. Department of Justice, Northern District of New York; Johns Hopkins University; The London School of Economics; The Royal Geographic Society; The Royal Institute of International Affairs; Bechtel Corporation; Banque Paribas; Credit Suisse; Arab Bank; the Rand Corporation; Claridge's; The Plaza; The Hay-Adams; the City of Hershey, Pennsylvania; and all sorts of other interesting places.

Miles opened a desk drawer and started handing me rubber stamps.

Backwards, I read:

"CLASSIFIED"

"Route To: _____"

"RCVD BY_____/DPTMT_____/DATE_____"

"TOP SECRET"

"SAIC_____"

"SECRET"

"FILE____-_____"

"EXPENDITURE ACCT _____"

I said, "I'm starting to be amazed."

Miles kept passing me stamps. He looked certain to slip into a burst of jazz. Any second now.

Instead he said, "We'll need those, but not the stationery. I just pulled those out to show you. But we won't need originals, and I've got all this stationery input into the computer."

To prove it, he typed a few commands into his keyboard.

A few seconds later, a blank United States Government Memorandum form emerged from the laser printer, followed immediately by a sheet of Treasury Department letterhead. I'd never seen anything like this before.

Miles said, "So what do you want to make of Mr. Dajani? A smuggler, or a tax cheat? A stooge for organized crime? How 'bout a pedophile?"

According to my journal, I said, "Don't ask me. I didn't even know his name until a few minutes ago." And Miles said, "You know, Larry . . . well, I don't have to tell you. Government leaders are *never* the Pollyannas they try to appear to be." And I said, "Thank God." And then Miles said, "Power politics is an amoral game. They all know it. And they all play it. In spite of the 'shock' and 'outrage' they profess whenever their opponents, or their own henchmen, are caught at it. If Dajani is a shrewd player, and we must assume he is to have gotten so far, then he's analyzed his new strategic importance on the gameboard, and he fully expects his opponents to attack him. They *must*. And since they must, I guarantee you Dajani will prefer a propaganda campaign to the other traditional Arab method of attacking politicians."

It was quiet for a moment. Then Miles said, "Larry, what I'm thinking is I could create a file. Probably an Interpol file, or maybe FBI, about an investigation into Dajani's suspected involvement in whatever the hell the client believes Dajani's been up to, in this case, arms dealing. Then I'd take the file to a reporter I've given stories before. I've got two or three in mind."

Miles's eyes skipped over me to the entrance hall, where Lorraine was just arriving from a walk. He greeted her with his eyes, then returned to me.

He said, "I'd let him see it, long enough to get the drift and to see enough detail to believe it's authentic. But I wouldn't give him a copy. We wouldn't want it under a microscope."

I said, "Why would he write about it?"

Miles said, "Because I've got credibility." Miles settled back in his chair. "Because the only hard details included in the file would all check out. Because I'd tantalize him. No pressure. If he didn't write about it I'd go on to the next reporter, and the first reporter would know that. Eventually somebody would write a cautiously worded story and Dajani would react."

I said, "And the closer you'd come to hitting a nerve, the more outraged Dajani's denial will be."

Miles said, "Probably so. And once the story is out, Dajani's enemies will crawl out of the woodwork. Everyone will recognize this as a good chance to pour a bucket of bullshit on his head. There'll be rumors, follow-up stories, investigations. Hell, if we're lucky someone will find *real* evidence. But that won't even matter much anymore. Because it won't be enough to dispute the story. He'll have to disprove it. And not by legal standards, but in the court of public opinion. And, when it's done right, that's impossible. It's all a matter of subtlety and finesse. If the wrong operator is running the campaign, even a true story comes off like a smear. But, if it's done right, it can be *very* effective. My friends in Washington tell me no one was ever better at it than Yuri Andropov."

Miles turned back to his computer keyboard, saying, "For now let's put together a few pages of a file on Dajani, and then take a look with fresh eyes and see how it plays."

Miles looked through a couple more binders. And finally selected an FBI case against a ring of Austrians illegally purchasing high-tech weapons and exporting them out of Charleston.

Then he started typing. He was mostly copying, but, as he typed, he turned the Austrians into Jordanians, and the port of Charleston into the port of New Orleans.

"Whenever possible," he explained, "it's much easier to copy text from real reports and just change the names and dates and things like that. Because it's the writing that's usually the hardest part. Until I figured out it was easiest to copy real files, I used to have to rewrite a document five or six times before it finally took on the authentic bloatedness of the U.S. Government's official style of writing."

He changed the name of the FBI man handling the case to Special Agent Thibodaux.

He said, "There's got to be at least one of them there. Half the people in Louisiana are named Thibodaux. In some parishes down there *everyone* is named Thibodaux."

He typed the revised text into the computer matching the typewriter fonts and formats of the originals. He copied the text onto the proper stationery. He printed out four pages of what, until that morning, would have seemed to me parts of an authentic FBI file. He applied rubber stamps, doodles, big loopy signatures, and cramped spidery signatures, and initials, and then he bent, folded, spindled, stapled, and otherwise mutilated the pages. He poured wine on one of them. He made six generations of photocopies of every page, then handed me the lowest-resolution copies of the documents, and said, "What do you think?"

I said, "I think no one is safe."

Miles said, "My first year in Damascus, it felt like I spent half my time forging love letters from Syrian politicians to thirteen-year-old boys."

Lorraine, who'd just appeared in the doorway, said, "Boys, I do hate to spoil your fun. But it's time for lunch."

Delilah led us to the dining room, where Lorraine seated us at an antique table and served a leg of lamb, fresh from the oven. Then she sat down and said, "Well, Larry, has Miles been showing you his toys?"

"I'm amazed," I said. "It's just dawning on me what an impact modern technology must be having on the forgery business."

Miles said, "Documentation's getting easier. But authenticization's getting harder."

Authenticizing the files, I knew, meant backstopping them—planting the documents in the real files and the real word-processing systems of whatever organization had purportedly issued them. So that, if an enterprising journalist or intelligence agency got an inside source to check to see if a document was authentic, it would indeed be found in the appropriate place. A second layer of verisimilitude.

Miles III had just bought a chateau in the Dordogne. We talked about that for a while, then about me. Miles and Lorraine always asked about me. A horse and rider were clopping by outside the window, and it was raining now, or misting. The sky was dove gray and the rain so fine that it seemed to be suspended in the air. "I read on the plane last night," I said, "that it takes about nine minutes for a snowflake to fall to earth from a height of a thousand feet."

That was the last thing any of us said before we began watching a glistening-black Austin Princess limousine curve its way toward us from the far side of the common green. Then Miles said, very casually, while reaching for his glass of claret, "What's a BBC car doing here?" And what Miles said after that was "Oh, hell! I totally forgot! I'm supposed to go on TV to talk about Iran-Iraq!"

He rose in pain and in a hurry, saying, "I've got to put on a suit."

Lorraine got up, saying, "I'll help you."

But then suddenly Miles was calm, and he said, "Oh, wait. Today's only radio. I can go like this. Tomorrow's TV."

We walked with Miles to the car. Lorraine helped him in. I passed him his wine. Miles said, "Sorry, Larry. I totally forgot."

And that was the last I ever heard of Ahmed Dajani.

Because, by the time Miles got home, I'd succumbed to jet lag, and retired to The Compleat Angler, an historic inn about ten miles away. Where, Lorraine had informed me before I left, "You can feel free to sleep in tomorrow, while Miles is doing breakfast telly."

So the next words I heard out of Miles's mouth were on the television the next morning, while I stared out my window at the Thames. Which wasn't all that wide there.

British TV presenter voice: "Have you ever met Saddam?"

Miles: "Just once. About ten years ago. Some of my friends sent me in to see him while I was in Baghdad."

British TV presenter voice: "Did you like him?"

Miles: "He was gracious enough. I wouldn't call him a merry fellow. But he's clever. And he's *not* crazy."

British TV presenter voice: "Of course, they bill him now as the successor to Nasser, the new Pan-Arab leader. How did he compare to Nasser?"

Miles: "I'll grant you he's wily. But, compared to Nasser, Saddam Hussein is a mental midget."

I loved Miles.

L ater that morning, I went back to Aston Rowant. Miles got home from the BBC just after I arrived. Then he proceeded to tell me that, in the early days of the CIA, his Political Action Staff had done a study of how world leaders made decisions. And were startled and fascinated to learn that more than seventy percent of them relied to some extent on the occult. They named their discovery OHP. Occultism in High Places. Astrologers were planning the daily schedules of Sukarno and Nkrumah. The Afghan Parliament was routinely settling deadlocks with cockfights. And this wasn't just going on in Asia and Africa and South America. Europe too.

"If you're finding this hard to believe," Miles said, "don't forget how greatly relieved all of us in the know were when we learned recently that President Reagan was listening to his wife's astrologer rather than the Secretary of State."

Next Miles told me that in the late 1950s the Political Action Staff launched an OHP offensive. They planted mystics, seers, witch doctors, palm readers, astrologers, and the like on national leaders. Or, in some cases, they didn't need to plant anyone. They simply went to the seers already in place and co-opted them.

"They were frauds, not fools," Miles said. "So a lot of them were more than happy to pass along, as predictions, the fairly solid information we gave them. It made them look like prophets. And gave us direct access to our targets' souls."

I said, "Did you actually implement this?"

Miles said, "Hell, yes. But I assure you it was all done in the *best* possible taste. And it worked very well, Larry. After we got the mystics hooked on our information, we could feed them whatever kind of bullshit we wanted and they'd pass it on. It was a great success."

Miles said, "So I was thinking . . . what about that swami of Adnan's? How tame's he?"

His Holiness Chandraswami Maharaj was a wild man, a great swirling devil of a holy man-tycoon who specialized in Hindu mysticism, tantric sex, and power politics. Miles had met him. But I knew him better. Owing primarily to the fact that, several times during the last few months, Adnan, who had enough on his plate as it was, had asked me to help keep His Holiness—or Swamiji for short—out of his hair. I'd done my share of babysitting lately.

And just last week Miles had asked me to be prepared to brief him on Swamiji when I came to England. Search your memory and your files, Miles had said. Focus on your personal observations. Think it through. Then organize it and write it all down.

But, in the end, I hadn't had time to finish it. When I arrived in Oxfordshire, I had it all laid out in bullet points, with long detailed passages beneath some of them, and blank spaces beneath the rest. So I remember reading some of my briefing to Miles and winging the rest of it. Probably it went something like this:

I first met Swamiji at a party on the roof garden of Adnan's penthouse in Monaco. It was someone's birthday. Some big-shot legal scholar from India.

After dinner and cake and speeches, Adnan led Swamiji and Lamia and me into the apartment. Trailed by my friend Schlimazel, of the enormous schlong—you remember hearing about him, Miles. That evening Schlimazel was artfully playing the role of my thick-necked guard. He stood in the doorway looking tough while the four of us went into a little den.

We sat down around a mahogany coffee table.

Adnan said, "What have you got for us?" He said it like I was the next act on that evening's entertainment bill. Which, come to think of it, maybe I was.

I pulled a little velvet pouch out of one of the front pockets of my suit jacket. Inside the pouch: twenty million dollars' worth of jewels.

It sounds like a lot, Miles, but that was at full retail.

I laid out on the table a marginally pigeon-blood-red Burma ruby of almost five carats. As good Burma rubies go, that's huge.

Next, a ninety-carat cornflower blue Ceylon sapphire. The best sapphires are from Burma, not Ceylon. Still, this one was quite a sapphire.

And then the Indore Pears. A matched set of pear-shaped white diamonds. H-color. About forty-six carats each. Old Mine. Golconda. Once the property of a maharajah who wore them in his turban. They'd been stolen more than once. During the Raj, lust for the Indore Pears provoked a sensational murder that rocked India. Now the Indore Pears are acknowledged to be the most fabulous set of earrings on earth.

Lamia took them into her hands, saying, "Oh look, Baba!" and you could tell she was in love, that she'd just decided she wanted the Indore Pears for herself.

Adnan broke her heart. "Yes, I think the President may like these."

The President in question being Mobutu Sese Seko.

Lamia lovingly put the Indore Pears back on the table. "Our appointment with the President," she said to me, "is tomorrow afternoon. His villa isn't far from here. Just you and I alone. No guards, okay?"

I said, "Fine," wondering how we were going to explain this to the insurance company.

Then I fished one more stone from the pouch. Oval-cut. Royal blue. Four-hundred-twenty-seven carats—nearly the size of a chicken egg. It seemed to glow from within. "This," I announced, "is the largest cut-and-faceted gem-quality Burma sapphire in captivity."

And, when he saw it, Swamiji's eyes went so huge that immediately I put the stone into his stubby fingers. He held it up toward a lamp and grinned. He said, "Has *wonderful* aura. *Very* special aura."

Adnan plucked the stone from Swamiji's fat fist. Adnan raised the stone to his eyes for a moment, and then, absentmindedly, like a bored baseball pitcher, began throwing the sapphire a few feet up in the air and letting it drop into his palm. Over and over.

Miles interrupted me there, said, "How much was it worth?"

I said, "Maybe three or four million. I'm not sure." Then I went back to the telling:

Swamiji's eyes never left the stone. You could tell that he, too, was in love.

Up, down, up, down, up, down, up, down, up, down, up, down—until finally I snatched the sapphire out of the air and returned it to my pocket.

Bullet point: *The Swami's Book of Memories.*

The next day I was summoned back to the penthouse for a private audience with His Holiness. I'd felt no great attraction to him the night before, had wondered what all the fuss was about. I'd heard he could be entrancing. I'd heard wondrous tales of how presidents, kings, and business moguls, who'd agreed to meet the holy man for just a few minutes, as a courtesy, had spent ten minutes with him and then suddenly cleared their schedules to give him hours, days, even weeks of their time. But even now I felt no attraction as Swamiji toddled into the living room to greet me.

I'd also heard his proudest possession was his photo album. He seemed to be carrying it toward me now. A thick book. Covered with gray velour. He handed it to me as he sat down in front of me, clumsily, and then he said, "Open. Look. Look."

I did, and inside were at least a hundred photographs of the swami. With the Sultan of Brunei. With Mobutu. Nixon. Mubarak. Jimmy Carter. Lynden

Pindling. Marcos. Kaunda. Suharto. Indira Gandhi. Rajiv Gandhi. Elizabeth Taylor. King Hussein. King Birenrda. King Tupou, of Tonga. Sheikh Isa of Bahrain. Sultan Qabus. Prince Rainier and Princess Stephanie. Jim Wright. John McEnroe. And in every photograph save one the image of Swamiji was of the man before me. Fat. His hair and beard long and black. Wearing a thick mala of hammered gold, and the flowing white *dhoti* skirt, shawl, and sandals of the Mahatma, but with a dark and brooding look about him.

But I flipped back to the photograph with Indira Gandhi. And, in that one, in place of the fat swami was a boy. A skinny teenager. Short-haired and smooth-faced. Dressed without guile in his best trousers and shirt. He was shy, spiritual, glowing with innocence.

I said, "What was your name then?"

A wistful smile. Very quietly, he said, "Nemmi Gandhi. Indira Gandhi loved me so much. When she heard I was riding on my bicycle to visit her, she waited outside her house for me. Sometimes when I arrived she garlanded me." He smiled again. But not at me. The swami no longer even saw me. He was twenty years and six thousand miles away, just discovering his power.

Miles was listening carefully.

I told him one day in New York I'd asked Adnan how Swamiji managed to enthrall so many heads of state. Adnan had thought about it carefully and replied, "It can be very lonely for a president or a king. He has no equal he can tell his problems. No one to tell him what to do. A link to God—even if it is only imagined—can be a very powerful appeal."

I said, another time in New York, when I was sitting around with my friend Bob Marx, telling him about the swami and his effect on leaders, Bob stopped me and said, "What's his secret?" And that I'd answered with the first true thing that came to my mind. Which was "He *talks down* to them."

Bullet point: *45-G.*

It's just twenty steps down from Adnan's celebrated apartment on the forty-sixth and forty-seventh floors of the Olympic Tower to the darkest reaches of the Third World. Apartment 45-G is where Adnan keeps Swamiji in New York.

The first time I went there, having been summoned by the swami for reasons unknown, Adnan led me down the back stairs and down the hall to the apartment. Adnan said, "Welcome to Delhi" as we entered, and the moment the door opened an invisible cloud of incense, sweat, snuff, and perfume oils, spiced with betel nut, chillies, coriander, cardamom, cloves, turmeric, and God knew what else hit you all at once. Just inside the doorway was a pile of shoes and sandals. To which we added our shoes.

Adnan had bought this separate two-bedroom apartment to put up guests he wanted to keep out of the flow of his own apartment. Swamiji and his entourage fit that bill. In fact, by now, even when Swamiji isn't in town, he usually has at least a few of his people staying there.

45-G is Indian Country. If they don't have squatter's rights yet, they will soon enough. And it's debatable whether anyone would want the apartment back when they leave anyway. A first-time visitor might get the impression Adnan didn't bother to furnish this place in his usual style. But I happen to remember visiting 45-G a few years before the Indian invasion. It was a beautiful little pad. Two bedrooms. Amber-colored marble, plush carpets, and really lovely couches and chairs covered in butter-soft tan suede. But on the day Adnan first took me there to see the swami, the place looked less like a tycoon's apartment than a fraternity house on the morning after the best party anyone could remember. In the dining room, plates, bowls, and glasses still bearing remnants of breakfast littered the table. The tabletop—once a perfect slice of shimmering crystal—was now chipped in several places. An enormous chunk was missing from one end. Wads of duct tape blunted the jagged edges. Evil brown food stains covered the satin chairs scattered around the table.

The central feature of the living room was now an ironing board. On which, when Adnan and I arrived, one of Swamiji's faithful band of helpers was pressing yards and yards of unstitched white muslin, to be swaddled around his master. Sconces hung on the walls sideways, or upside down, their shades dangling precariously or already fallen to the floor. Venetian blinds run terminally amok crazed what should have been a fabulous view of St. Patrick's Cathedral and lower Manhattan.

"Hello, gentlemen. Hello, hello," Adnan said to the six or seven disheveled members of Swamiji's entourage who sat listlessly in the living room.

The suede couches and chairs I remembered were still there. But now they were badly pocked and stained. Several cushions looked as if, well, as if they'd been gnawed. Adnan ignored the destruction and led me to Swamiji's room, the sanctum sanctorum where the holy man holds court. And we'll get there in a moment.

But first, the waiting room. The next few times I returned to 45-G, I went without Adnan, and was made to wait, as every other visitor was made to wait, crowded amongst the entourage on the drool-stained suede until the holy man sent for me.

The air had been breathed too many times. It was always hot. The heat was always turned on and the windows were always closed, simulating India. Even the most influential visitors I came across there—and we're talking mighty government officials and businessmen from India, U.S. congressmen, prime ministers, and deputy prime ministers from all over the Third World—were required to commune with the ironing board for several humbling minutes before one of the disciples would lead them down the passage to an audience with His Holiness. Lowlier supplicants sometimes sat waiting on the couch all day.

While you wait, you can read a pamphlet about His Holiness. There are little stacks of them conveniently all over the place. Swamiji, as it turns out, is a much bigger deal than I had imagined on meeting him. Not only is he one of the five spiritual kings of India, but, when he was born, in 1949, in a holy village in Rajasthan, to the Goddess Maa Durga—who to Hindus is none other than the female personification of God—the most renowned astrologers of the age predicted the newborn would become either a great king or a celebrated yogi. The tract goes on from there, about how our beloved Swamiji is the world's new savior, able to enchant all and sundry with his supernatural powers and magnetic personality, here amongst us to cleanse our souls and rid the world of chaos and corruption. And, I swear to God, Miles, it also says he's here to fight air pollution.

Swamiji calls his motley entourage "my disciples." I don't know where they come from, or where they go back to when they're not with him. An ever-changing cast, all Indians, most of them play multipurpose roles—as valets, secretaries, cooks, waiters, bearers, wipers, and general lackeys. But there are specialists among the ranks: The entourage usually seems to include at least one masseur and one nubile young female devotee, plus sometimes a religious scholar or two. With no apparent pattern, the entourage waxes or wanes almost daily. Usually five to ten of them are staying with Swamiji in 45-G at any one time.

My two favorites from the entourage are Dev Ketu—whom we'll come back to—and a sly old geezer who goes by the name of Achariyaji. Says he's a Sanskrit professor. Probably actually only in his late fifties, though he tries to act older.

Achariyaji is a gentle soul with a round funny face and a knack for making people laugh. Awake or asleep, he seems always to be sitting on the same spot on the same couch wearing a tan *kurta* shirt and matching pants, every time I arrive in 45-G. Unless he happens to have gone home to India, which he does from time to time.

Achariyaji speaks little *understandable* English. His delivery is Yogi Bear as Ben Kingsley as Mahatma Gandhi after somebody spiked his apple juice. A sage, crazy rhythm of hand and facial gestures, sighs, sudden bursts of pidgin English, chuckles, and unintelligible patches that just trail away. I've never actually conversed with Achariyaji. The best I've ever hoped for is to crack his code.

I don't know what drives Achariyaji, but it appears to me he could do with some more money. Probably he's corruptible—if that's where you're heading with this, Miles.

Some members of the entourage are wealthy. Some are penniless. Some of them are worldly sophisticates, some still mastering toilets. A few of them wear suits and ties. Most wear loose flowing *kurtas* and pajama pants. All of them are there to serve Swamiji.

And, if I arrive in 45-G before, say, nine-thirty most mornings, all of them are asleep, in their underwear or their wrinkled clothes, snoring, sweating, slavering on the suede and on the floor. And for that reason alone, I try never to visit 45-G before ten. But timing your descent from Adnan's palace into the netherworld of 45-G is a lot trickier than that.

Bullet point: *The Inner Sanctum.*

After several visits, I began to develop a sense of how much I could get away with in 45-G. Mysterious *sahib* that I am, I seem to be off-limits. I'm not sure why, but no member of the entourage will challenge me when I say I'm too busy to wait. Thus, I've effectively been granted the freedom to advance unannounced to Swamiji's room. But with that freedom comes certain risks.

Some days I hit it just right. Like the last time I was there. When I arrived, a few minutes after ten, I found Swamiji holding court in his big blue bedroom. He was sitting on a high-backed chair as if it were a throne, wearing a fresh red dot on his forehead, wrapped in white muslin, with his golden *mala*—prayer necklace—gleaming on his chest, and reeking with the tea rose perfume he wears by the quart.

His room is kept in better repair than the grubby outer chambers.

To Swamiji's left, atop a black dressing table, was a little shrine. Brightly colored prints of the Hindu god Shiva and his wife Shakti. A tiny pile of flower petals. Incense. A life-size brass head of Buddha with a fresh mark of sandalwood paste on his forehead.

In Swamiji's lap were tattered prayer booklets, wrapped together in a knotted saffron cloth.

At his right hand was a telephone, which, after the frequent calls for him had been screened by his disciples, he occasionally answered in torrents of fervent Hindi.

On entering the room, I brought my palms together in a *namaskar* salute while I said "*Namaste*," and, as has become our ritual, Swamiji laughed at my accent and then mimicked it back at me: "*Namaste.*"

His two visitors had already risen to show me respect. He told them to come back later.

I sat down in front of him, and he laughed his ass off and clapped his hand, while telling me, in exquisite detail, of news from India, news of the tribulations of one of his enemies. Not a religious enemy, Miles. Swamiji has political enemies, not religious ones.

We spoke uninterrupted for maybe ten minutes, and then I escaped. Straight up the back stairs to Adnan's apartment. It had been quick and painless.

But the timing can go horribly wrong.

For example, last month, arriving at around ten to eleven one day, I found the bloated holy man lying spread-eagled on the floor. Wearing only a white *dhoti*, a skirt, which was hiked up above his thighs and tied around his hips like a diaper. His enormous gray-brown belly and withering limbs shone with a light coat of oil. Anguish warped his face, and his mouth was opened wide. He was screaming for mercy.

Swamiji's morning massage is not a pleasant spectacle, for him or anyone who witnesses it.

Which brings us back to my other favorite member of the entourage, Dev Ketu. Swamiji's yogi masseur. Dev is a grinning, handsome, muscular young Indian with a slick red Porsche, a Ph.D. in Sanskrit, a house and family in Connecticut, and a Tom Sawyeresque sense of humor. Dev's English is fluent but distinctive. He pronounces every syllable and never uses contractions.

He has a genius for terrorism by massage. His method brooks no foreplay. His fingers go straight for the pressure points, hard as hell, and he is unmoved by threats, bribes, or pleas for compassion. The pain is terrifying until Dev lets go. But the result is magic.

Miles, I became a believer in Dev last year when I went to him with a bloodcurdling three-day-old headache. For a moment he looked assessingly at my head, like he could see the pain. Then he jabbed two fingertips just above and below my ear and the pain fucking quadrupled. After a few seconds of that, Dev jerked my neck down and around and instantly all the pain was gone.

But back to Swamiji on the floor, panting and blowing.

He began wailing now. "*Nahi, nahi, nahi,*" no, no, no. His face was ashen, and the outer edges of his lips were caking with dried foam. But Dev would not let go of the holy man's calf. How could such pathetically scrawny legs and arms be attached to a sumo torso? Now Swamiji was whimpering and struggling to roll himself into a fetal ball. And he was succeeding. Except for the one leg over which Dev had absolute control.

Dev said, "This will teach you to sit around and eat all day and never exercise! Why do you never do your yoga anymore?"

Swamiji hadn't seen me enter.

"*Namaste!*" I said loudly, mispronouncing it deliberately this time. His glazed eyes searched in the direction of my voice and he continued to writhe.

From the blackest region of his soul Swamiji saw in me a tiny glint of hope. "Stop. Stop. Must . . . talk to Larry . . . important . . .," he gasped and sputtered. But Dev did not let go. "Ooohhhhhh . . . *nahi, nahi . . . nahi!*" Swamiji began to twitch.

I said, "I'll wait in the living room." Suddenly I was lonesome for the ironing board and the entourage. But Swamiji flailed his free hand, the one Dev had not just pinned under his knee, and grunted a command that I stay and talk with him. Anything to divert his mind until the terror passed.

I stayed, but kept my eyes well above Swamiji. Too many times now I'd come across his screaming, thrashing, nearly naked body and I was afraid it would leave an indelible impression on me. Still, the way I figure it, Miles, between ten and eleven is the best time to risk a visit to 45-G. Because, in 45-G, lunch can begin anytime after eleven. And lunch with Swamiji is worse than attending his massage or tiptoeing across the snoring, dribbling disciples.

I can't tell you how many times I dodged Swamiji's invitations to lunch, but finally, once, he was leaving for India and said he didn't know when he'd be back, and he'd complained to Adnan that he kept inviting me to be his guest of honor for lunch and I kept making excuses. Adnan told me I'd better have lunch with Swamiji.

So on the appointed day, I got there about twenty minutes before noon. Swamiji was still in his inner sanctum. I found him talking on the speakerphone. "*Atcha, at-cha. . . . Atcha!*" Okay, okay, okay, he said, then he pushed a button to end the call.

"*Namaste,*" Swamiji greeted me with the smile I've learned is his genuine one. One of his disciples—I can never remember all their names—came in and handed him a tall glass of milk. Swamiji chugged it. Spice seeds streaked the glass like a chocolate syrup trail in a little kid's milk glass. Then Swamiji cut loose an enormous burp.

Swamiji said, "Are you ready for lunch?"

I said, "You know I'm always hungry."

Swamiji smiled and burped again and stood up and led me to the dining room.

He sat at the head of the table. Seated me at his right hand. Disciples filled in the seats farther down. Dev Ketu arrived last and got the duct-taped place at the far end, where a chunk of the glass tabletop is missing.

When the cooks had brought all the food to the table, for a moment Swamiji paused in silent prayer over his plates and bowls. Then he chugged down another glass of spiced milk and dug in. Literally.

Swamiji isn't one of those swamis you read about who are too good for food and live on nothing but air and sunshine. Nor is he one of those jolly fat men who eat like sparrows and leave you wondering *Could it be his glands?* And he's definitely not one of those etiquette-minded hosts who care which fork you use next. But he does bring to the task of eating a certain porcine gravitas. Meals are a serious matter to His Holiness, and it's best to stay out of his way when food is near.

Like most Hindus, Swamiji doesn't eat meat or eggs. To complicate things, he also doesn't eat potatoes, onions, radishes, coffee, chocolate, or many, many other things. What's left—besides the fruits and sweets with which he begins and ends his meals—are mostly dishes of rice, peas, beans, corn, tomatoes, cauliflower, okra, and other vegetables. Onto which Swamiji has his disciples pour thin yellow and brown sauces until everything is about the consistency of stew—which Swamiji eats with his fingers.

He holds the tips of his thumb and all four fingers of his right hand together—like an Italian holds his hand while speaking—and with just that hand he somehow balls rice, vegetables, and gravy into dripping lumps which he shovels and slurps into his mouth. Swamiji performs fantastic feats of gluttony every time I see him eating. He polishes off several plates at each sitting—pausing only to burp, rhapsodize over the food, or wait for a disciple to bring in more from the kitchen.

I'd seen all this but never actually had to eat with him, until now. His Holiness paused from his slurping for a moment to smile at me and gesture toward the food. "Good food, no? Eat more," he grunted happily, while a sticky yellowish paste of rice, peas, and sauce obscured parts of his contented face and coated his right hand up to his wrist.

"Indian food is delicious," I said honestly. *But not this Indian food.*

I love eating in Indian restaurants in London. And a few in New York. But I didn't enjoy Swamiji's food. All the slurping, burping, and farting put me off.

His burps are louder and longer than any I've ever heard. What prestige they must have given him as a boy! And, when he needs to fart, he lifts a cheek and farts. And nobody seems to notice.

When Swamiji had finished four or five plates and I'd finished the two I thought was the minimum I could politely get away with, he upped the ante on me. "Now," he said to me, "I have surprise for you. I have best *gulab jaman,* your favorite dessert, flown here for you from London."

Shit! Miles. Sometime before that lunch I must've made the blunder of telling Swamiji how much I loved *gulab jaman.* Past tense, not present. I may never eat another bite of *gulab jaman.* Swamiji cheered me on while I ate four bowls of the stuff.

Under all the layers of mystery, flowing white cotton, fat, and dripping vegetable curry with which Swamiji obscures himself, he can't lose the charm of obviously wanting to be loved by everyone. Nor his frustration that I haven't fallen in line. He's genuinely hospitable to me, and would be glad to have me eat lunch with him every day.

Bullet point: *Airports.*

When Swamiji left for India a few days after that lunch, Adnan asked me to go with him to the airport. The fat swami, four disciples, and I rode in a limo to JFK.

As His Holiness Chandraswami Maharaj toddled into Air India's VIP lounge on his silver-and-ebony cane, mouths dropped open and several passengers approached him, slowly, diffidently, to reverently touch his foot.

Swamiji was grinning at me like a proud child. "You see what I told you," he said to me. "In India I am like Pope."

And then there was a time I flew with Swamiji and a gaggle of disciples from Nice to London. They'd been staying on the boat and Adnan needed them off it. Asked me to go with them to London. That is, to make sure they left.

When we got to Heathrow, I was soon convinced I'd at last seen everything. I was beside Swamiji when we walked out of customs into the terminal. Where the usual throng of people was pressed along the rail waiting for arriving passengers. Chauffeurs were holding up signs with names on them. Swamiji stopped in his tracks—when out of the crowd emerged two men with the glow of veneration on their faces.

They were dressed in the finest bespoke suits from Saville Row, club ties and tasteful gold links at their starched white collars and cuffs. Their feet were laced into black oxfords. Lobbs, I thought. Very proper. Very expensive. And one of them was carrying an umbrella. They looked every bit the prosperous English gentlemen they seemed to wish they were, except for their inconvenient gray-brown skin and Indian features. Well, these two gentlemen silently approached Swamiji. And—I swear to God, Miles—one after the other, the two tycoons lay down flat on the filthy floor, stretched out in front of His Holiness, and then lovingly kissed his dirty, sandaled feet.

Swamiji at first feigned disinterest. Then he began to tap his cane as if he were impatient to get on his way. But I caught him checking me out of the corner of his eye—making sure I was taking it all in.

When we got outside, this unlikely pair helped Swamiji and me into their Rolls-Royce. Behind it was a convoy of Mercedes to carry disciples and baggage. They drove us about an hour north of London to their home, a huge Tudor manor house surrounded by several acres of gardens. They were Sindhis, they told me. And they were brothers. Both of them lived there. And a sister or two. And assorted spouses and children. There was plenty of room for all of them. And us.

We ate dinner in the banquet hall. Like a scene in a movie. At an ancient oak table so long that I was oblivious to Swamiji. While wives and sisters and disciples fawned over the holy man, I sat fifteen places away with the brothers and we talked about politics and business. Away from the swami, they seemed quite normal. They were in oil, and shares, they said. It was the damnedest thing, Miles. Whoever they were, they loved the swami. I still don't know what to make of it.

Miles had become the most appreciative of audiences. No more questions. No interruptions. No jazz. His eyes barely ever left me. Orange reflections from the fireplace glowed in his glasses. My father's glasses. And by now, Delilah and Lorraine had joined us.

Bullet point: *The Grand Yagna.*

I mustn't fail to mention Swamiji's fire act. We were in a house in Toronto. The home of one of Swamiji's followers. Not Ernie Miller, this was the home of someone who lived closer to the city center.

Out on this enormous balcony, Swamiji performed what the leaflets passed out by his friends described as a *Grand Yagna.* A fire ceremony. Several times that day he'd commanded me to be there. I'm sure he expected me to come up with some excuse to duck out of it at the last minute. But the truth was I wouldn't have missed it for anything. When I arrived, there were already several piles of shoes at the door and seventy or eighty Indian men, women, and children standing or sitting on the balcony.

Swamiji was wearing his finest white silk robes and sitting in front of a mound of burning sandalwood logs. From where I stood, his face kept fading in and out between wisps of smoke. Around the fire were little piles of joss sticks—that's incense—spices, fruits and nuts, flower petals, and silver cups of ghee, clarified butter. Almost everyone but Swamiji was chanting. His face brightened when he saw me. He nodded and motioned me to a seat of honor just behind him. A gorgeous girl in a rich blue sari stood up immediately. I was embarrassed, but she made me take the seat. Swamiji turned and smiled at me. Made sure I was noting all the love surrounding him. More than anything else, he wanted to be adored by everyone. And he knew he'd never won me over.

After a little while, Swamiji began to chant and everyone else went silent.

He stood up, lighted a sandalwood stick, and slowly circled the mound—touching the stick to the flames in several places. Then, still circling and chanting, he placed mangoes and bananas in the burning pile. Somehow it was as if, through his chanting, he was drinking up the concentrated intensity of the crowd and feeding it back to them, doubled. Soon his chant moved into a new propulsive phase that quickened him, and almost everyone else in the room stood up and started to move toward the flames. When Swamiji sat down and became very still, they formed a loose queue that snaked past the fire. There were more than a hundred of them now, circling the burning mound, chanting in unison, dropping offerings of fruits and cloves and nuts into the flames, staring with love at Swamiji as they passed by. Someone poured ghee onto the flames and a bank of sweet white smoke wafted over me. I closed my eyes and listened to the chanting.

"What a gift our Swamiji has!" one of his new followers said, while nudging me to open my eyes. Then he added a question he didn't expect me to answer: "Did you know that when he was young he performed a *yagna* in a place in south India where it had not rained for seven years, and then it rained for nearly a month!"

As to Swamiji's formative years, Lorraine, he says that when he was a teenager he lived up in a tree in the Himalayas. Meditating. But I read he was once a college student, in Hyderabad. And that he got his start selling cheap herbal antacids to nabobs and maharajas. Passing them off as precious aphrodisiacs. And there might be something to that. Because, one afternoon in France—it was on the boat, that day I flew with them to London and the Sindhi brothers met us—I had an ache in my shoulder and Dev was massaging me. Swamiji happened by the cabin we were in. He heard me and dropped in to watch.

While Dev held me down, I looked up at the blurry holy man as his hand dropped toward my face and then his fingertip jabbed into my jaw joint. It hurt. Not like Dev would make it hurt, because Swamiji's fingers are weak. But the thing was the holy man scored a direct hit on the pressure point.

Swamiji grinned at me and said, "You see. I know massage too."

"From Dev?" I asked.

"No, no, no. My guru. I study massage long ago."

And when the swami was gone, Dev said, "Swamiji was once a masseur and herbal healer."

I said, "In India?"

Dev said, "First in India. Then in Dubai. That is where he made his first big money. Healing sheikhs. Giving them sex-u-al power."

Here's a telling detail, Miles. You'll remember that when I was young and stupid—or some might say, stupider—out in California, I once knew a swami and his followers. And I learned to pray with them. They chanted, "*Om shanti shanti shanti shanti.*" Which means "God, give me peace."

But what Swamiji and his followers chant is *"Om shakti shakti shakti shakti."* Which means "God, give me power."

As you know, Miles, the swami has some money. Apparently, when Adnan met the swami, the attraction was not spiritual but financial. The swami had about a hundred million dollars socked away in Canada, managed by his disciple and front man Ernie Miller.

Ernie is billed as a wealthy benefactor of Swamiji; but it's all a façade. The ivied mansion on several acres in a tony suburb of Toronto, the Rolls-Royce, the Falcon 50, with just enough range to fly nonstop from Paris to New Delhi, the two factories in Toronto, the major ownership stake in EuroBank, of the Cayman Islands—all are owned in name only by Ernie Miller. All were purchased with the swami's money, as his trustee. When the swami's in Toronto, Ernie and his wife move into a guest bedroom to let the swami take over the master suite.

A hundred million dollars! Some of it paid to the swami by grateful sheikhs, for antacids, until they ran the swami out of Dubai. A few million of it paid by Tiny Rowland, as you may remember, for secret tapes of the swami talking Mohamed Al Fayed out of information about the true ownership of Harrods. But most of it paid by the Sultan of Brunei—to fund the swami's mission of promoting world peace—before the Sultan ran the swami out of Brunei.

But, if I may borrow a phrase, Miles, I'll grant you the swami's wily. But compared to Adnan, the swami's a mental midget. I've heard Adnan got seven million out of the swami the first week he knew him. And plenty more since. A hundred million doesn't go as far as it used to. Especially if you hang around with Adnan.

Now, Miles, when you asked me to write this, you said to end it with what I think makes the swami tick.

You don't see all that much about Swamiji in the press in the States. Sometimes over here you find him in the tabloids and some of the gossip magazines. But, in India, they either love Swamiji or hate him. He has his supporters, but most of the press there excoriates him. They call him the Godman. They call him a "Godman, bagman, con man—all in one."

But, Miles, I'm telling you: They're missing something important. The fundamental factor everybody misses is that Swamiji is a true believer. And that's why so many people fall for him. I've seen him enough to know he's telling the truth when he says that long ago he dedicated his life to God. Yes, he kept claiming to be a humble, penniless holy man even after he became a tycoon. But that doesn't mean he believes God is pleased with him for it. Yes, he's lying when he claims he's been celibate for the past twenty years. Had me fooled at first. I realize now he plays hide-the-holy-salami with those pretty young devotees he keeps around.

But, Miles, what if he was telling the truth when he said that at the age of eighteen he devoutly promised God he would be celibate for the rest of his life? Swamiji is a true believer who knows he's strayed. And that's the horrible joy of it.

Consider the possibility, Miles, that Swamiji is terrified of the wrath of God. I'm telling you, the man prays and preaches and chants praises for hours every day, while his face glows with religious joy. The story of Swamiji is the story of a spiritual boy who glowed with innocence until one day he discovered the key to worldly respect and riches. And all the temptation which came with them.

With the possible exception of the instant Jed Clampett's shot missed the possum, in no other single moment has such a flood of improbable power and wealth been released as when little Nemmi Gandhi finally understood the forces within him and changed his name to His Holiness Chandraswami Maharaj. The Vaticanesque air of godliness and infallibility which came with the new name and title brought him supremacy over men whose wealth and power were merely secular.

Now Swamiji could keep mere presidents and sultans waiting, lecture them on godliness and righteousness and charity, talk down to them. And no one was more impressed by the magnificence of it all, by the sound of his own voice, than Swamiji. Soon he began to see the deference and adulation bestowed on him as his natural due. With power came riches, and never-ending moral conflict. The story of Swamiji is the story of nothing less than the epic battle for his soul.

Miles said, "Holy shit! You've outdone yourself, Larry! And, as to the swami, he sounds perfect."

And so it came to pass: that Miles and I made a plan that day in Oxfordshire and, intelligence cell that we were, we kept it to ourselves; that Adnan, who was more than happy to send Swamiji off with me, loaned us a plane, though he didn't know the real reason why; that Swamiji and I and a whole troupe of his disciples flew off to Brasília, where we met all sorts of interesting people; and that I found myself in a hotel suite in Rio de Janeiro, high above Ipanema Beach, slurping down caipirinhas and reciting a lesser work of a lesser Metaphysical Poet while encoding a message bound to keep people up all night on both sides of the Atlantic.

W e got into Padre Miguel d'Escoto's white van, which was made in Japan, but at the moment happened to be on the tarmac beside Adnan's DC-9 at the Aeropuerto A. C. Sandino—just outside Managua, the capital of Nicaragua, where things had been a little tense lately. What with all the revolutions, counter-revolutions, death squads, assassinations, assassination attempts, harbor minings, blockades, literacy drives, volcanic eruptions, and, most recently, the presidential election almost everyone believed had been rigged by the CIA.

Inside the terminal, passport control was guaranteed to be a bitch. According to a report I'd received a few days earlier from someone in the know, the whole place was brimming with mysterious Cubans and East Germans and Russians, and some very sinister-looking Americans. Plus soldiers of fortune from all over the earth, journalists, Swedish diplomats, peaceniks, missionaries, and Contras slipping back into the capital. No matter what side you were on, you were sure to be within ten feet of an enemy agent while you waited, for at least two hours, probably closer to three or four, standing in line in the sweltering arrivals hall before they'd let you out of the airport.

But when the Foreign Minister of Nicaragua, and that's what Padre Miguel d'Escoto was, picks you up himself in his big white Japanese van, your passports are stamped and you're on your way in seconds.

Padre Miguel was shaped a bit like a teddy bear. He was bald, had a Friar Tuck beard, and was wearing jeans and a guayaberra shirt. In addition to his government duties, he was a leader in the international movement to free Nelson Mandela, and Padre Miguel was also a Maryknoll priest. That is, a Roman Catholic priest, of the Maryknoll order. Before he was called home to become Foreign Minister, he was a missionary working amongst the poor in Chile. Padre Miguel was also a moving target. Recently he'd been the intended victim of a spectacularly unsophisticated assassination attempt orchestrated by the CIA and the Contras. More on that later.

Padre Miguel sat up front beside his driver. Behind them were Swamiji and Dev. Next: Kim and me. And behind me sat the already mysterious Renee

Radka Ramirez. Blond hair, slim, mid-thirties, Eastern European accent, bright red lipstick. Wearing glasses and a flouncy skirt and blouse, with a pink scarf around her neck. She'd introduced herself as a cultural specialist from the Foreign Ministry. I took that to mean intelligence officer. Beside her sat a young Nicaraguan in blue jeans and a T-shirt, with an AK-47 laid casually across his legs and the safety off.

We passed rows of Soviet helicopter gunships—MI-24s—the fabled Hinds, which I counted. And rows of AN-2s, Antonov troop transports, biplanes, which I also counted. Not that there weren't plenty of other Americans passing by here regularly these days, but Miles had taught me to count such things whenever the opportunity arose, so I did.

We were waved through a checkpoint. We turned onto the road to Managua and took the scenic route. Padre Miguel kept up a running commentary from the moment we slipped out of the airport.

The vistas: brown mountain ridges; he gave them names. Tan and yellow plains; likewise. A smoking volcano, Volcán Momotombo. Quite an arresting sight. Peasant shanties by the hundreds, open spaces, then a barrio.

We'd reached the edge of the city. Campaign slogans elaborately painted on stucco walls. F.S.L.N. in red and black—the Sandinista colors. UNO in royal blue. Rusting beer signs.

At an intersection—walking through stopped traffic—women selling brightly colored bottled drinks. Kids selling *Barricada,* the Sandinista newspaper. A man balancing a tightly coiled garden hose on his head, with strings of candy, chewing gum, and what I took to be lottery coupons hanging from his shoulders. In one of his hands, a thick pack of Nicaraguan currency; in the other, a slim stack of greenbacks and a calculator. Padre Miguel, who had a subtle command of English, not to mention economic theory, said, "And that is a one-man conglomerate purveying garden supplies, confectionery, hope, and currency exchange."

Suddenly in view: Lake Managua. So big it looked like an ocean.

When we made it into the city proper, it wasn't a city. Most of Managua was rubble. Padre Miguel told us that, in the great earthquake of 1972, eighty percent of the city's structures were destroyed. Eighteen years later, with so much else going on, they still hadn't had time to clear it all. We saw what was left of the Managua Cathedral. We saw the Plaza de la Revolución, and the shiny new National Assembly building. We passed a broad green park on a gentle hill leading up from the lake. Padre Miguel said this used to be downtown. The biggest buildings in Managua were here.

By the way—like everybody else there—Padre Miguel said Managua with a silent *g.* And Nicaragua with a silent *g.*

Welcome to *Ma-na-wa, Ni-ca-ra-wa.* Rubble capital of Central America.

Padre Miguel said, "After the earthquake, Somoza left the fallen buildings here. We removed them, then built this park. We were planning to do more, but then . . ."

He didn't finish, and he didn't need to explain.

Through all of this, Swamiji had uttered not a word. Just before we'd left the plane, out of the blue he'd told me to announce to Padre Miguel that, throughout our time in Nicaragua, His Holiness would be fasting and meditating and praying for peace, while remaining silent except between the hours of seven and nine each night. He'd had me explain that he did this twice a year, for two weeks at a time, and that this was a discipline his guru had assigned to him when he was just a boy of twenty, and he'd never broken it since. He'd had me further explain that normally he stayed totally silent for the entire two weeks, but, because of the importance of his mission here, he'd been granted special permission to speak for two hours every night. What I was thinking while I said all this was: *Where does he come up with this shit?*

At the end of the park, we passed the Managua Inter-continental Hotel. It looked a bit like an Aztec pyramid. Except, at second glance, you saw it was made of concrete and actually rather ugly. It was Nicaragua's finest hotel. Inside it were three of Nicaragua's eleven working elevators. According to Miles, every phone in the hotel was tapped by multiple intelligence services. I remember that, while we drove by, I wondered how they managed that without bumping into one another.

We drove on.

Padre Miguel was so damn nice. He looked at me, very apologetically, and said, "We're going to pass by the Foreign Ministry office. There's a fax I've been waiting for, and I need to run in and get it. I promise you I won't be more than three minutes and then we'll be back on our way."

We passed through a security gate, then stopped in the converted strip mall that was now the Foreign Ministry of Nicaragua.

When Padre Miguel came back, true to his word, in a couple of minutes, and still apologizing profusely for delaying us, because we must be tired after our journey, quite suddenly I heard my father: repeating everything he'd ever told me about the loneliness and guilt of an infiltrator.

And then I heard Miles. *Keep smiling,* he said. *Act natural. It's only a game.*

When Swamiji and I'd set out in Adnan's DC-9 for Brasília, to attend the inauguration of Fernando Collor De Mello as President of Brazil, the plan Miles and I'd come up with was basically to dangle Swamiji in front of as many Latin

American leaders as we could get him in front of. Which could be quite a few, because every Latin head of state would be at the inauguration.

When we snared Daniel Ortega, when, in fact, Daniel was about the only Latin American leader who showed any interest at all in Swamiji, Miles and I had been shocked. Because, at that very moment, Daniel—who for the past decade had been the U.S. Government's Foreign Political Enemy No. 1, or 2, or 3, depending on whose list you looked at—had lost his country's presidential election just three weeks before and was constantly in the news while the world waited to see whether he would peaceably relinquish control of Nicaragua to the U.S.-backed winner, Violeta Chamorro.

It happened that Vice President Quayle, Fidel Castro, Daniel Ortega, Swamiji, Dev, and Kim and I had all been staying in the same hotel. And the one who seemed to have the largest security contingent of all was Ortega. Kim watched him pass through the lobby one afternoon, and told me about it when I got back to the hotel a few minutes later. She said Ortega was surrounded by at least fifty armed men, blocking traffic for him. I said, "I want to meet him." She said, "You'll never get to him."

It took me most of a day. After several politely tendered and politely rejected requests made through the proper protocol channels, through good luck and the hotel's back stairwell—I somehow got inside a cordon of Sandinista guards and was just about to knock on the door of Ortega's suite when he opened it and smiled up at me quizzically. At this moment, five or six guards were waving Kalashnikovs and pistols and hurrying down the hall toward me.

I prayed Ortega would remember me from my very brief encounter with him in New York a few years before. We'd literally bumped into each other on the sidewalk on Seventh Avenue when he hopped out of a limo. Most improbable, I know, given the carloads of Secret Service agents who escorted him everywhere he went throughout his visit to New York to deliver an address at the United Nations. But it had happened.

Ortega didn't remember. But he couldn't have been kinder to me.

I made sure everyone could see my hands were empty—just like I had when his Secret Service detail had surrounded me in New York.

Ortega shooed away his guards.

I asked him if he would meet briefly with a religious leader from India.

Ortega looked at his watch. He said something in Spanish, and a tall, pretty, and slightly chubby girl who said her name was Lourdes and that she was from the Foreign Ministry materialized beside me and translated. "The President said, 'I am very busy. But, if your friend can be here in five minutes, I will spend five minutes with him.'"

I ran down the stairs to Swamiji's bedroom. He was asleep when I got there. Four minutes later, he was wrapped in wrinkled white robes and a sincere smile, carrying his thick gray photo album like a preacher carries a Bible, and toddling humbly into the living room of Ortega's suite.

Ortega brought in a fat guy wearing bib overalls and a madras shirt. "Hi," he said. "I'm Father Miguel. I'm the Foreign Minister of Nicaragua, and I'm going to translate for you."

Swamiji seemed to know he was on the clock. Quickly, he opened his album and started showing Ortega pictures. When Swamiji got to the photo of himself with Rajiv Gandhi, Ortega told us he and Rajiv were friends.

To which Swamiji responded that he was Rajiv's spiritual advisor and I was one of Rajiv's closest friends, and that, since Mother Indira's assassination, we had all been working hard together to restore the power of the House of Nehru throughout India—just, Swamiji said, as our new brother Daniel must be restored to power in Nicaragua.

I cringed. Swamiji had known Ortega for all of two minutes when he'd sensed this commonality and pounced on it. Quite crudely, I thought, and this had to be the end of our meeting. But somehow Swamiji had forged a bond. And three minutes after he met Swamiji, Daniel Ortega had invited Swamiji and me to be his houseguests in Managua.

A few days later we'd met Daniel again in Rio, twice, for three or four hours each time.

Miles told me all this had raised the hackles of certain men in Washington who felt they had the Nicaragua situation well in hand; but that, in the end, it had been decided we should accept Daniel's invitation—because of my report on the enormous extent to which President Daniel Ortega Saavedra had opened up to His Holiness Chandraswami Maharaj.

When we passed what was once the headquarters of the dictator Somoza's goon squad, the Guarda Nacional, Padre Miguel said this was where Daniel spent each and every one of his years as a teenager. In jail.

Daniel didn't like to talk about it anymore. But his published poem "In the Prison" is perhaps instructive as to his experiences there.

> Kick him this way, like this
> in the balls, in the face, in the ribs.
> Pass me the hot iron, the billy-club.
> Talk! Talk, you son-of-a-bitch,
> try salt water,
> ta-a-alk, we don't want to mess you up.

In 1974, in Managua, a Sandinista commando unit wearing costumes and masks, and led by the famous Commandante Marcos, crashed a masquerade party at the home of a Somocista politician and took several of Somoza's cronies hostage. Eventually they swapped them for two million dollars in a suitcase, the release of fourteen political prisoners, including Daniel, radio and television broadcasts announcing this bold Sandinista victory, and a plane to fly them all to Cuba.

From whence, in 1976, Daniel returned to Nicaragua as one of the leaders of the Sandinista revolution. And three years later they finally overthrew Somoza—whereupon Daniel became President.

Free health clinics were opened all over Nicaragua. Free day care centers were opened all over Nicaragua. New schools were opened, and the national literacy rate was more than doubled. All that in just two years.

But then came the counterrevolution, the *Contrarevolución.* The Contras were aided and abetted by Ronald Reagan, Bill Casey, Oliver North, Mike Timpani, and Félix Rodríguez, among others. Reagan kept up covert support for the Contras, even after Congress prohibited it. The prohibition, as drafted, permitted continuing humanitarian aid to the Contras, and through that loophole passed humanitarian army helicopters with big red crosses painted on their sides, humanitarian mercenaries, humanitarian rifles with real bullets, humanitarian hand grenades and explosives, and, of course, humanitarian camouflage.

Low Intensity Conflict, in theory and practice, as explained to me by a friend of Miles before I left for Managua:

Since Vietnam, where we learned sending our own soldiers to fight local insurgencies in faraway civil wars can be very costly, very hard to win, and domestically very unpopular, we've developed a new kind of war. LIC. Low Intensity Conflict. Total war, without the visibility of total war. This is the way a superpower fights a guerrilla war. You don't have to actually win this kind of war. Stalemating the opposition can be enough. LIC knits psychological, economic, diplomatic, military, and political actions into a single system. The war in Nicaragua is a perfect example.

Psychologically, the United States pressures its enemy—in this case the FSLN, the *Frente Sandinista de Liberación Nacional,* also known as the Sandinistas— by constantly threatening to invade the target country. By conducting war games in neighboring countries. By making sure that every day nearly everyone in the target country hears sonic booms from U.S. fighter jets. And so on.

Economically, the U.S. punishes the target country through embargoes and boycotts and covert banking measures. Yes, covert banking measures. Encouraging American commercial banks—sometimes even paying American commercial banks—against their business interests, to call in loans, to engineer defaults, to denigrate the target country's credit in the international capital markets.

Diplomatically, the U.S. intensifies the pressure by inducing its Allies to expel the target country's ambassadors, by paying defectors, by promoting sham debates in international forums. The goal here is actually to force the target country to turn to Cuba and the Soviet Union for support. That's crucial. Because, once it's happened, the target country can be labeled "Marxist." And, with that, the U.S. Government can begin to build domestic support for its operations against the target country.

Militarily, the key is using proxies. Instead of sending our own troops in, we pay mercenaries to do the work. And if our Congress won't agree to pay or arm the mercenaries, we do it anyway, or get one of our friends to do it for us. Overtly, we send teams of military advisors to help the brave and oppressed locals in their valiant struggle against the Marxists—even when most of the brave, oppressed, and valiantly struggling locals aren't really locals. Covertly, we also send in small teams of saboteurs and assassins.

Politically, we insert covert operatives to ruin peace initiatives, spread disinformation, engineer public opinion, ghost-write for opposition newspapers. We generously support fundamentalist Christian missionaries willing to go to the target country and proselytize against the godless Marxists. And, as Miles can tell you, Larry, politically, if the enemy ever gets so vain or stupid as to hold a free election, we do all sorts of other shit.

Big rambling house. Terrazzo floors. Rocking chairs in every room. Primitivist paintings by Nicaraguan artists all over the walls. A wide verandah with more rocking chairs. The house is set near the crest of a hill, and surrounded by acres of jungle and a high wall.

Daniel had originally invited us to be his houseguests. But when he'd heard the size of Swamiji's entourage—two carloads of disciples and baggage had followed behind Padre Miguel's van on the way here—Daniel had decided to put us up in the Sandinista government's finest guest house, which had been confiscated from a Somocista and nationalized after the revolution. Fidel Castro had stayed here. Jimmy Carter too. I loved the place immediately.

The best part was that Swamiji was here, but silent. Every day, the great thespian swami would make a big show of fasting and keeping his mouth shut. Restricted to fruit juice and two hours per day for calls to India and meetings with Daniel, His Holiness meditated, napped, and lost ten pounds to the Central American heat.

By day I barely saw him, except every hour or two when he would appear briefly in the living room to mime to his disciples, or to Daniel's amused cooks, what type of fruit he wanted squeezed for him next. A watermelon was easy. He'd cradle his arms together over his stomach like he was holding and rocking a big fat baby, or a watermelon. A papaya was subtler and took rather longer to fathom.

I played *beisbol*, Nicaragua's national obsession, with Daniel's six young sons—to whom I forever became the *Yanqui Alto*. The Tall Yankee, who did magic tricks for them, and who sat an hour or two each day in a rocking chair beside a sun-splashed stucco wall, looking back at the house through palm fronds and banana trees, while methodically smoking his way through half a box of Cohibas Fidel Castro had given Daniel.

I toured Managua and the volcanic hinterlands. I saw the artists' village of Masaya. I saw the jail cells right inside the dictator Somoza's Presidential Palace.

I spent hours talking with Daniel's wonderful wife Comrade Rosario Murillo. Rosario had an impeccable Sandinista pedigree. Her grandfather was the great Augusto César Sandino himself, the rebel guerrilla leader, the man in the big white cowboy hat whose image was plastered all over Nicaragua, the general who'd not only founded but in death given his name to the struggle. Rosario had a beautiful face and dark hair, which at the time was cut very, very short. Rosario looked somehow like a leftist fairy godmother, without a wand, but she was also kind and smart and very friendly.

Of course, I also spent hours talking with Renee Radka Ramirez, my personal cultural specialist and Eastern European spy, who watched me like a hawk, and dogged me every time I left the house. Only once, while she was temporarily stunned by a Dev Ketu massage, was I able to give her the slip. I went out, found a florist, and bought her a bunch of flowers. Along with another for Rosario. And another for Kim.

One afternoon, Padre Miguel took Kim and me, and Renee Radka Ramirez, to a beautiful jungle spring to swim. Then he took us to his home. It was a marvelous old house on a yellow hill just outside Managua, filled with paintings, sculpture, and tropical birds. He walked us through his garden, then he took us inside to meet his ninety-year-old mother, and while we stood in her bedroom, and she lay on her side in her bed with great dignity but in pain, Padre Miguel told us the story of the bomb.

"A couple of years ago, Contras flew a little airplane just over the top of this house and opened a door and dropped out a bomb. It missed by fifty yards, and I wasn't home anyway. But my mother was home. And she was very brave. She walked out into the garden and raised her fist at the airplane when it flew back over."

Padre Miguel's mother had the darkest and prettiest eyes, and just then she smiled the sweetest smile at me.

To accommodate Swamiji's schedule, Daniel usually arrived where we were staying at around eight at night. He drove himself, in a black jeep with a whip antenna—he told me he didn't trust anyone else to drive him. Usually he wore an army shirt, jeans, and cowboy boots, and he was always trailed by a squad of guards. First, Daniel would pop into the kitchen for a mug of tea, or sometimes he'd grab a machete and prepare himself a concoction of gingerroot and Coca-Cola, and then he'd sit back in a rocking chair to chat with us.

Some nights, when Daniel arrived, Swamiji didn't even show his face, just sent someone out to say he was busy praying. *He talks down to them.* On those blessed nights, Daniel would sit around talking with Dev and Kim and me. Rosario usually did the translating, or sometimes Padre Miguel.

Even when he made himself available to Daniel, Swamiji never ate with us. Couldn't stand the sight of food because he couldn't have any. So Daniel usually sat next to me at dinner.

One night, over lentil beans and curry, he spent at least an hour giving me his version, complete with an elaborate map he drew in pencil on the tablecloth, of the history of U.S. involvement in Nicaragua.

Daniel's strange story began in the 1850s when a cowboy from the United States named William Walker arrived with a private army, proclaimed himself Emperor of Nicaragua, and then ruled the country for three years.

From there, Daniel moved on to the U.S. troops who landed at Corinto in 1912 and stayed in Nicaragua until 1925, and to the U.S. Government's announcement of its plan to build the Nicaragua Canal. The canal was actually begun, but eventually it was scrapped, leaving a scar halfway across Nicaragua, and an alternative canal was begun in Panama.

Daniel told me next about the U.S. troops who arrived again in Managua in 1927 and the six years of guerrilla warfare General Augusto César Sandino waged against them until the U.S. forces were beaten back and left the country in 1933. A few months later, Daniel said, General Sandino was lured into a peace pact. Then, after the banquet with the United States Ambassador to celebrate the signing of the pact, Sandino was assassinated on orders from the man who was soon to become the first President Somoza. This was the point at which Daniel first recited Pablo Neruda—*Se levantó Sandino y no sabía/ que su victoria había terminado/ y que el embajador lo señalaba*—and the point at which Rosario translated Pablo Neruda, on the subject of the murder of her own grandfather. They'd done this act before, I could tell, but they did it now with great sincerity, and it was riveting.

> *Sandino arose unaware*
> *that his victory was at an end*
> *that the Ambassador had fingered him,*
> *fulfilling his part in the deal:*
> *the murderers and North Americans*
> *made ready for the crime:*
> *and there at the door as they embraced him*
> *they saw him off and passed his sentence.*
> *A job well done. And Sandino took his leave*
> *with the executioner and began his walk with death . . .*

Daniel moved next to the U.S. companies which exported Nicaragua's natural wealth, giving nothing back, and to the dictator's hardworking torturers, the Guarda Nacional, and to the rebirth of the resistance spirit in the 1960s. More Neruda:

> *The guerrilla has begun again*
> *to murmur a name:*
> *Sandino, Sandino, Sandino.*

Daniel said the Sandinista Front grew strong first in the countryside, and that by the late Sixties it was organizing in the cities—in León and Managua and Matagalpa. Until in 1971, under the cover of earthquake relief, U.S. Army Rangers flew into Nicaragua and tried to squash the Sandinista Front. But did not succeed.

By 1978, Daniel told me, the second President Somoza suspected the United States was searching for his replacement, a substitute more acceptable in the opinion of the outside world. So Somoza ordered the assassination of the most likely candidate: Pedro Joaquín Chamorro, editor of *La Prensa*. Whose funeral turned into a mass demonstration against the dictator, and whose widow Doña Violeta Chamorro became a member of the Sandinista junta. General strikes were called. Sandinista Front commandos took several provinces on the Pacific coast and began moving toward the capital, Managua, seat of the hated dictator.

In 1979, Daniel said, Anastasio Somoza fled and the forty-four-year military dictatorship of the U.S.-backed Somoza family was finally over.

The next day Daniel rode into the capital looking scrawny and myopic— the most unlikely of conquerors—in a ragged uniform and Coke-bottle glasses. This was the point in Daniel's story at which he became the youngest head of state on earth. But he didn't even mention that.

He did tell me of his efforts to make friends with Ronald Reagan. "I did not want this small country to go to war with the huge United States," Daniel said. "We are neighbors, and we should be friends. But they have no right to squash us just because we say, 'This is *not* part of the empire of the United States. We are Americans too. This is *our* country.' Too many times we complied with the conditions Reagan and his man George Schultz had secretly told us would satisfy them. And, every time we did, they broke their promises and increased their demands."

Early in the 1980s, Doña Violeta broke with Daniel and the Sandinistas and went over to the opposition. She was from a moneyed elite. Daniel was a mestizo boy who'd fought in the mountains and the jungle. It hadn't been a good mix.

Then, Daniel told me, just a few months before the arrival in Managua of the *Hinduswami* and the *Yanqui Alto,* Doña Violeta had agreed to lead fourteen bickering, mosquito-sized political parties in a U.S.-funded coalition called UNO. In fact, UNO had been formed and named by none other than Oliver North. Then, against all polls and predictions, Doña Violeta had rather soundly defeated Daniel in a national election for the presidency of Nicaragua.

What had happened Daniel knew well. Why it had happened and where it would go from here seemed to be a sad mystery to him.

I'd had my own personal experience with Nicaraguan-American relations. Perhaps, I thought, it would help if I told Daniel and Rosario. Not the awkward bit about writing the plan for the Iran-Contra Affair; nothing to be gained by that. But perhaps, in the interest of international understanding, Commandante Daniel and Comrade Rosario would like to know about certain curious circumstances which had transpired while Kim and I lived in New York in the mid-1980s. I decided I'd tell them.

Our first apartment in New York was one floor of a grand old townhouse on East 73rd Street, just off Park Avenue. In which, on the floor upstairs from us, lived the famous Nicaraguan Bianca Jagger. Every once in a while water came through the ceiling of our bedroom, poured down a light fixture, pooled on our carpet, and stank. No one could figure out where it came from. Workmen repeatedly inspected the roof, the walls, the pipes, the electrical conduits, plugged every hole they could find. But still, every week or two, the acid rains fell.

This went on for more than a year. Until one afternoon, when I happened to be sitting in an armchair in our bedroom reading, and I happened to hear Bianca Jagger's footsteps coming down the hall above me, and I happened to hear Bianca Jagger sit down and pee, and then flush her toilet. And then the acid rains began.

The leak was directly under the toilet in Bianca Jagger's spare bathroom. She didn't use it all that often. But, every time she did, she flushed her toilet water straight onto our heads.

I told the story after dessert, and Daniel was delighted. "Then you know exactly how we feel," he said.

But a few minutes later Daniel casually took off his shirt, and I realized I could never know exactly how he felt. It was quite astonishing to see the web of scars that had covered his back since Daniel was a teenager, writing poetry in jail, and having the shit whipped out of him nearly every day. Look closely at Daniel's back and you couldn't see the conflict between the United States and the Sandinistas as purely good versus evil.

Once he got his shirt off, Daniel lay facedown on the floor in the living room. No cushions, no pad, no carpet. Daniel lay right on the hard terrazzo. Then, without whimpering even once, Daniel actually enjoyed a forty-five-minute Dev Ketu massage. An indisputable world record. No other human had ever endured Dev's singular massage technique for even a few minutes without at some point begging him to stop. In fact, when Dev tried to stop after fifteen minutes, Daniel politely asked for more. Dev went back to work and didn't stop for another half an hour. Then, while he was getting up off the floor, Daniel said, "Can you do it again tomorrow?"

A balmy afternoon.

Daniel and Padre Miguel were away at a meeting with Oscar Arias, the Costa Rican president. Daniel was still trying to figure out what to do about the election results.

Rosario and Kim and I were sitting on the verandah chatting, when all of a sudden the house began groaning and crackling. Then everything began to shake. You heard it before you felt it. It sounded like someone big and strong was shaking the metal tackle box my father and I used to take turns carrying when I was little and we went fishing. Shaking it hard.

And then Rosario was shrieking. *"Terremotto!"*

And various cooks and maids were also shrieking, *"Terremotto!"* *"Terremotto!"*

And then Kim and Renee Radka Ramirez, my wife and watcher respectively, joined in the chorus and they all ran gibbering and shrieking out of the house.

Swamiji had gone off to take a nap. His disciples were in town shopping at the hard-currency store. I ran in to Swamiji's bedroom to wake him and get him out. But Swamiji wasn't sleeping when I arrived in his room. He had his sandals in his hands, what appeared to be bread crumbs in his beard, and a wild look in his eyes, and he was running straight toward me with his head stuck out in front of him like a charging bull. He almost knocked me over. Then, at his door, he stopped, transmogrified himself into a feeble, disoriented holy man, and allowed me to take his arm and lead him shambling out.

When we got outside, Rosario said, "Oh, I am so glad you are safe, Your Holiness."

Swamiji smiled weakly and, breaking his vow of silence, said to the First Lady in his best broken English, "Larry wake me, and I feel bed moving, and I think maybe I am dreaming or luttle bit weak and dizzy because of fasting."

Then he sat down on the ground and looked so scared that Rosario took it upon herself to tell him that everything would be all right. And only then did Rosario allow herself to panic again. She took Kim and me aside and told us that in the last earthquake, the great Managua earthquake of 1972, she'd lost her first child, her baby girl. Rosario's voice was quavering. She said, "The ground opened up right in front of me and swallowed her, and there was nothing I could do."

Then Rosario became all business. She called for a guard to bring her a radio. Then she worked it like a pro until she had located every one of her children. "Bring them all to me!" she told their minders. Within twenty minutes of the earthquake, 6.5 on the Richter scale, little Ortegas began arriving. Within an hour, all of them were there. Their ages ranged from about three to about thirteen, and for the rest of the evening and the night, Rosario didn't let them out of her sight.

It was nearly midnight when Daniel got back. He was behind the wheel of his black jeep himself, as usual. Padre Miguel was dozing beside him, and three Sandinista guards were in the backseat. Just behind them were two more jeeps, stuffed with guards and radios and weapons.

Three sets of brakes squealed when Daniel's headlights revealed: Swamiji, Dev, Achariyaji, Kim, Rosario, all seven little Ortegas, Renee Radka Ramirez, and me sitting in a circle of chairs and couches and mattresses in the middle of the driveway.

Daniel flashed a questioning look at Rosario.

In rapid, comic Spanish, she informed her husband that since the earthquake the swami had refused to step back inside the house.

Daniel grinned.

And, Rosario added, the electricity was out.

Daniel shrugged. This was nothing new in Managua.

And, she concluded her report, His Holiness was afraid of the dark, and we had run out of flashlight batteries hours ago.

Daniel laughed. Like it was his first good laugh of the day.

Daniel looked up at the stars. Then he climbed out of his jeep, suddenly incandescent in the headlights from the second jeep. His shadow stretched a hundred feet down the drive and rose into the jungle as he steepled his hands and aimed a namaskar salute at Swamiji.

Then Daniel hurried into our dark circle and, while about half his kids tried to sit in his lap at once, he sat down beside his wife and quietly asked her how she was. Since early that evening, when we'd felt the first of several aftershocks, she'd kept all her children huddled around her.

Padre Miguel flopped down beside me while someone from one of the jeeps lit a lantern and carried it to the middle of our circle.

Guards with AK-47s and grenades and pistols and walkie-talkies hopped out of the jeeps and spread out around the grounds. As I watched the men moving through the jungle, the tips of their cigarettes glowing red-hot in the dark, a vague memory began to nag at me.

A name I'd heard long ago in California. Something Hispanic. Ramos? Not Ramos. Something chirpy. Maybe Pepé? No, that wasn't it.

Then I found it.

Chi Chi! Chi Chi Remon!

It was the story Bill Tharp had told me long ago in San Francisco, on the day he tried to recruit me for the CIA, while he sat across from me in a booth in a dark bar swirling his beer. The story of a bloody afternoon in Panama—not all that far from here. A sophisticated assassination, when you consider that Bill's life was spared. When he'd finished the story, Bill said, "I *told* Chi Chi we shouldn't go to that racetrack!"

I was in Nicaragua, but my mind was in Panama by way of San Francisco, until a command squawked over the radio and one by one Daniel's guards flipped their cigarettes away into the jungle.

I watched them disappearing into total darkness.

Padre Miguel was just starting to say something to me when we heard an enormous blast behind us. Instantly the invisible guards were yelling, and I heard boots thundering toward the noise, Daniel was on his feet and speaking faster than I could understand, and Swamiji was howling "Earthquake!" But my first impression was that it was a bomb. The noise seemed to have come from just the other side of the wall, near the gate. In my last split second of vision, before a guard shut off the lantern, all of us seemed to be frozen in anticipation—except for Achariyaji, who was holding his hands over his eyes and giggling hysterically, and Swamiji, who was flailing forward in a rocking chair, his eyes and mouth wide open. Then a voice came from the radio.

"It is a car accident," Rosario translated.

Daniel hopped into his jeep and was already starting to accelerate when I made it in beside him. The heavy wooden gate swung open and Daniel raced through it and then turned left. Three hundred yards away, on the crest of the hill, two trucks laden with peasants and driving without lights on the dark road had collided head-on.

In our headlights, dazed men stood speechless by the road and others wailed. I saw the bodies of two dead or unconscious in the dirt beside the road. Blood and gasoline were seeping down the pavement, and I saw men with lit cigarettes but couldn't remember how to say No Smoking in Spanish. Daniel stopped the jeep thirty yards short so all the wreckage would be illuminated in his headlights. He left the engine running, pulled on the parking brake, and ran to the two merged trucks. No one recognized him. Underneath the twisted metal someone was moaning, and in a moment Daniel and I were on the ground in blood and glass and metal, trying to pull a man out of the darkness.

We struggled at it for several minutes. But the man's legs were quite stuck and he soon stopped moaning. The guards had been busy with other catastrophes. But now one of them brought a flashlight and held it over us and I saw the dead young man whose head was resting on my thigh. His face was the palest white. And, beside him in the wreckage, Daniel's cheeks were wet with either sweat or tears.

I stared at Daniel while he looked away, and there was no doubt I loved him. He was as courageous as Muhammad. A hero. A warrior poet. A man of the people. And just then my father whispered in my ear. "*It's just not easy for a man to intentionally befriend and then betray another man,*" he said.

God damn it.

Then it happened. The next night, after dinner.

Daniel went to the bedroom that had become Swamiji's sanctum sanctorum.

I went with him.

We took off our boots at the door. Padre Miguel followed us in, absent his sandals, and closed the door on all the guards.

I was there as acolyte. Padre Miguel as translator, not priest. On a sign from Swamiji, who'd been sitting in the dark, I lit a single candle. Daniel sat down on an old wooden chair across from Swamiji, close but not too close, and by the light of the already guttering candle Swamiji chanted a prayer for Daniel. At the end of which there was an uncomfortable silence. It was a question of etiquette. None of us but Swamiji knew how to behave on an occasion such as this, and Swamiji wasn't saying.

Finally Daniel spoke. Said he'd never believed in fortune-telling, never in his entire life. But his father had. And recently he'd been thinking a lot about his father. And that was why Daniel had paid attention when he met me and I asked if he would meet a holy man from India.

In my pocket was a Walkman Miles had given me. It looked like any other Walkman, and in fact it was one of the models that came standard with a built-in microphone and RECORD function. The only modification to it, Miles had told me, was a tiny amplifier which increased the microphone's ability to pick up sounds by about eight times. I'd learned how to use it. It definitely worked as advertised, it was loaded with a fresh cassette, was set on Long Play, and part of me sensed where this was heading and thought now would be a good time to casually reach down and scratch myself and switch the recorder on.

But, having grown up watching my father's men sweep our houses for bugs, I recognized a microphone detector when I saw one. And twice that week already I'd watched Daniel's guards covertly sweep *this* house for bugs. They were just outside the door now, and any one of them might have a wand. If so, and if he turned it on while I was recording, we'd be blown and quite possibly dead. The penalty for espionage hasn't changed in centuries.

I sat in the dark, listening twice, building a memory tree, as Daniel talked, then Padre Miguel talked, and Swamiji listened quietly, lovingly, interjecting questions from time to time.

If the guards outside had had a bullshit detector and switched it on now, it wouldn't have registered a thing. I had this way of knowing whether Swamiji was working in his head or in his heart. Usually he worked in his head, and I could see it on his face and hear it in his voice. But not that night.

Most of all, Daniel was lost. Someplace far away, but close. Every time he faltered, Swamiji bucked him up, told him he would be restored to power soon. But how Swamiji charmed and coaxed so many confidences out of the oft-tortured and battle-hardened leader of the *Frente Sandinista* that night I'm still not sure—even though Muhammad and I once shared and studied a stack of stage magician's books on mentalism.

I won't tell you the things Daniel said and asked and prayed about his children and his wife. They were the normal concerns of a father and a husband, and Swamiji let Daniel talk through all of them for as long as he wanted, which was quite a while.

When Swamiji finally vectored the conversation to the subjects I wanted to know about, for a moment I imagined he knew what I was doing, what *we* were doing. He was asking all the right questions, and with a beautiful, carefree elicitation style, just the ticket to disarm suspicion. But he wasn't doing this for me, I realized. Swamiji, better than anyone, understood the power of possessing someone else's secrets.

For weeks now, Daniel had been negotiating with Violeta Chamorro over a possible transition of the presidency. And he'd given conflicting signals about what he intended to do.

Sometimes he said he would respect the election results, and Doña Violeta, in her wheelchair, would be inaugurated President. Other times he seemed to suggest otherwise. Daniel had the power to do whichever he chose.

He still controlled the army. His younger brother Humberto was its chief of staff. And Daniel had the justification, if he wanted it, to void the elections and declare martial law. It was already emerging in the international press just how much of a hand the CIA had played in engineering the recent elections. Elections which—Daniel told Swamiji—Fidel Castro had warned Daniel not to agree to.

"And what does Fidel say *now?*" said Swamiji.

To my ear, Daniel's voice grew defensive and humorless then. But Padre Miguel said that, on the occasion of Daniel's first meeting with his comrade and mentor after the election, Fidel said to Daniel, "You lost a *what?*" And Padre Miguel delivered this line so comically and beautifully that even Daniel laughed.

He was sitting there, only about four feet away from me—in total darkness now, for the candle had flamed out. "Fidel's advice now? In Rio, he told me, 'Go, but don't go.' And that was the last time we discussed it."

"And did you discuss with Gorbachev?" Swamiji wasn't fucking around.

"Gorbachev told me he will be in solidarity with my decision. Whatever I decide."

"But did Gorbachev make suggestion what to do?"

Pause.

"No."

Somewhere in the house a toilet was running, on and on, wasting more water than most Nicaraguans used in a month. Some crazy part of me wanted to get up and go fix it, or open the door and tell the guards to. That was the part of me that also wanted to stand up and switch on the lights to break the spell, make Daniel shut up.

I got up and lit a joss stick. There wasn't another candle.

"Mrs. Chamorro's son-in-law Antonio Lacayo is handling the negotiations for her," Daniel said. "Sometimes we think he is the real power. Not her. I have told him my position. My terms."

Miles had already told me this, and that Daniel had told Lacayo that, if the Contras turned in their weapons and disbanded, and if Humberto could remain the head of the army, Daniel would cede the presidency to Chamorro. *But the question,* Miles had told me, *the number-one question our friends in Washington want an answer to is Does Ortega really plan to give up the presidency—or is it all a ploy to disarm the Contras?*

"And has our brother Daniel made his decision?" said Swamiji. "Will you make Mrs. Chamorro the President?"

The room went almost totally silent now, except that somewhere that fucking toilet was still running, and the longer Daniel sat there without answering the question the louder my heart kept pounding in my ears. This was it, the money shot, and something told me Daniel wasn't being coy, sitting there in silence, he was making his decision right now. Even Padre Miguel seemed anxious for Daniel's answer. We all just sat there, waiting. There was a little sound Swamiji made with his hand when he got nervous, his tell, and I heard it now. Over and over.

Daniel finally spoke and Padre Miguel blew out a breath, and then translated. "Daniel says, 'If I give Doña Violeta the presidency, I give her some power. If I *do not* give her the presidency, I give her *more* power. So she will be President.'"

Gotcha! I thought in triumph, and an instant later another part of me felt ashamed.

"This is right," said Swamiji. "The right decision. And you will be President again in eight months!"

This stirred Daniel. "Eight months?" he said. "I had thought two years, or three. She will be President and I will control the National Assembly, and the army, and the streets, and we will see how much power she has."

Next Daniel proceeded to tell us every detail of his plan for bringing down the new government. There was another reason, he admitted now, why he'd been intrigued when the *Yanqui Alto* asked him if he'd like to meet a *Hinduswami*. And that was because, since the week after the election, Daniel had been studying the general strikes and the passive nonresistance with which the Mahatma Gandhi had paralyzed the Government of India. Daniel planned to do the same thing to Violeta's government. "We will give her four months," he said, "and then it will start." Swamiji's hand was making that noise again.

"But first," Daniel said, "before she is President, the Contras must give us their rifles. And their explosives." That was the launching point from which, for reasons I will never understand, Daniel then took it upon himself to tell us about the Contra safe house his security services had recently discovered in Managua. He told us the name of the district and even the name of the street the house was in, and then he said, "We're watching the house now, carefully. The Cuban intelligence are helping us with this. For now all we do is watch. We think the cell will bring in more men, more explosives. And we will arrest them, but not until just before the inauguration."

It occurred to me then, for a crazy moment, that maybe when I saw Miles I could get away with reporting only on this safe house. I was all for exfiltrating its occupants before they could be rolled up. The penalty for espionage hasn't changed in centuries.

The toilet stopped. Daniel rattled on.

He told us every secret thing, and when he was finished, stripped bare of fears and human frailties, Daniel felt better, I felt elated and sick, and Swamiji chanted a prayer for our souls.

A few days later I was back in Oxfordshire with Miles.

"You're back from the belly of the beast," he said.

"I'm back from the belly of the mouse that roared," I responded.

I had it all in my head, and written in code—laboriously dressed up as notes for a feasibility study on reviving the Nicaraguan fishing industry.

As much as I hurt and wanted to hold at least some of it back to protect my friend Daniel, I'd decided that I couldn't, that I would give it all up for my country, for my father's country. "He's really a terrific guy," I told Miles. "A warrior poet. You would love him, and I almost don't want to give you what I've got. But I'm going to."

Miles gave me a long, happy look and a smile. And then he said, "Forget it. Don't worry about it. My friends have already got it all on tape." He paused for a moment. "I'm proud of you," he said. "You were great. You kept the swami in line, the target talked, and we got every word."

PART FOUR

SWEET WHITE SMOKE

I f you've been wondering how I got into all the shit I'm in, how I managed to fuck myself so well and thoroughly that I wound up sentenced to this sunny shore for what by now seems like something close to eternity, listen up. If you're looking for a thoroughly modern way to self-destruct, this is how I did it.

I was in bed in another house in Florida.

Adnan was on the telephone saying something about a favor for a friend of his. I said, "Uh-huh." Adnan said, "There's a story we want the London newspapers to cover. You've got friends in the press there, don't you?"

I said, "Uh-huh."

I blinked at the bright light, and looked at my watch again. Still three in the morning. I should've hung up right then.

Adnan said, "Do you think you can help?"

I said, "Uh-huh. Probably. I can try." But I was way too sleepy to pretend to be enthusiastic about it.

Then I was starting to come to. Apparently Adnan's friend for whom he wanted to do the favor was my friend Rajiv. Because next Adnan said, "Mr. Gandhi sent one of his political men to London to work on this. Wait ten minutes and then call him. Ask for Dr. Channa. That's only a code name. But, if you use it, the Prime Minister's man will give you the details." Then Adnan read me a phone number.

I said, "All right, I'll call. Nice to hear from you. Are you in New York?" It was a stupid, sleep-induced question. Just about everyone who read newspapers knew that two weeks earlier—after three months in jail in Switzerland fighting extradition, and then ten days in jail in New York—Adnan had been released on ten million dollars bail, required to wear an electronic prisoner monitoring bracelet, and confined to the island of Manhattan until he stood trial with Ferdinand and Imelda Marcos.

Adnan chuckled and said, "Right now, I can't think of a better place to be. In fact, I've decided to stick around indefinitely." Then he told me he would tell Dr. Channa to expect my call, and I hung up and went to the kitchen to make some coffee. I didn't call in ten minutes. I waited probably half an hour until I was wide awake before I called. I should've never called.

"Dr. Channa" had an educated Indian voice. Whoever he was, he was polite, intelligent, probably in his mid-thirties—probably about my age. He told me national elections were to be held in India in four or five months, and that the leader of the opposition against Prime Minister Rajiv Gandhi was a man named V.P. Singh. He further told me that, before dramatically breaking away to lead the opposition, Singh had been a minister in Rajiv's government, and that Indian intelligence had recently discovered that, while he was Finance Minister, Singh had racked up about twenty million dollars in kickbacks and hidden the money in a bank on the Caribbean island of St. Kitts. "That," said Dr. Channa, "is what the P.M. wants exposed in an English newspaper."

I said, "Why not an Indian newspaper?"

The voice named Dr. Channa said, "To give the story credibility, it has to come from a foreign source. The newspapers in India are so corrupt, and everyone knows they are so corrupt that no one will believe the story if it originates there. Everyone knows the Prime Minister can walk into any pro-government newspaper in India and just tell the editor what story he wants, and it will be printed exactly as dictated. That's part of my problem," Dr. Channa went on, and now I could hear a hint of desperation rising in his voice. "I know how to deal with newspapers in India," he said. "But not here."

He told me he'd arrived in London five days earlier with proof of his story, but so far he'd only managed to meet with a reporter from *The Times,* which hadn't printed a word about what ought to be a huge scoop. Now the situation was becoming critical, because the Prime Minister needed the story broken before an important parliamentary session which was to begin in three days.

I asked him what sort of proof he had, and Dr. Channa said Indian intelligence had provided him certified copies of a St. Kitts bank's numbered account application signed by V.P. Singh and statements for the account.

I asked if the documents were strong enough to convince the editor of a major newspaper if I got Dr. Channa in to see him, and Dr. Channa said, "Yes, definitely."

"Let me make some calls to Fleet Street," I said, "and I'll call you back in an hour or two."

It was early morning in London, not the best time to reach the night owls who run morning newspapers. But eventually I was able to arrange for Dr. Channa to meet that afternoon with the editor of the *Daily Express.*

Dr. Channa's voice relaxed a lot when I called and told him he had an appointment, and assured him that, if he could prove his story, it would be published. For the next few minutes I coached him on how to behave at the meeting, and when I was finished, he asked if I was American.

"Yes."

"And a publicist?"

"No," I said, "I'm a businessman. But I know some people in the press, and I'd like to help. If I can."

My friend was running for reelection, and by now I'd seen enough to have a heightened understanding of all that might entail. Candidates smiling broadly in the sunshine, while in the shadows behind them secret wars were fought. In an age when image triumphs over substance, it's often the hit men, the character assassins, who're the most effective warriors. I'd never done such work before, but I was willing to try.

Hours later, at my request, a hidden photographer snapped a roll of photographs of Dr. Channa as he left the *Daily Express*. I wanted a record of what the mystery man looked like, and to know if I'd ever seen him around Rajiv. And while that record was being created, I got a call from a friend named Alun Rees, a *Daily Express* reporter, who told me the meeting had gone well and that, subject to some checking, the paper would likely run a story on V.P. Singh's secret bank account in the next morning's edition.

I called Adnan and told him the good news.

Mission accomplished, I thought. And, had it only been that simple, I wouldn't live on this beach today.

But some hours after that Alun Rees called me again. He said the story had been written and laid out in the next morning's paper, but had been withdrawn at the last minute. When the editor of *The Times* told the editor of the *Daily Express* that the story had been pitched to *The Telegraph* a few days before. And not by Dr. Channa, but by a public relations firm.

What I was thinking when I heard that was *It would've made things so much easier if you'd just told me the truth.* I called Dr. Channa and politely accused him. His voice broke in that uniquely Indian way while he swore he didn't know about an approach to *The Telegraph*. Yes, he said, he'd talked with a public relations firm about the story, but he hadn't known they discussed it with anyone else. He was almost crying. It sounded like he might be telling the truth and just totally out of his depth. "What do you normally do for a living?" I asked, and Dr. Channa said, "I'm a lawyer." Now he sounded more worried than sad.

Next I had to call Adnan. "This is so important for Rajiv," he said. "What can you do to fix it?"

"Your friends have so badly muddied the waters," I said, "that they might as well pack up and head for a different city. They're going to have to start all over again."

Adnan said: "Will you come up here and advise them on this, Your Excellency? We could use your help."

I had no business commitments for the next few weeks.

On the day after he was arrested I'd overnighted to Adnan in Bern a bright yellow GET OUT OF JAIL FREE card from the Community Chest in my Monopoly set along with a note offering to do anything I could to help. Since then, I'd felt so bad about Adnan languishing in jail that I'd sent three or four more notes wishing him well and offering to help if I could.

He'd responded only once—through Frank Morse—who called one morning from Switzerland and told me Adnan was asking me to try to sell his new house in Rome to Doris Duke. For twelve million dollars. I'd tried. She'd offered seven—not enough to consider—and I'd felt bad. This was another chance for me to help Adnan. How could I say no now?

"Sure," I said. "I'll be happy to. But only if everyone involved will level with me."

"Of course," he said. "Can you come to New York tonight?"

"Yes."

"*Yella!*" said Adnan, "*Yella!* We haven't much time."

Adnan's New York apartment filled the entire forty-sixth and forty-seventh floors of the Olympic Tower. It was a modern building, black steel and glass, rising over St. Patrick's Cathedral and just across Fifth Avenue from the gray-white stone towers of Rockefeller Center. The address was 641 Fifth Avenue, but the Olympic Tower's entrance was under a broad black awning on 51st Street, and it was guarded by a smiling doorman in full dress with epaulets and gleaming brass buttons and ropes of golden braid.

At nine in the morning, he opened the door for me and I walked into the lobby, and soon a concierge in a dove-gray uniform and white gloves escorted me in an elevator to the forty-sixth floor. He walked me down the carpeted hall, then knocked on the door to Adnan's private office. It might be that my whole life changed while I waited for that door to open. I still remember the lacquered blond wood and the soft light.

Eventually one of Adnan's aides, a handsome young Arab in a charcoal suit, opened the door, thanked the concierge, and then led me through the office and into the conference room. Before he disappeared, he told me Adnan would join me soon.

Kim and I had arrived in New York in the middle of the night, and spent the last five hours a block east of here in the Helmsley Palace. I was tired, and I'd been in this room plenty of times before. So I paid little attention to the framed photographs of Adnan with presidents and kings and sultans, the magazine covers from which Adnan smiled, the tall bookshelves filled with works on statecraft and art, the magnificent view. Extraordinary views through floor-to-ceiling windows wrapped around this entire apartment, which Adnan had fashioned out of sixteen separate apartments he'd bought years ago from his friend Aristotle Onassis.

I settled into a leather armchair at the round burled-wood conference table, and a few moments later a waiter appeared in a cream-colored tuxedo. I asked for espresso and maybe some fruit.

All around this apartment, I could be sure, were men in suits, Americans and Arabs and Frenchmen, maybe an Englishman or two—each either employed by Adnan or nebulously his partner—sitting beside open briefcases with phones in their hands, talking to London, Zurich, Paris, Riyadh, Dubrovnik, Beirut, Cairo, Perth. Working on deals. If Adnan was going to survive, he was going to have to keep working.

Probably I knew these men in suits, or most of them. Any other day, I likely would've been inclined to take an hour or so to stroll around the apartment, say hellos, pick up gossip. But today I had a chance to do a favor for Adnan and my friend Rajiv, a very important favor, judging by the sound of Adnan's voice. Today all I wanted to do was work.

I picked up a phone and tried to reach Miles. No luck. Ever since yesterday, his answering machine had been announcing that he and Lorraine were off doing a little shopping in the village and would be back in a few minutes. Covering fire. A burglar deterrent. It meant Miles and Lorraine could be almost anywhere. Including elsewhere on this floor. Or the one above it.

At Adnan's direction, this 110-room apartment had been designed and laid out as intricately as a honeycomb. For every grand staircase, imposing portal, and marble hallway there were back stairs, back doors, and hidden passages. All the better for Adnan to jovially flit between, say, in a salon, executives of one corporation, in the conference room, their competition, in the enormous living room, the prince who was their prospective customer, and in the other enormous living room, the banker who could finance the whole thing—with none of the visitors even aware of the presence of the others.

During my second cup of coffee, Adnan arrived.

"Ah, good. I see you made it, Larry." He slid the double doors closed behind him.

"You look no worse for wear," I said, and we shook hands.

Adnan was fifty-four now, officially at least, and sometimes I found it hard to believe he'd made his first huge deals more than thirty years earlier. Ever since then, all the yachts, jets, hotels, ranches, homes, and business operations around the planet he'd acquired had seen to it that he stayed in motion. For Adnan, like his nomadic ancestors, the traveling itself was home. Except for his hundred days in jail, he couldn't recall ever in the past twenty years staying in the same place for an entire week.

His dark tan was gone now, and his cheeks weren't as full as usual.

I said, "You've lost weight."

"Twenty-two pounds!" Adnan patted his still-prominent belly through a blue silk suit, silver tie, and sparkling white shirt. Fat is traditionally a status symbol for Arabs, an indication of wealth. But Adnan's doctors had been on him for years to lose weight. I looked for the electronic bracelet, but caught only the glint of a gold link on one of his starched white cuffs.

Adnan chuckled. "It's amazing what three months' enforced stay at a Swiss health spa will do for you."

A secretary knocked, and slid open the door. Behind her was a man in a rumpled plaid blazer and khaki pants. "Mr. Samghabadi is here," she said.

"Ah, Raji! Come in." We stood up and Adnan said, "Larry, this is Raji Samghabadi, the man who put me on the cover of *Time* magazine." Samghabadi, like Adnan, was about a foot shorter than me. He seemed to be about forty. "Raji, this is Larry Kolb," Adnan continued, as I shook Samghabadi's hand. "Larry is married to the daughter of my first wife, Soraya. So he's semi-family."

Raji Samghabadi spoke English in the quick dark rhythms of his native Iran. He told me he was a reporter on the staff of *Time* magazine, and that he had indeed written *Time*'s cover story on Adnan. While Samghabadi and I chatted, Adnan picked up a telephone and said, "Send in Mammaji."

Mammaji proved to be a short, almost-bald Indian. Probably in his early sixties. He had dark circles under his eyes and hadn't shaved for at least a couple of days. The stubble on his cheeks was silver, with flecks of bronze in places. He was wearing tan pajama pants and a wrinkled tan *kurta*—a long, loose Indian shirt—under a homespun vest. Something about his bearing suggested to me that this was a man who'd been in battle. He sat down directly across from me, squinting at the rich summer sunlight that poured in through the window at my back.

"Mammaji is a friend of Mr. Gandhi," Adnan said to me. "And he has close ties to Indian intelligence." Then Adnan looked at Mammaji and said, "Why don't you explain this to Mr. Kolb."

Mammaji didn't waste a beat.

"V.P. Singh is Lucifer, the Devil," he said. "He deals with mafias and terrorists and he has sold his soul to foreign powers. He was a trusted protégé of our Mother Indira and then Rajiv, but he has no loyalty. He saw his chance and joined the renegades, and now he leads them. Now he has become a moralist. He leads the charges against Rajiv over Bofors. He pretends to be patriotic and conscientious, but he is in truth an unmitigated village bandit."

I decided the little warrior before me *must* be a politician.

"In his moralizing he has found a source of power," Mammaji went on. "Too many in our gullible nation have become addicted to V.P. Singh's highly principled pronouncements. He is unscrupulous and corrupt, but he is such a sandman that already half the nation is nodding off and almost no one knows he is anything but squeaky clean. And if *we* do not burst his bubble, he could become Prime Minister of India."

Mammaji moved on to the St. Kitts case and it was then that I began to interrupt him. I wanted the facts in chronological order, but he seemed unable to deliver. He lurched forward and backward and talked in knots and parables and raw emotions. "Please, let's go back," I said. "Let's take it step by step."

After twenty minutes, I'd deduced that the story was that, while he was Rajiv's Finance Minister, V.P. Singh had allowed Citibank to open several branches in India and, in exchange, the bank had given his son Ajeya a job. According to Mammaji, Lucifer's thirty-three-year-old son Ajeya Singh now lived in luxury in New York, as a pampered Citibank executive. And while he was Finance Minister, V.P. Singh had also set up his evil crony S.V.S. Raghavan as chairman of the MMTC, Minerals and Metals Trading Corporation, a commodities purchasing company owned and operated by the Government of India.

That much, Mammaji said, was public knowledge. But, a few weeks earlier, Indian intelligence had discovered Raghavan had negotiated kickbacks when India bought copper and other metals from Africa, and that the sellers had funneled the payoffs to Ajeya Singh, who deposited them in a bank in St. Kitts.

"Are you following now?" said Mammaji, and then he said "Good" when I nodded.

Next he opened his briefcase, paused for effect, and passed me a sheet of paper. It was a photocopy of a *Numbered Account Agreement* on letterhead of *The First Trust Corporation Limited/ The Circus/ Basseterre/ St. Kitts and Nevis, West Indies*. It showed that account number 29479 was opened by Ajeya Singh for beneficiary V.P. Singh, and it set forth the procedures under which the secret account would be operated. I asked Mammaji to decipher the endorsements for me. He pointed out the signatures. "Here: Ajeya Singh. Here: V.P. Singh. And here: one George McLean. *He*," Mammaji said with gravity, "was the founder and managing director of the bank."

Moving on, Mammaji handed me a photocopy of a typed account statement, showing that the First Trust Corporation Limited's account 29479 was opened on September 16, 1986, and closed on February 13, 1988, after more than twenty-one million dollars had passed through the account. For several months after the last deposit, the balance had been more than fifteen million dollars.

"Where did the money go from St. Kitts?" I said.

"Our intelligence traced it as far as Norway. From there, it vanished."

I recognized, at the bottom of the page, under the legend *I certify the above to be a true record of the entries of account 29479,* the whorls and loops and flourishes Mammaji had said made up the signature of George McLean.

"Have handwriting experts verified all the signatures are authentic?"

"Yes," said Mammaji.

"Where did you get these?"

"Intelligence won't compromise its sources, of course," said Mammaji. "But it would be safe for you to assume these same documents were once in the possession of Ajeya Singh."

"You burgled him?"

Mammaji just smiled at me.

I turned to Adnan. "Are you convinced these are genuine?"

Adnan nodded. "In fact," he said, "Raji has just completed an investigation of the matter."

"Yes," Raji Samghabadi piped in on cue. "I'm certain the story is true."

"Do you intend to write about it for *Time*?"

"Yes."

I turned back to Adnan. "So why don't we just have *Time* break the story?"

"We can't wait," Adnan said. "The story must be published within two days."

"I'm on vacation," Samghabadi said. "Leaving this afternoon."

"So, we ask that you please arrange this for us," Mammaji said, looking straight into my eyes.

About then, the door slid open and in walked none other than His Holiness Chandraswami Maharaj.

"My brother A.K.! I looking for you *every*where," he said, smiling.

"Ah, Your Holiness," Adnan said. "I believe you've met Mammaji and Mr. Samghabadi. And here's your old friend Mr. Kolb."

Swamiji nodded at everyone, said, "Namaste."

"Please stay with us, Your Holiness," Adnan said. "We're discussing India. You might find this interesting."

About then I should've smelled a setup, left the room and headed back to Florida, and maybe taken my GET OUT OF JAIL FREE card with me. But I was very tired, and wanted to be helpful. And I just couldn't believe that—in his current situation, with the U.S. Government tapping his phones and monitoring his every move—Adnan would be fucking with this if it wasn't real.

He asked me to summarize the story for Swamiji and then explain how I planned to break it. When I finished, Adnan turned to the holy man and said, "So, what do you think?"

"I know God, not politics," Swamiji said quietly. "I think it better if my brother A.K. say what *he* think?"

"*I* think," Adnan said, arching one eyebrow and raising his voice to melodramatic tones, "that the fate of India is in Mr. Kolb's hands, and it's time for us to leave him alone so he can get to work."

Adnan walked out with the holy man, Samghabadi picked up a phone to make a call, and Mammaji and I went into the next room and asked a secretary to photocopy the bank documents. "Five sets, please," I said, and then we followed her into the copying room.

"How well do you know His Holiness?" I asked Mammaji, while he leaned against the refrigerator-sized, industrial-strength shredder that stood beside the copier.

Mammaji pondered the question at his leisure.

"Is it possible," he finally said, "for a lesser man to truly know a saint?"

I waited for Mammaji and Raji Samghabadi to leave, closed myself into the conference room, and then picked up the telephone. First, I rang Oxfordshire, looking for Miles again. The machine said he and Lorraine were still in the village doing a little shopping. Then I tried him in St. John's Wood. No answer. *Where are you, Miles?*

Next, I called the editorial offices of *Time* and asked for Mr. Samghabadi. His office said he was on leave, and suggested I try him at home.

Then I called a New York private investigator I knew and asked him if he could *quickly* get me a copy of any Citibank document signed by its executive Ajeya Singh. The investigator said he probably could, if I'd give him a couple of days. "I need it today," I said. "And I'll pay for the rush."

Next I called a friend in Washington who followed Indian politics. "What can you tell me about V.P. Singh?" I asked him.

"His power's growing, and right now he's even money in the next election," came the answer, over the sound of tapping on computer keys. "Let me see if I can get the basics for you." Pause. More tapping. "Here we go: 'Vishwanath Pratap Singh. Leader of the Janata Dal (People's Party). Born 1931. Natural son of the king of Daiya, a small feudal kingdom in northern India. Spent early years living in a walled palace surrounded by rice paddies and jungles. At age 5, adopted by a neighboring king who lacked an heir, becoming heir to the throne of the kingdom of Manda. Raised by a Scottish nanny and her husband. Bitter succession controversy upon death of adoptive father, so spent secondary-school years isolated and under the protection of armed bodyguards. Renounced throne and attended Allahabad University. Graduated with law degree. Married Sita Kumari 1955. Two children, both sons. Elected to Uttar Pradesh state assembly 1969. Elected to Indian parliament 1971, Congress party. Held several appointive posts in Indira Gandhi's governments as one of her most prominent protégés. Moved back to state government as Chief Minister of Uttar Pradesh state 1980 to '82. Indira Gandhi's Commerce Minister 1982 until her assassination in 1984. Rajiv Gandhi's Finance Minister 1984 to '86. Instituted aggressive anticorruption campaign while Finance Minister. Defense Minister 1986 to '87. Split with Gandhi and became opposition leader 1987.'"

"Do you know him?" I asked.

"Shook his hand once."

"What's he like?"

"Glasses, mustache, wiry. He's got this myopic grin, like maybe he needs to change the prescription of his glasses. Bit of a wimp on the surface. And sanctimonious. But he's got your handsome young Prime Minister friend and half his party on the defensive over Bofors. Here: 'Alleges that high-level Congress officials received more than sixty million dollars in kickbacks when Indian government bought howitzers from Swedish manufacturer Bofors.'"

I'd read of the Bofors scandal months before, but hadn't been aware it still plagued Rajiv's government. "That hasn't cooled down?"

"Not at all," said my friend. "It's getting worse, not better, for Congress."

So the stakes of the game were every bit as high as Adnan had said. To the winner went control of India.

I'd barely hung up when the telephone rang, and, as soon as I answered it, Adnan was speaking. "You and I will have a lunch guest," he said. "She is Lally Weymouth, the daughter of Mrs. Graham. Katharine Graham. You know, the owner of *The Washington Post*. Lally also writes for the paper. You should write a little report, just two or three pages, a sample newspaper story about this St. Kitts business to show her at lunch."

"In *one* hour?"

"*Yella!* . . . Can you do it?"

"I'll try," I said.

But I'd never written under a deadline with an editor breathing down my neck. Adnan paced in and out of the conference room every few minutes to stress the urgency, monitor my progress, and make exasperated suggestions.

I started with the background: V.P. Singh getting his start as Indira Gandhi's protégé, serving as a minister in Rajiv's government, dramatically breaking from the Congress party, now leading the assault against Rajiv over Bofors. Then, in the neutral language of newspapers, I described the certified bank documents I'd obtained from a highly placed source, and said the documents might raise suspicions that, while V.P. Singh was India's Finance Minister, his fifty-thousand-dollar-a-year-junior-executive son had deposited more than twenty-one million dollars in a bank in St. Kitts.

Adnan liked it.

With six minutes left before our lunch guest was due to arrive, I printed my story.

Then Mammaji arrived and read it and said the story was a travesty. Even the feeblest mind could see that the bank documents didn't merely raise suspicions. They irrefutably proved V.P. Singh stole twenty-one million dollars from the Government of India, and that he was a crook and a fraud and a traitor.

"You must change it after lunch," Adnan said, but he winked at me when Mammaji turned to leave.

The dining room was just down the corridor, through the marble entry hall, and past the largest living room in Manhattan—in just a corner of which was a miniature Amazon rain forest with jungle vegetation growing eighteen feet high. Lally Weymouth was waiting for us in the living room, and Adnan introduced me to her as a friend of Prime Minister Gandhi, just arrived from the Caribbean.

From the immense oval ebony and lapis-lazuli-inlaid table at which the three of us ate lunch, there was a marvelous view, an unforgettable view, through floor-to-ceiling windows, looking south over the spires of St. Patrick's Cathedral, straight down Fifth Avenue to the Empire State Building, on to the twin towers of the World Trade Center, and beyond to New York Harbor and the Statue of Liberty.

Charmed as she was, as almost everyone was, by Adnan, Lally Weymouth had a shrewd and patient look about her. Ten minutes into lunch I'd given up on selling her on immediately filing a *Washington Post* story about the St. Kitts account.

She said the story was interesting, but it would be impossible to run it in just a day or two. "I'll have some of our staff look into it," she promised, "but I should think that will take at least a week."

Wonderful food kept streaming from the kitchen—salmon and lobster and chicken and lamb elaborately arranged on beds of rice and borne on golden salvers—so I concentrated on eating. While Adnan launched sally after sally of spirited but doomed attempts to convince Lally Weymouth to reconsider.

After lunch, Adnan escorted his guest down to her waiting car, and while he did that, I went back to the conference room. Beside my briefcase on the table was a Manila envelope. Addressed to me. One of the secretaries said a messenger had delivered it a few minutes earlier.

I tore it open, and saw that my investigator had come through. The three Ajeya Singh signatures enclosed seemed to match the one on the Numbered Account Agreement given me by Mammaji.

By the way, the investigator added at the bottom of his cover memo, *Citibank says that Ajeya Singh is no longer employed there, and his whereabouts are now unknown.*

I tried Miles again, unsuccessfully. *Where the fuck are you when I need you, Miles?*

Then I called Mike Timpani in Washington. I think, at the time, he was officially working for a jet-trading company, advising them on the safety of their aviation operations, or some such story. Mike had never quite admitted to me who he really worked for. But I had no doubt it was an American intelligence service or some committee or task force closely linked to one. CIA. DIA. NSC. Take your pick. I didn't really care, as long as I could get Mike to get one of them to log in my query about whether there was any reason I shouldn't go ahead with publicizing this Singh business.

Mike said, "*Que pasa, hombre?*" as he picked up the phone, and after I told him what I wanted he said, "Standby fifteen." That was radio talk for: Stay there and I'll call you back within fifteen minutes. Which he did, saying, "I spoke to some friends of mine in the Agency. They checked around, and then they said to tell you, 'It's not like it's Nicaragua. We don't give a shit what happens in India. Go for it.'"

When I'd thanked Mike and hung up, I looked up and Adnan was there.

"We have just *two* more days!" he said, and his face was filled with urgency and something close to desperation. With all his other problems, I wondered why a favor for Rajiv should be so compelling to Adnan now. I'd taken off my suit jacket, unpacked my briefcase, foraged through Adnan's office supplies cabinets, and, with all the excessive neatness with which projects are begun, meticulously arranged on the conference table my address book, four pens, and two even stacks of yellow legal pads.

"It's *not* going to be in a paper tomorrow," I said. "So all I can do is work toward the day after."

"How will you do it?"

"I've got to get on the phone and start calling friends," I said. "Some of them I can push, and some I can't. But we don't want to look too anxious."

"If they owe you favors," Adnan said, lifting his right hand to demonstrate, "*squeeze* them like a lemon."

"That doesn't work," I said. "All this pounding on the press's door! This morning, in the hotel, I called my friend at the *Daily Express* to see if he would tell me any more about what went wrong. We were home free yesterday. But then—*twice* in three hours!—Dr. Channa called the editor. First to ask how much progress he'd made at verifying the story, and then to make sure it would be in today's paper."

Adnan frowned, and I went on: "That's what made the editor nervous enough to call his friend at *The Times,* and that was the end of that. These guys are independent. They'll allow you to use them. But on *their* terms. They love a scoop, but they won't be force-fed anything. What Dr. Channa should've done, instead of setting up in a plush hotel, was move in with a big Indian family somewhere on the edge of London, or maybe in Birmingham or Liverpool. And from there, in a curry take-away manager's voice, timidly call a newspaper and say his nephew, a clerk in government in New Delhi, had just arrived on holiday. He'd brought a big news story with him, and papers to prove it. And did they want to *buy* it?"

Adnan sat down across from me, warming to the subterfuge. "Why?"

"You've heard of it," I said. "You're the master of it. It's called cover, and a bit of cover would've added a new dimension to the story of the documents. And created a financial motive for why Dr. Channa wanted so urgently to arrange their publication. Right now, the only apparent motive for all this is to smear V.P. Singh.

"But it's too late for all of that," I added. "At least in London."

"So here's what you do," Adnan said. "I'm just out of jail and everyone wants my story. But I haven't spoken to the press about it. You tell your friends: Whichever one of them prints your story first, I'll give my first interview."

"That'll get their attention," I said.

"*Yella,* Larry! *Yella!*" Adnan stood up to leave, and nothing I'd said had swayed him.

Next I dialed a friend of mine who worked in the White House. His name isn't important here, and you wouldn't recognize it anyway. My friend was a survivor of several little wars, foreign and domestic, overt and covert. Over the years I'd run into him in some of the most unusual of places. "Who do you call," I said, "when you want to leak a story to the press?"

"*You* don't call anyone," he said. "We'll have him call you. When he does, you tell him what you've got to say, and then if he wants to tell you who he is and how to reach him, that's up to him."

"That's fine with me," I said, and then I gave him Adnan's switchboard number.

"We'll tell him he can trust you," said my friend. "And you can definitely trust him. You can tell him the background to help him understand, and he won't write it unless you tell him that he can."

"Good," I said. "So tell him I called you from Adnan Khashoggi's gilded jail cell high above New York. And that I'll stay by the phone for the next half hour."

The phone rang a few minutes later and the guy on the other end listened to my story and then he said his name was Steve Engelberg and that he worked for *The New York Times,* Washington bureau. He said he was very interested, and he asked me to fax him the bank documents. Which I did. And half an hour later he called back. "We like to move suspicion into the realm of unde-niable fact," he said. "Can you get me handwriting exemplars of these two fine gentlemen?"

"Messrs. Singh and Singh?"

"Yes."

"Yes," I said, "I'm sure I can."

"My editor likes this story. And what we want to do before we print is have handwriting experts verify the authenticity of the documents."

"How long will that take?" I asked.

"Don't know. At least a few days."

I didn't push him. That was the moment I decided to play some hands long, my way, and some hands Adnan's way. "I'll try to have a courier deliver handwriting samples to you within a day or two," I said, and made a note to ask Mammaji the Orator for a copy of any public-record document V.P. Singh had signed.

All the rest of that afternoon I called for bureau chiefs, editors, foreign af-fairs reporters, left messages, spoke with some, soft-sold, made appointments, sent out faxes, did my best to smile through interruptions. Dr. Channa called three times, "just to see how you're getting on." Mammaji dropped in to tell me that the quisling V.P. Singh should be thrown into a river of liquid fire for all eternity, and that it was up to me to make it happen. Before Mammaji left, I made him promise to get me an example of V.P. Singh's signature. "Since he was a minister," I said, "your embassy right here in New York must have plenty of things he signed."

"I'll try," said Mammaji unhappily.

Adnan's next visit was ostensibly to lead me down the hall to say hello to the famous photographer Norman Parkinson—whom we found in the living room wearing a maroon fez and setting up a Hasselblad on a tripod. But I sensed that Adnan really wanted our little walk together to find out if I'd made any progress, and so I told him about *The New York Times.*

An hour later, he popped into the conference room and handed me a slip of paper containing the name and phone number of a friend of his who owned a newspaper in Hong Kong. "As soon as it's morning there," Adnan said, "call him. Tell him you're my director of public relations, and I told you to call. Then send him your story and ask him to publish it."

Before the sun rose over Hong Kong, Adnan was back in the conference room. "Come, Larry," he said, waving his hands to speed me up. "Put your jacket on." He rushed me down the hall and, as we went, he said in lowered voice, "This woman is a famous Israeli journalist. She's got the power to print the story immediately. But we can't completely trust her. She's probably Mossad.

I don't want her writing that I'm involved in this, or that you're related to me."
That was all the briefing I got before we arrived on stage.

"Ahhh, *Yoni!*" Adnan said as we entered the living room and came upon a good-looking woman, tall, blond, and somewhere in her early thirties. She beamed at Adnan and rose from a chair to let him kiss her cheeks.

"*Adnan!*" Her voice was deep and Middle Eastern. "So you survived after all!"

"Of course," he said. "We must all endure. Yoni, this is Mr. Douglas. Larry Douglas. Larry is one of Rajiv Gandhi's campaign managers, and Rajiv has just sent him here to see me."

"I'm Yoni Sayar," she said, reaching out to shake my hand.

"Hello," I said. "Larry *Douglas*." In Adnan Khashoggi's theater of intrigue, one actor could play many roles in a single afternoon.

"Mr. Douglas has a story which you might be interested in." Adnan said it ever so casually. "Are you free for dinner tonight?"

"Sure," she said. She was lightly tanned, bare-shouldered in a summer dress.

"Good! You two can come together. And maybe you can have a cocktail together first."

The skirt of her dress draped to the middle of her knees. Her legs were bare and she wore white leather sandals. She took two steps back and made a show of looking me over. "Okay," she said.

"Stick out your wrists," she said to Adnan. He did.

"Take off your jacket," she commanded. He did.

"*Where's* this famous bracelet?" she cried.

"Ahhhhhh!" Adnan winked. "That's Top Secret!" Back then, nobody knew you'd wear an electronic monitoring "bracelet" on your ankle instead of your wrist. Adnan was the first person anyone had ever heard of wearing one.

"I *demand* a tour," Yoni said. "First I want to see the swimming pool."

Adnan took her arm and began to lead us toward the door. "I hope you'll excuse me," I said. "I have an important phone call to make." Adnan said dinner would be at half past nine. Yoni Sayar told me her address, and we agreed I'd pick her up around eight-fifteen. "I'm looking forward to it," she said. *And if you could only know,* I thought, *how much I'm looking forward to telling my wife I have a date with a sexy blond Mossad agent.*

Yoni Sayar and Larry Douglas stayed out late that night, drank whisky, told lies, dined at a Japanese restaurant with Adnan Khashoggi and his party of fourteen. After dinner, just the two of them now, in a dark romantic bar, the eminent journalist took notes in Hebrew while her swain touched her hair and whispered intimacies about Indian intelligence's recent chance discovery concerning a certain Mr. Singh and a tiny island called St. Kitts.

Yoni Sayar could've passed for a European that afternoon or earlier that evening. But the more we drank the more an accent poured out of her. "I tink maybe do you wanna go to my hapartment and haf hanother drink?" she finally said. Damn straight, I did. But first she wrote something down, on three or four pages, in big Hebrew letters, which I didn't understand, and asked me to take her back to Adnan's to fax them to her newspaper in Israel.

This, I thought, might be some sort of trick, an attempt to get Adnan's fax headers on a document relating to St. Kitts. Or whatever she'd written about. So instead I took her to the concierge's desk at the Helmsley Palace and gave him cash to fax the document from there. She made us wait until he gave her back the originals.

When I struggled out of bed early the next morning Yoni was still beside me, if only in my head. As I showered and shaved and dressed in a lightweight charcoal suit, she stayed with me. I could still smell the perfume on her neck, hear her voice, and the more I thought of her the worse I felt. *Lying to the press,* I told myself, *is the surest way to be burnt by them.* Promising to mend my ways, except of course when Yoni called for Mr. Douglas, I rushed downstairs for a meeting with Bill Felling.

I was nine minutes late, and Bill was the New York bureau chief for CBS Television News.

Yesterday he'd sounded interested in my story. Now, sitting across a pink tablecloth table from me in Le Trianon, he told me what I didn't want to hear. "We think it's intriguing," he said, "but we're not going to do it. What you're up against is that no one in the U.S. is interested in day-to-day Indian news." I was about to mount a protest but, before I could, he clinched his argument. "On American television news," he said, "when is the last time you saw a story about India if there wasn't a flood there the day before? Or an assassination?"

"Well, there was that time on the parade ground," I said, smiling in defeat, "when that Sri Lankan soldier tried to bash Rajiv Gandhi over the head with the butt of his rifle."

"Okay," said Felling. "Or an assassination *attempt*?"

I ate eggs Benedict and sausages while he ate something healthier and pitched me on a *60 Minutes* feature on Adnan. I asked if he would run the Indian story if I got him Adnan. He looked tempted, but said no. Well, I'd see what I could do, I said, but as far as I knew Adnan wasn't talking to the media.

After another cup of coffee Bill suggested I try *The Christian Science Monitor*.

"I spoke with them last night," I said.

"Then try London," he said. "They follow India. London's probably the natural place for this."

Yes, indeed it was.

Back in Adnan's conference room, I began to work the phone, and within two hours, I'd called five continents. As yesterday, as always, it was harder to reach people than I'd envisioned when I set out, even harder to accomplish anything. Most of the people I called for just weren't in. An intern from the *Miami Herald* rang me back and told me my friend there would be away for about five days. Friends of mine from NBC and ABC were away on assignments. Or vacations. Likewise other friends from other places.

Sometimes, when I gave my name and number, my quarry came on the line immediately, and other times they called right back. Still, I was relieved to know Adnan and his lawyers were inside a limousine, entombed in barely moving traffic on their way downtown to check in with Adnan's corrections officer. Beyond failures, vague hopes, and minor comedies that Adnan might not appreciate just then, I had nothing to report to him.

An *El Commercio* editor called me back from Peru to say "maybe" in that special Latin way I knew meant "no."

A reporter from *O Globo* of Rio promised to look into it just as soon as he got back from Buenos Aires, in a week or two.

A stringer I'd spoken with the day before called and told me the Toronto *Sun* was interested but noncommittal.

Down a clear line from Oslo, *Dag Blade*'s news editor promised to run a front-page story if I would provide him "confirmable details" about the Norwegian bank and the beneficiary who received the money once it was transferred from St. Kitts. Five minutes later, roused from bed and far too addled for elocution, Mammaji grumbled that he couldn't get what I needed for at least a week.

Funny thing, I realize now. Anytime I asked Mammaji for anything more, he didn't have it and couldn't get it.

Outside the window of Adnan's conference room and looking south, atop the forty-two-story Newsweek Building, under the magazine's bright red logo, the time and temperature were always on display. The glowing white numerals could be read from miles around, so, although the Newsweek clock was actually two blocks away, from where I sat it seemed to be just outside the window. Veterans of Adnan's office suite rarely checked their watches there.

That day the Newsweek clock became a presence for me to reckon with, a reminder of my deadline and my lack of progress. I knew it was unlikely the story would appear in the next morning's paper unless an editor had pretty well decided on it by his afternoon conference, and that those were usually held around four or five. As problems and rejections mounted, I was all the more frustrated because I knew I had a story that would rock India.

Spy or not, Yoni Sayar was a seasoned journalist. "My God, Larry!" she'd said last night. "This is going to be a *bombshell,* isn't it?!" But she'd also said she couldn't publish it for several days.

By late morning—11:47 Newsweek Time to be exact—I was reduced to making cold calls to wire services and dropping Adnan's name. Which got a lot of attention, but when I mentioned India, interest started petering out. Reuters New York said try Reuters New Delhi. AP's New York bureau chief said, "I'm supposed to refer you to our New Delhi bureau. But actually no one there files anything about India these days, because they're all so busy with Afghanistan." UPI's foreign editor said he would have to call me later.

The stringer, an Englishman, called back and said the *Sun* was looking better. "*Sun*'s a tabloid. Likes a juicy story," he said. "And Toronto's chock-ablock with Indians." Plus there was a local angle: The banker George McLean, they'd learned, was originally from Toronto. And now, apparently, he'd left St. Kitts and returned to Canada. "They think they've found him," said the stringer. "Should know in a couple hours." Dr. Channa had left five messages for me, so now I called him and told him about the *Sun.*

Around twelve-thirty, Adnan called me from his car. Although the day before he'd been something of a human ultimatum, pressing me at every chance, now he seemed much calmer, and I couldn't decide if it was because his lawyers were listening or he heard in my voice that already the challenge was beginning to possess me. Adnan gave me the telephone and fax numbers for Tiny Rowland's yacht, and asked me to call Tiny, tell him the story, and then fax him the details. Tiny owned, among many other things, London's venerable broadsheet *The Observer.*

I kept placing calls, and old friends and acquaintances were glad to hear from me—but not to hear me talking about shady Indian politicians.

"The problem," as Steve Dunleavy—who'd once planned to write a rather lurid book about me—put it at just past one, while we drank beers together in The Racing Club, a bar across the street from the studios of Fox TV, "quite simply, is that no one here gives a damn about India." Then Steve paused in thought. "London's your place for this one, mate," he said at last. "The Empire. The Commonwealth. London, that's your market."

On Steve's advice, half of my afternoon was devoted to acts of contrition, reopening the door to London. He gave me the names and private numbers of several friends of his from Fleet Street and suggested I call them and apologize that the story I wanted told had been handled so badly up to now. "Then," Steve said, "what you do is say, 'Look, mate, I'm sorry you've been mucked about on this. But it's still a hell of a story, you must admit. If you want it, I promise that you'll deal with me alone.'"

By five, I'd groveled to several London newsmen and, of the lot, I felt the foreign news editor of *The Times* had been the most receptive. Still, no London paper was going to help me meet my deadline, and I was already rationalizing an extension.

Since parliament met nearly every day, surely Rajiv could delay whatever he had up his sleeve for a day or two. Right?

Not so, said grim-faced Mammaji, an hour later when he arrived in the conference room and I told him that the Toronto *Sun* was my only remaining hope for the next morning. That the stringer had called and said the story had made it through the editorial conference, but they still hadn't found McLean, and their lawyers insisted they get a comment from him before they printed the story.

"So if they find McLean," said Mammaji, his eyes bright with excitement, "the story will be in?"

"Yes," I said. "If they find him fast enough."

"I'll be back!" said Mammaji, rushing toward the door. "I think I can help them find him!"

Where he'd been and what he'd done, I didn't know, but twenty minutes later Mammaji was back and triumphantly passing me a grubby little sheet of pencil scratchings—presumably his own excited handwriting. *Fat Man,* it said, and under that a telephone number with the Toronto area code.

"George McLean?" I asked.

Mammaji nodded. As I picked up the phone, he sat down beside me, staring out the window and clenching and unclenching his jaw. He listened to every word I said to the stringer, and then he dialed London and reported in excited Hindi to Dr. Channa.

"Now you call your friend," Mammaji said to me while he hung up, "and have him arrange for the newspaper to fax you the story as soon as it is laid out." I said no, and Mammaji's protest was soon so fierce that I called in Adnan. "One more ounce of pressure and we queer the deal," I told him. "Just like yesterday."

I remained that entire night in Adnan's office, unchanged, unshaven, reading at Adnan's desk, updating my contacts log, pacing around, waiting. Adnan, Mammaji, and I had finally agreed to send a man to wait that night outside the loading docks of the *Sun*'s printing plant and, when the first truck pulled out, to flag down the driver and offer him five dollars for a paper. Once our man had the paper—probably no later than one—he was to call me and then fax the story to me. As soon as I had it, I was to call Adnan and Mammaji.

But at two I was still waiting, and soon studying a row of framed photographs of Adnan with Richard Nixon, with Jimmy Carter, with Anwar Sadat, Jaafer Numeiri, the Sultan of Brunei, King Hussein, Pope Paul VI. *Who are you?* I wondered for the thousandth time, staring into Adnan's face for clues. *How did you pull all this off? Once I thought I knew, but I was wrong.* It hadn't escaped me that Adnan was far from home, under house arrest, facing decades in prison, his phones tapped, his faxes and his mail intercepted, and still he was exploding firecrackers under the parliament house of a very large country on the other side of the earth.

I meandered about the room, peering at other things that hung on the walls: a large portrait of Ronald Reagan matted and framed together with a friendly handwritten note to Adnan from the President; a platinum record album, *We Are the World,* a gift to Adnan from Quincy Jones; Adnan smiling at me winningly from the cover of *Time;* a framed front page of *The Wall Street Journal* containing a story about Adnan's construction of a refinery in Louisiana. Twelve years before that night, I'd managed to get a story about myself and my business on the front page of *The Wall Street Journal.* Since then I'd always felt I had an intuitive understanding of the news media's needs and how to mesh those with my own. So why hadn't Toronto called? It was 2:36 by the Newsweek clock when I settled into an armchair.

When the phone finally rang, I felt my heart throbbing against my shirt as I walked across the carpet toward Adnan's desk. I hadn't realized I was so anxious. It was 3:06.

"Hello," I said after a long, deep pause for breath.

"Mr. Larry?" asked an Indian voice.

"Yes."

"Mr. Larry, sir, there is nothing about India in this paper."

"Can you check again?" I said. "Look for V.P. Singh. Ajeya Singh. George McLean. St. Kitts."

"No, sir, Mr. Larry." His voice bordered on falsetto. "I have been checking for two hours. First edition and second edition. There is nothing about India in this paper."

So they didn't find McLean, I thought as I hung up, and then I laid my head down on the desk until something made me open my eyes, and I sat up and found Adnan standing in front of me. The room was lit with the flat gray light of early morning. Adnan was wearing a bright red track suit and his face was wrinkled with sleep.

"You work *hard,*" he said.

Then he looked at me with the smile that was part of his gift for listening. It said, *You can tell me anything, and I'll still be smiling when you finish.*

"What happened?" he asked sympathetically.

"We didn't make the paper." I turned my face away and rubbed my eyes. "I suppose they didn't find McLean, but I don't know for sure."

"I have a message from Rajiv," said Adnan. "Keep at it. Rajiv can wait for two more days."

And so the air of crisis which surrounded me, if anything, intensified. Adnan, Mammaji, and I met around noon each day, and each day was another disaster because V.P. Singh's secret was still not in print. The Orator's nerves were stretched to the breaking point, deadlines came and went, and he used our meetings to put my every move on trial.

Granted, his arguments always went, they had soiled things a bit in London before I began. But why had I not offered more journalists an interview with Adnan as just reward for defrocking the fiendish Mr. Singh? Or used Dr. Channa's rich and plentiful stock of inside material on Pamella Bordes as an inducement? True, he hadn't yet obtained for me the exemplars *The New York Times* had asked for, or the information requested by *Dag Blade.* But this story was so big that surely I could transcend all that. Surely it was time to abandon my high principles, which obviously didn't work.

Each day I held my line:

We're on the right track, I maintained.

We have the attention of several newspapers.

But if we push them they will run away. Like they did in London.

This is an important story. Yes, it's a scoop. But it's also a big black mark against the editor who runs it if he gets it wrong.

We must stay the course, I said.

Adnan always backed me up. And I suspected that meant that, behind the scenes, so did Rajiv.

One joyous afternoon Adnan and Mammaji listened in on a speakerphone while a reporter from a Fleet Street tabloid told me our story had made it unconditionally through the afternoon meeting and would be in the next day's paper.

Smiles, congratulations, and "I never doubted you"s were lavished on me.

But that night a crowded party boat sank sensationally in the River Thames. Several were drowned, including our story, and Mammaji looked at me as if it were all my fault.

Because my days were spent at infighting, sleeping, eating, taking care of the mundane, now all the key scenes played out at night. And they were remarkable nights up there above Manhattan, all alone but working feverishly. On the seventh night, after I'd lobbied half the bureau chiefs and editors and publishers on the planet, telephoned, faxed, and prayed toward every continent except Antarctica, missed two more strategic deadlines bewailed by Mammaji and Dr. Channa and even Adnan, suffered their scorn, eating by the phone, catnapping by the phone, while time blurred as I waited for a breakthrough, driven myself to exhaustion and exhilaration as publishing the story became my obsession, my quest, my only reason for living, and then, after three nights of working him, somehow satisfied the publisher of an English-language daily based in Kuwait that the story I'd told him was true, finally—in a long front-page story in its August 20, 1989 edition—The *Arab Times* broke the story of twenty-one million dollars in dirty money hidden in St. Kitts by Vishwanath Pratap Singh.

The *Arab Times* story electrified New Delhi.

Rajiv's supporters savaged V.P. Singh in parliament and in the press and on the government-controlled television news. They'd known all along that V.P. Singh was a crook, and here, finally, was proof. "Shame! Shame!" they taunted him in parliament.

Vishwanath Pratap Singh, the once putative King of Manda, responded with an open letter to Rajiv. "These St. Kitts charges are not fit for a dustbin," wrote the accused. "We are well aware that this canard was cooked up by the slander machine inside your Department of Diabolical Tricks," he raged on, and then challenged Rajiv to prosecute him. "But this would only reveal that there is a fatal lacuna in your charges. And that is that my son Ajeya Singh has never set foot in St. Kitts in his life. His passport proves that." In closing, V.P. Singh warned the contemptible curs behind the St. Kitts lies that he was on to them, that he knew that, for their next diabolical trick, they were plotting to kill him and make his death look like an accident.

This was all a bit too shrill and hysterical for Rajiv's Congress party brethren. They bayed for V.P. Singh's blood, or at least his arrest, and for the immediate extradition of his son Ajeya. But Rajiv remained above the fray. He delivered perfectly the lines I'd suggested for him when I faxed Dr. Channa the *Arab Times* story: "At the moment, these charges are nothing more than unsubstantiated press reports. As much as it might benefit me personally, it would not be appropriate for the prime minister of India to use the powers of his office against a political opponent without first receiving solid evidence of wrongdoing."

I slept through all of it.

As soon as I'd received a copy of the *Arab Times* story by fax from Kuwait, I'd faxed it on to Dr. Channa, who by then was back home in New Delhi. Then I'd sent copies to Adnan and Mammaji by hand, and gone back to my room in the Helmsley Palace and slept for twenty hours straight—while Kim watched two movies on television, went shopping, came home, had room service, puttered around the room, had room service again, checked once to make sure I was still breathing. When I woke, I ate a room-service steak with french fries, watched half a movie with Kim, and then slept for eight more hours.

All the while, the hotel operators told callers I'd asked not to be disturbed, by anyone. So there were two dozen messages when I finally came to—one of them from Kim saying she'd gone out with some friends, most of them from Adnan or Dr. Channa.

I called Adnan, and he invited me to dinner. "Come over for a cocktail in about an hour," he said. "We'll leave around nine-thirty."

The Helmsley Palace doormen wore most extraordinary hats, broad-brimmed and hairy things with one side folded up like Australian bush hats. I was contemplating just such a hat while I began to realize that tonight's dinner with Adnan would be the natural conclusion of the job, the small favor, I'd agreed to do for him, and I knew I was going to miss the adrenaline, the sense of being involved in something big.

Inside Adnan's apartment, I looked for A.K., but found instead—in a salon off the living room—Swamiji, seated regally in a big beige armchair and looking different than I'd ever seen him. Gone were the long, raven-black hair flowing straight back from his forehead to his shoulders, and the thick black beard brushing the top of his chest. Now he had a scraggly buzz cut and five or six days of beard. The holy man was smiling broadly at me, as were Mammaji and about a dozen more Indian men seated around the holy man on a couch and on the floor. All of them were wearing loose *dhotis* and *kurtas* and when they saw me they began to chant. I thought I'd walked into some sort of prayer meeting. But then I recognized my name, and realized they'd been waiting for me. "*Larry Kolb Zindabad! Larry Kolb Zindabad! Larry Kolb Zindabad! Larry Kolb Zindabad!*" they chanted.

"What does it mean?" I asked.

I already knew. But I wanted to hear it.

"Long live Larry Kolb!" said Mammaji in magisterial tones.

I was about to thank them when Swamiji spoke. "You do *very good* thing for our brother Rajiv. For India."

Mammaji beckoned me to an end table. He started dialing a telephone and the chanting started again. He hushed everyone, then handed me the phone, saying, "Dr. Channa has been waiting to congratulate you." I listened to the crackling and double-ring tones of the unpredictable Indian telephone system, and then to a series of clicks, and finally Dr. Channa: "Hello?"

"*Namaste,*" I said.

"Where have you been? I've been trying to get you forever."

"Sorry," I said. "How are things working out there?"

"Fabulous! And Rajiv sends his congratulations. He said to tell you, 'You've finally got the bastard on the run!'"

"So he's happy?"

"Oh yes!" said Dr. Channa. "And it's been a long time coming. I didn't want to discourage you before. So I told you I'd only been working on this for five days when you started. But we'd actually been trying to plant this story for almost three months. You did it in one week, and you did a great job. V.P. Singh is going *mad* with all this. And now Rajiv wants me to ask you to keep at it through the election. Pressuring V.P. Singh. Countering his denials. Working him over in the press. Giving Rajiv campaign advice."

I remember that what popped into my head just then was *In the land of the blind, the one-eyed man is king.* If Dr. Channa hadn't screwed things up before I got started, I could've placed the story in one day, not seven. Obviously Rajiv's team didn't have a clue when it came to running a propaganda war outside of India. "It *was* a much tougher job than I'd imagined," I said. "I'll discuss it with Adnan. Give Rajiv my best."

I said goodbye, then hung up and turned to Swamiji. "You had a haircut."

"Yes, yes," the holy man said. "When A.K. in jail, I vow to God that, when my brother A.K. is free, I shave my head and beard. And you see," he smiled, "I keep my vow."

"You *certainly* did."

"But this is easy vow." Swamiji beamed. "When I am eighteen, when I begin my mission for world peace through nonviolence, I also make vow, and now I am celibate for *twenty* years." He was so happy just then about Rajiv's good fortune and my good work, and so enthusiastic and positive. That's the word: positive. When I look back, I realize that somehow I still hadn't twigged to who was behind all this.

Mario, the butler, came in now and told me Adnan was upstairs in his personal quarters and had left word to send me up.

I found Adnan sitting back in the barber chair in his dressing room. Beside him stood George, a graying bear of a fellow, who was from Lebanon and had been Adnan's barber for thirty years. George was holding a straight razor and had just finished shaving his boss.

"Ah, India's national hero!" Adnan said when he saw me in the mirror ringed with large, bright lightbulbs—as in an actor's dressing room. He was wearing a white cotton *thobe*, unbuttoned at the neck. "You've made quite a stir over there."

"So I heard," I said. "I just talked to Dr. Channa, and he told me Rajiv is very pleased."

George adjusted the chair, and now I finally saw Adnan's new bracelet—

strapped around his right ankle. It was a rectangular block of black plastic with a rubbery plastic strap. It looked like something a scuba diver might wear on the ankle on which he didn't keep his dive knife.

"How does the bracelet work?" I said.

"They call here on a special phone two or three times a day," Adnan said. "And then I have to say my name and push this thing into a little slot next to the phone."

"And if you don't?"

"Heaven knows," he said, rolling his eyes as if he didn't want to find out.

I told Adnan Dr. Channa had just told me he'd actually been trying to plant the St. Kitts story for three months. "You didn't know that, did you?" I said, and then I watched for anything in Adnan's expression to change.

His face betrayed nothing. He shook his head at me quizzically. "No," he said. "Three months?"

Now George was combing what little hair was left atop the head of his only customer. Then he stood back to inspect, holding a pair of scissors out in front of him in that way that barbers do. He reached in and snipped once at the bottom of Adnan's thick black mustache.

"Rajiv wants me to keep working on this until after the election," I said. "What do you think?"

"Terrific!" Adnan said. "Accept it. I'm sure there'll be a big reward for you after the election."

Life could be so much more expensive than I'd ever imagined when I set out. In the past year, I'd grossed over sixteen million dollars—selling one big diamond and four used airliners, and those were big successes for me. But I was just a middleman, and my margins were relatively small. My annual expenses were now more than I'd once thought I could retire on forever. It had been dawning on me that to reach the level to which I now aspired I was going to have to graduate to doing hundred-million-dollar deals. This might be my chance. If, the next time Air India bought a new 747, I could be the broker, a five-percent commission on a three-hundred-twenty-five-million-dollar plane would suit me fine, even if I had to split it with Adnan. No need to rush into things, though. "I'm not really sure I want the job," I said. "I'll wait for you downstairs."

In the enormous living room, I waved off the waiter and fixed myself a Campari and soda, then settled down on a couch and nibbled shelled pistachios from a bowl of hammered gold. It was a beautiful room. The walls were hung with impressionist paintings, bronzes and carvings were everywhere. There were big comfortable armchairs and couches, jeweled boxes and figurines, there were fresh flowers all over the place, orchids, roses, birds-of-paradise. And there was the rain forest, climbing two stories high and lighted from within.

I got up and wandered past a Monet water lily canvas and a Picasso—one of those wild things he must've painted when he wasn't hungry anymore, a face with two noses and three eyes, and you saw them front and side at the same time. I stood at the window, staring north and wondering what I should do about helping Rajiv. Where was Miles? What would he say I should do? Central Park was a big black lake surrounded by the glowing cityscape. A million lights were twinkling out there.

Truth was, I'd never really had a job and a boss. Not since I was a lifeguard, at least, and that career had ended when I drowned. Since then, I'd been at various times founder, partner, promoter, agent, employer—but never employee. Miles and I were partners, collaborators. The more I thought about it, the more I realized I didn't want to take orders from *anyone* for the next five months, let alone Mammaji and Dr. Channa.

Soon—by Adnan's standards—he arrived in the living room in a spiffy black suit. "Ah, Your Excellency," he said as he shook my hand. "It's always so good to see you!" A waiter handed him a colorless drink in a frosted flute. Water? Vodka? Six months earlier, it would've been vodka, but I'd heard Adnan visited his prayer rug five times a day since jail, and hadn't touched alcohol.

Footsteps on marble, then rustling of silk, and Lamia appeared at Adnan's side. Her makeup and her hair were perfect. Jewels sparkled on her wrists, her hands, her ears, her throat. She was wearing a shapely emerald-green dress. "Va-va-va-voom!" I said before air-kissing Lamia's cheeks.

"Larry has just become our friend Mr. Gandhi's new campaign manager," Adnan announced to his wife. That was news to me.

Both of them were wonderful at small talk. The time passed seamlessly while we rode in a black limo to San Domenico, a luxe Italian restaurant up on Central Park South. Adnan was relaxed and happy in the car. Just as we arrived he became even more so. It was *the* Adnan Khashoggi, living legend, who swept into the dining room where one very long table and about twenty of Adnan's old classmates from Victoria College in Alexandria, plus some of their wives and sons and daughters, were waiting for us. They'd flown en masse to New York to show Adnan their support in this his most difficult time. It was obvious they loved him, admired him, had been marveling at his exploits for years. Adnan's eyes scintillated with charm and confidence as he greeted each person there, fussed over them, made sure they tasted every hors d'oeuvre. "The trick," Adnan had counseled Kim when she was a shy teenager, "is always to seem at ease, especially when you are not."

Halfway home from the restaurant, Adnan told the driver to stop and let us out. Then Adnan took his wife's hand and mine and led us on a stroll down Park Avenue. It's an Arab thing: Men hold men's hands. It's an American thing: Men don't hold men's hands. It isn't easy in Jiddah when you get into a taxi and the driver bids you into the front seat—the backseats are for women—and then holds your hand all the way to where you're going. But being as you have a diplomatic nature, you don't let go. In Jiddah, or on Park Avenue. After a minute or two, Adnan let go of my hand and took Lamia in both of his. He twirled her around through some dance steps for a moment, and then the three of us kept walking—unconnected. Up ahead, the Helmsley Building was bathed in lights and the Pan Am Building rose in perfect symmetry above it.

We turned right on 51st, and when we reached the door of the Helmsley Palace I felt like I'd lived there for years. "Come over tomorrow, before lunch," Adnan said. "I think it's important for us to talk about this job you're going to do for Rajiv."

The next morning was stinking hot. My shoes bit into the soft pavement when I set out across Madison Avenue. Inside Adnan's office, Mammaji was waiting for me with a curling stack of newspaper clippings just off the fax from New Delhi. He left as I began to read them.

Most of the Indian press coverage of the St. Kitts story was polemic and predictable. Singh's staunchest ally in the media war seemed to be the *Indian Express,* which was India's largest newspaper chain, with a dozen regional editions. I read V.P. Singh's open letter to Rajiv, and laughed at an opposition claim that The First Trust Corporation didn't even exist. Then I came across a three-paragraph story buried deep in the *Indian Express.*

I read it twice. Then another time. Holy shit!

I ran upstairs to look for Adnan.

His bedroom door was open, and his famous ten-foot-wide bed was made. Covered by his famous fourteen-foot-wide sable bedspread. Adnan wasn't there. Next I checked his dressing room. No luck.

I went down the hall to the swimming pool and, just past it, standing behind a massage table, was Werner, one of Adnan's masseurs. Werner was tall, young, fair, Belgian, wearing white pants and a white tennis shirt. Before him on the table was a stack of thick white towels, and in his hand and at his ear was a portable telephone coated with bright yellow rubber.

"Mr. Khashoggi is not here right now," Werner was saying in slightly accented English. "I'm not certain where he is."

Werner covered the phone, then whispered to me, "A.K.," pointing behind him toward the little window in the sauna door. I smelled chlorine from the pool. "Okay, sir, " said Werner. "I will have him call you. Yes, yes. In Paris."

I went to the window and tried to look in, but the glass was fogged. Werner grinned at me and said I should go on in. Adnan loved to summon his fully suited executives into his saunas or his steam baths for contrived emergency meetings. Such was the life of a courtier. I was wearing one of my favorite suits. Tropical wool. Muted Prince of Wales plaid. I said, "How long will he be?"

Werner shrugged. "Maybe five minutes. Maybe an hour."

Three minutes later, I was standing at the sauna door wearing nothing but a white towel around my waist. I knocked on the glass, then opened the door just wide enough to stick my face into the hot, resinous air.

"Ahh, Larry! Come in, come in," said Adnan.

"I've got something you need to read," I said while waving the fax as I stepped into the oven and closed the door behind me.

Of all the rooms in this vast apartment, the sauna was perhaps the simplest and most beautiful. A latticework grille of burnished redwood shaded the room and gave the effect of the screened rooms of old Arabia. Sunlight glared through thick windows glazed to keep the heat in, passed through the grille, and emerged to decorate the darkness with a thousand brilliant squares of light. It was spacious by the standards of a sauna, room enough for Adnan and fifteen men in suits. The walls and floor and ceiling were cedar. There were two long redwood-and-cedar beds topped with soft embroidered pallets and cushions.

The heat was set on the dry mode, so there was no steam. Adnan was sitting on one of the pallets, naked but for the electronic bracelet on his ankle and squares of light across his back and neck.

I tried to hand the fax to him, but he pushed it away. "Read it to me."

I sat on the end of the other bed, at an angle to catch some light. "The headline," I said, "is 'The Next Move Not a Forgery but an Account.' This was in the *Indian Express*'s August 20, 1989, edition, which had to have been printed a few hours *before* our *Arab Times* story."

I took a hot deep breath, then read to Adnan.

The first paragraph was about letters forged some time earlier to discredit V.P. Singh. It made no sense to me, so I read it quickly. "I've got no idea what that's all about," I said. "But, then, listen to this: '*However, this time it is much more diabolic than patently forged letters. Highly placed sources both in the government and among those who have been working with the government to smear Mr. Singh reveal that through the Department of Diabolical Tricks arrangements have been completed to open an account in a foreign bank which will be attributed to Mr. V.P. Singh. To make the arrangements look real, efforts are on to locate the accounts of Mr. V.P. Singh's two sons who live abroad so that some money from the account opened in Mr. V.P. Singh's name can be transferred into the accounts of his sons.* 'Express News Service understands that the first part of the plan has been completed and the smear will be formally launched within the next few days as soon as the transfer of money into the sons' accounts have been made.'"

Adnan leaned forward. He said, "So, Professor, what do you think?"

"I don't think it came from highly placed sources in the government at all," I said. "I think it came from V.P. Singh himself."

Go on, said Adnan with his eyes.

"On the nineteenth, the day before our story came out, an *Arab Times* reporter spoke with V.P. Singh. Told him, without going into specifics, that the newspaper had a story saying he had hidden money in a foreign bank account of one of his sons, and then asked for a comment."

"So Singh knew he was caught," said Adnan.

"Better than that," I said. "Why does the *Indian Express*—Singh's ally—say this is *not* a forgery, but *real* money in *real* accounts belonging to V.P. Singh's *sons*? And why the vague and tortured explanation of a smear that's soon to come?"

I handed him the fax so he could search for clues. But it wasn't Adnan's morning for playing along with anything. He leaned back and closed his eyes, and there came a long pause during which there was nothing I could do but listen to the *pat-pat-pat-pat* of our sweat hitting the floor. Eventually, in spite of Adnan's Delphic mood, I couldn't resist telling him my theory. "The more I read it," I said, "the more it seems the only explanation is that Mr. Singh has stashed money not only in Ajeya's Singh's name but in *both* his sons' names. When the *Arab Times* contacted him, the poor man knew he was caught, but he wasn't told enough details to know *which* of his dirty accounts had been discovered."

Adnan looked a very happy man then. "So you've cornered him," he said. "Now don't you want to stay around to finish him off?" That was when I said, okay, I'd take the job, through the election, but only if, right there and then, Adnan would tell me all about his time in jail. He said to pour some water on the stones, and I did. Then he told me, while staring straight ahead into the steam, seeing nothing but his story.

After that, a couple of weeks passed, while I stayed in New York and more than anything else what I did was wait—for a major Western publication to report the story of the St. Kitts account. The Indian news services had flashed all across India the report coming out of Kuwait, of course, and international wire services had picked the story up then. But, so far, not *The Washington Post* or *The New York Times* or *Time,* or any other major American or British news publication. When one of them did, it would increase the credibility of the story significantly. Lally Weymouth said the *Post* was still researching. Mammaji kept failing to deliver on the handwriting exemplars I'd promised Steve Engelberg of the *Times.* I couldn't reach Raji Samghabadi.

Kim flew home to Florida, incident-free. I called my friend Ahmed Jarallah, the owner and publisher of the *Arab Times.* Ahmed owned and published English- and Arabic-language papers in Kuwait, Saudi Arabia, and Morocco.

He was in his late forties, probably—like most Arabs of his era, he didn't really know for sure—and he was energetic, charismatic, a hell of a lot of fun. I'd traveled in Africa and Europe with him in his plane, which was not unlike one of Adnan's planes. Ahmed and I had talked about doing business together, but never had. He was a great guy, though, and a tough mother with ironclad balls.

We'd spent so much time together that I would've thought he'd have gone easier on me when I'd asked him to be first to publish an account of Ajeya Singh's St. Kitts bank account. But instead he'd grilled me about the story for three nights before he decided he believed it and would publish it.

A few years earlier, Ahmed had written an editorial which seriously pissed off one Hafez el-Assad, the President of Syria. Word had flowed down to Ahmed that he must stop writing such things or there would be consequences. Where-upon Ahmed had written and published more of such things, until one day a special Syrian delegation visited him in Kuwait. They got him coming out of his offices. He took something like a dozen bullets, they left him lying on the pavement, and yet he lived. "What were you thinking," I asked him once, "when you were lying there on the street believing you were dying, what was the last thing you thought about before it all went black?" I was expecting something spiritual, some epiphany Ahmed had hard earned, which I might borrow and benefit from for free. But his answer came quickly, and it was "I was thinking about the accounts and investments I had hidden and not told my family about yet. That this was a big mistake."

Ahmed told me he'd been taking a lot of heat for publishing the St. Kitts story, and that was fine with him. He agreed to let me write follow-up stories on the V.P. Singh case anonymously under the byline "Arab Times Special Caribbean Correspondent." This might be fun.

In my first dispatch, I named the scandal the St. Kitts Affair. It stuck. Every scandal needs a name. Every day, the St. Kitts Affair was covered in more than a thousand Indian newspapers. Every man in the street had an opinion on the twenty-one-million-dollar mystery. Every politician had a comment. Still nothing in *The Washington Post* or *The New York Times* or *Time*. But the story had its own momentum now, and the general elections were three or four months off. Even Mammaji the Orator agreed with me when I said there was time for patience now.

Miles turned up. He was, and for the past few weeks had been, in a hospital called The Paddock—the name of which I vowed to give him endless shit for once he made it out. Adnan and I sent him flowers, which I addressed to "*Mr. Miles Copeland/ Patient/ Stall 6/ The Paddock Veterinary Hospital*." He was there because of a flare-up of his arthritis and was hurting so badly that we didn't talk much. I did tell him I was now a superhero in India, an insider of the highest order, and we could expect to have their launch codes any day now.

What was that verse we memorized in Sunday school? *Pride goeth before destruction, and a haughty spirit before a fall.*

Yoni Sayar vanished, joining the list of people who'd once been involved in this story whom I could no longer locate. When I went to look for her, her apartment was nothing but bare floors and walls, and a broom leaning in a corner.

On a sunny afternoon, I went out for a walk. Right in front of the Olympic Tower, on the sidewalk, I was cut off by a tiny Indian dandy, who stepped out of a crowd of tourists milling around the corner of 50th and 51st. The little bastard stopped me with his furled umbrella, then bowed slightly and said, "Mr. Larry Kolb, we need to talk."

I hate it when people I don't know know my name. His face and hands glowed pink, like he'd just gotten out of a hot bath. He was meticulously dressed in a cheap pinstriped navy suit—the size you buy in the Teens department—a white shirt, and a bright red tie. His eyes were black and beady, sinister. But he was only about half my size. How much trouble could he be?

"Follow me," I said, and then I turned around and silently led him across 51st, down the sidewalk along the north wall of St. Patrick's, and across Madison and into the beautiful, old-world Villard House, the foundation of the Helmsley Palace. On the way into the Hunt Bar, you passed through a gilded rococo music chamber, and that day a woman was up on the balcony playing harp.

The dandy's well-polished black shoes didn't reach the footrail on his bar stool. He introduced himself, using a name that even five minutes later I wouldn't recall, because I was certain it was false.

"Let me buy you a drink," I said.

He ordered a Chivas and began to smoke, making a curious little popping sound each time he inhaled.

"Well, Mr. Kolb," he said, "you seem nice enough in person, but you're hell to find."

"Thanks." I looked away from him and took in the beautiful woodwork all around the room.

He was a chain smoker. As our drinks arrived, the dandy lit another cigarette—*pop.*

Then came an awkward silence while we drank, and after.

He'd already emptied his glass. But now he tried to drink more from it, then quickly set the glass down. I ordered him another. He waited until he'd had a sip, then smiled a most unpleasant smile. "You're in serious trouble," he said—*pop.* "You've been working in concert with Israeli and Indian intelligence."

Israeli intelligence. This startled me, and I tried hard not to show it. *Where are you, Yoni?*

"You're in *very* serious trouble," said the dandy, with the smuggest of grins. "If you tell me everything, maybe I can help you out of it."

I didn't say a word.

He fished into the inside breast pocket of his suit jacket and pulled out a folded piece of newspaper. "Read this cutting," he said.

Something about the way he'd said it all made me very angry. I slammed my glass down on the bar, took the newspaper clipping, told him I was late for a meeting, made a mockery of shaking his hand with the utmost courtesy, then left him there with the unpaid check.

I remember muttering under my breath, "*Ganduji!*—which means, basically, *You're an asshole!,* in Urdu, and has come into Hindi usage—as I turned and stared at him from across the room just before I passed out the door. His back was to me and he seemed to be working on his cigarette and ordering another drink.

I went to the Men's room and locked myself in a stall and read the clipping. An *India Abroad* story by someone named Lynn Hudson, dated September 1, 1989. Hudson said she'd been to St. Kitts the week before, and her nearly full-page report quoted The First Trust Corporation's solicitor and its former office manager, both dismissing the story of Ajeya Singh's secret bank account as nothing but a fraud.

I walked straight to the Olympic Tower and told Adnan what the little Indian fucker had told me, and then I showed him the newspaper clipping. This brought a certain tension to the person of Adnan M. Khashoggi, who, in the days since my success, had seemed about as relaxed and jolly as a man facing thirty-seven years in a federal penitentiary could be. But now I watched him change as he sat before me in the conference room and read Lynn Hudson's story. Anger, hope, resignation, puzzlement crossed Adnan's face somehow all at once. He pushed the paper aside. "Please wait here for me," he said politely, but without his air of confidence. Then he left the room for several minutes.

When Adnan came back he was troubled, but in control again. He pulled the big, wooden sliding door closed behind him and sat back down across from me. He said: "I'm afraid our Indian friends may have been sold a bill of goods. So I think you had better hurry down to St. Kitts and find out what you can about what's happened there."

"I thought you investigated this *before* we publicized it."

"Of course, well, yes, we did. But when Indian intelligence, or any intelligence service, brings you something, you just never can be . . ." Adnan's voice trailed off, and he looked away. "This story makes me worry."

I imagined the Caribbean in the last month of summer. A steam bath. "I hear it's nice there this time of year," I said.

"You'll have to be careful. There'll be Indians crawling all over the place by now. And greedy, dangerous people. These small Caribbean banks are for money launderers." Adnan paused, then added helpfully: "So remember to be polite."

It struck me that this was odd advice. But then it occurred to me that it was Adnan's formula for steering safely past all looming human hazards.

"Of course," I said.

"Tell them you're a journalist. No. I think you'd better go as a business-man. And when you call me, talk in code. Something simple related to busi-ness. Look into investment possibilities on the island. Maybe you'll actually find a deal for us. And when you find out what's going on down there, don't talk about the details on the telephone. Get back here and tell me."

Adnan pushed a paper sack in front of me. Said it was for my expenses. Ten thousand dollars in brand new hundred-dollar bills. I thumbed through the first few notes, then pushed the money back, halfway between Adnan and me. A wave of despair was washing over me.

But then the part of my mind that likes to stay positive lit on the little story in the *Indian Express*. The next move was not a forgery but a real account.

There was trouble coming, and I knew it. But as I write this, all these years later on the beach, I still believe what I believed at that moment in New York— that V.P. Singh had hidden money in offshore bank accounts of each of his children and when the *Arab Times* first approached him he assumed he was caught. Which is not to say I still believe either one of his sons ever had an ac-count in St. Kitts. I'm not so sure of that anymore.

"V.P. Singh hid money in *both* his sons' names," I told Adnan. "I'll leave to-morrow."

As I rode in the backseat of a taxi from the airport into Basseterre, the sweltering capital of the two-island Federation of St. Kitts and Nevis, nothing outside my window looked especially nefarious or prosperous. But the *International Herald Tribune* had recently called Basseterre "the new paradise for secret money." I was a wealthy plunger with far more money than sense, here to learn all about it, and to open an account at The First Trust Corporation Limited.

It was a small, dilapidated town. Most of the buildings seemed to be wooden, two stories with white walls. There were latticework balconies and porches and colonnades, bushes and climbing vines exploding with tangles of orange and purple blossoms, palm fronds and banana leaves hanging over low stone walls and iron gates and corrugated roofs, shady storefronts with doors open and wood-bladed fans spinning inside, flagstone alleys, sidewalks cracked with roots, and black men, women, and children glistening with sweat.

Waves of heat rose from the pavement as we entered the Circus—where the architecture became a bit more imposing, and where I had been told I would find The First Trust Corporation. I saw banks, tourist shops, restaurants, coconut palms ringing the plaza, but not V.P. Singh's favorite depository.

"Where's The First Trust Corporation?" I said to the driver. We eased past five or six pedestrians, two goats, and the little clock tower that stood in the center of the Circus.

"No such thin here mon."

"It's a private bank. The address is 'The Circus, Basseterre.'"

"It not here."

"Can you stop?"

"I not even gonna stop so you can ax. It not here." He turned right at the old stone customs house as I began to wonder what I'd gotten myself into. We followed the shore road around the gentle curve of Basseterre Bay, then climbed a switchback to the top of a green bluff. "Dat's a splendid view," he said. "De mountains, de peninsula, an blue water clear across to Nevis." But all I could think of was the possibility that the whole story was a fraud. Then he pulled up outside my hotel and earned a twenty-dollar tip. "De bank get close' down las' year mon."

I checked in to the Ocean Terrace Inn, took a shower, and put on a fresh linen suit. I was anxious to get to work and get the hell out of here. I hoped to meet as soon as possible with Prime Minister Kennedy Simmonds, Terence Byron, The First Trust Corporation's solicitor, and Anne Salvesen, its former office manager. How hard could that be in a little place like this?

I went back to the Circus, which was sort of a cross between a roundabout and the town square, and, I'd observed, it was also where taxi drivers congregated to wait for fares or radio calls. They sat around most of every day shooting the breeze and watching the comings and goings of the denizens of their nation's capital. I figured they had to know better than about anyone else—at least anyone else who would talk to me right now—what was going on around here.

I sat down across from an old driver and a young driver hard at thought over a game of checkers, using red bottle tops and white bottle tops for pieces, and seven or eight other drivers who were standing around watching.

"Where to mon?"

"Nowhere right now. Just watchin' the game."

"Watta mon say?"

"Anybody here know George McLean? The banker, from The First Trust Corporation?"

"We all know de Fat Man, yessiree," said one of them.

"Fat Man gone," said another.

"De Fat Man gone away home," said the young man playing with red bottle tops. "Bad luck dat Fat Man had here. But de mon hod it comin' too."

Everyone in Basseterre knew George Mclean, but no one in Basseterre liked George McLean. The five-hundred-pound man from Canada, alleged of late to have been V.P. Singh's secret banker, had arrived on the island four years earlier, in 1985, a big spender, flashing money, and promising to bring huge foreign investments into the country. But less than three years later he'd left the island, broke and in debt. How could you launder twenty-one million dollars and not make a profit off it?

"Does anybody here know Prime Minister Simmonds?"

"We all know Doctor Simmonds," said one man.

Before entering politics, they told me, Prime Minister Kennedy Simmonds had been a G.P. And nowadays, in spite of his exalted position, when enough emergencies arrived in the clinic at once, sometimes his old colleagues still called him in to assist with surgery.

But no sir, none of them knew how I could arrange to meet him. Maybe a bank director could help me. I could ax.

In the end, it took me more than a day to get a meeting with Prime Minister Simmonds. But I was a rich investor, after all, and I had an American congressman who was known in these parts, a dispenser of U.S. aid money, call the Prime Minister's secretary and put in a good word for me. After the congressman's call, the secretary called me herself and fixed an appointment for me for the next morning.

If I seem very clear about these next facts, it's because I have to be—as they are now the subject matter of certain criminal proceedings pending before the High Court in New Delhi.

Prime Minister Kennedy Simmonds met me at his door, and shook my hand when his grandmotherly secretary showed me into his small office in Government Headquarters, an ugly modern building that seemed to have evolved into equal parts concrete, rusted steel, and mildew.

Of all the offices of heads of state I'd seen around the world, his was probably the only one smaller than the Oval Office.

Simmonds was tall, fit, black, somewhere around fifty.

I told him I might want to buy a hotel, or maybe a bank. He said they might be available. He mentioned a company called DeeVee Hotels. That's my guess at how to spell it.

We talked about the business environment in his country and he told me St. Kitts and Nevis had enacted very strict banking-secrecy laws. I asked him what banks were operating in Basseterre, and he told me. The only name I remember is the Bank of Nova Scotia.

At some point, I dropped my veil, said something along the lines of "Look, I truly am very interested in investing in your beautiful islands. But I should tell you I'm also a friend of Rajiv Gandhi, who asked me to come here and privately find out if the recent allegations against Mr. Singh are true. If they are, Rajiv will pursue it. If they are not, he will immediately wash his hands of it."

The Prime Minister's only interest in the Singh matter seemed to be damage control. Speaking slowly, in deep, tranquil tones, he told me that for the past few days the opposition had been assailing him for involving St. Kitts in yet another international scandal. Last year, he said, they'd raised hell when they learned he'd innocently banked most of his government's money in the Cayman Islands branch of BCCI. Now they were on him about the Singh account. About which he said he knew absolutely nothing.

My first objective had to be challenging V.P. Singh's open letter to Rajiv.

I asked, "Is it possible that Ajeya Singh could have visited St. Kitts without having his passport stamped?"

Prime Minister Simmonds said, "Yes. If he presented a U.S. green card, he would be permitted to enter without a passport."

"But your immigration department would still have a record of his arrival?"

"Yes. He would still be required to fill out a landing card."

The Prime Minister's desk was covered with papers and Manila folders. Ten inches above the pile, he brought his hands together, perhaps in prayer that I would soon leave St. Kitts forever.

"Would it be possible for someone to visit this country without *any* immigration record?"

He looked over my shoulder toward the shuddering air conditioner before he answered. "Yes. I suppose it would be quite simple for someone to sneak on and off the island by boat. It's not as if we had an army of immigration officers patrolling our shores."

I did my best not to smile, hoping I'd gotten it all on the tape recorder in my pocket. *So much for your fatal lacuna, Mr. Singh.*

I didn't even know V.P. Singh. So why was I so hell-bent to bring him down? Simple. It was all a game, or so Miles kept reminding me in my head.

Outside, the sun burned down from a clear blue sky. The air was hot and sticky and there was no breeze. I heard reggae bouncing from a car stereo. I smelled ripe fruit that was stacked in crates in the shade under a latticework balcony across the street. Walking just two hundred yards from Government Headquarters to my next appointment, my face beaded with sweat and I felt the heat of the pavement through the soles of my shoes.

Terence Byron's law chambers filled the top floor of a ramshackle two-story wooden building on Fort Street, the closest thing to a main street in Basseterre.

There was something curiously resentful about Anne Salvesen as she came out to meet me and shook my hand in a hot waiting room full of sweating island folk. The next room, where she worked, was air-conditioned. She pulled up a folding metal chair for me, placed it in front of her desk, and then sat down on the other side.

She was in her early twenties, blond, damned good-looking, well shaped, almost tall, and one of the few Caucasians living on the island. Speaking perfect English, with just enough of a Nordic accent to charm, she told me that about four years ago she'd arrived from Norway looking for adventure and had never left. I thought how rosy-cheeked and beautiful she must have been when she left home. Now her long honey hair was sun-dried and her skin was so tanned it had lost most of its sheen. But still, damned good-looking.

She was wearing white shorts, white sandals, and a short-sleeved powder-blue blouse so billowy it was impossible for me to confidently gauge the size of her breasts. Her full mouth, little girl's turned-up nose, and pale blue eyes were friendly enough. But whenever I asked a question she didn't like, she became stiff and formal in that special way only Europeans can. Clearly, she despised her former boss George McLean, but at first she wouldn't say why.

The first thing of any substance I learned from Anne Salvesen was that Lynn Hudson was not a woman. The *India Abroad* investigative reporter who'd recently visited Basseterre and quoted Anne Salvesen and her current boss, Terence Byron, was a middle-aged man from New York named Lynn Hudson.

Anne was starting to loosen up to me. She said Hudson had perhaps stretched their quotes a bit. And George McLean was an asshole who picked his nose and ate his boogers right in front of her, he was pasty white, he weighed five hundred pounds, he was a liar, he owed her money, and, on the morning of the day he finally left Basseterre for good, he couldn't afford an air-line ticket until his daughter wire-transferred a small loan to him.

Still, Anne packed up what George had left behind in his apartment on Frigate Bay. Her family, visiting from Norway at the time, helped, and in the back of a closet one of them found a pair of George's enormous trousers. She gleefully showed me a photograph of herself, her sister, and her father all at once wearing the Fat Man's trousers. Anne and her teenage sister stood to-gether inside the right leg, their father inside the left—smiles on all their faces.

I wanted her to understand that money was going to be available if she could help me. I offered her a thousand dollars for that photograph. Peeled it out of my pocket and set it on her desk. She said no, it's a private picture, but her eyes stayed on the money for a moment. I wondered if I should just forget it and leave it on her desk when I left, but I decided she might be insulted. She still had an edge to her whenever the conversation didn't turn her way.

I said, look, I might be interested in buying the bank, if its charter is still valid, or at least buying some information about the bank. She said there were secrecy laws to be considered, but that I should talk to her boss, Terry. She said he wasn't in, and wouldn't be in today. At all.

So why was the waiting room full? I wondered.

For another day and a half, Mr. Terence Vincent Byron eluded me. But, late in my third afternoon in Basseterre, I finally met him. He was in his late thir-ties, medium height and build, wearing thick glasses, pencil-striped London bankers' trousers, scuffed brown shoes, and a fraying white dress shirt. No belt, no tie, no jacket. He wasn't handsome, but he was appealing in an unusual way. It was revealed, by his infectious smile, that one of his top front teeth had grown in shorter than the other, and, by his disheveled hair, that he'd had a nap somewhere recently.

"I must apologize for the cat and mouse," he said in a refined Islands ac-cent. "I wasn't going to see you at all, but then Miss Salvesen, Anne, said you're all right and I ought to hear what you and Mr. Gandhi have to say."

I hadn't mentioned Mr. Gandhi to Anne. Only to the Prime Minister.

Two photographs hanging on the wall showed Byron dressed formally and wearing sashes across his chest.

"What are those?"

I remember that when Byron turned his head to have a look, with the new angle of his glasses, his dark brown eyes suddenly became enormous. "Those were taken in Seoul and Taipei, on the days I presented my credentials to the heads of government. I am St. Kitts and Nevis's ambassador to South Korea and Taiwan."

The only other photograph on the wall was of an elderly black gentleman, who wore a dark suit and stood on a green lawn squinting out at Byron and me. "That," Byron said, "is Sir Clement Arrindell, the Governor General of St. Kitts. He is my uncle. His post is largely ceremonial, appointed by Her Britannic Majesty Queen Elizabeth II."

Outside, the waiting room had been full again today when Anne came out and whisked me through it.

I said, "Congratulations. It seems you have a thriving business here, Mr. Byron. What type of law do you practice?"

"Well," he said, "I am the Prime Minister's, Dr. Simmonds's, solicitor, I do work for offshore corporations and many local citizens, and, as all of the solicitors practicing here are required to, I serve in a rotation defending local citizens in criminal trials. Everything from stolen chickens to murder cases."

"And what about the bank?" I asked. "The First Trust Corporation." No sense messing around. With all those people waiting, there was no telling how short this meeting might be.

Mr. Byron's foil for deflecting unwanted questions was long bursts of Caribbean-accented King's Bench legalese which rambled artfully ever further from the subject. He told me, in rather more words than these: that he was only a nominal director of The First Trust Corporation, so he knew nothing about its operations, and he couldn't say much more because of bank-secrecy laws.

He did tell me, though, that all the records of The First Trust Corporation had been moved from the now famous bank's former offices in the Circus—just a hundred yards down Fort Street—to these very law chambers, and he pointed out to me, beside a credenza along the wall in Anne's office, a small, gray-steel safe. It was less than half as tall as me, a doily and a little vase of flowers sat atop it, on its flank was a bumper sticker from a Radio Shack in Miami, it wasn't nearly as strong or heavy as my father's safes had been, and according to Byron it was all that was left of The First Trust Corporation Limited.

I showed him the recent *Indian Express* articles that quoted him.

He read them, then wiped his glasses, looked at me, and slowly, carefully, said, "I am very certain that I could not have told Mr. Hudson that neither Mr. Ajeya Singh, nor his father, Mr. Vishwanath Pratap Singh, had accounts at The First Trust Corporation Limited, as I do not know who, if anyone, had accounts there, as I have never seen any books, in the sense of account books, of the corporation." He was speaking so formally and precisely, as he might address a judge in court, that I wondered if he suspected I was recording him.

We kept talking, and my eyes returned to the safe so many times while Byron spoke that eventually he stopped midsentence. "I am *not* going to open it for you," he told me.

One key to elicitation, I think, is to actually like people, and I liked Terry and Anne. That night we went to dinner, the three of us, out of town, at a little wooden restaurant on the beach on the Atlantic side of the island. We ate lobsters, more than one each. Anne drove, and didn't drink much. Terry and I drank a lot of cane—a clear white spirit made in St. Kitts, which produced in Terry a quite amiable intoxication.

Even under strict secrecy laws there are ways a smart lawyer can say things he wants to say to you, without violating any law. And that night Terry Byron said some very interesting things to me once he'd shaded their content with words like "perhaps," "probably," "maybe," "it might seem," and "one might gather."

"It just might be," Terry told me, "that, on the eve of George's penultimate departure from St. Kitts, his solicitor loaned him thirty thousand dollars, in cash, with which to go to Fort Lauderdale to pay some advance financing charges to obtain a capital infusion for The First Trust Corporation."

But, the story went on, the money had disappeared, apparently George had been scammed, and ever since then he'd been promising Terry he'd return with his money. George had promised it on the day he left for good, the day his sister wired enough money for him to beat it out of town, and since then he'd phoned Terry several times and promised the money.

"And perhaps," Terry added, "the last time I ever spoke with George, months ago, he actually swore to me he had my money and he had, in fact, that day dispatched it to me by courier."

We were moving in the right direction, but I didn't want to push it. You never want to put too much perfume in the air. Can't let a subject know just how valuable the information he has is to you. I hadn't asked a single question about McLean or the bank that night, and I wasn't about to start.

"This chap with your money isn't so late as couriers go," I said. "Not really. Not if you compare him with the world's worst carrier pigeon. You may be interested to know that that historic courier was released in Pembrokeshire,

England, in June 1953, expected to reach its base that evening. It returned eleven years later, dead, mailed from Brazil in a cardboard box. Its owner said, 'We had given it up for lost.'"

"My God," Terry wheezed with mirth. "Oh, my dear God! Larry, won't you have another drink?"

For a while we talked irreverently of politics. Indian, American, Scandinavian, and Caribbean. Miles had told me there was a school of thought within the CIA that elicitation works best when conducted one-on-one. But with Anne and Terry that never would've worked. They seemed to take confidence from each other. They seemed to be partners in this somehow.

When they'd had their say about politics, Terry shifted our gears to bawdy verse. Anne was turning out to be a go-getter. She made clear right away that she wasn't offended, by reciting one herself. Knowing and, fueled by cane, reciting the only known limerick in the English language with a triple-rhyming third verse, I quickly established my own proficiency in this arcane field.

> There was a young girl named Larue,
> Who said, as the parson withdrew,
> "'The vicar is quicker, and slicker, and thicker,
> And three inches longer than you.'"

My new mate Terry shook with laughter. "If we don't get out of here," he finally said, wiping tears out of his eyes, "I'm afraid I may start singing."

We drove home under a black sky wild with stars, and that night I was followed into my bungalow by a beautiful little gray brindle cat. For the next five nights, she ate my table scraps and rubbed against my ankles while I sat in my room, with the air conditioner going full blast, transcribing my tapes and writing up notes and speculations on whether or not Vishwanath Pratap Singh had actually been crazy enough to entrust twenty-one million dollars to a money launderer called the Fat Man. The jury was still out on that. I suppose, in a way, it still is. And that little cat is at my ankles now, under my desk in Florida, with the sun just beginning to rise through the slats of my window, as I sit here remembering.

My fifth night in Basseterre. Terry, seated across from me at an outdoor table, took a healthy swig of CSR, Cane Spirit Rothschild, then licked his lips and said, "You know, Larry, by now we probably should've told you that last week a young chap from Canada appeared in my chambers and offered to purchase The First Trust Corporation Limited and all its records."

"*What!*" I said. "*Who?* What was his name? And *why* did he want the bank? Did he say?"

"He called himself 'Roland St. Jacques,' and I thought that was an awfully funny name. You know, made up. So I delicately asked him if I might have a look at his passport and, true enough, it said his name was Roland St. Jacques."

"It's not all that hard," I said, "to get genuine passports with funny names, even from a big country like Canada."

Terry nodded knowingly. "Yes, one suspects."

"But why did he want the bank? Did he say? Did he mention India?"

"Not a word about India. What he said was he was looking for a dormant offshore bank with a valid license, he was willing to pay a hundred thousand dollars, and he'd heard The First Trust Corporation was available. I found that awfully strange."

"Has he left town?" I asked.

"I *honestly* don't know," Terry said, glancing at Anne.

I found that quite improbable. "Well, thanks for finally telling me," I said with a smile, while wondering *Who the fuck is Roland St. Jacques?* At least a couple of times every day since I'd been in town, I'd had a taxi drive me sedately down a long, empty stretch of Bay Road, then wind slowly up the switchbacks to Fort Thomas, and from there take me back into Basseterre on other roads. No one seemed to be following me. But had Roland St. Jacques left the island, or was he right behind me every day?

Was this something to add to my unified theory? In the secret world you fight against ghosts. Don't even know that they're there. Fuck! Who the hell was he working for? Indian intelligence? Mossad? V.P. Singh? Ernie Miller?

Nearly everyone on the island I'd talked to had seemed anxious to convince me the story of V.P. Singh's secret account was a fraud. Some of the time I'd believed them, and felt sick. But something kept telling me I was only getting half the truth, if that. I took a lot of tours of the island. I saw the cloud forest and the top of the mountain up close, the green vervet monkeys running riot out on the peninsula, the hairstyling techniques of Mr. Cool, the casinos, the forts, and I kept asking questions, until one day a taxi driver who apparently hadn't gotten the omerta memo said to me, "Yeah mon, dere been Indians coming here to see de Fat Man. Plenty of dem." We were in a sugarcane field at the time, and I remember looking out the window on the driver's side, down into Basseterre, where sunlight glared from iron rooftops beside the port.

So far I'd attempted to accomplish my objectives on the island without any dramatic flourishes. But that night, back on the beach, over more charcoal-grilled lobsters, I confronted Anne and Terry. "I hear there were Indians about.

Back when George was here," I said. "Lots of them. So why don't you just tell me what the fuck was going on here? What's the big secret?"

"Look," Terry said, "the reason the government doesn't want you poking around regarding The First Trust Corporation has nothing to do with Indian politics. It's all about Kittitian politics. Dr. Simmonds fell for George, and all his grand dreams, and helped him speed up the incorporation and licensing of The First Trust Corporation. A couple years ago, there was a big FBI investigation here, because George laundered several million dollars for a Canadian drug lord. Ever since then, the Prime Minister's been doing his best to dampen interest in the bank. The deeper anyone digs, the closer they get to his role, which was innocent and well-meaning, but doesn't look good. To the Prime Minister, you're just another potential source of trouble."

"Is Roland St. Jacques still here?" I asked.

"No."

"And there were Indians here from time to time dealing with George?"

"Yes."

That was all Terry or Anne would say on the subject that night. But I kept digging, all over the island, and a few nights later, in a truly melodramatic exchange at midnight in the moonless garden of the Ocean Terrace Inn, I acquired a rare first-edition brochure for The First Trust Corporation Limited's *Special Investment Program in Cooperation with Indian Nationals*. This was pricey, but seemed worth it to me. Because, if you read the text closely, it promoted a scheme under which Indian residents, whose financial lives are complicated by foreign-currency regulations out the *gandu*—which, as I alluded to earlier, is an anatomical term originally from the Urdu—could illegally but safely channel money, through their relatives or friends who reside outside of India, into accounts in The First Trust Corporation Limited. Just exactly what V.P. Singh was accused of having done through his son Ajeya.

For a separate fee, I also acquired a list of certain Indians who'd hidden money in The First Trust Corporation Limited. Ajeya Singh's name wasn't on it, but I knew that in advance. What I'd bought had been represented to be only partial—a sample, so to speak. And this rang true, for the list I received was alphabetized and I'd had only enough money on hand to buy the brochure and those names beginning with the letters A through R. The remaining names were going to cost a lot more. Apparently Roland St. Jacques was bidding by phone, driving up prices.

Still, the most important thing was that my source was now a little bit pregnant. And the information and documents I had were more than enough to send the Arab Times Special Caribbean Correspondent rocketing back to the comforts of New York to write a sensational exposé and request an increase in his operating funds.

When Frank Morse finished law school—second in his class at Harvard, according to what his younger brother Paul told me—he got himself a job as an assistant prosecutor working in the United States Attorney's office in Los Angeles. He was dynamite in court, won something like his first fifty-two cases in a row. Then, in a murder trial, under cross-examination, one of Frank's witnesses broke down and said, "Fuck yeah! I shot him!" Whereupon the *Los Angeles Times* wrote a story about young Frank Morse: fifty-two and zip, and then he finally lost a case. It happened that Howard Hughes read that news story, and called his chief of staff, and said, "Get me that lawyer!" And that was how Frank had managed to become Howard Hughes's general counsel at the tender age of twenty-eight. Within a few months, Frank was also running all of Hughes's Las Vegas operations.

"Or it was something like that. If you want to get the details right, you'll have to ask Frank when he gets here tomorrow," Paul Morse said. He said this to me on the night before Frank arrived at Paul's new house in North Palm Beach to begin shepherding me through my testimony before the Government of India.

"The even more interesting part," Paul said, "was what Frank did before he got to law school—when he was still an undergraduate at Stanford during the Freedom Summer. 1962. Frank and some of his friends from school drove down to Mississippi to do civil rights work, helping register black voters. Until one night four great big rednecks grabbed Frank and one of his buddies and drove them out into the middle of nowhere, tied them to trees, called them 'Nigger lovers!,' and beat the *absolute* shit out of them. Then left them there for dead. If you remember the two student civil rights workers who were kidnapped in Mississippi, and President Kennedy sent the National Guard and half of the FBI out to look for them, and it took a couple of days to find them, well, Frank was one of them. If you want to get those details right, you'll have to ask Frank about that too," Paul said. But I already knew I wouldn't be asking Frank to clarify anything about his background for me. All I needed to know was he was one hell of an attorney, who was only forty-five, and didn't even look that, but nonetheless had experience beyond his years.

When Frank arrived the next day, he immediately went about teaching me how little I actually know about anything. And that's a fact.

"You're under a federal subpoena," Frank said, "and even though you've managed not to be served, we've agreed to waive service and that you will voluntarily appear. So effectively you're under subpoena, and it's not anything to be taken lightly.

"Tomorrow morning we'll drive down to the U.S. Attorney's office in Miami. It's in a federal complex, so there'll be a federal court or at least a magistrate in the same building, or next door. And there'll be plenty of security.

"You'll be giving testimony pursuant to letters rogatory. Letters rogatory are similar to interrogatories in civil litigation, in that they are written questions. But in the case of letters rogatory the questions are posed by one government to a person in another country pursuant to a treaty between those two countries. Which means the questions you'll be asked were likely written down months ago and far away—which limits their flexibility. Typically, the questions will be posed to you in a courtroom in front of a judge or a magistrate. The U.S. Attorney will read the questions, an Indian government investigator or attorney will be there to assist the U.S. Attorney and put the evil eye on you, I'll be there to object if necessary, the federal judge or magistrate will referee, and a court stenographer will take everything down.

"You'll be sworn," Frank went on, "and you'll answer truthfully. But by that I mean truthfully according to the standards of the law, which means pursuant to the rules of evidence." This was the point at which Frank started smiling reassuringly. He was sitting there in his little brother's house, with his elbows up on a desk—which had once been Howard Hughes's private desk in his apartment in the Desert Inn in Las Vegas—wearing a track suit and increasingly looking about ready to leave me and go out for a run. But instead Frank said, "Just a minute," and then he hit the floor and did fifty push-ups, and when he finished, and sat back down in the big leather chair behind Howard Hughes's desk, there was only a little bit of pink in Frank's face and it didn't take him long at all to recover his breath.

"In everyday life," Frank said, "we accept things as true which aren't necessarily true," and just then, Paul Morse, Jr., Frank's blond six-year-old nephew, a/k/a P, stuck his head against one of the panes of the closed glass door of the study Frank and I were in and made some faces at us. Frank waved at P, I made some faces back at him, and Frank said, "If you were his father, and he asked you if he could eat a chocolate bar that was sitting here on the desk, and you said No, and then you left the room, and when you came back ten minutes later the chocolate wrapper was on the floor, and there was chocolate all over his lips and cheeks, you'd spank his ass. Even if he said he didn't eat the chocolate, you'd spank him. Because, by the standards of everyday life, you'd know he did eat the chocolate. But, according to the standards of the law, you'd only *suspect* he ate the chocolate, and that is meaningless. For all you'd *know*, he could've fallen and smashed his mouth on the chocolate bar, knocking the wrapper onto the floor. You weren't a percipient witness to Paul eating the chocolate bar. So, if you were asked in court if Paul ate the chocolate, the only truthful answer you could give would be *I don't know*."

Damn if Frank wasn't right. And that was a good thing, I was just beginning to realize. I'd testified a few times before under oath, in unrelated matters and under the advice and protection of expensive and what I thought was highly competent counsel. But in light of the new standards of truth, knowledge, beauty, and human frailty Frank was imparting to me now, it was quickly coming clear to me that my previous counsel had let me ramble and speculate shamelessly about things I didn't actually know.

"For example," Frank said to me now, "if you were asked, 'Why did Adnan Khashoggi ask you to help him with this matter?,' your answer would have to be 'I don't know.' Because you *don't* know. Most of us have enough trouble figuring out why we do things ourselves. There's no way we're competent to know why anybody else does anything. While testifying, don't ever let yourself be tricked into speculating about someone else's state of mind.

"If you happened to be asked, 'Why did Mr. Gandhi go to the restaurant?,' your answer could not be 'Because he was hungry' or 'To eat.' Your only truthful answer would be, 'I don't know.' Because, even if Rajiv told you he was hungry, that's just hearsay, and you don't know what went on in his mind that made him go into the restaurant. But, if you were asked, 'Did Mr. Gandhi eat in the restaurant?,' and you were in the restaurant when he was, and you saw him eat there, your answer would be?"

Finally a part for me. I said, "My answer would be 'Yes.'"

"Correct," said Frank. "Your answer would be 'Yes' and it would not be 'Yes, I saw him eating apple pie in the restaurant.' Because they didn't ask that, and it's not up to you to volunteer anything."

Frank did some more push-ups before he looked at me and said, "So, do you understand? Don't speculate about events to which you were not a percipient witness. Don't speculate about another person's state of mind. Don't volunteer anything. Don't ramble. Answer the questions, and only the questions, truthfully. And the only truthful answer you can give to a lot more questions than it might first seem is 'I don't know.'"

Then Frank spent several hours debriefing me on every pertinent thing I could tell him about what had happened. And in the process I quickly saw how little I actually knew about any of the really big questions surrounding the

St. Kitts Affair—a matter on which I might otherwise be considered somewhat of an authority. Did Ajeya Singh really stash more than twenty million dollars in The First Trust Corporation Limited? Were the account documents forged? Who was behind all this? Who was really doing what to whom, and for whom, and why? Truth be told, I didn't know.

Which made for some very fucking brief testimony the next day in Miami, while if I'd had another lawyer with me I might've rambled on all week.

So, before I go any further about this, I want to make sure you understand I don't claim to *know* much at all about the St. Kitts Affair—which soon, I hope, will be just another sordid footnote in the long and bloody history of Indian power politics. But if you can accept that in our everyday lives there are different standards of truth by which, for example, Paul Morse, Jr. might quite rightfully be punished for eating a chocolate bar after he'd been told not to, or under which His Holiness Chandraswami Maharaj might quite rightfully have his sorry tantric ass locked up on general principles, then I probably ought to tell you a little bit about what happened when I got back from my first trip to St. Kitts and during and between my next few visits there.

The first thing on my agenda back in New York was writing a long follow-up story poking holes in V.P. Singh's defenses, revealing that The First Trust Corporation Limited had been the focus of an FBI investigation for laundering drug money, and showing that Basseterre had once in the recent past been awash in rupees conveniently converted by the Fat Man into dollars.

Writing that took me a couple of days, and what I did next was dummy up some official-looking stationery for the Government of India's Department of Diabolical Tricks, sign a cover note "Minister of Propaganda," and send it and the report to Rajiv. Only then did I forward the story to Ahmed Jarallah, who the next day ran the Arab Times Special Caribbean Correspondent's report uncut on the front page of the *Arab Times*.

It was about then that Miles got into the action, in a limited way. He seemed pretty frail, but flew to New York, and Adnan and I briefed him on the wonders of the St. Kitts Affair. About which Miles scolded Adnan in a three-page memo the next day. *Over the telephone, before I got to New York, Adnan, you didn't make clear to me the extent to which a ruthless propaganda war is already under way, no holds barred, with much higher stakes and wider implications than I had imagined. Had I had these premises in mind, I could have done a much more pertinent job advising you recently. I am most impressed with the materials Larry has shown me, especially his own writings on the St. Kitts matter and his overall strategy for the operation at hand. Larry can make it work.*

Even Miles got things wrong sometimes. I only wish that in the end I'd fulfilled his vision. Or, better yet, that I could've lived an entire lifetime never hearing of the isle of St. Kitts.

On his way back to England from New York, Miles went to Washington to check in with his friends there and make sure it was true the United States really didn't give a shit what happened in India or what we did to help Rajiv. "Not only is it true," Miles reported back to me, "it's disgustingly true. The guys I talked to on the India desk said it *does* matter. India has the second-largest population on earth, for Christ's sake. It's perpetually on the brink of three different civil wars. And the Congress party and your friend Gandhi are the only forces there capable of *almost* keeping it stable. The natives could get awfully restless out there without strong leadership, and there are only about ten thousand different highly armed factions ready to blow at any one moment. So it *ought* to matter, and all the guys on the India desk are cheering for you, even though no one else in Washington pays any attention to what they have to say."

And with that ringing endorsement, Miles flew home to rest and I found myself suddenly alone again up in Adnan's offices through most of every night, running a propaganda war. Of the about thirty significant newspaper chains in India, nearly twenty of them by now were actively supporting V.P. Singh. The opposition press lampooned the St. Kitts charges at every opportunity, but my continuing dispatches as the Arab Times Special Caribbean Correspondent exposed a growing body of evidence linking Indians and dirty money to St. Kitts. Every new detail I published was sensationalized by pro-Gandhi newspapers and the government-controlled Indian television system, Doordarshan, to intensify the heat on V.P. Singh.

But Mr. Singh had some damned slick moves of his own. One day he and his entire Janata Dal party stood up in the middle of a session, walked out of Parliament, and called for a one-day general strike called *Bharat Bandh,* which means Close India. Almost all of India came to a halt on the appointed day. Singh's supporters refused to go to work. Rajiv's supporters stayed home too, afraid of violence if they tried to get to work. Armed gangs of thugs, called *goondas,* roamed the streets enforcing the strike. Twelve people were killed in factional fighting that day.

Bold and effective, I had to admit. But I kept going back to St. Kitts every week or two, and the Arab Times Special Caribbean Correspondent kept up his widely read reportage on the rupees of Basseterre, and when Rajiv finally announced he'd been shown enough evidence to order an official investigation into the St. Kitts Affair, that shifted the balance. We were in the lead again in the propaganda war, and Miles said I was doing him proud.

But then one morning in New York, I was abed in the blue suite, dreaming of Boeing 747 sales commissions, when I heard a portentous pounding on my door. For fuck sake, it was still dark outside. 4:57 Newsweek time. And when I opened my door the assholes standing there pounding on it were Mammaji and Swamiji.

Apparently they had to talk to Adnan right away and were afraid to pound on his door, but not afraid to pound on mine.

The first thing I did was call the special number Adnan's federal guardians used for waking him up in the middle of the night to verify he and his new bracelet were at home. When Adnan answered, I hung up on him. Then I led Mammaji and Swamiji upstairs to Adnan's bedroom door and made them knock. Whereupon Adnan soon emerged, yawning and with wrinkles all over his face and thobe.

Mammaji started talking fast and sounding desperate, and Adnan looked at me and said, Call Dev. Which I did, on a Miami number Mammaji supplied me.

What Dev told me was that the renowned investigator A.P. Nandey, the feared and respected Deputy Director of the Indian Enforcement Directorate, handpicked by Rajiv to travel to St. Kitts to deliver a fatal blow to the former King of Manda Vishwanath Pratap Singh, had arrived in Miami the previous evening howling drunk.

During his flight from New Delhi, excited by the most important case of his life and his first trip ever out of India, and flush with an expense advance, Nandey celebrated by buying bottles of Golconda—cheap Indian liquor named after a famous diamond market. As Nandey got drunk, it struck him that he was on a mission to destroy one of the two most powerful men in India. Suddenly seeing the danger this placed him in, Nandey drank lots more Golconda. By the time he'd changed planes in London and was crossing the Atlantic, he was certain he would be killed before he set foot on St. Kitts. This led Deputy Director Nandey to lock himself and his stock of Golconda into various aircraft lavatories throughout the remainder of his journey to Miami.

When Dev met Nandey's plane, Nandey was in a begging mood. "Please, please, please, boyo," he said, "please spirit me to safety. Because I have been seeing too many thugs on this flight and they are plotting to kill me to foil my investigation."

Dev checked Nandey into the Marriott by the airport and suggested he get a good night's sleep. Then Dev watched, amazed, as Nandey opened his last bottle of Golconda and, believing he was back home in India, spent the next two hours roaming the halls calling and searching for his faithful manservant. "Bipin, come quickly! Bipin, where are you? Bipin, I need you."

Finally convinced by Dev that he was not in India but in a strange and faraway land, Deputy Director Nandey remembered his mission, went to his room, and ordered a bottle of whisky. But when he checked his perimeters a few minutes later and saw two Bengali assassins shrouded in black creep into the room next to his, Nandey ran screaming to the lobby, telephoned the Miami police, and told them he was an Indian government agent on a secret mission and he was about to be killed. Hotel security came, the police came, room service came, the nice but confused black couple from Detroit which had just checked into the room next door to Nandey's was rousted, and Dev managed to avert a nasty little international incident by pointing out the obvious: Deputy Director A.P. Nandey was a drunken lunatic.

As the police left and Nandey began barricading his door around four o'clock of that balmy Miami night, Dev decided it was time to put out a Red Alert, waking Mammaji and Swamiji.

When I'd gotten all this from Dev and then related it to Adnan, he picked up a phone and scrambled his pilots, then he disappeared for a few minutes and came back to hand me three ten-thousand-dollar blocks of cash for fuel and expenses. Next he told me to call Dev back and tell him to feed Nandey lots of coffee and vitamins. And, an hour later, Swamiji, Mammaji, and I were in big comfortable beds in the DC-9, Victor Romeo Charlie Kilo Oscar, racing to Florida and trying to get back to sleep.

When we met Nandey he was better, but still seriously fucked up. Drunk, wild-eyed, and shaking like a very sick man. After bowing his scrawny brown frame and touching his hand to Swamiji's foot, Deputy Director Nandey looked up and matter-of-factly said, "Miami is nice and rather like paradise, I see, Your Holiness, and I'd really prefer not to go on to St. Kitts, because there are too many people waiting there to kill me."

Swamiji started working the phone. He dialed out several times and spoke in Hindi—until he got Rajiv on the phone and switched to English, apparently for my benefit. But real quickly Swamiji switched back to Hindi, and turned pale and desolate, and then he covered the phone and told me Rajiv urgently needed Nandey back home with the goods on Singh within four days. And that was when it suddenly dawned on me that Swamiji was as desperate as Rajiv to make the St. Kitts charges stick—they were Swamiji's ticket out of criminal tax-evasion charges in India.

Swamiji passed me the phone and Rajiv said, "Is Nandey really as bad as they're saying? What should we do?"

"Bad, Rajiv?" I said. "Bad? If this little cretin is your best man, we're all doomed!" I didn't mind talking like that in front of Nandey, because he was so totally fucking out of it. At the moment, he was across the room on a couch telling Dev about beautiful naked ladies he'd seen on Miami Beach that morning, and perhaps we should all go there this afternoon for some relaxation, but Dev, of course, kept telling Nandey he hadn't been to Miami Beach. "We've got to abort," I told Rajiv, "regroup, and then start over," and when I hung up Swamiji looked at me like he wanted to kill me.

A few minutes later, the phone rang, and Swamiji picked it up and started speaking highly agitated Hindi. I heard enough to get that Swamiji had been told to hold for someone, and Mammaji whispered to me: "P.C. Sharma.

Rajiv's hatchet man." Then I lost the thread of whatever Swamiji was talking about, until he hung up and announced triumphantly to me that the word from on high was: "You're to 'Go Anyway!'"

"Dev?" I yelled. "Dev, please take Mr. Nandey to his room and massage him within an inch of his life."

Nandey couldn't have weathered a commercial flight, and I still had just enough sense left to know not to get Adnan's plane spotted in St. Kitts. So I chartered a Lear-25, in which Nandey, Dev, Mammaji, and I flew to Basseterre, while His Holiness cooled his heels in Miami.

When our crack investigative unit got to Terry Byron's chambers, and Nandey presented his credentials and began questioning Anne Salvesen, he was doing fine. But soon he seemed to be drifting in and out of coherency and asking the occasional inappropriate question. Such as: "Where am I?"

This wasn't working. I took Deputy Director Nandey out onto Fort Street for some air, and while we were out there I asked him if it was within his powers to deputize me. "Oh, yes," he said, relief spreading across his face like a stain. "You are my deputy, instructed to please do the needful."

That was how it came to pass that I, Larry J. Kolb, son of a spy, Arab Times Special Caribbean Correspondent, Minister of Propaganda for the Prime Minister of the largest democracy on earth, newly commissioned Deputy-deputy Director of the Indian Enforcement Directorate, and one dumb mother soon to be hunted and in exile, gently led key witnesses Anne Salvesen and Terence Byron through a series of leading questions which, answered truthfully, would cast enormous suspicion over the leader of the Indian opposition, V.P. Singh.

When I was finished, Anne typed up their statements. Then she and Terry signed them and handed them to a thankful Deputy Director Nandey.

Next Mammaji wanted me to take Nandey to the Prime Minister's office. But I took a quick look at Nandey and his dancing eyes and knew better than to press our luck. "No fucking way," I told Mammaji. "Please be so kind as to go buy Mr. Nandey a six-pack of beer," I told Dev, which meant our mission in St. Kitts was at an end.

We were Wheels Up and heading back to Miami less than three hours after our arrival in Basseterre. When the plane reached altitude and settled into its humming and shuddering routine, I fell half to sleep, until there came a moment when I looked away from the horizon and the setting sun, and glanced at where Nandey and Mammaji were sitting side by side in front of me. And then I cringed, and tried to convince myself I'd only imagined what I'd just seen and heard. But, when I opened my eyes again, a can of beer was still trembling in Nandey's hand, and he was still excitedly inspecting the contents of a Manila file folder Mammaji had just produced from his briefcase, saying he'd found it "lying around Mr. Terence Byron's office."

They spent several minutes, heads together, poring over a stack of copies of canceled checks written and signed by you know who, and then Nandey stood up with joy all over his face and said, "I've caught him! I've caught the bandit red-handed!"

And now as a reward for Nandey's brilliant detective work, Mammaji reached into something and handed Nandey a large bottle of scotch. Nandey twisted off the cap slowly, then shot a happy grin my way. "Do you want a glass?" Dev said.

"Need for what?" Nandey mumbled, smiling at his bottle. "So, okay, boyo, give one glass now."

Dev handed Nandey a tumbler and walked disgustedly up to the front of the plane to talk with the pilots. And that's how I remember the end of the scene in which the crucial clinching evidence, the smoking checks, necessary to prove the Enforcement Directorate's criminal case against Messrs. Ajeya and V.P. Singh was obtained by Deputy Director Nandey not in "Camp Basseterre, St. Kitts and Nevis, West Indies," as he later reported, but in a Lear jet over the Caribbean Sea.

Now, of course, according to the rules of evidence, I don't actually know that the stack of documents Mammaji force-fed Nandey during our ride back to Miami was a stack of forgeries. I never saw anyone forge them. But, at the time, I sure thought they were fakes. And I remember trying to go to sleep while wondering whether the first batch of documents, the ones I'd arranged to be publicized in the *Arab Times*, were also forgeries. Maybe it was only vanity, but I was inclined to believe those were real, that Mammaji had merely succumbed to temptation to expedite delivery of the clinching evidence I hadn't been able to come up with yet. I couldn't sleep, and after awhile I sat up and looked around, and at that point things got worse. Mammaji was now sitting across the aisle from me, smiling ecstatically, and swigging on something himself. That was when he happily told me who we'd actually been doing all this shit for, and it wasn't Rajiv.

Miles had always told me most intelligence agents don't know who they're actually working for, but I'd always thought I was smart enough to be immune from that. Now Mammaji, who was exhausted and euphoric, and a little drunk and in a mood for confidences, told me, "Sure, that pompous asshole Rajiv, the premier, will benefit momentarily from all of this. He will knock out V.P. Singh with this. But the real beneficiary will be Chandrashekhar." And suddenly it all made perfect sense to me. Chandrashekhar was the second-most-powerful opposition leader in India and, with V.P. Singh discredited, would become the leader of the opposition. Now, of course, Chandrashekhar would certainly benefit from Singh's fall, but I had no evidence to make me think he had been involved in the framing. "Chandrashekhar is Swamiji's disciple," said Mammaji. "Chandrashekhar will do anything for Swamiji. Chandrashekhar is Swamiji's tea boy!" Mammaji was giddy now. "Since the inception of hostilities, we've been doing this for our friend and brother Chandrashekhar. Because when he is Prime Minister we will make a fortune!"

I don't *know* much at all about the St. Kitts Affair. But, these days, I look back on the whole thing, from the beginning to the end of my involvement in it, in a different light. I see the fine summer morning when I walked into the Olympic Tower so anxious to do a favor for Adnan and our mutual friend Rajiv. I see my introductions to Mr. Mammaji, the impassioned orator of Indian intelligence, and to Raji Samghabadi, the respected reporter from no less than *Time* magazine, another unwitting pawn of Swamiji, who's researched and verified the St. Kitts story but happens to be leaving on a vacation. I see the chance arrival of Swamiji, who professes not to be interested at all in whatever secular subject we're polluting our souls with. I see the big Newsweek clock looming outside the window and Adnan exhorting me to meet my deadlines, to work so fast that there wasn't time to think.

And I can't help but see myself as the smug Irish gangster in a brown suit and a homburg who limps into the betting parlor in the last reel of *The Sting,* carrying a suitcase stuffed with half a million dollars. He looks around at the fine walnut fixtures, at the brass and the potted palms, the tote boards, the horse prints in gilded frames, the silver trophies behind the bar, the tellers in tuxedos, the roomful of bettors in leather club chairs cheering as the live announcer reads the ticker tape over the radio. All that verisimilitude. It has to be real, right? So the dumb fuck bets it all on Lucky Dan to win in the third at Riverside.

H eathrow on a rainy afternoon.

I was on my way to see Rajiv. A beautiful stewardess in a turquoise sari was serving drinks. She'd closed the door of the 747 and we'd already taxied to the end of a runway. But this I'd barely noticed. Because, at first sight of all that sheer silk and her bare belly, my mind had transported me to India. As I'd been instructed, in my passport was an ordinary tourist visa and in my head were telephone numbers I'd memorized and then shredded in Adnan's huge gray shredder back in New York. And—this my own improvisation—in my carry-on bag was a long white robe I planned to change into before landing. As tall as I am, which means I'm always going to be noticed, it seems to me that sometimes the best disguise is to call attention to myself, give the impression that extra scrutiny doesn't worry me.

What I was thinking of—between peeks at the stewardess's navel while she floated around the First Class cabin dispensing champagne and juices—was what I planned to say to Rajiv. All he knew was that I'd accepted his invitation to "come say Hi in person and let me give you a pat on the back for all the help you've been to me lately." The pat on the back, and perhaps the beginnings of an Air India 747 contract, I certainly intended to get while I was in New Delhi. But I also planned to get Rajiv to someplace quiet and secure, just him and me, and tell him what I'd learned about Chandrashekhar's role, and Swamiji and Mammaji's true allegiance, in the St. Kitts Affair. Plus the fact that I thought at least the second batch of St. Kitts documents were fakes. Absent a preestablished code, which Rajiv and I didn't have, there's a certain class of secrets you can only tell in person. Sun Tzu called these "mouth-to-ear secrets."

Swamiji and Mammaji and Dr. Channa were all in New Delhi now, had organized the details of my schedule, and planned to go with me when I went to the Prime Minister's office. I could be certain they'd do their best to make sure I never got my mouth to Rajiv's ear.

Back in the rain at Heathrow. We were next in line for takeoff.

Until a police car with flashing lights came tearing out behind a FOLLOW ME truck and pulled us over. Planes began passing us.

The stewardess opened a door and lowered the automatic stairs. Two official-looking Englishmen in dripping macs and a plump Indian in an Air India blazer appeared at the top of the stairs and stepped into the First Class cabin. One of the Englishmen spoke quietly with a stewardess. For some reason, I had no doubt they'd come for me.

Still, I squirmed when the traitor in a turquoise sari scanned a list and then pointed straight at me. Very rude, pointing is. The courteous Englishmen escorted me down the stairs, into the rain, into the car, into their custody. I went cheerfully, doing my best Gee-whiz-I-get-to-ride-in-a-police-car-what's-all-this-about? Too bad I didn't have the long white robe on already. It might make a nice distraction.

They took me into a squalid little room somewhere in the bowels of Heathrow. They asked me for my passport. I patted all my pockets, a few of them twice, then finally pulled United States of America Passport No. Z5122852 from my briefcase, where I'd known it was all along. I gave it to them, then watched them inspect, in worrying detail and while taking notes, the dozens of entry stamps from Arab countries.

They searched me. They searched my bags. They asked me questions. Mostly obvious ones. Just like in the movies:

"Who are you?"

"Larry Kolb."

"What is your occupation?"

"Businessman."

"What sort of business?"

"Marketing and promotion."

"Why are you going to India?"

"To visit friends." *Don't mention Rajiv.*

"Who are you planning to see there?"

"Well, lots of people."

"Name one."

"Anup Jalota." India's Frank Sinatra. According to the *Guinness Book of World Records,* no one on earth had sold more records than the great ghazal singer and lover of beautiful women Anup Jalota. Whose name won me new respect from the Air India man who'd been lurking with his back against the door—which door, I'd already noted, would seem to require a key to open from this side. I'd actually met Anup Jalota the last time I was in New Delhi, and for some reason I'd been thinking about him lately, thinking maybe I'd see him there again on this trip.

"Are you carrying any explosives?"

"No."

"Have we removed all of your baggage and everything you took onto the aircraft?"

"It looks like it. Yes."

"Did you use a lavatory on the plane?"

"No."

"Do you know any reason it would not be safe for this flight to proceed to India?"

"No."

They asked me the same questions again. Then they asked me slightly different questions which were actually the same questions.

While all this was going on, the four of us occasionally watched a TV monitor which was against the wall on the end of the desk. Black-and-white picture. It seemed the Air India jet was somewhere just outside a hangar now.

All the passengers were out of the plane standing in the drizzle with their carry-ons while men in boilersuits removed every bag from the plane's belly.

Once all the checked luggage was out, one by one the passengers identified their own suitcases, and cardboard boxes, and antediluvian steamer trunks, then climbed back into the plane while porters humped the identified baggage back onto the plane.

Finally a new question: "When is the last time you spoke with your wife?"

With my wife? What the fuck is going on here? "This morning. Is she all right?"

"We'd like you to telephone her in New York."

"My wife is in Florida."

"We traced her call to New York. Please ring her on this number." The taller one handed me the phone and watched me dial. It was Adnan's number.

His secretary answered.

"Hi, Anna Paula. It's Larry Kolb. Is my wife there?" The Englishmen were listening on extensions, with their hands covering the mouthpieces.

"No, but I'll put you through to Mr. A.K.," she said in a nervous rush, and then she was gone.

Adnan picked up. "Where are you?"

"In the dungeon at Heathrow."

"Good. I'm glad they got you off the plane. Call me when you get to a hotel."

"But I think these nice gentlemen would like to ask you a few questions before they let me go to a hotel."

Adnan had already hung up.

One of the Englishmen said, "Who was that?"

I said, "Adnan Khashoggi."

That cost me another couple of hours, at least.

Finally they let me go.

That evening, in the West End, Lorraine's Volvo wagon pulled up in front of me.

I climbed into the backseat, saying: "As I live and breathe! Miles Copeland, back from the dead!"

"Good to see you too, Larry."

"But back too late to save me."

"It will pass."

Lorraine was driving. Miles was sitting beside her, with his head turned round to look at me, and my father's glasses reflecting all the lights of the high street as we drove by. We went to a hilarious play and then to dinner at a restaurant where a lot of people seemed to know Miles. And even more knew of him. Pretty soon Miles was holding court and buying drinks. Someone said, "Tell 'em about Lennie." So Miles did.

"When our little daughter Lennie was seven or eight and we lived in Beirut, she came home from school one day and found Oscar her parakeet dead in his cage."

Miles's tone became somber for a moment. "Poor Oscar was flat on his back," he said. "And Lennie went into *absolute* hysterics. She cried and cried on my arm, until I had a bright idea."

Miles sipped his gin and smiled.

"I walked her out onto the porch," he went on, "sat her down next to me, and tried to put her calamity into perspective. 'Look, Lennie,' I said. 'It's not the end of the world. Things like this *happen* to us. Death is a fact of life. Tell you what we'll do: We'll have Hagop build a coffin. Mommy will trim it with Damascus lace. And we'll have Father Pierre pray over Oscar while we put him in his coffin. Then we'll have a wake. We'll invite your friends for ice cream, candy, the *works*. . . . Next we'll put Oscar in your toy boat, and, while we stand on the shore singing and waving goodbye, we'll sail Oscar out into the Mediterranean. You know, a Vikings funeral.'

"Well, by that point," Miles said, "I was carried away with my own eloquence, and Lennie was eating it up. No more tears. She was grinning. But then an ominous sound came from the house. Squawking. Loud as hell. Lennie and I went back inside to check it out. And there was Oscar, staring at us from his perch. Good as new. We stared back at him in shock. Until little Lennie tugged at my sleeve. And she said"—Miles paused now—"'Daddy, let's *kill* him!'"

After a moment, Miles turned his attention just to me. "You see what I'm saying?" he said quietly. "If you dramatize it, Larry, if you see it as only an episode in a game, any disaster you encounter is bearable, even enjoyable. That's how you've got to live this life we're in."

Back in the car again. It was great to see Miles. I hadn't realized how much I'd missed him. He said, "So tell me again. Slower this time. Tell me what the hell happened at the airport?"

I told him again.

"Now tell me *why* it happened."

"I can't."

Miles said, "I talked to A.K., and here's what happened:

"Number one—early this morning he got a call from India. And as soon as he hung up the phone he told that little Portuguese spitfire of a secretary of his, Anna Paula Something or Other, to find you and tell you to stop your trip. A.K. said that was all he knew about how you were gotten off the plane. So later I talked to Anna Paula, and she said something like"—here Miles's voice rose an octave and he grew a Portuguese accent—"'Tell Mr. Larry I'm sorry if I made trouble for him. I called the airport and they told me he was already on the plane. So then I said I was his wife and it was very important for him to get out of that airplane. Fast. Then they put on another man and he asked me questions, and I said it would not be very good for him to go in that airplane. And when he asked me why, I wouldn't say, I only told him, "I have my reasons," and then everything got very nervous so I hung up.' Crude, but effective. Back to my conversation with A.K. now.

"Number two—today Rajiv Gandhi called the general elections for just three weeks from now. Apparently that's a big surprise. And, number three— as of today, all over India, you're blown. Every opposition newspaper in the country—and I hear there are lots of them—suddenly knows your name and is searching for a picture of you. They can't really do justice to burning you in effigy until they know what you look like. So for at least the next three weeks you're going to have to stay out of sight. Slip around in dark alleys after midnight while wearing sunglasses, and things like that. Got it?"

L *arry Jackson Kolb on the lam.*
   I thought about spending the next three weeks in Ibiza, but in the end decided I might not survive the liver damage. London was out of the question, because of the scene at Heathrow. Most every other place I thought of waiting out Rajiv's reelection, I'd have to go out occasionally to eat or buy supplies. So New York it would be—inside Adnan's apartment, which, as I'd heard said about certain ocean liners of comparable size, was a city in itself.

By the time I got there, a remarkable cast of intriguers had already assembled. Even Miles beat me there. He took the Concorde nonstop, while I went, not just by subsonic airliner, but, as he'd taught me to do in circumstances such as these, by a more circuitous route. All sorts of plots were well under way when I arrived, and I had some catching up to do if I was going to get in on the action.

Mostly Adnan needed money, and rather a lot of it. What he lacked in ready cash he'd been doing his best to make up for in charm and energy. Since his arrival in New York, his staff had gotten paid only with the greatest irregularity, but somehow failed to care all that much. When a revolt seemed imminent, he'd throw a staff party and hand out gifts so extravagant no one could imagine ever buying such fabulous things for themselves. Butlers, secretaries, maids, masseurs, valets, dogsbodies, and sundry others with fees in arrears kept coming back to work. And long-term staffers were endeared to know, from collective experience, that if ever they were truly in need—a child needing an operation, a mortgage about to be foreclosed—A.K. always came through with the cash, overpaying with generosity.

But Adnan's problem now wasn't coming up with the odd half million here or there due monthly to the staffs and crews of his many splendored residences and offices and boats and planes scattered around the world. Nor was he unable to keep paying American Express the million dollars or so a month he charged on his green AMEX card in the course of eating out and shopping all over Manhattan and throwing parties at home. Nor was he straitened by the few million dollars at a whack his lawyers dunned him for from time to time to keep managing his defense. The problem was the really big bills looming in the near term. Several of Adnan's crown jewels were in the pawnshop, so to speak. His Marbella estate. His Monaco penthouse. His townhouse in Paris. A couple of his houses in Cannes. Pay sums certain by dates certain or lose them, said writs served regularly on Adnan's lawyers.

The Marbella property alone was appraised at sixty million dollars, and mortgaged to the max. The sums due were huge, and making the balloon payments that were about to fall due wasn't going to be easy given that an army of U.S. Government bureaucrats had recently spent millions of dollars and thousands of manhours and womanhours plodding through Byzantine legal processes the world over in the course of attaching R.I.C.O. liens to as many of Adnan's bank accounts and assets as they could get their hooks into.

Refinancing was out of the question given the uncertainty of Adnan's future. Tiny Rowland and a few Saudi princes, including Talal bin Abdul Aziz, and Kamal Adham, the founder of the Saudi Mukhabarat, had been helping out with a few million here and there. But most of all the burden fell on Adnan to do what he'd always done best, make more money so he could spend it.

He'd always been a financial high-wire artist, but now he was reminding me of this guy my father and I watched once on television when I was a kid. This frantic, foreign-looking fellow who spun a whole bunch of plates on quivering shafts one Sunday evening on *The Ed Sullivan Show*. He'd nudge one plate just enough to regain stability here, quickly start another plate spinning, and then rush off just in time to save the next plate that seemed about to crash.

"Yella, Larry, yella!" Adnan said to me the day I arrived back in New York, and was assigned the blue suite, my favorite, to be my quarters for the duration. "Forget India for now. Come on, let's make some money!"

Across 51st, on the sidewalk on the St. Patrick's side of the street, the FBI seemed to manage to keep at least one touristy-looking agent hanging around at all hours to take pictures of the comings and goings through the front door of the Olympic Tower of all of Adnan's visitors, and incidentally every other visitor to the place. And, in court filings, the government had admitted that, for what it said were national security reasons, it was monitoring the telephone and fax traffic in and out of Adnan's apartment. Any and all of Adnan's old friends and associates willing to brave the FBI portraiture project and the wiretaps were welcome upstairs at Adnan's place to eat his food and swim in his pool and help him concoct new ways to make money.

For whatever it was worth, I'd entered the Olympic Tower this time via its underground parking garage, in the backseat of a limo with blackened windows and with my face buried in an *¡HOLA!* magazine. Not that it would fool the U.S. Government, with its wiretaps, and no doubt bugs in nearly every room of the apartment, but no representative of or vendor to the Indian opposition press had photographed me arriving at the Olympic Tower. All the staff were told to tell anyone who called for me that they thought I was in Florida.

During the first few weeks of the St. Kitts Affair, when I'd been up here almost constantly, the apartment had already been full of Adnan's friends and partners from all around the world, working the phones, trying to make deals, trying to make the center hold. As Adnan's deadlines approached, the human numbers present and the sense of urgency that possessed them had more than doubled.

Now in nearly every living room and conference room and salon and alcove and den and office in the apartment you could almost always find a man in a suit, usually speaking English, usually in a foreign accent, to someone on the other side of the world. There was a switchboard, and more than a hundred phone extensions throughout the apartment, with at least twenty outgoing lines, all of which were busy almost all the time. So Adnan had supplemented his landlines with mobile phones. I don't mean anything even resembling the little phone I slip into the back pocket of my surf baggies before I head out for a run down the beach these days. We're talking big-ass mobile phones.

The state-of-the-art mobile telephones of the day—about two dozen of which Adnan had recently bought to distribute to his visitors—were about the size of toasters, came with their own shoulder straps to lighten the strain they put on anyone trying to walk and talk with one at the same time, and had NYNEX branded across the straps in white letters you could read from a block away. Now Adnan's visitors were free to roam about the apartment as they made their deals. And roam they did, in small herds, men in suits, talking, talking, talking, and looking for Adnan.

I got the whole picture the day after I arrived in the apartment. Miles and I had breakfast with Adnan, and strategized about Miles's project of the moment, a campaign to orchestrate a liaison between the Saudi government and the White House—with the objective of arranging for President Bush to pardon Adnan on national security grounds. This sounded like fun to me, and I assumed I'd get to stick with Miles and work with him on it until he left town. But, when we finished breakfast, Adnan said he wanted me to follow him around the apartment all that day, pretending to be an executive who worked in his Geneva office. This, I pointed out, would be a really shitty cover given that at least half the people in the apartment knew me. So Adnan sent someone to bring me his slim black crocodile briefcase and some legal pads, and next he told me to sit at his right hand at every meeting, keep my mouth shut, and take notes on whatever was discussed.

Our first meeting was in the conference room, with the very-Mormon and very-old Bill Gay, who had been Howard Hughes's chief of staff for years, and now was a wrinkled and white-haired man in a gray suit and a white shirt, still tall, but stooped, and who still had quite a business mind and was using it for Adnan now, trying to save Marbella.

On one front, Bill had been attempting for several weeks to negotiate a new deal with the creditor who held the mortgage on Marbella. It was a Saudi bank, and you'd think it might take a little mercy on Adnan at this juncture in his life. But there are many competing factions within Saudi Arabia, and the bank wouldn't budge. So Bill was also working with a team of Danish developers on a plan to convert the Marbella ranch into a luxury resort and spa and golf club. Bill said the Danes would be in town next week with their bankers to sign a letter of intent. I was about to tell Bill that if he could conjure a golf course out of Adnan's Andalucian mountainside it would be about the hilliest and most unplayable golf course I'd ever seen in my life, and I'd seen quite a few. But then I remembered Adnan had told me to keep my mouth shut, and I did.

Our next meeting was in the West dining room—the one with the ebony and lapus lazuli table and the fabulous view of lower Manhattan—where we met a wiry little man in a black suit who Adnan had told me was from the mafia, but the guy told me he was in the waste-management business. He then proceeded to pitch a deal whereunder Adnan would receive a ten-million-dollar fee and an ongoing piece of the action if he would merely convince the King of Morocco to allow a certain European company to turn a certain Moroccan beach and the hillside behind it into a giant toxic waste site for consideration to the government of Morocco or its nominee in the amount of forty million dollars per annum. "I don't think the King's going to allow that," said Adnan. "But what about Equatorial Guinea—just a little farther down the coast?"

"I'll check," said the visitor, and indeed later that day he called and told Adnan and me, "Too far. How 'bout sixty million a year for Morocco?"

From our waste-management meeting, we went to the piano room for a meeting involving debt swaps and trade credits between Latin America and Eastern Europe, something Adnan had made a lot of money at in the past. For the entire ten minutes of the meeting, Adnan was full of energy and possibilities. He immediately saw linkages, connections, patterns, possibilities that his friends who'd come to pitch him had missed. He took my pen and legal pad and drew a vaguely Miroesque diagram of the way he saw a deal working, and everyone was getting very enthusiastic. But then, just when it felt like we were about to get somewhere with this, Anna Paula came in, interrupted, said we had to go see Frank Morse because he had a plane to catch. "We'll talk some more about this tomorrow," Adnan said to the debt-swap men on his way out the door.

Frank, who was waiting in the living room under a beautiful Kandinsky canvas, was just back from Europe, where, he told me, he'd flown all over the place for almost a week carrying in his briefcase a seventeen-million-dollar check endorsed to Adnan from an American defense contractor who'd owed Adnan big money for years. And had finally paid up at a hefty discount in exchange for a release from Adnan. Frank said he'd been trying like hell to get a banker to cash the check. Even for a small percentage, no bank in Western Europe was willing to do it, because of all the R.I.C.O. liens. Finally, Frank said rather triumphantly, yesterday, he'd gotten the check cashed in Yugoslavia. Adnan's eyes lit up. This was the best news he'd heard in awhile.

Next we met in the East dining room with a Chinaman, an old friend of Adnan, who wanted his help finding passports to sell in Hong Kong. The British handover of Hong Kong to the Chinese was only a few years away, and there were millions of Hong Kong residents who'd lived all their lives under British protection but were soon to become the proud holders of Red Chinese passports if they couldn't find alternative citizenships first. These people didn't necessarily actually want to leave Hong Kong. Just wanted different passports to facilitate their continuing travel, and enhance their legal rights—and to give them an escape route if they really needed it.

The Chinaman was a pudgy youngish guy, maybe forty at the most. He said most of the wealthiest Hong Kong residents had already bought themselves British or Canadian or American passports for something like a million U.S. dollars, each under various foreign-investment-for-citizenship programs. "That," said the Chinaman, "has left a huge second tier of prosperous but not super-rich Hong Kong residents who want new citizenships and passports, and could pay maybe seventy-five to a hundred thousand dollars each for them. If you can get the passports from someplace in the Caribbean or South America, maybe," the Chinaman told Adnan, "I could guarantee to move a thousand of them every month for two years." I did the math. The Chinaman was talking roughly a billion dollars a year. If Adnan could make ten percent of that, he'd be free and clear. And, if I could make ten percent of Adnan's ten percent, I'd be well and duly pleased.

Adnan said, "I'll think about where to get them. Nice to see you, Clive. I'm sorry I've got to hurry to another meeting now, but can you join us for dinner tonight?" And as we climbed the backstairs to our next meeting, Adnan wondered out loud if maybe I should call Terry Byron and Anne Salvesen to see if they wanted to be the St. Kitts and Nevis Special Citizenship Envoys to Hong Kong. It had a nice ring to it.

Up in Adnan's dressing room we met with three young Lebanese gentlemen, longtime employees of Adnan. They were, by trade, many things, but procurers of beautiful women more than any other thing. But what they were doing when we arrived was thumbing through boxes of snapshots—of Adnan and his family and guests in Marbella, and Paris, and Portofino, or on his planes, or at sea. "We think these ones, Mr. A.K.," said the tall one named Johnny, and he then laid out about forty of the pictures for Adnan's inspection. Adnan looked them over quickly, removed three or four, and said, "All right boys. The rest of these are fine. Divide them up and go to it. Yella! Bring me back some money!"

I left that meeting wondering what the fuck it was all about, until, with our footsteps echoing on the marble of the grand staircase, Adnan said the boys would be flying off that night to Europe. Where they would play the roles of disgruntled employees of Adnan Khashoggi with pictures and exclusive insider stories to sell to the sorts of magazines that pay big money for such things. Adnan figured that, if all three of the boys made their deals on the same day, so that each publisher believed it was getting an exclusive, they could get maybe a hundred thousand dollars each from three magazines. Of course, Adnan said, the boys would tell him they'd only gotten seventy-five thousand each, and they'd pocket the difference when they brought money back to him. But that was fine with Adnan. The trickle-down economics of Arabia.

Lunch was with Miles and Arthur Laffer, inventor of the Laffer Curve, Ronald Reagan's pet economist—and after that Adnan and I met in the conference room with a middle-aged New York real-estate developer who informed us that New York City's venerable and wonderfully located, but threadbare, Roosevelt Hotel was owned by the Government of Pakistan. "I'll pay you a five-and-a-half-million-dollar fee," he told Adnan, "if you can get the owner to sell me the hotel."

Then we met in the screening room with an earnest man in a Versace suit who wanted to trade bicycles made in Chicago for shiitake mushrooms grown outside Dubrovnik. Which I duly noted.

It wasn't even midafternoon yet, and it was already becoming clear to me there was no way Adnan could keep track of all this. And he didn't even really want to try. This was his Olympic Tower version of the rounds he'd perpetually made all about the earth until he was grounded on this island. What he was doing was keeping in touch, listening, sniffing for the real deals, the ones that could bring in the most money for the least work. Of today's meetings, the only ones that had really interested Adnan were the meetings with Bill Gay, about saving the Marbella ranch, and with Frank Morse, about the money.

The meeting with the boys about the photos was mostly a lark, something to keep their spirits up, and maybe bring in a couple hundred thousand bucks in pocket change. Just a few days' operating expenses. The debt swaps for trade credits might turn into something good. All the rest of the opportunities Adnan had heard about that day hadn't interested him—because he couldn't see a way to make them work. That didn't mean he wouldn't keep taking meeting after meeting, day after day. He knew that, if he kept moving and kept listening, eventually he'd hear of a deal that was made for him, for his connections, his expertise. Something he'd actually be able to make happen with a few calls to the right banker, or the right board member, or the right government official—and then there would be a cash inflow.

All around the apartment, the men in suits working the phones kept throwing shit up against the wall to see if any of it would stick. They were welcome to use Adnan's name, within reason, that was fine with him, and to try almost anything. And so Adnan and I kept going to meetings through the afternoon, about palm oil trading in the Philippines, about the financing of a petroleum refinery in Nigeria, about a hotel for sale in Buenos Aires, about computers made for export from South Korea.

At the start of the day, I'd been tacitly pissed off at Adnan for roping me into the St. Kitts Affair, which I'd come to figure he'd had to know from the beginning was based on a questionable set of documents. But, for Adnan, today had been just another day, and I'd seen there was no way he could stay aware of everything going on around him or that was being said or done in his name. Swamiji and Mammaji, I'd learned, had met Raji Samghabadi while he was working on the *Time* story on Adnan. Maybe they'd enlisted Samghabadi to give credibility to the story, rather than Adnan enlisting him. I decided to withhold judgment on that, pending further evidence.

When our meetings were over, Adnan spent a couple hours up in his private quarters and then got back to work over dinner around the big oval ebony and lapis lazuli table.

He ate with Miles, and Bill Gay, and Frank Morse—who'd missed his plane. With the mushroom farmer from Yugoslavia who wanted bicycles from Chicago. With the Chinaman in search of passports. With my old friend Bill Morrison, and his twenty-two-year-old son David, who'd just finished NYU with a degree in Middle Eastern politics and a profitable sideline in fashion models and nightlife. Which, come to think of it, made him Adnan's kind of guy. With Adnan's first wife Soraya, his current wife Lamia, and his soon-to-be third wife Shahpari. With the entire troupe of backup singers from Elton John's world tour. With, probably the most brilliant businessman in the room, the Lebanese financier Roger Tamraz. And with me. Somehow, as always, Adnan managed to keep the discussion flowing and everyone interested and involved.

While I was loading lobster kebabs onto my plate at the buffet table, Frank Morse told me more about the hassles he'd been through trying to get Adnan's check cashed. The Feds don't make it easy on their defendants. That's part of the game. And yet, in Adnan's case, they kept reminding him all he had to do in order to make all this insanity stop was bear witness against his friends.

The best part of the story Adnan had told me in the sauna about his jail time was once he got to New York. The jail in Bern had been pretty much a relaxation and weight-loss clinic for Adnan. He'd had his own cell, with a television, and they installed a bookshelf for him. He'd had wonderful low-calorie meals catered by the best chefs in the city and delivered to his cell. He'd been allowed to make phone calls all around the world all day. And there was a window box with red geraniums outside his window.

When he left Switzerland, he'd bought five first-class tickets, on Swissair, for himself, two of his lawyers, two Swiss plainclothes policemen. No handcuffs, and the Swiss took care to assure his security and shield him from the press. They sneaked him out of the jail in a bus, drove him a few miles from the jail, quietly switched him to a Mercedes limousine, drove straight to the side of the Swissair jet, and boarded him ahead of the other passengers. Next stop, John F. Kennedy International Airport. It was the first time Adnan had traveled on a commercial airliner in nearly thirty years.

The FBI agents who met Adnan at JFK coolly took him through immigration and customs, then handcuffed him and put him into the backseat of a car, which, it must be said, could have driven him the entire way to jail. But instead they perp-walked him. Stopped the car in front of a balcony packed with reporters and photographers, told him to get out and go to another car thirty yards away. The sole purpose of this vehicle change was obviously to give the photographers a choice view of Adnan in handcuffs, and he knew that, so he got out and raised his hands above his head to show off the cuffs and smiled and waved at everyone.

Next he found himself shuttled into the Metropolitan Correctional Facility, a maximum-security federal prison in lower Manhattan. There he faced a mug-shot camera and was fingerprinted. Then they led him through a gauntlet of screaming inmates to his cell. *God, protect me against the evils and bring me the good of this world* was the Muslim prayer Adnan recited in his head as he made his way past the other prisoners. "What a place this was, Larry!"

His cell was smaller than his Swiss cell, and had no television or bookshelf. While in Bern the cells had had doors, which made them like rooms, here the cells had bars, making them like cages. He could see the other prisoners. And he didn't take it as a coincidence that they had put him in a cell next to that of an enormous black man, who happened to be the most feared being, guard or prisoner, in the entire facility. His name was Sweet Pea, and he was a Muslim.

"I made him my friend," Adnan told me. "We prayed together, and he gave me some of his snack food. Because, until I had been there for three days on good behavior, I wouldn't have the privilege of ordering anything from the commissary.

"During our daily walks in the sun on the roof," Adnan said, "I met men I could have never imagined I could be near. Most of the inmates were here because, like Sweet Pea, they had committed murders while serving time in other places. And then there was me. I was in this maximum-security facility because the prosecutors wanted to scare me into testifying against my friends the Marcoses. Which was not something I would ever do.

"Sweet Pea and I prayed together five times a day. When Friday came, I thought we would have a gathering of all the Muslim prisoners to pray together. But Sweet Pea told me it wouldn't happen. 'We've tried and tried,' Sweet Pea said, 'but the guards won't listen.' So I had a word with the prison rabbi when I saw him passing, and an hour later an imam arrived, along with a guard to take us to another room—where the imam led the Friday prayer for me and seven other Muslim brothers.

"Sweet Pea said the imam obliged because of me. I disagree. A life of striking deals has taught me a lesson or two. A rabbi, not a guard, was the right person to ask."

A week later, a federal judge had released Adnan on ten million dollars bail and allowed him to ride uptown to this apartment. Before he left the prison, he gave Sweet Pea his prayer rug.

That was Adnan's story of why he was in New York that night. Mine you already know. Roger Tamraz's was something else entirely.

Roger—which is pronounced with the second *r* silent, just like Roget, as in *Roget's Thesaurus*—said nary a word at dinner that night, as I recall. And afterwards, when Adnan left with his wives and most of the rest of his guests to go out on the town, and Miles took a taxi uptown to his son Ian's apartment to get some rest, Roger Tamraz and I stayed in. I wasn't afraid, just avoiding photographers. Roger was petrified.

In the next few weeks, Adnan was out on the town almost every night. Gracing gala openings, balls, and dinner parties—living proof that, as the saying went that season, "If you're indicted, you're invited." Most of New York society treated Adnan like visiting royalty, and as long as he stayed within the confines of the island of Manhattan he was within his bail restrictions. Which made Roger and me the only full-time inmates in the Olympic Tower, and like prisoners everywhere, I imagine, we passed a lot of time together talking.

Roger was Lebanese, but not Muslim. He was forty-nine. Looked younger. Looked European. He was educated at Cambridge and at Harvard Business School. With his neatly parted dark blond hair and tortoiseshell glasses, he favored conservative business suits or tweedy blazers and striped ties. He owned the Hotel Meurice, the Grand Hôtel, and the Prince de Galles, in Paris, and the Casino Park, in Madeira, Portugal. He owned Tamoil, one of the largest oil refineries in Italy, which had a chain of petrol stations across the country. He owned merchant banks in Geneva, Lugano, and Paris, trade finance banks in the Central African Republic and Zaire, and two of the three largest retail banks in Lebanon. He was chairman of Middle East Airlines, the Lebanese passenger airline, and TMA, the Lebanese cargo airline. He was even chairman of the Casino du Liban. He was, according to *Newsweek,* "the very model of a modern Arab moneyman." Here in New York, he owned the Park Avenue Bank and an apartment on the Upper East Side.

But he wasn't about to leave the Olympic Tower.

Most of the time, while we talked, Roger seemed perfectly normal. And quite the brilliant financier he was. But then, for just a moment, his eyes would glaze over and I'd know he was back in chains and a blindfold in Lebanon.

Two weeks before his arrival here, Roger had been a hostage in Beirut, kidnapped and held by Hizballah until he negotiated and paid for his own release—bought his way out. He told me his abductors had let him make a series of telephone calls to Paris, by which he'd arranged to secretly wire-transfer several million dollars—all the unencumbered cash he had—into an account in Beirut.

More from *Newsweek*: "Daring and controversial, young Roger Tamraz has been involved in some of the most widely publicized international business transactions. Tamraz is typically cool about his successes and unperturbed by his flops. 'I'm interested in things they say can't be done.'"

After we'd spent enough days and nights talking for Roger to take the measure of me, he looked at me one night and said, "You know, Larry, I know the men who are holding the American and British hostages in Lebanon. They are the same people who held me, of course. Look, I know the psychology of how to deal with these people. I know which buttons to push and which ones to stay away from. I think I could get the hostages released."

Well, there I sat, an old hand at the American Government's covert attempts to negotiate the release of the American hostages. And what Roger was saying didn't seem all that outlandish to me. "How did you really do it, anyway?" I said to Roger. "Why did they release you instead of just taking your money?"

"Because I got inside their heads," Roger said. "I made it a point of honor. I spent hours, whole days, talking with them, engaging their minds. By the time I wired the money, I knew there was no conceivable way they would fail to keep their promises to me once they received the payment."

"And you know who these people are, the real players, and how to contact them?"

"Yes," said Roger, "I do."

"Have you talked with the CIA or the State Department about this?"

"No one from your government has even bothered to ask me how I got out."

That was strange, I thought, so I called Miles, who was back in Oxfordshire now, and told him about it. And the next day Miles called me back and said he'd asked around and the NSC wasn't interested. So I called Mike Timpani, who said this wasn't up his alley at all, of course, not working for an intelligence service himself. But he would talk to some friends of his who worked for the Agency and then get back to me. When Mike called back, he said the CIA wasn't interested in Roger's help either.

"Why?" I said.

"They said they feel they have the hostage situation under control."

"Under *control?* Half a dozen Americans in chains in Lebanon. They've been wasting away for years. The CIA station chief was flayed and skewered, and his colleagues say they have the situation under *control?*"

Mike said, "I'm just a soldier, taking orders. Plus I'm your friend, and don't shoot the fucking messenger, buddy. But the bottom line is I'd recommend you drop this immediately." And thus ended my third campaign to free the American hostages.

Roger didn't seem to be surprised at all.

Meanwhile, though Adnan was enjoying his nights, the shit he was in was piling higher by day. His criminal defense team was increasingly a presence in the apartment, while entrepreneurs from afar roamed the halls working deals, and Frank Morse held off creditors, and Bill Gay tried to pull a rabbit out of a hat, and Miles, when he was in town, kept cooking something grand and mysterious involving Riyadh and Washington. The apartment was on a full war footing now, something like Rick's American Café in Casablanca, it occurred to me one day. Except we were up in the sky, looking down on a world of trouble.

From my perspective, about the only good news was the Indian press hadn't gotten a picture of me. And that Swamiji was far away, in India. From which he kept calling and reporting that Rajiv seemed to have the election locked up. Which was odd, because Miles said the word he was getting was that Rajiv and V.P. Singh were running neck and neck.

In the last two weeks before the election, the nasty little Indian dandy, the pink-faced Ganduji I'd last seen in the bar in the Helmsley Palace, started calling Adnan's switchboard and asking for me. "Look, I know Mr. Kolb is in there," he told Anna Paula several times a day, "so please tell him it's for his own good to talk to me—*pop*—and put him on the line."

We had his calls traced and learned he was ringing from his home in Washington. Miles ran a background check on the little bastard, and found out he was four feet eleven inches tall, he worked for an Indian political magazine that supported Vishwanath Pratap Singh, and he had ties to, and was perhaps an agent of, the Indian government's poetically named Research and Analysis Wing, RAW—which was India's principal foreign intelligence service. Funny, he'd accused me of working with them. Soon Lynn Hudson also began calling the apartment and asking for me. Then another Indian reporter, named Balu.

They were closing in on me. Meanwhile Adnan was preparing to go to trial, even while I hid in his apartment and the financial pressures on him mounted. At this point, and for the next few months, his problems and mine began to knot together into such a tangled mess, with everything happening at once, that, when I look back, it's hard for even me to keep it all straight chronologically. So I think I should tell you the stories separately, starting with Adnan's escape from Manhattan.

Adnan retained new counsel. James Linn would be his new lead criminal attorney. Frank Morse would keep fighting a rearguard action against the creditors and serve as second chair to Linn at the trial. Robert Morvillo was out. He'd done a terrific job managing the extradition battle that resulted in Adnan now facing substantially reduced charges. But Morvillo was a gruff and no-nonsense New Yorker. I'd never once seen him at lunch or dinner in the apartment. He and Adnan just didn't get along that well together.

Jim Linn, on the day I met him, in Adnan's living room, told me he was from Oklahoma and it sure was nice to meet me. He was maybe fifty, tall and slender, rich brown hair, perfectly combed, silver sideburns, mustache, gentle eyes, wearing a beautifully tailored gray suit. And he was such a smooth talker. Just like the three other great trial attorneys I'd known—Melvin Belli, Racehorse Haynes, Paul Monzione. Jim Linn's voice was rich and resonant, soothing somehow. I knew immediately that I was in the presence of a master.

Rumors were flying all around the apartment that at the last minute the White House would block the trial. But Jim insisted the trial would not be averted. "Adnan can believe whatever he wants," he told me one day as we walked together toward the dining room for lunch. "And I know there are plenty of assholes running around telling him not to worry. But it's plain and simple. We're going to trial. There are no national security grounds to stay the trial. And every man I've ever seen who took immunity to testify against his friends lost his self-respect, and then just fell apart inside. I told the prosecutor, 'Mr. Khashoggi is the most positive and charming man I've ever met. You *can't* take away his dignity. You *may* be able to put him in prison. But, if you do, I guarantee you, within two weeks, every day he'll be sitting down with the warden for afternoon tea.'"

I liked Jim Linn. Not just for his plain talk. He seemed to value me, gave me useful things to do to take my mind off India—and best of all he was covert by nature. Talked one way inside Adnan's apartment, which we knew was bugged, another way inside Jim's thousand-dollar-a-day suite in the Waldorf Tower, which was probably bugged, and another way still while we walked together on the noisy, crowded sidewalks. Which were about the safest place available for us to have a confidential conversation, and Jim knew that. So we seemed to take a lot of walks together between the Olympic Tower and the Waldorf, varying our routes.

The Indian press weren't looking for me anymore, as you may have noticed. But we'll come back to that.

Jim had heard about the information I'd come up with about Rudy Giuliani vowing that one day he'd cut off A.K.'s nuts. "That was real good work," Jim said to me as we paced down Fifth Avenue at rush hour, "and, Larry, if you've got the right kind of contacts, and I hear you do, maybe you can help me out with something else. Something I've been trying to nail down but just haven't been able to seem to do. I've had several investigators on it. For weeks. But all we've got is a copy of one page of one government cable referring to it. That's all we can find about it."

"Referring to what? About what?" I said.

"Ferdinand Marcos's World War Two gold," Jim said, "and American attempts to help him cash it in. Once Marcos got to Honolulu, he told Adnan he had a load of gold so big it would fill a cargo ship. Sometimes he told Adnan it was already on a ship, and at sea, and all he needed was a safe port to store it in. Gold bullion worth billions of dollars. And that was how Marcos enticed Adnan to get into all this. It was probably all bullshit, but Adnan fell for it. And Adnan thinks so did Bush and a lot of others in the government. Because Marcos told him when Bush was Vice President he was trying to help him find a way to cash in all that gold. Marcos said members of the Congress got involved somehow too. Everybody wanted a piece of the deal and tried to help. Marcos was offering ten percent. And that's going to be part of Adnan's defense. He wasn't doing anything the U.S. Government wasn't doing too. And its leaders. But we've got one page of one government document referring to Marcos and gold, and that reference is oblique. There's got to be a lot more, Larry. Maybe you know how to get it, and it sure would help me, and Adnan even more than me, if you could."

That was the one and only thing Jim Linn had ever asked me for. It wasn't like he gave me a list of fifty items of interest and Marcos's gold happened to be on it. And it wasn't like he knew I had access to what he wanted. It was total serendipity. I know it's improbable and strains credibility, but fuck it, it's true: My answer to Jim, as we suddenly turned left onto 47th Street, was something along the lines of "Do you mean, Jim, for example, that: if I happened to have been in a hotel suite in Cairo one day with Muhammad Ali when Marcos called from Honolulu and told us about the gold and asked for Muhammad's help with it in exchange for a piece of the action; and if I could deliver Muhammad to testify to that; and if I also happened to know an American attorney by the name of Hirschfeld who was co-opted by the U.S. Government into going undercover to Hawaii to talk to Marcos about the gold, while tape-recording the whole thing; and if I could by, say, the end of this week, get you copies of the transcripts of Marcos talking about the gold and how he was going to cash it in and use the money to buy arms and invade the Philippines, landing first at Ilocos Norte and then fighting his way to Manila, plus, say, a copy of the U.S. Government's investigation into the whole mess, would that help?"

"No shit?" Jim said.

"No sir. No shit," I said.

And the next day I was in Washington picking up the transcripts and some other interesting documents, and the day after that I was in Chicago meeting with Jabir, who wrote a letter to James Linn saying Muhammad Ali would be pleased to testify for Mr. Adnan Khashoggi at trial. And the day after that, it had turned bitter cold, and I was in Michigan at Muhammad's farm and he kissed my cheeks and I kissed his, and we hugged like brothers and there was frost on our breath when we said it had been too long since we'd seen each other. Then Muhammad whispered in my ear, "You gettin' any lately?"

We went out for a ride in his Rolls. The same brown convertible we'd cruised the broad boulevards of Los Angeles in, and now we were driving through empty cornfields in it. When we got back to the gates of the farm, there were some very strange-looking people waiting out there.

When I got back to New York, Swamiji was there. Stinking up 45-G with tea rose and curry.

And soon thereafter a smiling, muscular Indian arrived from Dubai as a guest of Swamiji and one of his disciples.

The visitor from Dubai was named Dawood Ibrahim. And it didn't escape me that he had the good sense not to stay in 45-G. Took one look at it and then took three suites at the Helmsley Palace. Swamiji proudly told me, "Ibrahim is king of gold, king of hawala, king of Dubai smugglers."

There's a secret world all around us, and we just don't see it unless we know where to look. Hawala is the secret Indian banking system, sort of an underground Western Union arrangement for transferring funds without a trace. Give me twenty minutes, and I can find a hawala man in just about any town in America or anywhere else on earth.

My most vivid memories of Adnan's party on the night we met the king of gold and hawala are of Kim dancing with Anthony Quinn, who was doing his Zorba the Greek routine, and of the awe on Dawood Ibrahim's face when he met his hero and Muslim brother Adnan Khashoggi. So moved was Dawood by their first meeting that, as a token of respect, and in commiseration for Adnan's current plight, Dawood presented Adnan a gift, a check for one million dollars drawn on a bank in Dubai.

Adnan found that quite charming. As, I must admit, so did I.

But, to his everlasting grace and credit, later that night, Adnan's first son Mohamed, who'd just flown in from London, smelled a rat and said, "Wait a minute! Has anyone checked this guy out? Just who the fuck is he?"

And so it came to pass that, while several members of Adnan's team were assigned to find out just who the fuck Dawood Ibrahim was, I was assigned to entertain him.

Dawood was about my age and a very pleasant fellow. Though he barely spoke a word of English.

Kim and I took him to Tse Yang, and I hand-fed him minced squab wrapped in a lettuce leaf—in the style I'd learnt from Adnan. We took him and his crew to Au Bar and plied them with cognac.

Meanwhile, upon request for a reference, the chairman of the bank on which Dawood's check was drawn wrote back, "Not only is Mr. Dawood Ibrahim its biggest customer, but this bank could not survive without his business." Things were looking up. Having cut down on his spending dramatically, Adnan could now live for an entire two weeks, maybe even three, on a million dollars.

But then Miles reported that Dawood Ibrahim was the head of the Indian mafia, India's most wanted man, and was on everybody's radar screens because he could be particularly helpful in funneling money to the mujahideen.

"Get to know him, Larry," Miles said, and I said I already had.

On this beach, I've learned Dawood has moved now from Dubai to Pakistan, has become closely linked with India's second-most-wanted man, Osama bin Laden, and is allegedly bin Laden's main conduit for transportation of money, weapons, and covert operatives between Afghanistan, Pakistan, India, Saudi Arabia, Yemen, Dubai, and Europe.

With regret, I'm sure, Adnan declined the check. But he did it in a way that all parties could save face. Sometimes a little diplomacy's required, and Dawood Ibrahim was quite nice but apparently not the sort of fellow you wanted to insult. When I took him in a limo to JFK, he told me, "Now you are my brother, *Bhai!* So you must call me if ever you need anything." I said I would, but I haven't spoken with him since.

So what about the trial, the much-anticipated show trial of Imelda Marcos and Adnan Khashoggi? Three years and twenty-five million dollars in the making! What can I tell you about the scintillating exchanges between lawyers, the riveting courtroom drama? 'Tis the stuff of hour-long television programs, but not real life. Down in the federal courthouse, in the real world, the trial ground on month after month and was about as stupefyingly boring as anything you could ever sit through, and after one day of it I thanked God in his mercy that I didn't have to.

The real defendant was on ice in Honolulu while his widow awaited permission to send his body home to the Philippines. The Marcos and Khashoggi lieutenants said to have actually done the dirty deeds were on the lam, in Morocco and Thailand, outside the reach of the prosecutors. The only defendants present, Imelda, dressed in mourning clothes each day, and Adnan, wearing his owlish reading glasses, appeared to be a middle-aged odd couple who didn't have much to do with the alleged crimes.

Jim Linn's opening statement featured the Ship of Gold, and he was roundly mocked by the prosecutors and the press for telling fairy stories in open court. But I knew better.

Three weeks into the trial, I was in Florida and on the phone to Jim, to ask him how Adnan was faring. "So far, very well," Jim said. "Since the government's opening, they've hardly mentioned him. Their witnesses are talking only about the Marcoses."

"Do you cross-examine them?"

"Of course! I wander up there sort of sleepy-like and ask, 'Did Mr. Khashoggi have anything to do with any of this?' They say 'No.' And I go sit down again."

"And how's Mr. Spence doing for Imelda?" I said. Imelda was represented by the legendary Wyoming attorney Gerry Spence—who wore string ties and a cowboy hat, even in the big city.

"Sometimes he's brilliant," Jim said, "and sometimes I think he may have lost it. Just stands up there and talks and talks, babbling. But I don't think the government's hurt Mrs. Marcos much either. They're having a real hard time proving she even knew what her husband and his aides were doing."

Certain highlights of the remainder of the trial may be further condensed and adumbrated as follows:

Six weeks in, George Hamilton, who'd received immunity for what the government had touted as damning testimony, cried on the stand while telling the jury how Imelda once saved his mother's life with love and kindness.

A few weeks later, as the prosecution case droned into its third month, Imelda collapsed on the defense table spewing blood, and was rolled out of the courtroom on a gurney, put into an ambulance, and rushed to a hospital. This was the most exciting thing the jury had seen or heard in months. Something they would never, ever, forget, for as long as they lived. Though the judge told them to disregard it.

And when Imelda had recovered from her dramatic-but-not-life-threatening infirmity, and after several more weeks of testimony, the prosecution abruptly rested, and both stunned defense teams rested the same day without even putting on a witness.

The United States Government and a certain Rudolph Giuliani had spent more than twenty-five million dollars building this case, but the jury came back shortly with Not Guilty verdicts. Kim came flying up the stairs in Florida to tell me, I turned on CNN, and watched a woman juror telling a reporter, "This trial was held on the wrong side of the Pacific Ocean. We've got more than enough criminals here in New York than to be spending all this time and money on something that may or may not have happened in the Philippines."

Imelda went straight to St. Patrick's Cathedral and knee-walked her way up the center aisle, all the way to the altar. Adnan signed autographs and rode the subway home, then told his pilots to file a flight plan to Mecca, city of his birth. The next night, he threw a victory party at The Nile, an Egyptian restaurant in mid-Manhattan. As money rained down all around them, Adnan and Imelda and Jim Linn and Gerry Spence and several glistening belly dancers shimmied their way across a hardwood floor littered with hundred-dollar bills. I was there. I have pictures.

It took six or seven days to complete the paperwork of getting Adnan's bail money back and dismissing that portion of the original charges for which he'd not been extradited or tried. Technically, if he'd left the country before those additional charges were dismissed, he could've been arrested again and brought back to face another trial. So Adnan waited, and, though I didn't realize it yet, after that his last week of the many weeks he was stranded in New York, it would never be the same between us again. Once more he would become a nomad, and a moving target, and after that I would see him maybe twice or thrice a year.

Meanwhile my troubles were just beginning. And these many years later, I walk the beach pondering the start of my own trial, so far away it seems it might be a dream.

I n the fourth week of November 1989, in polling lasting five days, more than sixty-one percent of India's half a billion eligible souls voted in the biggest democratic exercise in the history of the world. Rajiv lost the election, but so did V.P. Singh. Congress won far more parliamentary seats than Singh's Janata Dal or any other party. But no one won a majority. In order to retain control of the government, Rajiv would have to form a coalition. He considered that, and decided to pass.

According to Swamiji, who was in New Delhi at the time, Rajiv told him, "The people are disenchanted. If I form another government now, I'll be gone for good within a year. If I let someone else fail now, I can come back in a year and stay for twenty more." Rajiv resigned to lead the opposition. For only the second time since independence, the House of Nehru had lost control of India. V.P. Singh formed a motley coalition—cobbled out of more than ten parties ranging from Communists to ultra-right Hindu fundamentalists—and on the second day of December, 1989, he became the Prime Minister of India.

Swamiji, in the breathless account he gave me back in New York a few days later, barely made it out alive. During the transition of power, there was a brief period before the new Prime Minister consolidated his control of India's security services, and it was during that blessed interregnum that His Holiness Chandraswami Maharaj, one of the five spiritual kings of India, and soon also to be one of its ten most-wanted men, slunk into Indira Gandhi International Airport and took the next flight out of the country.

While all that happened, Adnan was still in New York preparing for trial, Miles was still alive, and we all thought I was old news. Momentarily, there was no political advantage to be gained by the Indian press getting a picture of me, or a dossier on me. And that was when I flew off to Washington and Chicago and Muhammad's farm in Michigan, and then back to New York.

But, by the end of December, it emerged in the Indian press that V.P. Singh had a Hit List of the people he was most determined to get. And guess who was on it?

It took awhile for the rococo Indian bureaucracy to convert the new Prime Minister's personal will into a team of agents spreading out across America and the Caribbean to try to get me, but eventually they came.

One day Dr. Channa called from New Delhi, in a strained and reedy voice I've never forgotten, and told me, he wasn't exactly sure when, but two teams of agents from India's Central Bureau of Investigation, the CBI, were about to leave India to begin an investigation in St. Kitts and the United States, and their prime targets were Swamiji, Mammaji, and me. "Good luck, Larry," said the voice called Dr. Channa. "You may not hear from me again."

The next day Miles called me from England. He said friends of his from Washington had just told him the Indian Embassy had formally asked the American government for assistance in finding me.

Time to get the fuck out of New York, I thought, and Miles and Adnan agreed.

So during the dates when, according to Miles's sources, the first wave of CBI agents would be in New York and Connecticut and Florida looking for us, Swamiji, and Dev Ketu, and Kim and I, and a whole team of the holy man's wipers and flatterers, were in Lima and Callao, in Peru, and in Willemsted, in Curaçao, and in Toronto, in a snowstorm. It's our arrival in Toronto that I like to remember Swamiji by.

All week in Peru, he'd been cadging money off of me, telling me he'd lost his purse. I'd had to write checks and get friends of mine in Lima to cash them for me in order to pay our hotel bills. By the time we left Willemsted, in Adnan's DC-9, Swamiji owed me almost twelve thousand dollars. We filed a flight plan for Florida—having heard from Miles that it was now safe for us to go back there.

Remembering this now, I realize how much easier it was to hide from the Indians when Miles was around to tell me where they were and weren't, and when. To operate within the United States, the CBI agents were required to liaise with the Justice Department and other arms of our government. But, anyway, somewhere over Cuba, Swamiji got cold feet. Told me he didn't have a good feeling about Florida. So Captain Jerry called air traffic control and changed our flight plan and we flew straight to Toronto.

Where, after we landed, three Canadian customs and immigrations officers came on board. Quite routine. But instead of speaking briefly with just the crew and then stamping our passports, as they usually would, they insisted on entering the cabin to speak with all of us.

Swamiji gave me a little nudge that appointed me group spokesman. I answered several questions. Then one blond and slightly porky official spoke directly to Swamiji. I answered. "Let *him* answer," the official said to me. "I want to speak to *him*." He turned to Swamiji, who was sitting beside me on a couch. "Can you speak English?"

"Only speaking luttle bit Unglish," Swamiji said, sounding truly innocent and pathetic.

The official asked for Swamiji's passport, which I handed to the official. Then he asked for my passport, which I also gave him.

Next the three officials asked Swamiji and me to come with them while everyone else stayed on board.

This is it. V.P. Singh has got us was what I was thinking. In just fifty steps from the plane to the little immigration building, time stretched, and I felt curiously detached and alert. Part of my mind felt the icy wind and hoped the office would be well heated. Another cursed our stupidity, leapt to the assumption that we'd made a terrible mistake landing in a Commonwealth country, concluded that Commonwealth ties would make extradition between Canada and India easy, and then systematically sorted through a too-short list of people I could call who might be able to get me out of this. And still another part of my mind calmly noticed Swamiji toddling forlornly along beside me, with his white shawl waving in the breeze, and his black cane tapping and scraping, tapping and scraping.

Swamiji later told me he, too, had believed V.P. Singh had caught us. But, when we got inside, the officials only wanted to search us and our baggage. They went through everything we had. Starting with Swamiji's stuff. Inside His Holiness's white suitcase—under white *dhotis,* white shawls, white robes, white socks, white BVDs, and white sandals—a customs agent found a lumpy white pillowcase. He peeked inside and then held it up to Swamiji.

"Is this yours?"

"Uh, I dunno."

"You don't *know!* Is this yours?"

"I think . . . maybe."

"Do you remember what you packed inside here?"

"Uh . . ."

And then the customs man smiled and turned the pillowcase upside down and I watched as more than ninety thousand dollars poured out onto the table.

I would've really enjoyed that, except right about then Kim and Dev, the next pair selected for inspection, were arriving in the terminal. And Kim was spitting mad. Which is never a good thing when you're her husband.

She'd gone to bed in the back of the plane in Curaçao, thinking we were flying to Miami. And she'd slept through the whole flight, quite a blessing given that she can get a bit riled up around airplanes. But she'd also missed the news of our in-flight change of itinerary, and just moments earlier she'd stepped out of the plane wearing flip-flops and shorts and a T-shirt—into a blizzard, while accompanied by a nice Canadian who wouldn't let her go back into the plane to change. Somehow it was all my fault, I could already tell.

The pressure was rising, and I didn't see much of the holy man after that. But one day I got word he wanted to meet with me, in a hotel in Paris, where I spent the night in one of the five bedrooms in Swamiji's suite and, early the next morning, through my bedroom wall, I overheard him long-distance-shouting over a bad connection to India. "Yes. Yes. *Very* good homework Larry does. . . . No, no, no! *Mammaji and Fat Man* mess up St. Kitts. Not Larry." Several minutes after whatever all that was about, Swamiji came into my room and uncorked a burp for the ages. "Breakfast is ready," he said.

An hour later I had said my goodbyes to Swamiji and the disciples. I was just about to leave for Charles De Gaulle and a flight to Miami, when I heard Swamiji screaming. "Dev! Dev! *Dev!* Come here now!" Dev had just gone out the front door saying something about travelers checks. I went to see what the problem was.

When I got inside Swamiji's bedroom I realized the howling was coming from his bathroom. "Please come now, Mr. Ketu!" Swamiji bellowed, as if last-name formality might finally bring Dev running. "Mr. Ketu! Mr. Ketu! Mr. Ketu!" Swamiji screamed until he saw me opening the door. It was a large bathroom—gray marble walls and floor, half-fogged mirror, steel fixtures, sweating white porcelain bidet, toilet, sink, and bath. Steaming water tumbled out of the faucet into the tub. It was filled to the brim, beneath clouds of bubble bath billowing halfway to the ceiling.

Swamiji stood beside the tub, on tiptoes, bare except for a white *dhoti* gathered around his waist as a loincloth, clutching its hem to his groin like a woman who had just seen a mouse. "Please!" he said. "Can you help me? Turn off!"

I reached for the knobs to shut off the water, which was just beginning to stream over the side of the tub.

"No! No! Do not touch!" Swamiji said. "Is too hot!"

As I turned off the cold water and stretched for a washcloth to hold over the hot water knob, it occurred to me that the relentless swami, who would stop at nothing to reorganize the power structure of India, truly had no idea how to solve this simple problem with a bath tap. I shut off the water and left Swamiji contemplating what to do next.

"Thank you," he said as I closed the door. That was the last I ever saw of him.

When I got word from Miles that a second wave of CBI agents was on its way to try to find me, Kim and I blew out of New York in a thirty-two-foot Winnebago.

A rolling safe house, in which we lollygagged our way to Florida, sleeping in state parks and highway rest areas and campgrounds along the way. In Florida, we ditched the mobile home and took up residence in a succession of ill-lit cinder-block motels with names like Briny Breezes and The Beachcomber.

"Vary your normal patterns on the run," Tex had taught me one long ago day in London. "If you're used to flying First Class, fly Coach. If you're used to taking private jets, take a Greyhound. If you're used to staying in grand hotels, stay in dumps. And keep moving until you know you're in a safe place. Then stay put."

It was after the cheap motels, which I didn't feel safe in, that I took up residence on this beach—thinking I'd be here maybe five or six weeks while a deal was struck for my testimony. But in the end, of course, I spent more than a year here before I testified. And during that year, Miles went radio-silent on me one last time. He stayed out of touch for nearly two weeks, during which I left him four or five messages. And then one day I came inside from a swim and found an ominous message on my answering machine: Lorraine sounding brave and efficient and giving me *her* new telephone number. Though I didn't know, I knew. When I called her, Lorraine told me Miles had gone back into The Paddock hospital in terrible pain with another arthritis flare-up. Eventually his heart failed. He died a day before the first American coalition air assault on Baghdad, the beginning of Operation Desert Storm.

I couldn't go to Miles's funeral, and that hurt. I kept thinking of things I wanted to tell him. I wanted to tell him I missed him. I wanted to tell him he'd forgotten to tell me the contingency plan to be executed upon his death or incapacitation. And I think what I really wanted—given how badly fucked and useless I feel here on this beach—was one last pat on the head. I wanted to be sure Miles knew that, in spite of my recent troubles, he'd been right all along in his assessment that I was, in the special language of the secret world he'd helped create, a "well-informed private individual."

How else could you explain two items of unassailable intelligence that wafted down to me, even while I lived on this beach, all the way from Baghdad. First this:

On the opening night of the war, in January 1991, when the skies over Baghdad lit up with tracers and antiaircraft fire and Bernard Shaw described the action to the whole world live on CNN, the first man through the triple-A, the pilot of the lead coalition jet who dropped the first bomb on Baghdad at the start of Operation Desert Storm, was none other than Saudi superhero, fighter jock, and Ambassador of the Kingdom of Saudi Arabia to the United States of America His Royal Highness Bandar bin Sultan al Saud.

And this:

The first President Bush telephoned the leaders of most of the world's major countries twenty-four hours before the start of the air attack to confidentially notify them of when it would begin. Except he didn't call Mikhail Gorbachev until one hour before the attack. And that was because, while he liked and trusted Gorbachev personally, he knew there was a leak somewhere in Gorbachev's inner circle. And sure enough, in the hour before the bombardment began, before Bandar arrived over Baghdad, our intelligence intercepted a warning call to Baghdad from Moscow.

Top-shelf material. Even if, by definition, there were certain parties in Washington already witting of these facts, there were others with the clearance to know, who didn't know. It was gossipy, and not about to change the fate of the world, but just the sort of information Miles would've traded on and dined off for a week in Georgetown and Foggy Bottom. Had he only gotten the chance. In his absence I've waited a suitable interval, more than ten years, before telling anyone.

Of course, by the time I testified behind bulletproof glass in the federal building in Miami, on the very day coalition tanks rolled into Kuwait City just six weeks after Miles died, Frank Morse had made painfully clear to me the rules of evidence and just how little I unequivocally knew about almost anything. So my testimony was brief, and not all that informative. Which, strangely, seemed to be all right with the government of India. This, I believed at the time, was because for V.P. Singh there'd been certain complications.

The Babri Masjid, V.P. Singh's personal Temple of Doom, was a tumbledown mosque in Ayodhya—a dusty Uttar Pradesh village so small its telephone numbers had only two digits. When India was partitioned, nearly all of Ayodhya's Muslims had left for Pakistan. For forty years after that the Babri Masjid was abandoned, chained shut due to lack of interest.

Then a group of Hindu activists decided the little gray mosque stood on the birthplace of the blue-skinned god Rama—the most popular hero of the Hindu pantheon. Hindus went to court and got an order unchaining the mosque's doors. They moved in and redecorated: Out went prayer rugs and Qurans; in went bells, candles, incense pots, saffron-colored flags, and icons of the blue baby. For Muslims, there could be no greater abomination than men bowing down before idols. One famous day in Mecca, the Prophet Muhammad had stormed into the Kabbah and personally smashed the hundreds of idols his tribe had prayed to for centuries. Now, from all across India, pilgrims were flocking to a mosque to prostrate themselves before the graven image of a little blue god.

Battle lines were drawn. Hindus asked a court for a permit to tear down the Babri Masjid and build in its place the Temple of Rama. Muslims asked the court to throw out the holy men who occupied the mosque. The house of worship remained open, but was ringed with concertina wire, steel barricades, sandbags, and hundreds of troops. The Hindu pilgrims who visited had to pass through metal detectors to get in. By court order Muslims were also allowed inside, but none dared.

All that began before V.P. Singh became Prime Minister, but the tension at Ayodhya intensified during his government—mostly due to the fact that the Hindu-fundamentalist BJP party was a key element of the coalition that kept Singh in office. Ten months into his government, the holy men encamped inside the Babri Masjid called a press conference and cordially announced they'd determined the most astrologically auspicious time to begin work there on the new Temple of Rama was between 9:44 o'clock and 11:48 o'clock on the morning of October 30th, 1990. R.S.V. P.

BJP volunteers streamed to Ayodhya, massed outside the Babri Masjid, sharpened swords, daggers, axes, made gasoline bombs, chanted praises to the blue-skinned baby, and made ready to tear down the mosque at the ordained time. Then V.P. Singh did an amazing thing. He sided with the Muslims, point-blank, didn't even leave the Hindus a graceful way out. There will be no Temple of Rama, no Hindu construction whatsoever, at the mosque site, Singh proclaimed. Then he sent thousands of troops to protect the mosque, blocked all roads leading to Ayodhya, and arrested BJP leader L.K. Advani as he attempted to reach the village for a rally.

Advani, it should be noted, was astride a truck, retrofitted and decorated to look like Lord Krishna's chariot from the Hindu epics, in which he had wound his way through India, more than six thousand miles, on his way to Ayodhya. Accompanying Advani along the entire route were native dancers and activists in epic costumes, with loudspeakers blaring Hindu songs. Inside the chariot, Advani received a jar filled with an offering of the blood of a hundred men.

His arrest only increased the BJP's fervor. By 9:44 on the morning of the appointed day, more than a hundred thousand Hindus had massed outside the Babri Masjid. They raised a saffron-colored flag, chanted *Jai Shri Rama!*—Hail Lord Rama!—and stormed the mosque in a screaming cloud of dust. With bricks and rocks and clubs and sheer numbers they overwhelmed the outer ring of defenders. In a mass religious trance they broke down barricades and passed through razor-sharp wire fences without pain. When they reached the Muslim walls they began tearing them down with their bare hands, and then—when the more heavily laden of their brothers got through—with their bare hands and sledgehammers and pickaxes.

The army regrouped and fought back, launched tear gas into the orgy, bashed heads with the butts of Sten rifles, lashed BJP backs with bamboo poles, fired rubber bullets, and, when all that failed, cut down their Hindu brothers with lead. At last light, the Babri Masjid was damaged but intact and back in the army's hands. But by then rioting had spread into several Indian states. When order was finally restored, more than a thousand were dead and the government of V.P. Singh was dying.

Swamiji deployed to Singapore, ready to swoop in to New Delhi the moment Singh fell. The holy man stopped returning my calls. When he happened to answer his phone himself and find me cluttering his line, he got rid of me as fast as he could. "Cannot talk now," he dismissed me. "Chandrashekhar need me. Must call. Goodbye." Click.

Swamiji's tea boy Chandrashekhar called for a no-confidence vote and began a campaign to replace the Prime Minister. Singh searched for a power base but found only the residue of the Faustian bargains he'd made to form his government. On the morning before the vote, Rajiv announced he'd agreed to cooperate with Chandrashekhar. By the time I testified in Miami, Chandrashekhar was the new Prime Minister in India.

I bring this up for two reasons. First, you would think that, with Chandrashekhar as Prime Minister, Swamiji would've been able to get the St. Kitts investigators to stop looking for me. But he didn't and, on the day Frank Morse and I drove through a rainstorm down to the federal building in Miami to give my testimony, our biggest concern was that Swamiji planned to make me his patsy. Second, it's important to understand just what crazy motherfuckers the BJP are.

A year after V.P. Singh's fall, three hundred thousand Hindus surrounded the Babri Masjid, and this time they were not restrained. They swarmed over the mosque and pounded it into rubble. In a country founded on secularism and the nonviolence of the Mahatma Gandhi, a country in which more than a hundred twenty million Muslims reside, BJP allies routinely make speeches such as this one which made it out into the Western press: "Indian Muslims are cancer for this country. Cancer is an incurable disease. Its only cure is operation. O Hindus, take weapons in your hands and remove this cancer from the roots!" Anti-Muslim agitation has been a key to the rise of the BJP, and now, incredibly, they control India, and have developed and tested an arsenal of nuclear missiles. L.K. Advani, the BJP's man in the golden chariot, is now the Deputy Prime Minister of India and among his brethren in the BJP leadership Advani is considered a moderate. It's as if, in the 1960s, the Ku Klux Klan had somehow taken control of the White House, the Justice Department, the Supreme Court, the Pentagon, and the Strategic Air Command. Maybe it's just me, but something tells me we might've been better off in the 1980s and early 1990s keeping our eye on the ball in India and Pakistan rather than devoting so much talent and energy to kicking ass in Nicaragua and El Salvador. And, oh, by the way, it's the BJP that's kept me on this beach for what seems like a thousand extra years now. But I'm getting ahead of myself. There've been so many complications I can barely keep them all straight.

Frank Morse and I were pleasantly surprised by the tenor of my interrogation in Miami. After all the drama of getting me there, the questions seemed perfunctory, carefully framed to close out the investigation. We thought it was over, that I was free to travel the world again. Which was what I planned to do. Except that first I went to Los Angeles to see Muhammad, as I mentioned earlier. Then, when I was about to leave for Europe and Africa, something came up. I went to Las Vegas instead.

You'll probably remember that, in 1984, when I was in the hospital in New York with Muhammad, Jesse Jackson came to visit. I suggested he and Muhammad go downstairs and announce they were forming a ticket to run for President. We went downstairs and, when we got there, I blinked.

When we got there, I blinked, and became, you guessed it: Elvis Presley. An AP photo of Muhammad and Jesse and me ran in newspapers all over the world, and five years later someone reading an old paper noticed that a man in the photo, taken seven years after Elvis Presley's funeral, looked just like Elvis. There I was, frozen in time in a grainy black-and-white image, between Muhammad and Jesse, my face tilted down, my eyes closed, somehow looking so much like the King of Rock-'n'-Roll that Elvis's own stepbrother identified the man in the picture as Elvis.

Soon a forensic scientist who worked for Scotland Yard opined that the photo was not a fake and that, based on biometrics, minute measurements of the facial features of the man in the picture—*my* facial features—compared with known photographs of Elvis's facial features, it was almost certain the man in the picture was Elvis Presley.

Someone found an old interview in which Elvis had said, when he wanted to chill out and get away from his fans, he used to go stay in a cabin owned by his friend Muhammad Ali. From there it wasn't much of a stretch for fans, who'd said for years that Elvis had faked his death, to conclude that Muhammad was harboring the King. The picture appeared on the cover of supermarket tabloids all over the world. "Elvis: Dead or Alive?" became the bestselling videotape at Wal-Mart and the gift shop at Graceland, and guess whose picture was on the box?

Larry King Live devoted an hour to the photo. Fans began waiting outside the gates of Muhammad's farm in Michigan, not for his autograph, but to hand him letters or jars of jam or fried-banana-and-peanut-butter sandwiches. "Give this to the King," they'd say. Commando squads with my picture in their pockets spread out over Muhammad's hundred acres by night, looking for the King. I was the mother of all Elvis sightings, and things were getting out of hand. So I went to Las Vegas and—live from the Elvis Stage in the highest-rated prime-time special of that year—I was the mystery guest, the man in the picture, to be interviewed by Bill Bixby.

Backstage, I peeked through the curtains, and the place was filling up with crazies expecting the second coming of Elvis. But I went out and announced to my millions of new fans that I am not Elvis Presley, and please stay out of Muhammad's barns.

How can I make sense of that? I can't. But I can distill from the experience these two observations useful to my unified theory. First, biometrics and digital facial recognition technology, then and now, have a long way to go. If you think we're going to keep known terrorists outside our borders using biometrics, think again. Second, appearing live on a television special aired around the world isn't a good idea for an international fugitive.

Of course, I'd done it only because I hadn't known I was still wanted. The night of the broadcast happened to be Bill Bixby's birthday, and that of Joe Esposito, Elvis's best friend going all the way back to when the King was robbing the cradle at my junior high school in Wiesbaden. Joe appeared on the show after me, and later we all went out to dinner and then out on the town. I seem to remember Joe putting me on the phone to Colonel Tom Parker around midnight, and most of the rest of that night has faded now to a blur of neon and really-long limos and a troupe of Elvis impersonators who arrived from somewhere to congratulate me, and ask me, "How'd you do it, man?"

When I finally rolled out of bed the next afternoon and went downstairs, I immediately saw I had a problem. Stepping out of an elevator onto the casino floor, I scanned the crowd, the whole crowd first, before any individuals. What I was looking for was any reaction to me, and what I saw was: at eleven o'clock, and perfectly positioned to see everyone coming and going from the elevator bank, an Indian muscleman with crow-black hair and a mustache, wearing a white shirt, a black tie, and a black leather jacket, the kind that's cut like a suit coat; and, at two o'clock and a little farther back, ready to pick up anyone who came out of the elevators and headed toward the front door, another fit young Indian, in a white V-neck sweater, with three gold chains around his neck; and, at ten o'clock, behind a little cloud of cigarette smoke, perfectly situated to cut off anyone heading toward the back door, and turning away from me now, trying not to meet my eyes, the little pink-faced Indian fucker I'd last seen in the Hunt Bar in the Helmsley Palace in New York. A friend of the Research and Analysis Wing, Miles had said. Ganduji.

It's all about escape routes, I heard Tex telling me.

These guys looked serious. Bore no resemblance, in style, or purpose, or competence, to Deputy Director A. P. Nandey. I didn't lock eyes with any one of them. Or turn and run. Instead I kept walking out of the elevator bank, and then patted my chest anxiously like I was looking for my wallet. And then I stopped and patted both sides of the top of my suit jacket again, and swore at myself, and turned around and stepped into an elevator. Which I rode to the floor above mine, and then took three stairs at a time on my way back down to my room.

Being an international celebrity now, I wasn't registered in my own name. And the TV production company I was there for had about twenty rooms on several floors on its tab. I assumed the Indians didn't know yet what room I was staying in. But also that, if I didn't go back downstairs again soon, they'd start finding out.

I feel calm remembering it now, but I wasn't then. I remember my heart was pounding hard while I decided what to do. I had a friend named John who'd driven in from California to see me. He was on his own tab. Not on a list of rooms I could be traced to. I grabbed my suitcase and every piece of paper I'd written on and went by the stairs to his room. He was holding a four-inch stack of five-hundred-dollar chips when he opened the door.

"Good work, old boy," I said. "Now let me in. And chain the door behind me."

Next a little charade.

I sent John downstairs, first to a pay phone to ring the hotel and ask them to page Mr. Larry Kolb in the casino. That was to perk up the ears of everyone down there looking for me. Then John—who I knew would do a good job because he was a bullshit artist extraordinaire, he was a movie executive for God's sake—went to a house phone right behind the little Indian dandy, to talk over a dial tone, while pretending to call me and loudly tell me he'd booked me onto a Delta flight that evening, and that a limo would pick me up in the parking garage at six-forty to take me to the airport.

And, at six thirty-seven, by my watch, after John had loaded his stuff and mine into his DeLorean, and had made relatively sure no Indians were following him, at just about the same time that in the parking garage on the other side of the hotel a limo driver was holding a sign that said "Mr. Kolb" and a porter was putting a bag stuffed with newspapers into the limo and telling the driver Mr. Kolb would be there shortly—I walked right out the front door of the casino in the middle of a small crowd, knees bent slightly to make me a lit- tle shorter, and stepped straight into John's car, which was idling on the Strip with a wing door open, and off we drove. Quite demurely, until we hit the desert, where John floored it and took me to a small airport. From which I chartered a single-engine plane to fly me to Phoenix feeling like a thief in the night. It took all the cash I had on me, and John had on him, but I wasn't about to use a credit card. Cash leaves no trail. The pilot gave me a break because he'd seen me on TV the night before.

By the time I made it back to Florida, I'd had plenty of time to turn over in my head half a dozen conflicting theories of what was going on, and why—and the only thing I was certain of was that somehow Swamiji was behind this. Probably looking to lay his guilt off on me.

I called Frank. He said he didn't get it. What the fuck was I talking about, Indians after me in Las Vegas? Elvis Presley sightings? Maybe he thought I was joking. Or drunk. It seemed obvious to me what the Indians were up to. They were going to frame me. My testimony had been just a preliminary round for gathering information to be woven into the epic story of Larry Kolb the master criminal who tried to corrupt India. Forgers were probably on the job already.

"Whatever they're trying to do," Frank said eventually, "it's going to take them awhile. If they do it through the courts and treaties, it won't be fast. I'll look into extradition procedures between the United States and India. Hang tight."

Kim was still in Africa, so I had no one to talk to except our cats. I fed myself and the cats. I dialed Dr. Channa's New Delhi number several times, but he didn't answer. I wanted to call Miles. I've rarely had trouble sleeping. But that night I was a full-blown insomniac. I read until the alphabet began to swim around the page, but I couldn't doze off. I stared at the ceiling and then looked at the clock on my nightstand. Three-fourteen. The last time I'd looked it had been three-twelve. What the fuck is Chandrashekhar up to? I rolled over and punched my pillow. Not quite. I punched it again. Why now? I stared at the ceiling for half an hour. My chest got hot so I pushed down the comforter. It got cold so I pulled the comforter back up. I rearranged my legs. I looked at the clock. Three-eighteen.

I got up and opened a window. Moonlight shone on the water. Somewhere frogs were droning. I got back into bed. The last of the cats who'd been trying to sleep on the bed gave up and left indignantly for another room. I tried reading again, but the words wouldn't stay in line. I went downstairs to the kitchen, while picturing a joint CBI-RAW task force arriving in Miami, stone cold sober, to hunt me down. Back in bed, I wondered if Swamiji had had a falling-out with Chandrashekhar. Tea boys could get mighty uppity when they became heads of state, I imagined. Or were Swamiji and Chandrashekhar now running the St. Kitts investigation themselves? I thought myself into a dark box I couldn't think myself out of.

Three forty-six. Eight forty-six in London.

Miles was dead, but I still had friends. I called one, from MI6, and around noon, my time, while I was finally sleeping, he called me back and told me he'd checked around, as I'd requested, and he'd found out the Indian authorities had lodged an Interpol Red Notice against me. "Larry, I'm afraid there *is* a problem with any movement at the moment, especially across any border, and

I don't know how we get round it," he said, sounding apologetic and embarrassed at once. Like he was the one who'd done it to me, regretfully, and he'd be there now to help me through it. Quite the winning bedside manner for a spymaster. I still have it all on tape.

For the next few months it felt like I had a low-grade fever.

But suddenly things got better. Chandrashekhar's government collapsed, thanks in part to Swamiji. Two days before he submitted his resignation, Prime Minister Chandrashekhar stood awkwardly before Parliament and announced that two constables, officially on leave from the police of Haryana state, had been arrested for spying outside Rajiv's house. In the great Nixonian tradition, Chandrashekhar promised a thorough, unbiased investigation into the matter and punishment of everyone involved.

But lawyers for the arrested policemen soon complained that just hours after the arrests, without interrogation, the government had forced their clients to sign confessions they hadn't even read. Then it emerged that the espionage campaign against Rajiv was entirely political in scope, was run by the general secretary of the Janata Dal, Chandrashekhar's party, and that on the day of the arrests the general secretary was in London staying with Swamiji at Claridges.

Rajiv smelled a cover-up, and announced that his entire Congress party would boycott Parliament until acceptable action was taken on the spying case. The next day, Chandrashekhar resigned.

I heard about that all at once, on the morning after Chandrashekhar quit. India was plunging into a nearly perpetual state of political chaos. Chandrashekhar was the third Indian Prime Minister to fall in the last seventeen months.

Indian President Venkataraman, a figurehead without much in the way of real power except in times such as these, asked Chandrashekhar to stay on as caretaker Prime Minister until another election could be held. That meant he got to keep the nice big office a few more months, and Swamiji's tea boy eagerly agreed.

The analyses I read over the next few months said the general election would be a three-horse race between Congress, the BJP, and an alliance between the Janata Dal and the Communist Party. Everyone said Rajiv was going to win, and suddenly India was the magical place I'd always loved until St. Kitts. I had visions of sitting once again before the Taj Mahal, and riding elephants, and dancing girls, and selling an entire fleet of 747s. I even called Rajiv's office and made plans to visit him not long after the election. What was that verse from Sunday school again? *Pride goeth before destruction, and a haughty spirit before a fall.*

The election would be spread over a week, with voting in different parts of India on three separate days, to allow the movement of more than a million troops between polling sites in an attempt to limit violence. More than a hundred people had already been killed during the campaign. The Indian security services feared a whole lot more would die before the election was over.

Late one hot, bright morning, I was reading *The New York Times* and sipping iced tea in my study. On the front page was a picture of Rajiv. He had a half-smile on his face as he dropped his vote into a ballot box on the first day of polling. I'd made my way into the Sports section when my phone rang, and it was my mother calling. There was something almost frantic in her voice, "Are you sitting down?"

"Yes," I said. "What's wrong?"

"I just saw on CNN that they murdered Rajiv. With a bomb. They blew his head off. At a campaign rally. In South India."

Fuck!

I turned on Headline News. It said Rajiv had been killed, apparently by a bomb, during a campaign rally near Madras. No further information was available yet.

All that afternoon and evening, while my phone kept ringing with people telling me Rajiv was dead, I watched television wanting more details. But all I learned was that Rajiv and several others had been killed by a bomb just after he arrived to give a speech at an evening rally in the town of Sriperumbudur in the southern state of Tamil Nadu. Mobs were rioting in New Delhi now, and the Indian military was on Red Alert.

I went to bed thinking about the last time I saw Rajiv, that quick meeting in New Delhi. He'd sent me to No. 1, Safdarjung Road, his mother's house. On a gray path in the garden where I met her, the chalk outline of her body. The little piles of flower petals. And then for some reason my mind drifted to Bill Tharp and the death of his friend Chi Chi Remon. I'd turned Bill down, but somehow slipped anyway into the life I set out to avoid. Now my friend Rajiv was dead.

I barely slept that night, and before dawn I went downstairs to watch the news and read the papers. A week of national mourning in India had been declared and the remainder of the elections were postponed until June. On my television screen, Rajiv's wife Sonia and their daughter Priyanka arrived in New Delhi with his body. Prime Minister Chandrashekhar met them at the airport.

Sonia I hardly knew. I doubted she even remembered my name—unless she'd read it recently in some scandalous Indian press report. For a while there, I'd been quite the whipping boy in the Indian yellow press. I'd shaken Sonia's hand once, or greeted her by folding my hands—a namaskar. That was all. But I'd liked her immediately. Not only because of the sly smile she gave me but also because Rajiv had told me she was quite handy in the kitchen. In 1977, when the Janata Dal had first, and ever so briefly, succeeded in defeating the House of Nehru, and police arrived to arrest Indira at the house she shared with her sons Sanjay and Rajiv and their wives, Indira delayed a search of the house by posing for press photographers on her verandah while loudly demanding that the police handcuff her. Meanwhile Sonia took charge in the kitchen, shredding documents with a noodle-cutting machine she'd brought from Italy. Or at least that was what Rajiv had told me, and I'd always felt a special affection for her because of it. Sonia Gandhi. Widow.

In *The New York Times,* I finally got a sense of what had happened.

Rajiv rode to his last rally in a little Ambassador car, smiling and waving to adoring crowds, shaking hands and accepting garlands through the windows.

Rajiv got out of the car and plunged into a crowd of well-wishers. He was making his way to a platform to deliver a speech when he was consumed in a blinding flash. All that was left of him were his feet and a little piece of his head. At least a dozen others were killed around him. Bodies, and parts of bodies, fell in a bloody circle around the epicenter of the blast—the spot where Rajiv last stood. He was smiling, leaning forward to accept a garland around his neck, when a beatific little girl holding a ring of flowers and wearing a belt of plastic explosives killed them all. In India, politics is a blood sport.

As yet no one had claimed responsibility for the assassination. But mobs raging through New Delhi, Bombay, and Calcutta blamed the CIA. The Indian Government's chief suspects were the Sikh separatists, who'd gunned down Rajiv's mother and since declared war on the Congress party, and militant Tamil separatists—who were active around Madras and had a history of using bombs as assassination weapons.

On television, I saw thousands of mourners in line outside Teen Murti House in New Delhi—waiting to enter to pay their last respects to my friend. What little remained of Rajiv was wrapped in a shroud and lay in state under a large photograph of him. In the photograph, Rajiv was wearing a garland.

Another dead friend whose funeral I couldn't attend.

Rajiv was cremated at Shantivana, the sacred spot on the bank of the Jamuna River where his grandfather Jawaharlal Nehru, and his mother Indira Gandhi, and, before them, Mahatma Gandhi, were also cremated. Of the four of them, only one had not been murdered.

Heads of state and diplomats and a sea of Indians watched in person as Hindu priests in flowing white robes helped Rajiv's twenty-year-old son Rahul light a sandalwood stick and circle the body nine times, touching the flame to his father's head each time he passed it. When the ninth circle was completed, he lit the body. Then Sonia and Priyanka joined Rahul to cover Rajiv's body with sandalwood logs and sprinkle flowers and cloves and fruits and ghee on the pyre. Priests chanted while hundreds of mourners circled the body and added offerings to the flames. I scanned the crowd for Swamiji or Adnan, but didn't see them. The television cut to a tight shot of just the pyre and Rajiv's family, standing together, staring into the flames, watching everything Rajiv ever was or dreamed of being vanish in curling wisps of smoke.

Fuck!

I didn't used to swear as much before I washed up here. If it offends you, please accept my apology. Probably, I imagine, I swear more now because I used to spend more time in polite society than circumstances have allowed me recently; I can't remember wearing shoes anytime in the last few months. Or maybe it's just because I'm really pissed off at my circumstances.

That very night was when I started digging in. Now that my departure from this house no longer seemed imminent, as it always had before, there were some home improvements I wanted to make. Involving walls and a gun and Krugerrands and escape routes, as I believe I related to you earlier. Or maybe I didn't. Fuck it. I'm so tired of remembering all this and writing it down. After Rajiv's death, for months at a time, I felt not fear but dread. A relentless, numbing dread that attached itself to me moments after I awoke, and that I could never quite shake.

I spent most of my time inside this house, my redoubt; or out on the beach. My telephones were listed and billed in the name of a corporation. When I did go out, and unimaginative people insisted on my business card, I yielded one which gave just a name and phone and fax numbers in New York and Rio de Janeiro. To communicate with friends, Kim and I used a Palm Beach answering service at first, and then a voicemailbox. I returned calls. I never answered my phones unless the caller knew the signal. The nearest bank in which I kept an account was three counties away. I never used a credit card. My cars were leased by corporations. On the road, in town, on the beach, everywhere I went, I watched for watchers. My father would've been proud of me. Or would he? The Indian muck into which I'd fallen was sucking me down.

Eventually Swamiji was suspected of being behind Rajiv's assassination, paying for it in fact. But he was not charged. The Jain Commission, sort of India's Warren Commission, which investigated Rajiv's murder, said it was the work of a Tamil terrorist group, the LTTE—the Liberation Tigers of Tamil Eelam. Which is not to say Swamiji didn't benefit in a way from Rajiv's death. It's been said that, had Rajiv become Prime Minister again, Swamiji would've slunk out of India, lickety-split. But, recently, someone I trust has told me that, in those last few months of Rajiv's life, Swamiji and Rajiv had patched things up, were friends again. Regardless, when the election was completed, and Rajiv's Congress party won handily, his replacement as party leader, Narasimha Rao, became the new Prime Minister of India. Rao was even more of a devotee of Swamiji than Chandrashekhar had ever been.

When Rao's government finally fell five years later, it was over Swamiji. That, as my father could've pointed out to you, was clearly part of a pattern of Indian governments falling over Swamiji. For years the CBI had been investigating him for all sorts of things, St. Kitts included. But in the last weeks before the first Indian national elections since the one that killed Rajiv, Rao finally succumbed to pressure and allowed the CBI to arrest the holy man on charges he'd swindled an Indian pickle manufacturer out of a mere hundred thousand dollars many years earlier. For months, opposition leaders had so relentlessly accused Prime Minister Rao of protecting his friend that finally he had to let the arrest happen.

Swamiji didn't go quietly. As the cries for his arrest grew louder, he did what he does best, one king-hell of a magic trick, a diversion. Perhaps you caught his act. Or read about it, as I did. Swamiji's Great Ganpati Milk Frenzy got coverage worldwide.

No one was quite sure where it all started. Mumbai? New Delhi? Calcutta? Madras? But somehow Swamiji allowed word to get out that stone idols of the god Ganesh, the elephant god, were drinking milk offered to them by worshipers in temples all across India. The rumor spread like wildfire. Hindus thronged temples to see for themselves. Prominent citizens swore they'd witnessed the miracle. "Ganeshji drank the milk!" Scientists called it absurd. Vans with loudspeakers circled temples trying to disperse the crowds, telling the people it wasn't true. But, no, even when skeptics went to see, they agreed: The stone idols really did seem to be drinking the milk. Touch a spoonful lovingly to the little idol's mouth, and the liquid slowly disappeared. It was the damnedest thing. Amazing.

Long, serpentine queues, congeries of true believers formed outside temples all across India, to give offerings to the god. Traffic ground to a halt. Schools closed early. Police leaves were canceled. So many people wanted in on the act that milkmen were running out of milk. Within a day, the chaos spread to temples in Los Angeles, London, Dubai, all over the earth.

Then a new rumor started moving through the temples. "It's Chandraswami's miracle! Our god Ganesh is drinking the milk for Chandraswami!" When contacted at his ashram by reporters, the humble holy man shyly allowed that, yes, on the day it had all started, during his morning prayers he had "invoked god Ganesha" for help. And he added, "This is only the beginning!"

For the next few months, demands for Swamiji's arrest were lost in the mass ecstasy and the Godman's glory. And how did he make it happen? It's simple physics, actually. Capillary action—which I learned about in grade school, and I suppose Swamiji did too. But in spite of his devotees in high places and his proven talents for inspiring the masses, eventually the CBI arrested Swamiji, and then his henchman Mammaji, and charged them with defrauding the Indian pickle and chutney king of London. When all the ruckus Swamiji made in the process was over, the Congress party had lost control of India and the BJP was in power.

India's new Hindu-fundamentalist government tested a nuclear bomb, kicked a lot of Muslim ass, launched a new investigation into Swamiji's role in Rajiv's murder, and repudiated the deal its predecessors had made regarding me. Three times India requested my extradition, and three times the United States Government refused to extradite me to India. The unseen hand. Swamiji, Mammaji, and Narasimha Rao were all arrested on St. Kitts conspiracy charges. Three key witnesses in the government's St. Kitts case died—A.P. Nandey, George McLean, Ernie Miller. Miller, just a week before he was supposed to give his deposition. A trial date was set. Indian prosecutors went into the trial court and said they had no evidence against me and the charges against me should be dismissed. But the Supreme Court of India intervened, said no.

And so I've wound up back where I began, a man on a beach, hiding and waiting, trying to make sense of it all, longing to fly away. If I traveled due east from here, the first point of land I'd reach is Morocco. After that—Algeria, Libya, Egypt, Saudi Arabia, Iran, Pakistan, and then India. In fact, I was surprised to discover recently that my beach and the capital of India are on virtually identical latitudes. I stand on the shore behind my house and stare out across the ocean toward New Delhi, where the trial in the curious matter of the St. Kitts Affair is finally under way.

EPILOGUE

I look out over the black beach. In a few minutes I'll be able to discern between the black ocean and the almost black sky. Then strips of orange cloud will appear out over the water and the stars will melt away. In the palmettos, birds will begin to chitter and sing, and out on the sand a great blue heron will arrive from his roost in the tall trees on the other side of my house.

My kitchen is filling up with smells of coffee and buttered toast and fresh-sliced mangoes, and soon its bare white walls will be covered with slats of golden light. Or will they be pink today? On certain mornings the shadows are pale and blue and the kitchen wall glows as pink as a rose.

I close my briefcase and sip my coffee.

If our lives had all the perfection of a novel, my story would've ended with Rajiv's death and I never would've known this place so well. But human lives are anything but perfect. There are always loose ends, complications, unexpected currents.

So this house has for several years now been the property of a Panamanian corporation, whose only address is a post office box in Panama, and whose only shareholders, officers, and directors of record are a pair of nominee attorneys, both named Franco, of the venerable and eponymous firm Franco & Franco, attorneys and secret keepers.

I haven't heard from Swamiji in years—not since he left me four urgent messages asking me to call him at a number in Houston. I didn't return his calls. But a few weeks later I called Dev, who told me Swamiji had gone to Houston for the Republican National Convention as a guest of Neil Bush, son of the President. That was 1992. Did the amazing swami meet and charm George Bush, the elder or the younger? The answer lies inside a thick gray photo album I hope I never see again.

Dev said Swamiji was eager to talk to me because I was the last witness necessary to clear his name in the St. Kitts investigation. Soon thereafter, the U.S. Attorney's office in New York contacted me, and then the State Department, and then the U.S. Attorney's office in Miami. None of them knew where to find me; they reached me through my attorneys. Indian investigators arrived in the United States expecting to interrogate me again, but went home without a glimpse of me.

I butter another piece of toast, slather on some marmalade. Might as well use it all up. I hope it's rancid by the time I see this jar again.

Today is the first day I've worn a suit since the day several months ago when I sneaked out of town to have dinner with Muhammad. He was fine and in good spirits. Looking older, but aren't we all? During my tenure on this beach, Muhammad lit the Olympic flame in Atlanta, and he finally went to Vietnam—on a goodwill mission, just one of many he's undertaken. Blessed are the peacemakers. Anymore, I dream of Muhammad more often than I actually see him. So much has happened since I came here. There's plenty of evidence the world is moving on without me. The Soviet Union disappeared. A great comet came and hung in the sky for weeks for us to marvel at. A woman in New York gave birth to a son, a prince, I suppose, reportedly fathered by His Holiness Chandraswami Maharaj. Bill Clinton became our President, followed by George W. Bush. And, more recently, four American airliners were quite ingeniously turned into flying bombs directed from mission control in a cave in Afghanistan.

That faint sucking sound you heard beneath all the cheering and the martial music while the hammer-and-sickle flag was lowered for the last time in Red Square was the power vacuum created when the Soviet empire collapsed. We live now in an asymmetrical world. The mighty Soviet Union was brought down not by American might, but more than anything else by two stubborn men from Poland and that tent full of Afghan elders I met with Muhammad at the Khyber Pass. America backed them, it's true. And now all the training in tactics and tradecraft, demolition and insurgency we gave the mujahideen and their Muslim brothers, and the guns and bombs and shoulder-fired missiles we passed out to them, are deployed against us.

So much has happened since I came here.

Adnan lost his ranch in Marbella, *La Baraka*—which is Arabic for "good fortune." He's still at work, though, rebuilding, making deals. Four years after his trial, he made it back onto the front page of *The Wall Street Journal,* when he and an Israeli partner, a former Mossad officer, announced that, in cooperation with the World Bank and private investors, they'd put together five hundred million dollars in funding for development projects in Gaza and the West Bank, to be jointly owned by Arabs and Israelis. I don't see all that much of Adnan anymore, but we speak every once in awhile. He carries a cell phone that works almost everywhere, and usually when I call him he seems to be in Saudi Arabia or London or France. He lives mostly in Cannes these days. A couple years ago, Kim and I had Christmas dinner with him here in Florida. Adnan still believes the key to lasting Mideast peace lies in economics, and I can't say he's wrong.

Forty years ago, Adnan began telling the West the underlying problems of the Middle East are the whole world's problems. Back then, to most Americans those problems seemed a world away. Now they know better, and are more inclined to listen. But is it too late? Adnan doesn't think so.

Roger Tamraz became an American citizen. Even started pronouncing the *r* at the end of his first name. American immigrants dream big, and Roger was no exception. Roger's dream was to build an oil pipeline from the Caspian Sea port of Baku in Azerbaijan, through Nakhichivan, Nagorno Karabakh, Armenia, and Turkey to the Mediterranean. This, Roger argued, would significantly decrease American dependence on Arab oil, and would take control of the vast Azerbaijani oil reserves out of the hands of the Russians. For at the moment it is Russian pipelines the Azerbaijani output flows through. But Big Oil, in the form of a consortium between Amoco and BP, had a different plan in mind— and had paid an army of Washington power brokers to convince the State Department and the National Security Council to back their plan.

So Roger exercised his constitutional right to have his business proposal personally considered and endorsed by the President of the United States. Roger did this by donating three hundred thousand dollars to the Democratic National Committee, and soon he was having coffee with President Clinton in the White House. Roger explained his project to the President, who seemed interested, and later Roger discussed the plan in detail with White House Chief of Staff Mac McLarty. McLarty gave his tentative thumbs-up on the plan, and Roger became a frequent visitor to the White House.

Which turned into quite a stink when the Republicans got wind of it. The Senate Governmental Affairs Committee subpoenaed Roger to appear before it to answer charges that he'd contributed to the DNC to attempt to influence U.S. policy toward Central Asia. I don't know what level of contrition they were expecting, but, when Roger appeared, he was calm and unapologetic. I watched it live on C-SPAN, and saw the highlights again later on all the networks and in the newspapers.

For a time, Roger became quite the media darling because he spoke the plain truth.

He said it was all true, and that he'd done nothing wrong, this is how the system works in our country. "Look," he told the senators, "when it comes to money and politics, *you* make the rules." When they asked him if he was frustrated that his attempts had failed, he said, "I've been in much worse positions in my life," and he reminded them he'd once been kidnapped, poisoned, tortured, beaten, and held hostage in Lebanon and that he was happy now to be an American citizen free to dream big and act on his dreams. When they asked him if he'd learned a lesson from this, he said, "I think next time I'll give six hundred thousand dollars."

The senators gave up when they realized they couldn't lay a glove on him, and, worse, that the American public was getting a civics lesson it didn't need. Roger went home to New York, to dream.

Daniel never regained the presidency of Nicaragua. He's lost two elections so far. But still leads the Sandinistas in opposition in the national assembly. We've spoken by phone. A few years ago, a couple of right-wing senators enlisted me to serve as a back channel to engage in confidential discussions with Daniel. It was great talking to him again. I did not confess.

Mike Timpani vanished on me, which wasn't unusual. But this time he stayed missing for quite a while. We'd stayed in touch and spoken often while Mike was in Kuwait and Baghdad, working for the Kuwaiti royal family—his mission, which he accomplished: planning and running an operation to recover from Baghdad the Kuwaiti crown jewels and gold bars and certain other assets Saddam Hussein had stolen from Kuwait. "Sounds like fun," I told Mike. "Count me in." But Mike said he needed guys slightly more accustomed than I to dressing all in black, including balaclava hoods, and with demonstrated proficiency in night optics, flash-bang entry, and throat-slicing. So I didn't see Mike again until he went to work, at least officially, for the United Nations, where he said his job was advising them on the safety of their aviation operations. His office was in the United Nations Building in New York, and he lived in an apartment a few blocks away. We drank some wine together one night in midtown, and Mike really seemed to love New York.

But the next time I heard from him, he'd moved to Singapore, where officially he was working for an aviation services company based at an airport used exclusively by executive jets and military aircraft. When he went missing, I heard from a mutual acquaintance of ours that, though he was nominally based in Singapore, Mike was actually spending most of his time in Cambodia. Doing what, they wouldn't say. But that was about the time Pol Pot was run to ground and put under house arrest. Funny how Mike always seemed to be in or around the hot spots.

On MacDill Air Force Base, in Tampa, Florida—where my father once arrested a maintenance crew chief who'd been sabotaging B-26s—there's a Covert Operations Memorial Wall styled after the Vietnam Veterans Memorial in Washington, D.C. And that was where I finally found Mike, or at least his name. He died, I am told, in 1998. Though part of me still harbors a suspicion Mike is alive and spending his nights in a dark and highly sophisticated helicopter flying through canyons in Afghanistan, I've learned enough now to accept that that isn't so.

Mike lived in the secret world that's all around us. Even right here in the United States. Where secret wars are fought in the shadows, just out of view. If you've ever doubted that, look at what you saw of the fighting over the outcome of the 2000 presidential election. That was just the tip, not the whole iceberg. What we saw was ugly. But you can bet that what we weren't allowed to see was uglier.

For the benefit of conspiracy theorists, I should mention here Adnan's stewardess Theresa LePore, whom you may remember from my descriptions of certain flights on Adnan's DC-9. Theresa went on to fame and glory as the Palm Beach County Elections Commissioner. She was the designer of the butterfly ballot which gave the presidency to the son of Adnan's old friend the first President Bush. Adnan has been involved in nearly every major American political scandal since the Second World War. I doubt he had anything to do with the election, but we'll never know. Miles taught me not to believe in coincidences.

For the further benefit of conspiracy theorists, I should also mention that packed in one of my two suitcases, which stand now just inside the front door, is a postcard from Dodi's aunt which Kim and I received here on the morning after his death. It ends: *Adnan's locked in a room in France and the world's press is waiting for his words and mine on Dodi who may well marry Di. When they have a kid, your brothers and sister will have the same blood as Princes W and H!* That, I suppose, had to be very disconcerting to certain people.

I'm not the sort to automatically disbelieve every conspiracy theory I hear, and you wouldn't be either if you'd seen what I've seen. But I've also spent plenty of time in cars chased by photographers, and it is dangerous. I'd hate to think Dodi and Diana were murdered, but we'll never know. There's a secret world all around us.

A couple years ago, Kim's youngest sister, Octavia, was on her way to a little town in Africa to spend her gap year teaching English in a mission. Maybe you heard about it. Approaching Nairobi, the British Airways 747 Octavia and three hundred ninety-seven others were aboard dived three miles in a few seconds when a man forced his way into the cockpit and tried to crash the plane. The cabin lights went out, the passengers were screaming and bouncing off the walls and ceiling, and everyone on board thought they were going to die. Until the crew and a few passengers overpowered the madman, pulled the plane out of its death spiral with only a couple of seconds to spare, kicked the shit out of the asshole who'd tried to kill them, and tied him to a seat.

That was the end of Octavia's year as a teacher in Africa. I'm sure she'd spent months thinking of the place she was going, a little town called George.

She'd seen photographs of the town and of the school where she'd be teaching. Probably, she'd already spent so much time imagining the land, the town, the school, the quarters she would live in, and what it would feel like standing up in front of her class, that, in her mind at least, she already knew the place where she would spend the next year. In a certain way, she was already there. Then, in less than a minute, everything changed. Octavia decided to go home to London, and she never saw the place she'd dreamed of.

Our lives are wildly contradictory and fundamentally uncertain. I thought I'd never stop traveling. I could've never imagined spending ten years living on this beach. But here I am. Charged with substantive offences under Sections 120, 182, 193, 218, 465, 468, 469, 471, and 500 of the Indian Penal Code, as amended. These equate essentially to forgery, conspiracy to commit forgery, and attempting to use a forgery for my own gain and to harm another.

Notwithstanding the expert lessons in forgery Miles gave me one day in Oxfordshire—with the exception of stacks of photographs one of my clients required me to autograph for her when I was just starting as a sports agent, and a note to my junior high school principal in which, in the guise of my mother, I explained that my son Larry had been sick and therefore absent from school the previous day—I've never forged anything. As to conspiring to forge, if The First Trust Corporation documents I brought to light were forged, they were forged before I ever laid eyes on them. I'd like to tell this to the Indians who would like to arrest me. But, of course, I already told them once, under oath, and since then I'm just not convinced they're looking to winnow falsehood from truth.

So this beach is where I live, and have lived for way too long now.

Apparently I'm not the only one who came here looking to escape from the covert world I was born into, thought I could leave, still want to leave.

You may remember a certain tall, blond American spy—the American Air Attaché to Finland—who was a friend of my father, until the attaché happened to be spied dancing in a gay bar in Helsinki with a Russian agent. The last I'd heard he'd been bundled into an Air Force cargo plane and flown to Washington in a hurry. He was forced into early retirement from the Air Force.

And where did he go from there? To this beach. Where he lives today, not five miles from me. How do I know? My mother told me.

Her house, the house my father bought when he retired, is only about an hour away from mine. If there's been any blessing in this exile I've lived through, it's that it's given me a chance to see more of my mother in these last years. Near her home, there's a base pharmacy where she's been entitled to fill her prescriptions for free because of my father's years of military service. She told me she ran into the former attaché and his wife one day in that pharmacy.

They didn't talk much, my mother said, because it was awkward. But they did tell her where they live.

On the mainland, just across the causeway from my mother's house is a Publix supermarket, where I've stopped often with her to buy her groceries on our way back from our many trips to her doctors' appointments. One of the baggers, an old guy, almost as old as my mother, used to get my attention and make me sad, because, as he seemed to tell everyone he helped out to their cars with their groceries, he was a retired U.S. Army colonel, after all, only sacking to help make ends meet.

I tried to give him big tips. Until he was arrested and became the highest-ranking American military officer ever charged with espionage.

His name, it turned out, was George Trofimoff. He was born to Russian parents, joined the U.S. Army just after the Second World War, and became a naturalized U.S. citizen three years later. His job for the U.S. Army was de-briefing defectors and refugees from the Soviet bloc. But over twenty-five years he also delivered more than fifty thousand pages of classified documents to his KGB handler, a cardinal in the Russian Orthodox church. He was caught be-cause of information that leaked out of the Lubyanka after the Soviet Union collapsed. According to documents produced at his trial, KGB chief Yuri An-dropov called Trofimoff the Soviet Union's single most productive intelligence agent.

He was tried and convicted, and sentenced to life in prison. George Trofi-moff, KGB agent, my grocery bagger.

But he wasn't the only shuffleboard player around here with a dark secret.

There was also John Forrester Gedney. Mr. Gedney retired recently after more than twenty sober years as a code inspector, inspecting houses, like mine, for compliance with building codes. You may have heard his name in the movie *J.F.K.*, or read it in a book. For, as Mr. Gedney announced, and proved, last year, he was one of the three railway tramps arrested behind the grassy knoll in Dallas on November 22, 1963. He was the tall one in the grainy, mys-terious photograph used so often by conspiracy theorists as evidence that the CIA and other dark forces were behind the assassination of our president.

Gedney shared a cell block with Lee Harvey Oswald. Unlike Oswald, Ged-ney made it out alive. He spent the next several years on muscatel, but then cleaned his life up, moved here, and became a model citizen. He could've cleared the mystery of the railway tramps up a lot earlier, Gedney said, when he finally broke his silence. But he was just too damned embarrassed to admit to the fine people of his community he was once a wino and a bum, and not a trigger man for the CIA.

My kitchen wall is turning pink. I look at my watch.

There's just enough time for one more cup of coffee. If I drink it fast, and keep remembering, I won't have time to reconsider what I've been planning.

When the trial began in India, I went native on this beach. That tall man in a Hawaiian shirt with wild hair and a wilder beard and a tan you passed last year on the beach, that was me. That short-haired guy in the geek glasses and a nondescript gray car you noticed last month in the turn lane beside you while you waited for a traffic light outside the surf shop, that was me too. That clean-cut guy you saw running up and down the same stretch of beach every day for a couple of months four years ago—also me.

All over India, the BJP still pushes its platform of Hindu nationalism, to the exclusion of anyone not so fervent. Hindu-Muslim rioting has become an electoral tool, used to stir up the hostility of the Hindu majorities before state elections that take place around the country from time to time. Nothing else gets out the vote quite like torching Muslim neighborhoods. Meanwhile, the rump of the Indian secular state refuses to allow Hindus to construct a Temple of Rama on the Ayodhya killing ground, where the Babri Masjid once stood, until a court has decided on the matter. *Jai Shri Rama!* is still the battle cry. Tensions are high, and the court is dithering.

Nothing in India moves quickly. In New Delhi, holy cows and elephants roam the streets, snarling traffic, as they always have. But now a plague of monkeys, rhesus macaques, has descended on the beautiful complex of colon-naded buildings that form the seat of the Indian government. By night, the monkeys tear down power and telephone lines, overrun offices, ransack files, shit in the corners. In the mornings, they're escorted outside, where they screech at visitors, hang from window ledges, and pound on office windows. The lawmakers and jurists and bureaucrats who work there own the day, barely. But the monkeys own the night, and have become increasingly brazen pickpockets and lunchbox thieves by day. The Supreme Court of India has de-creed that New Delhi is to be a monkey-free city. But certain Hindus believe the monkeys in the halls of power are manifestations of the monkey god Hanuman, so they feed them and pray to them, and plans to relocate the mon-keys to forests outside the city are going nowhere fast.

All of which perhaps explains the continuing delays in the resolution of a certain Indian trial I have a vested interest in. The only other thing I can figure is that perhaps the prosecutors know they don't have sufficient evidence to con-vict anyone, so they've decided the trial itself should be the punishment. I never could've believed that the St. Kitts trial would still be going on five fucking years after it began. But it is. The prosecution hasn't even rested yet. When they're finally done, the defense will have their turn. The trial could trickle on forever.

Do you believe that all these things have been written in the stars since the moment of my birth? Swamiji would tell you that they have, and I always would've told you that I doubted that. But since one afternoon a few months ago, I'm not so sure. In the back of my mother's closet, in a box of my father's papers I'd never seen before, I found a book written by Miles. In which, in a passage on how CIA field officers protect each other from their bureaucratic bosses, he revealed the identity of his own protector: *Each time I ran into trouble, a wonderful man named Bill Tharp would save me.* Maybe it was all meant to be. Who can say? Who knows anything for sure?

When I came to this beach, I still felt young. And I never stopped feeling young until I watched my mother die a slow and awful death from cancer. It took almost four years.

One day in the middle years, I was sitting talking with my mother in her house. Probably we'd been that day to a doctor's appointment somewhere. Probably she'd just told me, "I don't know what I'd do without you," because she told me that often in those days.

There was a knock on her front door. The mailman, with a package from my older brother, who was a perfect child, is a natural horseman, and can sing with perfect pitch.

"Oh, wonderful, it's from Jerry," my mother said brightly. "Open it."

I did.

Inside a big blue-leather presentation folder was a parchment with lots of seals and calligraphy, commemorating my brother's retirement. "Read it to me," said my mother.

I did.

It ended, *Now, therefore, I, Kay Barnes, Mayor of Kansas City, Missouri, do hereby thank Jerry Kolb for his great service to the community. Reverend Kolb's tireless dedication to the citizens of Kansas City and to Saint Luke's Hospital has been a treasure, and we are appreciative. Therefore, I proclaim September 8, 1999 to be Reverend Jerry Kolb Day in Kansas City, Missouri.*

I can't win.

But I learned as much from my mother in the end as I did in the beginning. Until she died, I'd always managed to look at the inevitability of death as nothing more than an ugly rumor. I thought I could wait patiently on this beach forever if I had to. Now I have this sense that I've been left behind and the world is spinning out its destiny without me. I have to get out of here or I will die of this place.

Kim's been away in Africa most of the last two years, taking care of her father while I took care of my mother. I'd like to see Kim. I'd like to see my friends. I'd like to see the world I grew up in. So much has happened since I came here.

I check my passport and slip it back into my pocket. What I decided when my mother died was that I would wait six more months for the trial to end, and, depending on how things went, the passport I carried when I left here would either bear my name or someone else's. It would take me either one day or three to get to the city I long to visit most. But, eight months later, the trial is never-ending. That much is clear now.

I look at my watch.

As you will have guessed because I'm wearing a suit today, a sincere blue suit chosen for the effect I hope it will have on immigration officers and policemen, today is the day. Inside this house on a beach in Florida, I finish my coffee and take one last look at the ocean and the red morning sky. It's time to go now. Wish me well.

ACKNOWLEDGMENTS

One night, years ago, in the fine dining room of a pub which plies its trade not quite in the middle of nowhere, but where two roads meet near the confluence of the Chiltern Hills and the Oxfordshire countryside, Miles Copeland told me, "You really should write a book some day, you know, Larry. Tell how historical events *really* happened. It'll make a fine contrast to the stories of tireless patriotism, courage, and moral clarity the politicians involved will wheel out in their autobiographies."

I cannot know whether Miles would've approved of my attempt here to follow that advice, but I hope he would've, and I am indebted to Miles for the experiences he gave me, and for the many wonderful stories he told me, in person, and in his books and other writings. Thank you, Miles. And thank you, Lorraine Copeland, for recently sharing with me a few of your memories of my friend, your husband. Thank you, too, Miles A. Copeland III, for reading an early draft of this book and graciously answering my many questions about your father and mother.

Encouragement and advice from three extraordinary authors gave me the confidence to write this book. Thank you, Herb Wind, for, half my lifetime ago, telling me I should become a writer, and, all these years later, kindly writing me your thoughts on how to make this book work. Thank you, James Ellroy, for reading an early outline hereof and offering several sagacious suggestions on structuring this story. Thank you, Norman Mailer, for, even while working against a deadline of your own, taking time to consider my questions and convey to me your insights into the life and writings of a certain recurring character in your great CIA novel, *Harlot's Ghost*: Miles Copeland.

I am indebted to my mother and father for all the experiences they gave me, every thing they did for me, and the lessons they taught me. Thank you, Mom and Dad. My brothers have each kindly answered my questions about their memories of certain aspects of our family lore, and have shared with me photographs and documents which aided me as I wrote. Thank you, Jerry and

Bill. Thank you, too, Watt and Aleen Redfield, for all the encouragement and help you gave me throughout your lives.

Muhammad Ali graciously took it upon himself to hammer home to me the fact that this book would well and duly suck if it did not include at least a couple chapters about him. Thank you, Muhammad, for that, and everything else.

Adnan Khashoggi, during the height of my efforts to break the news story that launched the St. Kitts Affair, told me that some day I should write a book about it all. "I think the story behind the story is always the most interesting," he said. "Don't you agree, Your Excellency?" Thank you, Adnan.

This would not be the book it is had not Noah Lukeman, one of my literary agents, suggested I make Part I a father-and-son memoir. Thank you, Noah. And thank you, Joel Gotler, proprietor of Intellectual Property Group, literary managers, for your advice and counsel. Thanks, too, to Joel's colleagues Justin Manask and Maria Ruvalcaba Hackett.

Thank you, Mark Canton, Mark Kimsey, Steve Barnett, Ray Kimsey, Lynwood Spinks, Silenn Thomas, and Andy Ziskin, of Atmosphere Entertainment, for, to my great astonishment, actually paying me money for the motion picture rights to the story told herein.

Thank you, Oliver Stone, Kathleen Kennedy, Paula Wagner, Craig Zadan, David Fincher, Dick Christie, Tony Peck, and Mike Ovitz for reading early outlines or drafts and telling me this was a story worth telling.

Nearly an entire pride of Morrisons—Bill Morrison, Dave Morrison, Stephen Morrison, and Sandra Butter Morrison—each in his or her own way played a part in helping me turn this story into a book. Thanks to all of you.

Thank you, Tom Dugan, for your great literary taste and advice. Thank you, Dan Barber, for the same. Thank you, Bob Marx, for your legal advice, and a lot more.

Thank you, Tom Mullins, for all you taught me about the Middle East. Most of my best lines, I got from you. Thank you, Michael Oatley, for saving me, and then, in accordance with the protocols of the secret world, disappearing. Thank you, Sylvie Patrick and Jerry Stalnaker, for sharing with me your memories of your father, my Uncle George. Thank you, Anne Sither, for taking the time to help me verify my memories of your husband, my Uncle Charley. Thank you, John Lepre, for detailing for me the Tumpane Company's history in Saudi Arabia, and a certain American court. Thank you, Asa Candler and David Candler, for sharing memories of your father, who was my father's friend and protector. Thank you, Kathleen Tharp and Sarah Tharp, for answering my many questions about your father, my Uncle Bill Tharp.

Thank you, Duval A. Edwards, former Counter Intelligence Corps special agent for telling me of the mission my father sent you on during World War II.

Thank you, Tim Trewhella, for graciously sharing with me all of your research on Operation Pastorius. Thank you, Robert Rynerson, for helping me verify my memories of the U.S. Army troop trains that connected West Berlin and West Germany. Thank you, Geoffrey Cribb, for answering my many questions about yachts.

Thank you Kari Nordgaard-Tveit and Tore John Andreassen for helping me keep my Norway geography straight. Thank you, Neil Hamilton, for sharing with me your photos and knowledge of Carpenders Park. Thank you, Bill Stoner, for patiently answering my questions about police procedures. Thank you to Arthur M. Mitchell and Bonnie Elliott for politely parsing my Japanese. Thank you, Sandra van Essche, for fixing my French. Thank you, Dev Ketu, soon to be an M.D., for answering my many questions. Thank you, Mike Timpani. Thank you, Mary Dunham. Thank you, Judith McNally. Thank you, Linda Permann. Thank you, Bob Wittek. Thank you, Dianna Edwards. Thank you, Jocelyn Arsht. Thank you, Melanie West. Thank you, Mike Dixon. Thank you, Adrian Wadey. Thank you to Scott Gough, former F-16 pilot, now an airline pilot, for verifying that it wasn't an hallucination: a multitude of Cairenes with nothing more than muscles and a rope could indeed move a fully-fueled and loaded Boeing-747.

Thank you, Helen Morris, Marc Joubert, Fiona Waterstreet, Nancy Conrad, Robert Ducas, Paul Monzione, Rene Chun, Ross Galbraith, Marin Conde, Lynda Rufo, Lucas Meyers, Karen Palacios-Jansen, Allan Sonnenschein, Bruce Schwack, and Denise Waterbury, among others, for reading various portions of my manuscript, and giving me valuable suggestions. Thank you, John Alexander, not only for reading and commenting on an early draft, but also for advising me that, in artistic endeavors, it's best not to get started until around midnight, when the spirits come out to help us.

Thank you, Marc Zimmerman, for graciously allowing me to use your beautiful translations of the beautiful poetry of Pablo Neruda.

There is a Cyrus International Ltd. operating today in London. I am told, and I have no reason to disbelieve, that, though it is run by a former officer of MI6, and is in the business of providing commercial intelligence and risk management, the present-day Cyrus International Ltd. has nothing to do with the Cyrus International that Miles Copeland and I in 1985 concluded was a front for Iranian intelligence interests.

In December 2003, in New Delhi, His Holiness Chandraswami Maharaj, Mammaji, and former Indian prime minister Narasimha Rao were acquitted of all charges relating to CBI allegations that they had defrauded the Indian pickle and chutney king of London, Mr. Lakhubhai Pathak. In rendering its verdict, the Court stated that it had found Mr. Pathak's evidence unreliable and uncorroborated.

In the second week of August 2004, Chandraswami gave evidence in the St. Kitts trial. He said the government of Vishwanath Pratap Singh had falsely implicated him, Chandraswami, in the St. Kitts case because of his close proximity to former prime ministers Rajiv Gandhi and Narasimha Rao. Chandraswami further testified that he was falsely accused of involvement in the St. Kitts Affair because V.P. Singh's government had targeted its political enemies. Mammaji, through his legal counsel, told the Court he was falsely implicated in the case because he is a close associate of Chandraswami. The Court fixed August 21, 2004, as the date for commencement of final arguments in the case.

Given all that I know now, I can find no convincing evidence, nearly-convincing evidence, or even slightly-convincing evidence, that either V.P. Singh or his son Ajeya Singh ever banked money on the many-splendored isle of St. Kitts.

The quotation which begins "Indian Muslims are cancer for this country" is a quotation of Bal Thackeray, founder and leader of the Shiv Sena, ally of the BJP, which I took from "The Strongman: Where is Hindu-nationalist violence leading?" by Larissa MacFarquhar, published in the May 26, 2003 edition of *The New Yorker*. I learned from Muhammad Ali never to disrespect another man's religion, and, notwithstanding my opinions of the BJP, I've got nothing against any Hindu, Muslim, Christian, Jew, Buddhist, or anyone else who comes by his religion honestly.

Dan Schwartz, once the general counsel of the world's largest spy agency, the NSA, assisted me in eliminating classified information from this book, and in other ways complying with laws pertaining to the disclosure of intelligence sources and methods and the identities of American intelligence officers and agents. Thank you, Dan. And thank you to Dan's colleague Coleen Reddan.

Toward compliance with those laws, or for other reasons, the names of a few of the characters in this book have been changed. Much of the dialogue in this book is recreated.

Thank you, Sean McDonald, Cindy Spiegel, Julie Grau, Susan Petersen Kennedy, Megan Lynch, Alexander Gigante, Peter Grennen, Marilyn Ducksworth, Steve Oppenheim, Andrea Ho, and Noelle Murrain, of Riverhead Books and/or its parent Penguin Group USA. Thank you, too, Chris Knutsen, formerly of Riverhead Books, for your faith in this story and my ability to tell it, and for all of your advice. And thank you, Gary Mailman, outside counsel for Penguin Group USA for your assistance. Thank you, Doug Young, Bill Scott-Kerr, Sally Gaminara, and Simon Thorogood, of my United Kingdom publisher, Transworld Books. This book was edited by Sean McDonald and Doug Young. All errors or omissions herein are entirely their fault.

Thank you to my son.

And, most of all, thank you to Kim—who brought me back to books.